Pro MERN Stack

Full Stack Web App Development with
Mongo, Express, React, and Node

Second Edition

Vasan Subramanian

Apress®

Pro MERN Stack

Vasan Subramanian
Bangalore, Karnataka, India

ISBN-13 (pbk): 978-1-4842-4390-9   ISBN-13 (electronic): 978-1-4842-4391-6
https://doi.org/10.1007/978-1-4842-4391-6

Managing Director, Apress Media LLC: Welmoed Spahr
Acquisitions Editor: Nikhil Karkal
Development Editor: Matthew Moodie
Coordinating Editor: Divya Modi

Cover designed by eStudioCalamar

Cover image designed by Freepik (www.freepik.com)

Distributed to the book trade worldwide by Springer Science+Business Media New York, 233 Spring Street, 6th Floor, New York, NY 10013. Phone 1-800-SPRINGER, fax (201) 348-4505, e-mail orders-ny@springer-sbm.com, or visit www.springeronline.com. Apress Media, LLC is a California LLC and the sole member (owner) is Springer Science + Business Media Finance Inc (SSBM Finance Inc). SSBM Finance Inc is a **Delaware** corporation.

For information on translations, please e-mail rights@apress.com, or visit http://www.apress.com/rights-permissions.

Apress titles may be purchased in bulk for academic, corporate, or promotional use. eBook versions and licenses are also available for most titles. For more information, reference our Print and eBook Bulk Sales web page at http://www.apress.com/bulk-sales.

Any source code or other supplementary material referenced by the author in this book is available to readers on GitHub via the book's product page, located at www.apress.com/978-1-4842-4390-9. For more detailed information, please visit http://www.apress.com/source-code.

Printed on acid-free paper

To all the full-stack developers of the world.

Table of Contents

About the Author

Vasan Subramanian has experience with all kinds of programming, from 8-bit, hand-assembled code on an 8085 to AWS Lambda. He not only loves to solve problems using software, but he also looks for the right mix of technology and processes to make a software product team most efficient. He learned software development at companies such as Corel, Wipro, and Barracuda Networks, not just as a programmer but also as a leader of teams at those companies.

Vasan studied at IIT Madras and IIM Bangalore. In his current job as CTO at Accel, he mentors startups on all things tech. His Twitter handle is @vasansr. While not mentoring or coding (or writing books!), Vasan runs half marathons and plays five-a-side soccer.

About the Technical Reviewer

Anshul Chanchlani is a full-stack developer at Wipro Digital, delivering solutions using various upcoming and existing technologies like MERN stack, GraphQL, and micro-services. He currently lives in London and loves traveling. In his leisure time, he watches films and directs short movies.

Acknowledgments

This book would not have been possible without the official reviewers. But the most I owe to is my wife, Keerthana, for the illustrations. Not just for drawing them, but for designing them as well. And to do that, she had to read each chapter, understand it in detail, and try out the code in it. Honestly, this book would not have been possible without her.

Preface

Pro MERN Stack is for full-stack developers, architects, and team leads wanting to learn about this stack built with Mongo, Express, React, and Node.

It was in late December 2016 that I finished the manuscript of the first edition. But within just a few months after the book was out, it was outdated. React Router released a new version, 3.0, and this alone was enough to warrant a new edition. I tried to communicate to readers via GitHub issues, asking them to use the older version of React Router. It worked for a while, but this was less than satisfactory.

That was not all. Within another few months, there was a new Node.js LTS version, then React 16, and then a new version of MongoDB, and then Babel. Almost every module used in the MERN stack was upgraded and soon *Pro MERN Stack* became outdated. This pace of change amazed me. Although every new change was great, it did no good for technical authors like me.

I did wait for things to stabilize a bit before initiating the second edition of *Pro MERN Stack*. And I am glad I did, because I believe the current set of tools that form the MERN stack have reached a good level of maturity and therefore will be reasonably stable for some time to come.

Compared to the first edition, there are the expected newer versions of all the tools and libraries. But importantly, I have introduced more modern *ways* of doing things.

I have replaced REST APIs with GraphQL, which I believe is a superior way of implementing APIs. There is a new architecture that separates the user interface and the APIs into two different servers. Instead of using in-memory sessions to track logged-in users, I used JSON Web Tokens. I have simplified server rendering by using a global store instead of the deprecated React Context. Finally, I introduced a new chapter on deployment using Heroku.

I also changed many things that one needs to do as an author to enhance the readers' experiences. I added illustrations and more explanations to code snippets and increased the granularity of the sections. All these changes, in my opinion, will make *Pro MERN Stack*, Second Edition, far superior to the first edition. It's not just an up-to-date version of the first edition, but it enhances the learning experience significantly.

CHAPTER 1

■ ■ ■

Introduction

Web application development is not what it used to be, even a few years back. Today, there are so many options, and the uninitiated are often confused about what's good for them. There are many choices; not just the broad *stack* (the various tiers or technologies used), but also for tools that aid in development. This book stakes a claim that the MERN stack is great for developing a complete web application and takes the reader through all that is necessary to get that done.

In this chapter, I'll give a broad overview of the technologies that the MERN stack consists of. I won't go into details or examples in this chapter, instead, I'll just introduce the high-level concepts. I'll focus on how these concepts affect an evaluation of whether MERN is a good choice for your next web application project.

What's MERN?

Any web application is built using multiple technologies. The combinations of these technologies is called a "stack," popularized by the LAMP stack, which is an acronym for Linux, Apache, MySQL, PHP, which are all open-source software. As web development matured and their interactivity came to the fore, Single Page Applications (SPAs) became more popular. An SPA is a web application paradigm that avoids fetching the contents of an entire web page from the server to display new contents. It instead uses lightweight calls to the server to get some data or snippets and changes the web page. The result looks quite nifty as compared to the old way of reloading the page entirely. This brought about a rise in front-end frameworks, since a lot of the work was done on the front-end. At approximately the same time, though completely unrelated, NoSQL databases also started gaining popularity.

The MEAN (MongoDB, Express, AngularJS, Node.js) stack was one of the early open-source stacks that epitomized this shift toward SPAs and adoption of NoSQL. AngularJS, a front-end framework based on the Model View Controller (MVC) design pattern, anchored this stack. MongoDB, a very popular NoSQL database, was used for persistent data storage. Node.js, a server-side JavaScript runtime environment, and Express, a web-server built on Node.js, formed the middle-tier, or the web server. This stack was arguably the most popular stack for any new web application until a few years back.

Not exactly competing, but React, an alternate front-end technology created by Facebook, has been gaining popularity and offers an alternative to AngularJS. It thus replaces the "A" with an "R" in MEAN, to give us the MERN Stack. I said "not exactly" since React is not a full-fledged MVC framework. It is a JavaScript library for building user interfaces, so in some sense, it's the View part of the MVC.

Although we pick a few defining technologies to define a stack, these are not enough to build a complete web application. Other tools are required to help the process of development, and many libraries are needed to complement React. This book is about building a complete web application based on the MERN stack and all these related tools and libraries.

© Vasan Subramanian 2019
V. Subramanian, *Pro MERN Stack*, https://doi.org/10.1007/978-1-4842-4391-6_1

Who Should Read This Book

Developers and architects who have prior experience in any web app stack other than the MERN stack will find the book useful for learning about this modern stack. Prior knowledge of how web applications work is required. Knowledge of JavaScript is also required. It is further assumed that the reader knows the basics of HTML and CSS. It will greatly help if you are also familiar with the version control tool git; you could try out the code just by cloning the git repository that holds all the source code described in this book and running each step by checking out a branch.

The code in the book uses the latest features of JavaScript (ES2015+), and it is assumed that you well-versed in these features such as classes, fat-arrow functions, `const` keyword, etc. Whenever I first use any of these modern JavaScript features, I will point it out using a note so that you are aware that it is a new feature. In case you are not familiar with a particular feature, you can read up on it as and when you encounter it.

If you have decided that your new app will use the MERN stack, then this book is a perfect enabler for you that lets you quickly get off the ground. Even if you have not, reading the book will get you excited about MERN and equip you with enough knowledge to make a choice for a future project. The most important thing you will learn is to put together multiple technologies and build a complete, functional web application, and you can be called a full-stack developer or architect on MERN.

Structure of the Book

Although the focus of the book is to let you learn how to build a complete web application, most of the book revolves around React. That's just because, as is true of most modern SPAs, the front-end code forms the bulk. And in this case, React is used for the front-end.

The tone of the book is tutorial-like and designed for learning by doing. We will build a web application during the course of the book. I use the term "we" because you will need to write code just as I show you the code that is to be written as part of the plentiful code listings. Unless you write the code yourself alongside me and solve the exercises, you will not get the full benefit of the book. I encourage you *not* to copy-paste; instead please type out the code. I find this very valuable in the learning process. There are very small nuances—e.g., types of quotes—that can cause a big difference. When you type out the code, you are much more conscious of this than when you are just reading it.

Sometimes, you may run into situations where what you typed in doesn't work. In such cases, you may want to copy-paste to ensure that the code is correct and overcomes any typos you may have made. In such cases, do *not* copy-paste from the electronic version of the book, as the typesetting may not be faithful to the actual code. I have created a GitHub repository at `https://github.com/vasansr/pro-mern-stack-2` for you to compare, and in unavoidable circumstances, to copy-paste from.

I have also added a checkpoint (a git branch in fact) after every change that can be tested in isolation so that you can look at the exact diffs between two checkpoints, online. The checkpoints and links to the diffs are listed in the home page (the README) of the repository. You may find this more useful than looking at the entire source, or even the listings in the text of this book, as GitHub diffs are far more expressive than what I can show in print.

Rather than cover one topic or technology per section, I have adopted a more practical and problem-solving approach. We will have developed a full-fledged working application by the end of the book, but we'll start small with a Hello World example. Just as in a real project, we will add more features to the application as we progress. When we do this, we'll encounter tasks that need additional concepts or knowledge to proceed. For each of these, I will introduce the concept or technology that can be used, and I'll discuss that in detail.

Thus, you may not find every chapter or section devoted purely to one topic or technology. Some chapters may focus on a technology and others may address a set of goals we want to achieve in the application. We will be switching between technologies and tools as we progress.

I have included exercises wherever possible, which makes you either think or look up various resources on the Internet. This is so that you know where to get additional information for things that are not covered in the book, typically very advanced topics or APIs.

I have chosen an issue-tracking application as the application that we'll build together. It's something most developers can relate to, at the same time has many of the attributes and requirements that any enterprise application will have, commonly referred to as a "CRUD" application (CRUD stands for Create, Read, Update, Delete of a database record).

Conventions

Many of the conventions used in the book quite obvious, so I'll not explain all of them. I'll only cover some conventions with respect to how the sections are structured and how changes to the code are shown because it's not very obvious.

Each chapter has multiple sections, and each section is devoted to one set of code changes that results in a working application that can be run and tested. A section can have multiple listings, but each of them may not be testable by itself. Every section will also have a corresponding entry in the GitHub repository, where you can see the complete source of the application as of the end of that section, as well as the differences between the previous and the current section. You will find the difference view very useful to identify the changes made in the section.

All code changes will appear in listings within the section, but please do not rely on their accuracy. The reliable and working code can be found in the GitHub repository, which could even have undergone last-minute changes that couldn't make it to the printed book in time. All listings will have a listing caption, which will include the name of the file being changed or created.

You may use the GitHub repository to report problems in the printed book. But before you do that, do check the existing list of issues to see if anyone else has reported the same. I will monitor the issues and post resolutions and, if necessary, correct the code in the GitHub repository.

A listing is a full listing if it contains a file, a class, a function, or an object in its entirety. A full listing may also contain two or more classes, functions, or objects, but not multiple files. In such a case, if the entities are not consecutive, I'll use ellipses to indicate chunks of unchanged code.

Listing 1-1 is an example of a full listing, the contents of an entire file.

Listing 1-1. server.js: Express Server

```
const express = require('express');

const app = express();
app.use(express.static('static'));

app.listen(3000, function () {
  console.log('App started on port 3000');
});
```

A partial listing, on the other hand, will not list complete files, functions, or objects. It will start and end with an ellipsis, and may have ellipses in the middle to skip chunks of code that have not changed. The new code added will be highlighted in bold, and the unchanged code will be in the normal font. Listing 1-2 is an example of a partial listing that has small additions.

Listing 1-2. package.json: Adding Scripts for Transformation

```
...
  "scripts": {
    "compile": "babel src --presets react --out-dir static",
    "watch": "babel src --presets react --out-dir static --watch",
    "test": "echo \"Error: no test specified\" && exit 1"
  },
...
```

Deleted code will be shown using strikethrough, like in Listing 1-3.

Listing 1-3. package.json: Changes for Removing Polyfill

```
...
  "devDependencies": {
    "babel-polyfill": "^6.13.0",
    ...
  }
...
```

Code blocks are used within regular text to extract changes in code for discussion and are usually a repetition of code in listings. These are not listings and often are just a line or two. Here is an example, where the line is extracted out of a listing and one word is highlighted:

```
...
const contentNode = ...
...
```

All commands that need to be executed on the console will be in the form a code block starting with $. Here is an example:

```
$ npm install express
```

All commands used in the book can also be found in the GitHub repository in a file called commands.md. This is so that errors in the book can be corrected after the book has been published, and also to be a more reliable source for copy-pasting. Again, you are encouraged not to copy-paste these commands, but if you are forced to because you find something is not working, then please copy-paste from the GitHub repository rather than the book's text.

In later chapters in the book, the code will be split across two projects or directories. To distinguish in which directory the command should be issued, the command block will start with a cd. For example, to execute a command in the directory called api, the following will be used:

```
$ cd api
$ npm install dotenv@6
```

All commands that need to be executed within a MongoDB shell will be in the form of a code block starting with >. For example:

```
> show collections
```

These commands are also collected in one file, called mongoCommands.md in the GitHub repository.

What You Need

You will need a computer that can run your server and do other tasks such as compilation. You will also need a browser to test your application. I recommend a Linux-based computer such as Ubuntu, or a Mac as your development server, but with minor changes, you could also use a Windows PC.

Running Node.js directly on Windows will also work, but the code samples in this book assume a Linux-based PC or Mac. If you choose to run directly on a Windows PC, you may have to make appropriate changes, especially when running commands in the shell, using a copy instead of using soft links, and in rare cases, to deal with \ vs. / in path separators.

One option would be to try to run an Ubuntu server Virtual Machine (VM) using Vagrant (https:// www.vagrantup.com/). This is helpful because you will eventually deploy your code on a Linux-based server, and it is best to get used to that environment from the beginning. But you may find it difficult to edit files, because in an Ubuntu server, you only have a console. An Ubuntu desktop VM may work better for you, but it will need more memory.

Further, to keep the book concise, I have not included installation instructions for packages, and they are different for different operating systems. You will need to follow the installation instructions from the package providers' websites. And in many cases, I have not included direct links to websites and I ask you to look them up. This is due to a couple of reasons. The first is to let you learn by yourself how to search for these. The second is that any link I provide may have moved to another location due to the fast-paced changes that the MERN stack was experiencing at the time of writing this book.

MERN Components

I'll give a quick introduction to the main components that form the MERN stack, and a few other libraries and tools that we'll be using to build our web application. I'll just touch upon the salient features and leave the details to other chapters where they are more appropriate.

React

React anchors the MERN stack. In some sense, this is the defining component of the MERN stack.

React is an open-source JavaScript library maintained by Facebook that can be used for creating views rendered in HTML. Unlike AngularJS, React is not a framework. It is a library. Thus, it does not, by itself, dictate a framework pattern such as the MVC pattern. You use React to render a view (the V in MVC), but how to tie the rest of the application together is completely up to you.

Not just Facebook itself, but there are many other companies that use React in production like Airbnb, Atlassian, Bitbucket, Disqus, Walmart, etc. The 120,000 stars on its GitHub repository is an indication of its popularity.

I'll discuss a few things about React that make it stand out.

Why Facebook Invented React

The Facebook folks built React for their own use, and later they made it open-source. Now, why did they have to build a new library when there are tons of them out there?

React was born not in the Facebook application that we all see, but in Facebook's Ads organization. Originally, they used a typical client-side MVC model to start with, which had all the regular two-way data binding and templates. Views would listen to changes on models, and they would respond to those changes by updating themselves.

Soon, this got pretty hairy as the application became more and more complex. What would happen was that a change would cause an update, that would cause another update (because something changed due to that update), which would cause yet another, and so on. Such cascading updates became difficult to maintain, because there would be subtle differences in the code to update the view, depending on the root cause of the update.

Then they thought, why do we need to deal with all this, when all the code to depict the model in a view is already there? Aren't we replicating the code by adding smaller and smaller snippets to manage transitions? Why can't we use the *templates* (that is, the views) themselves to manage state changes?

That's when they started thinking of building something that's *declarative* rather than *imperative*.

Declarative

React views are declarative. What this really means is that you, as a programmer, don't have to worry about managing the effect of changes in the view's state or the data. In other words, you don't worry about transitions or mutations in the DOM caused by changes to the view's state. Being declarative makes the views consistent, predictable, easier to maintain, and simpler to understand. It's someone else's problem to deal with transitions.

How does this work? Let's compare how things work in React and how things work in the conventional approach, say, using jQuery.

A React component *declares* how the view looks, given the data. When the data changes, if you are used to the jQuery way of doing things, you'd typically do some DOM manipulation. If, for example, a new row has been inserted in a table, you'd create that DOM element and insert it using jQuery. But not in React. You just don't do anything! The React library figures out how the new view looks and renders that.

Won't this be too slow? Will it not cause the entire screen to be refreshed on every data change? Well, React takes care of this using its *Virtual DOM* technology. You declare how the view looks and React builds a virtual representation, an in-memory data structure, out of it. I'll discuss more about this in Chapter 2, but for now, just think of the Virtual DOM as an intermediate representation, somewhere between an HTML and the actual DOM.

When things change, React builds a new virtual DOM based on the new truth (state) and compares it with the old (before things changed) virtual DOM. React then computes the differences in the old and the changed Virtual DOM, then applies these changes to the actual DOM.

Compared to manual updates as you would have performed in the jQuery way of doing things, this adds very little overhead because the algorithm to compute the differences in the Virtual DOM has been optimized to the hilt. Thus, we get the best of both worlds: not having to worry about implementing transitions and also the performance of minimal changes.

Component-Based

The fundamental building block of React is a component that maintains its own state and renders itself.

In React, all you do is build components. Then, you put components together to make another component that depicts a complete view or page. A component encapsulates the state of data and the view, or how it is rendered. This makes writing and reasoning about the entire application easier, by splitting it into components and focusing on one thing at a time.

Components talk to each other by sharing state information in the form of read-only properties to their child components and by callbacks to their parent components. I'll dig deeper into this concept in a later chapter, but the gist of it is that components in React are very cohesive, but the coupling with one another is minimal.

No Templates

Many web application frameworks rely on templates to automate the task of creating repetitive HTML or DOM elements. The templating language in these frameworks is something that the developer will have to learn and practice. Not in React.

React uses a full-featured programming language to construct repetitive or conditional DOM elements. That language is none other than JavaScript. For example, when you want to construct a table, you'd write a for(...) loop in JavaScript or use the map() function of Array.

There is an intermediate language to represent a Virtual DOM, and that is JSX (short for JavaScript XML), which is very much like HTML. This lets you create nested DOM elements in a familiar language rather than hand-construct them using JavaScript functions. Note that JSX is not a programming language; it is a representational markup like HTML. It's also very similar to HTML so you don't have to learn too much. More about this later.

In fact, you don't have to use JSX—you can write pure JavaScript to create your virtual DOM if you prefer. But if you are used to HTML, it's simpler to just use JSX. But don't worry about it; it's really not a new language that you'll need to learn.

Isomorphic

React can be run on the server too. That's what *isomorphic* means: the same code can run on the server and the browser. This allows you to create pages on the server when required, for example, for SEO purposes. I'll talk discuss how this works in a bit more detail later, in Chapter 12, which deals with server-side rendering. But to be able to run React code on the server, we do need something that can run JavaScript, and this is where I introduce Node.js.

Node.js

Simply put, Node.js is JavaScript outside of a browser. The creators of Node.js just took Chrome's V8 JavaScript engine and made it run independently as a JavaScript runtime. If you are familiar with the Java runtime that runs Java programs, you can easily relate to the JavaScript runtime: the Node.js runtime runs JavaScript programs.

Although you may find people who don't think Node.js is fit for production use, claiming it was meant for the browser, there are many industry leaders who have chosen Node.js. Netflix, Uber, and LinkedIn are a few companies that use Node.js in production, and that should lend credibility as a robust and scalable environment to run the back-end of any application.

Node.js Modules

In a browser, you can load multiple JavaScript files, but you need an HTML page to do all that. You cannot refer another JavaScript file from one JavaScript file. But for Node.js, there is no HTML page that starts it all. In the absence of the enclosing HTML page, Node.js uses its own module system based on CommonJS to put together multiple JavaScript files.

Modules are like libraries. You can include the functionality of another JavaScript file (provided it's written to follow a module's specifications) by using the require keyword (which you won't find in a browser's JavaScript). You can therefore split your code into files or modules for the sake of better organization and load them using require. I'll talk about the exact syntax in a later chapter; at this point it's enough to note that compared to JavaScript on the browser, there is a cleaner way to modularize your code using Node.js.

Node.js ships with a bunch of core modules compiled into the binary. These modules provide access to the operating system elements such as the file system, networking, input/output, etc. They also provide some utility functions that are commonly required by most programs.

Apart from your own files and the core modules, you can also find a great amount of third-party open-source libraries available for easy installation. That brings us to npm.

Node.js and npm

npm is the default package manager for Node.js. You can use npm to install third-party libraries (packages) and manage dependencies between them. The npm registry (www.npmjs.com) is a public repository of all modules published by people for the purpose of sharing.

Although npm started off as a repository for Node.js modules, it quickly transformed into a package manager for delivering other JavaScript based modules, notably, those that can be used in the browser. jQuery, by far the most popular client-side JavaScript library, is available as an npm module. In fact, even though React is largely client-side code and can be included directly in your HTML as a script file, it is recommended instead that React is installed via npm. But once it's installed as a package, we need something to put all the code together that can be included in the HTML so that the browser can get access to the code. For this, there are build tools such as Browserify or Webpack that can put together your own modules as well as third-party libraries in a bundle that can be included in the HTML.

As of writing this book, npm tops the list of modules or package repositories, having more than 450,000 packages (see Figure 1-1). Maven, which used to be the biggest two years back, has fewer than half the number now. This shows that npm is not just the largest, but also the fastest growing repository. It is often said that the success of Node.js is largely owed to npm and the module ecosystem that has sprung around it.

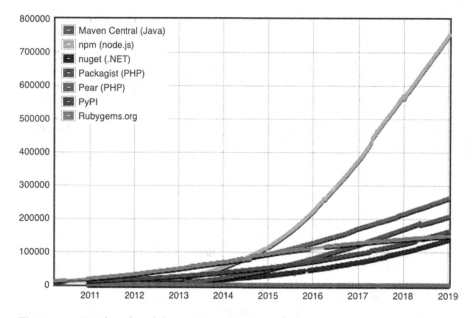

Figure 1-1. *Number of modules in various languages (source: www.modulecounts.com)*

npm is not just easy to use both for creating and using modules; it also has a unique conflict resolution technique that allows multiple conflicting versions of a module to exist side-by-side to satisfy dependencies. Thus, in most cases, npm just works.

Node.js is Event Driven

Node.js has an asynchronous, event driven, non-blocking input/output (I/O) model, as opposed to using threads to achieve multi-tasking.

Most other languages depend on threads to do things simultaneously. But in fact, there is no such thing as simultaneous when it comes to a single processor running your code. Threads give the feeling of simultaneousness by letting other pieces of code run while one piece waits (blocks) for some event to complete. Typically, these are I/O events such as reading from a file or communicating over the network. For example, on one line, you make a call to open a file, and on the next line, you have your file handle ready. What really happens is that your code is *blocked* (doing nothing) while the file is being opened. If you have another thread running, the operating system or the language will switch out this code and start running some other code during the blocked period.

Node.js, on the other hand, has no threads. It relies on *callbacks* to let you know that a pending task is completed. So, if you write a line of code to open a file, you supply it with a callback function to receive the results—the file handle. On the next line, you continue to do other things that don't require the file handle. If you are used to asynchronous Ajax calls, you will immediately know what I mean. Event driven programming is natural to Node.js due to the underlying language constructs of JavaScript such as closures.

Node.js achieves multi-tasking using an *event loop*. This is nothing but a queue of events that need to be processed, and callbacks to be run on those events. In the previous example, the file being ready to be read will be an event that will trigger the callback you supplied while opening it. If you don't understand this completely, don't worry. The examples in the rest of this book should make you comfortable about how it really works.

On the one hand, an event-based approach makes Node.js applications fast and lets the programmer be blissfully oblivious of semaphores and locks that are utilized to synchronize multi-threaded events. On the other hand, writing code that is inherently asynchronous takes some learning and practice.

Express

Node.js is just a runtime environment that can run JavaScript. To write a full-fledged web server by hand on Node.js directly is not easy, neither is it necessary. Express is a framework that simplifies the task of writing the server code.

The Express framework lets you define *routes*, specifications of what to do when an HTTP request matching a certain pattern arrives. The matching specification is regular expression (regex) based and is very flexible, like most other web application frameworks. The what-to-do part is just a function that is given the parsed HTTP request.

Express parses the request URL, headers, and parameters for you. On the response side, it has, as expected, all functionality required by web applications. This includes determining response codes, setting cookies, sending custom headers, etc. Further, you can write Express *middleware*, custom pieces of code that can be inserted in any request/response processing path to achieve common functionality such as logging, authentication, etc.

Express does not have a template engine built in, but it supports any template engine of your choice such as pug, mustache, etc. But, for an SPA, you will not need to use a server-side template engine. This is because all dynamic content generation is done on the client, and the web server only serves static files and data via API calls.

In summary, Express is a web server framework meant for Node.js. It's not very different from many other web server frameworks in terms of what you can achieve with it.

MongoDB

MongoDB is the database used in the MERN stack. It is a NoSQL document-oriented database, with a flexible schema and a JSON-based query language. Not only do many modern companies (including Facebook and Google) use MongoDB in production, but some older established companies such as SAP and Royal Bank of Scotland have adopted MongoDB.

I'll discuss a few things that MongoDB is (and is not) here.

NoSQL

NoSQL stands for "non-relational," no matter what the acronym expands to. It's essentially *not* a conventional database where you have tables with columns and rows and strict relationships among them. I find that there are two attributes of NoSQL databases that differentiate them from the conventional.

The first is their ability to horizontally scale by distributing the load over multiple servers. They do this by sacrificing an important (for some) aspect of the traditional databases: strong consistency. That is, the data is not necessarily consistent for very brief amounts of time across replicas. For more information, read up on the "CAP theorem" (https://en.wikipedia.org/wiki/CAP_theorem). But in reality, very few applications require web-scale, and this aspect of NoSQL databases comes into play very rarely.

The second, and according to me more important, aspect is that NoSQL databases are not necessarily relational databases. You don't have to think of your objects in terms of rows and columns of tables. The difference between the representation in the application (objects) and on disk (rows in tables) is sometimes called *impedance mismatch*. This is a term borrowed from electrical engineering, which means, roughly, that we're not talking the same language. Because of the impedance mismatch, we have to use a layer that translates or maps between objects and relations. These layers are called Object Relational Mapping (ORM) layers.

In MongoDB, instead, you can think of the persisted data just as you see them in your application code, that is, as objects or documents. This helps you avoid the ORM layer and think of the persisted data as naturally as you would in the application's memory.

Document-Oriented

Compared to relational databases where data is stored in the form of relations, or tables, MongoDB is a document-oriented database. The unit of storage (comparable to a row) is a *document*, or an object, and multiple documents are stored in *collections* (comparable to a table). Every document in a collection has a unique identifier, using which it can be accessed. The identifier is indexed automatically.

Imagine the storage structure of an invoice, with the customer name, address, etc. and a list of items (lines) in the invoice. If you had to store this in a relational database, you would use two tables, say, invoice and invoice_lines, with the lines or items referring to the invoice via a foreign-key *relation*. Not so in MongoDB. You would store the entire invoice as a single document, fetch it, and update it in an atomic operation. This applies not just to line items in an invoice. The document can be any kind of deeply nested object.

Modern relational databases have started supporting one level of nesting by allowing array fields and JSON fields, but it is not the same as a true document database. MongoDB has the ability to index on deeply nested fields, which relational databases cannot do.

The downside is that the data is stored de-normalized. This means that data is sometimes duplicated, requiring more storage space. Also, things like renaming a master (catalog) entry name would mean sweeping through the database and updating all occurrences of the duplicated data. But then, storage has become relatively cheap these days, and renaming master entries are rare operations.

Schema-Less

Storing an object in a MongoDB database does not have to follow a prescribed schema. All documents in a collection need not have the same set of fields.

This means that, especially during early stages of development, you don't need to add/rename columns in the schema. You can quickly add fields in your application code without having to worry about database migration scripts. At first this may seem a boon, but in effect all it does is transfers the responsibility of data sanity from the database to your application code. I find that in larger teams and more stable products, it is better to have a strict or semi-strict schema. Using Object Document Mapping libraries such as mongoose (not covered in this book) alleviates this problem.

JavaScript Based

MongoDB's language is JavaScript.

For relational databases, we had a query language called SQL. For MongoDB, the query language is based on JSON. You create, search for, make changes, and delete documents by specifying the operation in a JSON object. The query language is not English-like (you don't SELECT or say WHERE), and therefore much easier to construct programmatically.

Data is also interchanged in JSON format. In fact, the data is natively stored in a variation of JSON called BSON (where B stands for Binary) in order to efficiently utilize space. When you retrieve a document from a collection, it is returned as a JSON object.

MongoDB comes with a shell that's built on top of a JavaScript runtime like Node.js. This means that you have a powerful and familiar scripting language (JavaScript) to interact with the database via command line. You can also write code snippets in JavaScript that can be saved and run on the server (equivalent of stored procedures).

Tools and Libraries

It's hard to build any web application without using tools to help you on your way. Here's a brief introduction to the other tools apart from the MERN stack components that we will be using to develop the sample application in this book.

React-Router

React gives us only the View rendering capability and helps manage interactions in a single component. When it comes to transitioning between different views of the component and keeping the browser URL in sync with the current state of the view, we need something more.

This capability of managing URLs and history is called *routing*. It is similar to server-side routing that Express does: a URL is parsed and based on its components, a piece of code is associated with the URL. React-Router not only does this, but also manages the browser's Back button functionality so that we can transition between what seem as pages without loading the entire page from the server. We could have built this ourselves, but React-Router is a very easy-to-use library that manages this for us.

React-Bootstrap

Bootstrap, the most popular CSS framework, has been adapted to React and the project is called React-Bootstrap. This library not only gives us most of the Bootstrap functionality, but the components and widgets provided by this library also give us a wealth of information on how to design our own widgets and components.

11

There are other component/CSS libraries built for React (such as Material-UI, MUI, Elemental UI, etc.) and also individual components (such as react-select, react-treeview, and react-date-picker). All these are good choices too, depending on what you are trying to achieve. But I have found that React-Bootstrap is the most comprehensive single library with the familiarity of Bootstrap (which I presume most of you know already).

Webpack

This tool is indispensable when it comes to modularizing code. There are other competing tools such as Bower and Browserify which also serve the purpose of modularizing and bundling all the client code, but I found that Webpack is easier to use and does not require another tool (like gulp or grunt) to manage the build process.

We will be using Webpack not just to modularize and build the client-side code into a bundle to deliver to the browser, but also to "compile" some code. We need the compilation step to generate pure JavaScript from React code written in JSX.

Other Libraries

Very often, we'll feel the need for a library to address a seemingly common problem that all of us would face. In this book, we'll use libraries such as body-parser (to parse POST data in the form of JSON, or form data) and ESLint (for ensuring our code follows conventions), all on the server side, and some more like react-select on the client side.

Other Popular Libraries

Although we will not be using these libraries as part of this book, some that are very popular additions to the MERN stack and are used together are:

- *Redux*: This is a state management library that also combines the Flux programming pattern. It's typically used in larger projects where even for a single screen, managing the state becomes complex.

- *Mongoose*: If you are familiar with Object Relational Mapping layers, you may find Mongoose somewhat similar. This library adds a level of abstraction over the MongoDB database layer and lets the developer see objects as such. The library also provides other useful conveniences when dealing with the MongoDB database.

- *Jest*: This is a testing library that can be used to test React applications easily.

Versions

Although the MERN stack is a robust, production-ready stack as of today, improvements happen in every single component of the stack at a blistering pace. I have used the latest version of all tools and libraries available at the time of writing the book.

But without doubt, by the time you get to read this book, a lot would have changed and the latest version will not be the same as what I used when writing the book. So, in the instructions for installing any package, I have included the major version of the package.

▨ **Note**   To avoid surprises due to changes in packages, install the same major version of a package as mentioned in the book rather than the latest version of a package available.

Minor version changes are supposed to be backward compatible. For example, if the book has used version 4.1.0 of a package, and while installing you get the latest as 4.2.0, the code should work without any changes. But there is a small chance that the maintainers of the package have erroneously introduced an incompatible change in a minor version upgrade. So, if you find that something is not working despite copy-pasting the code from the GitHub repository, as a last resort, switch to the *exact* version as used in the book, which can be found in the package.json file in the root of the repository.

Table 1-1 lists the major versions of the important tools and libraries used as part of this book.

Table 1-1. *Versions of Various Tools and Libraries*

Component	Major Version	Remarks
Node.js	10	This is an LTS (long term support) release
Express	4	--
MongoDB	3.6	Community Edition
React	16	--
React Router	4	--
React Bootstrap	0.32	There is no 1.0 release yet, things may break with 1.0
Bootstrap	3	This is compatible with React Bootstrap 0 (and 1 when released)
Webpack	4	--
ESLint	5	--
Babel	7	--

Note that the JavaScript specification itself has many versions and the support for various versions and features varies across browsers and Node.js. In this book, we will use all new features supported by the tool that is used to compile JavaScript to the lowest common denominator: ES5. This set of features includes JavaScript features from ES2015 (ECMAScript 2015), ES2016, and ES2017. Collectively, these are called ES2015+.

Why MERN?

So now you have a fair idea of the MERN stack and what it comprises. But is it really far superior to any other stack, say, LAMP, MEAN, etc.? By all means, any of these stacks are good enough for most modern web applications. All said and done, familiarity is the crux of productivity in software, so I wouldn't advise a MERN beginner to blindly start their new project on MERN, especially if they have an aggressive deadline. I'd advise them to choose the stack that they are already familiar with.

But MERN does have its special place. It is ideally suited for web applications that have a large amount of interactivity built into the front-end. Go back and re-read the section on "Why Facebook Built React," as it will give you some insights. You could perhaps achieve the same with other stacks, but you'll find that it is most convenient to do so with MERN. So, if you do have a choice of stacks, and the luxury of a little time to get familiar, you may find that MERN is a good choice. I'll talk about a few things that I like about MERN, and these may help you decide.

JavaScript Everywhere

The best part about MERN that I like is that there is a single language used everywhere. We use JavaScript for client-side code as well as server-side code. Even if you have database scripts (in MongoDB), you write them in JavaScript. So, the only language you need to know and be comfortable with is JavaScript.

This is kind of true of all other stacks based on MongoDB and Node.js at the back-end, especially the MEAN stack. But what makes the MERN stack stand out is that you don't even need to know a template language that generates pages. In the React way, the way to programmatically generate HTML (actually DOM elements) is using JavaScript. So, not only do you avoid learning a new language, you also get the full power of JavaScript. This is in contrast to a template language, which will have its own limitations. Of course, you will need to know HTML and CSS, but these are not programming languages, and there is no way you can avoid learning HTML and CSS (not just the markup, but the paradigm and the structure).

Apart from the obvious advantage of not having to switch contexts while writing client-side and server-side code, having a single language across tiers also lets you share code between these. I can think of functions that execute business logic, do validation etc. that can be shared. They need to be run on the client side so that user experience is better by being more responsive to user inputs. They also need to be run on the server side to protect the data model.

JSON Everywhere

When using the MERN stack, object representation is JSON (JavaScript Object Notation) everywhere—in the database, in the application server and on the client, and even on the wire.

I have found that this often saves me a lot of hassle in terms of transformations. No Object Relational Mapping (ORM), not having to force fit an object model into rows and columns, no special serializing and de-serializing code. An Object Document Mapper (ODM) such as mongoose may help enforce a schema and make things even simpler, but the bottom line is that you save a *lot* of data transformation code.

Further, it just lets me *think* in terms of native objects and see them as their natural selves even when inspecting the database directly using a shell.

Node.js Performance

Due to its event-driven architecture and non-blocking I/O, the claim is that Node.js is very fast and a resilient web server.

Although it takes a little getting used to, I have no doubt that when your application starts scaling and receiving a lot of traffic, this will play an important role in cutting costs and savings in terms of time spent in trouble-shooting server CPU and I/O problems.

The npm Ecosystem

I've already discussed the huge number of npm packages available freely for everyone to use. Most problems that you face will have an npm package already as a solution. Even if it doesn't fit your needs exactly, you can fork it and make your own npm package.

npm has been developed on the shoulders of other great package managers and has therefore built into it a lot of best practices. I find that npm is by far the easiest to use and fastest package manager I have used up to now. Part of the reason is that most npm packages are so small, due to the compact nature of JavaScript code.

Isomorphic

SPAs used to have the problem hat they were not SEO friendly, because a search engine would not make Ajax calls to fetch data or run JavaScript code to render the page. One had to use workarounds like running PhantomJS on the server to pseudo-generate HTML pages, or use Prerender.io services that did the same for us. This introduced additional complexity.

With the MERN stack, serving complete pages out of the server is natural and doesn't require tools that are after-thoughts. This is possible because React runs on JavaScript, which is the same on the client or the server. When React-based code runs on the browser, it gets data from the server and constructs the page (DOM) in the browser. This is the SPA way of rendering the UI. If we wanted to *generate* the same page in the server for search engine bots, the same React-based code can be used to get the data from an API server and construct the page (this time, as an HTML) and stream that back to the client. This is called *server-side rendering* (SSR).

Figure 1-2 compares these two modes of operation. What makes this possible is the fact that the same language is used to run the UI construction code in the server and the browser: JavaScript. This is what is meant by the term isomorphic: the same code can be run on the browser or the server. We'll discuss SSR in depth and how it works in Chapter 12. At this point, it is sufficient to appreciate that the *same code* can be run on the browser and the client to achieve the two different modes of operation.

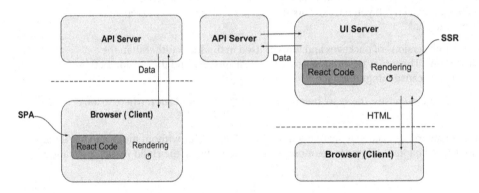

Figure 1-2. *Comparison of the SPA way of doing things and server-side rendering using React*

In fact, React Native has taken it to another extreme: it can even produce a mobile application's UI. I don't cover React Native in this book, but this fact should give you a feel of how React is structured and what it can do for you in the future.

It's Not a Framework!

Not many people like or appreciate this, but I really like the fact that React is a library, not a framework.

A framework is opinionated; it has a set way of doing things. The framework asks you to fill in variations of what it thinks all of us want to get done. A library, on the other hand, gives you tools to construct your application. In the short term, a framework helps a lot by getting most of the standard stuff out of the way. But over time, vagaries of the framework, its assumptions about what we want to get done, and the learning curve will make you wish you had some control over what's happening under the hood, especially when you have some special requirements.

With a library, experienced architects can design their own applications with complete freedom to pick and choose from the library's functions and build their own frameworks that fit their application's unique needs and vagaries. So, for an experienced architect or very unique application needs, a library is better, even though a framework can get you started quickly.

Summary

This book lets you experience what it takes, and what it is like, to develop an application using the MERN stack.

In this chapter, we discussed the reasons that make MERN a compelling choice for any web application, which included the advantages of a single programming language throughout the stack, characteristics of a NoSQL database, and the isomorphism of React. I hope these reasons convince you to try out the MERN stack if not adopt it.

This book encourages you to do, think, and experiment rather than just read. Therefore, please remember the following tips so that you get the maximum out of this book:

- Avoid copy-pasting code from the book or the GitHub repository. Instead, type out the code yourself. Resort to copy-pasting only when you are stuck and find that things are not working as expected.

- Use the GitHub repository (`https://github.com/vasansr/pro-mern-stack-2`) to view code listing and changes; it is more convenient because of the way GitHub shows differences.

- Do not rely on the accuracy of code listing in the book, instead, rely on the code in the GitHub repository. If you have to copy-paste, do so from the GitHub repository, not from the book.

- Use the same versions of packages and tools as used in this book rather than the latest versions. There may be differences in the latest versions and the version in this book that may cause things to break.

- Do not skip the exercises: these are meant to make you think and learn where to look for further resources.

Finally, I hope you are really excited to learn about the MERN stack. So, without much ado, we'll jump into code right in the next chapter and create the most basic of applications: the Hello World application.

CHAPTER 2

Hello World

As is customary, we will start with a Hello World application, something that is a bare minimum and uses most of the MERN components. The main purpose of any Hello World is to show the basic characteristics of the technology or stack that we are using, and the tools required to get it up and running.

In this Hello World application, we'll use React to render a simple page and use Node.js and Express to serve that page from a web server. This will let you learn the fundamentals of these technologies. This will also give you some basic familiarity with nvm, npm, and JSX transformation—some tools that we'll use a lot as we go along.

Server-Less Hello World

To quickly get off the ground, let's write a simple piece of code in a single HTML file that uses React to display a simple page on the browser. No installations, downloads, or server! All you need is a modern browser that can run the code that we write.

Let's start creating this HTML file and call it index.html. You can use your favorite editor and save this file anywhere on your file system. Let's start with the basic HTML tags such as <html>, <head>, and <body>. Then, let's include the React library.

No surprise, the React library is available as a JavaScript file that we can include in the HTML file using the <script> tag. It comes in two parts: the first is the React core module, the one that is responsible for dealing with React components, their state manipulation, etc. The second is the ReactDOM module, which deals with converting React components to a DOM that a browser can understand. These two libraries can be found in unpkg, a Content Delivery Network (CDN) that makes all open-source JavaScript libraries available online. Let's use the development (as opposed to production) version of the libraries from the following URLs:

- React: https://unpkg.com/react@16/umd/react.development.js

- ReactDOM: https://unpkg.com/react-dom@16/umd/react-dom.development.js

These two scripts can be included in the <head> section using <script> tags like this:

```
...
  <script src="https://unpkg.com/react@16/umd/react.development.js"></script>
  <script src="https://unpkg.com/react-dom@16/umd/react-dom.development.js"></script>
...
```

Next, within the body, let's create a <div> that will eventually hold any React elements that we will create. This can be an empty <div>, but it needs an ID, say, content, to identify and get a handle in the JavaScript code.

© Vasan Subramanian 2019

V. Subramanian, *Pro MERN Stack*, https://doi.org/10.1007/978-1-4842-4391-6_2

```
...
  <div id="content"></div>
...
```

To create the React element, the `createElement()` function of the React module needs to be called. This is quite similar to the JavaScript `document.createElement()` function, but has an additional feature that allows nesting of elements. The function takes up to three arguments and its prototype is as follows:

```
React.createElement(type, [props], [...children])
```

The type can be any HTML tag such as the string `'div'`, or a React component (which we will start creating in the next chapter). `props` is an object containing HTML attributes or custom component properties. The last parameter(s) is zero or more children elements, which again are created using the `createElement()` function itself.

For the Hello World application, let's create a very simple nested element—a `<div>` with a title attribute (just to show how attributes work) that contains a heading with the words "Hello World!" Here is the JavaScript code snippet for creating our first React element, which will go inside a `<script>` tag within the body:

```
...
    const element = React.createElement('div', {title: 'Outer div'},
      React.createElement('h1', null, 'Hello World!')
    );
...
```

■ **Note** We are using ES2015+ features of JavaScript in this book, and in this snippet, we used the `const` keyword. This should work in all modern browsers as is. If you are using an older browser such as Internet Explorer 10, you will need to change `const` to `var`. Toward the end of the chapter, we will discuss how to support older browsers, but until then, please use one of the modern browsers to test.

A React element (the result of a `React.createElement()` call) is a JavaScript object that represents what is shown on screen. Since it can be a nested collection of other elements and can depict everything on the entire screen, it is also called the *virtual DOM*. Note that this is not yet the real DOM, which is in the browser's memory and that is why it is called a virtual DOM. It resides in the JavaScript engine's memory as a deeply nested set of React elements, which are also JavaScript objects. A React element contains not just the details of what DOM elements need to be created, but also some additional information about the tree that helps in optimization.

Each of these React elements needs to be transferred to the real DOM for the user interface to be constructed on screen. To do this, a series of `document.createElement()` calls needs to be made corresponding to each of the React elements. The ReactDOM does this when the `ReactDOM.render()` function is called. This function takes in as arguments the element that needs to be rendered and the DOM element that it needs to be placed under.

We already constructed the element that needs to be rendered using `React.createElement()`. As for the containing element, we have a `<div>` that we created in the body, which is the target where the new element needs to be placed. We can get the parent's handle by calling `document.getElementByID()`, as we would have done using regular JavaScript. Let's do that and render the Hello World React element:

```
...
    ReactDOM.render(element, document.getElementById('content'));
...
```

Let's put all this together in index.html. The contents of this file is shown in Listing 2-1.

Listing 2-1. index.html: Server-less Hello World

```html
<!DOCTYPE HTML>
<html>

<head>
  <meta charset="utf-8">
  <title>Pro MERN Stack</title>

  <script src="https://unpkg.com/react@16/umd/react.development.js"></script>
  <script src="https://unpkg.com/react-dom@16/umd/react-dom.development.js"></script>
</head>

<body>
  <div id="contents"></div>

  <script>
    const element = React.createElement('div', {title: 'Outer div'},
      React.createElement('h1', null, 'Hello World!')
    );

    ReactDOM.render(element, document.getElementById('content'));
  </script>
</body>

</html>
```

You can test this file by opening it in a browser. It may take a few seconds to load the React libraries, but soon enough, you should see the browser displaying the caption, as seen in Figure 2-1. You should also be able to hover over the text or anywhere to its right side within the boundaries of the outer div, and you should be able to see the tooltip "Outer div" pop up.

Figure 2-1. *A Hello World written in React*

EXERCISE: SERVER-LESS HELLO WORLD

1. Try to add a class to the h1 element (you will also need to define the class in a
   <style> section within the <head> section to test whether it works). Hint: Search
   for "how to specify class in jsx" in stackoverflow.com. Can you explain this?

2. Inspect the element variable in the developer console. What do you see? If you
   were to call this tree something, what would you call it?

Answers are available at the end of the chapter.

JSX

The simple element that we created in the previous section was easy to write using React.createElement()
calls. But imagine writing a deeply nested hierarchy of elements and components: it can get pretty complex.
Also, the actual DOM can't be easily visualized when using the function calls as it can be visualized if it were
plain HTML.

To address this, React has a markup language called JSX, which stands for *JavaScript XML*. JSX looks
very much like HTML, but there are some differences. So, instead of the React.createElement() calls, JSX
can be used to construct an element or an element hierarchy and make it look very much like HTML. For the
simple Hello World element that we created, in fact, there is no difference between HTML and JSX. So, let's
just write it as HTML and assign it to the element, replacing the React.CreateElement() calls:

```
...
  const element = (
    <div title="Outer div">
      <h1>Hello World!</h1>
    </div>
  );
...
```

Note that although it is strikingly close to HTML syntax, it is *not* HTML. Note also that the markup is not
enclosed within quotes, so it is not a string that can be used as an innerHTML either. It is JSX, and it can be
freely mixed with JavaScript.

Now, given all the differences and the complexity in comparison to HTML, why do you need to learn
JSX? What value does it add? Why not write the JavaScript itself directly? One of the things I talked about in
the Introduction chapter is that MERN has just one language throughout; isn't this contrary to that?

As we explore React further, you will soon find that the differences between HTML and JSX are not
earth-shaking and they are very logical. You will not need to remember a lot or need to look up things as long
as you understand and internalize the logic. Though writing JavaScript directly to create the virtual DOM
elements is indeed an option, I find that it is quite tedious and doesn't help me visualize the DOM.

Further, since you probably already know the basic HTML syntax, writing JSX will probably work best.
It is easy to understand how the screen will look when you read JSX, because it is very similar to HTML. So,
for the rest of the book, we use JSX.

But browsers' JavaScript engines don't understand JSX. It has to be transformed into regular JavaScript
based React.createElement() calls. To do this, a compiler is needed. The compiler that does this (and can
do a lot more, in fact) is Babel. We should ideally pre-compile the code and inject it into the browser, but

for prototyping purposes, Babel provides a standalone compiler that can be used in the browser. This is available as a JavaScript file, as usual, at unpkg. Let's include this script within the <head> section of index.html like this:

```
...
  <script src="https://unpkg.com/@babel/standalone@7/babel.min.js"></script>
...
```

But the compiler also needs to be told which scripts have to be transformed. It looks for the attribute type="text/babel" in all scripts and transforms and runs any script with this attribute. So let's add this attribute to the main script for Babel to do its job. Here is the code snippet for doing that:

```
...
  <script type="text/babel">
...
```

The complete set of changes to use JSX is shown in Listing 2-2.

Listing 2-2. index.html: Changes for Using JSX

```
<!DOCTYPE HTML>
<html>

<head>
  <meta charset="utf-8">
  <title>Pro MERN Stack</title>

  <script src="https://unpkg.com/react@16/umd/react.development.js"></script>
  <script src="https://unpkg.com/react-dom@16/umd/react-dom.development.js"></script>

  <script src="https://unpkg.com/@babel/standalone@7/babel.min.js"></script>
</head>

<body>
  <div id="contents"></div>

  <script type="text/babel">
    const element = React.createElement('div', {title: 'Outer div'},
      React.createElement('h1', null, 'Hello World!')
    );
    const element = (
      <div title="Outer div">
        <h1>Hello World!</h1>
      </div>
    );

    ReactDOM.render(element, document.getElementById('contents'));
  </script>
</body>

</html>
```

■ **Note** Although no effort has been spared to ensure that all code listings are accurate, there may be typos or even corrections that did not make it to the book before it went to press. So, always rely on the GitHub repository (https://github.com/vasansr/pro-mern-stack-2) as the tested and up-to-date source for all code listings, especially if something does not work as expected.

When you test this set of changes, you will find no difference in the appearance of the page, but it could be a wee bit slower due to the compilation done by Babel. But don't worry. We'll soon switch to compiling JSX at build-time rather than at runtime to get rid of the performance impact. Note that the code will not work on older browsers yet; you may get errors in the script babel.min.js.

The file index.html can be found under a directory called public in the GitHub repository; this is where the file will eventually end up.

EXERCISE: JSX

1. Remove type="text/babel" from the script. What happens when you load index. html? Can you explain why? Put back type="text/babel" but remove the Babel JavaScript library. What happens now?

2. We used the minified version of Babel, but not for React and ReactDOM. Can you guess why? Switch to the production minified version and introduce a runtime error in React (check out the unpkg.com website for the names of the production versions of these libraries). For example, introduce a typo in the ID of the content node so there is no place to mount the component. What happens?

Answers are available at the end of the chapter.

Project Setup

The server-less setup allowed you to get familiarized with React without any installations or firing up a server. But as you may have noticed, it's good neither for development nor for production. During development, some additional time is introduced for loading the scripts from a Content Delivery Network or CDN. If you take a look at the size of each of the scripts using the Network tab of the browser's developer console, you'll see that the babel compiler (even the minified version) is quite large. On production, especially in larger projects, runtime compilation of JSX to JavaScript will slow down the page loading and affect user experience.

So, let's get a little organized and serve all files from an HTTP server. We will, of course, use some other components of the MERN stack to achieve this. But before we do all that, let's set up our project and folders in which we will be saving the files and installing libraries.

The commands that we will be typing in the shell have been collected together in a file called commands.md in the root of the GitHub repository.

■ **Note**   If you find that something is not working as expected when typing a command, cross-check the commands with the same in the GitHub repository (`https://github.com/vasansr/pro-mern-stack-2`). This is because typos may have been introduced during the production of the book, or last-minute corrections may have missed making it to the book. The GitHub repository, on the other hand, reflects the most up-to-date and tested set of code and commands.

---

nvm

To start, let's install nvm. This stands for Node Version Manager, that tool makes installation and switching between multiple versions of Node.js easy. Node.js can be installed directly without nvm, but I've found that having nvm installed at the very beginning made my life easier when I had to start a new project and I wanted to use the latest and greatest version of Node.js at that point in time. At the same time, I did not want to switch to the newest version for some other of my large projects, for fear of breaking things in those projects.

To install nvm, if you are using Mac OS or any Linux-based distribution, follow the instructions on nvm's GitHub page. This can be found at `https://github.com/creationix/nvm`. Windows users can follow nvm for Windows (search for it in your favorite search engine) or install Node.js directly without nvm. Generally, I advise Windows users to install a Linux virtual machine (VM), preferably using Vagrant, and do all the server-side coding within the VM. This usually works best, especially because the code is finally deployed almost always on a Linux server, and having the same environment for development works best.

One tricky thing about nvm is knowing how it initializes your PATH. This works differently on different operating systems, so make sure you read up the nuances. Essentially, it adds a few lines to your shell's initialization scripts so that the next time you open a shell, your PATH is initialized and executes nvm's initialization scripts. This lets nvm know about the different versions of Node.js that are installed, and the path to the default executable.

For this reason, it's always a good idea to start a new shell right after you install nvm rather than continue in the shell that you installed it. Once you get the right path for your nvm, things follow smoothly.

You may choose to install Node.js directly, without nvm, and that is fine too. But the rest of the chapter assumes that you have installed nvm.

Node.js

Now that we have installed nvm, let's install Node.js using nvm. There are many versions of Node.js available (do check out the website, `https://nodejs.org`), but for the purpose of the book, we'll choose the latest Long Term Support (LTS), which happens to be a minor version of 10:

```
$ nvm install 10
```

The LTS version is assured to have support for a longer term than other versions. This means that although feature upgrades cannot be expected, security and performance fixes that are backward compatible can be expected. Also newer minor versions can be installed without worrying about breaking existing code.

Now that we have installed Node.js, let's make that version the default for the future.

```
$ nvm alias default 10
```

Otherwise, the next time you enter the shell, node will not be in the PATH, or we make pick the previously installed default version. You can confirm the version of node that's been installed as your default by typing the following in a new shell or terminal:

```
$ node --version
```

Also, do make sure that any *new* shell also shows the newest version. (Note that the Windows version of nvm does not support the alias command. You may have to do nvm use 10 each time you open a new shell.)

Installing Node.js via nvm will also install npm, the package manager. If you are installing Node.js directly, ensure that you have installed a compatible version of npm as well. You can confirm this by noting down the version of npm that was installed along with Node.js:

```
$ npm --version
```

It should show version 6 something. npm may prompt you that there is a newer version of npm available and ask you to install that. In any case, let's install the npm version that we wish to use in the book by specifying the version like this:

```
$ npm install -g npm@6
```

Please ensure you don't miss the -g flag. It tells npm to install itself *globally*, that is, available to all projects. To double check, run npm --version again.

Project

Before we install any third-party packages with npm, it's a good idea to initialize the project. With npm, even an application is considered a package. A package defines various attributes of the application. One such important attribute is a list of other packages that the application depends upon. This will change over time, as we find a need to use libraries as we make progress with the application.

To start with, we need at least a placeholder where these things will be saved and initialized. Let's create a directory called pro-mern-stack-2 to host the application. Let's initialize the project from within this directory like this:

```
$ npm init
```

Most questions that this command asks of you should be easy to answer. The defaults will work fine too. From now on, you should be in the project directory for all shell commands, especially npm commands (which I'll describe next). This will ensure that all changes and installations are localized to the project directory.

npm

To install anything using npm, the command to be used is npm install <package>. To start off, and because we need an HTTP server, let's install Express using npm. Installing Express is as simple as:

```
$ npm install express
```

Once done, you will notice that it says many packages are installed. This is because it installs all other packages that Express depends upon as well. Now, let's uninstall and install it again with a specific version. In this book, we use version 4, so let's specify that version when installing.

```
$ npm uninstall express
$ npm install express@4
```

■ **Note**   Specifying the major version alone (in this case 4) will suffice while installing a package. Which means that you may install a minor version that is not the same as what was used when writing this book. In the rare case that this is causing a problem, look up the specific version of the package within `package.json` in the GitHub repository. Then, specify that exact while installing the package, for example, `npm install express@4.16.4`.

---

npm is extremely powerful, and its options are vast. For the moment, we will concern ourselves only with the installation of packages and a few other useful things. The location of the installed files under the project directory is a conscious choice that the makers of npm made. This has the following effect:

1. All installations are *local* to the project directory. This means that a different project can use a different version of any of the installed packages. This may, at first, seem unnecessary and feel like a lot of duplication. But you will really appreciate this feature of npm when you start multiple Node.js projects and don't want to deal with a package upgrade that you don't need. Further, you will notice that the entire Express package, including all dependencies, is just 1.8MB. With packages being so tiny, excessive disk usage is not a concern at all.

2. A package's dependencies are also isolated within the package. Thus, two packages depending on different versions of a common package could be installed, and they would each have their own copy and therefore work flawlessly.

3. Administrator (superuser) rights are not needed to install a package.

There is, of course, an option to install packages globally, and sometimes it is useful to do this. One use case is when a command-line utility is packaged as an npm package. In such cases, having the command-line available regardless of the working directory is quite useful. In such cases, the –g option of npm install can be used to install a package globally and made available everywhere.

If you had installed Node.js via nvm, a global install will use your own home directory and make the package available to all projects within your home directory. You don't need superuser or administrator rights to install a package globally. On the other hand, if you had installed Node.js directly, making it available for all users on your computer, you will need superuser or administrator rights.

At this point in time, it is a good idea to look at the GitHub repository (`https://github.com/vasansr/pro-mern-stack-2`) again, especially to view the differences from the previous step. In this section we only added new files, so the only differences you will see are the new files.

EXERCISE: PROJECT SETUP

---

1. When was `package.json` created? If you can't guess, inspect the contents; that should give you a hint. Still can't figure out? Go back and re-do your steps. Start with creation of the project directory and look at the directory contents at each step.

2. Uninstall Express, but use the option `--no-save`. Now, just type `npm install`. What happens? Add another dependency, say, MongoDB, manually to `package.json` this time. Use version as "latest". Now, type `npm install`. What happens?

3. Use `--save-dev` while installing any new package. What difference do you see in `package.json`? What difference do you think it will make?

4. Where do you think the packages files are installed? Type `npm ls --depth=0` to check all the currently installed packages. Clean up any packages you do not need.

Play around with npm installation and un-installation a bit. This will be useful in general. Learn more about npm version syntax from the documentation: `https://docs.npmjs.com/files/package.json#dependencies`.

Answers are available at the end of the chapter.

■ **Note**   Although it is a good practice to check in the `package.json.lock` file so that the exact versions installed can be shared among team members, I have excluded it from the repository to keep the diffs concise and readable. When you start a team project using the MERN stack, you should check in this file in your Git repository.

Express

Express, if you remember in the introduction in the previous chapter, is the best way to run an HTTP server in the Node.js environment. For starters, we'll use Express to serve only static files. This is so that we get used to what Express does, without getting into a lot of server-side coding. We'll serve the `index.html` file that we created in the previous section via Express.

We had installed Express in the previous step, but to ensure it's there, let's execute the npm command for installing it again. This command does nothing if the package is installed, so when in doubt, we can always run it again.

```
$ npm install express@4
```

To start using Express, let's import the module and use the top-level function that the module exports, in order to instantiate an application. This can be done using the following code:

```
...
const express = require('express');
...
```

require is a JavaScript keyword specific to Node.js, and this is used to import other modules. This keyword is not part of browser-side JavaScript because there was no concept of including other JavaScript files. All needed scripts were included directly in HTML files only. ES2015 specification came up with a way to include other files using the import keyword, but before the specification came out, Node.js had to invent its own using require. It's also known as the CommonJS way of including other modules.

In the previous line, we loaded up the module called express and saved the top-level *thing* that the module exports, in the constant named express. Node.js allows the *thing* to be a function, an object, or whatever can fit into a variable. The type and form of what the module exports is really up to the module, and the documentation of the module will tell you how to use it.

In the case of Express, the module exports a function that can be used to instantiate an application. We just assigned this function to the variable express.

■ **Note**   We used the ES2015 const keyword to define the variable express. This makes the variable non-assignable after the first declaration. For variables that may be assigned a new value, the keyword let can be used in place of const.

An Express application is web server that listens on a specific IP address and port. Multiple applications can be created, which listen on different ports, but we won't do that, as we need just a single server. Let's instantiate the one and only application by calling the express() function:

```
...
const app = express();
...
```

Now that we have a handle to the application, let's set it up. Express is a framework that does minimal work by itself; instead, it gets most of the job done by functions called *middleware*. A middleware is a function that takes in an HTTP request and response object, plus the next middleware function in the chain. The function can look at and modify the request and response objects, respond to requests, or decide to continue with middleware chain by calling the next middleware function.

At this point in time, we need something that looks at a request and returns the contents of a file based on the request URL's path. The built-in express.static function generates a middleware function that does just this. It responds to a request by trying to match the request URL with a file under a directory specified by the parameter to the generator function. If a file exists, it returns the contents of the file as the response, if not, it chains to the next middleware function. This is how we can create the middleware:

```
...
const fileServerMiddleware = express.static('public');
...
```

The argument to the static() function is the directory where the middleware should look for the files, relative to where the app is being run. For the application we'll build as part of this book, we'll store all static files in the public directory under the root of our project. Let's create this new directory, public, under the project root and move index.html that we created in the previous section to this new directory.

Now, for the application to use the static middleware, we need to *mount* it on the application. Middleware in an Express application can be mounted using the use() method of the application. The first argument to this method is the base URL of any HTTP request to match. The second argument is the middleware function itself. Thus, to use the static middleware, we can do this:

```
...
app.use('/', fileServerMiddleware);
...
```

The first argument is optional and defaults to '/' if not specified, so we could skip it too.

Finally, now that the application is set up, we'll need to start the server and let it serve HTTP requests. The listen() method of the application starts the server and waits eternally for requests. It takes in a port number as the first argument. Let's use the port 3000, an arbitrary port. We won't use port 80, the usual HTTP port, because to listen to that port we need to have administrative (superuser) privileges.

The listen() method also takes another argument, an optional callback that can be called when the server has been successfully started. Let's supply an anonymous function that just prints a message that the server has been started, like this:

```
...
app.listen(3000, function () {
  console.log('App started on port 3000');
});
...
```

Let's put all this together in a file called server.js in the root directory of the project. Listing 2-3 shows the final server code, with the use() call merged with the creation of the middleware in a single line, and skipping the optional first argument, the mount point.

Listing 2-3. server.js: Express Server

```
const express = require('express');

const app = express();

app.use(express.static('public'));

app.listen(3000, function () {
  console.log('App started on port 3000');
});
```

Now, we are ready to start the web server and serve index.html. If you are looking at the GitHub repository for the code, you will find server.js under a directory called server. But at this point, the file needs to be in the root of the project directory.

To start the server, run it using the Node.js runtime like this, at the root directory of the project:

```
$ node server.js
```

You should see a message saying the application has started on port 3000. Now, open your browser and type http://localhost:3000/index.html in the URL bar. You should see the same Hello World page that we created in the previous section. If you see a 404 error message, maybe you have not moved index.html to the public directory.

The static middleware function served the contents of the index.html file from the public directory, as it matched the request URL. But it is also smart enough to translate a request to / (the root of the website) and respond by looking for an index.html in the directory. This is similar to what other static web servers such as Apache do. Thus, typing just http://localhost:3000/ is good enough to get the Hello World page.

To start the server, we had to supply the name of the entry point (server.js) to Node.js. This may not be something that is easy to remember or to tell other users of the project. If there were many files in our project, how does anyone know which is the file that starts the server? Fortunately, there is a convention used in all Node.js projects: npm scripts are used to do common tasks. The following command line is an alternative way to start the server:

```
$ npm start
```

When this is executed, npm looks for the file server.js and runs it using Node.js. So, let's stop the server (using Ctrl+C on the command shell) and restart the server using npm start. You should see the same message saying the server has been started.

But what if we had a different starting point for the server? In fact, we want all the server-related files to go into a directory called server. So, let's create that directory and move server.js into that directory.

Now, if you run npm start, it will fail with an error. That's because npm looks for server.js in the root directory and doesn't find it. In order to let npm know that the entry point for the server is server.js within the sub-directory called server, an entry needs to be added to the scripts section of package.json. Listing 2-4 shows these changes.

Listing 2-4. package.json: Changes for Start Script

```
...
  "main": "index.js",
  "scripts": {
    "start": "node server/server.js",
    "test": "echo \"Error: no test specified\" && exit 1"
  },
...
```

Thus, if the server starting point is anything other than server.js in the root directory, the full command line has to be specified in the scripts section of package.json.

Note that there is also a field called main in package.json. When we initialized this file, the value of this field was set to index.js automatically. This field is *not* meant for indicating the starting point of the server. Instead, if the package was a module (as opposed to an application), index.js would have been the file to load when the project is imported as a module using require() in other projects. Since this project is not a module that can be imported in other projects, this field is not of any interest to us, and neither do we have index.js in the source code.

Now, we can use npm start and see the familiar application started message and test it out one final time. At this point in time, it's good to check out the GitHub repository and look at the diffs for this section. In particular, take a look at changes in an existing file, package.json, to familiarize yourself with how changes within a file are shown in the book and how the same changes are seen in GitHub as diffs.

EXERCISE: EXPRESS

1. Change the name of the index.html file to something else, say, hello.html. How does this affect the application?

2. If you wanted all static files to be accessed by a prefixed URL, for example /public, what change would you make? Hint: Take a look at the Express documentation for static files at https://expressjs.com/en/starter/static-files.html.

Answers are available at the end of the chapter.

Separate Script File

In all the previous sections, the transformation of JSX to JavaScript happens at runtime. This is inefficient and quite unnecessary. Let's instead move the transformation to the build stage in our development, so that we can deploy a ready-to-use distribution of the application.

As the first step, we need to separate out the JSX and JavaScript from the all-in-one index.html and refer to it as an external script. This way, we can keep the HTML as pure HTML and all the script that needs compilation in a separate file. Let's call this external script App.jsx and place it in the public directory, so that it can be referred to as /App.jsx from the browser. The contents of the new script file, of course, won't have the <script> tag enclosing it. And, within index.html, let's replace the inline script with a reference to an external source like this:

```
...
  <script type="text/babel" src="/App.jsx"></script>
...
```

Note that the script type text/babel continues to be needed, since the JSX compilation happens in the browser using the Babel library. The newly modified files are listed in Listings 2-5 and 2-6.

Listing 2-5. index.html: Separate HTML and JSX

```
<!DOCTYPE HTML>
<html>

<head>
  <meta charset="utf-8">
  <title>Pro MERN Stack</title>

  <script src="https://unpkg.com/react@16/umd/react.development.js"></script>
  <script src="https://unpkg.com/react-dom@16/umd/react-dom.development.js"></script>

  <script src="https://unpkg.com/@babel/standalone@7/babel.min.js"></script>
</head>

<body>
  <div id="contents"></div>

  <script type="text/babel" src="/App.jsx"></script>
</body>

</html>
```

Listing 2-6. App.jsx: JSX Part Separated Out from the HTML

```
const element = (
  <div title="Outer div">
    <h1>Hello World!</h1>
  </div>
);

ReactDOM.render(element, document.getElementById('contents'));
```

At this point, the app should continue to work as before. If you point your browser to http://localhost:3000, you should see the same Hello World message. But we have only separated the files; we have not moved the transform to build time. The JSX continues to get transformed by the Babel library script, which was executed in the browser. We'll move the transform to build time in the next section.

JSX Transform

Let's now create a new directory to keep all the JSX files, which will be transformed into plain JavaScript and into the public folder. Let's call this directory src and move App.jsx into this directory.

For the transformation, we'll need to install some Babel tools. We need the core Babel library and a command-line interface (CLI) to do the transform. Let's install these using the command:

```
$ npm install --save-dev @babel/core@7 @babel/cli@7
```

To ensure we have the Babel compiler available as a command-line executable, let's try to execute the command babel on the command line and check the version that is installed using the --version option. Since it is not a global install, Babel will not be available in the path. We have to specifically invoke it from its installed location like this:

```
$ node_modules/.bin/babel --version
```

This should give an output similar to this, but the minor version may be different for you, for example, 7.2.5 instead of 7.2.3:

```
7.2.3 (@babel/core 7.2.2)
```

We could have installed @babel/cli globally using the --global (or -g) option of npm. That way, we would have had access to the command in any directory, without having to prefix the path. But as discussed earlier, it's good practice to keep all installations local to a project. This is so that we don't have to deal with version differences of a package across projects. Further, the latest version of npm gives us a convenient command called npx, which resolves the correct *local* path of any executable. This command is available only in npm version 6 onwards. Let's use this command to check the Babel version:

```
$ npx babel --version
```

Next, to transform JSX syntax into regular JavaScript, we need a preset (a kind of plugin that Babel uses). That's because Babel is capable of doing a lot of other transforms (which we'll cover in the next section) and many presets not part of the Babel core library are shipped as a different package. The JSX transform preset is one such preset called preset-react, so let's install it.

```
$ npm install --save-dev @babel/preset-react@7
```

Now we're ready to transform App.jsx into pure JavaScript. The babel command-line takes an input directory with the source files and the presets that are applicable and the output directory as options. For the Hello World application, the source files are in the src directory, so we want the output of the transform to be in the public directory and we want to apply the JSX transform preset, @babel/react. Here's the command line for that:

```
$ npx babel src --presets @babel/react --out-dir public
```

If you look at the output directory `public`, you will see that there is a new file called `App.js` in there. If you open the file in your editor, you can see that the JSX elements have been converted to `React.createElement()` calls. Note that the Babel compilation automatically used the extension `.js` for the output file, which indicates that it is pure JavaScript.

Now, we will need to change the reference in `index.html` to reflect the new extension and remove the script type specification since it is pure JavaScript. Further, we'll no longer need the runtime transformer to be loaded in `index.html`, so we can get rid of the `babel-core` script library specification. These changes are shown in Listing 2-7.

Listing 2-7. index.html: Change in Script Name and Type

```
...
  <script src="https://unpkg.com/@babel/standalone@7/babel.min.js"></script>
...
  <body>
    <div id="contents"></div
    <script src="/App.jsx" type="text/babel"></script>
    script src="/App.js"></script>
  </body>
...
```

If you test this set of changes, you should see that things work as before. For good measure, you could use the browser's developer console to ensure it is `App.js` that's being fetched, and not `App.jsx`. The developer console can be found on most browsers; you may need to look at your browser's documentation for instructions to get to it.

EXERCISE: JSX TRANSFORM

1. Inspect the contents of `App.js`, the output of the transform. You'll find it in the `public` directory. What do you see?

2. Why did we use `--save-dev` while installing `babel-cli`? Hint: Read the npm documentation for the CLI command for install at `https://docs.npmjs.com/cli/install`.

Answers are available at the end of the chapter.

Older Browsers Support

I'd mentioned earlier that the JavaScript code will work in all modern browsers that support ES2015. But what if we need to support older browsers, for example, Internet Explorer? The older browsers don't support things like Arrow Functions and the `Array.from()` method. In fact, running the code at this point in IE 11 or earlier should throw a console error message saying `Object.assign` is not a function.

Let's make some changes to the JavaScript and React to use some of these advanced ES2015 features. Then, let's make changes to support all these features in older browsers as well. To use ES2015 features, instead of showing a message with Hello World in it, let's create an array of continents and construct a message with each continent included in it.

```
...
const continents = ['Africa','America','Asia','Australia','Europe'];
...
```

Now, let's use the `Array.from()` method to construct a new array with a Hello in front of each continent's name and exclamation mark at the end. To do this, we will use the `map()` method of array, taking in an arrow function. We will use string interpolation instead of concatenating the strings. `Array.from()`, Arrow Functions, and string interpolation are both ES2015 features. Using the new mapped array, let's construct the message, which just joins the new array. Here's the code snippet:

```
...
const helloContinents = Array.from(continents, c => `Hello ${c}!`);
const message = helloContinents.join(' ');
...
```

Now, instead of the hard-coded Hello World message, let's use the constructed `message` variable inside the heading element. Similar to ES2015 string interpolation using back-ticks, JSX lets us use any JavaScript expression by enclosing it in curly braces. These will be replaced by the value of the expression. This works not only for HTML text nodes but also within attributes. For example, the class name for an element can be a JavaScript variable. Let's use this feature to set the message to be displayed in the heading.

```
...
    <h1>{message}</h1>
...
```

The full source code of the modified `App.jsx` is shown in Listing 2-8.

Listing 2-8. App.jsx: Changes to Show the World with ES2015 Features

```
const continents = ['Africa','America','Asia','Australia','Europe'];
const helloContinents = Array.from(continents, c => `Hello ${c}!`);
const message = helloContinents.join(' ');

const element = (
  <div title="Outer div">
    <h1>{message}</h1>
  </div>
);

ReactDOM.render(element, document.getElementById('contents'));
```

If you transform this using Babel, restart the server and point a browser at it. You will find that it works on most modern browsers. But, if you look at the transformed file, `App.js`, you will see that the JavaScript itself has not been changed, only the JSX has been replaced with `React.createElement()` calls. This is sure to fail on older browsers that neither recognize the arrow function syntax or the `Array.from()` method.

Babel comes to the rescue again. I talked about other transforms that Babel is capable of, and this includes transforming newer JavaScript features into older JavaScript, that is, ES5. Just like the `react` preset for JSX transformation, there is a plugin for each of these features. For example, there is a plugin called `plugin-transform-arrow-functions`. We can install this plugin and use it in addition to the React preset like this:

```
$ npm install --no-save @babel/plugin-transform-arrow-functions@7
```

We used the --no-save install option because this is a temporary installation, and we don't want package.json to change because of the temporary installation. Let's use this plugin and transform the source file like this:

```
$ npx babel src --presets @babel/react ↵
--plugins=@babel/plugin-transform-arrow-functions --out-dir public
```

Now if you inspect the output of the transform, App.js, you will see that arrow functions have been replaced with regular functions.

That's great, but how does one know which plugins have to be used? It's going to be tedious to find out which browsers support what syntax and what transforms we've to choose for each. Fortunately, Babel does the job of automatically figuring this out via a preset called preset-env. This preset lets us specify the target browsers that we need to support and automatically applies all the transforms and plugins that are required to support those browsers.

So, let's uninstall the transform-arrow-function preset and install instead the env preset that includes all the other plugins.

```
$ npm uninstall @babel/plugin-transform-arrow-functions@7
$ npm install --save-dev @babel/preset-env@7
```

Instead of using the command-line (which can get quite lengthy if we do use it), let's specify the presets that need to be used in a configuration file. Babel looks for this in a file called .babelrc. In fact, there can be a .babelrc file in different directories, and the settings for files in that directory can be specified in each of those separately. Since we have all the client-side code in the directory called src, let's create this file in that directory.

The .babelrc file is a JSON file, which can contain presets as well as plugins. Presets are specified as an array. We can specify both the presets as strings in this array like this:

```
...
{
  "presets": ["@babel/preset-env", "@babel/preset-react"]
}
```

The preset preset-env needs further configuration to specify target browsers and their versions. This can be done by using an array with the first element as the preset name followed by its options. For preset-env, the option that we will use is called targets, which is an object with the key as the browser name and the value as its targeted version:

```
["@babel/preset-env", {
  "targets": {
    "safari": "10",
    ...
  }
}]
```

Let's include support for IE version 11 and slightly older versions of the other popular browsers. The complete configuration file is shown in Listing 2-9.

Listing 2-9. src/.babelrc: Presets Configured for JSX and ES5 Transform

```
{
  "presets": [
    ["@babel/preset-env", {
      "targets": {
        "ie": "11",
        "edge": "15",
        "safari": "10",
        "firefox": "50",
        "chrome": "49"
      }
    }],
    "@babel/preset-react"
  ]
}
```

Now, the babel command can be run without specifying any presets on the command-line:

```
$ npx babel src --out-dir public
```

If you run this command and then inspect the generated App.js, you will find that the arrow function has been replaced with a regular function and also that the string interpolation has been replaced with a string concatenation. If you take out the line ie: "11" from the configuration file and re-run the transform, you'll find that these transformations are no longer there in the output file, because the browsers that we're targeting already support these features natively.

But even with these transformations, if you test on an Internet Explorer version 11, the code will still not work. That's because it's not just the transformations; there are some built-ins such as Array.find() that just aren't there in the browser. Note that no amount of compilation or transformation can add a bunch of code like the Array.find() implementation. We really need these implementations to be available at runtime as a library of functions.

All such function implementations to supplement the missing implementation in older browsers are called *polyfills*. Babel transforms can only deal with syntactic changes, but these polyfills are required to add these new functions' implementations. Babel provides these polyfills too, which can just be included in the HTML file to make these functions available. The Babel polyfill can be found in unpkg, so let's include that in index.html. Listing 2-10 shows the changes to index.html for including the polyfill.

Listing 2-10. index.html: Changes for Including Babel Polyfill

```
...
  <script src="https://unpkg.com/react-dom@16/umd/react-dom.development.js"></script>

  <script src="https://unpkg.com/@babel/polyfill@7/dist/polyfill.min.js"></script>
</head>
...
```

Now, the code can work on Internet Explorer as well. Figure 2-2 shows how the new Hello World screen should look.

Figure 2-2. *The new Hello World screen*

EXERCISE: OLDER BROWSER SUPPORT

1. Try to format the message as one per line by using `<br />` to join the individual messages instead of a space. Are you able to do it? Why not?

Answers are available at the end of the chapter.

Automate

Apart from being able to start the project using `npm start`, npm has the ability to define other custom commands. This is especially useful when there are many command line parameters for the command and typing them out on the shell becomes tedious. (Didn't I say npm was powerful? This is one of the things that it does, even though this is not real package manager functionality.) These custom commands can be specified in the scripts section of `package.json`. These can then be run using `npm run <script>` from the console.

Let's add a script called `compile` whose command line is the Babel command line to do all the transforms. We don't need the `npx` prefix because npm automatically figures out the location of commands that are part of any locally installed packages. The addition we'll need to do in `package.json` is thus:

```
...
    "compile": "babel src --out-dir public",
...
```

The transform can now be run like this:

```
$ npm run compile
```

After this, if you run `npm start` again to start the server, you can see any changes to `App.jsx` reflected in the application.

> ■ **Note** Avoid using npm sub-command names that are also npm first-level commands such as `build` and `rebuild`, as this leads to silent errors if and when you leave out the `run` in the npm command.

When we work on the client-side code and change the source files frequently, we have to manually recompile it for every change. Wouldn't it be nice if someone could detect these changes for us and recompile the source into JavaScript? Well, Babel supports this out of the box via the `--watch` option. To make use of it, let's add another script called `watch` with this additional option to the Babel command line:

```
...
    "watch": "babel src --out-dir public --watch --verbose"
...
```

It is essentially the same command as compile, but with two extra command line options, `--watch` and `--verbose`. The first option instructs Babel to watch for changes in source files, and the second one causes it to print out a line in the console whenever a change causes a recompilation. This is just to give a reassurance that a compile has in fact taken place whenever a change is made, provided you keep a watch on the console running this command.

A similar restart on changes to the server code can be affected by using a wrapper command called nodemon. This command restarts Node.js with the command specified whenever there is a change in a set of files. You may also find by searching the Internet that `forever` is another package that can be used to achieve the same goal. Typically, `forever` is used to restart the server on crashes rather than watch for changes to files. The best practice is to use nodemon during development (where watching for changes is the real need) and forever on production (where restarting on crashes is the need). So, let's install nodemon now:

```
$ npm install nodemon@1
```

Now, let's use nodemon to start the server instead of Node.js in the script specification for `start` in `package.json`. The command nodemon also needs an option to indicate which files or directory to watch changes for using the `-w` option. Since all the server files are going to be in the directory called `server`, we can use `-w server` to make nodemon restart Node.js when any file in that directory changes. So, the new command for the start script within `package.json` will now be:

```
...
    "start": "nodemon -w server server/server.js"
...
```

The final set of scripts added or changed in `package.json` is shown in Listing 2-11.

Listing 2-11. Package.json: Adding Scripts for Transformation

```
...
  "scripts": {
    "start": "node server/server.js",
    "start": "nodemon -w server server/server.js",
    "compile": "babel src --out-dir public",
    "watch": "babel src --out-dir public --watch --verbose",
    "test": "echo \"Error: no test specified\" && exit 1"
  },
...
```

If you now run the new command using `npm run watch`, you will notice that it does one transform, but it doesn't return to the shell. It's actually waiting in a permanent loop, watching for changes to the source files. So, to run the server, another terminal is needed, where `npm start` can be executed.

If you make make a small change to `App.jsx` and save the file, you'll see that `App.js` in the `public` directory is regenerated. And, when you refresh the browser, you can see those changes without having to manually recompile. You can also make any changes to `server.js` and see that the server starts, with a message on the console that says the server is being restarted.

Summary

In this chapter, you learned the basics of how React applications can be built. We started with a simple piece of code written in React JSX that we compiled at runtime, then we moved the compilation as well as serving the file to the server.

We used nvm to install Node.js; you saw how npm can be used not just to install Node.js packages, but also to save command-line instructions in conventional or easy-to-spot scripts. We then used Babel, to *transpile*, that is, transform or compile from one specification of the language to another to support older browsers. Babel also helped us transform JSX into pure JavaScript.

You also got a whiff of what Node.js with Express can do. We did not use MongoDB, the M in the MERN stack, but I hope you got a good view of the other components of the stack.

By now, you should also have gotten familiar with how the book's GitHub repository is organized and the conventions used in the book. For every section, there is a testable set of code that you can compare your own typed out code with. Importantly, the diffs between each step are valuable to understand the exact changes that were made in each step. Once again, note that the code in the GitHub repository is the one to rely on, with up-to-date changes that couldn't make it to the printed book. If you find that you have followed the book verbatim, yet things don't work as expected, do consult the GitHub repository to see if the printed book's errors have been corrected there.

In the next two chapters, we'll dive deeper into React, then surface up to look at the big picture, dealing with APIs, MongoDB, and Express in later chapters.

Answers to Exercises

Exercise: Server-less Hello World

1. To specify a class in `React.createElement()`, we need to use `{ className: <name>}` instead of `{class: <name>}`. This is because `class` is a reserved word in JavaScript, and we cannot use it as a field name in objects.

2. The `element` variable contains a nested tree of elements, which reflects what the DOM would contain. I would call this a *virtual DOM*, which is what it is indeed popularly referred to as.

Exercise: JSX

1. Removing the script type will cause the browser to treat it as regular JavaScript and we will see syntax errors on the console because JSX is not valid JavaScript. Removing the Babel compiler instead will cause the script to be ignored, since the browser does not recognize scripts of type `text/babel`, and it will ignore it. In either case, the application will not work.

2. A minified version of React hides or shortens runtime errors. A non-minified version gives full errors and helpful warnings as well.

Exercise: Project Setup

1. package.json was created when we created the project using npm init. In fact, all our responses to the prompts when we ran npm init were recorded in package.json.

2. When using --no-save, npm keeps the file package.json unchanged. Thus, package.json would have retained the dependency of Express. Running npm install without any further options or parameters installs all dependencies listed in package.json. Thus, you could add dependencies manually to package.json and just use npm install.

3. The --save-dev option adds the package in devDependencies instead of dependencies. The list of dev dependencies will not be installed in production, which is indicated by the environment variable NODE_ENV being set to the string production.

4. Package files are installed under the directory node_modules under the project. npm ls lists all the packages installed, in a tree-like manner. --depth=0 restricts the tree depth to the top-level packages. Deleting the entire node_modules directory is one way of ensuring you start clean.

Exercise: Express

1. The static file middleware does not specially treat hello.html as it did index.html, so you will have to access the application with the name of the file like this: http://localhost:3000/hello.html.

2. For accessing static files via a different mount point, specify that prefix in the middleware generated helper function as the first parameter. For example, app.use('/public', express.static('/public')).

Exercise: JSX Transform

1. App.js now contains pure JavaScript, with all JSX elements converted to React.createElement() calls. We couldn't see this transform earlier when the transform happened in the browser.

2. When we deploy the code, we will only deploy a pre-built version of the application. That is, we will transform the JSX on a build server or our development environment and push out the resulting JavaScript to our production server. Thus, on the production server, we will not need the tools that are required to build the application. Therefore, we used --save-dev so that, on the production server, the package need not be installed.

Exercise: Older Browsers Support

1. React does this on purpose, to avoid cross-site scripting vulnerabilities. It is not easy to insert HTML markup, although there is a way using the dangerouslySetInnerHTML attribute of an element. The correct way to do this would be to compose an array of components. We will explore how to do this in later chapters.

## CHAPTER 3

React Components

In the Hello World example, we created a very basic React native component, using pure JSX. However, in the real world, you will want to do much more than what a simple single-line JSX can do. That is where React components come in. React components can be composed using other components and basic HTML elements; they can respond to user input, change state, interact with other components, and much more.

But, before going into all that detail, let me first describe the application that we will build as part of this book. At every step that we take in this as well as the following chapters, we'll take features of the application or tasks that need to be performed one by one and address them. I like this approach because I've learned things the best when I put them to immediate use. This approach not only lets you appreciate and internalize the concepts because you put them to use, but also brings the more useful and practical concepts to the forefront.

The application I've come up with is something that most developers can relate to.

Issue Tracker

I'm sure that most of you are familiar with GitHub Issues or Jira. These applications help you create a bunch of issues or bugs, assign them to people, and track their statuses. These are essentially CRUD applications (Create, Read, Update, and Delete a record in a database) that manage a list of objects or entities. The CRUD pattern is so useful because pretty much all enterprise applications are built around the CRUD pattern on different entities or objects.

In the case of the Issue Tracker, we'll only deal with a single object or record, because that's good enough to depict the pattern. Once you grasp the fundamentals of how to implement the CRUD pattern in MERN, you'll be able to replicate the pattern and create a real-life application.

Here's the requirement list for the Issue Tracker application, a simplified or toned-down version of GitHub Issues or Jira:

- The user should be able to view a list of issues, with an ability to filter the list by various parameters.

- The user should be able to add new issues, by supplying the initial values of the issue's fields.

- The user should be able to edit and update an issue by changing its field values.

- The user should be able delete an issue.

An issue should have following attributes:

- A title that summarizes the issue (freeform long text)

- An owner to whom the issue is assigned (freeform short text)

- A status indicator (a list of possible status values)

- Creation date (a date, automatically assigned)

- Effort required to address the issue (number of days, a number)

- Estimated completion date or due date (a date, optional)

Note that I've included different types of fields (lists, date, number, text) to make sure you learn how to deal with different data types. We'll start simple, build one feature at a time, and learn about the MERN stack as we go along.

In this chapter, we'll create React classes and instantiate components. We'll also create bigger components by putting together smaller components. Finally, we'll pass data among these components and create components dynamically from data. In terms of features, the objective in this chapter is to lay out the main page of the Issue Tracker: a list of issues. We'll hard-code the data that is used to display the page and leave retrieval of the data from the server to a later chapter.

React Classes

In this section, the objective is to convert the single-line JSX into a simple React component instantiated from a React class, so that we can later use the full power of the first class React components.

React classes are used to create real components (as opposed to templated HTML where we created a Hello World message based on a variable, which we created in the previous chapter). These classes can then be reused within other components, handle events, and so much more. To start with, let's replace the Hello World example with a simple class forming the starting point for the Issue Tracker application.

React classes are created by extending `React.Component`, the base class from which all custom classes must be derived. Within the class definition, at the minimum, a `render()` method is needed. This method is what React calls when it needs to display the component in the UI.

There are other methods with special meaning to React that can be implemented, called the Lifecycle methods. These provide hooks into various stages of the component formation and other events. We'll discuss other Lifecycle functions in later chapters. But `render()` is one that *must* be present, otherwise the component will have no screen presence. The `render()` function is supposed to return an element (which can be either a native HTML element such as a `<div>` or an instance of another React component).

Let's change the Hello World example from a simple element to use a React class called `HelloWorld`, extended from `React.Component`:

```
...
class HelloWorld extends React.Component {
  ...
}
...
```

■ **Note**   We used the ES2015 `class` keyword and the `extends` keyword to define a JavaScript class. React recommends the use of ES2015 classes. If you are not familiar with JavaScript classes, read up and learn about classes starting at `https://developer.mozilla.org/en-US/docs/Web/JavaScript/Reference/Classes`.

Now, within this class, a render() method is needed, which should return an element. We'll use the same JSX <div> with the message as the returned element.

```
...
  render() {
    return (
      <div title="Outer div">
        <h1>{message}</h1>
      </div>
    );
...
```

Let's also move all the code for message construction to within the render() function so that it remains encapsulated within the scope where it is needed rather than polluting the global namespace.

```
...
  render() {
    const continents = ['Africa','America','Asia','Australia','Europe'];
    const helloContinents = Array.from(continents, c => `Hello ${c}!`);
    const message = helloContinents.join(' ');

    return (
      ...
    );
...
```

In essence, the JSX element is now returned from the render() method of the component class called Hello World. The brackets around the JSX representation of the Hello World element are not necessary, but it is a convention that is normally used to make the code more readable, especially when the JSX spans multiple lines.

Just as an instance of a div element was created using JSX of the form <div></div>, an instance of the HelloWorld class can be created like this:

```
...
const element = <HelloWorld />;
...
```

Now, this element can be used in place of the <div> element to render inside the node called contents, as before. It's worth noting here that div and h1 are built-in internal React components or elements that could be directly instantiated. Whereas HelloWorld is something that *we* defined and later instantiated. And within HelloWorld, we used React's built-in div component. The new, changed App.jsx is shown in Listing 3-1.

In the future, I may use component and component class interchangeably, like sometimes we tend to do with classes and objects. But it should be obvious by now that HelloWorld and div are actually React component classes, whereas <HelloWorld /> and <div /> are tangible components or instances of the component class. Needless to say, there is only one HelloWorld class, but many HelloWorld components can be instantiated based on this class.

Listing 3-1. App.jsx: A Simple React Class and Instance

```
class HelloWorld extends React.Component {
  render() {
    const continents = ['Africa','America','Asia','Australia','Europe'];
    const helloContinents = Array.from(continents, c => `Hello ${c}!`);
    const message = helloContinents.join(' ');

    return (
      <div title="Outer div">
        <h1>{message}</h1>
      </div>
    );
  }
}

const element = <HelloWorld />;

ReactDOM.render(element, document.getElementById('contents'));
```

By now you should be running npm run watch in a console and have started the server using npm start in a separate console. Thus, any changes to App.jsx should have been automatically compiled. So, if you refresh your browser, you should see the greeting with all the continents, just as before.

EXERCISE: REACT CLASSES

1. In the render function, instead of returning one <div>, try returning two <div> elements placed one after the other. What happens? Why, and what's the solution? Ensure you look at the console running npm run watch.

2. Create a runtime error for the React library by changing the string 'contents' to 'main' or some other string that doesn't identify an element in the HTML. Where can one see the error? What about JavaScript runtime errors like undefined variable references?

Answers are available at the end of the chapter.

Composing Components

In the previous section, you saw how to build a component by putting together built-in React components that are HTML element equivalents. It's possible to build a component that uses other user-defined components as well, and that's what we will explore in this section.

Component composition is one of the most powerful features of React. This way, the UI can be split into smaller independent pieces so that each piece can be coded and reasoned in isolation, making it easier to build and understand a complex UI. Using components rather than building the UI in a monolithic fashion also encourages reuse. We'll see in a later chapter how one of the components that we built could easily be reused, even though we hadn't thought of reuse at the time of building the component.

A component takes inputs (called properties) and its output is the rendered UI of the component. In this section, we will not use inputs, but put together fine-grained components to build a larger UI. Here are a few things to remember when composing components:

- Larger components should be split into fine-grained components when there is a logical separation possible between the fine-grained components. In this section we'll create logically separated components.

- When there is an opportunity for reuse, components can be built which take in different inputs from different callers. When we build specialized widgets for user inputs in Chapter 10, we will be creating reusable components.

- React's philosophy prefers component composition in preference to inheritance. For example, a specialization of an existing component can be done by passing properties to the generic component rather than inheriting from it. You can read more about this at https://reactjs.org/docs/composition-vs-inheritance.html.

- In general, remember to keep coupling between components to a minimum (coupling is where one component needs to *know* about the details of another component, including parameters or properties passed between them).

Let's design the main page of the application to show a list of issues, with an ability to filter the issues and create a new issue. Thus, it will have three parts: a filter to select which issues to display, the list of issues, and finally an entry form for adding an issue. We're focusing on composing the components at this point in time, so we'll only use placeholders for these three parts. The structure and hierarchy of the user interface is shown in Figure 3-1.

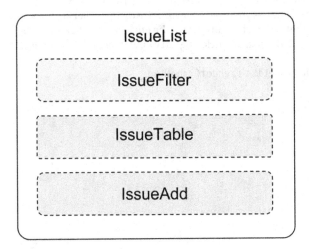

Figure 3-1. *Structure of the Issue List page*

Let's define three placeholder classes—IssueFilter, IssueTable, and IssueAdd—with just a placeholder text within a <div> in each. The IssueFilter component will look like this:

```
...
class IssueFilter extends React.Component {
  render() {
    return (
      <div>This is a placeholder for the issue filter.</div>
    );
  }
}
...
```

The other two classes—IssueTable and IssueAdd—will be similar, with a different placeholder message each:

```
...
class IssueTable extends React.Component {
    ...
        <div>This is a placeholder for a table of issues.</div>
...
class IssueAdd extends React.Component {
    ...
        <div>This is a placeholder for a form to add an issue.</div>
...
```

To put these together, let's remove the Hello World class and add a class called IssueList.

```
...
class IssueList extends React.Component {
}
...
```

Now let's add a render() method. Within this method, let's add an instance of each of the new placeholder classes separated by a <hr> or horizontal line. As you saw in the exercise of the earlier section, since the return of render() has to be a single element, these elements have to be enclosed within a <div> or a React Fragment component. The Fragment component is like an enclosing <div> but it has no effect on the DOM.

Let's use a Fragment component like this in the IssueList's render() method:

```
...
  render() {
    return (
      <React.Fragment>
        <h1>Issue Tracker</h1>
        <IssueFilter />
        <hr />
        <IssueTable />
        <hr />
        <IssueAdd />
      </React.Fragment>
    );
  }
...
```

Finally, instead of instantiating a HelloWorld class, let's instantiate the IssueList class, which we will place under the contents div.

```
...
const element = <HelloWorld />;
const element = <IssueList />;
...
```

46

Ideally, each component should be written as an independent file. But at the moment, we only have placeholders, so for the sake of brevity, we'll keep all the classes in the same file. Also, you haven't learned how to put multiple class files together. At a later stage, when the classes are expanded to their actual content and we also have a way of building or referring to once class from another, we'll separate them out.

Listing 3-2 shows the new contents of the App.jsx file with all the component classes.

Listing 3-2. App.jsx: Composing Components

```
class IssueFilter extends React.Component {
  render() {
    return (
      <div>This is a placeholder for the issue filter.</div>
    );
  }
}

class IssueTable extends React.Component {
  render() {
    return (
      <div>This is a placeholder for a table of issues.</div>
    );
  }
}

class IssueAdd extends React.Component {
  render() {
    return (
      <div>This is a placeholder for a form to add an issue.</div>
    );
  }
}

class IssueList extends React.Component {
  render() {
    return (
      <React.Fragment>
        <h1>Issue Tracker</h1>
        <IssueFilter />
        <hr />
        <IssueTable />
        <hr />
        <IssueAdd />
      </React.Fragment>
    );
  }
}

const element = <IssueList />;

ReactDOM.render(element, document.getElementById('contents'));
```

The effect of this code will be an uninteresting page, as shown in Figure 3-2.

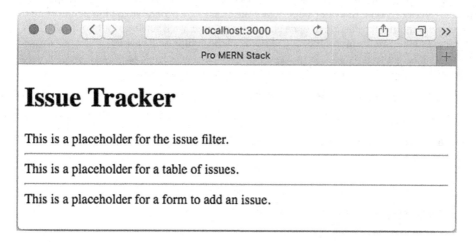

Figure 3-2. *Issue Tracker by composing components*

EXERCISE: COMPOSING COMPONENTS

1. Inspect the DOM in the developer console. Do you see any HTML element corresponding to the `React.Fragment` component? How do you think this can be useful as compared to using a `<div>` element to enclose the various elements?

Answers are available at the end of the chapter.

Passing Data Using Properties

Composing components without any variables is not so interesting. It should be possible to pass different input data from a parent component to a child component and make it render differently on different instances. In the Issue Tracker application, one such component that can be instantiated with different inputs is a table-row showing an individual issue. Depending on the inputs (an issue), the row can display different data. The new structure of the UI is shown in Figure 3-3.

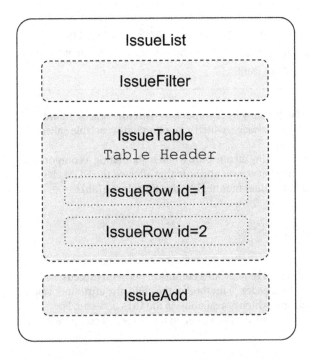

Figure 3-3. Issue List UI hierarchy with issue rows

So, let's create a component called IssueRow, and then use this multiple times within IssueTable, passing in different data to show different issues, like this:

```
...
class IssueTable extends React.Component {
  render() {
    return (
      <table>
        <thead>
          <tr>
            <th>ID</th>
            <th>Title</th>
          </tr>
        </thead>
        <tbody>
          <IssueRow /> {/* somehow pass Issue 1 data to this */}
          <IssueRow /> {/* somehow pass Issue 2 data to this */}
        </tbody>
      </table>
    );
  }
}
...
```

> ■ **Note** JSX does not support comments natively. In order to add comments, a JavaScript snippet has to be added that has JavaScript style comments. Thus, the form {/* ... */} can be used to place comments within JSX. Using HTML style comments like <!-- ... --> will not work.

In fact, the way to switch to the JavaScript world within any JSX snippet is to use curly braces. In the previous chapter, we used this to display the Hello World message, which was a JavaScript variable called message using the syntax {message}.

The easiest way to pass data to child components is using an attribute when instantiating a component. We used the title attribute in the previous chapter, but that was an attribute that affected the DOM element in the end. Any custom attribute can also be passed in a similar manner like this from IssueTable:

```
...
    <IssueRow issue_title="Title of the first issue" />
...
```

We used the name issue_title rather than simply title to avoid a confusion between this custom attribute and the HTML title attribute. Now, within the render() method of the child, the attribute's value can be accessed via a special object variable called props, which is available via the this accessor. For example, this is how the value of issue_title can be displayed within a cell in the IssueRow component:

```
...
    <td>{this.props.issue_title}</td>
...
```

In this case, we passed across a simple string. Other data types and even JavaScript objects can be passed this way. Any JavaScript expression can be passed along, by using curly braces ({}) instead of quotes, because the curly braces switches into the JavaScript world.

So, let's pass the issue's title (as a string), its ID (as a number), and the row style (as an object) from IssueTable to IssueRow. Within the IssueRow class, we'll use these passed-in properties to display the ID and title and set the style of the row, by accessing these properties through this.props.

The code for the complete IssueRow class is shown in Listing 3-3.

Listing 3-3. App.jsx: IssueRow Component, Accessing Passed-in Properties

```
class IssueRow extends React.Component {
  render() {
    const style = this.props.rowStyle;
    return (
      <tr>
        <td style={style}>{this.props.issue_id}</td>
        <td style={style}>{this.props.issue_title}</td>
      </tr>
    );
  }
}
```

We used the attribute style for the table-cell just as we would have used it in regular HTML. But note that this is not really an HTML attribute. Instead, it is a *property* being passed on to the built-in React component <td>. It's just that the style property in the td component is interpreted and set as the HTML style attribute. In most cases, like `style`, the name of the attribute is the same as the HTML attribute, but for a few attributes causing conflict with JavaScript reserved words, naming requirements are different. Thus, the `class` HTML attribute needs to be `className` in JSX. Also, hyphens in the HTML attributes need to be replaced by camel cased names, for example, `max-length` becomes `maxLength` in JSX.

A complete list of DOM elements and how attributes for these need to be specified can be found in the React Documentation at `https://reactjs.org/docs/dom-elements.html`.

Now that we have an `IssueRow` component receiving the properties, let's pass them from the parent, `IssueTable`. The ID and the title are straightforward, but the style we need to pass on has a special convention of specification in React and JSX.

Rather than a CSS kind of string, React needs it to be specified as an object with a specific convention containing a series of JavaScript key-value pairs. The keys are the same as the CSS style name, except that instead of dashes (like `border-collapse`), they are camel cased (like `borderCollapse`). The values are CSS style values, just as in CSS. There is also a special shorthand for specifying pixel values; you can just use a number (like 4) instead of a string `"4px"`.

Let's give the rows a silver border of one pixel and some padding, say four pixels. The style object that would encapsulate this specification would be as follows:

```
...
    const rowStyle = {border: "1px solid silver", padding: 4};
...
```

This can be passed on to the `IssueRow` component using `rowStyle={rowStyle}` when instantiating it. This, and the other variables, can be passed to `IssueRow` while instantiating it like this:

```
...
<IssueRow rowStyle={rowStyle} issue_id={1}
  issue_title="Error in console when clicking Add" />
...
```

Note that we are not using string-like quotes for the Issue ID since it is a number or for `rowStyle` since it is an object. We instead use the curly braces, which makes it a JavaScript expression.

Now, let's construct the `IssueTable` component, which is essentially a `<table>`, with a header row and two columns (ID and title), and two hard-coded `IssueRow` components. Let's also specify an inline style for the table to indicate a collapsed border and use the same `rowStyle` variable to specify the header row styles, to make it look uniform.

Listing 3-4 shows the modified `IssueTable` component class.

Listing 3-4. App.jsx: IssueTable Passing Data to IssueRow

```
class IssueTable extends React.Component {
  render() {
    const rowStyle = {border: "1px solid silver", padding: 4};
    return (
      <table style={{borderCollapse: "collapse"}}>
        <thead>
          <tr>
            <th style={rowStyle}>ID</th>
            <th style={rowStyle}>Title</th>
          </tr>
        </thead>
```

```
      <tbody>
        <IssueRow rowStyle={rowStyle} issue_id={1}
          issue_title="Error in console when clicking Add" />
        <IssueRow rowStyle={rowStyle} issue_id={2}
          issue_title="Missing bottom border on panel" />
      </tbody>
    </table>
  );
  }
}
```

Figure 3-4 shows the effect of these changes in the code.

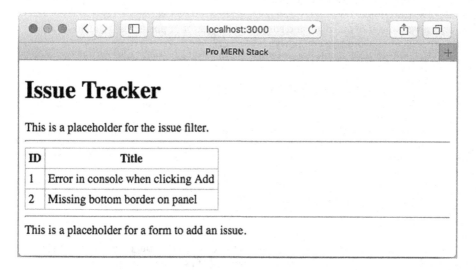

Figure 3-4. *Passing data to child components*

EXERCISE: PASSING DATA USING PROPERTIES

1. Try adding an attribute border=1 for the table, as we would in regular HTML. What happens? Why? Hint: Read up the section titled "All Supported HTML Attributes" in the "DOM Elements" section of the React API Reference.

2. Why is there a double curly brace in the inline style for the table? Hint: Compare it to the other style, where we declared a variable and used that instead of specifying it inline.

3. The curly braces are a way to escape into JavaScript in the middle of JSX markup. Compare this to similar techniques in other templating languages such as PHP.

Answers are available at the end of the chapter.

Passing Data Using Children

There is another way to pass data to other components, using the contents of the HTML-like node of the component. In the child component, this can be accessed using a special field of this.props called this. props.children.

Just like in regular HTML, React components can be nested. In the Hello World example, we nested a <h1> element inside a <div>. When the components are converted to HTML elements, the elements nest in the same order. React components can act like the <div> and take in nested elements. In such cases, the JSX expression will need to include both the opening and closing tags, with *child* elements nested in them.

But then, when the parent React component renders, the children are not automatically under it because the structure of the parent React component needs to determine where exactly the children will appear. So, React lets the parent component access the children element using this.props.children and lets the parent component determine where it needs to be displayed. This works great when one needs to wrap other components within a parent component. For example, a wrapper <div> that adds a border and a padding can be defined like this:

```
...
class BorderWrap extends React.Component {
  render() {
    const borderedStyle = {border: "1px solid silver", padding: 6};
    return (
      <div style={borderedStyle}>
        {this.props.children}
      </div>
    );
  }
}
...
```

Then, during the rendering, *any* component could be wrapped with a padded border like this:

```
...
  <BorderWrap>
    <ExampleComponent />
  </BorderWrap>
...
```

Thus, instead of passing the issue title as a property to IssueRow, this technique could be used to embed it as the child contents of <IssueRow> like this:

```
...
  <IssueRow issue_id={1}>Error in console when clicking Add</IssueRow>
...
```

Now, within the render() method of IssueRow, instead of referring to this.props.issue_title, it will need to be referred to as this.props.children, like this:

```
...
  <td style={borderedStyle}>{this.props.children}</td>
...
```

Let's modify the application to use this method of passing data from IssueTable to IssueRow. Let's also pass in a nested title element as children, one that is a <div> and includes an emphasized piece of text. This change is shown in Listing 3-5.

Listing 3-5. App.jsx: Using Children Instead of Props

```
...
class IssueRow extends React.Component {
...
    return (
      <tr>
        <td style={style}>{this.props.issue_id}</td>
        <td style={style}>{this.props.issue_title}</td>
        <td style={style}>{this.props.children}</td>
      </tr>
    );
...
}
...
...
class IssueTable extends React.Component {
...
        <tbody>
          <IssueRow rowStyle={rowStyle} issue_id={1}
            issue_title="Error in console when clicking Add" />
          <IssueRow rowStyle={rowStyle} issue_id={2}
            issue_title="Missing bottom border on panel" />
          <IssueRow rowStyle={rowStyle} issue_id={1}>
            Error in console when clicking Add
          </IssueRow>
          <IssueRow rowStyle={rowStyle} issue_id={2}>
            <div>Missing <b>bottom</b> border on panel</div>
          </IssueRow>
        </tbody>
...
```

The result of these changes on the output will be minimal, just a little formatting in the title of the second issue will be visible. This is shown in Figure 3-5.

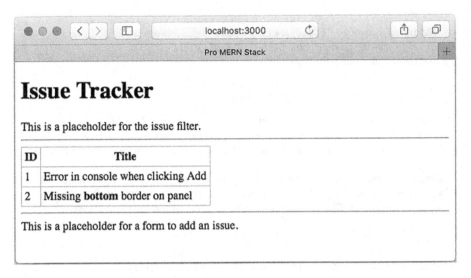

Figure 3-5. *Passing data to child components*

Dynamic Composition

In this section, we'll replace our hard-coded set of `IssueRow` components with a programmatically generated set of components from an array of issues. In later chapters we'll get more sophisticated by fetching the list of issues from a database, but for the moment, we'll use a simple in-memory JavaScript array to store a list of issues.

Let's also expand the scope of the issue from just an ID and a title to include as many fields of an issue as we can. Listing 3-6 shows this in-memory array, declared globally at the beginning of the file `App.jsx`. It has just two issues. The field due is left undefined in the first record, to ensure that we handle the fact that this is an optional field.

Listing 3-6. App.jsx: In-Memory Array of Issues

```
const issues = [
  {
    id: 1, status: New', owner: 'Ravan', effort: 5,
    created: new Date('2018-08-15'), due: undefined,
    title: 'Error in console when clicking Add',
  },
```

```
  {
    id: 2, status: 'Assigned', owner: 'Eddie', effort: 14,
    created: new Date('2018-08-16'), due: new Date('2018-08-30'),
    title: 'Missing bottom border on panel',
  },
];
```

You can add more example issues, but two issues are enough to demonstrate dynamic composition. Now, let's modify the IssueTable class to use this array of issues rather than the hard-coded list. Within the IssueTable class' render() method, let's iterate over the array of issues and generate an array of IssueRows from it.

The map() method of Array comes in handy for doing this, as we can map an issue object to an IssueRow instance. Also, instead of passing each field as a property, let's pass the issue object itself because there are many fields as part of the object. This is one way to do it, in-place within the table's body:

```
...
  <tbody>
    {issues.map(issue => <IssueRow rowStyle={rowStyle} issue={issue}/>)}
  </tbody>
...
```

If you wanted to use a for loop instead of the map() method, you can't do that within the JSX, as JSX is not really a templating language. It only can allow JavaScript expressions within the curly braces. We'll have to create a variable in the render() method and use that in the JSX. Let's create that variable for the set of issue rows like that anyway for readability:

```
...
  const issueRows = issues.map(issue => <IssueRow rowStyle={rowStyle} issue={issue}/>);
...
```

Now, we can replace the two hard-coded issue components inside IssueTable with this variable within the <tbody> element like this:

```
...
  <tbody>
    {issueRows}
  </tbody>
...
```

In other frameworks and templating languages, creating multiple elements using a template would have required a special for loop construct (e.g., ng-repeat in AngularJS) within that templating language. But in React, regular JavaScript can be used for all programmatic constructs. This not only gives you the full power of JavaScript to manipulate templates, but also a lesser number of constructs to learn and remember.

The header row in the IssueTable class will now need to have one column for each of the issue fields, so let's do that as well. But by now, specifying the style for each cell is becoming tedious, so let's create a class for the table, name it table-bordered, and use CSS to style the table and each table-cell instead. This style will need to be part of index.html, and Listing 3-7 shows the changes to that file.

Listing 3-7. index.html: Styles for Table Borders

```
...
  <script src="https://unpkg.com/@babel/polyfill@7/dist/polyfill.min.js"></script>
  <style>
    table.bordered-table th, td {border: 1px solid silver; padding: 4px;}
    table.bordered-table {border-collapse: collapse;}
  </style>
</head>
...
```

Now, we can remove rowStyle from all the table-cells and table-headers. One last thing that needs to be done is to identify each instance of IssueRow with an attribute called key. The value of this key can be anything, but it has to uniquely identify a row. React needs this key so that it can optimize the calculation of differences when things change, for example, when a new row is inserted. We can use the ID of the issue as the key, as it uniquely identifies the row.

The final IssueTable class with a dynamically generated set of IssueRow components and the modified header is shown in Listing 3-8.

Listing 3-8. App.jsx: IssueTable Class with IssueRows Dynamically Generated and Modified Header

```
class IssueTable extends React.Component {
  render() {
    const issueRows = issues.map(issue =>
      <IssueRow key={issue.id} issue={issue} />
    );

    return (
      <table className="bordered-table">
        <thead>
          <tr>
            <th>ID</th>
            <th>Status</th>
            <th>Owner</th>
            <th>Created</th>
            <th>Effort</th>
            <th>Due Date</th>
            <th>Title</th>
          </tr>
        </thead>
        <tbody>
          {issueRows}
        </tbody>
      </table>
    );
  }
}
```

The changes in IssueRow are quite simple. The inline styles have to be removed, and a few more columns need to be added, one for each of the added fields. Since React does not automatically call toString() on objects that are to be displayed, the dates have to be explicitly converted to strings. The toString() method results in a long string, so let's use toDateString() instead. Since the field due is optional, we need to also check for its presence before calling `toDateString()` on it. An easy way to do this is to use the ternary ? - : operator in an expression like this:

```
...
  issue.due ? issue.due.toDateString() : ''
...
```

The ternary operator is handy because it is a JavaScript expression, and it can be used directly in place of the display string. Otherwise, to use an `if-then-else` statement, the code would have to be outside the JSX part, in the beginning of the `render()` method implementation. The new `IssueRow` class is shown in Listing 3-9.

Listing 3-9. App.jsx: New IssueRow Class Using Issue Object Property

```
class IssueRow extends React.Component {
  render() {
    const issue = this.props.issue;
    return (
      <tr>
        <td>{issue.id}</td>
        <td>{issue.status}</td>
        <td>{issue.owner}</td>
        <td>{issue.created.toDateString()}</td>
        <td>{issue.effort}</td>
        <td>{issue.due ? issue.due.toDateString() : ''}</td>
        <td>{issue.title}</td>
      </tr>
    );
  }
}
```

After these changes, the screen should look like Figure 3-6.

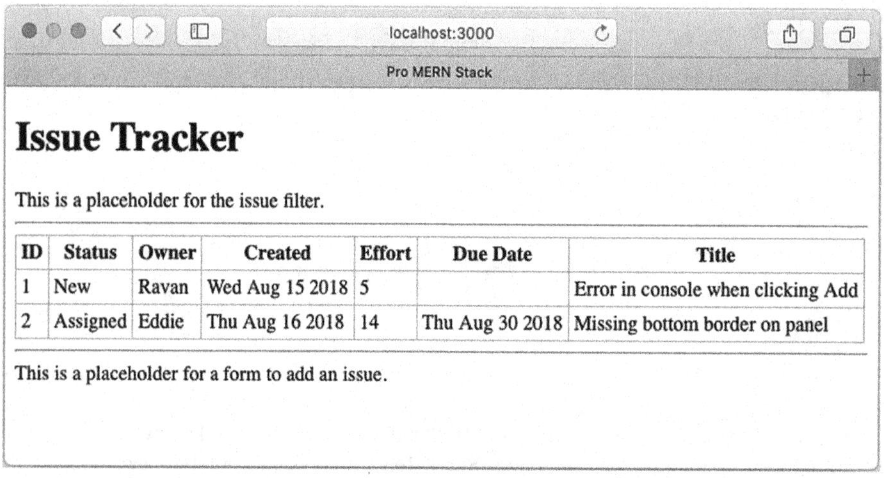
localhost:3000
Pro MERN Stack
Issue Tracker
This is a placeholder for the issue filter.
ID Status Owner Created Effort Due Date Title
1 New Ravan Wed Aug 15 2018 5 Error in console when clicking Add
2 Assigned Eddie Thu Aug 16 2018 14 Thu Aug 30 2018 Missing bottom border on panel
This is a placeholder for a form to add an issue.

Figure 3-6. *Issue Rows constructed programmatically from an array*

EXERCISE: DYNAMIC COMPOSITION

1. We used the issue's id field as the value of key. What other keys could have been used? Which one would you choose?

2. In the previous section, we passed every field of an issue as a separate property to IssueRow. In this section, we passed the entire issue object. Why?

3. Instead of using a local variable issueRows, try using the map expression directly inside the <tbody>. Does it work? What does it tell us?

Answers are available at the end of the chapter.

Summary

In this chapter, we created a barebones version of the main page of the Issue Tracker. We started using React classes instead of simple elements, some of which were just placeholders to depict components that we have not yet developed. We did this by writing fine-grained individual components and putting them together (composing) in an enclosing component. We also passed parameters or data from an enclosing component to its children, and thus reused a component class and rendered it differently with different data, dynamically using a map() to generate components based on an array of input data.

The components didn't do much apart from rendering themselves based on the input data. In the next chapter, we'll see how user interaction can affect the data and change the appearance of a component.

Answers to Exercises

Exercise: React Classes

1. Compilation will fail with an error, "Adjacent JSX elements must be wrapped in an enclosing tag". The render() method can only have a single return value, thus, it can return only one element. Enclosing the two <div>s in another <div> is one solution, or as the error message suggests, using a Fragment component is another solution, which we will discuss in later sections.

2. React prints an error in the browser's JavaScript console when it is a React error. Regular JavaScript errors are also shown in the console, but the code displayed is not the original code; it is the compiled code. We'll learn how to debug using the original source in later chapters.

Exercise: Composing Components

1. No, there is no enclosing element. All the elements returned by IssueList appear directly under the contents div. In this case, we could have easily used a <div> to enclose the elements.

    But imagine a situation where a list of table-rows needs to be returned, like this:

    ```
    ...
      <tr> {/* contents of row 1 */} </tr>
      <tr> {/* contents of row 2 */} </tr>
    ...
    ```

Then, the calling component would place these rows under a `<tbody>` element. Adding a `<div>` to enclose these rows would result in an invalid DOM tree, as `<tbody>` cannot have a `<div>` within it. A fragment is the only option in this case.

Exercise: Passing Data Using Properties

1. A border will not be displayed. How React interprets each element's attribute is different from how an HTML parser does it. The border attribute is not one of the supported attributes. React completely ignores the border attribute.

2. The outer braces denote that the attribute value is a JavaScript expression. The inner braces specify an object, which is the attribute's value.

3. The curly braces of React are similar to `<?php ... ?>` of PHP, with a slight difference. The contents within a `<?php ... ?>` tag are full-fledged programs, whereas in JSX, you can only have JavaScript expressions. All programming constructs like for loops are written outside the JSX in plain JavaScript.

Exercise: Passing Data Using Children

1. `props` are flexible and useful for passing in any kind of data. On the other hand, `children` can only be an *element*, which can also be deeply nested. Thus, if you have simple data, pass it as `props`. If you have a component to pass, you could use `children` if it is deeply nested and naturally appears within the child component. Components can also be passed as `props`, typically when you want to pass multiple components or when the component is not a natural child content of the parent.

Exercise: Dynamic Composition

1. Another choice for the key property is the array index, as it is also unique. If the key is a large value like a UUID, you may think that it is more efficient to use the array index, but in reality it is not. React uses the key to *identify* the row. If it finds the same key, it assumes it is the same row. If the row has not changed, it does not re-render the row.

   Thus, if you insert a row, React will be more efficient in shuffling existing rows rather than re-rendering the entire table if the rows' keys were the ID of the object. If you used the array index instead, it would think that every row after the inserted row has changed and re-render each of them.

2. Passing the entire object is obviously more concise. I would choose to pass individual properties only if the number of properties being passed is a small subset of the full set of properties of the object.

3. It works, despite the fact that we have JSX within the expression. Anything within the curly braces is parsed as a JavaScript expression. But since we are using a JSX transform on JavaScript expressions, these snippets will also go through the transform. It is possible to nest this deeper and use another set of curly braces within the nested piece of JSX and so on.

CHAPTER 4

React State

Until now, we only saw static components, that is, components that did not change. To make components that respond to user input and other events, React uses a data structure called *state* in the component. In this chapter, we will explore how to use React State and how it can be manipulated to change how the component looks and what it shows on screen.

The state essentially holds the data, something that can change, as opposed to the immutable properties in the form of `props` that you saw earlier. This state needs to be used in the `render()` method to build the view. It is only the change of state that can change the view. When data or the state changes, React automatically rerenders the view to show the new changed data.

For this chapter, the goal is to add a button and append a row to the initial list of issues on click of that button. We'll add this button in place of the placeholder text in the `IssueAdd` component. By doing that, you'll learn about a component's state, how to manipulate it, how to handle events, and how to communicate between components.

We'll start by appending a row without user interaction. We'll do this using a timer rather than a button so that we focus on the state and modifications and not deal with things like user input. Toward the end of the chapter, we will replace the timer with an actual button and a form for user input.

Initial State

The state of a component is captured in a variable called `this.state` in the component's class, which should be an object consisting of one or more key-value pairs, where each key is a state variable name and the value is the current value of that variable. React does not specify what needs to go into the state, but it is useful to store in the state anything that affects the rendered view and can change due to any event. These are typically events generated due to user interaction.

For the `IssueTable` component, the list of issues being displayed is definitely one such piece of data that both affects the rendered view and can also change when an issue is added, edited, or deleted. The array of issues is therefore an ideal state variable.

Other things, such as the size of the window, also can change, but this is not something that affects the DOM. Even though the display changes (for example, a line may wrap because the window is narrower), the change is handled by the browser directly based on the same DOM. So, we don't need to capture this in the state of the component. There may be cases where it does affect the DOM; for example, if the height of the window determines *how many* issues we display, we may store the height of the window in a state variable and restrict the number of `IssueRow` components being constructed. In those cases, the height of the window, or a derived value, for example, the number of issues being shown, could also be stored in the state.

Things that don't change, for example, the border style of the table, also don't need to go into the state. That's because user interaction or other events do not affect the style of borders.

© Vasan Subramanian 2019
V. Subramanian, *Pro MERN Stack*, https://doi.org/10.1007/978-1-4842-4391-6_4

For now, let's just use an array of issues as the one and only state of the component and use that array to construct the table of issues. Thus, in the render() method of IssueTable, let's change the loop that creates the set of IssueRows to use the state variable called issues rather than the global array like this:

```
...
  const issueRows = this.state.issues.map(issue =>
      <IssueRow key={issue.id} issue={issue} />
...
```

As for the initial state, let's use a hard-coded set of issues and set it to the initial state. We already have a global array of issues; let's rename this array to initialIssues, just to make it explicit that it is only an initial set.

```
...
const initialIssues = [
  ...
];
...
```

Setting the initial state needs to be done in the constructor of the component. This can be done by simply assigning the variable this.state to the set of state variables and their values. Let's use the variable initialIssues to initialize the value of the state variable issues like this:

```
...
    this.state = { issues: initialIssues };
...
```

Note that we used only one state variable called issues. We can have other state variables, for instance if we were showing the issue list in multiple pages, and we wanted to also keep the page number currently being shown as another state variable, we could have done that by adding another key to the object like page: 0.

The set of all changes to use the state to render the view of IssueTable is shown in Listing 4-1.

Listing 4-1. App.jsx: Initializing and Using State

```
...
const issues = [
const initialIssues = [
  {
    id: 1, status: 'New', owner: 'Ravan', effort: 5,
    created: new Date('2018-08-15'), due: undefined,
  },
...
class IssueTable extends React.Component {
  constructor() {
    super();
    this.state = { issues: initialIssues };
  }

  render() {
    const issueRows = issues.map(issue =>
```

```
const issueRows = this.state.issues.map(issue =>
  <IssueRow key={issue.id} issue={issue} />
);
...
```

Running and testing this piece of code should show no change in the application; you will still see a table containing two rows of issues, just as before.

EXERCISE: INITIAL STATE

---

1. If you needed to display each row in a different background color based on the status of the issue, how would you go about it? Would you have a list of colors corresponding to each issue also stored in the state? Why or why not?

Answers are available at the end of the chapter.

Async State Initialization

Although we set the initial state in the constructor, it is highly unlikely that regular SPA components will have the initial state available to them statically. These will typically be fetched from the server. In the case of the Issue Tracker application, even the initial list issues to be displayed would have to be fetched via an API call.

The state can only be assigned a value in the constructor. After that, the state can be modified, but only via a call to React.Component's this.setState() method. This method takes in one argument, which is an object containing all the changed state variables and their values. The only state variable that we have is the one called issues, which can be set to any list of issues in a call to this.setState() like this:

```
...
  this.setState({ issues: newIssues });
...
```

If there were additional state variables, setting only one variable (issues) will cause it to get *merged* with the existing state. For example, if we had stored the current page as another state variable, the new value of the state variable issues will be merged into the state, keeping the value of the current page unchanged.

Since at the time of constructing the component, we don't have the initial data, we will have to assign an empty array to the issues state variable in the constructor.

```
...
  constructor() {
    this.state = { issues: [] };
...
```

We will not fetch the data from the server just yet, but to explore the changes to the state initialization, let's simulate such a call. The key difference between a global array of issues and a call to the server is that the latter needs an asynchronous call. Let's add a method to the IssueTable class that asynchronously returns an array of issues. Eventually, we'll replace this with an API call to the server, but for the moment, we'll use a setTimeout() call to make it asynchronous. In the callback to the setTimeout() call (which will eventually be an Ajax call), let's call this.setState() with the static array of initial issues like this:

```
...
  loadData() {
    setTimeout(() => {
      this.setState({ issues: initialIssues });
    }, 500);
  }
...
```

The timeout value of 500 milliseconds is somewhat arbitrary: it's reasonable to expect a real API call to fetch the initial list of issues within this time.

Now, it is very tempting to call loadData() within the constructor of IssueTable. It may even seem to work, but the fact is that the constructor only constructs the *component* (i.e., does all the initialization of the object in memory) and does not render the UI. The rendering happens later, when the component needs to be shown on the screen. If this.setState() gets called before the component is ready to be rendered, things will go awry. You may not see this happening in simple pages, but if the initial page is complex and takes time to render, and if the Ajax call returns before rendering is finished, you will get an error.

React provides many other methods called *lifecycle methods* to cater to this and other situations where something needs to be done depending on the stage, or changes in the status of the component. Apart from the constructor and the render() methods, the following lifecycle methods of a component could be of interest:

- componentDidMount(): This method is called as soon as the component's representation has been converted and inserted into the DOM. A setState() can be called within this method.

- componentDidUpdate(): This method is invoked immediately after an update occurs, but it is not called for the initial render. this.setState() can be called within this method. The method is also supplied the previous props and previous state as arguments, so that the function has a chance to check the differences between the previous props and state and the current props and state before taking an action.

- componentWillUnmount(): This method is useful for cleanup such as cancelling timers and pending network requests.

- shouldComponentUpdate(): This method can be used to optimize and prevent a rerender in case there is a change in the props or state that really doesn't affect the output or the view. This method is rarely used because, when the state and props are designed well, there will rarely be a case when the state or props change but an update is not required for the view.

The best place to initiate the loading of data in this case is the componentDidMount() method. At this point in time, the DOM is guaranteed to be ready, and setState() can be called to rerender the component. componentDidUpdate() is an option as well, but since it may not be called for the initial render, let's not use it. Let's add the componentDidMount() method in IssueTable and load the data within this method:

```
...
  componentDidMount() {
    this.loadData();
  }
...
```

The complete set of changes in the `IssueTable` class is shown in Listing 4-2.

Listing 4-2. App.jsx, IssueTable: Loading State Asynchronously

```
...
class IssueTable extends React.Component {
  constructor() {
    super();
    this.state = { issues: initialIssues };
    this.state = { issues: [] };
  }

  componentDidMount() {
    this.loadData();
  }

  loadData() {
    setTimeout(() => {
      this.setState({ issues: initialIssues });
    }, 500);
  }
}
...
```

If you refresh the browser (assuming you're still running `npm run watch` and `npm start` on two different consoles), you will find that the list of issues is displayed as it used to be in the previous steps. But, you will also see that for a fraction of a second after the page is loaded, the table is empty, as shown in Figure 4-1.

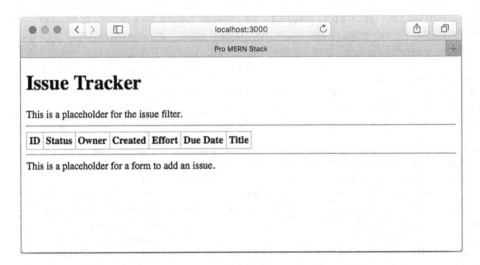

Figure 4-1. *Empty table shown for a fraction of a second*

It gets filled soon after, but still, there is a flicker. When we explore server-side rendering in later chapters, we will get rid of this ungainly flicker. For the moment, let's live with this minor UI unpleasantness.

Updating State

In the previous sections, you saw how to set the initial state, using a direct assignment in the constructor as well as setting a value in other lifecycle methods using this.setState(). In this section, let's make a minor change to the state rather than set a completely new value to it. Let's add a new issue and thus change, not the complete state, but only a portion of it.

To start, let's add a method in IssueTable to add a new issue. This can take in as an argument an issue object, to which we'll assign a new ID and set the creation date. The new ID can be calculated from the existing length of the array.

```
...
  createIssue(issue) {
    issue.id = this.state.issues.length + 1;
    issue.created = new Date();
  }
...
```

Note that the state variable cannot be set directly, nor can it be mutated directly. That is, setting this.state.issues to a new value or modifying its elements is not allowed. The variable this.state in the component should always be treated as immutable. For example, the following should not be done:

```
...
    this.state.issues.push(issue);     // incorrect!
...
```

The reason is that React does not automatically identify such changes to the state because it is a plain JavaScript variable. The only way to let React know something has changed, and to cause a rerender, is to call this.setState(). Further, this.setState() may cause the changes that are done directly to the state variable to be overwritten. So, the following should not be done either:

```
...
    issues = this.state.issues;
    issues.push(issue);          // same as this.state.issues.push()!
    this.setState({ issues: issues });
...
```

It may seem to work, but it will have unexpected consequences in some of the lifecycle methods within this as well as descendent components. Especially in those methods that compare the old and new properties, the difference between the old state and the new one will not be detected.

What is needed in the setState() call is a fresh array of issues, say a copy of the state variable. If any existing array element, say an issue itself, is changing, not only is the copy of the array needed, but also the copy of the object that is being changed is needed. There are libraries called *immutability helpers,* such as immutable.js (http://facebook.github.io/immutable-js/), which can be used to construct the new state object. When a property of the object is modified, the library creates a copy optimally.

But we will only append an issue, and not change an existing issue. It's fairly straightforward to make a shallow copy of the array, and this will suffice for the moment. So, we won't be using the library—there isn't much extra code we need to write to handle it. If, in your application, you find that you have to make lots of copies because of deep nesting of objects in the state, you could consider using immutable.js.

The simple way to make a copy of an array is using the `slice()` method. So let's create a copy of the `issues` array like this:

```
...
    issues = this.state.issues.slice();
...
```

Later in the chapter, we will create a user interface to add a new issue. But for now, rather than dealing with the complexity of UI and event handling, let's just add a timer, on the expiry of which, a hard-coded sample issue will be appended to the list of issues. Let's first declare this hard-coded sample issue object globally, right after the global `initialIssues`:

```
...
const sampleIssue = {
  status: 'New', owner: 'Pieta',
  title: 'Completion date should be optional',
};
...
```

Let's use this object in a call to `createIssue()`, after the expiry of a timer of two seconds, in the constructor of `IssueTable`:

```
...
    setTimeout(() => {
      this.createIssue(sampleIssue);
    }, 2000);
...
```

This should automatically add the sample issue to the list of issues after the page is loaded. The final set of changes—for using a timer to append a sample issue to the list of issues—is shown in Listing 4-3.

Listing 4-3. App.jsx: Appending an Issue on a Timer

```
...
const initialIssues = [
  ...
];

const sampleIssue = {
  status: 'New', owner: 'Pieta',
  title: 'Completion date should be optional',
};

...

class IssueTable extends React.Component {
  constructor() {
    super();
    this.state = { issues: [] };
    setTimeout(() => {
      this.createIssue(sampleIssue);
    }, 2000);
  }
```

...

```
createIssue(issue) {
  issue.id = this.state.issues.length + 1;
  issue.created = new Date();
  const newIssueList = this.state.issues.slice();
  newIssueList.push(issue);
  this.setState({ issues: newIssueList });
}
}
```

...

On running this set of changes and refreshing the browser, you'll see that there are two rows of issues to start with. After two seconds, a third row is added with a newly generated ID and the contents of the sample issue. A screenshot of the three-row table is shown in Figure 4-2.

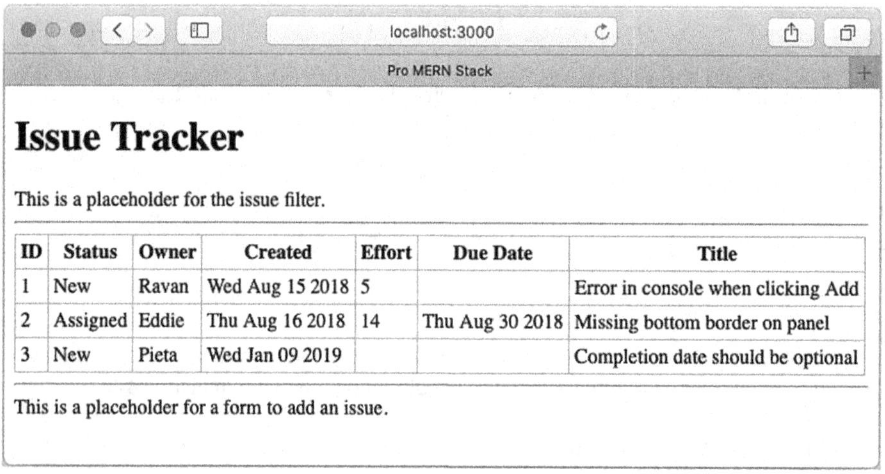

Figure 4-2. *Appended row to initial set of issues*

Note that we did not explicitly call a setState() on the IssueRow components. React automatically propagates any changes to child components that depend on the parent component's state. Further, we did not have to write any code for inserting a row into the DOM. React calculated the changes to the virtual DOM and inserted a new row.

At this point, the hierarchy of the components and the data flow can be visually depicted, as shown in Figure 4-3.

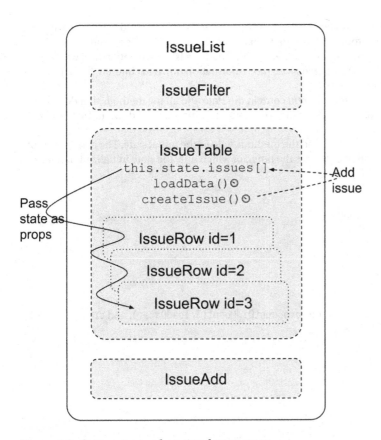

Figure 4-3. Setting state and passing data as props

EXERCISE: UPDATING STATE

1. Set up another timer at say, three seconds, right after the first timer to add yet another issue based on sampleIssue. Do you notice something going wrong when the second new issue is added? Hint: Look at the ID of the first new issue. Why do you think this is happening? How can you correct it?

2. Add a console.log in the IssueRow's render() method. How many times do you expect render() to be called? How many console logs do you see? (Make sure you undo the changes you did in the previous exercise!)

Answers are available at the end of the chapter.

Lifting State Up

Before we add user interface elements to create new issues, let's move the initiation of the creation to where it really belongs: in the IssueAdd component. This will allow us to deal with the changes one step at a time, because moving the timer for adding a new issue from the IssueTable component to the IssueAdd component is not as trivial as it first appears.

If you do try to move it, you will immediately realize that the createIssue() method will also have to move, or we need to have a variant within IssueAdd that can communicate back to IssueTable and call the createIssue() method, which continues to remain there. But there is no straightforward way to communicate between siblings in React. Only parents can pass information down to children; horizontal communication seems hard, if not impossible.

The way around this is to have the *common parent* contain the state and all the methods that deal with this state. By lifting the state up on level to IssueList, information can be propagated down to IssueAdd as well as to IssueTable.

Let's start by moving the state to IssueList and the methods to load the initial state. The constructor of IssueTable had both the state initialization as well as the timer, of which only the state initialization needs to move (the timer will move to IssueAdd):

```
...
class IssueList extends React.Component {
  constructor() {
    super();
    this.state = { issues: [] };
  }
...
```

The other methods that deal with the state are componentDidMount(), loadData(), and createIssue(). Let's move these also to the IssueList class:

```
...
class IssueList extends React.Component {
  ...
  componentDidMount() {
    ...
  }
  loadData() {
    ...
  }
  createIssue(issue) {
    ...
  }
  ...
}
```

Now, IssueTable doesn't have a state to construct the IssueRow components from. But you have already seen how data can be passed in from a parent to a child in the form of props. Let's use that strategy and pass the array of issues from the state within IssueList to IssueTable via props:

```
...
        <IssueTable issues={this.state.issues} />
...
```

And, within IssueTable, instead of referring to the state variable issues, we'll need to get the same data from props:

```
...
    const issueRows = this.state.issues.map(issue =>
    const issueRows = this.props.issues.map(issue =>
...
```

As for `IssueAdd`, we need to move the timer into the constructor of this class and trigger the addition of a new issue from within this component. But we don't have the `createIssue()` method available here. Fortunately, since a parent component can pass information down to a child component, we'll pass the *method* itself as part of the props to `IssueAdd` from `IssueList`, so that it can be called from `IssueAdd`. Here's the changed instantiation of the `IssueAdd` component within `IssueList`:

```
...
        <IssueAdd createIssue={this.createIssue} />
...
```

This lets us make a call to `createIssue()` from `IssueAdd` using `this.props.createIssue()` as part of the timer callback. So let's create a constructor in `IssueAdd` and move the timer set up with a minor change to use the `createIssue` callback passed in via props like this:

```
...
    setTimeout(() => {
      this.props.createIssue(sampleIssue);
    }, 2000);
...
```

We still have to take care of one more thing before we can say we are done with this set of changes. All this while, we have been using the arrow function syntax to set up timers. In ES2015, the arrow function has the effect of setting the context (the value of this) to the *lexical scope*. This means that this within the callback will refer to whatever this was in the lexical scope, that is, outside of the anonymous function, where the code is present.

That worked as long as the called function was within the same class as the timer callback. It still works, in the `loadData()` method, because this refers to the `IssueList` component where the timer was fired, and therefore, `this.state` refers to the state within `IssueList` itself.

But, when `createIssue` is called from a timer within `IssueAdd`, this will refer to the `IssueAdd` component. But what we really want is for `createIssue` to be always called with this referring to the `IssueList` component. Otherwise, `this.state.issues` will be undefined.

The way to make this work is to *bind* the method to the `IssueList` component before passing it around. We could make this change when instantiating `IssueAdd` like this:

```
...
        <IssueAdd createIssue={this.createIssue.bind(this)} />
...
```

But then, if we need to ever refer to the same method again and pass it to some other child component, we'd have to repeat this code. Also, there is never going to be a case where we will need the method to be not bound, so it is best to replace the definition of `createIssue` with a bound version of itself. The recommended way to do this is in the constructor of the class where this method is implemented.

So, instead of binding during the instantiation of `IssueAdd`, let's bind it in the constructor of `IssueList`.

```
...
    this.createIssue = this.createIssue.bind(this);
...
```

The new versions of each of these classes, after making all these changes, are shown in the following listings. Listing 4-4 shows the new `IssueTable` class; Listing 4-5 shows the new `IssueAdd` class; and Listing 4-6 shows the new `IssueList` class.

Listing 4-4. App.jsx: New IssueTable Class

```
class IssueTable extends React.Component {
  render() {
    const issueRows = this.props.issues.map(issue =>
      <IssueRow key={issue.id} issue={issue} />
    );

    return (
      <table className="bordered-table">
        <thead>
          <tr>
            <th>ID</th>
            <th>Status</th>
            <th>Owner</th>
            <th>Created</th>
            <th>Effort</th>
            <th>Due Date</th>
            <th>Title</th>
          </tr>
        </thead>
        <tbody>
          {issueRows}
        </tbody>
      </table>
    );
  }
}
```

Listing 4-5. App.jsx, IssueAdd: New IssueAdd Class

```
class IssueAdd extends React.Component {
  constructor() {
    super();
    setTimeout(() => {
      this.props.createIssue(sampleIssue);
    }, 2000);
  }
  render() {
    return (
      <div>This is a placeholder for a form to add an issue.</div>
    );
  }
}
```

Listing 4-6. App.jsx, IssueList: New IssueList Class

```
class IssueList extends React.Component {
  constructor() {
    super();
    this.state = { issues: [] };
```

```
      this.createIssue = this.createIssue.bind(this);
  }

  componentDidMount() {
    this.loadData();
  }

  loadData() {
    setTimeout(() => {
      this.setState({ issues: initialIssues });
    }, 500);
  }

  createIssue(issue) {
    issue.id = this.state.issues.length + 1;
    issue.created = new Date();
    const newIssueList = this.state.issues.slice();
    newIssueList.push(issue);
    this.setState({ issues: newIssueList });
  }

  render() {
    return (
      <React.Fragment>
        <h1>Issue Tracker</h1>
        <IssueFilter />
        <hr />
        <IssueTable issues={this.state.issues} />
        <hr />
        <IssueAdd createIssue={this.createIssue} />
      </React.Fragment>
    );
  }
}
```

The effect of these changes will not be seen in the user interface. The application will behave as it used to. On refreshing the browser, you will see an empty table to start with, which will soon be populated with two issues and after two seconds, another issue will be added.

But this sets us up nicely for the change where we can replace the timer in IssueAdd with a button that the user can click to add a new issue.

EXERCISE: LIFTING STATE UP

1. Remove the binding of the method createIssue(). What error do you see in the console? What does it tell you?

Answers are available at the end of the chapter.

Event Handling

Let's now add an issue interactively, on the click of a button rather than use a timer to do this. We'll create a form with two text inputs and use the values that the user enters in them to add a new issue. An Add button will trigger the addition.

Let's start by creating the form with two text inputs in the render() method of IssueAdd in place of the placeholder div.

```
...
    <div>This is a placeholder for a form to add an issue.</div>
    <form>
      <input type="text" name="owner" placeholder="Owner" />
      <input type="text" name="title" placeholder="Title" />
      <button>Add</button>
    </form>
...
```

At this point, we can remove the timer that creates an issue from the constructor.

```
...
  constructor() {
    super();
    setTimeout(() => {
      this.props.createIssue(sampleIssue);
    }, 2000);
  }
...
```

If you run the code, you'll see a form being displayed in place of the placeholder in IssueAdd. The screenshot of how this looks is shown in Figure 4-4.

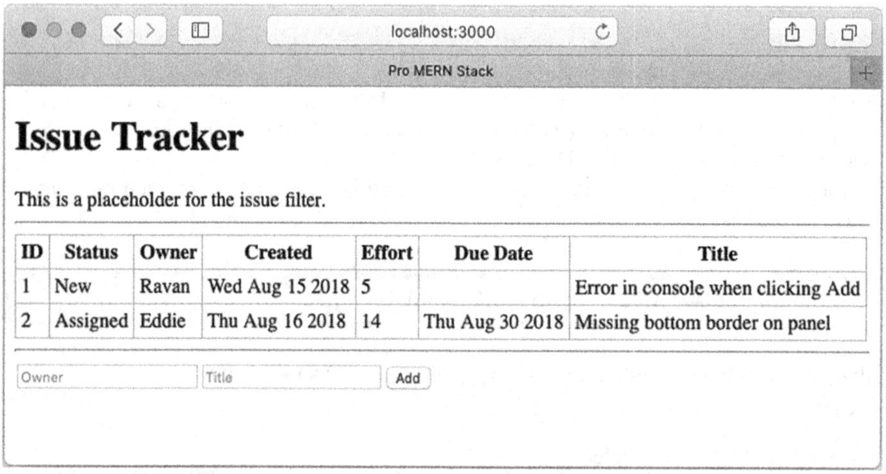

Figure 4-4. IssueAdd placeholder replaced with a form

At this point, clicking Add will submit the form and fetch the same screen again. That's not what we want. Firstly, we want it to call createIssue() using the values in the owner and title fields. Secondly, we want to prevent the form from being submitted because we will handle the event ourselves.

To handle events such as onclick and onsubmit, the properties that we need to supply to the elements are, simply, onClick and onSubmit. As in plain HTML and JavaScript, these properties take functions as values. We'll create a class method called handleSubmit() to receive the submit event from the form when the Add button is clicked. Within this method, we'll need a handle to the form, so as in regular HTML, let's give the form a name, say, issueAdd which can then be referred to in JavaScript using document.forms. issueAdd.

So, let's rewrite the form declaration with a name and an onSubmit handler like this.

```
...

        <form name="issueAdd" onSubmit={this.handleSubmit}>
...
```

Now, we can implement the method handleSubmit() in IssueAdd. This method receives the event that triggered the submit as an argument. In order to prevent the form from being submitted when the Add button is clicked, we need to call the preventDefault() function on the event. Then, using the form handle via documents.forms.issueAdd, we can get the values of the text input fields. Using these, we'll create a new issue by calling createIssue(). After the call to createIssue(), let's keep the form ready for the next set of inputs by clearing the text input fields.

```
...
  handleSubmit(e) {
    e.preventDefault();
    const form = document.forms.issueAdd;
    const issue = {
      owner: form.owner.value, title: form.title.value, status: 'New',
    }
    this.props.createIssue(issue);
    form.owner.value = ""; form.title.value = "";
  }
...
```

■ **Note** At this point, we are using the conventional way of taking user input, using named inputs and getting their value using the value property of the DOM element. React has another way of dealing with user input by way of *controlled* components, where the value of the input is tied to a state variable. We'll explore this in later chapters.

Since handleSubmit will be called from an event, the context, or this will be set to the object generating the event, which is typically the window object. As you saw in the previous section, to let this method have access to the object variables via this, we need to bind it to this in the constructor:

```
...
  constructor() {
    super();
    this.handleSubmit = this.handleSubmit.bind(this);
  }
...
```

The new full code of the IssueAdd class, after these changes, is shown in Listing 4-7.

Listing 4-7. App.jsx, IssueList: New IssueAdd Class

```
class IssueAdd extends React.Component {
  constructor() {
    super();
    this.handleSubmit = this.handleSubmit.bind(this);
  }

  handleSubmit(e) {
    e.preventDefault();
    const form = document.forms.issueAdd;
    const issue = {
      owner: form.owner.value, title: form.title.value, status: 'New',
    }
    this.props.createIssue(issue);
    form.owner.value = ""; form.title.value = "";
  }

  render() {
    return (
      <form name="issueAdd" onSubmit={this.handleSubmit}>
        <input type="text" name="owner" placeholder="Owner" />
        <input type="text" name="title" placeholder="Title" />
        <button>Add</button>
      </form>
    );
  }
}
```

The global object sampleIssue is no longer required, so we can get rid of it. This change is shown in Listing 4-8.

Listing 4-8. App.jsx, Removal of sampleIssue

```
...
const sampleIssue = {
  status: 'New', owner: 'Pieta',
  title: 'Completion date should be optional',
};
...
```

You can now test the changes by entering some values in the owner and title fields and clicking Add. You can add as many rows as you like. If you add two issues, you'll get a screen like the one in Figure 4-5.

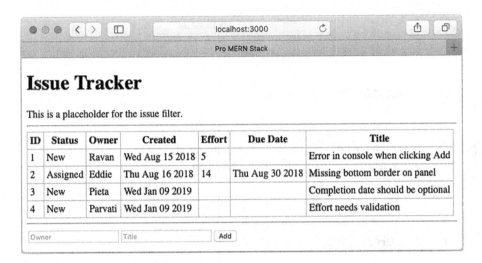

Figure 4-5. Adding new issues using the IssueAdd form

At the end of all this, we have been able to encapsulate and initiate the creation of a new issue from the IssueAdd component itself. To do this, we "lifted the state up" to the least common ancestor, so that all children have access to it directly via passed-in props or via callbacks that can modify the state. This new UI hierarchy data and function flow is depicted in Figure 4-6. Compare this with the situation where the state was maintained in IssueTable, as in Figure 4-3.

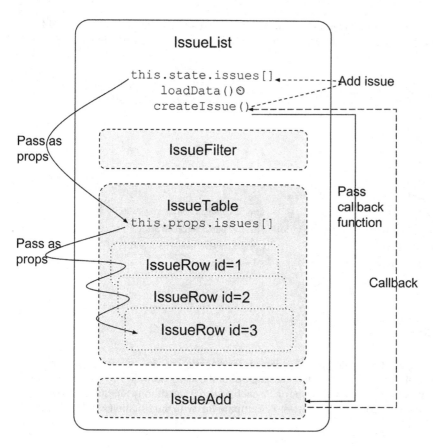

Figure 4-6. Component hierarchy and data flow after lifting state up

EXERCISE: EVENT HANDLING

1. Refresh the browser; you'll see that the added issues are gone. How does one persist the changes?

2. Remove e.preventDefault(). Click the Add button with some values for owner and title. What happens? What do you see in the URL bar? Can you explain this?

3. Use the developer console to inspect the table and add a breakpoint on the <tbody> element as "break on subtree modification". Now, add a new issue. How many times is the subtree being modified? Compare this with exercise #2 in "Updating State," where you traced the number of render() calls in a IssueRow.

Answers are available at the end of the chapter.

Stateless Components

We have three functioning React components (IssueAdd, IssueRow and IssueTable) composed hierarchically into IssueList (another one, the IssueFilter, is still a placeholder). But there is a difference among these functioning component classes.

IssueList has lots of methods, a state, initialization of the state, and functions that modify the state. In comparison, IssueAdd has some interactivity, but no state[1]. But, if you notice, IssueRow and IssueTable have nothing but a render() method. For performance reasons and for clarity of code, it is recommended that such components are written as functions rather than classes: a function that takes in props and just renders based on it. It's as if the component's view is a pure function of its props, and it is stateless. The render() function itself can be the component.

If a component does not depend on props, it can be written as a simple function whose name is the component name. For example, consider the following Hello World class we wrote in the beginning of Chapter 2 (React Components):

```
...
class HelloWorld extends React.Component {
  render() {
    return (
      <div title="Outer div">
        <h1>Hello World!</h1>
      </div>
    );
  }
}
...
```

This can be rewritten as a pure function like this:

```
...
function HelloWorld() {
  return (
    <div title="Outer div">
      <h1>Hello World!</h1>
    </div>
  );
}
...
```

If the rendering depends on the props alone (more often than not, this will indeed be the case), the function can be written with one argument as the props, which can be accessed within the function's JSX body. Say the Hello World component takes in a message as part of the props. The component can be rewritten as follows:

```
...
function HelloWorld(props) {
  return (
    <div title="Outer div">
```

---

[1]This is not entirely true. There is, in fact, state in this component: the state of the input fields as the user is typing. But we have not captured them as React State and have let the browser's native handlers maintain it. So we don't really treat it as a regular state.

```
      <h1>{props.message}</h1>
    </div>
  );
}
...
```

An even more concise form using an arrow function can be used when the rendered output can be represented as a JavaScript expression, that is, a function with no other statement than just the return statement:

```
...
const HelloWorld = (props) => (
  <div title="Outer div">
    <h1>{props.message}</h1>
  </div>
);
...
```

This HelloWorld component could have been instantiated like this:

```
...
  <HelloWorld message="Hello World" />
...
```

Since IssueRow and IssueTable are stateless components, let's change them to pure functions. The new components are shown in Listing 4-9 and Listing 4-10, respectively.

Listing 4-9. App.jsx, IssueRow as a Stateless Component

```
function IssueRow(props) {
  const issue = props.issue;
  return (
    <tr>
      <td>{issue.id}</td>
      <td>{issue.status}</td>
      <td>{issue.owner}</td>
      <td>{issue.created.toDateString()}</td>
      <td>{issue.effort}</td>
      <td>{issue.due ? issue.due.toDateString() : ''}</td>
      <td>{issue.title}</td>
    </tr>
  );
}
```

Listing 4-10. App.jsx, IssueTable as a Stateless Component

```
function IssueTable(props) {
  const issueRows = props.issues.map(issue =>
    <IssueRow key={issue.id} issue={issue} />
  );
```

```
  return (
    <table className="bordered-table">
      <thead>
        <tr>
          <th>ID</th>
          <th>Status</th>
          <th>Owner</th>
          <th>Created</th>
          <th>Effort</th>
          <th>Due Date</th>
          <th>Title</th>
        </tr>
      </thead>
      <tbody>
        {issueRows}
      </tbody>
    </table>
  );
}
```

Designing Components

Most beginners will have a bit of confusion between state and props, when to use which, what granularity of components should one choose, and how to go about it all. This section is devoted to discussing some principles and best practices.

State vs. Props

Both state and props hold model information, but they are different. The props are immutable, whereas state is not. Typically, state variables are passed down to child components as props because the children don't maintain or modify them. They take in a read-only copy and use it only to render the view of the component. If any event in the child affects the parent's state, the child calls a method defined in the parent. Access to this method should have been explicitly given by passing it as a callback via props.

Anything that *can* change due to an event anywhere in the component hierarchy qualifies as being part of the state. Avoid keeping computed values in the state; instead, simply compute them when needed, typically inside the render() method.

Do not copy props into state, just because props are immutable. If you feel the need to do this, think of modifying the original state from which these props were derived. One exception is when props are used as *initial* values to the state, and the state is truly disjointed from the original state after the initialization.

You can use Table 4-1 as a quick reference to the differences.

Table 4-1. *State vs. Props*

Attribute	State	Props
Mutability	Can be changed using `this.setState()`	Cannot be changed
Ownership	Belongs to the component	Belongs to an ancestor, the component gets a read-only copy
Information	Model information	Model information
Affects	Rendering of the component	Rendering of the component

Component Hierarchy

Split the application into components and subcomponents. Typically, this will reflect the data model itself. For example, in the Issue Tracker, the issues array was represented by the `IssueTable` component, and each issue was represented by the `IssueRow` component.

Decide on the granularity just as you would for splitting functions and objects. The component should be self-contained with minimal and logical interfaces to the parent. If you find it doing too many things, just like in functions, it should probably be split into multiple components, so that it follows the Single Responsibility principle (that is, every component should be responsible for one and only one thing). If you are passing in too many `props` to a component, it is an indication that either the component needs to be split, or it need not exist: the parent itself could do the job.

Communication

Communication between components depends on the direction. Parents communicate to children via `props`; when state changes, the `props` automatically change. Children communicate to parents via callbacks.

Siblings and cousins can't communicate with each other, so if there is a need, the information has to go up the hierarchy and then back down. This is called *lifting the state up*. This is what we did when we dealt with adding a new issue. The `IssueAdd` component had to insert a row in `IssueTable`. It was achieved by keeping the state in the least common ancestor, `IssueList`. The addition was initiated by `IssueAdd` and a new array element added in `IssueList`'s state via a callback. The result was seen in `IssueTable` by passing the `issues` array down as `props` from `IssueList`.

If there is a need to know the state of a child in a parent, you're probably doing it wrong. Although React does offer a way using `refs`, you shouldn't feel the need if you follow the one-way data flow strictly: state flows as props into children, events cause state changes, which flows back as props.

Stateless Components

In a well-designed application, most components would be stateless functions of their properties. All states would be captured in a few components at the top of the hierarchy, from where the props of all the descendants are derived.

We did just that with the `IssueList`, where we kept the state. We converted all descendent components to stateless components, relying only on props passed down the hierarchy to render themselves. We kept the state in `IssueList` because that was the least common component above all the descendants that depended on that state. Sometimes, you may find that there is no logical common ancestor. In such cases, you may have to invent a new component just to hold the state, even though visually the component has nothing.

Summary

In this chapter, you learned how to use state and make changes to it on user interactions or other events. The more interesting aspect was how state values are propagated down the component hierarchy as props. You also had a glimpse of user interaction: the click of a button to add a new issue, and how that causes the state to change, and in turn, how the props in the descendant components changed, causing them to rerender as well. Further, you learned how a child can communicate with its parent via callbacks.

We used simulated asynchronous calls and data local to the browser to achieve all this. In the next chapter, instead of using local data, we'll fetch the data from the server. When an issue is added, we'll send the data to the server to persist it.

Answers to Exercises

Exercise: Initial State

1. You could store the background color of each row as part of the state, but then, the values will have to be calculated at some point in time. When is a good time to do this? Just before setting the state? How about when setting the initial state?

   Since this is a *derived* value, it is better and more efficient to just calculate these values within the render() method and use them then and there rather than save them in the state.

Exercise: Updating State

1. When the second timer fires and another issue is added, you will find that it gets an ID of 4 but the ID of the third row also changes to 4. Further, in the console, you will see an error to the effect that two children with the same key were found.

   This happens because we are using the same object as the first to create the second issue, and setting the ID to 4 sets it in the one and only object: sampleIssue. To avoid this, you have to create a copy of the object before using it to create a new issue, say, using Object.assign().

2. Each row is rendered once when initialized (two renders, one for each row). After the new row is inserted, each row is rendered once again (three renders, one for each row). Although a render is called, this does not mean that the DOM is updated. Only the virtual DOM is recreated on each render. Real DOM update happens only where there are differences.

Exercise: Lifting State Up

1. On removing the bind() call, you'll see an error that says *undefined is not an object*, while evaluating this.state.issues. This should tell you that this. state is undefined, and lead you to think about whether this is the correct this in this call sequence.

   In future, if you see a similar error, it should trigger off a thought that maybe a bind() call is missing somewhere.

Exercise: Event Handling

1. To persist the changes, we could either save the issues in local storage on the browser, or save it in the server. Modifying the global `initialIssues` variable will not work because when the page is refreshed, this variable is recreated.

2. The page is refreshed as if a new request to / has been made. In the URL bar, you can see URL query parameters for owner and title like `?owner=&title=`. This is because the default action of a form is a GET HTTP request with the values of the form, and what you see in the URL bar is just the result of this call. (The values in the URL parameters are blank because they were assigned to empty strings in `handleSubmit()`).

3. You will see that the subtree under `<tbody>` is being modified only once. In the details of the modification, you can see that a child is being added, but none of the other existing children are being modified. If you compare it with the number of `render()` method calls, you will find that even though `render()` was being called for each row, only the new row is being added to the DOM.

Express and GraphQL

Now that you have learned about creating components and building a workable user interface using React, in this chapter, we'll spend some time integrating with the back-end server for the data.

Until now, the only resource the Express and Node.js server was serving was static content in the form of index.html. In this chapter, we'll start fetching and storing the data using APIs from the Express and Node.js server in addition to the static HTML file. This will replace the hard-coded array of issues in the browser's memory. We will be making changes to both front-end and back-end code, as we'll be implementing as well as consuming the APIs.

We will not persist the data on disk; instead, we'll just use a simulated database in the server's memory. We will leave actual persistence to the next chapter.

Express

I briefly touched upon Express and how to serve static files using Express in the Hello World chapter. But Express can do much more than just serve static files. Express is a minimal, yet, flexible web application framework. It's minimal in the sense that by itself, Express does very little. It relies on other modules called *middleware* to provide the functionality that most applications will need.

Routing

The first concept is that of routing. At the heart of Express is a router, which essentially takes a client request, matches it against any routes that are present, and executes the handler function that is associated with that route. The handler function is expected to generate the appropriate response.

A route specification consists of an HTTP method (GET, POST, etc.), a path specification that matches the request URI, and the route handler. The handler is passed in a request object and a response object. The request object can be inspected to get the various details of the request, and the response object's methods can be used to send the response to the client. All this may seem a little overwhelming, so let's just start with a simple example and explore the details.

We already have an Express application in the which we created using the express() function. We also installed a middleware for handling static files. A middleware function deals with *any* request matching the path specification, regardless of the HTTP method. In contrast, a route can match a request with a specific

HTTP method. So, instead of `app.use()`, `app.get()` has to be used in order to match the GET HTTP method. Further, the handler function, the second argument that the routing function takes, can set the response to be sent back to the caller like this:

```
...
app.get('/hello', (req, res) => {
  res.send('Hello World!');
});
...
```

Request Matching

When a request is received, the first thing that Express does is match the request to one of the routes. The request method is matched against the route's method. In the previous example, the route's method is `get()` so any HTTP request using the GET method will match it. Further, the request URL is matched with the path specification, the first argument in the route, which is `/hello`. When a HTTP request matches this specification, the handler function is called. In the previous example, we just responded with a text message.

The route's method and path need not be specific. If you want to match all HTTP methods, you could write `app.all()`. If you needed to match multiple paths, you could pass in an array of paths, or even a regular expression like `'/*.do'` will match any request ending with the extension `.do`. Regular expressions are rarely used, but route parameters are often used, so I'll discuss that in a little more detail.

Route Parameters

Route parameters are named segments in the path specification that match a part of the URL. If a match occurs, the value in that part of the URL is supplied as a variable in the request object.

This is used in the following form:

```
app.get('/customers/:customerId', ...)
```

The URL `/customers/1234` will match the route specification, and so will `/customers/4567`. In either case, the customer ID will be captured and supplied to the handler function as part of the request in `req.params`, with the name of the parameter as the key. Thus, `req.params.customerId` will have the value `1234` or `4567` for each of these URLs, respectively.

■ **Note** The query string is not part of the path specification, so you cannot have different handlers for different parameters or values of the query string.

Route Lookup

Multiple routes can be set up to match different URLs and patterns. The router does not try to find a best match; instead, it tries to match all routes in the order in which they are installed. The first match is used. So, if two routes are possible matches to a request, it will use the first defined one. So, the routes have to be defined in the order of priority.

Thus, if you add patterns rather than very specific paths, you should be careful to add the more generic pattern after the specific paths in case a request can match both. For example, if you want to match everything that goes under `/api/`, that is, a pattern like `/api/*`, you should add this route only after all the more specific routes that handle paths such as `/api/issues`.

Handler Function

Once a route is matched, the handler function is called, which in the previous example was an anonymous function supplied to the route setup function. The parameters passed to the handler are a request object and a response object. The handler function is not expected to return any value. But it can inspect the request object and send out a response as part of the response object based on the request parameters.

Let's briefly look at the important properties and methods of the request and response objects.

Request Object

Any aspect of the request can be inspected using the request object's properties and methods. A few important and useful properties and methods are listed here:

- req.params: This is an object containing properties mapped to the named route parameters as you saw in the example that used :customerId. The property's key will be the name of the route parameter (customerId in this case) and the value will be the actual string sent as part of the HTTP request.

- req.query: This holds a parsed query string. It's an object with keys as the query string parameters and values as the query string values. Multiple keys with the same name are converted to arrays, and keys with a square bracket notation result in nested objects (e.g., order[status]=closed can be accessed as req.query.order. status).

- req.header, req.get(header): The get method gives access to any header in the request. The header property is an object with all headers stored as key-value pairs. Some headers are treated specially (like Accept) and have dedicated methods in the request object for them. That's because common tasks that depend on these headers can be easily handled.

- req.path: This contains the path part of the URL, that is, everything up to any ? that starts the query string. Usually, the path is part of the route specification, but if the path is a pattern that can match different URLs, you can use this property to get the actual path that was received in the request.

- req.url, req.originalURL: These properties contain the complete URL, including the query string. Note that if you have any middleware that modifies the request URL, originalURL will hold the URL as it was received, before the modification.

- req.body: This contains the body of the request, valid for POST, PUT, and PATCH requests. Note that the body is not available (req.body will be undefined) unless a middleware is installed to read and optionally interpret or parse the body.

There are many other methods and properties; for a complete list, refer to the Request documentation of Express at http://expressjs.com/en/api.html#req as well as Node.js' request object at https://nodejs.org/api/http.html#http_class_http_incomingmessage, from which the Express Request is extended.

Response Object

The response object is used to construct and send a response. Note that if no response is sent, the client is left waiting.

- `res.send(body)`: You already saw the `res.send()` method briefly, which responded with a string. This method can also accept a buffer (in which case the content type is set as `application/octet-stream` as opposed to `text/html` in case of a string). If the body is an object or an array, it is automatically converted to a JSON string with an appropriate content type.

- `res.status(code)`: This sets the response status code. If not set, it is defaulted to 200 OK. One common way of sending an error is by combining the `status()` and `send()` methods in a single call like `res.status(403).send("Access Denied")`.

- `res.json(object)`: This is the same as `res.send()`, except that this method forces conversion of the parameter passed into a JSON, whereas `res.send()` may treat some parameters like `null` differently. It also makes the code readable and explicit, stating that you are indeed sending out a JSON.

- `res.sendFile(path)`: This responds with the contents of the file at `path`. The content type of the response is guessed using the extension of the file.

There are many other methods and properties in the response object; you can look at the complete list in the Express documentation for Response at `http://expressjs.com/en/api.html#res` and Node.js' Response object in the HTTP module at `https://nodejs.org/api/http.html#http_class_http_serverresponse`. But for most common use, the previous methods should suffice.

Middleware

Express is a web framework that has minimal functionality of its own. An Express application is essentially a series of middleware function calls. In fact, the Router itself is nothing but a middleware function. The distinction is that middleware usually works on generic handling of requests and/or things that need to be done for all or most requests, but not necessarily be the last in the chain, that sends out a response. A route, on the other hand, is meant to be used for a specific path+method combination and is expected to send out a response.

Middleware functions are those that have access to the request object (`req`), the response object (`res`), and the next middleware function in the application's request-response cycle. The next middleware function is commonly denoted by a variable named `next`. I won't go into the details of how to write your own middleware function, since we will not be writing new middleware in the application. But we will use some middleware for sure, so it's handy to understand how any middleware works at a high level.

We already used one middleware called `express.static` in the Hello World example, to serve static files. This is the only built-in middleware (other than the router) available as part of Express. But there are other very useful middleware supported by the Express team, of which we will be using body-parser in this chapter, though indirectly. Third-party middleware is available via npm.

Middleware can be at the application level (applies to all requests) or at a specific path level (applies to specific request path patterns). The way to use a middleware at the application level is to simply supply the function to the application, like this:

```
app.use(middlewareFunction);
```

In the case of the static middleware, we constructed a middleware function by calling express.static() method. This not only returned a middleware function, but also configured it to use the directory called public to look for the static files.

In order to use the same middleware for only requests matching a certain URL path, say, /public, the app.use() method would have to be called with two arguments, the first one being the path, like this:

```
app.use('/public', express.static('public'));
```

This would have *mounted* the static middleware on the path /public and all static files would have to be accessed with the prefix /public, for example, /public/index.html.

REST API

REST (short for representational state transfer) is an architectural pattern for application programming interfaces (APIs). There are other older patterns such as SOAP and XMLRPC, but of late, the REST pattern has gained popularity.

Since the APIs in the Issue Tracker application are only for internal consumption, we could use any API pattern or even invent our own. But let's not do that because using an existing pattern forces you to think and organize the APIs and schema better and encourages some good practices.

Although we won't be using the REST pattern, I'll discuss it briefly since it is one of the more popular choices due to its simplicity and small number of constructs. It'll let you appreciate the differences and the logic for the choice that I'll make eventually, to use GraphQL.

Resource Based

The APIs are resource based (as opposed to action based). Thus, API names like getSomething or saveSomething are not normal in REST APIs. In fact, there are no API *names* in the conventional sense, because APIs are formed by a combination of resources and actions. There are really only resource names called *endpoints*.

Resources are accessed based on a Uniform Resource Identifier (URI), also known as an endpoint. Resources are nouns (not verbs). You typically use two URIs per resource: one for the collection (like /customers) and one for an individual object (like /customers/1234), where 1234 uniquely identifies a customer.

Resources can also form a hierarchy. For example, the collection of orders of a customer is identified by /customers/1234/orders, and an order of that customer is identified by /customers/1234/orders/43.

HTTP Methods as Actions

To access and manipulate the resources, you use HTTP methods. While resources were nouns, the HTTP methods are verbs that operate on them. They map to CRUD (Create, Read, Update, Delete) operations on the resource. Table 5-1 shows commonly used mapping of CRUD operations to HTTP methods and resources.

Table 5-1. *CRUD Mapping for HTTP Methods*

Operation	Method	Resource	Example	Remarks
Read – List	GET	Collection	`GET /customers`	Lists objects (additional query string can be used for filtering and sorting)
Read	GET	Object	`GET / customers/1234`	Returns a single object (query string may be used to specify which fields)
Create	POST	Collection	`POST /customers`	Creates an object with the values specified in the body
Update	PUT	Object	`PUT / customers/1234`	Replaces the object with the one specified in the body
Update	PATCH	Object	`PATCH / customers/1234`	Modifies some properties of the object, as specified in the body
Delete	DELETE	Object	`DELETE / customers/1234`	Deletes the object

Some other operations such as DELETE and PUT in the collection may also be used to delete and modify the entire collection in one shot, but this is not common usage. HEAD and OPTIONS are also valid verbs that give out information about the resources rather than actual data. They are used mainly for APIs that are externally exposed and consumed by many different clients.

Although the HTTP method and operation mapping are well mapped and specified, REST by itself lays down no rules for the following:

- Filtering, sorting, and paginating a list of objects. The query string is commonly used in an implementation-specific way to specify these.

- Specifying which fields to return in a READ operation.

- If there are embedded objects, specifying which of those to expand in a READ operation.

- Specifying which fields to modify in a PATCH operation.

- Representation of objects. You are free to use JSON, XML, or any other representation for the objects in both READ and WRITE operations.

Given the fact that different API sets use different ways of dealing with these issues, most REST API implementations are more REST-*like* than strict REST. This has affected common adoption and there are, therefore, a lack of tools that can help do much of the common things that need to be done to implement a REST-based API.

GraphQL

Although the REST paradigm is quite useful in making APIs predictable, the shortcomings discussed previously have made it hard to use it when different clients access the same set of APIs. For example, how an object is displayed in a mobile application and the same is displayed in a desktop browser can be quite different, and therefore, a more granular control as well as aggregation of different resources may work better.

GraphQL was developed to address just these concerns. As a result, GraphQL is a far more elaborate specification, with the following salient features.

Field Specification

Unlike REST APIs, where you have little control on what the server returns as part of an object, in GraphQL, the properties of an object that need to be returned must be specified. Specifying no fields of an object would, in a REST API, return the entire object. In contrast, in a GraphQL query, it is invalid to request nothing.

This lets the client control the amount of data that is transferred over the network, making it more efficient, especially for lighter front-ends such as mobile applications. Further, addition of new capabilities (fields or new APIs) does not require you to introduce a new version of the API set. Given a query, since the shape of the returned data is determined by it, the effect of it is the same, regardless of changes to the API.

A downside to this that there is a bit of a learning curve for the GraphQL query language, which must be used to make any API call. Fortunately, the specification of the language is quite simple and easy to master.

Graph Based

REST APIs were resource based, whereas GraphQL is graph based. This means that relationships between objects are naturally handled in GraphQL APIs.

In the Issue Tracker application, you could think of Issues and Users having a relation: An issue is assigned to a user, and a user has one or more issues assigned to them. When querying for a user's properties, GraphQL makes it natural to query for some properties associated with all the issues assigned to them as well.

Single Endpoint

GraphQL API servers have a *single* endpoint in contrast to one endpoint per resource in REST. The name of the resource(s) or field(s) being accessed is supplied as part of the query itself.

This makes it possible to use a single query for *all* the data that is required by a client. Due to the graph-based nature of the query, all related objects can be retrieved as part of a query for one object. Not only that, even unrelated objects can be queried in a single call to the API server. This obviates the need for "aggregation" services whose job was to put together multiple API results into one bundle.

Strongly Typed

GraphQL is a strongly typed query language. All fields and arguments have a type against which both queries and results can be validated and give descriptive error messages. In addition to types, it is also possible to specify which fields and arguments are required and which others are optional. All this is done using the GraphQL schema language.

The advantage of a strongly typed system is that it prevents errors. This is a great thing, considering that APIs are written and consumed by different teams and there is bound to be communication gaps due to this.

The type system of GraphQL has its own language for specifying the details of the types that you wish to support in your API. It supports the basic scalar types such as integer and string, objects composed of these basic data types, and custom scalar types and enumerations.

Introspection

A GraphQL server can be queried for the types it supports. This creates a powerful platform for tools and client software to build atop this information. This includes code-generation utilities in statically typed languages and explorers that let developers test and learn an API set quickly, without grepping the codebase or wrangling with cURL.

We will be using one such tool, called the Apollo Playground, to test our APIs before integrating them into the application's UI.

Libraries

Parsing and dealing with the type system language (also called the GraphQL Schema Language) as well as the query language is hard to do on your own. Fortunately, there are tools and libraries available in most languages for this purpose.

For JavaScript on the back-end, there is a reference implementation of GraphQL called GraphQL.js. To tie this to Express and enable HTTP requests to be the transport mechanism for the API calls, there is a package called `express-graphql`.

But these are very basic tools that lack some advanced support such as modularized schemas and seamless handling of custom scalar types. The package `graphql-tools` and the related `apollo-server` are built on top of GraphQL.js to add these advanced features. We will be using the advanced packages for the Issue Tracker application in this chapter.

I will cover only those features of GraphQL that are needed for the purpose of the application. For advanced features that you may need in your own specific application, do refer to the complete documentation of GraphQL at `https://graphql.org` and the tools at `https://www.apollographql.com/docs/graphql-tools/`.

The About API

Let's start with a simple API that returns a string, called About. In this section, we'll implement this API as well as another API that lets us change the string that is returned by this API. This will let you learn the basics of simple reads as well as writes using GraphQL.

Before we start writing the code for it, we need the npm packages for `graphql-tools`, `apollo-server`, and the base package `graphql` that these depend on. The package `graphql-tools` is a dependency of `apollo-server-express`, so we don't have to specify it explicitly, whereas `graphql` is a peer dependency that needs to be installed separately. Here is the command to install these:

```
$ npm install graphql@0 apollo-server-express@2
```

Now, let's define the schema of the APIs that we need to support. The GraphQL schema language requires us to define each type using the `type` keyword followed by the name of the type, followed by its specification within curly braces. For example, to define a `User` type containing a string for the user's name, this is the specification in the schema language:

```
...
type User {
  name: String
}
...
```

For the About API, we don't need any special types, just the basic data type String is good enough. But GraphQL schema has two special types that are entry points into the type system, called Query and Mutation. All other APIs or fields are defined hierarchically under these two types, which are like the entry points into the API. Query fields are expected to return existing state, whereas mutation fields are expected to change something in the application's data.

A schema must have at least the Query type. The distinction between the query and mutation types is notional: there is nothing that you can do in a query or mutation that you cannot do in the other. But a subtle difference is that whereas query fields are executed in parallel, mutation fields are executed in series. So, it's best to use them as they are meant to be used: implement READ operations under Query and things that modify the system under Mutation.

The GraphQL type system supports the following basic data types:

- Int: A signed 32-bit integer.

- Float: A signed double-precision floating-point value.

- String: A UTF-8 character sequence.

- Boolean: true or false.

- ID: This represents a unique identifier, serialized as a string. Using an ID instead of a string indicates that it is not intended to be human-readable.

In addition to specifying the type, the Schema Language has a provision to indicate whether the value is optional or mandatory. By default, all values are optional (i.e., they can be null), and those that require a value are defined by adding an exclamation character (!) after the type.

In the About API, all we need is a field called about under Query, which is a string and a mandatory one. Note that the schema definition is a string in JavaScript. We'll use the template string format so that we can smoothly add newlines within the schema. Thus, the schema definition of the about field that can be queried is written like this:

```
...
const typeDefs = `
  type Query {
    about: String!
  }
`;
...
```

We'll use the variable typeDefs when we initialize the server, but before that, let's also define another field that lets us change the message and call this setAboutMessage. But this needs an input value for the new message that we will receive. Such input values are specified just like in function calls: using parentheses. Thus, to indicate that this field needs a mandatory string input called message, we need to write:

```
...
  setAboutMessage(message: String!)
...
```

Note that all arguments must be named. There are no positional arguments in the GraphQL Schema Language. Also, all fields must have a type, and there is no void or other type that indicates that the field returns nothing. To overcome this, we can just use any data type and make it optional so that the caller does not expect a value.

Let's use a string data type as the return value for the setAboutMessage field and add it to the schema under the Mutation type. Let's also name the variable that contains the schema typeDefs and define it as a string in server.js:

```
...
const typeDefs = `
  type Query {
    about: String!
  }
  type Mutation {
    setAboutMessage(message: String!): String
  }
`;
...
```

Note that I stopped calling these APIs, rather I am calling even something like setAboutMessage a *field*. That's because all of GraphQL has only fields, and accessing a field can have a side effect such as setting some value.

The next step is to have handlers or functions that can be called when these fields are accessed. Such functions are called *resolvers* because they resolve a query to a field with real values. Although the schema definition was done in the special Schema Language, the implementation of resolvers depends on the programming language that we use. For example, if you were to define the About API set, say, in Python, the schema string would look the same as in JavaScript. But the handlers would look quite different from what we are going to write in JavaScript.

In the Apollo Server as well as in graphql-tools, resolvers are specified as nested objects that follow the structure of the schema. At every leaf level, the field needs to be resolved using a function of the same name as the field. Thus, at the topmost level, we'll have two properties named Query and Mutation in the resolver. Let's start defining this:

```
...
const resolvers = {
  Query: {
  },
  Mutation: {
  },
};
...
```

Within the Query object, we'll need a property for about, which is a function that returns the About message. Let's first define that message as a variable at the top of the file. Since we will change the value of the message within the setAboutMessage field, we'll need to use the let keyword rather than const.

```
...
let aboutMessage = "Issue Tracker API v1.0";
...
```

Now, all the function needs to do is return this variable. A simple arrow function that takes no arguments should do the trick:

```
...
  Query: {
    about: () => aboutMessage,
  },
...
```

The setAboutMessage function is not so simple since we'll need to receive input arguments. All resolver functions are supplied four arguments like this:

```
fieldName(obj, args, context, info)
```

The arguments are described here:

- obj: The object that contains the result returned from the resolver on the parent field. This argument enables the nested nature of GraphQL queries.

- args: An object with the arguments passed into the field in the query. For example, if the field was called with setAboutMessage(message: "New Message"), the args object would be: { "message": "New Message" }.

- context: This is an object shared by all resolvers in a particular query and is used to contain per-request state, including authentication information, dataloader instances, and anything else that should be taken into account when resolving the query.

- info: This argument should only be used in advanced cases, but it contains information about the execution state of the query.

The return value should be of the type that is specified in the schema. In the case of the field setAboutMessage, since the return value is optional, it can choose to return nothing. But it's good practice to return *some* value to indicate successful execution of the field, so let's just return the message input value. We will also not be using any properties of the parent object (Query) in this case, so we can ignore the first argument, obj, and use only the property within args. Thus, the function definition for setAboutMessage looks like this:

```
...
function setAboutMessage(_, { message }) {
  return aboutMessage = message;
}
...
```

■ **Note** We used the ES2015 Destructuring Assignment feature to access the message property present inside the second argument called args. This is equivalent to naming the argument as args and accessing the property as args.message rather than simply message.

Now, we can assign this function as the resolver for setAboutMessage within the Mutation top-level field like this:

```
...
  Mutation: {
    setAboutMessage,
  },
...
```

■ **Note** We used the ES2015 Object Property Shorthand to specify the value of the setAboutMessage property. When the property name and the variable name assigned to it are the same, the variable name can be skipped. Thus, { setAboutMessage: setAboutMessage } can be simply written as { setAboutMessage }.

Now that we have the schema defined as well as the corresponding resolvers, we are ready to initialize the GraphQL server. The way to do this is to construct an ApolloServer object defined in the apollo-server-express package. The constructor takes in an object with at least two properties—typeDefs and resolvers—and returns a GraphQL server object. Here's the code to do that:

```
...
const { ApolloServer } = require('apollo-server-express');
...
const server = new ApolloServer({
  typeDefs,
  resolvers,
});
...
```

Finally, we need to install the Apollo Server as a middleware in Express. We need a path (the single endpoint) where we will mount the middleware. But, the Apollo Server is not a single middleware; there are in fact a group of middleware functions that deal with different HTTP methods differently. The ApolloServer object gives us a convenience method that does all this for us, called applyMiddleware. It takes in a configuration object as its argument that configures the server, of which two important properties are app and path. Thus, to install the middleware in the Express application, let's add the following code:

```
...
server.applyMiddleware({ app, path: '/graphql' });
...
```

After putting all this together, we should have a working API server. The new contents of server.js are shown in Listing 5-1, which includes all the code snippets.

Listing 5-1. server.js: Implementing the About API Set

```
const express = require('express');
const { ApolloServer } = require('apollo-server-express');

let aboutMessage = "Issue Tracker API v1.0";
```

```
const typeDefs = `
  type Query {
    about: String!
  }
  type Mutation {
    setAboutMessage(message: String!): String
  }
`;

const resolvers = {
  Query: {
    about: () => aboutMessage,
  },
  Mutation: {
    setAboutMessage,
  },
};

function setAboutMessage(_, { message }) {
  return aboutMessage = message;
}

const server = new ApolloServer({
  typeDefs,
  resolvers,
});

const app = express();

app.use(express.static('public'));

server.applyMiddleware({ app, path: '/graphql' });

app.listen(3000, function () {
  console.log('App started on port 3000');
});
```

■ **Note** Although no effort has been spared to ensure that all code listings are accurate, there may be typos, formatting errors such as type of quotes, or even corrections that did not make it to the book before it went to the press. So, always rely on the GitHub repository (`https://github.com/vasansr/pro-mern-stack-2`) as the tested and up-to-date source for all code listings, especially if something does not work as expected.

As I pointed out earlier, GraphQL schema and introspection allows tools to be built that can let developers explore the API. The tool called *Playground* is available by default as part of the Apollo Server and can be accessed simply by browsing the API endpoint. Thus, if you type `http://localhost:3000/graphql` in your browser's URL bar, you'll find the Playground UI.

The default for the Playground is a dark theme. Using the settings function (gear icon in the top-right corner), I have changed it to a light theme as well as reduced the font size to 12. If you also make these changes, you may see the UI as shown in Figure 5-1.

Figure 5-1. *The GraphQL Playground*

Before we test the APIs, it's a good idea to explore the schema using the green SCHEMA button on the right side of the UI. On doing that, you'll find that the about and setAboutMessage fields are described in the schema. To make a query, you can type the query in the left-side window and see the results on the right side after clicking on the Play button, as described in the UI.

The query language has to be used to write the query. The language is JSON-like, but is not JSON. The query needs to follow the same hierarchical structure of the schema and is similar to it. But we don't specify the types of the fields, just their names. In case of input fields, we specify the name and value, separated by a colon (:). Thus, to access the about field, a top-level query has to be used, which contains nothing but the field we need to retrieve, that is about. Here's the complete query:

```
query {
  about
}
```

Note that there is an autocompletion feature in the Playground, which may come in handy as you type. The Playground also shows errors in the query using red underlines. These features use the schema to know about the available fields, arguments, and their types. The Playground queries the schema from the server, so whenever the schema changes, if you rely on autocompletion, you need to refresh the browser so that the changed schema is retrieved from the server.

Since by default all queries are of type Query (as opposed to Mutation), we can skip the keyword query and just type { about }. But to keep it clear, let's always include the query keyword. On clicking the Play button, you will find the following output on the results window on the right side:

```
{
  "data": {
    "about": "Issue Tracker API v1.0"
  }
}
```

The output is a regular JSON object unlike the query, which followed the query language syntax. It also reflects the structure of the query, with "data" as the root object in the result.

Now to test the setAboutMessage field, you can replace the query with a mutation, or better still, you can open a new tab using the + symbol in the UI and type in the mutation query like this:

```
mutation {
  setAboutMessage(message: "Hello World!")
}
```

Running this query should result in returning the same message as the result, like this:

```
{
  "data": {
    "setAboutMessage": "Hello World!"
  }
}
```

Now, running the original about query (in the first tab) should return the new message, "Hello World!" to prove that the new message has been successfully set in the server. To assure ourselves that there is no magic that the Playground is doing, let's also run a query using cURL on the command line for the about field.

A quick way to do this is to copy the command using the COPY CURL button in the Playground and paste it in the command shell. (On a Windows system, the shell does not accept single quotes, so you have to manually edit and change single quotes to double quotes and then escape the double quotes within the query using a backslash.) The command and its output will be as follows:

```
$ curl 'http://localhost:3000/graphql' -H 'Accept-Encoding: gzip, deflate, br' -H
'Content-Type: application/json' -H 'Accept: application/json' -H 'Connection: keep-alive'
-H 'DNT: 1' -H 'Origin: http://localhost:3000' --data-binary '{"query":"query {\n  about\
n}\n"}' -compressed
{"data":{"about":"Hello World!"}}
```

Note that the cURL query was sent as a JSON, with the actual query encoded as a string value for the property query. You can see that something similar happens when using the Playground, by inspecting the Network tab of the Developer Console in your browser. The JSON contains at the minimum a property called query (as seen in the curl command), and optionally the operationName and variables properties. The JSON object looks like this:

```
{
  "operationName":null,
  "variables":{},
  "query": "{\n  about\n}\n"
}
```

Further, if you look at the headers (or understand the curl command), you will also find that for both the setAboutMessage mutation as well as the about query, the HTTP method used was the same: POST. It may feel a little disconcerting to use a POST method for fetching values from the server, so if you prefer a GET, you could use that instead. The query string of the GET URL can contain the query like this:

```
$ curl 'http://localhost:3000/graphql?query=query+\{+about+\}'
```

Note that this is not a JSON object, as in the POST operation. The query is sent as a plain URL encoded string. We had to escape the curly braces because these have special meaning for cURL, so in a regular Ajax call from the browser, you need not do this. If you execute this command, you should see the same results as the POST command before:

```
$ curl 'http://localhost:3000/graphql?query=query+\{+about+\}'
{"data":{"about":"Hello World!"}}
```

EXERCISE: THE ABOUT API

1. Use the same URL in the browser as well as command line for cURL. For example, type curl http://localhost:3000/graphql, which is the same URL as we used in the browser to invoke the Playground. Or, copy paste the curl command we used for doing a GET request for the about field. What do you see? Can you explain the difference? Hint: Compare the request headers.

2. What are the pros and cons of using GET vs. POST for read-only API calls?

Answers are available at the end of the chapter.

GraphQL Schema File

In the previous section, we specified the GraphQL schema within the JavaScript file. If and when the schema grows bigger, it would be useful to separate the schema into a file of its own. This will help keep the JavaScript source files smaller, and IDEs may be able to format these files and enable syntax coloring.

So, let's move the schema definition to a file of its own rather than a string in the source file. Moving the contents per se is simple; let's create a file called schema.graphql and move the contents of the string typeDefs into it. The new file, schema.graphql, is shown in in Listing 5-2.

Listing 5-2. schema.graphql: New File for GraphQL Schema

```
type Query {
  about: String!
}

type Mutation {
  setAboutMessage(message: String!): String
}
```

Now, to use this instead of the string variable, this file's contents have to be read into a string. Let's use the fs module and the readFileSync function to read the file. Then, we can use the string that readFileSync returned as the value for the property typeDefs when creating the Apollo Server. The changes in the server.js file are shown in Listing 5-3.

Listing 5-3. server.js: Changes for Using the GraphQL Schema File

```
const fs = require('fs');
const express = require('express');
...

const typeDefs = `
  type Query {
    about: String!
  }
  type Mutation {
    setAboutMessage(message: String!): String!
  }
`;

...

const server = new ApolloServer({
  typeDefs: fs.readFileSync('./server/schema.graphql', 'utf-8'),
  resolvers,
});
...
```

There's just one other thing that needs a change: the nodemon tool that restarts the server on detecting changes to files by default only looks for changes to files with a .js extension. To make it watch for changes to other extensions, we need to add an -e option specifying all the extensions it needs to watch for. Since we added a file with extension .graphql, let's specify js and graphql as the two extensions for this option.

The changes to package.json are shown in Listing 5-4.

Listing 5-4. package.json: Changes to nodemon to Watch GraphQL Files

```
...
  "scripts": {
    "start": "nodemon -w server -e js,graphql server/server.js",
    "compile": "babel src --out-dir public",
...
```

If you restart the server using npm start now, you will be able to test the APIs using the Playground and ensure that they behave as before.

The List API

Now that you have learned the basics of GraphQL, let's make some progress toward building the Issue Tracker application using this knowledge. The next thing we'll do is implement an API to fetch a list of issues. We'll test it using the Playground and, in the next section, we'll change the front-end to integrate with this new API.

Let's start by modifying the schema to define a custom type called Issue. It should contain all the fields of the issue object that we have been using up to now. But since there is no scalar type to denote a date in GraphQL, let's use a string type for the time being. We'll implement custom scalar types later in this chapter. So, the type will have integers and strings, some of which are optional. Here's the partial schema code for the new type:

```
...
type Issue {
  id: Int!
  ...
  due: String
}
...
```

Now, let's add a new field under Query to return a list of issues. The GraphQL way to specify a list of another type is to enclose it within square brackets. We could use [Issue] as the type for the field, which we will call issueList. But we need to say not only that the return value is mandatory, but also that each element in the list cannot be null. So, we have to add the exclamation mark after Issue as well as after the array type, as in [Issue!]!.

Let's also separate the top-level Query and Mutation definitions from the custom types using a comment. The way to add comments in the schema is using the # character at the beginning of a line. All these changes are listed in Listing 5-5.

Listing 5-5. schema.graphql: Changes to Include Field issueList and New Issue Type

```
type Issue {
  id: Int!
  title: String!
  status: String!
  owner: String
  effort: Int
  created: String!
  due: String
}

##### Top level declarations

type Query {
  about: String!
  issueList: [Issue!]!
}

type Mutation {
  setAboutMessage(message: String!): String
}
```

In the server code, we need to add a resolver under Query for the new field, which points to a function. We'll also have an array of issues (a copy of what we have in the front-end code) that is a stand-in for a database. We can immediately return this array from the resolver. The function could be in-place like that for the about field, but knowing that we'll expand this function to do more than just return a hard-coded array, let's create a separate function called issueList for it.

This set of changes in server.js is shown in Listing 5-6.

Listing 5-6. server.js: Changes for issueList Query Field

```
...
let aboutMessage = "Issue Tracker API v1.0";

const issuesDB = [
  {
    id: 1, status: 'New', owner: 'Ravan', effort: 5,
    created: new Date('2019-01-15'), due: undefined,
    title: 'Error in console when clicking Add',
  },
  {
    id: 2, status: 'Assigned', owner: 'Eddie', effort: 14,
    created: new Date('2019-01-16'), due: new Date('2019-02-01'),
    title: 'Missing bottom border on panel',
  },
];

const resolvers = {
  Query: {
    about: () => aboutMessage,
    issueList,
  },
  Mutation: {
    setAboutMessage,
  },
};

function setAboutMessage(_, { message }) {
  return aboutMessage = message;
}

function issueList() {
  return issuesDB;
}
...
```

To test this in the Playground, you will need to run a query that specifies the issueList field, with subfields. But first, a refresh of the browser is needed so that the Playground has the latest schema and doesn't show errors when you type the query.

The array itself need not be expanded in the query. It is implicit (due to the schema specification) that issueList returns an array, and therefore, subfields of the field are automatically expanded within the array.

Here is one such query that you can run to test the issueList field:

```
query {
  issueList {
    id
    title
    created
  }
}
```

This query will result in an output like this:

```
{
  "data": {
    "issueList": [
      {
        "id": 1,
        "title": "Error in console when clicking Add",
        "created": "Tue Jan 15 2019 05:30:00 GMT+0530 (India Standard Time)"
      },
      {
        "id": 2,
        "title": "Missing bottom border on panel",
        "created": "Wed Jan 16 2019 05:30:00 GMT+0530 (India Standard Time)"
      }
    ]
  }
}
```

If you add more subfields in the query, their values will also be returned. If you look at the date fields, you will see that they have been converted from a Date object to a string using the toString() method of the Date JavaScript object.

EXERCISE: THE LIST API

1. Try to specify no subfields for the issueList field, like query { issueList }, like we did for the about field and click the Play button. What do you observe as the result? Try to specify an empty field list using query { issueList { } } instead and play the request. What do you see now? Can you explain the difference?

2. Add an invalid subfield (say, test) to the query under issueList. What error do you expect when you click the Play button? In particular, would Playground send the request to the server? Try it out in the Playground, with the Developer Console open.

3. How would an aggregated query look, one that includes the list of issues as well as the about field?

Answers are available at the end of the chapter.

List API Integration

Now that we have the List API working, let's get it integrated into the UI. In this section, we will replace the implementation of the loadData() method in the IssueList React component with something that fetches the data from the server.

To use the APIs, we need to make asynchronous API calls, or Ajax calls. The popular library jQuery is an easy way to use the $.ajax() function, but including the entire jQuery library just for this purpose seems like overkill. Fortunately, there are many libraries that provide this functionality. Better still, modern browsers support Ajax calls natively via the Fetch API. For older browsers such as Internet

Explorer, a polyfill for the Fetch API is available from whatwg-fetch. Let's use this polyfill directly from a CDN and include it in index.html. We'll use the same CDN we used before, unpkg.com, for this purpose. These changes are shown in Listing 5-7

Listing 5-7. index.html: Changes for Including whatwg-fetch Polyfill

```
...
  <script src="https://unpkg.com/@babel/polyfill@7/dist/polyfill.min.js"></script>
  <script src="https://unpkg.com/whatwg-fetch@3.0.0/dist/fetch.umd.js"></script>
  <style>
...
```

■ **Note**   The polyfill is required only for Internet Explorer and older versions of other browsers. All latest versions of popular browsers—such as Chrome, Firefox, Safari, Edge, and Opera—support fetch() natively.

Next, within the loadData() method, we need to construct a GraphQL query. This is a simple string like what we used in the Playground to test the issueList GraphQL field. But we've to ensure that we're querying for all subfields of an issue, so the following can be the query for fetching all issues and all subfields:

```
...
  const query = `query {
    issueList {
      id title status owner
      created effort due
    }
  }`;
...
```

We'll send this query string as the value for the query property within a JSON, as part of the body to the fetch request. The method we'll use is POST and we'll add a header that indicates that the content type is JSON. Here's the complete fetch request:

```
...
  const response = await fetch('/graphql', {
    method: 'POST',
    headers: { 'Content-Type': 'application/json'},
    body: JSON.stringify({ query })
  });
...
```

■ **Note**   We used the await keyword to deal with asynchronous calls. This is part of the ES2017 specification and is supported by the latest versions of all browsers except Internet Explorer. It is automatically handled by Babel transforms for older browsers. Also, await can only be used in functions that are marked async. We will have to add the async keyword to the loadData() function soon. If you are not familiar with the async/await construct, you can learn about it at https://developer.mozilla.org/en-US/docs/Web/JavaScript/Reference/Statements/async_function.

Once the response arrives, we can get the JSON data converted to a JavaScript object by using the response.json() method. Finally, we need to call a setState() to supply the list of issues to the state variable called issues, like this:

```
...
    const result = await response.json();
    this.setState({ issues: result.data.issueList });
...
```

We will also need to add the keyword async for the function definition of loadData() since we have used awaits within this function.

At this point, you will be able to refresh the Issue Tracker application in the browser, but you will see an error. This is because we used a string instead of Date objects, and a call to convert the date to a string using toDateString() in the IssueRow component's render() method throws an error. Let's remove the conversions and use the strings as they are:

```
...
      <td>{issue.created}</td>
      ...
      <td>{issue.due}</td>
...
```

We can also now remove the global variable initialIssues, as we no longer require it within loadData(). The complete set of changes in App.jsx is shown in Listing 5-8.

Listing 5-8. App.jsx: Changes for Integrating the List API

```
const initialIssues = [
  {
    id: 1, status: 'New', owner: 'Ravan', effort: 5,
    created: new Date('2018-08-15'), due: undefined,
    title: 'Error in console when clicking Add',
  },
  {
    id: 2, status: 'Assigned', owner: 'Eddie', effort: 14,
    created: new Date('2018-08-16'), due: new Date('2018-08-30'),
    title: 'Missing bottom border on panel',
  },
];

function IssueRow(props) {
  const issue = props.issue;
  return (
    <tr>
      ...
      <td>{issue.created.toDateString()}</td>
      <td>{issue.effort}</td>
      <td>{issue.due ? issue.due.toDateString() : ''}</td>
      ...
  );
}
...
```

106

```
async loadData() {
  setTimeout(() => {
    this.setState({ issues: initialIssues });
  }, 500);
  const query = `query {
    issueList {
      id title status owner
      created effort due
    }
  }`;

  const response = await fetch('/graphql', {
    method: 'POST',
    headers: { 'Content-Type': 'application/json'},
    body: JSON.stringify({ query })
  });
  const result = await response.json();
  this.setState({ issues: result.data.issueList });
}
```

That completes the changes required for integrating the List API. Now, if you test the application by refreshing the browser, you will find a screen similar to the screenshot shown in Figure 5-2. You will notice that the dates are long and ungainly, but otherwise, the screen looks the same as it did at the end of the previous chapter. An Add operation will not work, because it uses `Date` objects rather than strings when adding a new issue. We will address these two issues in the next section.

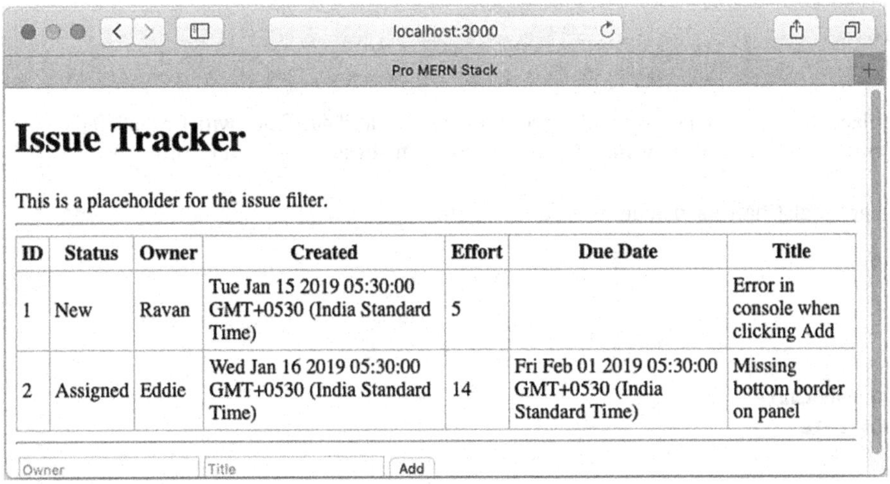
localhost:3000
Pro MERN Stack
Issue Tracker
This is a placeholder for the issue filter.
ID | Status | Owner | Created | Effort | Due Date | Title
1 | New | Ravan | Tue Jan 15 2019 05:30:00 GMT+0530 (India Standard Time) | 5 | | Error in console when clicking Add
2 | Assigned | Eddie | Wed Jan 16 2019 05:30:00 GMT+0530 (India Standard Time) | 14 | Fri Feb 01 2019 05:30:00 GMT+0530 (India Standard Time) | Missing bottom border on panel
Owner
Title
Add

***Figure 5-2.** After List API integration*

Custom Scalar Types

Storing dates as strings may seem to work most times, but not always. For one, sorting and filtering on dates makes it harder, because one has to convert from string to Date types every time. Also, dates should ideally be displayed in the user's time zone and locale, regardless of where the server is. Different users may see the same dates differently based on where they are, and even see dates in the form of "2 days ago" etc.

To achieve all that, we need to store dates as JavaScript's native Date objects. It should ideally be converted to a locale-specific string at the time of displaying it to the user only. But unfortunately, JSON does not have a Date type, and thus, transferring data using JSON in API calls also must convert the date to and from strings.

The recommended string format for transferring Date objects in a JSON is the ISO 8601 format. It is concise and widely accepted. It is also the same format used by JavaScript Date's toJSON() method. In this format, a date such as 26 January 2019, 2:30 PM UTC would be written as 2019-01-26T14:30:00.000Z. It is easy and unambiguous to convert a date to this string using either the toJSON() or the toISOString() methods of Date, as well as to convert it back to a date using new Date(dateString).

Although GraphQL does not support dates natively, it has support for custom scalar types, which can be used for creating a custom scalar type date. To be able to use a custom scalar type, the following has to be done:

1. Define a type for the scalar using the `scalar` keyword instead of the `type` keyword in the schema.

2. Add a top-level resolver for all scalar types, which handles both serialization (on the way out) as well as parsing (on the way in) via class methods.

After these, the new type can be used just as any native scalar type like String and Int would be used. Let's call the new scalar type GraphQLDate. The scalar type has to be defined as such in the schema using the scalar keyword followed by the name of the custom type. Let's put this in the beginning of the file:

```
...
scalar GraphQLDate
...
```

Now, we can replace the String type association with the created and due fields with GraphQLDate. The changes for the scalar definition and the new data types for the date fields are shown in Listing 5-9.

Listing 5-9. schema.graphql: Changes in Schema for Scalar Date

```
scalar GraphQLDate

type Issue {
  id: Int!
  ...
  created: StringGraphQLDate!
  due: StringGraphQLDate
}
...
```

A scalar type resolver needs to be an object of the class GraphQLScalarType, defined in the package graphql-tools. Let's first import this class in server.js:

```
...
const { GraphQLScalarType } = require('graphql');
...
```

The constructor of GraphQLScalarType takes an object with various properties. We can create this resolver by calling new() on the type like this:

```
...
const GraphQLDate = new GraphQLScalarType({ ... });
...
```

Two properties of the initializer—name and description—are used in introspection, so let's set them to the appropriate values:

```
...
  name: 'GraphQLDate',
  description: 'A Date() type in GraphQL as a scalar',
...
```

The class method serialize() will be called to convert a date value to a string. This method takes the value as an argument and expects a string to be returned. All we need to do, thus, is call toISOString() on the value and return it. Here's the serialize() method:

```
...
  serialize(value) {
    return value.toISOString();
  },
...
```

Two other methods, parseValue() and parseLiteral(), are needed to parse strings back to dates. Let's leave this parsing to a later stage when it is really needed for accepting input values, since these are optional methods.

Finally, we need to set this resolver at the same level as Query and Mutation (at the top level) as the value for the scalar type GraphQLDate. The complete set of changes in server.js is shown in Listing 5-10.

Listing 5-10. server.js: Changes for Adding a Resolver for GraphQLDate

```
...
const { ApolloServer } = require('apollo-server-express');
const { GraphQLScalarType } = require('graphql');
...

const GraphQLDate = new GraphQLScalarType({
  name: 'GraphQLDate',
  description: 'A Date() type in GraphQL as a scalar',
  serialize(value) {
    return value.toISOString();
  },
});

const resolvers = {
  Query: {
    ...
  },
```

```
  Mutation: {
    ...
  },
  GraphQLDate,
};
...
```

At this point, if you switch to the Playground and refresh the browser (due to schema changes), and then test the List API. You will see that dates are being returned as the ISO string equivalents rather than the locale-specific long string previously used. Here's a query for testing in the Playground:

```
query {
  issueList {
    title
    created
    due
  }
}
```

Here are the results for this query:

```
{
  "data": {
    "issueList": [
      {
        "title": "Error in console when clicking Add",
        "created": "2019-01-15T00:00:00.000Z",
        "due": null
      },
      {
        "title": "Missing bottom border on panel",
        "created": "2019-01-16T00:00:00.000Z",
        "due": "2019-02-01T00:00:00.000Z"
      }
    ]
  }
}
```

Now, in App.jsx, we can convert the string to the native Date type. One way to do this is to loop through the issues after fetching them from the server and replace the fields due and created with their date equivalents. A better way do this is to pass a *reviver* function to the JSON parse() function. A reviver function is one that is called for parsing all values, and the JSON parser gives it a chance to modify what the default parser would do.

So, let's create such a function that looks for a date-like pattern in the input and converts all such values to a date. We'll use a regular expression to detect this pattern, and a simple conversion using new Date(). Here's the code for the reviver:

```
...
const dateRegex = new RegExp('^\\d\\d\\d\\d-\\d\\d-\\d\\d');
```

```
function jsonDateReviver(key, value) {
  if (dateRegex.test(value)) return new Date(value);
  return value;
}
...
```

The conversion function response.json() does not have the capability to let us specify a reviver, so we have to get the text of the body using response.text() and parse it ourselves using JSON.parse() by passing in the reviver, like this:

```
...
    const body = await response.text();
    const result = JSON.parse(body, jsonDateReviver);
...
```

Now, we can revert our changes to display the dates to what we had before: using toDateString() to render the dates in IssueRow. Including this change, the complete set of changes for using the Date scalar type in App.jsx is shown in Listing 5-11.

Listing 5-11. App.jsx: Changes for Receiving ISO Formatted Dates

```
const dateRegex = new RegExp('^\\d\\d\\d\\d-\\d\\d-\\d\\d');

function jsonDateReviver(key, value) {
  if (dateRegex.test(value)) return new Date(value);
  return value;
}

function IssueRow(props) {
  const issue = props.issue;
  return (
    <tr>
      ...
      <td>{issue.created.toDateString()}</td>
      <td>{issue.effort}</td>
      <td>{issue.due ? issue.due.toDateString() : ' '}</td>
...
    );
}
...
class IssueList extends React.Component {
  async loadData() {
    ...
    const result = await response.json();
    const body = await response.text();
    const result = JSON.parse(body, jsonDateReviver);
    this.setState({ issues: result.data.issueList });
  }
  ...
}
...
```

With this set of changes, the application should appear as before, at the end of the previous chapter. The dates will look nicely formatted. Even adding an issue should work, but on refreshing the browser, the added issue will disappear. That's because we have not saved the issue in the server—all we have done is changed the local state of the issue list in the browser, which will be reset to the initial set of issues on a refresh.

EXERCISE: CUSTOM SCALAR TYPES

1. In `server.js`, remove the resolver that associates the type `GraphQLDate` to the resolver object. Make the API request for `issueList` to be called. Is there any difference in the output? What do you think could explain the difference or lack of difference?

2. How can you be sure that the scalar type resolver is indeed being used?

Answers are available at the end of the chapter.

The Create API

In this section, we will implement an API for creating a new issue in the server, which will be appended to the list of issues in the server's memory.

To do this, we have to first define a field in the schema under `Mutation` called `issueAdd`. This field should take arguments, just as the `setAboutMessage` field did. But this time, we need multiple arguments, one for each property of the issue being added. Alternatively, we can define a new type as an object that has the fields we need for the input. This can't be the same as the `Issue` type because it has some required fields (`id` and `created`) that are not part of the input. These are values that are set by the server only. Further, GraphQL needs a different specification when it comes to input types. Instead of using the `type` keyword, we have to use the `input` keyword.

Let's first define this new input type called `IssueInputs` in the schema:

```
...
input IssueInputs {
  # ... fields of Issue
}
...
```

We discussed how to add comments in the schema. But these comments are not formal descriptions of the types or subfields. For real documentation that is shown part of the schema explorer, a string above the field needs to be added. When the schema is shown to an exploring developer, these descriptions will appear as helpful hints. So, let's add a description for `IssueInputs` as well as for the property `status`, saying it will be defaulted to the value `'New'` if not supplied:

```
...
"Toned down Issue, used as inputs, without server generated values."
input IssueInputs {
  ...
  "Optional, if not supplied, will be set to 'New'"
  status: String
  ...
}
...
```

112

Now, we can use the type `IssueInputs` as the argument type to the new `issueAdd` field under `Mutation`. The return value of this field can be anything. It is usually good practice to return the values generated at the server, typically the ID of the new object. In this case, since both the ID and the created date are set at the server, let's return the entire issue object that was created.

The complete set of changes to the schema is shown in Listing 5-12.

Listing 5-12. schema.graphql: Changes for New Type IssueInputs and New Field issueAdd

```
...
"Toned down Issue, used as inputs, without server generated values."
input IssueInputs {
  title: String!
  "Optional, if not supplied, will be set to 'New'"
  status: String
  owner: String
  effort: Int
  due: GraphQLDate
}

##### Top level declarations
...
type Mutation {
  setAboutMessage(message: String!): String
  issueAdd(issue: IssueInputs!): Issue!
}
```

Next, we need a resolver for `issueAdd` that takes in an `IssueInput` type and creates a new issue in the in-memory database. Just like we did for `setAboutMessage`, we can ignore the first argument and use a destructuring assignment to access the issue object, which is the input:

```
...
function issueAdd(_, { issue }) {
  ...
}
```

In the function, let's set the ID and the created date as we did in the browser:

```
...
  issue.created = new Date();
  issue.id = issuesDB.length + 1;
...
```

Further, let's also default the status, if not supplied (since we have not declared it as a required subfield) to the value `'New'`:

```
...
  if (issue.status == undefined) issue.status = 'New';
...
```

Finally, we can append the issue to the global variable issuesDB and return the issue object as is:

```
...
  issuesDB.push(issue);
  return issue;
...
```

This function now can be set as the resolver for the issueAdd field under Mutation:

```
...
  Mutation: {
    setAboutMessage,
    issueAdd,
  },
...
```

We had postponed implementing the parsers for the custom scalar type GraphQLDate because we didn't need it then. But now, since the type IssueInputs does have a GraphQLDate type, we must implement the parsers for receiving date values. There are two methods that need to be implemented in the GraphQLDate resolver: parseValue and parseLiteral.

The method parseLiteral is called in the normal case, where the field is specified in-place in the query. The parser calls this method with an argument ast, which contains a kind property as well as a value property. The kind property indicates the type of the token that the parser found, which can be a float, an integer, or a string. For GraphQLDate, the only type of token we'll need to support is a string. We can check this using a constant defined in the Kind package in graphql/language. If the type of token is string, we will parse the value and return a date. Otherwise, we'll return undefined. Here's the implementation of parseLiteral:

```
...
  parseLiteral(ast) {
    return (ast.kind == Kind.STRING) ? new Date(ast.value) : undefined;
  },
...
```

A return value of undefined indicates to the GraphQL library that the type could not be converted, and it will be treated as an error.

The method parseValue will be called if the input is supplied as a variable. I will cover variables in the query input in a later section in this chapter, but at the moment, consider it as an input in the form of a JavaScript object, a pre-parsed JSON value. This method's argument will be the value directly, without a kind specification, so all we need to do is construct a date out of it and return it like this:

```
...
  parseValue(value) {
    return new Date(value);
  },
...
```

The complete set of changes to server.js is shown in Listing 5-13.

Listing 5-13. server.js: Changes for the Create API

```
...
const { GraphQLScalarType } = require('graphql');
const { Kind } = require('graphql/language');
...

const GraphQLDate = new GraphQLScalarType({
  ...
  parseValue(value) {
    return new Date(value);
  },
  parseLiteral(ast) {
    return (ast.kind == Kind.STRING) ? new Date(ast.value) : undefined;
  },
});
...

const resolvers = {
  ...
  Mutation: {
    setAboutMessage,
    issueAdd,
  },
  GraphQLDate,
};
...

function issueAdd(_, { issue }) {
  issue.created = new Date();
  issue.id = issuesDB.length + 1;
  if (issue.status == undefined) issue.status = 'New';
  issuesDB.push(issue);
  return issue;
}
...
```

Now we are ready to test the Create API using the Playground. If you explore the schema in the Playground (a browser refresh may be needed) and drill down to the status field of IssueInputs, you will find the descriptions that we provided in the schema. A screenshot of this is shown in Figure 5-3.

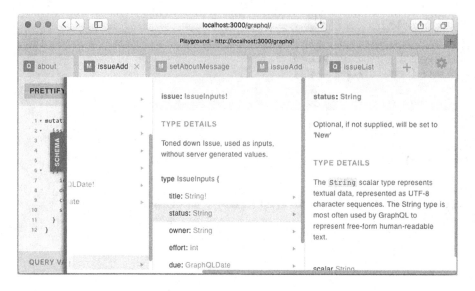

Figure 5-3. *Schema showing descriptions of IssueInputs and status*

To test the addition of a new issue, you can use the following query in the Playground:

```
mutation {
  issueAdd(issue:{
    title: "Completion date should be optional",
    owner: "Pieta",
    due: "2018-12-13",
  }) {
    id
    due
    created
    status
  }
}
```

Running this query should give the following result in the result window of the Playground:

```
{
  "data": {
    "issueAdd": {
      "id": 4,
      "due": "2018-12-13T00:00:00.000Z",
      "created": "2018-10-03T14:48:10.551Z",
      "status": "New"
    }
  }
}
```

This shows that the due date has been properly parsed and converted. The status field also has been defaulted to 'New' as expected. You can also confirm that the issue has been created by running a query for issueList in the Playground and checking the results.

EXERCISE: THE CREATE API

1. We used an `input` complex type to supply the values for `issueAdd`. Compare this with passing each field individually, like `issueAdd(title: String!, owner: String ...)`. What are the pros and cons of each method?

2. Instead of a valid date string, try passing a valid integer like `due: 2018` for the field. What do you think the value of `ast.kind` will be in `parseLiteral`? Add a `console. log` message in `parseLiteral` and confirm this. What other values of `ast.kind` do you think are possible?

3. Pass a string, but an invalid date, like `"abcdef"` for the `due` field. What happens? How can one fix this?

4. Is there another way of specifying default values for the `status` field? Hint: Read up on passing arguments in the GraphQL schema documentation at `http://graphql. github.io/learn/schema/#arguments`.

Answers are available at the end of the chapter.

Create API Integration

Let's start the integration of the Create API with a minor change in the defaulting of the new issue in the UI. Let's remove setting the status to 'New' and set the due date to 10 days from the current date. This change can be done in the `handleSubmit()` method in the `IssueAdd` component in `App.jsx`, like this:

```
...
    const issue = {
      owner: form.owner.value, title: form.title.value, status: 'New',
      due: new Date(new Date().getTime() + 1000*60*60*24*10),
    }
...
```

Before making the API call, we need a query with the values of the fields filled in. Let's use a template string to generate such a query within the `createIssue()` method in `IssueList`. We can use the title and owner properties of the passed-in issue object as they are, but for the date field `due`, we have to explicitly convert this to a string as per the ISO format, because that's the format we decided for passing dates.

On the return path, we won't be needing any of the new issue's values, but since the subfields cannot be empty, let's just specify the id field. So, let's form the query string as follows:

```
...
    const query = `mutation {
      issueAdd(issue:{
        title: "${issue.title}",
```

```
      owner: "${issue.owner}",
      due: "${issue.due.toISOString()}",
    }) {
      id
    }
  }`;
```
...

Now, let's use this query to execute `fetch` asynchronously as we did for the Issue List call:

...

```
const response = await fetch('/graphql', {
  method: 'POST',
  headers: { 'Content-Type': 'application/json'},
  body: JSON.stringify({ query })
});
```
...

We could use the complete issue object that is returned and add it to the array in the state as we did before, but it's simpler (although less performant) to just refresh the list of issues, by calling `loadData()` after sending the new issue off to the server. It is also more accurate, just in case there were errors and the issue couldn't be added, or even if more issues were added by some other user in the meantime.

...

```
this.loadData();
```
...

The complete set of changes to integrate the Create API is shown in Listing 5-14.

Listing 5-14. App.jsx: Changes for Integrating the Create API

```
...
class IssueAdd extends React.Component {
  ...
  handleSubmit(e) {
    ...
    const issue = {
      owner: form.owner.value, title: form.title.value, status: 'New',
      due: new Date(new Date().getTime() + 1000*60*60*24*10),
    }
    ...
  }
  ...
}
...
  async createIssue(issue) {
    issue.id = this.state.issues.length + 1;
    issue.created = new Date();
    const newIssueList = this.state.issues.slice();
    newIssueList.push(issue);
    this.setState({ issues: newIssueList });
    const query = `mutation {
```

```
  issueAdd(issue:{
    title: "${issue.title}",
    owner: "${issue.owner}",
    due: "${issue.due.toISOString()}",
  }) {
      id
    }
  }`;

  const response = await fetch('/graphql', {
    method: 'POST',
    headers: { 'Content-Type': 'application/json'},
    body: JSON.stringify({ query })
  });
  this.loadData();
}
```

On testing this set of changes by adding a new issue using the UI, you will find that the due date is set to 10 days from the current date. Also, if you refresh the browser, you will find that the added issue stays, because the new issue has now been saved on the server.

EXERCISE: CREATE API INTEGRATION

1. Add a new issue with a title that has quotes in it, for example, `Unable to create issue with status "New"`. What happens? Inspect the console as well as the request and response in the Developer Console of the browser. How do you think this can be fixed?

Answers are available at the end of the chapter.

Query Variables

For both the mutation calls, we have specified the arguments to the fields inside the query string. When trying out an API in the Playground, as we did for setAboutMessage, this works great. But in most applications, the arguments will be dynamic, based on user input. And that's exactly what happened with issueAdd, and we had to construct the query string using a string template.

This isn't a great idea, firstly because of the small overhead of converting a template to the actual string. A more important reason is that special characters such as quotes and curly braces will need to be escaped. This is quite error-prone, and easy to miss. Since we have not done any escaping, if you test the Issue Tracker application at this point in time by adding an issue that has a double quote in say, the title, you will find that it doesn't work correctly.

GraphQL has a first-class way to factor dynamic values out of the query and pass them as a separate dictionary. These values are called *variables*. This way of passing dynamic values is quite similar to prepared statements in SQL queries.

To use variables, we have to name the operation first. This is done by specifying a name right after the query or mutation field specification. For example, to give a name to a setAboutMessage mutation, the following will have to be done:

```
mutation setNewMessage { setAboutMessage(message: "New About Message") }
```

Next, the input value has to be replaced with a variable name. Variable names start with the $ character. Let's call the variable $message and replace the string "New About Message" with this variable. Finally, to accept the variable, we need to declare it as an argument to the operation name. Thus, the new query will be:

```
mutation setNewMessage($message: String!) { setAboutMessage(message: $message) }
```

Now, to supply the value of the variable, we need to send it across in a JSON object that is *separate* from the query string. In the Playground, there is a tab called QUERY VARIABLES in the bottom-right corner. Clicking on this will split the request window and allow you to type in the query variables in the bottom half. We need to send across the variables as a JSON object with the name of the variable (without the $) as a property and its value as the property's value.

A screenshot of the Playground is shown in Figure 5-4, with the value of the message as "Hello World!".

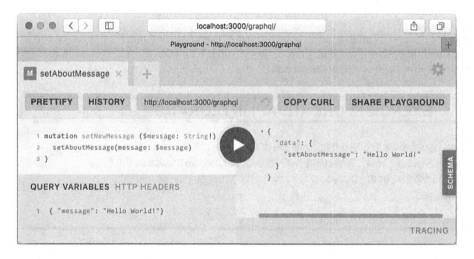

Figure 5-4. *Playground with query variables*

If you inspect the request data in the Developer Console, you will find that the request JSON has three properties—operationName, variables, and query. While we were using only the query until now, to take advantage of variables, we've had to use the other two as well.

■ **Note** GraphQL specification allows multiple operations to be present in the same query string. But only one of these can be executed in one call. The value of operationName specifies which of those operations needs to be executed.

We are now ready to replace the template string with a regular string in the query, using the operation name and variable specification format. The new query string will now be like this:

```
...
  const query = `mutation issueAdd($issue: IssueInputs!) {
    issueAdd(issue: $issue) {
      id
    }
  }`;
...
```

Then, while constructing the body for the fetch() request, in addition to the query property, let's specify the variables property as well, which will contain one variable: issue. The complete set of changes in App.jsx, including this, is shown in Listing 5-15.

Listing 5-15. App.jsx: Changes for Using Query Variables

```
...
  async createIssue(issue) {
    const query = `mutation {
      issueAdd(issue:{
        title: "${issue.title}",
        owner: "${issue.owner}",
        due: "${issue.due.toISOString()}",
      }) {
        id
      }
    }`;
    const query = `mutation issueAdd($issue: IssueInputs!) {
      issueAdd(issue: $issue) {
        id
      }
    }`;

    const response = await fetch('/graphql', {
      method: 'POST',
      headers: { 'Content-Type': 'application/json'},
      body: JSON.stringify({ query, variables: { issue } })
    });
    this.loadData();
  }
...
```

On testing these changes in the Issue Tracker application, you will find that adding a new issue works as before. Further, you should be able to use double quotes in the title of a newly added issue without causing any errors.

EXERCISE: QUERY VARIABLES

1. In the custom scalar type `GraphQLDate`, now that we are using variables, which one of the parsing methods do you think will be called? Will it be `parseLiteral` or `parseValue`? Add a temporary `console.log` statement in both these functions and confirm your answer.

Answers are available at the end of the chapter.

Input Validations

We have kind of ignored validation up until now. But all applications have some typical validations required, not just to prevent invalid input from the UI, but also to prevent invalid inputs from direct API calls. In this section we will add a few validations that are typical for most applications.

A common validation is where the set of allowed values is restricted, one that can be shown in a dropdown. The `status` field in the Issue Tracker application is one such field. One way to implement this validation is adding a check against an array of allowed values as part of the `issueAdd` resolver. But the GraphQL schema itself gives us an automatic way of doing this via enumeration types or *enums*. An enum definition in the schema looks like this:

```
...
enum Color {
  Red
  Green
  Blue
}
...
```

Note that while the definition may translate to actual enum types in other languages, since JavaScript does not have enum types, these will be dealt with as strings, both in the client as well as in the server. Let's add this enum type for status called `StatusType`:

```
...
enum StatusType {
  New
  Assigned
  Fixed
  Closed
}
...
```

Now, we can replace the type `String` with `StatusType` in the `Issue` type:

```
...
type Issue {
  ...
  status: StatusType!
  ...
}
```

The same can be done in the `IssueInput` type. But one notable feature of the GraphQL schema is that it allows us to supply default values in case the input has not given a value for an argument. This can be done by adding an = symbol and the default value after the type specification, like `owner: String = "Self"`. In the case of `status`, the default value is an enum, so it can be specified without the quotes like this:

```
...
  status: StatusType = New
...
```

Now, we can remove the defaulting of `issue.status` to `'New'` within the `issueAdd` resolver in `server.js`. The set of all changes to the `schema.graphql` file is shown in Listing 5-16.

Listing 5-16. schema.graphql: Changes for Using Enums and Default Values

```
scalar GraphQLDate

enum StatusType {
  New
  Assigned
  Fixed
  Closed
}

type Issue {
  ...
  status: StringStatusType!
  ...
}
...
input IssueInputs {
  ...
  status: StringStatusType = New
  owner: String
  effort: Int
  due: GraphQLDate
}
...
```

As for programmatic validations, we have to have them before saving a new issue in `server.js`. We'll do this in a separate function called `validateIssue()`. Let's first create an array to hold the error messages of failed validations. When we find multiple validation failures, we'll have one string for each validation failure message in this array.

```
...
function validateIssue(_, { issue }) {
  const errors = [];
...
```

Next, let's add a minimum length for the issue's title. If that check fails, we'll push a message into the errors array.

```
...
  if (issue.title.length < 3) {
    errors.push('Field "title" must be at least 3 characters long.')
  }
...
```

Let's also add a conditional mandatory validation, one that checks for the owner being required when the status is set to Assigned. The UI has no way of setting the status field at this stage, so to test this, we will use the Playground.

```
...
  if (issue.status == 'Assigned' && !issue.owner) {
    errors.push('Field "owner" is required when status is "Assigned"');
  }
...
```

We could add more validations, but for demonstrating programmatic validations, this is enough. At the end of the checks, if we find that the errors array is not empty, we'll throw an error. The Apollo Server recommends using the UserInputError class to generate user errors. Let's use that to construct an error to throw:

```
...
  if (errors.length > 0) {
    throw new UserInputError('Invalid input(s)', { errors });
  }
...
```

Now, let's add one more validation that we missed doing earlier: catch invalid date strings while parsing the value on the way in. The new Date() constructor does not throw any errors when the date string is invalid. Instead, it creates a date object, but the object contains an invalid date. One way to detect input errors is by checking if the constructed date object is a valid value. It can be done using the check isNaN(date), after constructing the date. Let's implement this check in parseValue as well as parseLiteral:

```
...
  parseValue(value) {
    const dateValue = new Date(value);
    return isNaN(dateValue) ? undefined : dateValue;
  },
  parseLiteral(ast) {
    if (ast.kind == Kind.STRING) {
      const value = new Date(ast.value);
      return isNaN(value) ? undefined : value;
    }
  },
...
```

Note that returning undefined is treated as an error by the library. If the supplied literal is not a string, the function will not return anything, which is the same as returning undefined.

124

Finally, you'll find that though all errors are being sent to the client and shown to the user, there is no way to capture these at the server for analysis at a later point in time. In addition, it would be nice to monitor the server's console and see these errors even during development. The Apollo Server has a configuration option called formatError that can be used to make changes to the way the error is sent back to the caller. We can use this option to print out the error on the console as well:

```
...
  formatError: error => {
    console.log(error);
    return error;
  }
...
```

All the changes in server.js for adding programmatic validations and proper validation of GraphQLDate type are shown in Listing 5-17.

Listing 5-17. server.js: Programmatic Validations and Date Validations

```
...
const { ApolloServer, UserInputError } = require('apollo-server-express');
...

const GraphQLDate = new GraphQLScalarType({
  ...
  parseValue(value) {
    return new Date(value);
    const dateValue = new Date(value);
    return isNaN(dateValue) ? undefined : dateValue;
  },
  parseLiteral(ast) {
    return (ast.kind == Kind.STRING) ? new Date(ast.value) : undefined;
    if (ast.kind == Kind.STRING) {
      const value = new Date(ast.value);
      return isNaN(value) ? undefined : value;
    }
  },
});
...

function validateIssue(_, { issue }) {
  const errors = [];
  if (issue.title.length < 3) {
    errors.push('Field "title" must be at least 3 characters long.')
  }
  if (issue.status == 'Assigned' && !issue.owner) {
    errors.push('Field "owner" is required when status is "Assigned"');
  }
  if (errors.length > 0) {
    throw new UserInputError('Invalid input(s)', { errors });
  }
}
```

```
function issueAdd(_, { issue }) {
  issueValidate(issue);
  issue.created = new Date();
  issue.id = issuesDB.length + 1;
  if (issue.status == undefined) issue.status = 'New';
  issuesDB.push(issue);
  return issue;
}
...

const server = new ApolloServer({
  typeDefs: fs.readFileSync('./server/schema.graphql', 'utf-8'),
  resolvers,
  formatError: error => {
    console.log(error);
    return error;
  },
});
```

Testing these changes using the application is going to be hard, requiring temporary code changes, so you can use the Playground to test the validations. Note that since status is now an enum, the value should be supplied as a literal, i.e., without quotes in the Playground. A valid call to issueAdd will look like this:

```
mutation {
  issueAdd(issue:{
    title: "Completion date should be optional",
    status: New,
  }) {
    id
    status
  }
}
```

On running this code, Playground results should show the following new issue added:

```
{
  "data": {
    "issueAdd": {
      "id": 5,
      "status": "New"
    }
  }
}
```

If you change the status to an invalid enum like Unknown, you should get back an error like this:

```
{
  "error": {
    "errors": [
```

```
    {
        "message": "Expected type StatusType, found Unknown.",
...
```

If you use a string "New" instead, it should show a helpful error message like this:

```
{
  "error": {
    "errors": [
      {
        "message": "Expected type StatusType, found \"New\"; Did you mean the enum value
        New?",
...
```

Finally, if you remove the status altogether, you will find that it does default the value to New as seen in the result window.

For testing the programmatic validations, you can try to create an issue where both checks will fail. The following query should help with that:

```
mutation {
  issueAdd(issue:{
    title: "Co",
    status: Assigned,
  }) {
    id
    status
  }
}
```

On running this query, the following error will be returned, where both the messages are listed under the exception section.

```
{
  "data": null,
  "errors": [
    {
      "message": "Invalid input(s)",
      ...
      "extensions": {
        "code": "BAD_USER_INPUT",
        "exception": {
          "errors": [
            "Field \"title\" must be at least 3 characters long.",
            "Field \"owner\" is required when status is \"Assigned\""
          ],
...
```

To test the date validations, you need to test both using literals and query variables. For the literal test, you can use the following query:

```
mutation {
  issueAdd(issue:{
    title: "Completion data should be optional",
    due: "not-a-date"
  }) {
    id
  }
}
```

The following error will be returned:

```
{
  "error": {
    "errors": [
      {
        "message": "Expected type GraphQLDate, found \"not-a-date\".",
        ...
        "extensions": {
          "code": "GRAPHQL_VALIDATION_FAILED",
```

As for the query variable based test, here's the query that can be used:

```
mutation issueAddOperation($issue: IssueInputs!) {
  issueAdd(issue: $issue) {
    id
    status
    due
  }
}
```

And this is the query variables:

```
{"issue":{"title":"test", "due":"not-a-date"}}
```

On running this, you should see the following error in the result window:

```
{
  "error": {
    "errors": [
      {
        "message": "Variable \"$issue\" got invalid value {\"title\":\"test\",\"due\":\"not-
        a-date\"}; Expected type GraphQLDate at value.due.",
        ...
```

```
      "extensions": {
        "code": "INTERNAL_SERVER_ERROR",
```

Displaying Errors

In this section, we'll modify the user interface to show any error messages to the user. We'll deal with transport errors due to network connection problems as well as invalid user input. Server and other errors should normally not occur for the user (these would most likely be bugs), and if they do, let's just display the code and the message as we receive them.

This is a good opportunity to create a common utility function that handles all API calls and report errors. We can replace the fetch calls within the actual handlers with this common function and display to the user any errors as part of the API call. Let's call this function graphQLFetch. This will be an async function since we'll be calling fetch() using await. Let's make the function take the query and the variables as two arguments:

```
...
async function graphQLFetch(query, variables = {}) {
...
```

■ **Note** We used the ES2015 Default Function parameter to assign {} to the parameter variables in case it was not passed in by the caller. Read more about this feature at https://developer.mozilla.org/en-US/docs/Web/JavaScript/Reference/Functions/Default_parameters.

All transport errors will be thrown from within the call to fetch(), so let's wrap the call to fetch() and the subsequent retrieval of the body and parse it within a try-catch block. Let's display errors using alert in the catch block:

```
...
  try {
    const response = await fetch('/graphql', {
      ...
    });
  ...
  } catch (e) {
    alert(`Error in sending data to server: ${e.message}`);
  }
...
```

The fetch operation is the same as originally implemented in issueAdd. Once the fetch is complete, we'll look for errors as part of result.errors.

```
...
  if (result.errors) {
    const error = result.errors[0];
...
```

The error code can be found within `error.extensions.code`. Let's use this code to deal with each type of error that we are expecting, differently. For `BAD_USER_INPUT`, we'll need to join all the validation errors together and show it to the user:

```
...
    if (error.extensions.code == 'BAD_USER_INPUT') {
      const details = error.extensions.exception.errors.join('\n ');
      alert(`${error.message}:\n ${details}`);
...
```

For all other error codes, we'll display the code and the message as they are received.

```
...
    } else {
      alert(`${error.extensions.code}: ${error.message}`);
    }
...
```

Finally, in this new utility function, let's return `result.data`. The caller can check if any data was returned, and if so, use that. The method `loadData()` in `IssueList` is the first caller. After building the query, all the code to fetch the data can be replaced with a simple call to `graphQLFetch` with the query. Since it is an async function, we can use the `await` keyword and receive the results directly to a variable called data. If the data is non-null, we can use it to set the state like this:

```
...
  async loadData() {
    ...
    const data = await graphQLFetch(query);
    if (data) {
      this.setState({ issues: data.issueList });
    }
  }
...
```

Let's make a similar change to `createIssue` method in the same class. Here, we also need to pass a second argument, the variables, which is an object containing the `issues` variable. On the return path, if the data is valid, we know that the operation was successful and so we can call `this.loadData()`. We don't use the return value of data except for knowing that the operation was successful.

```
...
    const data = await graphQLFetch(query, { issue });
    if (data) {
      this.loadData();
    }
...
```

The complete set of changes in `App.jsx` to display errors is shown in Listing 5-18.

Listing 5-18. App.jsx: Changes for Displaying Errors

```
...
async function graphQLFetch(query, variables = {}) {
  try {
    const response = await fetch('/graphql', {
      method: 'POST',
      headers: { 'Content-Type': 'application/json'},
      body: JSON.stringify({ query, variables })
    });
    const body = await response.text();
    const result = JSON.parse(body, jsonDateReviver);

    if (result.errors) {
      const error = result.errors[0];
      if (error.extensions.code == 'BAD_USER_INPUT') {
        const details = error.extensions.exception.errors.join('\n ');
        alert(`${error.message}:\n ${details}`);
      } else {
        alert(`${error.extensions.code}: ${error.message}`);
      }
    }
    return result.data;

  } catch (e) {
    alert(`Error in sending data to server: ${e.message}`);
  }
}
...
class IssueList extends React.Component {
  ...

  async loadData() {
    const query = `query {
      ..
    }`;

    const response = await fetch('/graphql', {
      method: 'POST',
      headers: { 'Content-Type': 'application/json'},
      body: JSON.stringify({ query })
    });
    const body = await response.text();
    const result = JSON.parse(body, jsonDateReviver);
    this.setState({ issues: result.data.issueList });
    const data = await graphQLFetch(query);
    if (data) {
      this.setState({ issues: data.issueList });
    }
  }
```

```
async createIssue(issue) {
    const query = `mutation issueAdd($issue: IssueInputs!) {
        issueAdd(issue: $issue) {
            id
        }
    }`;

    const response = await fetch('/graphql', {
        method: 'POST',
        headers: { 'Content-Type': 'application/json' },
        body: JSON.stringify({ query, variables: { issue } })
    });
    this.loadData();
    const data = await graphQLFetch(query, { issue });
    if (data) {
        this.loadData();
    }
}
```

To test transport errors, you can stop the server after refreshing the browser and then try to add a new issue. If you do that, you will find the error message like the screenshot in Figure 5-5.

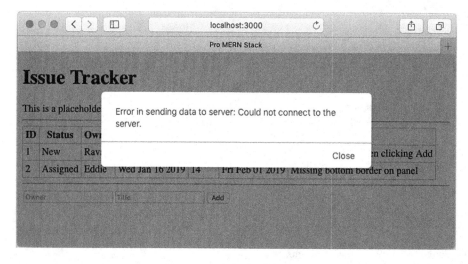

Figure 5-5. *Transport error message*

As for the other messages, the length of title can be tested by typing a small title in the user input. The other validations have to be tested only by temporarily changing the code, for example, by setting the `status` to the desired value and setting the due field to an invalid date string etc. within the `IssueAdd` component's `handleSubmit()` method.

Summary

In this chapter, we compared two API standards: REST and GraphQL. Although REST is widely used, we chose GraphQL for the features and ease of implementation, given that there are tools and libraries to help us build the APIs.

GraphQL is an extremely structured API standard and is quite extensive. I covered only the basics of GraphQL, which only included the features that were required for the Issue Tracker application at this stage. I encourage you to read more on GraphQL at `https://graphql.org/`. There are advanced features such as directives and fragments, which can be helpful in reusing code for building queries. These can be quite handy in a larger project, but I will not cover these as part of this book as they are not really required for the Issue Tracker application.

Using GraphQL, you saw how to build the C and R part of CRUD in this chapter. You also saw how easy some of the validations were to implement and how the strong type system of GraphQL helps avoid errors and makes the APIs self-documenting. We will deal with U and D part of CRUD in later chapters, as and when we build those features.

In the meantime, it would be a good idea to see how to persist the data. We moved the array of issues from the browser's memory to the server's memory. In the next chapter, we'll move it further, to a real database, MongoDB.

Answers to Exercises

Exercise: The About API

1. The same URL in the browser and the cURL command line cause different results. In the browser, the Playground UI is returned, whereas in the command line, the API is executed. The Apollo Server makes the distinction by looking at the `Accept` header. If it finds `"text/html"` (which is what browsers send), it returns the Playground UI. You can check this out by adding `--header "Accept: text/html"` to the cURL command line and executing it.

2. The browser can cache GET requests and return the response from the cache itself. Different browsers behave differently and it's hard to predict the right behavior. Normally, you would want API results to never be cached, instead always fetched from the server. In such cases, using POST is safe, since browsers don't cache the results of a POST.

    But in case you really want the browser to cache certain API responses where possible, because the result is large and doesn't change (e.g., images), GET is the only option. Or, you could use POST but deal with caching yourself (e.g., by using local storage) rather than let the browser handle it.

Exercise: The List API

1. In the first case, the query has a valid syntax, but it does not conform to the schema. The Playground sent the request, and the server responded with an error to that effect.

    In the second case, the Playground did not send the query to the server (you can see an error using the Developer Console in the console logs), because it found that the query does not have a valid syntax: a subfield name is expected within the curly braces.

In both cases, the Playground does show the errors as red underlines in the query. Hovering the cursor on the red underlines will show the actual error message regardless of whether it is a syntax error or a schema error.

2. Adding an invalid subfield does not make the query syntactically invalid. The request is sent to the server, which validates the query and returns an error saying that the subfield is invalid.

3. The query can be like `query { about issueList { id title created } }`. In the result, you can see that both `about` and `issueList` are returned as properties of the `data` object.

Exercise: Custom Scalar Types

1. The output is identical to the case whether or not the resolver for the scalar type is being used. The fact that the schema defined `GraphQLDate` as a scalar type has made the default resolver for the `Date` object use `toJSON()` instead of `toString()`.

2. A `console.log()` message could be added in the serialize function. Alternatively, if you temporarily change the conversion to use `Date.toString()` instead of `Date.toISOString()`, you can see that the conversion is being done differently.

Exercise: The Create API

1. In terms of verbosity, both methods are the same, all the common properties have to be repeated between `Issue` and `IssueInputs` or the argument list. If the list of properties change, for example, if we add a new field called `severity`, the change has to be made in two places: in the `Issue` type and in the `IssueInputs` type *or* the argument list to `issueAdd`.

   One advantage of defining an input type is that the same type can be reused. This can come in handy if, for example, both the Create and the Update operations can take in the same input type.

2. Passing an integer will set `ast.kind` to `Kind.INT` (which is set to the string `'IntValue'`, as seen in the console log). Other possible values are `Kind.FLOAT`, `Kind.BOOLEAN`, and `Kind.ENUM`.

3. Passing a valid string but an invalid date will not throw any errors during the creation of the issue, but the issue will be saved with an invalid `Date` object, which is the result of `new Date()` using an invalid date string. The effect of this will be seen when an issue is returned; there will be errors that show that the date object cannot be converted to a string. We will add validations later in this chapter.

4. A default value can be specified in the schema by adding an = symbol and the default value after the type specification, like `status: String = "New"`. We will switch to this method later in this chapter.

Exercise: Create API Integration

1. The issue is not created, and the console will have an error indicating a bad request. You will find that the request is malformed because the quote ends the string, which is the value for the title, and everything after that is unrecognized by the GraphQL query parser.

   One way to remedy this is to look for quotes within string values and escape them using a backslash (\) character. But as you will see in the next section, there is a better way to do this.

Exercise: Query Variables

1. Since the values are not being passed as literals within the query string, it is `parseValue` that will be called now.

CHAPTER 6

MongoDB

In this chapter, I'll take up MongoDB, the database layer and the M in the MERN stack. Until now, we had an array of issues in the Express server's memory that we used as the database. We'll replace this with real persistence and read and write the list of issues from a MongoDB database.

To achieve this, we'll need to install or use MongoDB on the cloud, get used to its shell commands, install a Node.js driver to access it from Node.js, and finally modify the server code to replace the API calls to read and write from a MongoDB database instead of the in-memory array of issues.

MongoDB Basics

This is an introductory section, where we will not be modifying the application. We'll look at these core concepts in this section: MongoDB, documents, and collections. Then, we'll set up MongoDB and explore these concepts with examples using the mongo shell to read and write to the database.

Documents

MongoDB is a document database, which means that the equivalent of a record is a document, or an object. In a relational database, you organize data in terms of rows and columns, whereas in a document database, an entire object can be written as a document.

For simple objects, this may seem no different from a relational database. But let's say you have objects with nested objects (called *embedded* documents) and arrays. Now, when using a relational database, this will typically need multiple tables. For example, in a relational database, an Invoice object may be stored in a combination of an invoice table (to store the invoice details such as the customer address and delivery details) and an invoice_items table (to store the details of each item that is part of the shipment). In MongoDB, the entire Invoice object would be stored as one document. That's because a document can contain arrays and other objects in a nested manner and the contained objects don't have to be separated out into other documents.

A document is a data structure composed of field and value pairs. The values of fields may include objects, arrays, and arrays of objects and so on, as deeply nested as you want it to be. MongoDB documents are similar to JSON objects, so it is easy to think of them as JavaScript objects. Compared to a JSON object, a MongoDB document has support not only for the primitive data types—Boolean, numbers, and strings—but also other common data types such as dates, timestamps, regular expressions, and binary data.

An Invoice object may look like this:

```
{
  "invoiceNumber" : 1234,
  "invoiceDate" : ISODate("2018-10-12T05:17:15.737Z"),
  "billingAddress" : {
```

© Vasan Subramanian 2019

V. Subramanian, *Pro MERN Stack*, https://doi.org/10.1007/978-1-4842-4391-6_6

```
      "name" : "Acme Inc.",
      "line1" : "106 High Street",
      "city" : "New York City",
      "zip" : "110001-1234"
  },
  "items" : [
    {
      "description" : "Compact Flourescent Lamp",
      "quantity" : 4,
      "price" : 12.48
    },
    {
      "description" : "Whiteboard",
      "quantity" : 1,
      "price" : 5.44
    }
  ]
}
```

In this document, there are numbers, strings, and a date data type. Further, there is a nested object (`billingAddress`) and an array of objects (`items`).

Collections

A collection is like a table in a relational database: it is a set of documents. Just like in a relational database, the collection can have a primary key and indexes. But there are a few differences compared to a relational database.

A primary key is mandated in MongoDB, and it has the reserved field name _id. Even if _id field is not supplied when creating a document, MongoDB creates this field and auto-generates a unique key for every document. More often than not, the auto-generated ID can be used as is, since it is convenient and guaranteed to produce unique keys even when multiple clients are writing to the database simultaneously. MongoDB uses a special data type called the `ObjectId` for the primary key.

The _id field is automatically indexed. Apart from this, indexes can be created on other fields, and this includes fields within embedded documents and array fields. Indexes are used to efficiently access a subset of documents in a collection.

Unlike a relational database, MongoDB does not require you to define a schema for a collection. The only requirement is that all documents in a collection must have a unique _id, but the actual documents may have completely different fields. In practice, though, all documents in a collection do have the same fields. Although a flexible schema may seem very convenient for schema changes during the initial stages of an application, this can cause problems if some kind of schema checking is not added in the application code.

As of version 3.6, MongoDB has supported a concept of schema, even though it is optional. You can read all about MongoDB schemas at https://docs.mongodb.com/manual/core/schema-validation/index.html. A schema can enforce allowed and required fields and their data types, just like GraphQL can. But it can also validate other things like string length and minimum and maximum values for integers.

But the errors generated because of schema violations do not give enough details as to which of the validation checks fail as of version 3.6. This may improve in future versions of MongoDB, at which point in time it is worth considering adding full-fledged schema checks. For the Issue Tracker application, we'll not use the schema validation feature of MongoDB, instead, we'll implement all necessary validations in the back-end code.

Databases

A database is a logical grouping of many collections. Since there are no foreign keys like in a SQL database, the concept of a database is nothing but a logical partitioning namespace. Most database operations read or write from a single collection, but $lookup, which is a stage in an aggregation pipeline, is equivalent to a join in SQL databases. This stage can combine documents within the same database.

Further, taking backups and other administrative tasks work on the database as a unit. A database connection is restricted to accessing only one database, so to access multiple databases, multiple connections are required. Thus, it is useful to keep all the collections of an application in one database, though a database server can host multiple databases.

Query Language

Unlike the universal English-like SQL in a relational database, the MongoDB query language is made up of *methods* to achieve various operations. The main methods for read and write operations are the CRUD methods. Other methods include aggregation, text search, and geospatial queries.

All methods operate on a collection and take parameters as JavaScript objects that specify the details of the operation. Each method has its own specification. For example, to insert a document, the only argument needed is the document itself. For querying, the parameters are a query filter and a list of fields to return (also called the *projection*).

The query filter is a JavaScript object consisting of zero or more properties, where the property name is the name of the field to match on and the property value consists of another object with an operator and a value. For example, to match all documents with the field invoiceNumber that are greater than 1,000, the following query filter can be used:

```
{ "invoiceNumber": { $gt: 1000 } }
```

Since there is no "language" for querying or updating, the query filters can be very easily constructed programmatically.

Unlike relational databases, MongoDB encourages denormalization, that is, storing related parts of a document as embedded subdocuments rather than as separate collections (tables) in a relational database. Take an example of people (name, gender, etc.) and their contact information (primary address, secondary address etc.). In a relational database, this would require separate tables for People and Contacts, and then a join on the two tables when all of the information is needed together. In MongoDB, on the other hand, it can be stored as a list of contacts *within* the same People document. That's because a join of collections is not natural to most methods in MongoDB: the most convenient find() method can operate only on one collection at a time.

Installation

Before you try to install MongoDB on your computer, you may want to try out one of the hosted services that give you access to MongoDB. There are many services, but the following are popular and have a free version that you can use for a small test or sandbox application. Any of these will do quite well for the purpose of the Issue Tracker application that we'll build as part of this book.

- MongoDB Atlas (https://www.mongodb.com/cloud/atlas): I refer to this as Atlas for short. A small database (shared RAM, 512 MB storage) is available for free.

- mLab (previously MongoLab) (https://mlab.com/): mLab has announced an acquisition by MongoDB Inc. and may eventually be merged into Atlas itself. A sandbox environment is available for free, limited to 500 MB storage.

- Compose (https://www.compose.com): Among many other services, Compose offers MongoDB as a service. A 30-day trial period is available, but a permanently free sandbox kind of option is not available.

Of these three, I find Atlas the most convenient because there are many options for the location of the host. When connecting to the database, it lets me choose one closest to my location, and that minimizes the latency. mLab does not give a cluster—a database can be created individually. Compose is not permanently free, and it is likely that you may need more than 30 days to complete this book.

The downside of any of the hosted options is that, apart from the small extra latency when accessing the database, you need an Internet connection. Which means that you may not be able to test your code where Internet access is not available, for example, on a flight. In comparison, installing MongoDB on your computer may work better, but the installation takes a bit more work than signing up for one of the cloud-based options.

Even when using one of the cloud options, you will need to download and install the mongo shell to be able to access the database remotely. Each of the services come with instructions on this step as well. Choose version 3.6 or higher of MongoDB when signing up for any of these services. Test the signup by connecting to the cluster or database using the mongo shell, by following instructions given by the service provider.

If you choose to install MongoDB on your computer (it can be installed easily on OS X, Windows, and most distributions based on Linux), look up the installation instructions, which are different for each operating system. You may install MongoDB by following the instructions at the MongoDB website (https://docs.mongodb.com/manual/installation/ or search for "mongodb installation" in your search engine).

Choose MongoDB version 3.6 or higher, preferably the latest, as some of the examples use features introduced only in version 3.6. Most local installation options let you install the server, the shell, and tools all in one. Check that this is the case; if not, you may have to install them separately.

After a local installation, ensure that you have started MongoDB server (the name of the daemon or service is mongod), if it is not already started by the installation process. Test the installation by running the mongo shell like this:

```
$ mongo
```

On a Windows system, you may need to append .exe to the command. The command may require a path depending on your installation method. If the shell starts successfully, it will also connect to the local MongoDB server instance. You should see the version of MongoDB printed on the console, the database it is connecting to (the default is test), and a command prompt, like this, if you had installed MongoDB version 4.0.2 locally:

```
MongoDB shell version v4.0.2
connecting to: mongodb://127.0.0.1:27017
MongoDB server version: 4.0.2
>
```

The message you see can be slightly different from this, especially if you have installed a different version of MongoDB. But you do need to see the prompt > where you can type further commands. If, instead, you see an error message, revisit the installation and the server starting procedure.

The Mongo Shell

The mongo shell is an interactive JavaScript shell, very much like the Node.js shell. In the interactive shell, a few non-JavaScript conveniences are available over and above the full power of JavaScript. In this section, we'll discuss the basic operations that are possible via the shell, those that are most commonly used. For a full reference of all the capabilities of the shell, you can take a look at the mongo shell documentation at `https://docs.mongodb.com/manual/mongo/`.

The commands that we will be typing in the mongo shell have been collected together in a file called `mongo_commands.txt`. These commands have been tested to work as is on Atlas or a local installation, but you may find variations in the other options. For example, mLab lets you connect only to a database (as opposed to a cluster), so it does not allow of switching between databases in mLab.

■ **Note** If you find that something is not working as expected when typing a command, cross-check the commands with the same in the GitHub repository (`https://github.com/vasansr/pro-mern-stack-2`). This is because typos may have been introduced during the production of the book, or last-minute corrections may have missed making it to the book. The GitHub repository, on the other hand, reflects the most up-to-date and tested set of code and commands.

To work with MongoDB, you need to connect to a database. Let's start with finding which databases are available. The command to show the current databases is:

```
> show databases
```

This will list the databases and the storage occupied by them. For example, in a fresh local installation of MongoDB, this is what you will see:

```
admin      0.000GB
config     0.000GB
local      0.000GB
```

These are system databases that MongoDB uses for its internal book keeping, etc. We will not be using any of these to create our collections, so we'd better change the current database. To identify the current database, the command is:

```
> db
```

The default database a mongo shell connects to is called `test` and that is what you are likely to see as the output to this command. Let's now see what collections exist in this database.

```
> show collections
```

You will find that there are no collections in this database, since it is a fresh installation. Further, you will also find that the database `test` was not listed when we listed the available databases. That's because databases and collections are really created only on the first write operation to any of these.

Let's switch to a database called `issuetracker` instead of using the default database:

```
> use issuetracker
```

This should result in output that confirms that the new database is `issuetracker`:

```
switched to db issuetracker
```

Let's confirm that there are no collections in this database either:

```
> show collections
```

This command should return nothing. Now, let's create a new collection. This is done by creating one document in a collection. A collection is referenced as a property of the global object db, with the same name as the collection. The collection called `employees` can be referred to as `db.employees`. Let's insert a new document in the `employees` collection using the `insertOne()` method. This method takes in the document to be inserted as an argument:

```
> db.employees.insertOne({ name: { first: 'John', last: 'Doe' }, age: 44 })
```

The result of this command will show you the result of the operation and the ID of the new document that was created, something like this:

```
{
    "acknowledged" : true,
    "insertedId" : ObjectId("5bbc487a69d13abf04edf857")
}
```

Apart from the `insertOne()` method, many methods are available on any collection. You can see the list of available methods by pressing the Tab character twice after typing `"db.employees."` (the period at the end is required before pressing Tab). You may find an output like the following:

```
db.employees.addIdIfNeeded(          db.employees.getWriteConcern(
db.employees.aggregate(              db.employees.group(
db.employees.bulkWrite(              db.employees.groupcmd(
db.employees.constructor             db.employees.hasOwnProperty
db.employees.convertToCapped(        db.employees.hashAllDocs(
db.employees.convertToSingleObject(  db.employees.help(
db.employees.copyTo(                 db.employees.initializeOrderedBulkOp(
db.employees.count(                  db.employees.initializeUnorderedBulkOp(
db.employees.createIndex(            db.employees.insert(
db.employees.createIndexes(          db.employees.insertMany(
db.employees.dataSize(               db.employees.insertOne(
...
```

This is the auto-completion feature of the mongo shell at work. Note that you can let the mongo shell auto-complete the name of any method by pressing the Tab character after entering the beginning few characters of the method.

Let's now check if the document has been created in the collection. To do that, we can use the `find()` method on the collection. Without any arguments, this method just lists all the documents in the collection:

```
> db.employees.find()
```

This should result in displaying the document we just created, but it is not "pretty" formatted. It will be printed all in one line and may wrap around to the next line inconveniently. To get a more legible output, we can use the pretty() method on the result of the find() method:

```
> db.employees.find().pretty()
```

That should show a much more legible output, like this:

```
{
    "_id" : ObjectId("5bbc487a69d13abf04edf857"),
    "name" : {
            "first" : "John",
            "last" : "Doe"
    },
    "age" : 44
}
```

At this point in time, if you execute show collections and show databases, you will find that the employees collection and the issuetracker database have indeed been created and are listed in the output of their respective commands. Let's insert another document in the same collection and try to deal with multiple documents in the collection:

```
> db.employees.insertOne({ name: { first: 'Jane', last: 'Doe' }, age: 54 })
```

Now, since we have the full power of JavaScript in the shell, let's try to exercise some of it to get a taste. Instead of printing the results onscreen, let's collect the results into a JavaScript array variable. The result of the find() method was a cursor that could be iterated. In the cursor object, there are methods other than pretty(), one of which is toArray(). This method reads all the documents from the query and places them in an array. So, let's use this method and assign its result to an array variable.

```
> let result = db.employees.find().toArray()
```

Now, the variable result should be an array with two elements, each an employee document. Let's use the JavaScript array method forEach() to iterate through them and print the first names of each employee:

```
> result.forEach((e) => print('First Name:', e.name.first))
```

This should give an output like this:

```
First Name: John
First Name: Jane
```

In Node.js, the console.log method is available for printing objects on the console. The mongo shell, on the other hand, provides the print() method for the same purpose, but this prints only strings. Objects need to be converted to strings before printing, using the utility function tojson(). There is also another method, called printjson(), which prints objects as JSON. Let's use that to inspect the contents of the nested document name instead of only the first name:

```
> result.forEach((e) => printjson(e.name))
```

Now, you should see the name object expanded into first and last names, like the following:

```
{ "first" : "John", "last" : "Doe" }
{ "first" : "Jane", "last" : "Doe" }
```

The shell by itself does very little apart from providing a mechanism to access methods of the database and collections. It is the JavaScript engine, which forms the basis of the shell and gives a lot of flexibility and power to the shell.

In the next section, we will discuss more methods on the collection, such as insertOne() that you just learned about. These methods are accessible from many programming languages via a driver. The mongo shell is just another tool that can access these methods. You will find that the methods and arguments available in other programming languages are very similar to those in the mongo shell.

EXERCISE: MONGODB BASICS

1. Using the shell, display a list of methods available on the cursor object. Hint: Look up the mongo shell documentation for mongo Shell Help at https://docs. mongodb.com/manual/tutorial/access-mongo-shell-help/.

Answers are available at the end of the chapter.

MongoDB CRUD Operations

Since the mongo shell is the easiest to try out, let's explore the CRUD operations available in MongoDB using the shell itself. We will continue to use the issuetracker database we created in the previous section. But let's clear the database so that we can start fresh. The collection object provides a convenient method for erasing itself called drop():

```
> db.employees.drop()
```

This should result in an output like this:

```
true
```

This is different from removing all the documents in the collection, because it also removes any indexes that are part of the collection.

Create

In the previous section, you briefly saw how to insert a document, and as part of that, you found how MongoDB automatically created the primary key, which was a special data type called ObjectID. Let's now use our own ID instead of letting MongoDB auto-generate one.

```
> db.employees.insertOne({
  _id: 1,
  name: { first: 'John', last: 'Doe' },
  age: 44
})
```

This will result in the following output:

```
{ "acknowledged" : true, "insertedId" : 1 }
```

Note that the value of insertedId reflected the value that we supplied for _id. Which means that, instead of an ObjectID type of value, we were able to supply our own value. Let's try to create a new identical document (you can use the Up Arrow key to repeat the previous command in the mongo shell). It will fail with the following error:

```
WriteError({
    "index" : 0,
    "code" : 11000,
    "errmsg" : "E11000 duplicate key error collection: issuetracker.employees index:
    _id_ dup key: { : 1.0 }",
    "op" : {
            "_id" : 1,
            "name" : {
                    "first" : "John",
                    "last" : "Doe"
            },
            "age" : 44
    }
})
```

This shows that the _id field continues to be a primary key and it is expected to be unique, regardless of whether it is auto-generated or supplied in the document. Now, let's add another document, but with a new field as part of the name, say, the middle name:

```
> db.employees.insertOne({
  name: {first: 'John', middle: 'H', last: 'Doe'},
  age: 22
})
```

This works just fine, and using find(), you can see that two documents exist in the collection, but they are not necessarily the same schema. This is the advantage of a flexible schema: the schema can be enhanced whenever a new data element that needs to be stored is discovered, without having to explicitly modify the schema.

In this case, it is implicit that any employee document where the middle field under name is missing indicates an employee without a middle name. If, on the other hand, a field was added that didn't have an implicit meaning when absent, its absence would have to be handled in the code. Or a migration script would have to be run that defaults the field's value to something.

You will also find that the format of the _id field is different for the two documents, and even the data type is different. For the first document, the data type is an integer. For the second, it is of type ObjectID (which is why it is shown as ObjectID(...)). Thus, it's not just the presence of fields that can differ between two documents in the same collection, even the data types of the same field can be different.

In most cases, leaving the creation of the primary key to MongoDB works just great, because you don't have to worry about keeping it unique: MongoDB does that automatically. But, this identifier is not human-readable. In the Issue Tracker application, we want the identifier to be a number so that it can be easily remembered and talked about. But instead of using the _id field to store the human-readable identifier, let's use a new field called id and let MongoDB auto-generate _id.

So, let's drop the collection and start creating new documents with a new field called id.

```
> db.employees.drop()
```

```
> db.employees.insertOne({
  id: 1,
  name: { first: 'John', last: 'Doe' },
  age: 48
})
```

```
> db.employees.insertOne({
  id: 2,
  name: { first: 'Jane', last: 'Doe'} ,
  age: 16
})
```

The collection has a method that can take in multiple documents in one go. This method is called insertMany(). Let's use that to create a few more documents in a single command:

```
> db.employees.insertMany([
  { id: 3, name: { first: 'Alice', last: 'A' }, age: 32 },
  { id: 4, name: { first: 'Bob', last: 'B' }, age: 64 },
])
```

The response to this would have shown that multiple insertedIds that were created as opposed to a single insertedId for the insertOne() method, like this:

```
{
    "acknowledged" : true,
    "insertedIds" : [
          ObjectId("5bc6d80005fb87b8f2f5cf6f"),
          ObjectId("5bc6d80005fb87b8f2f5cf70")
    ]
}
```

Read

Now that there are multiple documents in the collection, let's see how to retrieve a subset of the documents as opposed to the full list. The find() method takes in two more arguments. The first is a filter to apply to the list, and the second is a projection, a specification of which fields to retrieve.

The filter specification is an object where the property name is the field to filter on, and the value is its value that it needs to match. Let's fetch one employee's document, identified by the id being equal to 1. Since we know that there can only be one employee for the given ID, let's use findOne() rather than find(). The method findOne() is a variation of the method find(), and it returns a single object rather than a cursor.

```
> db.employees.findOne({ id: 1 })
```

This should return the first employee document that we created, and the output will look like this:

```
{
        "_id" : ObjectId("5bc6d7e505fb87b8f2f5cf6d"),
        "id" : 1,
        "name" : {
                "first" : "John",
                "last" : "Doe"
        },
        "age" : 48
}
```

Note that we did not use pretty() here, yet, the output is prettified. This is because findOne() returns a single object and the mongo shell prettifies objects by default.

The filter is actually a shorthand for { id: { $eq: 1 } }, where $eq is the operator signifying that the value of the field id has to be *equal* to 1. In the generic sense, the format of a single element in the filter is fieldname: { operator: value }. Other operators for comparison are available, such as $gt for greater than, etc. Let's try the $gte (greater than or equal to) operator for fetching a list of employees aged 30 or older:

```
> db.employees.find({ age: { $gte: 30 } })
```

That command should return three documents, because we inserted those many whose age was more than 30. If multiple fields are specified, then all of them have to match, which is the same as combining them with an *and* operator:

```
> db.employees.find({ age: { $gte: 30 }, 'name.last': 'Doe' })
```

The number of documents returned now should be reduced to only one, since there is only one document that matched both the criteria, the last name being equal to 'Doe' as well as age being greater than 30. Note that we used the dot notation for specifying a field embedded in a nested document. And this also made us use quotes around the field name, since it is a regular JavaScript object property.

To match multiple values of the same field—for example, to match age being greater than 30 *and* age being less than 60—the same strategy cannot be used. That's because the filter is a regular JavaScript object, and two properties of the same name cannot exist in a document. Thus, a filter like { age: { $gte: 30 }, age: { $lte: 60 } } will not work (JavaScript will not throw an error, instead, it will pick just one of the values for the property age). An explicit $and operator has to be used, which takes in an array of objects specifying multiple field-value criteria. You can read all about the $and operator and many more operators in the operators section of the reference manual of MongoDB at https://docs.mongodb.com/manual/reference/operator/query/.

When filtering on a field is a common occurrence, it's typically a good idea to create an index on that field. The createIndex() method on the collection is meant for this purpose. It takes in an argument specifying the fields that form the index (multiple fields will form a composite index). Let's create an index on the age field:

```
> db.employees.createIndex({ age: 1 })
```

With this index, any query that uses a filter that has the field age in it will be significantly faster because MongoDB will use this index instead of scanning through all documents in the collection. But this was not a unique index, as many people can be the same age.

147

The age field is probably not a frequently used filter, but fetching a document based on its identifier is going to be very frequent. MongoDB automatically creates an index on the _id field, but we have used our own identifier called id, and this field is what is more likely to be used to fetch individual employees. So let's create an index on this field. Further, it has to be unique since it identifies the employee: no two employees should have the same value for id. The second argument to createIndex() is an object that contains various attributes of the index, one of them specifying whether the index is unique. Let's use that to create a unique index on id:

```
> db.employees.createIndex({ id: 1 }, { unique: true })
```

Now, not only will the find() method perform much better when a filter with id is supplied, but creation of a document with a duplicate id will be prevented by MongoDB. Let's try that by re-running the insert command for the first employee:

```
> db.employees.insertOne({
  id: 1,
  name: { first: 'John', last: 'Doe' },
  age: 48
})
```

Now, you should see an error in the mongo shell like this (the ObjectID will be different for you):

```
WriteError({
    "index" : 0,
    "code" : 11000,
    "errmsg" : "E11000 duplicate key error collection: issuetracker.employees index:
    id_1 dup key: { : 1.0 }",
    "op" : {
        "_id" : ObjectId("5bc04b8569334c5ff5bb7e8c"),
        "id" : 1
        ...
    }
})
```

Projection

All this while, we retrieved the entire document that matched the filter. In the previous section, when we had to print only a subset of the fields of the document, we did it using a forEach() loop. But this means that the entire document is fetched from the server even when we needed only some parts of it for printing. When the documents are large, this can use up a lot of network bandwidth. To restrict the fetch to only some fields, the find() method takes a second argument called the *projection*. A projection specifies which fields to include or exclude in the result.

The format of this specification is an object with one or more field names as the key and the value as 0 or 1, to indicate exclusion or inclusion. But 0s and 1s cannot be combined. You can either start with nothing and include fields using 1s, or start with everything and exclude fields using 0s. The _id field is an exception; it is always included unless you specify a 0. The following will fetch all employees but only their first names and age:

```
> db.employees.find({}, { 'name.first': 1, age: 1 })
```

Note that we specified an empty filter, to say that all documents have to be fetched. This had to be done since the projection is the second argument. The previous request would have printed something like this:

```
{ "_id" : ObjectId("5bbc...797855"), "name" : { "first" : "John" }, "age" : 48 }
{ "_id" : ObjectId("5bbc...797856"), "name" : { "first" : "Jane" }, "age" : 16 }
{ "_id" : ObjectId("5bbc...797857"), "name" : { "first" : "Alice" }, "age" : 32 }
{ "_id" : ObjectId("5bbc...797858"), "name" : { "first" : "Bob" }, "age" : 64 }
```

Even though we specified only the first name and age, the field _id was automatically included. To suppress the inclusion of this field, it needs to be explicitly excluded, like this:

```
> db.employees.find({}, { _id: 0, 'name.first': 1, age: 1 })
```

Now, the output will exclude the ID and look like this:

```
{ "name" : { "first" : "John" }, "age" : 48 }
{ "name" : { "first" : "Jane" }, "age" : 16 }
{ "name" : { "first" : "Alice" }, "age" : 32 }
{ "name" : { "first" : "Bob" }, "age" : 64 }
```

Update

There are two methods—updateOne() and updateMany()—available for modifying a document. The arguments to both methods are the same, except that updateOne() stops after finding and updating the first matching document. The first argument is a query filter, the same as the filter that find() takes. The second argument is an update specification if only some fields of the object need to be changed.

When using updateOne(), the primary key or any unique identifier is what is normally used in the filter, because the filter can match only one document. The update specification is an object with a series of $set properties whose values indicate another object, which specifies the field and its new value. Let's update the age of the employee identified by the id 2:

```
> db.employees.updateOne({ id: 2 }, { $set: {age: 23 } })
```

This should result in the following output:

```
{ "acknowledged" : true, "matchedCount" : 1, "modifiedCount" : 1 }
```

The matchedCount returned how many documents matched the filter. If the filter had matched more than one, that number would have been returned. But since the method is supposed to modify only one document, the modified count should always be 1, unless the modification had no effect. If you run the command again, you will find that modifiedCount will be 0, since the age was already 23 for the employee with ID 2.

To modify multiple documents in one shot, the updateMany() method has to be used. The format is the same as the updateOne() method, but the effect is that *all* documents that match will be modified. Let's add an organization field to all employees using the updateMany() method:

```
> db.employees.updateMany({}, { $set: { organization: 'MyCompany' } })
```

Note that even though the field `organization` did not exist in the documents, the new value `MyCompany` would have been applied to all of them. If you execute the command `find()` to show the companies alone in the projection, this fact will be confirmed.

There is also a method to *replace* the complete document called `replaceOne()`. Instead of specifying which fields to modify, if the complete modified document is available, it can be used to just replace the existing document with the new one. Here's an example:

```
> db.employees.replaceOne({ id: 4 }, {
  id: 4,
  name : { first : "Bobby" },
  age : 66
});
```

This command will replace the existing document with ID 4, with the new one. The fact that the `organization` and `name.last` fields were not specified will have the effect that these fields will not *exist* in the replaced document, as opposed to not *changed* using `updateOne()`. Getting the replaced object should show proof of that:

```
> db.employees.find({ id: 4 })
```

This should result in a document that looks as follows:

```
{ "_id" : ObjectId("5c38ae3da7dc439456c0281b"), "id" : 4, "name" : { "first" : "Bobby" },
"age" : 66 }
```

You can see that it no longer has the fields `name.last` and `organization`, because these were not specified in the document that was supplied to the command `replaceOne()`. It just replaces the document with the one supplied, except for the field `ObjectId`. Being the primary key, this field cannot be changed via an `updateOne()` or a `replaceOne()`.

Delete

The `delete` operation takes a filter and removes the document from the collection. The filter format is the same, and the variations `deleteOne()` and `deleteMany()` are both available, just as in the `update` operation.

Let's delete the last document, with ID 4:

```
> db.employees.deleteOne({ id: 4 })
```

This should result in the following output, confirming that the deletion affected only one document:

```
{ "acknowledged" : true, "deletedCount" : 1 }
```

Let's also cross-check the deletion by looking at the size of the collection. The `count()` method on the collection tells us how many documents it contains. Executing that now should return the value 3, because we originally inserted four documents.

```
> db.employees.count()
```

Aggregate

The find() method is used to return all the documents or a subset of the documents in a collection. Many a time, instead of the list of documents, we need a summary or an aggregate, for example, the count of documents that match a certain criterion.

The count() method can surely take a filter. But what about other aggregate functions, such as sum? That is where the aggregate() comes into play. When compared to relational databases supporting SQL, the aggregate() method performs the function of the GROUP BY clause. But it can also perform other functions such as a join, or even an unwind (expand the documents based on arrays within), and much more.

You can look up the advanced features that the aggregate() function supports in the MongoDB documentation at https://docs.mongodb.com/manual/reference/operator/aggregation-pipeline/ but for now, let's look at the real aggregation and grouping construct that it provides.

The aggregate() method works in a pipeline. Every *stage* in the pipeline takes the input from the result of the previous stage and operates as per its specification to result in a new modified set of documents. The initial input to the pipeline is, of course, the entire collection. The pipeline specification is in the form of an array of objects, each element being an object with one property that identifies the pipeline stage type and the value specifying the pipeline's effect.

For example, the find() method can be replicated using aggregate() by using the stages $match (the filter) and $project (the projection). To perform an actual aggregation, the $group stage needs to be used. The stage's specification includes the grouping key identified by the property _id and other fields as keys, whose values are aggregation specifications and fields on which the aggregation needs to be performed. The _id can be null to group on the entire collection.

Let's try this by getting the total age of all employees in the entire collection. There will be only one element in the array of pipelines, an object with a single property $group. In the value, _id will be set to null because we don't want to group by any field. We'll need to sum (using the aggregate function $sum) the field age into a new field called total_age like this:

```
> db.employees.aggregate([
  { $group: { _id: null, total_age: { $sum: '$age' } } }
])
```

This should result in an output like this:

```
{ "_id" : null, "total_age" : 103 }
```

The same function, $sum, can be used to get a count of the records by simply summing the value 1:

```
> db.employees.aggregate([
  { $group: { _id: null, count: { $sum: 1 } } }
])
```

To group the aggregate by a field, we'll need to specify the name of the field (prefixed by a $) as the value of _id. Let's use the organization field, but before that, let's insert a new document with an organization different from the rest of the documents (which were all set to MyCompany):

```
> db.employees.insertOne({
  id: 4,
  name: { first: 'Bob', last: 'B' },
  age: 64,
  organization: 'OtherCompany'
})
```

Now, here's the command that aggregates the age using sum across different organizations:

```
> db.employees.aggregate([
  { $group: { _id: '$organization', total_age: { $sum: '$age' } } }
])
```

This should result in an output like this:

```
{ "_id" : "OtherCompany", "total_age" : 64 }
{ "_id" : "MyCompany", "total_age" : 103 }
```

Let's also try another aggregate function, say average, using $avg:

```
> db.employees.aggregate([
  { $group: { _id: '$organization', average_age: { $avg: '$age' } } }
])
```

This should now result in an output like this:

```
{ "_id" : "OtherCompany", "average_age" : 64 }
{ "_id" : "MyCompany", "average_age" : 34.333333333333336 }
```

There are other aggregation functions, including minimum and maximum. For the complete set, refer to the documentation at https://docs.mongodb.com/manual/reference/operator/aggregation/group/#accumulator-operator.

EXERCISE: MONGODB CRUD OPERATIONS

1. Write a simple statement to retrieve all employees who have middle names. Hint: Look up the MongoDB documentation for query operators at https://docs.mongodb.com/manual/reference/operator/query/.

2. Is the filter specification a JSON? Hint: Think about date objects and quotes around field names.

3. Say an employee's middle name was set mistakenly, and you need to remove it. Write a statement to do this. Hint: Look up the MongoDB documentation for update operators at https://docs.mongodb.com/manual/reference/operator/update/.

4. During index creation, what did the 1 indicate? What other valid values are allowed? Hint: Look up the MongoDB indexes documentation at https://docs.mongodb.com/manual/indexes/.

Answers are available at the end of the chapter.

MongoDB Node.js Driver

This is the Node.js driver that lets you connect and interact with the MongoDB server. It provides methods very similar to what you saw in the mongo shell, but not exactly the same. Instead of the low-level MongoDB driver, we could use an Object Document Mapper called Mongoose, which has a higher level of abstraction and more convenient methods. But learning about the lower-level MongoDB driver may give you a better handle on the actual working of MongoDB itself, so I've chosen to use the low-level driver for the Issue Tracker application.

To start, let's install the driver:

```
$ npm install mongodb@3
```

Let's also start a new Node.js program just to try out the different ways that the driver's methods can be used. In the next section, we'll use some code from this trial to integrate the driver into the Issue Tracker application. Let's call this sample Node.js program trymongo.js and place it in a new directory called scripts, to distinguish it from other files that are part of the application.

The first thing to do is make a connection to the database server. This can be done by first importing the object MongoClient from the driver, then creating a new client object from it using a URL that identifies a database to connect to, and finally calling the connect method on it, like this:

```
...
const { MongoClient } = require('mongodb');

const client = new MongoClient(url);
client.connect();
...
```

The URL should start with mongodb:// followed by the hostname or the IP address of the server to connect to. An optional port can be added using : as the separator, but it's not required if the MongoDB server is running on the default port, 27017. It's good practice to separate the connection parameters into a configuration file rather than keep them in a checked-in file, but we'll do this in the next chapter. For the moment, let's hard code this. If you have used one of the cloud providers, the URL can be obtained from the corresponding connection instructions. For the local installation, the URL will be mongodb://localhost/issuetracker. Note that the MongoDB Node.js driver accepts the database name as part of the URL itself, and it is best to specify it this way, even though a cloud provider may not show this explicitly.

Let's add the local installation URL to trymongo.js and a commented version of cloud providers' URLs.

```
...
const url = 'mongodb://localhost/issuetracker';

// Atlas URL - replace UUU with user, PPP with password, XXX with hostname
// const url = 'mongodb+srv://UUU:PPP@cluster0-XXX.mongodb.net/issuetracker?retryWrites=true';

// mLab URL - replace UUU with user, PPP with password, XXX with hostname
// const url = 'mongodb://UUU:PPP@XXX.mlab.com:33533/issuetracker';
...
```

Further, the client constructor takes in another argument with more settings for the client, one of which is whether to use the new style parser. Let's change the constructor to pass this also, to avoid a warning in the latest Node.js driver (version 3.1).

```
...
const client = new MongoClient(url, { useNewUrlParser: true });
...
```

The connect() method is an asynchronous method and needs a callback to receive the result of the connection. The callback takes in two arguments: an error and the result. The result is the client object itself. Within the callback, a connection to the database (as opposed a connection to the server) can be obtained by calling the db method of the client object. Thus, the callback and connection to the database can be written like this:

```
...
client.connect(function(err, client) {
  const db = client.db();
...
```

The connection to the database, db, is similar to the db variable we used in the mongo shell. In particular, it is the one that we can use to get a handle to a collection and its methods. Let's get a handle to the collection called employees that we were using in the previous section using the mongo shell.

```
...
  const collection = db.collection('employees');
...
```

With this collection, we can do the same things we did with the mongo shell's equivalent db.employees in the previous section. The methods are also very similar, except that they are all asynchronous. This means that the methods take in the regular arguments, but also a callback function that's called when the operation completes. The convention in the callback functions is to pass the error as the first argument and the result of the operation as the second argument. You already saw this pattern of callback in the previous connection method.

Let's insert a document and read it back to see how these methods work within the Node.js driver. The insertion can be written using the insertOne method, passing in an employee document and a callback. Within the callback, let's print the new _id that was created. Just as in the mongo shell insertOne command, the created ID is returned as part of the result object, in the property called insertedId.

```
...
  const employee = { id: 1, name: 'A. Callback', age: 23 };
  collection.insertOne(employee, function(err, result) {
    console.log('Result of insert:\n', result.insertedId);
...
```

Note that accessing the collection and the insert operation can only be called within the callback of the connection operation, because only then do we know that the connection has succeeded. There also needs to be some amount of error handling, but let's deal with this a little later.

Now, within the callback of the insert operation, let's read back the inserted document, using the ID of the result. We could use either the ID we supplied (id) or the auto-generated MongoDB ID (_id). Let's use _id just to make sure that we are able to use the result values.

```
...
    collection.find({ _id: result.insertedId})
      .toArray(function(err, docs) {
        console.log('Result of find:\n', docs);
      }
...
```

Now that we are done inserting and reading back the document, we can close the connection to the server. If we don't do this, the Node.js program will not exit, because the connection object is waiting to be used and listening to a socket.

```
...
    client.close();
...
```

Let's put all this together in a function called testWithCallbacks(). We will soon also use a different method of using the Node.js driver using async/await. Also, as is customary, let's pass a callback function to this function, which we will call from the testWithCallbacks() function once all the operations are completed. Then, if there are any errors, these can be passed to the callback function.

Let's first declare this function:

```
...
function testWithCallbacks(callback) {
  console.log('\n--- testWithCallbacks ---');
  ...
}
...
```

And within each callback as a result of each of the operations, on an error, we need to do the following:

- Close the connection to the server
- Call the callback
- Return from the call, so that no more operations are performed

We also need to do the same when all operations are completed. The pattern of the error handling is like this:

```
...
    if (err) {
      client.close();
      callback(err);
      return;
    }
...
```

Let's also introduce a call to the testWithCallbacks() function from the main section, supply it a callback to receive any error, and print it if any.

```
...
testWithCallbacks(function(err) {
  if (err) {
```

```
    console.log(err);
  }
});
...
```

With all the error handling and callbacks introduced, the final code in the `trymongo.js` file is shown in Listing 6-1.

 Note   Although no effort has been spared to ensure that all code listings are accurate, there may be typos or even corrections that did not make it to the book before it went to press. So, always rely on the GitHub repository (`https://github.com/vasansr/pro-mern-stack-2`) as the tested and up-to-date source for all code listings, especially if something does not work as expected.

Listing 6-1.   trymongo.js: Using Node.js driver, Using the Callbacks Paradigm

```
const { MongoClient } = require('mongodb');

const url = 'mongodb://localhost/issuetracker';

// Atlas URL  - replace UUU with user, PPP with password, XXX with hostname
// const url = 'mongodb+srv://UUU:PPP@cluster0-XXX.mongodb.net/issuetracker?retryWrites=true';

// mLab URL - replace UUU with user, PPP with password, XXX with hostname
// const url = 'mongodb://UUU:PPP@XXX.mlab.com:33533/issuetracker';

function testWithCallbacks(callback) {
  console.log('\n--- testWithCallbacks ---');
  const client = new MongoClient(url, { useNewUrlParser: true });
  client.connect(function(err, client) {
    if (err) {
      callback(err);
      return;
    }
    console.log('Connected to MongoDB');

    const db = client.db();
    const collection = db.collection('employees');

    const employee = { id: 1, name: 'A. Callback', age: 23 };
    collection.insertOne(employee, function(err, result) {
      if (err) {
        client.close();
        callback(err);
        return;
      }
      console.log('Result of insert:\n', result.insertedId);
      collection.find({ _id: result.insertedId})
        .toArray(function(err, docs) {
```

```
      if (err) {
        client.close();
        callback(err);
        return;
      }
      console.log('Result of find:\n', docs);
      client.close();
      callback(err);
    });
  });
 });
}

testWithCallbacks(function(err) {
  if (err) {
    console.log(err);
  }
});
```

Let's clean up the collection before we test this. We could open another command shell, run the mongo shell in it, and execute db.employees.remove({}). But the mongo shell has a command line way of executing a simple command using the --eval command line option. Let's do that instead and pass the database name to connect to; otherwise, the command will be executed on the default database test. For the local installation, the command will look like this:

```
$ mongo issuetracker --eval "db.employees.remove({})"
```

If you are using a remote server from one of the hosting providers, instead of the database name, use the connection string including the database name as suggested by the hosting provider. For example, the Atlas command may look like this (replace the hostname, user, and password with your own):

```
$ mongo "mongodb+srv://cluster0-xxxxx.mongodb.net/issuetracker" --username atlasUser
--password atlasPassword --eval "db.employees.remove({})"
```

Now, we are ready to test the trial program we just created. It can be executed like this:

```
$ node scripts/trymongo.js
```

This should result in output like this (you will see a different ObjectID, otherwise the output should be the same):

```
--- testWithCallbacks ---
Connected to MongoDB
Result of insert:
 5bbef955580a2c313d4052f6
Result of find:
 [ { _id: 5bbef955580a2c313d4052f6,
     id: 1,
     name: 'A. Callback',
     age: 23 } ]
```

As you probably felt yourself, the callback paradigm is a bit unwieldy. But the advantage is that it works in the older JavaScript version (ES5), and therefore, older versions of Node.js. The callbacks are bit too deeply nested and the error handling makes for repetitive code. ES2015 started supporting Promises, which is supported by the Node.js MongoDB driver as well, and this was an improvement over callbacks. But in ES2017 and Node.js from version 7.6, full support for the async/await paradigm appeared, and this is the recommended and most convenient way to use the driver.

Let's implement another function called testWithAsync() within trymongo.js that uses the async/await paradigm. All asynchronous calls with a callback can now be replaced by a call to the same method, but without supplying a callback. Using await before the method call will simulate a synchronous call by *waiting* for the call to complete and return the results. For example, instead of passing a callback to the connect() method, we can just wait for it to complete like this:

```
...
    await client.connect();
...
```

Right in the next line, we can do whatever needs to be done after the operation is completed, in this case, get a connection to the database:

```
...
    await client.connect();
    const db = client.db();
...
```

The same pattern can be used for the other asynchronous calls, with one change: the result of the call, which was originally the second argument of the callback, can directly be assigned to a variable like a return value from the function call. So, the result of insertOne() can be captured like this:

```
...
    const result = await collection.insertOne(employee);
...
```

Errors will be thrown and can be caught. We can place all the operations in a single try block and catch any error in one place (the catch block) rather than after each call. There is no need for the function to take a callback, because if the caller needs to wait for the result, an await can be added before the call to this function, and errors can be thrown.

The new function using await before each of the operations—connect(), insertOne(), and find()—is shown in Listing 6-2.

Listing 6-2. trymongo.js, testWithAsync Function

```
async function testWithAsync() {
  console.log('\n--- testWithAsync ---');
  const client = new MongoClient(url, { useNewUrlParser: true });
  try {
    await client.connect();
    console.log('Connected to MongoDB');
    const db = client.db();
    const collection = db.collection('employees');

    const employee = { id: 2, name: 'B. Async', age: 16 };
    const result = await collection.insertOne(employee);
    console.log('Result of insert:\n', result.insertedId);
```

```
    const docs = await collection.find({ _id: result.insertedId })
      .toArray();
    console.log('Result of find:\n', docs);
  } catch(err) {
    console.log(err);
  } finally {
    client.close();
  }
}
```

Finally, let's modify the main part of the program to call testWithAsync() within the callback that handles the return value from testWithCallbacks():

```
...
testWithCallbacks(function(err) {
  if (err) {
    console.log(err);
  }
  testWithAsync();
});
...
```

If you clear the collection using remove() as described previously and test these changes, you will see this result (the ObjectIDs that you see will be different than the ones shown here):

```
--- testWithCallbacks ---
Connected to MongoDB
Result of insert:
 5bbf25dcf50e97340be0f01f
Result of find:
 [ { _id: 5bbf25dcf50e97340be0f01f,
     id: 1,
     name: 'A. Callback',
     age: 23 } ]

--- testWithAsync ---
Connected to MongoDB
Result of insert:
 5bbf25dcf50e97340be0f020
Result of find:
 [ { _id: 5bbf25dcf50e97340be0f020,
     id: 2,
     name: 'B. Async',
     age: 16 } ]
```

A good way to test whether errors are being caught and displayed is by running the program again. There will be errors because we have a unique index on the field id, so MongoDB will throw a duplicate key violation. If you have dropped the collection after creating the index, you could run the createIndex() command to reinstate this index.

As you can see, the async/await paradigm is much smaller in terms of code, as well as a lot clearer and easier to read. In fact, although we caught the error within this function, we didn't have to do it. We could as well have let the caller handle it.

Given the benefits of the async/await paradigm, let's use this in the Issue Tracker application when interacting with the database.

Schema Initialization

The mongo shell is not only an interactive shell, but is also a scripting environment. Using this, scripts can be written to perform various tasks such as schema initialization and migration. Because the mongo shell is in fact built on top of a JavaScript engine, the power of JavaScript is available in the scripts, just as in the shell itself.

One difference between the interactive and the non-interactive mode of working is that the non-interactive shell does not support non-JavaScript shortcuts, such as use <db> and show collections commands. The script has to be a regular JavaScript program adhering to the proper syntax.

Let's create a schema initialization script called init.mongo.js within the script directory. Since MongoDB does not enforce a schema, there is really no such thing as a schema initialization as you may do in relational databases, like creation of tables. The only thing that is really useful is the creation of indexes, which are one-time tasks. While we're at it, let's also initialize the database with some sample documents to ease testing. We will use the same database called issuetracker that we used to try out the mongo shell, to store all the collections relevant to the Issue Tracker application.

Let's copy the array of issues from server.js and use the same array to initialize the collection using insertMany() on a collection called issues. But before that, let's clear existing issues it by calling a remove() with an empty filter (which will match all documents) on the same collection. Then, let's create a few indexes on useful fields that we will be using to search the collection with.

Listing 6-3 shows the complete contents of the initialization script, init.mongo.js. There are comments in the beginning of the file that indicate how to run this script for different types of databases—local, Atlas, and mLab.

Listing 6-3. init.mongo.js: Schema Initialization

```
/*
 * Run using the mongo shell. For remote databases, ensure that the
 * connection string is supplied in the command line. For example:
 * localhost:
 *    mongo issuetracker scripts/init.mongo.js
 * Atlas:
 *    mongo mongodb+srv://user:pwd@xxx.mongodb.net/issuetracker ↵
      scripts/init.mongo.js
 * MLab:
 *    mongo mongodb://user:pwd@xxx.mlab.com:33533/issuetracker ↵
      scripts/init.mongo.js
 */

db.issues.remove({});

const issuesDB = [
  {
    id: 1, status: 'New', owner: 'Ravan', effort: 5,
    created: new Date('2019-01-15'), due: undefined,
    title: 'Error in console when clicking Add',
  },
```

```
  {
    id: 2, status: 'Assigned', owner: 'Eddie', effort: 14,
    created: new Date('2019-01-16'), due: new Date('2019-02-01'),
    title: 'Missing bottom border on panel',
  },
];

db.issues.insertMany(issuesDB);
const count = db.issues.count();
print('Inserted', count, 'issues');

db.issues.createIndex({ id: 1 }, { unique: true });
db.issues.createIndex({ status: 1 });
db.issues.createIndex({ owner: 1 });
db.issues.createIndex({ created: 1 });
```

You should be able to run this script using the mongo shell, with the name of the file as an argument in the command line, if you are using the local installation of MongoDB like this:

```
$ mongo issuetracker scripts/init.mongo.js
```

For the other methods of using MongoDB, there are instructions as comments on the top of the script. In essence, the entire connection string has to be specified in the command line, including the username and password that you use to connect to the hosted service. Following the connection string, you can type the name of the script, `scripts/init.mongo.js`.

You can run this any time you wish to reset the database to its pristine state. You should see an output that indicates that two issues were inserted, among other things such as the MongoDB version and the shell version. Note that creating an index when one already exists has no effect, so it is safe to create the index multiple times.

EXERCISE: SCHEMA INITIALIZATION

1. The same schema initialization could have been done using a Node.js script and the MongoDB driver. What are the pros and cons of each of these methods: using the mongo shell vs. the Node.js MongoDB driver?

2. Are there any other indexes that may be useful? Hint: What if we needed a search bar in the application? Read about MongoDB index types at `https://docs. mongodb.com/manual/indexes/#index-types`.

Answers are available at the end of the chapter.

Reading from MongoDB

In the previous section, you saw how to use the Node.js driver to perform basic CRUD tasks. With this knowledge, let's now change the List API to read from the MongoDB database rather than the in-memory array of issues in the server. Since we've initialized the database with the same initial set of issues, while testing, you should see the same set of issues in the UI.

In the trial that we did for the driver, we used the connection to the database in a sequence of operations and closed it. In the application, instead, we will maintain the connection so that we can reuse it for many operations, which will be triggered from within API calls. So, we'll need to store the connection to the database in a global variable. Let's do that in addition to the import statement and other global variable declarations and call the global database connection variable db:

```
...
const url = 'mongodb://localhost/issuetracker';

// Atlas URL  - replace UUU with user, PPP with password, XXX with hostname
// const url = 'mongodb+srv://UUU:PPP@cluster0-XXX.mongodb.net/issuetracker?retryWrites=true';

// mLab URL - replace UUU with user, PPP with password, XXX with hostname
// const url = 'mongodb://UUU:PPP@XXX.mlab.com:33533/issuetracker';

let db;
...
```

Next, let's write a function to connect to the database, which initializes this global variable. This is a minor variation of what we did in trymongo.js. Let's not catch any errors in this function, instead, let the caller deal with them.

```
...
async function connectToDb() {
  const client = new MongoClient(url, { useNewUrlParser: true });
  await client.connect();
  console.log('Connected to MongoDB at', url);
  db = client.db();
}
...
```

Now, we have to change the setup of the server to first connect to the database and then start the Express application. Since connectToDb() is an async function, we can use await to wait for it to finish, then call app.listen(). But since await cannot be used in the main section of the program, we have to enclose it within an async function and execute that function immediately.

```
...
(async function () {
  await connectToDb();
  app.listen(3000, function () {
    console.log('App started on port 3000');
  });
})();
...
```

But we also have to deal with errors. So, let's enclose the contents of this anonymous function within a try block and print any errors on the console in the catch block:

```
...
(async function () {
  try {
    ...
  } catch (err) {
    console.log('ERROR:', err);
  }
})();
...
```

Now that we have a connection to the database set up in the global variable called db, we can use it in the List API resolver issueList() to retrieve a list of issues by calling the find() method on the issues collection. We need to return an array of issues from this function, so let's just use the toArray() function on the results of find() like this:

```
...
  const issues = await db.collection('issues').find({}).toArray();
...
```

The changes to server.js are shown in Listing 6-4.

Listing 6-4. server.js: Changes for Reading the Issue List from MongoDB

```
...
const { Kind } = require('graphql/language');
const { MongoClient } = require('mongodb');

const url = 'mongodb://localhost/issuetracker';

// Atlas URL  - replace UUU with user, PPP with password, XXX with hostname
// const url = 'mongodb+srv://UUU:PPP@cluster0-XXX.mongodb.net/issuetracker?retryWrites=true';

// mLab URL - replace UUU with user, PPP with password, XXX with hostname
// const url = 'mongodb://UUU:PPP@XXX.mlab.com:33533/issuetracker';

let db;

let aboutMessage = "Issue Tracker API v1.0";
...

async function issueList() {
  return issuesDB;
  const issues = await db.collection('issues').find({}).toArray();
  return issues;
}
...

async function connectToDb() {
  const client = new MongoClient(url, { useNewUrlParser: true });
  await client.connect();
  console.log('Connected to MongoDB at', url);
  db = client.db();
}

const server = new ApolloServer({
...

(async function () {
  try {
    await connectToDb();
```

```
    app.listen(3000, function () {
      console.log('App started on port 3000');
    });
  } catch (err) {
    console.log('ERROR:', err);
  }
})();
```

■ **Note**   We did not have to do anything special due to the fact that the resolver `issueList()` is now an async function, which does not immediately return a value. The `graphql-tools` library handles this automatically. A resolver can return a value immediately or return a Promise (which is what an async function returns immediately). Both are acceptable return values for a resolver.

Since the issues from the database now contain an _id in addition to the id field, let's include that in the GraphQL schema of the type Issue. Otherwise, clients who call the API will not be able to access this field. Let's use ID as its GraphQL data type and make it mandatory. This change is shown in Listing 6-5.

Listing 6-5.   schema.graphql: Changes to add _id as a Field in Issue

```
...
type Issue {
  _id: ID!
  id: Int!
  ...
}
...
```

Now, assuming that the server is still running (or that you have restarted the server and the compilation), if you refresh the browser, you will find that the two initial sets of issues are listed in a table, as before. The UI itself will show no change, but to convince yourself that the data is indeed coming from the database, you could modify the documents in the collection using the mongo shell and the `updateMany()` method on the collection. If, for example, you update effort to 100 for all the documents and refresh the browser, you should see that the effort is indeed showing 100 for all the rows in the table.

EXERCISE: READING FROM MONGODB

1. We are saving the connection in a global variable. What happens when the connection is lost? Stop the MongoDB server and start it again to see what happens. Does the connection still work?

2. Shut down the MongoDB server, wait for a minute or more, and then start the server again. Now, refresh the browser. What happens? Can you explain this? What if you wanted a longer period for the connection to work even if the database server is down? Hint: Look up the connection settings parameters at `http://mongodb.github.io/node-mongodb-native/3.1/reference/connecting/connection-settings/`.

3. We used `toArray()` to convert the list of issues into an array. What if the list is too big, say, a million documents? How would you deal with this? Hint: Look up the documentation for the MongoDB Node.js driver's `Cursor` at http://mongodb. github.io/node-mongodb-native/3.1/api/Cursor.html. Note that the `find()` method returns a `Cursor`.

Writing to MongoDB

In order to completely replace the in-memory database on the server, we'll also need to change the Create API to use the MongoDB database. As you saw in the MongoDB CRUD Operations section, the way to create a new document is to use the `insertOne()` method on the collection.

We used the size of the in-memory array to generate the new document's `id` field. We could do the same, using the `count()` method of the collection to get the next ID. But there is a small chance when there are multiple users using the application that a new document is created between the time we call the `count()` method and the time we call the `insertOne()` method. What we really need is a reliable way of generating a sequence of numbers that cannot give us duplicates, much like sequences in popular relational databases.

MongoDB does not provide such a method directly. But it does support an atomic update operation, which can return the result of the update. This method is called `findOneAndUpdate()`. Using this method, we can update a counter and return the updated value, but instead of using the `$set` operator, we can use the `$inc` operator, which increments the current value.

Let's first create a collection with the counter that holds a value for the latest Issue ID generated. To make it a bit generic, let's assume we may have other such counters and use a collection with an ID set to the name of the counter and a value field called `current` holding the current value of the counter. In the future, we could add more counters in the same collections, and these would translate to one document for each counter.

To start, let's modify the schema initialization script to include a collection called `counters` and populate that with one document for the counter for issues. Since there are insertions that create a few sample issues, we'll need to initialize the counter's value to the count of inserted documents. The changes are in `init.mongo.js`, and Listing 6-6 shows this file.

Listing 6-6. init.mongo.js: Initialize Counters for Issues

```
...
print('Inserted', count, 'issues');

db.counters.remove({ _id: 'issues' });
db.counters.insert({ _id: 'issues', current: count });
...
```

Let's run the schema initialization script again to make this change take effect:

```
$ mongo issuetracker scripts/init.mongo.js
```

Now, a call to `findOneAndUpdate()` that increments the `current` field is guaranteed to return a unique value that is next in the sequence. Let's create a function in `server.js` that does this, but in a generic manner. We'll let it take the ID of the counter and return the next sequence. In this function, all we have to do is call `findOneAndUpdate()`. It identifies the counter to use using the ID supplied, increments the field called `current`, and returns the new value. By default, the result of the `findOneAndUpdate()` method returns the original document. To make it return the new, modified document instead, the option returnOriginal has to be set to false.

The arguments to the method findOneAndUpdate() are (a) the filter or match, for which we used _id, then (b) the update operation, for which we used a $inc operator with value 1, and finally, (c) the options for the operation. Here's the code that will do the needful:

```
...
async function getNextSequence(name) {
  const result = await db.collection('counters').findOneAndUpdate(
    { _id: name },
    { $inc: { current: 1 } },
    { returnOriginal: false },
  );
  return result.value.current;
}
...
```

■ **Note**　The option for returning the current or new value is called differently in the Node.js driver and in the mongo shell. In the mongo shell, the option is called returnNewDocument and the default is false. In the Node. js driver, the option is called returnOriginal and the default is true. In both cases, the default behavior is to return the original, so the option must be specified to return the new document.

Now, we can use this function to generate a new ID field and set it in the supplied issue object in the resolver issueAdd(). We can then write to the collection called issues using insertOne(), and then read back the newly created issue using findOne().

```
...
  issue.id = await getNextSequence('issues');

  const result = await db.collection('issues').insertOne(issue);
  const savedIssue = await db.collection('issues')
    .findOne({ _id: result.insertedId });
  return savedIssue;
...
```

Finally, we can get rid of the in-memory array of issues in the server. Including this change, the complete set of changes in server.js is represented in Listing 6-7.

Listing 6-7.　server.js: Changes for Create API to Use the Database

```
...
const issuesDB = [
  {
    id: 1, status: 'New', owner: 'Ravan', effort: 5,
    ...
  },
  ...
  },
];
```

```
...
async function getNextSequence(name) {
  const result = await db.collection('counters').findOneAndUpdate(
    { _id: name },
    { $inc: { current: 1 } },
    { returnOriginal: false },
  );
  return result.value.current;
}

async function issueAdd(_, { issue }) {
  const errors = [];
  ...
  issue.created = new Date();

  issue.id = issuesDB.length + 1;
  issue.id = await getNextSequence('issues');

  issuesDB.push(issue);
  const result = await db.collection('issues').insertOne(issue);

  return issue;
  const savedIssue = await db.collection('issues')
    .findOne({ _id: result.insertedId });
  return savedIssue;
...
```

Testing this set of changes will show that new issues can be added, and even on a restart of the Node.js server, or the database server, the newly added issues are still there. As a cross-check, you could use the mongo shell to look at the contents of the collection after every change from the UI.

EXERCISE: WRITING TO MONGODB

1. Could we have just added the _id to the passed-in object and returned that instead of doing a find() for the inserted object?

Answers are available at the end of the chapter.

Summary

In this chapter, you learned about the installation and other ways of getting access to an instance of a database in MongoDB. You saw how to use the mongo shell and the Node.js driver to access the basic operations in MongoDB: the CRUD operations. We then modified the Issue Tracker application to use some of these methods to read and write to the MongoDB database, thus making the issue list persistent.

I covered only the very basics of MongoDB, only the capabilities and features that will be useful to build the Issue Tracker application, which is a rather simple CRUD application. In reality, the capabilities of the database as well as the Node.js driver and the mongo shell are vast, and many more features of MongoDB may be required for a complex application. I encourage you to take a look at the MongoDB documentation (https://docs.mongodb.com/manual/) and the Node.js driver documentation (http://mongodb.github.io/node-mongodb-native/) to familiarize yourself with what else the database and the Node.js drivers are capable of.

Now that we have used the essentials of the MERN stack and have a working application, let's take a break from implementing features and get a bit organized instead. Before the application gets any bigger and becomes unwieldy, let's modularize the code and use tools to improve our productivity.

We'll do this in the next chapter, by using Webpack, one of the best tools that can be used to modularize both the front-end and the back-end code.

Answers to Exercises

Exercise: MongoDB Basics

1. As per the mongo shell documentation under "Access the mongo shell Help", you can find that there is a method called help() on many objects, including the cursor object. The way to get help on this is using db.collection.find().help().

    But since this is also a JavaScript shell like Node.js, pressing Tab will auto-complete and a double-Tab will show a list of possible completions. Thus, if you assign a cursor to a variable and press Tab twice after typing the variable name and a dot after that, the shell will list the possible completions, and that is a list of methods available on the cursor.

Exercise: MongoDB CRUD Operations

1. This can be done using the $exists operator like this:

    ```
    > db.employees.find({ "name.middle": { $exists: true } })
    ```

2. The filter specification is not a JSON document, because it is not a string. It is a regular JavaScript object, which is why you are able to skip the quotes around the property names. You will also be able to have real Date objects as field values, unlike a JSON string.

3. The $unset operator in an update can be used to unset a field (which is actually different from setting it to null). Here is an example:

    ```
    > db.employees.update(({_id: ObjectId("57b1caea3475bb1784747ccb")},
    {"name.middle": {$unset: null}})
    ```

    Although we supplied null as the value for $unset, this value is ignored. It can be anything.

4. The 1 indicates an ascending sort order for traversing the index. -1 is used to indicate a descending sort order. This is useful only for compound (aka composite) indexes, because a simple index on one field can be used to traverse the collection in both directions.

Exercise: Schema Initialization

1. The advantage of using the Node.js driver is that there is one way of doing things across the application and the scripts, and the familiarity will help prevent errors. But running the program requires a proper Node.js environment, including npm modules installed, whereas the mongo shell script can be run from anywhere, provided the machine has the mongo shell installed.

2. A search bar is quite helpful when searching for issues. A text index (an index based on the words) on the title field would be useful in this case. We'll implement a text index toward the end of the book.

Exercise: Reading from MongoDB

1. The connection object is in fact a connection pool. It automatically determines the best thing to do: reuse an existing TCP connection, reestablish a new connection when the connection is broken, etc. Using a global variable (at least, reusing the connection object) is the recommended usage.

2. If the database is unavailable for a short period (less than 30 seconds), the driver retries and reconnects when the database is available again. If the database is unavailable for a longer period, the read throws an error. The driver is also unable to reestablish a connection when the database is restored. The application server needs to be restarted in this case.

   The default interval of 30 seconds can be changed using the connection settings reconnectTries or reconnectInterval.

3. One option is to use limit() on the result to limit the return value to a maximum number of records. For example, find().limit(100) returns the first 100 documents. If you were to paginate the output in the UI, you could also use the skip() method to specify where to start the list.

   If, on the other hand, you think the client can handle large lists but you don't want to expend that much memory in the server, you could deal with one document at a time using hasNext() and next() and stream the results back to the client.

Exercise: Writing to MongoDB

1. Adding the _id and returning the object passed in would have worked, so long as you know for a fact that the write was a success and the object was written to the database as is. In most cases, this would be true, but it's good practice to get the results from the database, as that is the ultimate truth.

■ ■ ■

## CHAPTER 7

Architecture and ESLint

In this chapter and the next, we'll take a break from adding features. Instead, we'll get a bit more organized in preparation for when the application grows larger and larger.

In this chapter, we'll look again at the architecture and make it more flexible so that it can cater to larger applications with lots of traffic. We'll use a package called dotenv to help us run the same code on different environments using different configurations for each environment, such as development and production.

Finally, we'll add checks to verify that the code we write follows standards and good practices and catches possible bugs earlier in the testing cycle. We'll use ESLint for this purpose.

UI Server

Until now, we did not pay too much attention to the architecture of the application and the one and only server dealt with two functions. The Express server not only serves static content, but also serves API calls. The architecture is depicted in Figure 7-1.

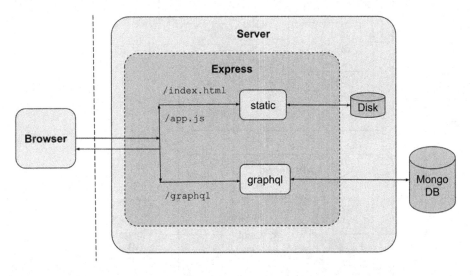

Figure 7-1. *Single server architecture*

All requests land on the same physical server, and within that is the one and only Express application. Then, the requests are routed into two different middleware depending on the request. Any request-matching files in the `public` directory are matched by the middleware called `static`. This middleware uses the disk

© Vasan Subramanian 2019

V. Subramanian, *Pro MERN Stack*, https://doi.org/10.1007/978-1-4842-4391-6_7

to read files and serve the file's contents. Other requests that match the /graphql path are dealt with by the Apollo Server's middleware. This middleware, using resolvers, gets the data from the MongoDB database.

This works great for small applications, but one or more of the following starts happening as the application grows:

- The API has other consumers, not just the browser-based UI. For example, the API may be exposed to third parties or mobile applications.

- The two parts have different scaling requirements. Typically, as more consumers of the API appear, you may need multiple servers for the API and a load-balancer. Whereas, since most static content can and will be cached in the browsers, having many servers for static assets may be overkill.

Further, the fact that both functions are being done on the same server, both inside the same Node.js and Express process, makes it harder to diagnose and debug performance issues. A better option is to separate the two functions into two servers: one that serves static content, and another that hosts just the API.

In later chapters, I introduce *server rendering*, wherein complete pages will be generated from the server as opposed to being constructed on the browser. This helps search engines index the pages correctly, because search engine bots do not necessarily run JavaScript. When we implement server rendering, it will help if all the API code and the UI code are kept separate.

Figure 7-2 depicts a new-generation architecture with the UI and the API server separated. It also shows where server-side rendering will fit in eventually, when we do implement it.

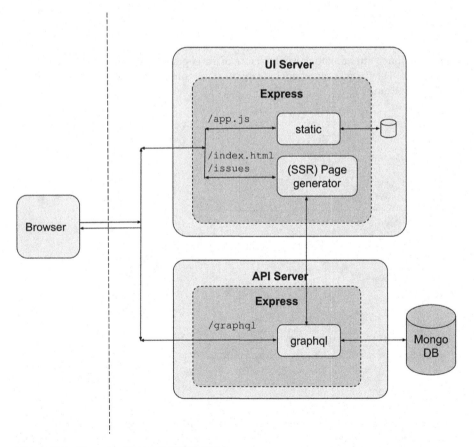

Figure 7-2. *Separate UI server architectures*

In the diagram in Figure 7-2, you can see that there are two servers: the UI server and the API server. These can be physically different computers, but for development purposes, we'll run these on the same computer but on different ports. These will be run using two different Node.js processes, each with its own instance of Express.

The API server will now be responsible for handling *only* the API requests, and therefore, it will respond only to URLs matching /graphql in the path. Thus, the Apollo server middleware and its requests to the MongoDB database will be the only middleware in the API server.

The UI server part will now contain *only* the static middleware. In the future, when we introduce server rendering, this server will be responsible for generating HTML pages by calling the API server's APIs to fetch the necessary data. For the moment, we'll be using the UI server only for serving all static content, which consists of index.html and the JavaScript bundle that contains all the React code.

The browser will be responsible for using the appropriate server based on the type of request: all API calls will be directed to the API server, whereas the static files will be referred to the UI server.

The first thing we'll do to achieve this is create a new directory structure that cleanly separates the UI and the API code.

■ **Note**   Ideally, the UI and API code would belong in two different repositories, because there is nothing that is shared among them. But for the convenience of reading this book and referring to Git diffs from the GitHub repository (https://github.com/vasansr/pro-mern-stack-2), I have kept the code together but in different directories at the top-most level.

Let's rename the server directory api rather than create a new one.

```
$ mv server api
```

■ **Note**   The commands that are shown (which can also be found in the GitHub repository (https://github. com/vasansr/pro-mern-stack-2 in the file commands.md) are meant for execution in MacOS or the bash shell in a Linux-based distribution. If you are using a Windows PC, you will have to use the Windows equivalent commands.

Since all the scripts that we have are meant only for the API server, let's move the scripts directory under the new directory api as well.

```
$ mv scripts api
```

For the UI code, let's create a new directory called ui under the project root and move the UI-related directories public and src under this.

```
$ mkdir ui
$ mv public ui
$ mv src ui
```

But just moving the directories is not enough; we need a package.json file in each of these directories ui and api, both for saving npm dependencies as well as for creating convenient scripts for running the server. With the new package.json files and after installing all the dependencies, the new directory structure will look like Figure 7-3.

Figure 7-3. *New directory structure for UI server separation*

Let's now create two new `package.json` files in the two new directories. You could also copy this file from the root project directory for convenience and make changes.

In the file corresponding to the API, let's use the word API in the name (for example, `pro-mern-stack-2-api`) and the description (for example, `"Pro MERN Stack (2nd Edition) API"`). As for the scripts, we'll have just one script to start the server. Since the location of the files has changed from `server` to the current directory, we can remove the `-w` option to `nodemon` in this script.

```
...
    "start": "nodemon -e js,graphql server.js",
...
```

As for the dependencies, we'll not have any `devDependencies`, but all the regular dependencies that were needed for running the server. The complete `package.json` file is shown in Listing 7-1.

Listing 7-1. api/package.json: New File

```
{
  "name": "pro-mern-stack-2-api",
  "version": "1.0.0",
  "description": "Pro MERN Stack (2nd Edition) API",
  "main": "index.js",
  "scripts": {
    "start": "nodemon -e js,graphql server.js",
    "test": "echo \"Error: no test specified\" && exit 1"
  },
  "repository": {
    "type": "git",
    "url": "git+https://github.com/vasansr/pro-mern-stack-2.git"
  },
```

```
    "author": "vasan.promern@gmail.com",
    "license": "ISC",
    "homepage": "https://github.com/vasansr/pro-mern-stack-2",
    "dependencies": {
      "apollo-server-express": "^2.3.1",
      "express": "^4.16.4",
      "graphql": "^0.13.2",
      "mongodb": "^3.1.10",
      "nodemon": "^1.18.9"
    }
}
```

■ **Note**   Although no effort has been spared to ensure that all code listings are accurate, there may be typos or even corrections that did not make it into the book before it went to press. So, always rely on the GitHub repository (`https://github.com/vasansr/pro-mern-stack-2`) as the tested and up-to-date source for all code listings, especially if something does not work as expected.

Let's now install all the npm dependencies based on the new package.json file in the api directory.

```
$ cd api
$ npm install
```

Since we'll be running the server from within this new api directory, we will need to load schema.graphql from the current directory. So let's change code in server.js to remove the /server/ prefix from the path of schema.graphql being loaded.

```
...
const server = new ApolloServer({
  typeDefs: fs.readFileSync('./server/schema.graphql', 'utf-8'),
...
```

We can also remove loading of the static middleware and call the new server the API server rather than the App server in the console message. The full set of changes for api/server.js are shown in Listing 7-2.

Listing 7-2.   api/server.js: Changes for New Location of schema.graphql

```
...
const server = new ApolloServer({
  typeDefs: fs.readFileSync('./server/schema.graphql', 'utf-8'),
...
const app = express();

app.use(express.static('public'));

server.applyMiddleware({ app, path: '/graphql' });
...
    app.listen(3000, function () {
      console.log('AppAPI server started on port 3000');
    });
...
```

At this point in time, you should be able to run the API server using npm start. Further, if you test the APIs using the GraphQL Playground, you should find that the APIs are working as before.

The UI server changes are a bit more involved. We'll need a new package.json that has both server and transformation npm packages, such as Babel. Let's create a new package.json in the UI directory. You could do this either by copying from the project root directory or by running npm init. Then, in the dependencies section, let's add Express and nodemon:

```
...
  "dependencies": {
    "express": "^4.16.4",
    "nodemon": "^1.18.9"
  },
...
```

As for devDependencies, let's keep the original set from the package.json in the root directory.

```
...
  "devDependencies": {
    "@babel/cli": "^7.2.3",
    "@babel/core": "^7.2.2",
    "@babel/preset-env": "^7.2.3",
    "@babel/preset-react": "^7.0.0"
  }
...
```

Let's install all the dependencies that are needed for the UI server.

```
$ cd ui
$ npm install
```

Now, let's create an Express server to serve the static files, called uiserver.js, in the directory ui. This is very similar to the server we created for Hello World. All we need is the Express app with the static middleware. The contents of the file are shown in Listing 7-3.

Listing 7-3. ui/uiserver.js: New Server for Static Content

```
const express = require('express');

const app = express();

app.use(express.static('public'));

app.listen(8000, function () {
  console.log('UI started on port 8000');
});
```

To run this server, let's create a script for starting it in package.json. It is the usual nodemon command that you have seen in other server start scripts. This time, we'll only watch for the uiserver.js file since we have other files not related to the server per se.

```
...
  "scripts": {
    "start": "nodemon -w uiserver.js uiserver.js",
  },
...
```

Further, to generate the transformed JavaScript file, let's add the compile and watch scripts, as in the original package.json file. The complete contents of this file, including the compile and watch scripts, are shown in Listing 7-4.

Listing 7-4. ui/package.json: New File for the UI Server

```
{
  "name": "pro-mern-stack-2-ui",
  "version": "1.0.0",
  "description": "Pro MERN Stack (2nd Edition) - UI",
  "main": "index.js",
  "scripts": {
    "start": "nodemon -w uiserver.js uiserver.js",
    "compile": "babel src --out-dir public",
    "watch": "babel src --out-dir public --watch --verbose"
  },
  "repository": {
    "type": "git",
    "url": "git+https://github.com/vasansr/pro-mern-stack-2.git"
  },
  "author": "vasan.promern@gmail.com",
  "license": "ISC",
  "homepage": "https://github.com/vasansr/pro-mern-stack-2",
  "dependencies": {
    "express": "^4.16.3",
    "nodemon": "^1.18.4"
  },
  "devDependencies": {
    "@babel/cli": "^7.0.0",
    "@babel/core": "^7.0.0",
    "@babel/preset-env": "^7.0.0",
    "@babel/preset-react": "^7.0.0"
  }
}
```

Now, you can test the application by running both the UI and API servers using npm start within each corresponding directory. As for the transformation, you could, within the ui directory, either run npm run compile or npm run watch. But the API calls will fail because the endpoint /graphql has no handlers in the UI server. So, instead of making API calls to the UI server, we need to change the UI to call the API server. This can be done in the App.jsx file, as shown in Listing 7-5.

Listing 7-5. ui/src/App.jsx: Point to a Different API Server

```
...
async function graphQLFetch(query, variables = {}) {
  try {
    const response = await fetch('http://localhost:3000/graphql', {
      method: 'POST',
...
```

Now, if you test the application, you will find that it is working as before. We can also clean up the root directory. The file package.json and the directory node_modules are no longer required and can be removed. The Linux and MacOS commands for doing this are as follows:

```
$ rm package.json
$ rm -rf node_modules
```

EXERCISE: UI SERVER

1. Open a new browser tab and type http://localhost:3000. What do you see, and why? Do we need to do anything about this? What are the options? Hint: Browse to GitHub's API endpoint host in a similar manner, at https://api.github.com.

Answers are available at the end of the chapter.

Multiple Environments

We postponed removing hard-coded things such as the port numbers and MongoDB URL. Now that the directory structure has been finalized, it's perhaps a good time to remove all hard-coding and keep these as variables that can be changed more easily.

Typically, there would be three deployment environments: development, staging, and production. The server ports and MongoDB URL for each of these would be quite different. For example, the ports of both the API server and the UI server would be 80. We used two different ports because both servers were run on the same host, and two processes cannot listen on the same port. Also, we used ports like 8000 because using port 80 requires administrative privileges (superuser rights).

Rather than predetermine the ports and the MongoDB URL based on possible deployment targets such as development, staging, and production, let's keep the variables flexible so that they can be set to anything at runtime. A typical way of supplying these is via environment variables, especially for remote targets and production servers. But during development, it's nice to be able to have these in some configuration file so that the developers don't need to remember to set these up every time.

Let's use a package called dotenv to help us achieve this. This package can convert variables stored in a file into environment variables. Thus, in the code, we only deal with environment variables, but the environment variables can be supplied via real environment variables or configuration files.

The dotenv package looks for a file called .env, which can contain variables defined like in a shell. For example, we could have the following line in this file:

```
...
DB_URL=mongodb://localhost/issuetracker
...
```

In the code, all we'd have to do is look for the environment variable DB_URL using process.env.DB_URL and use the value from it. This value can be overridden by an actual environment variable defined before starting the program, so it is not necessary to have this file. In fact, most production deployments would take the value only from the environment variable.

Let's now install the package, first in the API server:

```
$ cd api
$ npm install dotenv@6
```

To use this package, all we need to do is to require it and immediately call config() on it.

```
...
require('dotenv').config();
...
```

Now, we can use any environment variable using process.env properties. Let's first do that in server.js, for the MongoDB URL. We already have a variable url, which we can set to DB_URL from process.env and default it to the original localhost value if it is undefined:

```
...
const url = process.env.DB_URL || 'mongodb://localhost/issuetracker';
...
```

Similarly, for the server port, let's use an environment variable called API_SERVER_PORT and use a variable called port within server.js like this:

```
...
const port = process.env.API_SERVER_PORT || 3000;
...
```

Now we can use the variable port to start the server.

```
...
    app.listen(3000port, function () {
      console.log('API server started on port 3000');
      console.log(`API server started on port ${port}`);
...
```

Note the change of quote style from a single quote to back-ticks because we used string interpolation. The complete set of changes to the api/server.js file are shown in Listing 7-6.

Listing 7-6. api/server.js: Changes to Use Environment Variables

```
...
const fs = require('fs');
require('dotenv').config();
const express = require('express');
...
const url = process.env.DB_URL || 'mongodb://localhost/issuetracker';
```

```
// Atlas URL - replace UUU with user, PPP with password, XXX with hostname
// const url = 'mongodb+srv://UUU:PPP@cluster0-XXX.mongodb.net/issuetracker?retryWrites=true';

// mLab URL - replace UUU with user, PPP with password, XXX with hostname
// const url = 'mongodb://UUU:PPP@XXX.mlab.com:33533/issuetracker';
...

const port = process.env.API_SERVER_PORT || 3000;

(async function () {
  try {
    ...
    app.listen(3000port, function () {
      console.log('API server started on port 3000');
      console.log(`API server started on port ${port}`);
    });
    ...
  ...
```

Let's also create a file called .env in the api directory. There is a file called sample.env that I have included in the GitHub repository that you may copy from and make changes to suit your environment, especially the DB_URL. The contents of this file are shown in Listing 7-7.

Listing 7-7. api/sample.env: Sample .env File

```
## DB
# Local
DB_URL=mongodb://localhost/issuetracker

# Atlas - replace UUU: user, PPP: password, XXX: hostname
# DB_URL=mongodb+srv://UUU:PPP@XXX.mongodb.net/issuetracker?retryWrites=true

# mLab - replace UUU: user, PPP: password, XXX: hostname, YYY: port
# DB_URL=mongodb://UUU:PPP@XXX.mlab.com:YYY/issuetracker

## Server Port
API_SERVER_PORT=3000
```

It is recommended that the .env file itself not be checked into any repository. Each developer and deployment environments must specifically set the variables in the environment or in this file as per their needs. This is so that changes to this file remain in the developer's computer and others' changes don't overwrite a developer's settings.

It's also a good idea to change the nodemon command line so that it watches for changes to this file. Since the current command line does not include a watch specification (because it defaults to ".", that is, the current directory), let's include that as well. The changes to this script in package.json are shown in Listing 7-8.

Listing 7-8. api/package.json: nodemon to Watch for .env

```
...
  "scripts": {
    "start": "nodemon -e js,graphql -w . -w .env server.js",
    "test": "echo \"Error: no test specified\" && exit 1"
  },
...
```

Now, if you specify `API_SERVER_PORT` as 4000 in the file `.env` and restart the API server (because nodemon needs to know the new watch files), you should see that it now uses port 4000. You could undo this change and instead define an environment variable (do not forget to use `export` in the bash shell to make the variable available to sub-processes) and see that the change has indeed been made. Note that the actual environment variables take precedence over (or override) the same variable defined in the `.env` file.

Let's also make a similar set of changes to `api/scripts/trymongo.js` to use the environment variable `DB_URL`. These changes are shown in Listing 7-9. There are also changes to print out the URL after connecting, to cross-check that the environment variable is being used.

Listing 7-9. api/scripts/trymongo.js: Read DB_URI from the Environment Using dotenv

```
require('dotenv').config();
const { MongoClient } = require('mongodb');

const url = process.env.DB_URL || 'mongodb://localhost/issuetracker';

// Atlas URL - replace UUU with user, PPP with password, XXX with hostname
// const url = 'mongodb+srv://UUU:PPP@cluster0-XXX.mongodb.net/issuetracker?retryWrites=true';

// mLab URL - replace UUU with user, PPP with password, XXX with hostname
// const url = 'mongodb://UUU:PPP@XXX.mlab.com:33533/issuetracker';

...
  client.connect(function(err, client) {
    ...
    console.log('Connected to MongoDB');
    console.log('Connected to MongoDB URL', url);
...
    await client.connect();
    console.log('Connected to MongoDB');
    console.log('Connected to MongoDB URL', url);
```

You can now test the script using the command line and Node.js as before, and you'll see the effect of different environment variables, both in the shell as well as in the `.env` file.

We need to make a similar set of changes for the UI server. In this case, the variables we need to use are:

- The UI server port
- The API endpoint to call

The UI server port changes are similar to the API server port changes. Let's get that done first. Just as for the API server, let's install the dotenv package.

```
$ cd ui
$ npm install dotenv@6
```

Then, in the ui/uiserver.js file, let's require and configure dotenv:

```
...
require('dotenv').config();
...
```

Let's also change the hard-coded port to use the environment variable.

```
...
const port = process.env.UI_SERVER_PORT || 8000;

app.listen(8000 port, function () {
  console.log('UI started on port 8000');
  console.log(`UI started on port ${port}`);
});
...
```

Unlike these changes, the API endpoint has to somehow get to the browser in the form of JavaScript code. It is not something that can be read from an environment variable, because that is not transmitted to the browser.

One way to do this is to replace a predefined string within the code with the variable's value as part of the build and bundle process. I'll describe this method in the next section. Although this is a valid and preferred choice for many people, I have chosen to make the configuration a *runtime* variable as opposed to a compile-time one. That's because on the real UI servers, the way to set the server port and the API endpoint will be uniform.

To do this, let's *generate* a JavaScript file and inject that into index.html. This JavaScript file will contain a global variable with the contents of the environment. Let's call this new script file env.js and include it in index.html. This is the only change to index.html in this section, and it's shown in Listing 7-10.

Listing 7-10. ui/public/index.html: Include the Script /env.js

```
...
  <div id="contents"></div>

  <script src="/env.js"></script>
  <script src="/App.js"></script>
...
```

Now, within the UI server, let's generate the contents of this script. It should result in setting a global variable called ENV with one or more properties that are set to environment variables, something like this:

```
...
window.ENV = {
  UI_API_ENDPOINT: "http://localhost:3000"
}
...
```

182

When the JavaScript is executed, it will initialize the global variable ENV to the object. When the variable is needed in any other place, it can be referred from the global variable. Now, in the UI server code, let's first initialize a variable for the API endpoint and default it if not found. Then we'll construct an object with just this one variable as a property.

```
...
const UI_API_ENDPOINT = process.env.UI_API_ENDPOINT || 'http://localhost:3000';
const env = { UI_API_ENDPOINT };
...
```

Now, we can create a route in the server that responds to a GET call for env.js. Within the handler for this route, let's construct the string as we need, using the env object, and send it as the response:

```
...
app.get('/env.js', function(req, res) {
  res.send(`window.ENV = ${JSON.stringify(env)}`)
})
...
```

The complete changes to ui/uiserver.js are shown in Listing 7-11.

Listing 7-11. ui/uiserver.js: Changes for Environment Variable Usage

```
require('dotenv').config();
const express = require('express');

const app = express();

app.use(express.static('public'));

const UI_API_ENDPOINT = process.env. UI_API_ENDPOINT || 'http://localhost:3000/graphql';
const env = { UI_API_ENDPOINT };

app.get('/env.js', function(req, res) {
  res.send(`window.ENV = ${JSON.stringify(env)}`)
})

const port = process.env.UI_SERVER_PORT || 8000;

app.listen(8000port, function () {
  console.log('UI started on port 8000');
  console.log(`UI started on port ${port}`);
});
```

Just like for the API server, let's create an .env file to hold two variables, one for the server's port and the other for the API endpoint the UI needs to access. You could use a copy of the sample.env file, whose contents are shown in Listing 7-12.

Listing 7-12. ui/sample.env: Sample .env File for the UI Server

```
UI_SERVER_PORT=8000
UI_API_ENDPOINT=http://localhost:3000/graphql
```

Finally, in App.jsx, where the API endpoint is hard-coded, let's replace the hard-coding with a property from the global ENV variable. This change is shown in Listing 7-13.

Listing 7-13. ui/src/App.jsx: Replace Hard-Coding of API Endpoint

```
...
async function graphQLFetch(query, variables = {}) {
  try {
    const response = await fetch('http://localhost:3000/graphql', {
    const response = await fetch(window.ENV.UI_API_ENDPOINT, {
    ...
  ...
}
...
```

Let's also make nodemon watch for changes in the .env file. Since we are specifying individual files to watch in the UI server, this requires us to add another file to watch for using the -w command line option. The changes to ui/package.json are shown in Listing 7-14.

Listing 7-14. ui/package.json: nodemon to Watch for Changes in .env

```
...
  "scripts": {
    "start": "nodemon -w uiserver.js -w .env uiserver.js",
...
```

Now, if you test the application with the default ports and endpoints, the application should be working as before. If you have been running npm run watch in a console, the changes to App.jsx would have been automatically recompiled.

You can also ensure that a change to any of the variables, both via an actual environment variable and a change in the .env file (if you have one), do take effect. If you change a variable via an environment variable do remember to export it if you are using the bash shell. Also, the server has to be restarted since nodemon does not watch for changes to any environment variable.

EXERCISE: MULTIPLE ENVIRONMENTS

1. In the browser, manually type http://localhost:8000/env.js. What do you see? Set the environment variable UI_API_ENDPOINT to a different location and restart the UI server. Check the contents of env.js.

Answers are available at the end of the chapter.

Proxy-Based Architecture

If you had your Network tab open in the Developer Console while testing, you would have noticed that there are *two* calls to /graphql instead of just one. The HTTP method for the first call is OPTIONS. The reason is that the API call is to a host (http://localhost:3000) that is different from the origin of the application (http://localhost:8000). Due to the Same-origin policy, such requests are normally blocked by the browser unless the server specifically allows it.

The Same-origin policy exists to prevent malicious websites from gaining unauthorized access to the application. You can read the details of this policy at https://developer.mozilla.org/en-US/docs/Web/Security/Same-origin_policy. But the gist of it is that since cookies set by one origin are automatically attached with any request to that origin, it is possible that a malicious website can make a call to the origin from the browser and the browser will attach the cookie.

Say you are logged into a bank's website. In another browser tab, you are browsing some news website that has some malicious JavaScript running in it, maybe via an advertisement on the website. If this malicious JavaScript makes an Ajax call to the bank's website and the cookies are sent as part of the request, the malicious JavaScript can end up impersonating you and maybe even transferring funds to the hacker's account!

So, browsers prevent this by requiring that such requests be explicitly permitted. The kind of requests that can be permitted is controlled by the Same-origin policy as well as parameters controlled by the server, which determines if the request can be allowed. This mechanism is called *cross-origin resource sharing* or CORS for short. The Apollo GraphQL server, by default, allows unauthenticated requests across origins. The following headers in the response to the OPTIONS request shows this:

```
Access-Control-Allow-Headers: content-type
Access-Control-Allow-Methods: GET,HEAD,PUT,PATCH,POST,DELETE
Access-Control-Allow-Origin: *
```

Let's disable the default behavior of the Apollo server (using, of course, an environment variable) and check out the new behavior of the API server. Let's call this environment variable ENABLE_CORS and set the api/.env file to false (the default being true, the current behavior).

```
...
## Enable CORS (default: true)
ENABLE_CORS=false
...
```

Now, in server.js in the API, let's look for this environment variable and set an option called cors to true or false, depending on this variable. The changes to api/server.js are shown in Listing 7-15.

Listing 7-15. api/server.js: Option for Enabling CORS

```
...
const app = express();

const enableCors = (process.env.ENABLE_CORS || 'true') == 'true';
console.log('CORS setting:', enableCors);
server.applyMiddleware({ app, path: '/graphql', cors: enableCors });
...
```

If you test the application, you will find that the OPTION request fails with an HTTP response of 405. Now, the application is safe from malicious cross-site attacks. But this also means that we need some other mechanism to make API calls.

I'll discuss CORS in more detail and why it's safe to enable CORS at the current stage of the application, where all resources are publicly available without authentication. But let's also look at alternatives for the sake of security. In this section, we'll change the UI to make even API requests to the UI server, where we will install a proxy so that any request to /graphql is routed to the API server. This new architecture is depicted in Figure 7-4.

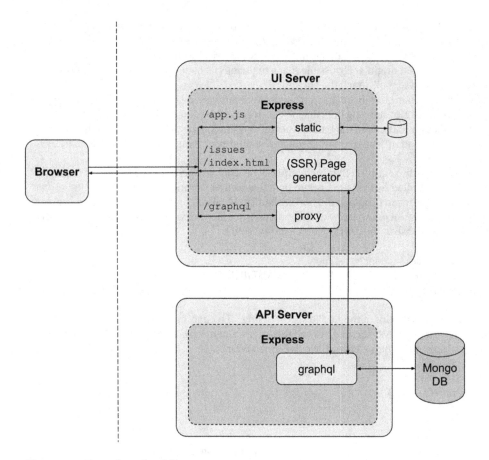

Figure 7-4. *Proxy-based architecture*

Such a proxy can be easily implemented using the `http-proxy-middleware` package. Let's install this package:

```
$ cd ui
$ npm install http-proxy-middleware@0
```

Now, a proxy can be used as a middleware that the package provides, mounted on the path /graphql, using app.use(). The middleware can be created with just a single option: the target of the proxy, which is the base URL of the host where the requests have to be proxied. Let's define another environment variable called API_PROXY_TARGET and use its value as the target. If this variable is undefined, we can skip installing the proxy rather than default it.

The changes to ui/uiserver.js are shown in Listing 7-16.

Listing 7-16. ui/uiserver.js: Changes to Install Proxy

```
...
require('dotenv').config();
const express = require('express');
const proxy = require('http-proxy-middleware');
...
```

```
const apiProxyTarget = process.env.API_PROXY_TARGET;
if (apiProxyTarget) {
  app.use('/graphql', proxy({ target: apiProxyTarget }));
}

const UI_API_ENDPOINT = process.env.UI_API_ENDPOINT ||
...
```

Let's now change the environment variable that specifies the API endpoint in ui/.env to set it to /graphql, which means /graphql on the same host as the origin. Further, let's define the target of the proxy, the variable API_PROXY_TARGET as http://localhost:3000.

```
...
UI_API_ENDPOINT=http://localhost:3000/graphql
API_PROXY_TARGET=http://localhost:3000
...
```

Now, if you test the application and look at the Network tab in the browser's Developer Console, you will find that there is only one request going to the UI server (port 8000) for each of the API calls, which successfully execute.

You can use the proxy method as described in this section or let the UI make direct calls to the API server and enable CORS in the API server. Both options are equally good and your actual choice depends on various things, such as your deployment environment and the security needs of your application.

For the purpose of following this book, let's revert the changes to the .env files we did as part of this section so that we use the direct API call mechanism. You may copy the sample.env file in both the API and the UI directories from the GitHub repository to your own .env files, which reflects the direct API way of working.

ESLint

A *linter* (something that *lints*) checks for suspicious code that could be bugs. It can also check whether your code adheres to conventions and standards that you want to follow across your team to make the code predictably readable.

While there are multiple opinions and debates on what is a good standard (tabs vs. spaces, for example), there has been no debate on whether there needs to be a standard in the first place. For one team or one project, adopting one standard is far more important than adopting the right standard.

ESLint (https://eslint.org) is a very flexible linter that lets you define the rules that you want to follow. But we need something to start off with and the rule set that has appealed to me the most has been that of Airbnb. Part of the reason for its appeal has been its popularity: if more people adopt it, the more standardized it gets, so more people end up following it, becoming a virtuous cycle.

There are two parts to the Airbnb ESLint configuration: the base configuration applies to plain JavaScript and the regular configuration includes rules for JSX and React as well. In this section, we'll use ESLint for the back-end code alone, which means we'll need to install the base configuration only, along with ESLint and other dependencies that the base configuration needs:

```
$ cd api
$ npm install --save-dev eslint@5 eslint-plugin-import@2
$ npm install --save-dev eslint-config-airbnb-base@13
```

ESLint looks for a set of rules in the `.eslintrc` file, which is a JSON specification. These are not the definition of rules, instead, a specification of which rules need to be enabled or disabled. Rule sets also can be inherited, which is what we'll do using the `extends` property in the configuration. Using a `.eslintrc` file makes the rules apply to all the files in that directory. For overrides in a single file, rules can be specified within comments in that file, or even just a single line.

Rules in the configuration file are specified under the property `rules`, which is an object containing one or more rules, identified by the rule name, and the value being the error level. The error levels are `off`, `warning`, and `error`. For example, to specify that the rule `quotes` (which checks for single vs. double quotes for strings) should show a warning, this is how the rule needs to be specified:

```
...
  rules: {
    "quotes": "warning"
  }
...
```

Many rules have options, for example, the rule `quotes` has an option for whether the quote type to be enforced is single or double. When specifying these options, the value needs to be an array with the first element as the error level and the second (or more, depending on the rule) is the option. Here's how the quotes rule can take an option indicating a check for double quotes:

```
...
    "quotes": ["warning", "double"]
...
```

Let's start with a basic configuration that only inherits from the Airbnb base configuration, without any rules. Let's also be specific about where the code is going to be run using the env property. Since all the back-end code is meant only to be run on Node.js (and only on Node.js), this property will have a single entry for `node` with a value `true`. Here's how the `.eslintrc` file will look at this stage:

```
{
  "extends": "airbnb-base",
  "env": {
    "node": "true"
  }
}
```

Now, let's run ESLint on the entire `api` directory. The command line to do this is as follows:

```
$ cd api
$ npx eslint .
```

Alternatively, you can install a plugin in your editor that shows lint errors in the editor itself. The popular code editors Atom and Sublime do have plugins to handle this; follow the instructions on their respective websites to install the plugins. Then, we'll look at every type of error or warning and deal with it.

For most of the errors, we are just going to change the code to adhere to the suggested standard. But in a few cases, we will make exceptions to the Airbnb rule. This could be for the entire project or, in some cases, for a specific file or line in a file.

Let's look at each type of error and fix them. Note that I am only discussing the errors that ESLint would have found in the code we've written up to now. As we write more code, we'll fix any lint errors reported then and there, so an editor plugin to report errors while we type is highly recommended.

Stylistic Issues

JavaScript is quite flexible in syntax, so there are many ways to write the same code. The linter rules report some errors so that you use a consistent style throughout the project.

- *Indentation*: Consistent indentation is expected throughout; this needs no justification. Let's fix any violations.

- *Keyword spacing*: Spaces between a keyword (`if`, `catch`, etc.) and the opening parenthesis is recommended. Let's change the code wherever this is reported.

- *Missing semicolon*: There's a lot of debate on whether semicolons everywhere or semicolons nowhere is better. Both work, except for a few cases where the absence of semicolons causes a behavior change. If you follow the no-semicolons standard, you must remember those special cases. Let's go with the Airbnb default, which is to require a semicolon everywhere.

- *Strings must use single quotes*: JavaScript allows both single and double quotes. In order to standardize, it's better to consistently use one and only one style. Let's use the Airbnb default, single quotes.

- *Object properties on a new line*: Either all properties of an object have to be in one line, or each property in a new line. It just makes it more predictable, especially when a new property has to be inserted. There is no doubt as to whether to append the new property to one of the existing lines or in a new line.

- *Space after { and before } in objects*: This is just for readability; let's change it wherever the linter reports an error.

- *Arrow function style*: The linter recommends using either parentheses around a single argument and a function body in curly braces, or no parentheses around the argument and a return expression (i.e., not a function body). Let's make the suggested corrections.

Best Practices

These rules are related to better ways of doing things, which typically helps you avoid errors.

- *Functions must be named*: Omitting function names makes it harder to debug because the stack trace cannot identify the function. But this applies only to regular functions, not the arrow-style functions, which are expected to be short pieces of callbacks.

- *Consistent return*: Functions should always return a value or never return a value, regardless of conditions. This reminds developers to add a return value or be explicit about it, just in case they have forgotten to return a value outside a condition.

- *Variables must be defined before use*: Although JavaScript *hoists* definitions such that they are available throughout the file, it's good practice to define them before use. Otherwise, it can get confusing while reading the code top to bottom.

- *Console*: Especially in the browser, these are typically leftover debug messages, and therefore are not suitable to be shown in the client. But these are fine in a Node.js application. So, let's switch this rule off in the API code.

- *Returning in assignments*: Though it is concise, a return and an assignment together can be confusing to the reader. Let's avoid it.

Possible Errors

Consider these possible errors you might run across:

- *Redeclaring variables*: It's hard to read and understand the intent of the original coder when a variable shadows (overwrites) another variable in a higher scope. It's also impossible to access the variable in the higher scope, so it's best to give different names to variables.

- *Undeclared variables*: It's best to avoid a variable in an inner scope having the same name as one in the outer scope. It's confusing, and it hides access to the outer scope variable in case it is required to be accessed. But in the mongo script, we do have variables that are really global: db and print. Let's declare these as global variables in a comment so that ESLint knows that these are not errors:

```
...
/* global db print */
...
```

- *Prefer arrow callback*: When using anonymous functions (as when passing a callback to another function), it's better to use the arrow function style. This has the added effect of setting the variable this to the current context, which is desirable in most cases, and the syntax is also more concise. If the function is large, it's better to separate it out to a named regular function.

- *Triple-equals*: Usage of triple-equals ensures that the values are not coerced before comparison. In most cases, this is what is intended, and it avoids errors due to coerced values.

- *Assignment to function parameters*: Mutating passed-in parameters may cause the caller to be unaware of the change and therefore unexpected behavior. Let's avoid changing function parameters' values and instead make a copy of the parameter.

- *Restricted globals*: iNaN is considered a restricted global function because it coerces non-numbers to numbers. The function Number.isNaN() is recommended, but it works only on numbers, so let's do a getTime() on the date objects before checking with Number.isNaN(). Also, print() is a restricted global, but its use in the mongo script is valid, so let's switch off this rule only for the mongo script like this:

```
...
/* eslint no-restricted-globals: "off" */
...
```

- *Wrap immediately invoked function expressions (IIFE)*: An immediately invoked function expression is a single unit. Wrapping it in parentheses not only makes it clearer, but also makes it an expression rather than a declaration.

The contents of the final .eslintrc file under the API directory are shown in Listing 7-17.

Listing 7-17. api/.eslintrc: Settings for ESLint in the API Directory

```
{
  "extends": "airbnb-base",
  "env": {
```

```
    "node": "true"
  },
  rules: {
    "no-console": "off"
  }
}
```

The changes to the JavaScript files under the API directory are shown in Listings 7-18 to 7-20.

Listing 7-18. api/scripts/init.mongo.js: Fixes for ESLint Errors

```
/*
 ...
*/

/* global db print */
/* eslint no-restricted-globals: "off" */

db.issues.remove({});

const issuesDB = [
  {
    id: 1, status: 'New', owner: 'Ravan', effort: 5,
    created: new Date('2019-01-15'), due: undefined,
    id: 1,
    status: 'New',
    owner: 'Ravan',
    effort: 5,
    created: new Date('2019-01-15'),
    due: undefined,
    title: 'Error in console when clicking Add',
  },
  {
    id: 2, status: 'Assigned', owner: 'Eddie', effort: 14,
    created: new Date('2019-01-16'), due: new Date('2019-02-01'),
    id: 2,
    status: 'Assigned',
    owner: 'Eddie',
    effort: 14,
    created: new Date('2019-01-16'),
    due: new Date('2019-02-01'),
    title: 'Missing bottom border on panel',
  },
...
```

Listing 7-19. api/scripts/trymongo.js: Fixes for ESLint Errors

```
function testWithCallbacks(callback) {
  console.log('\n--- testWithCallbacks ---');
  const client = new MongoClient(url, { useNewUrlParser: true });
  client.connect(function(err, client) {
  client.connect((connErr) => {
```

```
    if (err connErr) {
      callback(errconnErr);
      return;
    }
    console.log('Connected to MongoDB URL', url);
...
    const employee = { id: 1, name: 'A. Callback', age: 23 };
    collection.insertOne(employee, function(err, result) {
    collection.insertOne(employee, (insertErr, result) => {
      if (err insertErr) {
        client.close();
        callback(err insertErr);
        return;
      }
      console.log('Result of insert:\n', result.insertedId);
      collection.find({ _id: result.insertedId})
      collection.find({ _id: result.insertedId })
        .toArray(function(err, docs) {
        .toArray((findErr, docs) => {
        if (err) {
          client.close();
          callback(err);
          return;
        }
          if (findErr) {
            client.close();
            callback(findErr);
            return;
          }
        console.log('Result of find:\n', docs);
        client.close();
        callback(err);
      });
          console.log('Result of find:\n', docs);
          client.close();
          callback();
        });
...

async function testWithAsync() {
  ...
  } catch(err) {
  } catch (err) {
  ...
}

testWithCallbacks(function(err) {
testWithCallbacks((err) => {
  ...
}
```

Listing 7-20. api/server.js: Fixes for ESLint Errors

```
let db;

~~let aboutMessage = "Issue Tracker API v1.0";~~
let aboutMessage = 'Issue Tracker API v1.0';
...

const GraphQLDate = new GraphQLScalarType({
  ...
  parseValue(value) {
    ...
    ~~return isNaN(dateValue) ? undefined : dateValue;~~
    return Number.isNaN(dateValue.getTime()) ? undefined : dateValue;
  },
  parseLiteral(ast) {
    if (ast.kind === Kind.STRING) {
      const value = new Date(ast.value);
      ~~return isNaN(value) ? undefined : value;~~
      return Number.isNaN(value.getTime()) ? undefined : value;
    }
    return undefined;
  },
});
...

~~const resolvers = {~~
  ~~...~~
~~};~~
...

function setAboutMessage(_, { message }) {
  ~~return aboutMessage = message;~~
  aboutMessage = message;
  return aboutMessage;
}
...

async function issueAdd(_, { issue }) {
  ...
    ~~errors.push('Field "title" must be at least 3 characters long.')~~
    errors.push('Field "title" must be at least 3 characters long.');
  ...
  ~~if (issue.status == 'Assigned' && !issue.owner) {~~
  if (issue.status === 'Assigned' && !issue.owner) {
  ...
  const newIssue = Object.assign({}, issue);
  ~~issue~~ newIssue.created = new Date();
  ~~issue~~ newIssue.id = await getNextSequence('issues');
```

```
  const result = await db.collection('issues').insertOne(issue newIssue);
  ...
}
...

const resolvers = {
  ...
};
...

const server = new ApolloServer({
  ...
  formatError: error => {
  formatError: (error) => {
  ...
});
...

const enableCors = (process.env.ENABLE_CORS || 'true') == 'true';
const enableCors = (process.env.ENABLE_CORS || 'true') === 'true';
...

(async function start() {
  ...
    app.listen(port, function () => {
    ...
  ...
})();
}());
```

Finally, let's add an npm script that will lint all the files in the API directory. The command line is similar to what we used before to lint the entire directory. The changes to this are shown in Listing 7-21, in package.json.

Listing 7-21. api/package.json: New Script for lint

```
...
  "scripts": {
    "start": "nodemon -e js,graphql -w . -w .env server.js",
    "lint": "eslint .",
    "test": "echo \"Error: no test specified\" && exit 1"
  },
...
```

ESLint for the Front-End

In this section, we'll add ESLint checking to the UI directory. This time we'll install not just the airbnb-base package, but the complete Airbnb configuration, which includes the React plugin.

```
$ cd ui
$ npm install --save-dev eslint@5 eslint-plugin-import@2
$ npm install --save-dev eslint-plugin-jsx-a11y@6 eslint-plugin-react@7
$ npm install --save-dev eslint-config-airbnb@17
```

Next, let's start with a .eslintrc for the server code, by extending airbnb-base. Since this is Node.js code, let's also set the environment to node and set the rule no-console to off, just as in the API configuration. The entire contents of .eslintrc are shown in Listing 7-22.

Listing 7-22. ui/.eslintrc: New ESLint Configuration for UI Server Code

```
{
  "extends": "airbnb-base",
  "env": {
    "node": true
  },
  "rules": {
    "no-console": "off"
  }
}
```

To run the linter, we can execute the command with the current directory (.) as the command line argument. But, executing on the current directory will cause ESLint to run in sub-directories as well, and that includes the compiled file under the public directory. The compiled file will have lots of lint errors, because it is not source code. So let's exclude that from the ESLint purview by using the --ignore-pattern command line option of ESLint to exclude the public directory.

```
$ npx eslint . --ignore-pattern public
```

Another way of ignoring patterns of files is to add them as lines to a text file called .eslintignore. This is useful when there are many patterns to be ignored. Since we need only one directory to be ignored, we'll use the command line option.

The uiserver.js file, at this stage in the development, will throw up errors similar to what were detected for the API server.js. file. These are stylistic issues, including missing semicolons, preference for arrow functions, and line-break style for long lines. The changes to server.js after fixing these errors are shown in Listing 7-23.

Listing 7-23. ui/uiserver.js: Fixes for ESLint Errors

```
...
const UI_API_ENDPOINT = process.env.UI_API_ENDPOINT ||
  'http://localhost:3000/graphql';
const UI_API_ENDPOINT = process.env.UI_API_ENDPOINT
  || 'http://localhost:3000/graphql';
...

app.get('/env.js', function(req, res) {
app.get('/env.js', (req, res) => {
...

app.listen(port, function () {
app.listen(port, () => {
...
```

Now, let's start with a simple configuration for the React code under the src directory. The .eslintrc file will have to extend airbnb rather than airbnb-base. In the environment, we can specify support for browser instead of Node.js. The starting .eslintrc file will look like this:

```
...
{
  "extends": "airbnb",
  "env": {
    "browser": true
  }
}
...
```

Now, we can run ESLint to check the React code. In the earlier invocation of ESLint, the React code in App.jsx was not checked because by default ESLint does not match files with the extension jsx. To include this extension, ESLint needs the complete list of extensions in a command line option --ext.

```
$ npx eslint . --ext js,jsx --ignore-pattern public
```

The errors that are thrown on this command include some issues that we have already discussed as part of the previous section. These are:

- Object properties on a new line
- Missing semicolon
- Strings must use single quotes
- Consistent return
- Spacing around curly braces in object definitions
- Space after { and before } in objects
- Triple-equals

Let's discuss the rest of the issues shown by ESLint.

Stylistic Issues

- *Implicit arrow line break*: This is a stylistic issue, to maintain consistency of line breaks. It is recommended to keep the expression returned from an arrow function on the same line as the arrow. If the expression is long and cannot fit on one line, it can be enclosed in parentheses starting on the same line. Let's make this change.

- *Infix operators must be spaced*: For readability, operators need spaces around them. Let's make the change as suggested.

Best Practices

- *'React' must be in scope*: When ESLint detects JSX, it expects that React be defined. At this stage, we are including React from the CDN. Soon, we will be using this and other modules by installing them using npm. Until then, let's disable these checks. We'll do these inline, keeping the .eslintrc contents free of such temporary workarounds. Let's add the following comments for this in the App.jsx file:

```
...
/* eslint "react/react-in-jsx-scope": "off" */
/* globals React ReactDOM */
/* eslint "react/jsx-no-undef": "off" */
...
```

- *Stateless functions*: The component `IssueFilter` currently is just a placeholder. When we do add functionality to it, it will become a stateful component. Until then, let's disable the ESLint check, but only for this component.

```
...
// eslint-disable-next-line react/prefer-stateless-function
class IssueFilter extends React.Component {
...
```

- *Prefer destructuring, especially props assignment*: Not only is the new style of assigning variables from objects more concise and readable, it also saves temporary references for those properties being created. Let's change the code as recommended.

- *One component per file*: Declaring only one component per file improves readability and reusability of components. At the moment, we have not discussed how to create multiple files for the React code. We will do that in the next chapter; until then, let's disable the check for the file.

```
...
/* eslint "react/no-multi-comp": "off" */
...
```

- *No alerts*: The original intention of this rule was to weed out debugging messages that were left unpruned. We'll be converting alert messages to nicely styled messages within the document. Until then, let's disable this check, but only in files where we are showing error messages.

- *Missing trailing comma*: Requiring a comma for the last item in a multi-line array or object is really handy when inserting new items. In addition, when looking at the difference between two versions in say, GitHub, the fact that a comma is added to the last line suggests that the line has changed, whereas in reality, it hasn't.

Possible Errors

- *Props validation*: It's good practice to check for the types of properties being passed in to a component, both to make it explicit to the user of the component, and to avoid errors in input. Although I'll discuss this briefly, I'll not be adding the props validation in React code, purely to avoid distraction in the code listings. Let's switch off this rule globally for the Issue Tracker application, but I encourage you to keep this enabled in your own application.

```
...
  "rules": {
    "react/prop-types": "off",
  }
...
```

- *Button type:* Although the default type of a button is submit, it is better to ensure that it is explicitly stated, just in case this is not the behavior that is intended, and the developer has missed adding a type. Let's follow the recommendation and add submit to the type of the button.

- *Function parameter reassignment:* Assigning to a function parameter can make the original parameter inaccessible and lead to confusing behavior. Let's use a new variable rather than reuse the function parameter.

After making these changes to the .eslintrc file, the final contents of this file are shown in Listing 7-24.

Listing 7-24. ui/src/.eslintrc: New ESLint Configuration for UI Code

```
{
  "extends": "airbnb",
  "env": {
    "browser": true
  },
  rules: {
    "react/prop-types": "off"
  }
}
```

Listing 7-25 is a consolidation of all changes to uiserver.js for addressing ESLint errors.

Listing 7-25. ui/src/App.jsx: Fixes for ESLint Errors

```
...
/* eslint "react/react-in-jsx-scope": "off" */
/* globals React ReactDOM */
/* eslint "react/jsx-no-undef": "off" */
/* eslint "no-alert": "off" */
...

// eslint-disable-next-line react/prefer-stateless-function
class IssueFilter extends React.Component {
...

function IssueRow(props{ issue }) {
  const issue = props.issue;
...

function IssueTable(props{ issue }) {
  const issueRows = props.issues.map(issue =>
  const issueRows = issues.map(issue => (
    <IssueRow key={issue.id} issue={issue} />
  ));
...

    const issue = {
      owner: form.owner.value, title: form.title.value,
      title: form.title.value,
      due: new Date(new Date().getTime() + 1000*60*60*24*10),
```

```
      due: new Date(new Date().getTime() + 1000 * 60 * 60 * 24 * 10),
    }
    this.props.createIssue(issue);
    const { createIssue } = this.props;
    createIssue(issue);
    form.owner.value = ""; form.title.value = "";
    form.owner.value = ''; form.title.value = '';
...


        <button type="submit">Add</button>
...

async function graphQLFetch(query, variables = {}) {
...

      headers: { 'Content-Type': 'application/json'},
      headers: { 'Content-Type': 'application/json' },
      body: JSON.stringify({ query, variables })
      body: JSON.stringify({ query, variables }),
...


      if (error.extensions.code == 'BAD_USER_INPUT') {
      if (error.extensions.code === 'BAD_USER_INPUT') {
...

  } catch (e) {
    alert(`Error in sending data to server: ${e.message}`);
    return null;
  }
}

class IssueList extends React.Component {
  ...
  render() {
    const { issues } = this.state;
    return (
      ...
        <IssueTable issues={this.state.issues} />
      ...
    )
...
```

Finally, for convenience, let's add an script to package.json in the UI directory to perform lint on all the relevant files. The command line is the same as we used before to check the entire directory. This is shown in Listing 7-26.

Listing 7-26. ui/package.json: Command for Running ESLint on the UI Directory

```
...
  "scripts": {
    "start": "nodemon -w uiserver.js -w .env uiserver.js",
    "lint": "eslint . --ext js,jsx --ignore-pattern public",
    ...
  },
...
```

Now, the command `npm run lint` will check the current set, and any other files that will be added under the UI directory. After these code changes, the command should return no errors or warnings.

React PropTypes

In strongly typed languages such as Java, the type of parameters is always predetermined and specified as part of the function declaration. This ensures that the caller knows the list and the types of parameters and ensures that passed-in parameters are validated against this specification.

Similarly, the properties being passed from one component to another can also be validated against a specification. This specification is supplied in the form of a static object called `propTypes` in the class, with the name of the property as the key and the validator as the value. The validator is one of the many constants exported by `PropTypes`, for example, `PropTypes.string`. When the property is a required one, `.isRequired` can be added after the data type. The object `PropTypes` is available as a module called prop-types, which can be included in `index.html` from the CDN as we did for React itself. This change is shown in Listing 7-27.

Listing 7-27. ui/public/index.html: Changes to Include PropTypes Library

```
...
  <script src="https://unpkg.com/react-dom@16/umd/react-dom.development.js"></script>
  <script src="https://unpkg.com/prop-types@15/prop-types.js"></script>
...
```

The `IssueTable` and `IssueRow` components need an object and an array of objects as properties, respectively. Although `PropTypes` supports data types such as arrays and objects, ESLint considers these to be too vague. Instead, the actual *shape* of the object has to be described, which means each field of the object and its data type has to be specified to avoid the ESLint warning.

Let's add a simpler check for ensuring that `IssueAdd` is passed a `createIssue` function. We'll need to define an `IssueAdd.propTypes` object, with `createIssue` as a key and `PropTypes.func.isRequired` as its type. Further, since `PropTypes` is a global object (due to inclusion as a script from the CDN), it has to be declared as a global to avoid ESLint errors. These changes to `App.jsx` are shown in Listing 7-28.

Listing 7-28. ui/src/App.jsx: Adding PropType Validation for IssueAdd Component

```
...
/* globals React ReactDOM PropTypes */
...
class IssueAdd extends React.Component {
  ...
}
```

```
IssueAdd.propTypes = {
  createIssue: PropTypes.func.isRequired,
};
```

At runtime, property validation is checked only in development mode, and a warning is shown in the console when any validation fails. If you remove the passing of the createIssue property when the IssueAdd component is being constructed, you'll find the following in the Developer Console as an error:

```
Warning: Failed prop type: The prop `createIssue` is marked as required in `IssueAdd`, but
its value is `undefined`.
    in IssueAdd (created by IssueList)
    in IssueList
```

Though it is a great idea to add PropTypes-based validation for all components, for the purpose of this book, I'll be skipping this. The only reason is that it makes the code more verbose and could distract readers from the main focus of changes.

Summary

Although we did not add any features to the application in this chapter, we made a big architectural change by separating the UI and the API servers. We discussed implications of CORS and coded an option for dealing with it using a proxy.

Then, you saw how to make the application configurable for different deployment environments like staging and production. We also sanitized the code by adding checks for adhering to coding standards, best practices, and validations.

In the next chapter, we will continue to improve developer productivity by modularizing the code (i.e., splitting single large files into smaller, reusable pieces) and adding support for debugging and other tools useful during the development process.

Answers to Exercises

Exercise: UI Server

1. You should see a message in the browser like Cannot GET /. This is a message returned by the Express server since there is no route present for /. By itself, it's not a problem since the only consumer of the API is the web UI, and within our control. If, on the other hand, the API were exposed to others like GitHub's API, it would indeed be better to return a helpful message indicating where the real API endpoints are.

    Another option is to host the API on the root (/) rather than on /graphql. But having /graphql as the endpoint name makes it explicit that it's a GraphQL API.

Exercise: Multiple Environments

1. The contents of env.js will show a JavaScript assignment of window.ENV to an object with the UI_API_ENDPOINT property. Restarting the UI server after changes to the environment will cause the contents to reflect the new value.

CHAPTER 8

▓ ▓ ▓

Modularization and Webpack

We started to get organized in the previous chapter by changing the architecture and adding checks for coding standards and best practices. In this chapter, we'll take this a little further by splitting the code into multiple files and adding tools to ease the process of development. We'll use Webpack to help us split front-end code into component-based files, inject code into the browser incrementally, and refresh the browser automatically on front-end code changes.

Some of you may find this chapter not worth your time because it is not making any progress on the real features of the application, and/or because it discusses nothing about the technologies that make up the stack. That's a perfectly valid thought if you are not too concerned about all these, and instead rely on someone else to give you a template of sorts that predefines the directory structure as well as has configuration for the build tools such as Webpack. This can let you focus on the MERN stack alone, without having to deal with all the tooling. In that case, you have the following options:

- Download the code from the book's GitHub repository (`https://github.com/vasansr/pro-mern-stack-2`) as of the end of this chapter and use that as your starting point for your project.

- Use the starter-kit `create-react-app` (`https://github.com/facebook/create-react-app`) to start your new React app and add code for your application. But note that `create-react-app` deals only with the React part of the MERN stack; you will have to deal with the APIs and MongoDB yourself.

- Use `mern.io` (`http://mern.io`) to create the entire application's directory structure, which includes the entire MERN stack.

But if you are an architect or just setting up the project for your team, it is important to understand how tools help developer productivity and how you can have finer control over the whole build and deployment process as well. In which case, I encourage you *not* to skip this chapter, even if you use one of these scaffolding tools, so that you learn about what exactly happens under the hood.

Back-End Modules

You saw all this while in `api/server.js` how to include modules in a Node.js file. After installing the module, we used the built-in function `require()` to include it. There are various standards for modularization in JavaScript, of which Node.js has implemented a slight variation of the CommonJS standard. In this system, there are essentially two key elements to interact with the module system: `require` and `exports`.

The require() element is a function that can be used to import symbols from another module. The parameter passed to require() is the ID of the module. In Node's implementation, the ID is the name of the module. For packages installed using npm, this is the same as the name of the package and the same as the sub-directory inside the node_modules directory where the package's files are installed. For modules within the same application, the ID is the path of the file that needs to be imported.

For example, to import symbols from a file called other.js in the same directory as api/server.js, the ID that needs to be passed to require() is the path of this file, that is, './other.js', like this:

```
const other = require('./other.js');
```

Now, whatever is *exported* by other.js will be available in the other variable. This is controlled by the other element we talked about: exports. The main symbol that a file or module exports must be set in a global variable called module.exports within that file, and that is the one that will be returned by the function call to require(). If there are multiple symbols, they can be all set as properties in an object, and we can access those by dereferencing the object or by using the destructuring assignment.

To start, let's separate the function GraphQLDate() from the main server.js file and create a new file called graphql_date.js for this. Apart from the entire function itself, we also need the following in the new file:

1. require() statements to import GraphQLScalarType and Kind from the other packages.

2. The variable module.exports to be set to the function, so that it can be used after importing the file.

The contents of this file are shown in Listing 8-1, with changes from the original in api/server.js highlighted in bold.

Listing 8-1. api/graphql_date.js: Function GraphQLDate() in a New File

```
const { GraphQLScalarType } = require('graphql');
const { Kind } = require('graphql/language');

const GraphQLDate = new GraphQLScalarType({
  ...
});

module.exports = GraphQLDate;
```

Now, in the file api/server.js, we can import the symbol GraphQLDate like this:

```
...
const GraphQLDate = require('graphql_date.js');
...
```

As you can see, whatever was assigned to module.exports is the value that a call to require() returns. Now, this variable, GraphQLDate can be seamlessly used in the resolver, as before. But we won't be making this change in server.js just yet, because we'll be making more changes to this file.

The next set of functions that we can separate out are the functions relating to the about message. Though we used an anonymous function for the resolver about, let's now create a named function so that it can be exported from a different file. Let's create a new file that exports the two functions getMessage() and setMessage() called about.js in the API directory. The contents of this file are quite straightforward, as listed in Listing 8-2. But instead of exporting just one function as we did in graphql_date.js, let's import both the setMessage and getMessage as two properties in an object.

Listing 8-2. api/about.js: Separated About Message Functionality to New File

```
let aboutMessage = 'Issue Tracker API v1.0';

function setMessage(_, { message }) {
  ...
}

function getMessage() {
  return aboutMessage;
}

module.exports = { getMessage, setMessage };
```

Now, we can import the about object from this file and dereference about.getMessage and about.setMessage when we want to use them in the resolver, like this:

```
...
const about = require('about.js');
...
const resolvers = {
  Query: {
    about: about.getMessage,
    ...
  },
  Mutation: {
    setAboutMessage: about.setMessage,
    ...
  },
  ...
};
```

This change could be in server.js, but we'll be separating all this into one file that deals with Apollo Server, the schema, and the resolvers. Let's create that file now and call it api/api_handler.js. Let's move the construction of the resolvers object and the creation of the Apollo server into this file. As for the actual resolver implementations, we'll import them from three other files—graphql_date.js, about.js, and issue.js.

As for the export from this file, let's export a function that will do what applyMiddleware() did as part of server.js. We can call this function installHandler() and just call applyMiddleware() within this function.

The full contents of this new file are shown in Listing 8-3, with changes compared to the original code in server.js highlighted.

Listing 8-3. api/api_handler.js: New File to Separate the Apollo Server Construction

```
const fs = require('fs');
require('dotenv').config();
const { ApolloServer, UserInputError } = require('apollo-server-express');

const GraphQLDate = require('./graphql_date.js');
const about = require('./about.js');
const issue = require('./issue.js');

const resolvers = {
  Query: {
    about: about.getMessage,
    issueList: issue.list,
  },
  Mutation: {
    setAboutMessage: about.setMessage,
    issueAdd: issue.add,
  },
  GraphQLDate,
};

const server = new ApolloServer({
  ...
});

function installHandler(app) {
  const enableCors = (process.env.ENABLE_CORS || 'true') === 'true';
  console.log('CORS setting:', enableCors);
  server.applyMiddleware({ app, path: '/graphql', cors: enableCors });
}

module.exports = { installHandler };
```

We have not created issue.js yet, which is needed for importing the issue-related resolvers. But before that, let's separate the database connection creation and a function to get the connection handler into a new file. The issue.js file will need this DB connection, etc.

Let's call the file with all database-related code db.js and place it in the API directory. Let's move the functions connectToDb() and getNextSequence() into this file, as also the global variable db, which stores the result of the connection. Let's export the two functions as they are. As for the global connection variable, let's expose it via a getter function called getDb(). The global variable url can also now be moved into the function connectDb() itself.

The contents of this file are shown in Listing 8-4, with changes from the original in server.js highlighted in bold.

Listing 8-4. api/db.js: Database Related Functions Separated Out

```
require('dotenv').config();
const { MongoClient } = require('mongodb');

let db;
```

```
async function connectToDb() {
  const url = process.env.DB_URL || 'mongodb://localhost/issuetracker';
  ...
}

async function getNextSequence(name) {
  ...
}

function getDb() {
  return db;
}

module.exports = { connectToDb, getNextSequence, getDb };
```

Now, we are ready to separate the functions related to the Issue object. Let's create a file called issue.js under the API directory and move the issue related to this file. In addition, we'll have to import the functions getDb() and getNextSequence() from db.js. to use them. Then, instead of using the global variable db directly, we'll have to use the return value of getDb(). As for exports, we can export the functions issueList and issueAdd, but now that they are within the module, their names can be simplified to just list and add. The contents of this new file are shown in Listing 8-5.

Listing 8-5. api/issue.js: Separated Issue Functions

```
const { UserInputError } = require('apollo-server-express');
const { getDb, getNextSequence } = require('./db.js');

async function issueListlist() {
  const db = getDb();
  const issues = await db.collection('issues').find({}).toArray();
  return issues;
}

function issueValidatevalidate(issue) {
  const errors = [];
  ...

}

async function issueAddadd(_, { issue }) {
  const db = getDb();
  validate(issue);
  ...
  return savedIssue;
}

module.exports = { list, add };
```

Finally, we can make changes to the file api/server.js to use all this. After all the code has been moved out to individual files, what's left is only the instantiation of the application, applying the Apollo Server middleware and then starting the server. The contents of this entire file are listed in Listing 8-6. The removed code is not explicitly shown. New code is highlighted in bold.

Listing 8-6. api/server.js: Changes After Moving Out Code To Other Files

```
require('dotenv').config();
const express = require('express');
const { connectToDb } = require('./db.js');
const { installHandler } = require('./api_handler.js');

const app = express();

installHandler(app);

const port = process.env.API_SERVER_PORT || 3000;

(async function () {
  try {
    await connectToDb();
    app.listen(port, function () {
      console.log(`API server started on port ${port}`);
    });
  } catch (err) {
    console.log('ERROR:', err);
  }
}());
```

Now, the application is ready to be tested. You can do that via the Playground as well as using the Issue Tracker application UI to ensure that things are working as they were before the modularization of the API server code.

Front-End Modules and Webpack

In this section, we'll deal with the front-end, or the UI code, which is all in one big file, called App.jsx. Traditionally, the approach to using split client-side JavaScript code was to use multiple files and include them all (or whichever are required) using <script> tags in the main HTML file or index.html. This is less than ideal because the dependency management is done by the developer, by maintaining a certain order of files in the HTML file. Further, when the number of files becomes large, this becomes unmanageable.

Tools such as Webpack and Browserify provide alternatives. Using these tools, dependencies can be defined using statements equivalent to require() that we used in Node.js. The tools then automatically determines not just the application's own dependent modules, but also third-party library dependencies. Then, they put together these individual files into one or just a few bundles of pure JavaScript that has all the required code that can be included in the HTML file.

The only downside is that this requires a build step. But then, the application already has a build step to transform JSX and ES2015 into plain JavaScript. It's not much of a change to let the build step also create a bundle based on multiple files. Both Webpack and Browserify are good tools and can be used to achieve the goals. But I chose Webpack, because it is simpler to get all that we want done, which includes separate bundles for third-party libraries and our own modules. It has a single pipeline to transform, bundle, and watch for changes and generate new bundles as fast as possible.

If you choose Browserify instead, you will need other task runners such as gulp or grunt to automate watching and adding multiple transforms. This is because Browserify does only one thing: bundle. In order to combine bundle and transform (using Babel) and watch for file changes, you need something that puts all of them together, and gulp is one such utility. In comparison, Webpack (with a little help from loaders, which we'll explore soon) can not only bundle, but can also do many more things such as transforming and watching for changes to files. You don't need additional task runners to use Webpack.

Note that Webpack can also handle other static assets such as CSS files. It can even split the bundles such that they can be loaded asynchronously. We will not be exercising those aspects of Webpack; instead, we'll focus on the goal of being able to modularize the client-side code, which is mainly JavaScript at this point in time.

To get used to what Webpack really does, let's use Webpack from the command line just like we did for the JSX transform using the Babel command linel. Let's first install Webpack, which comes as a package and a command line interface to run it.

```
$ cd ui
$ npm install --save-dev webpack@4 webpack-cli@3
```

We are using the option --save-dev because the UI server in production has no need for Webpack. It is only during the build process that we need Webpack, and all the other tools we will be installing in the rest of the chapter. To ensure we can run Webpack using the command line, let's check the version that was installed:

```
$ npx webpack --version
```

This should print out the version like 4.23.1. Now, let's "pack" the App.js file and create a bundle called app.bundle.js. This can be done simply by running Webpack on the App.js file and specifying an output option, which is app.bundle.js, both under the public directory.

```
$ npx webpack public/App.js --output public/app.bundle.js
```

This should result in output like the following:

```
Hash: c5a639b898efcc81d3f8
Version: webpack 4.23.1
Time: 473ms
Built at: 10/25/2018 9:52:25 PM
        Asset      Size  Chunks             Chunk Names
app.bundle.js  6.65 KiB       0  [emitted]  main
Entrypoint main = app.bundle.js
[0] ./public/App.js 10.9 KiB {0} [built]

WARNING in configuration
The 'mode' option has not been set, webpack will fallback to 'production' for this value.
Set 'mode' option to 'development' or 'production' to enable defaults for each environment.

You can also set it to 'none' to disable any default behavior. Learn more: https://
webpack.js.org/concepts/mode/
```

To get rid of the warning message, let's supply the mode as development in the command line:

```
$ npx webpack public/App.js --output public/app.bundle.js --mode development
```

The differences between the two modes are the various things Webpack does automatically, such as removing the names of modules, minifying, etc. It's good to have all these optimizations when building a bundle for deploying in production, but these may hamper debugging and efficient development process.

The resulting file app.bundle.js is hardly interesting and is not very different from App.js itself. Note also that we didn't run it against the React file App.jsx, because Webpack cannot handle JSX natively. All it did in this case was minify App.js. We did it just to make sure we've installed Webpack correctly and are able to run it and create output. To actually let Webpack figure out dependencies and put together multiple files, let's split the single file App.jsx into two, by taking out the function graphQLFetch and placing it in a separate file.

We could, just as in the back-end code, use the require way of importing other files. But you will notice that most front-end code examples on the Internet use the ES2015-style modules using the import keyword. This is a newer and more readable way of importing. Even Node.js has support for the import statement, but as of version 10 of Node.js, it is experimental. If not, it could have been used for the back-end code as well. Using import makes it mandatory to use Webpack. So, let's use the ES2015-style import for the front-end code only.

To import another file, the import keyword is used, followed by the element or variable being imported (which would have been the variable assigned to the result of require()), followed by the keyword from, and then the identifier of the file or module. For example, to import graphQLFetch from the file graphQLfetch.js, this is what needs to be done:

```
...
import graphQLFetch from './graphQLFetch.js';
...
```

Using the new ES2015 style to export a function is as simple as prefixing the keyword export before the definition of whatever is being exported. Further, the keyword default can be added after export if a single function is being exported, and it can be the result of the import statement directly (or a top-level export). So, let's create a new file ui/src/graphQLFetch.js with the contents of the same function copied over from App.jsx. We'll also need the implementation of jsonDateReviver along with the function The contents of this file are shown in Listing 8-7, with export default added to the definition of the function.

Listing 8-7. ui/src/graphQLFetch.js: New File with Exported Function graphQLFetch

```
const dateRegex = new RegExp('^\\d\\d\\d\\d-\\d\\d-\\d\\d');

function jsonDateReviver(key, value) {
  if (dateRegex.test(value)) return new Date(value);
  return value;
}

export default async function graphQLFetch(query, variables = {}) {
  ...
}
```

Now, let's remove the same set of lines from ui/src/App.jsx and replace them with an import statement. This change is shown in Listing 8-8.

Listing 8-8. ui/src/App.jsx: Replace graphQLFetch with an Import

```
...
/* eslint "react/no-multi-comp": "off" */
/* eslint "no-alert": "off" */

import graphQLFetch from './graphQLFetch.js';

const dateRegex = new RegExp('^\\d\\d\\d\\d-\\d\\d-\\d\\d');

function jsonDateReviver(key, value) {
  if (dateRegex.test(value)) return new Date(value);
  return value;
}

class IssueFilter extends React.Component {
  ...
}

async function graphQLFetch(query, variables = {}) {
  ...
}
...
```

At this point, ESLint will show an error to the effect that extensions (`.js`) in an `import` statement are unexpected, because this extension can be automatically detected. But it turns out that the `import` statement is good only to detect `.js` file extensions, and we'll soon be importing `.jsx` files as well. Further, in the back-end code we used the extensions in `require()` statements. Let's make an exception to this ESLint rule and always include extensions in `import` statements, except, of course, for packages installed via npm. This change to the `.eslintrc` file in the `ui/src` directory is shown in Listing 8-9.

Listing 8-9. ui/src/.eslintrc: Exception for Including Extensions in Application Modules

```
...
  "rules": {
    "import/extensions": [ "error", "always", { "ignorePackages": true } ],
    "react/prop-types": "off"
  }
...
```

If you are running `npm run watch`, you'll find that both `App.js` and `graphQLFetch.js` have been created after the Babel transformation in the `public` directory. If not, you can run `npm run compile` in the `ui` directory. Now, let's run the Webpack command again and see what happens.

```
$ npx webpack public/App.js --output public/app.bundle.js --mode development
```

This should result in output like this:

```
Hash: 4207ff5d100f44fbf80e
Version: webpack 4.23.1
Time: 112ms
```

```
Built at: 10/25/2018 10:21:06 PM
        Asset    Size  Chunks                Chunk Names
app.bundle.js  16.5 KiB    main  [emitted]  main
Entrypoint main = app.bundle.js
[./public/App.js] 9.07 KiB {main} [built]
[./public/graphQLFetch.js] 2.8 KiB {main} [built]
```

As you can see in the output, the packing process has included both App.js and graphQLFetch.js. Webpack has automatically figured out that App.js depends on graphQLFetch.js due to the import statement and has included it in the bundle. Now, we'll need to replace App.js in index.html with app.bundle.js because the new bundle is the one that contains all the required code. This change is shown in Listing 8-10.

Listing 8-10. ui/public/index.html: Replace App.js with app.bundle.js

```
...
  <script src="/env.js"></script>
  <script src="/App.js/app.bundle.js"></script>
</body>
...
```

If you test the application at this point, you should find it working just as before. For good measure, you could also check in the Network tab of the Developer Console in the browser that it is indeed app.bundle.js that is being fetched from the server.

So, now that you know how to use multiple files in the front-end code, we could possibly create many more files like graphQLFetch.js for convenience and modularization. But the process was not simple, as we had to manually Babel transform the files first, and then put them together in a bundle using Webpack. And any manual step can be error prone: one can easily forget the transform and end up bundling an older version of the transformed file.

Transform and Bundle

The good news is that Webpack is capable of combining these two steps, obviating the need for intermediate files. But it can't do that on its own; it needs some helpers called *loaders*. All transforms and file types other than pure JavaScript require loaders in Webpack. These are separate packages. To be able to run Babel transforms, we'll need the Babel loader.

Let's install this now.

```
$ cd ui
$ npm install --save-dev babel-loader@8
```

It's a bit cumbersome to use this loader in the command line of Webpack. To make the configuration and options easier, Webpack can be supplied configuration files instead. The default file that it looks for is called webpack.config.js. Webpack loads this file as a module using Node.js require(), so we can treat this file as a regular JavaScript, which includes a module.exports variable that exports the properties that specify the transformation and bundling process. Let's start building this file under the ui directory, with one property: mode. Let's default it to development as we did in the command line previously.

```
...
module.exports = {
  mode: development,
}
...
```

The entry property specifies the file that is the starting point from which all dependencies can be determined. In the Issue Tracker application, this file is App.jsx under the src directory. Let's add this next.

```
...
  entry: './src/App.jsx',
...
```

The output property needs to be an object with the filename and path as two properties. The path has to be an absolute path. The recommended way to supply an absolute path is by constructing it using the path module and the path.resolve function.

```
...
const path = require('path');

module.exports = {
  ...
  output: {
    filename: 'app.bundle.js',
    path: path.resolve(__dirname, 'public'),
  },
...
```

Loaders are specified under the property module, which contains a series of rules as an array. Each rule at the minimum has a test, which is a regex to match files and a use, which specifies the loader to use on finding a match. We'll use a regex that matches both .jsx and .js files and the Babel loader to run transforms when a file matches this regex, like this:

```
...
    {
      test: /\.jsx?$/,
      use: 'babel-loader',
    },
...
```

The complete file, ui/webpack.config.js, is shown in Listing 8-11.

Listing 8-11. ui/webpack.config.js: Webpack Configuration

```
const path = require('path');

module.exports = {
  mode: 'development',
  entry: './src/App.jsx',
  output: {
    filename: 'app.bundle.js',
    path: path.resolve(__dirname, 'public'),
  },
```

```
  module: {
    rules: [
      {
        test: /\.jsx?$/,
        use: 'babel-loader',
      },
    ],
  },
};
```

Note that we did not have to supply any further options to the Babel loader, since all Webpack did was use the existing Babel transformer. And this used the existing configuration from .babelrc in the src directory.

At this point, you can quickly run the Webpack command line without any parameters and see that the file app.bundle.js is created, without creating any intermediate files. You may have to delete the intermediate files App.js and graphQLFetch.js in the public directory to ensure that this is happening. The command line for doing this is as follows:

$ npx webpack

This may take a bit of time. Also, just like the --watch option for Babel, Webpack too comes with a --watch option, which incrementally builds the bundle, transforming only the changed files. Let's try this:

$ npx webpack --watch

This command will not exit. Now, if you change one of the files, say graphQLFetch.js, you will see the following output on the console:

```
Hash: 3fc38bc043fafe268e06
Version: webpack 4.23.1
Time: 53ms
Built at: 10/25/2018 11:09:49 PM
        Asset     Size  Chunks          Chunk Names
app.bundle.js  16.6 KiB    main  [emitted]  main
Entrypoint main = app.bundle.js
[./src/graphQLFetch.js] 2.71 KiB {main} [built]
    + 1 hidden module
```

Note the last line in the output: +1 hidden module. What this really means is that App.jsx was not transformed when only graphQLFetch.js was changed. This is a good time to change the npm scripts for compile and watch to use the Webpack command instead of the Babel command.

Webpack has two modes, production and development, which change the kind of optimizations that are added during transformation. Let's assume that during development we'll always use the watch script and to build a bundle for deployment, we'll use the mode as production. The command line parameters override what is specified in the configuration file, so we can set the mode accordingly in the npm scripts.

The changes needed to do this are shown in Listing 8-12.

Listing 8-12. ui/package.json: Changes to npm Scripts to Use Webpack Instead of Babel

```
...
  "scripts": {
    "start": "nodemon -w uiserver.js -w .env uiserver.js",
    "compile": "babel src --out-dir public",
    "compile": "webpack --mode production",
    "watch": "babel src --out-dir public --watch --verbose"
    "watch": "webpack --watch"
  },
...
```

Now, we are ready to split the App.jsx file into many files. It is recommended that each React component be placed in its own file, especially if the component is a stateful one. Stateless components can be combined with other components when convenient and when they belong together.

So, let's separate the component IssueList from App.jsx. Then, let's also separate the first level of components in the hierarchy—IssueFilter, IssueTable, and IssueAdd—into their own files. In each of these, we will export the main component. App.jsx will import IssueList.jsx, which in turn will import the other three components. IssueList.jsx will also need to import graphQLFetch.js since it makes the Ajax calls.

Let's also move or copy the ESLint exceptions to the appropriate new files. All files will have an exception for declaring React as global; IssueFilter will also have the exception for stateless components.

The new file IssueList.jsx is described in Listing 8-13.

Listing 8-13. ui/src/IssueList.jsx: New File for the IssueList Component

```
/* globals React */
/* eslint "react/jsx-no-undef": "off" */

import IssueFilter from './IssueFilter.jsx';
import IssueTable from './IssueTable.jsx';
import IssueAdd from './IssueAdd.jsx';
import graphQLFetch from './graphQLFetch.js';

export default class IssueList extends React.Component {
  ...
}
```

The new IssueTable.jsx file is shown in Listing 8-14. Note that this contains two stateless components, of which only IssueTable is exported.

Listing 8-14. ui/src/IssueTable.jsx: New File for the IssueTable Component

```
/* globals React */

function IssueRow({ issue }) {
  ...
}

export default function IssueTable({ issues }) {
  ...
}
```

The new `IssueAdd.jsx` file is shown in Listing 8-15.

Listing 8-15. ui/src/IssueAdd.jsx: New File for the IssueAdd Component

```
/* globals React PropTypes */

export default class IssueAdd extends React.Component {
  ...
}
```

The new `IssueFilter.jsx` file is shown in Listing 8-16.

Listing 8-16. ui/src/IssueFilter.jsx: New File for the IssueFilter Component

```
/* globals React */
/* eslint "react/prefer-stateless-function": "off" */

export default class IssueFilter extends React.Component {
  ...
}
```

Finally, the main class `App.jsx` will have very little code, just an instantiation of the `IssueList` component and mounting it in the contents `<div>`, and the necessary comment lines to declare React and ReactDOM as globals for ESLint. This file is shown in its entirety (deleted lines are not shown for the sake of brevity) in Listing 8-17.

Listing 8-17. ui/src/App.jsx: Main File with Most Code Moved Out

```
/* globals React ReactDOM  */

import IssueList from './IssueList.jsx';

const element = <IssueList />;

ReactDOM.render(element, document.getElementById('contents'));
```

If you run `npm run watch` from the `ui` directory, you will find that all the files are being transformed and bundled into `app.bundle.js`. If you now test the application, it should work just as before.

EXERCISE: TRANSFORM AND BUNDLE

1. Save any JSX file with only a spacing change, while running `npm run watch`. Does Webpack rebuild the bundle? Why not?

2. Was it necessary to separate the mounting of the component (in `App.jsx`) and the component itself (`IssueList`) into different files? Hint: Think about what other pages we'll need in the future.

3. What would happen if the `default` keyword was not used while exporting a class, say `IssueList`? Hint: Look up Mozilla Developer Network (MDN) documentation on the JavaScript `export` statement at `https://developer.mozilla.org/en-US/docs/web/javascript/reference/statements/export#Using_the_default_export`.

Answers are available at the end of the chapter.

Libraries Bundle

Until now, to keep things simple, we included third-party libraries as JavaScript directly from a CDN. Although this works great most times, we have to rely on the CDN services to be up and running to support our application. Further, there are many libraries that need to be included, and these too have dependencies among them.

In this section, we'll use Webpack to create a bundle that includes these libraries. If you remember, I discussed that npm is used not only for server-side libraries, but also client-side ones. What's more, Webpack understands this and can deal with client-side libraries installed via npm.

Let's first use npm to install the client-side libraries that we have used until now. This is the same list as the list of `<script>`s in `index.html`.

```
$ cd ui
$ npm install react@16 react-dom@16
$ npm install prop-types@15
$ npm install whatwg-fetch@3
$ npm install babel-polyfill@6
```

Next, to use these installed libraries, let's import them in all the client-side files where they are needed, just like we imported the application's files after splitting `App.jsx`. All the files with React components will need to import React. App.jsx will need to import ReactDOM in addition. The polyfills—babel-polyfill and whatwg-fetch—can be imported anywhere, since these will be installed in the global namespace. Let's do this in `App.jsx`, the entry point. This, and the other components' changes, are shown in Listings 8-18 to 8-22.

Listing 8-18. App.jsx: Changes for Importing Third-Party Libraries

```
/* globals React ReactDOM */
import 'babel-polyfill';
import 'whatwg-fetch';
import React from 'react';
import ReactDOM from 'react-dom';

import IssueList from './IssueList.jsx';
...
```

Listing 8-19. IssueList.jsx: Changes for Importing Third-Party Libraries

```
-/* globals React */
-/* eslint "react/jsx-no-undef": "off" */
import React from 'react';

import IssueFilter from './IssueFilter.jsx';
...
```

Listing 8-20. IssueFilter.jsx: Changes for Importing Third-Party Libraries

```
/* globals React */
/* eslint "react/prefer-stateless-function": "off" */

import React from 'react';

export default class IssueFilter extends React.Component {
...
```

Listing 8-21. IssueTable.jsx: Changes for Importing Third-Party Libraries

```
-/* globals React */
import React from 'react';

function IssueRow(props) {
...
```

Listing 8-22. IssueAdd.jsx: Changes for Importing Third-Party Libraries

```
/* globals React PropTypes */
import React from 'react';
import PropTypes from 'prop-types';

export default class IssueAdd extends React.Component {
...
```

If you have npm run watch already running, you will notice in its output that the number of hidden modules has shot up from a few to a few hundred and that the size of app.bundle.js has increased from a few KBs to more than 1MB. The new output of the Webpack bundling will now look like this:

```
Hash: 2c6bf561fa9aba4dd3b1
Version: webpack 4.23.1
Time: 2184ms
Built at: 10/26/2018 11:51:01 AM
        Asset      Size  Chunks            Chunk Names
app.bundle.js  1.16 MiB    main  [emitted]  main
Entrypoint main = app.bundle.js
[./node_modules/webpack/buildin/global.js] (webpack)/buildin/global.js 492 bytes {main}
[built]
    + 344 hidden modules
```

The fact that the bundle includes all of the libraries is a minor problem. The libraries will not change often, but the application code will, especially during the development and testing. Even when the application code undergoes a small change, the entire bundle is rebuilt, and therefore, a client will have to fetch the (now big) bundle from the server. We're not taking advantage of the fact that the browser can cache scripts when they are not changed. This not only affects the development process, but even in production, users will not have the optimum experience.

A better alternative is to have two bundles, one for the application code and another for all the libraries. It turns out we can easily do this in Webpack using an optimization called splitChunks. To use this optimization and automatically name the different bundles it creates, we need to specify a variable in the filename. Let's use a named entry point and the name of the bundle as a variable in the filename in the Webpack configuration for the UI like this:

```
...
  entry: './src/App.jsx',
  entry: { app: './src/App.jsx' },
  output: {
    filename: 'app.bundle.js',
    filename: '[name].bundle.js',
    path: path.resolve(__dirname, 'public'),
  },
...
```

Next, let's save some time by excluding libraries from transformation: they will already be transformed in the distributions that are provided. To do this, we need to exclude all files under node_modules in the Babel loader.

```
...
        test: /\.jsx?$/,
        exclude: /node_modules/,
        use: 'babel-loader',
...
```

Finally, let's enable the optimization splitChunks. This plugin does what we want out of the box, that is, it separates everything under node_modules into a different bundle. All we need to do is to say that we need all as the value to the property chunks. Also, for a convenient name of the bundle, let's give a name in the configuration, like this:

```
...
    splitChunks: {
      name: 'vendor',
      chunks: 'all',
    },
...
```

The complete set of changes to webpack.config.js under the ui directory is shown in Listing 8-23.

Listing 8-23. ui/webpack.config.js: Changes for Separate Vendor Bundle

```
module.exports = {
  mode: 'development',
  entry: './src/App.jsx',
  entry: { app: './src/App.jsx' },
```

```
  output: {
    filename:  'app.bundle.js',
    filename: '[name].bundle.js',
    path: path.resolve(__dirname, 'public'),
  },
  module: {
    rules: [
      {
        test: /\.jsx?$/,
        exclude: /node_modules/,
        use: 'babel-loader',
      },
    ],
  },
  optimization: {
    splitChunks: {
      name: 'vendor',
      chunks: 'all',
    },
  },
};
```

Now, if you restart npm run watch, it should spew out two bundles—app.bundle.js and vendor. bundle.js—as can be seen in the sample output of this command:

```
Hash: 0d92c8636ffc24747d70
Version: webpack 4.23.1
Time: 1664ms
Built at: 10/26/2018 2:32:34 PM
           Asset      Size  Chunks                 Chunk Names
    app.bundle.js  29.7 KiB     app  [emitted]  app
 vendor.bundle.js  1.24 MiB  vendor  [emitted]  vendor
Entrypoint app = vendor.bundle.js app.bundle.js
[./node_modules/webpack/buildin/global.js] (webpack)/buildin/global.js 489 bytes {vendor}
[built]
[./src/App.jsx] 307 bytes {app} [built]
[./src/IssueAdd.jsx] 3.45 KiB {app} [built]
[./src/IssueFilter.jsx] 2.67 KiB {app} [built]
[./src/IssueList.jsx] 6.02 KiB {app} [built]
[./src/IssueTable.jsx] 1.16 KiB {app} [built]
[./src/graphQLFetch.js] 2.71 KiB {app} [built]
    + 338 hidden modules
```

Now that we have all the third-party libraries included in the bundle, we can remove the loading of these libraries from the CDN. Instead, we can include the new script vendor.bundle.js. The changes are all in index.html, as shown in Listing 8-24.

Listing 8-24. ui/public/index.html: Removal of Libraries Included Directly from CDN

```
...
<head>
  <meta charset="utf-8">
  <title>Pro MERN Stack</title>

  <script src="https://unpkg.com/react@16/umd/react.development.js"></script>
  <script src="https://unpkg.com/react-dom@16/umd/react-dom.development.js"></script>
  <script src="https://unpkg.com/prop-types@15/prop-types.js"></script>

  <script src="https://unpkg.com/@babel/polyfill@7/dist/polyfill.min.js"></script>
  <script src="https://unpkg.com/whatwg-fetch@3.0.0/dist/fetch.umd.js"></script>
  <style>
    ...
  </style>
</head>

<body>
  ...
  <script src="/env.js"></script>
  <script src="/vendor.bundle.js"></script>
  <script src="/app.bundle.js"></script>
</body>
...
```

If you now test the application (after starting the API and the UI servers, of course), you will find that the application works just as before. Further, a quick look at the Network tab in the Developer Console will show that the libraries are no longer being fetched from the CDN; instead, the new script vendor.bundle.js is being fetched from the UI server.

If you make a small change to any of the JSX files and refresh the browser, you will find that fetching vendor.bundle.js returns a "304 Not Modified" response, but the application's bundle, app.bundle.js, is indeed being fetched. Given the sizes of the vendor.bundle.js file, it is a great saving of both time and bandwidth.

Hot Module Replacement

The watch mode of Webpack works well for client-side code, but there is a potential pitfall with this approach. You must keep an eye on the console that is running the command npm run watch to ensure that bundling is complete, before you refresh your browser to see the effect of your changes. If you press refresh a little too soon, you will end up with the previous version of your client-side code, scratch your head wondering why your changes didn't work, and then spend time debugging.

Further, at the moment, we need an extra console for running npm run watch in the UI directory to detect changes and recompile the files. To solve these issues, Webpack has a powerful feature called Hot Module Replacement (HMR). This changes modules in the browser while the application is running, removing the need for a refresh altogether. Further, if there is any application state, that will also be retained, for example, if you were in the middle of typing in some text box, that will be retained because there is no page refresh. Most importantly, it saves time by updating only what is changed, and it removes the need for switching windows and pressing the refresh button.

There are two ways to implement HMR using Webpack. The first involves a new server called `webpack-dev-server`, which can be installed and run from the command line. It reads the contents of `webpack.config.js` and starts a server that serves the compiled files. This is the preferred method for applications without a dedicated UI server. But since we already have a UI server, it's better to modify this slightly to do what the `webpack-dev-server` would do: compile, watch for changes, and implement HMR.

HMR has two middleware packages that can be installed within the Express application, called `webpack-dev-middleware` and `webpack-hot-middleware`. Let's install these packages:

```
$ cd ui
$ npm install --save-dev webpack-dev-middleware@3
$ npm install --save-dev webpack-hot-middleware@2
```

We'll use these modules within the Express server for the UI, but only when explicitly enabled because we don't want to do this in production. We'll have to import these modules and mount them in the Express app as middleware. But these modules need special configuration, different from the defaults in `webpack.config.js`. These are:

- They need additional entry points (other than `App.jsx`) so that Webpack can build the client-side code necessary for this extra functionality into the bundle.

- A plugin needs to be installed that generates incremental updates rather than entire bundles.

Rather than create a new configuration file for this, let's instead modify the configuration *on the fly*, when HMR is enabled. Since the configuration itself is a Node.js module, this can be easily done. But we do need one change in the configuration, one that does not affect the original configuration. The entry point needs to be changed to an array so that a new entry point can be pushed easily. This change is shown in Listing 8-25.

Listing 8-25. ui/webpack.config.js: Change Entry to an Array

```
...
  entry: { app: './src/App.jsx' },
  entry: { app: ['./src/App.jsx'] },
...
```

Now, let's add an option for the Express server to enable HMR. Let's use an environment variable called `ENABLE_HMR` and default it to `true`, as long as it is not a production deployment. This gives developers a chance to switch it off in case they prefer the `webpack --watch` way of doing things.

```
...
const enableHMR = (process.env.ENABLE_HMR || 'true') === 'true';
if (enableHMR && (process.env.NODE_ENV !== 'production')) {
  console.log('Adding dev middleware, enabling HMR');
  ...
}
...
```

To enable HMR, the first thing we'll do is import the modules for Webpack and the two new modules we just installed. We'll also have to let ESLint know that we have a special case where we are installing development dependencies conditionally, so a couple of checks can be disabled.

```
...
  /* eslint "global-require": "off" */
  /* eslint "import/no-extraneous-dependencies": "off" */
  const webpack = require('webpack');
  const devMiddleware = require('webpack-dev-middleware');
  const hotMiddleware = require('webpack-hot-middleware');
...
```

Next, let's import the configuration file. This is also just a `require()` call, as the configuration is nothing but a Node.js module:

```
...
  const config = require('./webpack.config.js');
...
```

In the `config`, let's add a new entry point for Webpack that will install a listener for changes to the UI code and fetch the new modules when they change.

```
...
  config.entry.app.push('webpack-hot-middleware/client');
...
```

Then, let's enable the plugin for HMR, which can be instantiated using `webpack.HotModuleReplacementPlugin()`.

```
...
  config.plugins = config.plugins || [];
  config.plugins.push(new webpack.HotModuleReplacementPlugin());
...
```

Finally, let's create a Webpack compiler from this config and create the dev middleware (which does the actual compilation of the code using the config and sends out the bundles) and the hot middleware (which incrementally sends the new modules to the browser).

```
...
  const compiler = webpack(config);
  app.use(devMiddleware(compiler));
  app.use(hotMiddleware(compiler));
...
```

Note that the dev and hot middleware have to be installed *before* the static middleware. Otherwise, in case the bundles exist in the `public` directory (because `npm run compile` was executed some time back), the `static` module will find them and send them as a response, even before the dev and hot middleware get a chance.

The changes to the `uiserver.js` file are shown in Listing 8-26.

Listing 8-26. ui/uiserver.js: Changes for Hot Module Replacement Middleware

```
...
const app = express();

const enableHMR = (process.env.ENABLE_HMR || 'true') === 'true';

if (enableHMR && (process.env.NODE_ENV !== 'production')) {
  console.log('Adding dev middleware, enabling HMR');
  /* eslint "global-require": "off" */
  /* eslint "import/no-extraneous-dependencies": "off" */
  const webpack = require('webpack');
  const devMiddleware = require('webpack-dev-middleware');
  const hotMiddleware = require('webpack-hot-middleware');

  const config = require('./webpack.config.js');
  config.entry.app.push('webpack-hot-middleware/client');
  config.plugins = config.plugins || [];
  config.plugins.push(new webpack.HotModuleReplacementPlugin());

  const compiler = webpack(config);
  app.use(devMiddleware(compiler));
  app.use(hotMiddleware(compiler));
}

app.use(express.static('public'));
...
```

At this point, the following are different ways that the UI server can be started:

- npm run compile + npm run start: In production mode (the NODE_ENV variable is defined to production), starting of the server requires that npm run compile has been run and app.bundle.js and vendor.bundle.js have been generated and are available in the public directory.

- npm run start: In development mode (NODE_ENV is either not defined or set to development), this starts the server with HMR enabled by default. Any changes to the source files will be *hot* replaced in the browser instantly.

- npm run watch + npm run start, ENABLE_HMR=false: In development or production mode, these need to be run in two consoles. The watch command looks for changes and regenerates the JavaScript bundles, and the start command runs the server. Without ENABLE_HMR, the bundles will be served from the public directory, as generated by the watch command.

Let's add these as comments before the scripts in package.json in the UI. Since a JSON file cannot have comments like JavaScript, we'll just use properties prefixed with # to achieve this. The changes to ui/package.json are shown in Listing 8-27.

Listing 8-27. ui/package.json: Comments to Define Each Script

```
...
  "scripts": {
    "#start": "UI server. HMR is enabled in dev mode.",
    "start": "nodemon -w uiserver.js -w .env uiserver.js",
    "#lint": "Runs ESLint on all relevant files",
    "lint": "eslint . --ext js,jsx --ignore-pattern public",
    "#compile": "Generates JS bundles for production. Use with start.",
    "compile": "webpack --mode production",
    "#watch": "Compile, and recompile on any changes.",
    "watch": "webpack --watch"
  },
...
```

Now, if you run npm start in the UI as well as npm start in the API server, you'll be able to test the application. If you are running npm run watch, you may stop it now. The application should work as before. You will also see the following in the browser's Developer Console, assuring you that HMR has indeed been activated:

```
[HMR] connected
```

But when a file changes, say IssueFilter.jsx, you will see a warning in the browser's console to this effect:

```
[HMR] bundle rebuilding
HMR] bundle rebuilt in 102ms
[HMR] Checking for updates on the server...
Ignored an update to unaccepted module ./src/IssueFilter.jsx -> ./src/IssueList.jsx ->
./src/App.jsx -> 0
[HMR] The following modules couldn't be hot updated: (Full reload needed)
This is usually because the modules which have changed (and their parents) do not know how
to hot reload themselves. See https://webpack.js.org/concepts/hot-module-replacement/ for
more details.
[HMR]  - ./src/IssueFilter.jsx
```

This means that although the module was rebuilt and received in the browser, it couldn't be *accepted*. In order to accept the changes to a module, its parent needs to accept it using the HotModuleReplacementPlugin's accept() method. The plugin's interface is exposed via the module.hot property. Let's accept all changes unconditionally right at the top of the hierarchy of modules, App.jsx. The change for this is shown in Listing 8-28.

Listing 8-28. ui/src/App.jsx: Changes to Accept HMR

```
...
ReactDOM.render(element, document.getElementById('contents'));

if (module.hot) {
  module.hot.accept();
}
...
```

Now, if you change the contents of say, IssueFilter.jsx, you will see in the Developer Console that not just this module, but all modules that include this and upwards in the chain of inclusions, are updated: IssueList.jsx and then App.jsx. One effect of this is that the App.jsx module is loaded again (an equivalent of import is executed) by the HMR plugin. This has the effect of running the entire code in the contents of this file, which includes the following:

```
...
const element = <IssueList />;
ReactDOM.render(element, document.getElementById('contents'));
..
```

Thus, the IssueList component is constructed again and rendered, and almost everything gets refreshed. This can potentially lose local state. For example, if you had typed something in the text boxes for Owner and Title in the IssueAdd component, the text will be lost when you change IssueFilter.jsx.

To avoid this, we should ideally look for changes in every module and mount the component again, but preserve the local state. React does not have methods that make this possible, and even if it did, it would be tedious to do this in every component. To solve these problems, the react-hot-loader package was created. At compile time, it replaces a component's methods with *proxies*, which then call the real methods such as render(). Then, when a component's code is changed, it automatically refers to the new methods without having to remount the component.

This could prove to be useful in applications where local state is indeed important to preserve across refreshes. But for the Issue Tracker application, let's not implement react-hot-loader, instead, let's settle for the entire component hierarchy reloading when some code changes. It does not take that much time, in any case, and saves the complexity of installing and using react-hot-loader.

EXERCISE: HOT MODULE REPLACEMENT

1. How can you tell that the browser is not being fully refreshed when a module's code is changed? Use the Network section of your browser's developer tools and watch what goes on.

Answers are available at the end of the chapter.

Debugging

The unpleasant thing about compiling files is that the original source code gets lost, and if you have to put breakpoints in the debugger, it's close to impossible, because the new code is hardly like the original. Creating a bundle of all the source files makes it worse, because you don't even know where to start.

Fortunately, Webpack solves this problem by its ability to give you source maps, things that contain your original source code as you typed it in. The source maps also connect the line numbers in the transformed code to your original code. Browsers' development tools understand source maps and correlate the two, so that breakpoints in the original source code are converted breakpoints in the transformed code.

Webpack configuration can specify what kind of source maps can be created along with the compiled bundles. A single configuration parameter called devtool does the job. The kind of source maps that can be produced varies, but the most accurate (and the slowest) is generated by the value source-map. For this application, because the UI code is small enough, this is not discernably slow, so let's use it as the value for devtool. The changes to webpack.config.js in the UI directory are shown in Listing 8-29.

Listing 8-29. ui/webpack.config.js: Enable Source Map

```
...
  optimization: {
    ...
  },
  devtool: 'source-map'
};
...
```

If you are using the HMR-enabled UI server, you should see the following output in the console that is running the UI server:

```
webpack built dc6a1e03ee249e546ffb in 2964ms
[wdm]: Hash: dc6a1e03ee249e546ffb
Version: webpack 4.23.1
Time: 2964ms
Built at: 10/27/2018 12:08:12 AM
              Asset      Size  Chunks           Chunk Names
       app.bundle.js  54.2 KiB     app  [emitted]  app
   app.bundle.js.map  41.9 KiB     app  [emitted]  app
    vendor.bundle.js  1.26 MiB  vendor  [emitted]  vendor
vendor.bundle.js.map   1.3 MiB  vendor  [emitted]  vendor
Entrypoint app = vendor.bundle.js vendor.bundle.js.map app.bundle.js app.bundle.js.map
[0] multi ./src/App.jsx webpack-hot-middleware/client 40 bytes {app} [built]
[./node_modules/ansi-html/index.js] 4.16 KiB {vendor} [built]
[./node_modules/babel-polyfill/lib/index.js] 833 bytes {vendor} [built]
...
```

As you can see, apart from the package bundles, there are accompanying maps with the extension .map. Now, when you look at the browser's Developer Console, you will be able to see the original source code and be able to place breakpoints in it. A sample of this in the Chrome browser is shown in Figure 8-1.

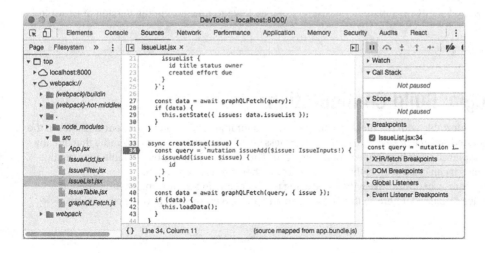

Figure 8-1. *Breakpoints in the original source code using source maps*

You will find the sources in other browsers in a roughly similar manner, but not exactly the same. You may have to look around a little to locate them. For example in Safari, the sources can be seen under Sources -> app.bundle.js -> "" -> src.

If you are using the Chrome or Firefox browser, you will also see a message in the console asking you to install the React Development Tools add-on. You can find installation instructions for these browsers at https://reactjs.org/blog/2015/09/02/new-react-developer-tools.html. This add-on provides the ability to see the React components in a hierarchical manner like the DOM inspector. For example, in the Chrome browser, you'll find a React tab in the developer tools. Figure 8-2 shows a screenshot of this add-on.

Figure 8-2. *React Developer Tools in the Chrome browser*

■ **Note**   The React Developer Tools has a compatibility problem with React version 16.6.0 at the time of writing this book. If you do face an issue (there will be an error in the console like `Uncaught TypeError: Cannot read property 'displayName' of null`), you may have to downgrade the version of React to 16.5.2.

DefinePlugin: Build Configuration

You may not be comfortable with the mechanism that we used for injecting the environment variables in the front-end: a generated script like `env.js`. For one, this is less efficient than generating a bundle that already has this variable replaced wherever it needs to be replaced. The other is that a global variable is normally frowned upon, since it can clash with global variables from other scripts or packages.

Fortunately, there is an option. We will not be using this mechanism for injecting environment variables, but I have discussed it here so that it gives you an option to try out and adopt if convenient.

To replace variables at build time, Webpack's `DefinePlugin` plugin comes in handy. As part of `webpack.config.js`, the following can be added to *define* a predefined string with the value like this:

```
...
  plugins: [
    new webpack.DefinePlugin({
      __UI_API_ENDPOINT__: "'http://localhost:3000/graphql'",
    })
  ],
...
```

Now, within the code for `App.jsx`, instead of hard-coding this value, the `__UI_API_ENDPOINT__` string can be used like this (note the absence of quotes; it is provided by the variable itself):

```
...
    const response = await fetch(__UI_API_ENDPOINT__, {
...
```

When Webpack transforms and creates a bundle, the variable will be replaced in the source code, resulting in the following:

```
...
    const response = await fetch('http://localhost:3000/graphql', {
...
```

Within `webpack.config.js`, you can determine the value of the variable by using `dotenv` and an environment variable instead of hard-coding it there:

```
...
require('dotenv').config();
...
    new webpack.DefinePlugin({
      __UI_API_ENDPOINT__: `'${process.env.UI_API_ENDPOINT}'`,
    })
...
```

Although this approach works quite well, it has the downside of having to create different bundles or builds for different environments. It also means that once deployed, a change to the server configuration, for example, cannot be done without making another build. For these reasons, I have chosen to stick with the runtime environment injection via `env.js` for the Issue Tracker application.

Production Optimization

Although Webpack does all that's necessary, such as minifying the output JavaScript when the mode is specified as production, there are two things that need special attention from the developer.

The first thing to be concerned about is the *bundle size*. At the end of this chapter, the third-party libraries are not many, and the size of the vendor bundle is around 200KB in production mode. This is not big at all. But as we add more features, we'll be using more libraries and the bundle size is bound to increase. As we progress along in the next few chapters, you will soon find that when compiling for production,

Webpack starts showing a warning that the bundle size for vendor.bundle.js is too big and that this can affect performance. Further, there will also be a warning that the combined size for all assets required for the entry point app is too large.

The remedy to these issues depends on the kind of application. For applications that are frequently used by users such as the Issue Tracker application, the bundle size is not of much concern because it will be cached by the user's browser. Except for the first time, the bundles will not be fetched unless they have changed. Since we have separated the application bundle from the libraries, we've more or less ensured that most of the JavaScript code, which is part of the vendor bundle, does not change and hence need not be fetched frequently. Thus, the Webpack warning can be ignored.

But for applications where there are many infrequent users, most of them visiting the web application for the first time, or after a long time, the browser cache will have no effect. To optimize the page load time for such applications, it's important to not just split the bundles into smaller pieces, but also to load the bundles only when required using a strategy called *lazy loading*. The actual steps to split and load the code to improve performance depends on the way the application is used. For example, it would be pointless to postpone loading of the React libraries upfront because without this, any page's contents will not be shown. But in later chapters you will find that this is not true, when the pages are constructed using server rendering and React can indeed be lazy loaded.

For the Issue Tracker application, we'll assume that it's a frequently used application and therefore the browser cache will work great for us. If your project's needs are different, you will find the Webpack documentation on code splitting (https://webpack.js.org/guides/code-splitting/) and lazy loading (https://webpack.js.org/guides/lazy-loading/) useful.

The other thing to be concerned about is *browser caching*, especially when you don't want it to cache the JavaScript bundle. This happens when the application code has changed and the version in the user's browser's cache is the wrong one. Most modern browsers handle this quite well, by checking with the server if the bundle has changed. But older browsers, especially Internet Explorer, aggressively cache script files. The only way around this is to change the name of the script file if the contents have changed.

This is addressed in Webpack by using content hashes as part of the bundle's name, as described in the guide for caching in the Webpack documentation at https://webpack.js.org/guides/caching/. Note that since the script names are generated, you will also need to generate index.html itself to contain the generated script names. This too is facilitated by a plugin called HTMLWebpackPlugin.

We won't be using this for the Issue Tracker application, but you can read more about how to do this in the Output Management guide of Webpack (https://webpack.js.org/guides/output-management/) and the documentation of HTMLWebpackPlugin itself starting at https://webpack.js.org/plugins/html-webpack-plugin/.

Summary

Continuing in the spirit of coding hygiene in the previous chapter, we modularized the code in this chapter. Since JavaScript was not originally designed for modularity, we needed the tool Webpack to put together and generate a few bundles from a handful of small JavaScript files and React components.

We removed the dependency on the CDN for runtime libraries such as React and the polyfills. Again, Webpack helped resolve dependencies and create bundles for these. You also saw how Webpack's HMR helped us increase productivity by efficiently replacing modules in the browser. You then learned about source maps that help in debugging.

In the next chapter, we'll come back to adding features. We'll explore an important concept of client-side routing that will allow us to show different components or pages and navigate between them in a seamless manner, even though the application will continue to be single page application (SPA) practically.

Answers to Exercises

Exercise: Transform and Bundle

1. No, Webpack does not rebuild if you save a file with just an extra space. This is because the preprocessing or loader stage produces a normalized JavaScript, which is no different from the original. A rebundling is triggered only if the normalized script is different.

2. As of now, we have only one page to display, the Issue List. Going forward, we'll have other pages to render, for example, a page to edit the issue, maybe another to list all users, yet another to show one's profile information, and so on. The App.jsx file will then need to mount different components based on user interaction. Thus, it's convenient to keep the application separate from each top-level component that may be loaded.

3. Not using the `default` keyword has the effect of exporting the class as a property (rather than itself) of the object that's exported. It is equivalent to doing this after defining the exportable element:

    ```
    export { IssueList };
    ```

    In the `import` statement, you would have to do this:

    ```
    import { IssueList } from './IssueList.jsx';
    ```

Note the destructuring assignment around the LHS. This allows multiple elements to be exported from a single file, each element you want from the import being separated by a comma. When only a single element is being exported, it's easiest to use the `default` keyword.

Exercise: Hot Module Replacement

1. There are many logs in the browser's console that tell you that HMR is being invoked. Further, if you look at the network requests, you will find that for a browser refresh, requests are made to all of the assets. Take a look at the sizes of these assets. Typically, `vendor.bundle.js` is not fetched again when client-side code changes (it would return a 304 response), but `app.bundle.js` will be reloaded.

    But when HMR succeeds, you will see that the entire assets are not fetched; instead, incremental files, much smaller than `app.bundle.js`, are being transferred.

CHAPTER 9

■ ■ ■

React Router

Now that we've organized the project and added development tools for productivity, let's get back to adding more features to the Issue Tracker.

In this chapter, we'll explore the concept of routing, or handling multiple pages that we may need to display. Even in a single-page application (SPA), there are in fact multiple *logical* pages (or views) within the application. It's just that the page load happens only the first time from the server. After that, each of the other views is displayed by manipulating or changing the DOM rather than fetching the entire page from the server.

To navigate between different views of the application, *routing* is needed. Routing links the state of the page to the URL in the browser. It's not only an easy way to reason about what is displayed in the page based on the URL, it has the following very useful properties:

- The user can use the forward/back buttons of the browser to navigate between visited pages (actually, *views*) of the application.

- Individual pages can be bookmarked and visited later.

- Links to views can be shared with others. Say you want to ask someone to help you with an issue, and you want to send them the link that displayed the issue. Emailing them the link is far easier and more convenient for the recipient than asking them to navigate through the user interface.

Before SPAs really matured, this was rather difficult, or sometimes impossible. SPAs had just a single page, which meant a single URL. All navigation had to be interactive: the user had to go through the application via predefined steps. For example, a link to a specific issue couldn't be sent to someone. Instead, they had to be told to follow a sequence of steps on the SPA to reach that issue. But modern SPAs handle this gracefully.

In this chapter, we'll explore how to use React Router to ease the task of setting up navigations between views. We'll start with another view to the application, one where the user can see and edit a single issue. Then, we'll create links between the views so that the user can navigate between them. On the hyperlinks that we create, we'll add parameters that can be passed to the different views, for example, the ID of the issue that needs to be shown, to a view that shows a single issue. Finally, we'll see how to nest components and routes.

© Vasan Subramanian 2019

V. Subramanian, *Pro MERN Stack*, https://doi.org/10.1007/978-1-4842-4391-6_9

In order to affect routing, any page needs to be connected to something that the browser recognizes and indicates that "this is the page that the user is viewing." In general, for SPAs, there are two ways to make this connection:

- *Hash-based:* This uses the anchor portion of the URL (everything following the #). This method is natural in the sense that the # portion can be interpreted as a location within the page, and there is only one page in an SPA. This location then determines what section of the page is displayed. The portion before the # never changes from the one and only page (index.html) that comprises the entire application. This is simple to understand and works well for most applications. In fact, implementing hash-based routing ourselves, without using a routing library, is quite simple. But we won't do it ourselves, we will use React Router to do that.

- *Browser history:* This uses a new HTML5 API that lets JavaScript handle the page transitions, at the same time preventing the browser from reloading the page when the URL changes. This is a little more complex to implement even with help from React Router (because it forces you to think about what happens when the server gets a request to the different URLs). But it's quite handy when we want to render a complete page from the server itself, especially to let search engine crawlers get the content of the pages and index them.

We'll start with the hash-based technique because it's easy to understand, and then switch over to the browser history technique because we'll implement server-side rendering in a later chapter.

Simple Routing

In this section, we'll create two views, one for the issue list that we've been working on all along, and another (a placeholder) for a report section. We'll also ensure that the home page, that is, /, redirects to the issue list. To start, let's install the package that will help us do all this: React Router.

```
$ cd ui
$ npm install react-router-dom@4
```

Let's also create a placeholder component for the report view. We'll save this along with other components in the ui/src directory. Let's call this component's file IssueReport.jsx, the entire contents of which is listed in Listing 9-1.

Listing 9-1. ui/src/IssueReport.jsx: New File for Report Placeholder

```
import React from 'react';

export default function IssueReport() {
  return (
    <div>
      <h2>This is a placeholder for the Issue Report</h2>
    </div>
  );
}
```

Let's now split the application's main page into two sections: a header section containing a navigation bar with hyperlinks to different views, and a contents section, which will switch between the two views depending on the hyperlink selected. The navigation bar will remain regardless of the view that is shown. In the future, we may have other views in the contents section. Let's create a component for the contents and place it in a file called Contents.jsx under the ui/src directory. This component will be responsible for switching between views.

To achieve routing or switching between different components based on the hyperlink that is clicked, React Router provides a component called Route. It takes in as a property the path that the route needs to match, and the component that needs to be shown when the path matches the URL in the browser. Let's use the path /issues to show the issue list and /report to show the report view. The following code snippet will achieve this:

```
...
    <Route path="/issues" component={IssueList} />
    <Route path="/report" component={IssueReport} />
...
```

To redirect the home page to /issues, we can further add a Redirect component that redirects from / to /issues, like this:

```
...
    <Redirect from="/" to="/issues" />
...
```

And finally, let's add a message that is shown when none of the routes match. Note that when the property path is not specified for the Route component, it implies that it matches *any* path.

```
...
const NotFound = () => <h1>Page Not Found</h1>;
...
    <Route component={NotFound} />
...
```

The four routes need to be enclosed in a wrapper component, which can be just a <div>. But to indicate that only *one* of these components needs to be shown, they should be enclosed in a <Switch> component so that only the first match's component will be rendered. In this case, we do need the switch because the last route will match any path.

Note also that the match is a *prefix* match. For example the path / will match not only / but also /issues and /report. Therefore, the order of routes is also important. The Redirect has to come after /issues and /report, and the catch-all route will need to come last. Alternatively, the exact property can be added to any route to indicate that it needs to be an exact match.

Note that the matching is not like the Express router in two ways. Firstly, in Express, the match is exact by default, and an * has to be added to match anything that follows. Secondly, in Express, a route match stops further processing (unless it's middleware, which can add value to the request-response process and continue), whereas in React Router, a <Switch> is explicitly needed to make it stop at the first match. Otherwise, *all* components whose routes match will be rendered.

Let's use an exact match for the Redirect and let the catch-all route be the last one. The final contents of Contents.jsx are shown in Listing 9-2, after adding the necessary import statements and the <Switch> wrapper.

Listing 9-2. ui/src/Contents.jsx: New File for the Contents Section

```
import React from 'react';
import { Switch, Route, Redirect } from 'react-router-dom';

import IssueList from './IssueList.jsx';
import IssueReport from './IssueReport.jsx';

const NotFound = () => <h1>Page Not Found</h1>;

export default function Contents() {
  return (
    <Switch>
      <Redirect exact from="/" to="/issues" />
      <Route path="/issues" component={IssueList} />
      <Route path="/report" component={IssueReport} />
      <Route component={NotFound} />
    </Switch>
  );
}
```

Next, let's create the page that shows the navigation bar and the contents component. A stateless component that displays the NavBar and the Contents component one after the other like this will do the needful. (A <div> is needed to enclose these two since a component's render method can return only one element) :

```
...
    <div>
      <NavBar />
      <Contents />
    </div>
...
```

As for the navigation bar, we'll need a series of hyperlinks. Since we are going to use the HashRouter, the pages will all have the main URL as /, followed by an in-page anchor that starts with the # symbol and has the actual path of the route. For example, to match the /issues path as specified in the Route specification, the URL will be /#/issues, where the first / is the one and only page of the SPA, # is the delimiter for the anchor, and /issues is the path of the route.

Thus, a link to the issue list will be of the form /#/issues, like this:

```
...
    <a href="/#/issues">Issue List</a>
...
```

Let's have three hyperlinks, one each for Home, Issue List and Reports. To separate them with a bar (|) character, we'll need to use a JavaScript expression like this:

```
...
    {' | '}
...
```

This is because whitespaces are stripped by the JSX transform, and we cannot otherwise naturally add the bar with spaces around it. Let's create the navigation bar as a stateless component with the three hyperlinks and place it along with the Page component, also stateless, in a new file called Page.jsx. The contents of this new file are shown in Listing 9-3.

Listing 9-3. ui/src/Page.jsx: New File for Composite Page

```
import React from 'react';

import Contents from './Contents.jsx';

function NavBar() {
  return (
    <nav>
      <a href="/">Home</a>
      {' | '}
      <a href="/#/issues">Issue List</a>
      {' | '}
      <a href="/#/report">Report</a>
    </nav>
  );
}

export default function Page() {
  return (
    <div>
      <NavBar />
      <Contents />
    </div>
  );
}
```

Finally, in App.jsx, we'll need to render this page instead of the original IssueList component into the DOM. Further, the page itself needs to be wrapped around a router, as all routing functionality must be within this for routing to work. We'll use the HashRouter component from the react-router-dom package. These changes to App.jsx are shown in Listing 9-4.

Listing 9-4. ui/src/App.jsx: Changes to Mount Page Instead of IssueList

```
...
import ReactDOM from 'react-dom';
import { HashRouter as Router } from 'react-router-dom';

import IssueList from './IssueList.jsx';
import Page from './Page.jsx';

const element = <IssueList />;
const element = (
  <Router>
    <Page />
  </Router>
);
...
```

■ **Note** Although no effort has been spared to ensure that all code listings are accurate, there may be typos or even corrections that did not make it into the book before it went to press. So, always rely on the GitHub repository (https://github.com/vasansr/pro-mern-stack-2) as the tested and up-to-date source for all code listings, especially if something does not work as expected.

Now, if you test the application in the browser by navigating to localhost:8000, you will find that the URL of the browser changes automatically to http://localhost:8000/#/issues. This is because of the Redirect route. On screen, you will see a navigation bar and the usual issue list below it. A screenshot is shown in Figure 9-1.

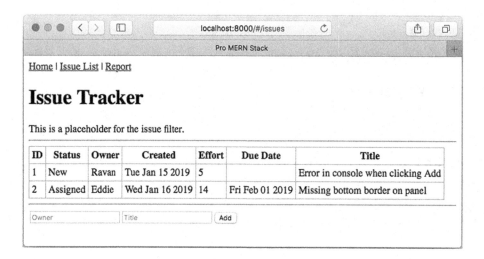

Figure 9-1. *Navigation bar and usual issue list*

You should also now be able to switch between the three views by clicking on the hyperlinks in the navigation bar. Clicking on Home will redirect to the issue list, and clicking on Report will show the placeholder like for the report view, as shown in Figure 9-2.

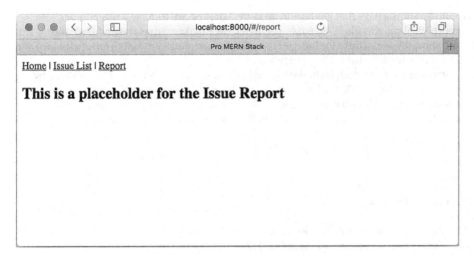

Figure 9-2. *The issue report placeholder*

If you type any other text instead of report or issues, you should see the Page Not Found message as well. Importantly, you should be able to navigate using the forward and back buttons through the history of your navigation. A refresh on the browser should also show the current page.

EXERCISE: SIMPLE ROUTING

1. Remove exact from the Redirect's list of properties. What happens? Can you explain the behavior? Can you achieve what is required without the exact property? (Remember to revert the change after this exercise.)

2. Replace <Switch> with a <div>. Now what happens? Can you explain this as well? (Revert the code to restore the original behavior after this exercise.)

3. When viewing the issue list, if you append some extra text to the URL, for example, /#/issues000, what do you expect to happen? Try it out to confirm your answer. Now, try the same but with a / before the extra text, for example, /#/issues/000. Now what do you expect, and what do you see? Also try adding exact to the route. What does it tell you about the matching algorithm?

Answers are available at the end of the chapter.

Route Parameters

As you just saw (that is, if you had done the exercise in the previous section), the URL's path and the route's path need not be a perfect match. Whatever follows the matched part in the URL is the *dynamic* part of the path, and it can be accessed as a variable in the routed component. This is one way of supplying parameters to the component. The other way is using the URL's query string, which we will explore in the next section.

Let's use this facility to show a page that lets us edit an issue. For now, we'll create a placeholder, just like we did for the report. We'll call this file IssueEdit.jsx. Later, we'll make an Ajax call and fetch the details of the issue and show them as a form for the user to make changes and save. Just to ensure that we are receiving the right ID of the issue, let's display it in the placeholder.

Specifying parameters in the route path is similar to that in Express, using the : character followed by the name of the property that will receive the value. Let's call the base of the path that edits an issue, /edit. Then, the path specification /edit/:id will match a URL path like /edit/1, /edit/2, etc. This change to the routes, and the import of the component, are shown in Listing 9-5, in the Contents.jsx file.

Listing 9-5. ui/src/Contents.jsx: Changes for IssueEdit Route

```
...
import IssueReport from './IssueReport.jsx';
import IssueEdit from './IssueEdit.jsx';
...
      <Route path="/issues" component={IssueList} />
      <Route path="/edit/:id" component={IssueEdit} />
...
```

Via props, all routed components are provided an object called match that contains the result of the match operation. This contains a field called params that holds the route parameter variables. Thus, to access the trailing portion of the URL's path containing the id, match.params.id could be used. Let's use it and create the placeholder Edit component in IssueEdit.jsx. The contents of this file are shown in Listing 9-6.

Listing 9-6. ui/src/IssueEdit.jsx: New File for Placeholder IssueEdit Component

```
import React from 'react';

export default function IssueEdit({ match }) {
  const { id } = match.params;
  return (
    <h2>{`This is a placeholder for editing issue ${id}`}</h2>
  );
}
```

Now, you could type /#/edit/1 etc. in the browser's URL bar and test it out, but let's create a hyperlink in every row in the issue list as a convenience. We'll create a new column for this purpose called Action and fill it with a hyperlink to /edit/<issue id>. These changes are in IssueTable.jsx, as shown in Listing 9-7.

Listing 9-7. ui/src/IssueTable.jsx

```
...
function IssueRow({ issue }) {
...
      <td>{issue.title}</td>
      <td><a href={`/#/edit/${issue.id}`}>Edit</a></td>
    </tr>
...
}
...
```

```
export default function IssueTable({ issues }) {
...
        <th>Title</th>
        <th>Action</th>
      </tr>
...
}
...
```

Now, if you test the application and go to the Issue List page, you will see an extra column at the right of the table with a link called Edit. Clicking on this link should show the placeholder page for editing an issue, with the ID of the issue that you clicked on. To get back to the Issue List page, you could use the back button of the browser, or click on the Issue List hyperlink in the navigation bar. A screenshot of the placeholder Edit page is shown in Figure 9-3.

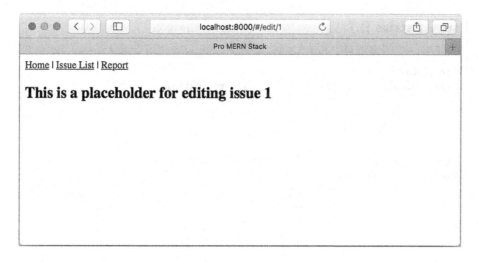

Figure 9-3. *The Edit page placeholder*

Query Parameters

It's quite simple and natural to add variables such as the ID of the issue being edited as route parameters like we saw in the previous section. But there will be cases where the variables are many and not necessarily in some order.

Let's take the case of the issue list. Until now, we were showing all the issues in the database. This is obviously not a great idea. Ideally, we will have many ways of filtering the issues to be shown. For example, we'd like to filter on status, assignee etc., be able to search the database for issues containing certain text, and have additional parameters for sorting and paginating the list. The Query String part of the URL is an ideal way to deal with these issues.

We'll not implement all the possible filters, sort and pagination right now. But to understand how query parameters work, let's implement a simple filter based on the status field so that the user can list only issues that have a particular status. Let's first change the List API to accept this filter. Let's start by changing the GraphQL schema. This is a simple change; all we need to do is add a parameter called status to the issueList query, of type StatusType. This change is shown in Listing 9-8.

Listing 9-8. api/schema.graphql: Addition of a Filter to issueList API

```
...
type Query {
  about: String!
  issueList(status: StatusType): [Issue!]!
}
...
```

Let's accept this new argument in the API implementation in the file issue.js, in the function list(). This function will now take an argument called status similar to the add() function. Since the argument is optional, we'll conditionally add a filter on status and pass it to the collection's find() method. These changes are shown in Listing 9-9, all part of issue.js.

Listing 9-9. api/issue.js: Handle Filtering on Issue Status

```
...
async function list(_, { status }) {
  const db = getDb();
  const filter = {};
  if (status) filter.status = status;
  const issues = await db.collection('issues').find(filter).toArray();
  return issues;
}
...
```

At this point, it's good to run a quick test using the Playground. You can test filtering of the issue list on issues with a New status with a query like this:

```
{
  issueList(status: New) {
    id status title
  }
}
```

You should get a response that contains only new issues. Further, you can ensure that the original query (without any filter) also works correctly, returning all issues in the database.

Now, let's replace the placeholder for the filter with three hyperlinks: All Issues, New Issues, and Assigned Issues. Let's use one query string variable, called status, with the value indicating which status to filter on, and add hyperlinks just as we did in the navigation bar. The new component with hyperlinks instead of a placeholder is shown in Listing 9-10 as the entire contents of the IssueFilter.js file.

Listing 9-10. ui/src/IssueFilter.js: New Component with Filter Links

```
/* eslint "react/prefer-stateless-function": "off" */

import React from 'react';

export default class IssueFilter extends React.Component {
  render() {
    return (
      <div>This is a placeholder for the issue filter.</div>
```

```
    <div>
      <a href="/#/issues">All Issues</a>
      {' | '}
      <a href="/#/issues?status=New">New Issues</a>
      {' | '}
      <a href="/#/issues?status=Assigned">Assigned Issues</a>
    </div>
  );
 }
}
```

The query string will need to be handled by the IssueList component as part of the loadData()
function. Just like the match property, the React Router also supplies as part of props, an object called
location that includes the path (in the field pathname) and the query string (in the field search). The React
Router does not parse the query string and leaves it to the application to determine how this field needs to
be parsed. Let's follow the conventional interpretation and parsing of the query string, which can easily be
done by the JavaScript API URLSearchParams(), like this, within the loadData() method:

```
...
    const { location: { search } } = this.props;
    const params = new URLSearchParams(search);
...
```

The API URLSearchParams() may need a polyfill for older browsers, especially Internet Explorer,
as described in the MDN documentation at https://developer.mozilla.org/en-US/docs/Web/API/
URLSearchParams. Since we have committed to support IE also, let's install the polyfill.

```
$ cd ui
$ npm install url-search-params@1
```

To include the polyfill, we'll have to import it in IssueList.jsx.

```
...
import URLSearchParams from 'url-search-params';
...
```

After parsing the query string, we'll have access to the status parameter using the get() method
of URLSearchParams, like params.get('status'). Let's create a variable that we can supply to the
GraphQL as a query variable. The params.get() method returns null if the parameter is not present,
but we want to skip setting the variable in this case. So, we'll add a check to see if the status is defined
before adding it to the variables.

```
...
    const vars = {};
    if (params.get('status')) vars.status = params.get('status');
...
```

Let's modify the simple GraphQL query to one that is a named operation with variables:

```
...
    const query = `query issueList($status: StatusType) {
      issueList (status: $status) {
        id title status owner
        created effort due
      }
    }`;
...
```

Now, we can modify the call to graphQLFetch() to include the query variable that has the status filter parameter:

```
...
    const data = await graphQLFetch(query, vars);
...
```

At this point in time, if you try the application and apply a filter by clicking on each of the filter hyperlinks, you'll find that the list of issues doesn't change. But on a browser refresh with an existing filter in the URL, it does show the correct filtered list of issues. You'll also find that navigating to another route, for example, the report page or the edit page, and using the back button makes the filter take effect. This indicates that loadData() is being called on the initial render, but a change in the query string doesn't cause loadData() to be called.

I talked briefly about component lifecycle methods earlier. These are hooks into various changes that React does on the component. We used the lifecycle method componentDidMount() to hook into the initially ready state of the component. Similarly, we need to hook into a method that tells us that the query string has changed, so that we can reload the list. The complete set of lifecycle methods is very nicely described in this diagram: http://projects.wojtekmaj.pl/react-lifecycle-methods-diagram/.

From the diagram, it is clear that the lifecycle method componentDidUpdate() is good for taking action whenever some properties change. A render() is automatically called when this happens, but that's not enough. We also need to refresh the state by making a call to loadData().

Let's implement the lifecycle hook componentDidUpdate(), and reload the data if necessary, by comparing the old and the new query string in IssueList. This method is passed the previous props. The current props can be accessed using this.props. We can detect a change in the filter by comparing the location.search property of the previous and the current props and reloading the data on a change:

```
...
  componentDidUpdate(prevProps) {
    const { location: { search: prevSearch } } = prevProps;
    const { location: { search } } = this.props;
    if (prevSearch !== search) {
      this.loadData();
    }
  }
...
```

The complete changes to `IssueList` component, including these most recent ones, are shown in Listing 9-11.

Listing 9-11. ui/src/IssueList.jsx: Changes for Handling a Query String Based Filter

```
...
import React from 'react';
import URLSearchParams from 'url-search-params';
...

  componentDidUpdate(prevProps) {
    const { location: { search: prevSearch } } = prevProps;
    const { location: { search } } = this.props;
    if (prevSearch !== search) {
      this.loadData();
    }
  }
...

  async loadData() {
    const { location: { search } } = this.props;
    const params = new URLSearchParams(search);
    const vars = {};
    if (params.get('status')) vars.status = params.get('status');

    const query = `query {
      issueList {
    const query = `query issueList($status: StatusType) {
      issueList (status: $status) {
        id title status owner
        created effort due
      }
    }`;

    const data = await graphQLFetch(query, vars);
    if (data) {
      ...
    }
  }
...
```

Now, if you navigate between the different filter hyperlinks, you will find that the issue list refreshes based on the filter selected.

EXERCISE: QUERY PARAMETERS

---

1. Navigate between two different issues' edit pages, by changing the Issue ID in the URL bar, or by creating a bookmark for one of them. The two different pages are shown correctly. Compare this with the Issue List page, where a `componentDidUpdate()` method was needed. Why is this so? Hint: Think about how a change in properties affected the issue list vis-à-vis the Issue Edit page.

2. Within `componentDidUpdate()`, there is a check for old and new properties being the same. Is this needed? One reason, is of course, that it avoids an unnecessary `loadData()`. But why not just reload the data when properties change? Try it out and see for yourself. (Remember to revert the changes after the exercise.)

3. Add a breakpoint in the `render()` method of `IssueAdd` and switch between filters. You will find that this component is being rendered again when the filter changes. What are the performance implications? How can this be optimized? Hint: Read the "Component Lifecycle" section in the documentation on React at `https://reactjs.org/docs/react-component.html`.

Answers are available at the end of the chapter.

Links

We used `hrefs` until now to create hyperlinks. Although this works, React Router provides a better and more convenient way to create links via the `Link` component. This component is very much like an `href`, but it has the following differences:

- The paths in a `Link` are always absolute; it does not support relative paths.

- The query string and the hash can be supplied as separate properties to the `Link`.

- A variation of `Link`, `NavLink` is capable of figuring out if the current URL matches the link and adds a class to the link to show it as active.

- A `Link` works the same between different kinds of routers, that is, the different ways of specifying the route (using the # character, or using the path as is) are hidden from the programmer.

Let's take advantage of these properties of the Link component and change all `hrefs` to `Links`. This component takes one property, `to`, which can be a string (for simple targets) or an object (for targets with query strings, etc.). Let's start with the change in the `IssueRow` component, where the target is a simple string. We need to change the name of the component from `<a>` to `<Link>` and the property `href` to `to`, while maintaining the same string as the target. The changes to `IssueTable.jsx` are shown in Listing 9-12.

Listing 9-12. ui/src/IssueTable.jsx: Changes to IssueRow to Use Link

```
...
import React from 'react';
import { Link } from 'react-router-dom';
```

```
function IssueRow({ issue }) {
...
    <td>{issue.title}</td>
    <td><a href={`/#/edit/${issue.id}`}>Edit</a></td>
    <td><Link to={`/edit/${issue.id}`}>Edit</Link></td>
...
}
...
```

We can take up `IssueFilter` next, where there are query strings. This time, instead of a string, let's supply an object containing the path and the query string separately. The object properties for these are `pathname` and `search`, respectively. Thus, for the link to new issues, the `to` property will contain the pathname as `/issues`, and the query string as `?status=New`.

Note that React Router does not make assumptions about the query string, as you saw in the previous section. In the same spirit, it requires the `?` prefix to be supplied as part of the query string too. These changes to `IssueFilter` are shown in Listing 9-13.

Listing 9-13. ui/src/IssueFilter.jsx: Change to Convert hrefs to Links

```
...
import React from 'react';
import { Link } from 'react-router-dom';

export default class IssueFilter extends React.Component {
...
        <a href="/#/issues">All Issues</a>
        <Link to="/issues">All Issues</Link>
        ...
        <a href="/#/issues?status=New">New Issues</a>
        <Link to={{ pathname: '/issues', search: '?status=New' }}>
          New Issues
        </Link>
        ...
        <a href="/#/issues?status=Assigned">Assigned Issues</a>
        <Link to={{ pathname: '/issues', search: '?status=Assigned' }}>
          Assigned Issues
        </Link>
...
}
...
```

As for the navigation bar in `Page.jsx`, let's use a `NavLink` instead, which will allow us to highlight the currently active navigation link. Note that the `NavLink` will highlight any path that *partially* matches the URL's path based on segments separated by a `/`. This is useful when the entire hierarchy of navigation paths can be highlighted, or when the navigation link has further variations within the page. For the navigation bar we have currently in the application, the `Home` link, whose target is just `/`, will match any path in the browser's URL. To avoid it being highlighted always, `NavLink` has a `exact` property, just like the same property for the `Route` component, that enforces an exact match instead of a prefix match. Let's use that property for the `Home` link alone and convert the others simply as we did for the `IssueRow` component. These changes are shown in Listing 9-14.

Listing 9-14. ui/src/Page.jsx: Change to Replace hrefs with NavLinks

```
...
import React from 'react';
import { NavLink } from 'react-router-dom';
...

function NavBar() {
...
      <a href="/">Home</a>
      <NavLink exact to="/">Home</NavLink>
      ...
      <a href="/#/issues">Issue List</a>
      <NavLink to="/issues">Issue List</NavLink>
      ...
      <a href="/#/report">Report</a>
      <NavLink to="/report">Report</NavLink>
...
}
...
```

NavLink only adds a class called `active` when the link matches the URL. In order to change the look of active links, we need to define a style for the class. Let's use a light blue background for an active link in the styles specification. This change in `index.html` is shown in Listing 9-15.

Listing 9-15. ui/public/index.html: Style for Active NavLinks

```
...
  <style>
    ...
    a.active {background-color: #D8D8F5;}
  </style>
...
```

Now, when you test the application, you should not only see it working as before but also see one of the Navigation links highlighted based on the current page being shown: the Issue List page or the Report page. The edit page, however, not having any corresponding navigation link, does not result in any of the links being highlighted. A screenshot of the application when viewing the issue list is shown in Figure 9-4.

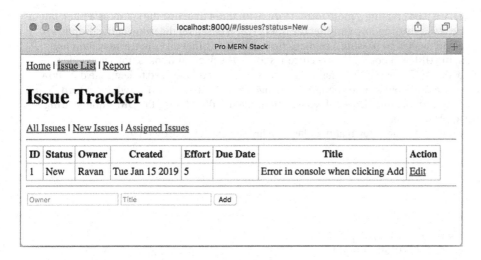

Figure 9-4. *The Issue List link highlighted when viewing the list*

If you click on the same link twice, you may also see a warning in the Developer Tools console saying "Hash history cannot PUSH the same path..." This message is seen only in development mode and is shown just in case we are programmatically pushing in a route path that is the same as before. You can safely ignore this warning. In any case, we'll be transitioning to the browser history router soon, where this warning will not be seen.

EXERCISE: LINKS

1. You'd have noticed that we did not use NavLinks for the filter links. Try changing these also to NavLinks. What do you observe when you navigate between the filters? Can you explain this? (Remember to revert the changes after you are done with the experiment.)

2. Let's say you are using a third-party CSS library, and the way to highlight a link using this library is to add the current class rather than the active class. How would you do this? Hint: Look up the documentation of NavLink at https://reacttraining.com/react-router/web/api/NavLink.

Answers are available at the end of the chapter.

Programmatic Navigation

Query strings are typically used when the variables' values are dynamic and could have many combinations that cannot be predetermined. They are also typically a result of an HTML form. A form would require that the query string be constructed dynamically, as opposed to a predetermined string that we used in the Links until now.

In later chapters, we'll be creating a more formal form with more than just the status as a filter, but in this section, we'll add a simple dropdown and set the query string based on the value of the dropdown. We could directly reload the list, by passing a callback from IssueList that takes in the new filter as a parameter. But then, the URL will not reflect the current state of the page, and that's not a good idea, since if the user refreshes the browser, the filter will be cleared. It's recommended to keep the data flow unidirectional: when the dropdown value changes, it changes the URL's query string, which in turn applies the filter. The same would work even if we started in the middle: change the URL's query string directly, and it will apply the filter.

Let's first create this simple dropdown and replace the links in IssueFilter with it.

```
...
    <div>
      Status:
      {' '}
      <select>
        <option value="">(All)</option>
        <option value="New">New</option>
        ...
      </select>
    </div>
...
```

■ **Note** The compiler strips all whitespaces within JSX at element boundaries, so a space after the label Status: will have no effect. One way to add a space after the label is using the HTML non-breaking space using . Another way to insert an element is to add it as JavaScript text, and that's what we've used in this example.

Next, let's trap the event when the dropdown value is changed, and predictably, the property for this in onChange. Let's add this property and set it to a class method called onChangeStatus.

```
...
      <select onChange={this.onChangeStatus}>
...
```

In the implementation of the method onChangeStatus, we can get the value of selected item in the dropdown using the event's target (which will be a handle to the dropdown itself), via the value property:

```
...
  onChangeStatus(e) {
    const status = e.target.value;
}
...
```

Just like the location property that React Router added to the IssueList component, it also adds some more properties, one of which is history. Using this, the location, query string, etc. of the browser's URL can be set. But, unlike IssueList, since IssueFilter is not directly part of any route, React Router cannot automatically make these available. To do that, we'll have to inject these additional properties into the IssueFilter component explicitly. This can be done using a wrapper function provided by React Router called withRouter(). This function takes in a component class as an argument and returns a new component class that has history, location, and match available as part of props. So, instead of exporting the component, we'll just export the wrapped component like this:

```
...
~~export default~~ class IssueFilter extends React.Component {
  ...
}
...
export default withRouter(IssueFilter);
...
```

Now, within onChangeStatus(), we'll have access to this.props.history, which can be used to push the new location based on the changed filter. But to access this within the handler, we'll have to ensure that the handler is bound to this within the constructor.

```
...
  constructor() {
    super();
    this.onChangeStatus = this.onChangeStatus.bind(this);
  }
...
```

Now, within the handler, we can use the push() method of history to push the new location. This method takes in an object just like the object that we used for Link to specify a location, that is, a pathname and a search. Let's also deal with the empty status option, for which we will have no search.

```
...
  onChangeStatus(e) {
    ...
    const { history } = this.props;
    history.push({
      pathname: '/issues',
      search: status ? `?status=${status}` : '',
    });
  }
...
```

The complete source code of IssueFilter.jsx is shown in Listing 9-16. The deleted code is not shown since pretty much all of the previous code has been removed.

Listing 9-16. ui/src/IssueFilter.jsx: New Implementation of IssueFilter

```
import React from 'react';
import { withRouter } from 'react-router-dom';

class IssueFilter extends React.Component {
  constructor() {
    super();
    this.onChangeStatus = this.onChangeStatus.bind(this);
  }
```

```
onChangeStatus(e) {
  const status = e.target.value;
  const { history } = this.props;
  history.push({
    pathname: '/issues',
    search: status ? `?status=${status}` : '',
  });
}

render() {
  return (
    <div>
      Status:
      {' '}
      <select onChange={this.onChangeStatus}>
        <option value="">(All)</option>
        <option value="New">New</option>
        <option value="Assigned">Assigned</option>
        <option value="Fixed">Fixed</option>
        <option value="Closed">Closed</option>
      </select>
    </div>
  );
}
}

export default withRouter(IssueFilter);
```

If you test the application now, you'll find that the issue list changes when a different item is selected in the dropdown. To see whether it works for statuses other than New and Assigned, you will have to add more issues with other statuses directly in to MongoDB or via the Playground. A screenshot of the application with the issue list filtered on new issues is captured in Figure 9-5.

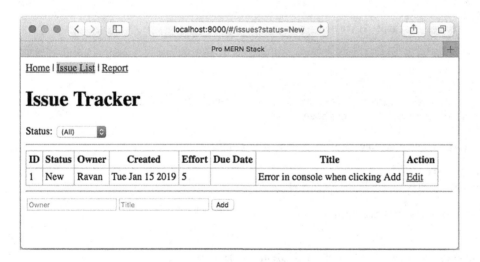

Figure 9-5. *The issue list filtered using a dropdown*

EXERCISE: PROGRAMMATIC NAVIGATION

1. We used the push() method of history. What other method could have been used, and what would be the difference in the effect? Hint: Look up the documentation of history at https://reacttraining.com/react-router/web/api/history. Try it out. (Remember to revert the changes after the exercise.)

2. Filter the issue list on say, New. Now, keep the developer console open and click refresh in the browser. Does the dropdown reflect the status of the filter? Select New in the dropdown again. What do you see? What does it mean?

3. The IssueList component has access to the history object. So, instead of using withRouter on IssueFilter, you could either pass the history object from IssueList to IssueFilter, or pass a callback to IssueFilter that sets a new filter and call that from the child component. Compare these alternatives. What are the pros and cons as compared to the original method using withRouter?

Answers are available at the end of the chapter.

Nested Routes

A common pattern for displaying details of one object while displaying a list of objects is using the header-detail UI pattern. This is the same as some email clients, notably Outlook and Gmail with a vertical or horizontal split use. A list of objects is shown with brief information about them (the sender and subject of each email), and on selecting one of them, further detail of the selected object (the message itself) is shown in a detail area.

An Issue Tracker is not of much use unless it had the ability to store a detailed description and comments by various users along with each issue. So, similar to the email clients, let's add a description field to an issue, which can be lengthy text and not suitable for displaying within the table of issues. Let's also make it so that on selecting an issue, the lower half of the page shows the description of the issue.

This calls for *nested routes*, wherein the beginning part of the path depicts one section of a page, and based on interaction within that page, the latter part of the path depicts variation, or further definition of what's shown additionally in the page. In the case of the Issue Tracker application, we will have /issues showing a list of issues (and no detail), and /issues/1 showing the detail section with the description of issue with ID 1, in addition to the issue list.

React Router makes this easy to do this by way of its *dynamic routing* philosophy. At any point in the hierarchy of components, a Route component can be added which will be rendered if the URL matches the route's path. In the Issue Tracker application, we can define such a Route with the actual component being the Issue Detail, within the IssueList, right after the IssueAdd section. The path can be of the form /issues/<id>, similar to the path match for the IssueEdit component, like this:

```
...
        <IssueAdd createIssue={this.createIssue} />
        <hr />
        <Route path="/issues/:id" component={IssueDetail} />
...
```

Thus, unlike Express routes, React Router's routes don't all need to be predeclared; they can be placed at any level and are evaluated during the process of rendering.

But before we make this change, let's modify the schema to add a description field. We'll do this both in the type Issue and the type IssueInputs. We'll also need a new API that can retrieve a single issue given its ID. This API is what the component IssueDetail will use to fetch the description, which the IssueTable will not fetch. Let's call this API simply issue, which takes in an integer as an argument to specify the ID of the issue to fetch. The changes to schema.graphql are listed in Listing 9-17.

Listing 9-17. api/schema.graphql: Changes for a New Field in Issue and a New Get API

```
...
type Issue {
  ...
  description: String
}
...

input IssueInputs {
  ...
  description: String
}
...

type Query {
  ...
  issue(id: Int!): Issue!
}
...
```

Next, let's implement the API to get a single issue. This is fairly straightforward: all we need to do is use the id argument to create a MongoDB filter and call findOne() on the issues collection with this filter. Let's call this function get() and export it along with the other exported functions from issue.js. This set of changes is shown in Listing 9-18.

Listing 9-18. api/issue.js: Implementation of New Function get() to Fetch a Single Issue

```
...
async function get(_, { id }) {
  const db = getDb();
  const issue = await db.collection('issues').findOne({ id });
  return issue;
}

async function list(_, { status }) {
  ...
}
...

module.exports = { list, add, get };
...
```

254

Finally, we'll need to tie up the new function in the resolvers we supply to the Apollo Server. This change to api_handler.js is shown in Listing 9-19.

Listing 9-19. api/api_handler.js

```
const resolvers = {
  Query: {
    ...
    issue: issue.get,
  },
...
```

At this point in time, you could test the new API using the Playground. You could create a new issue with a description field, fetch it using the issue query, and see if the description is being returned. For convenience, let's also modify the schema initializer script to add a description field to the initial set of issues. This change to init.mongo.js is shown in Listing 9-20.

Listing 9-20. api/scripts/init.mongo.js: Addition of Description to Sample Issues

```
...
const issuesDB = [
  {
    ...
    description: 'Steps to recreate the problem:'
      + '\n1. Refresh the browser.'
      + '\n2. Select "New" in the filter'
      + '\n3. Refresh the browser again. Note the warning in the console:'
      + '\n   Warning: Hash history cannot PUSH the same path; a new entry'
      + '\n   will not be added to the history stack'
      + '\n4. Click on Add.'
      + '\n5. There is an error in console, and add doesn\'t work.',
  },
  {
    ...
    description: 'There needs to be a border in the bottom in the panel'
      + ' that appears when clicking on Add',
  },
];
...
```

You could run this script using the usual command to initialize the database so that the description matches your tests and the screenshots in this chapter:

```
$ mongo issuetracker api/scripts/init.mongo.js
```

You may have to start from the Home link if you ran the script, since it may have removed some issues that you had created manually. Otherwise, if the UI is referring to these issues, you'll probably get a GraphQL error to the effect that Query.issue cannot be null.

Now, we can implement the IssueDetail component. We'll do the following as part of this component:

1. We'll maintain the state, which will contain an issue object.

2. The ID of the issue object will be retrieved from match.params.id like in the IssueEdit component.

3. The issue object will be fetched using the issue GraphQL query using the fetch() API, in a method called loadData(), and set as the state.

4. The method loadData() will be called after the component mounted (for the first time), or when the ID changes (in componentDidUpdate()).

5. In the render() method, we'll just display the description using the <pre> tag so that newlines are maintained in the display.

The complete code for the component, in a new file called IssueDetail.jsx, is shown in Listing 9-21.

Listing 9-21. ui/src/IssueDetail.jsx: New Component to Show the Description of an Issue

```
import React from 'react';

import graphQLFetch from './graphQLFetch.js';

export default class IssueDetail extends React.Component {
  constructor() {
    super();
    this.state = { issue: {} };
  }

  componentDidMount() {
    this.loadData();
  }

  componentDidUpdate(prevProps) {
    const { match: { params: { id: prevId } } } = prevProps;
    const { match: { params: { id } } } = this.props;
    if (prevId !== id) {
      this.loadData();
    }
  }

  async loadData() {
    const { match: { params: { id } } } = this.props;
    const query = `query issue($id: Int!) {
      issue (id: $id) {
        id description
      }
    }`;

    const data = await graphQLFetch(query, { id });
    if (data) {
      this.setState({ issue: data.issue });
```

```
    } else {
      this.setState({ issue: {} });
    }
  }

  render() {
    const { issue: { description } } = this.state;
    return (
      <div>
        <h3>Description</h3>
        <pre>{description}</pre>
      </div>
    );
  }
}
```

To integrate the IssueDetail component into the IssueList component, we'll need to add a route, as discussed in the beginning of this section. But, instead of hardcoding /issues, let's use the path as matched in the parent component, using this.props.match.path. This is so that even if the parent path changes for any reason, the change is isolated to one place.

This change, along with the necessary imports, is shown in Listing 9-22.

Listing 9-22. ui/src/IssueList.jsx: Changes for Including IssueDetail in a Route

```
...
import URLSearchParams from 'url-search-params';
import { Route } from 'react-router-dom';
...

import IssueAdd from './IssueAdd.jsx';
import IssueDetail from './IssueDetail.jsx';
...

  render() {
    const { issues } = this.state;
    const { match } = this.props;
    ...
        <IssueAdd createIssue={this.createIssue} />
        <hr />
        <Route path={`${match.path}/:id`} component={IssueDetail} />
    ...
  }
...
```

To select an issue, let's create another link beside the Edit link in the table of issues. This time, let's use a NavLink to highlight the selected issue. Ideally, we should be able to select by clicking anywhere in the row, and it should be highlighting the entire row when selected. But let's keep that for a later chapter, where we will have better tools to implement this effect. The NavLink will point to /issues/<id>, where <id> is the ID of the issue in the row being selected.

Further, to not lose the query string part of the URL, we'll have to add the current query string as the search property to the target of the link. But, to access the current query string, we'll need access to the current location, and since `IssueRow` is not displayed as part of a `Route`, we'll have to inject the location by wrapping the component with `withRouter`.

The changes to the `IssueTable.jsx` file are shown in Listing 9-23.

Listing 9-23. ui/src/IssueTable.jsx: Addition of a Link to Select an Issue for Display in the Details Section

```
...
import React from 'react';
import { Link, NavLink, withRouter } from 'react-router-dom';
...

function IssueRow({ issue }) {
const IssueRow = withRouter(({ issue, location: { search } }) => {
  const selectLocation = { pathname: `/issues/${issue.id}`, search };
  ...
      <td>{issue.title}</td>
      <td><Link to={`/edit/${issue.id}`}>Edit</Link></td>
      <td>
        <Link to={`/edit/${issue.id}`}>Edit</Link>
        {' | '}
        <NavLink to={selectLocation}>Select</NavLink>
      </td>
    </tr>
  ...
}
});
```

If you now test the application, you'll find a Select link next to the Edit link for every issue. Clicking on this link should change the URL so that the ID of the issue is appended to the main path, but before the query string (if any). You should try this with and without filters to make sure it works in both cases, and that a refresh continues to show the description of a selected issue.

A screenshot of the page with the ID 1 issue selected is shown in Figure 9-6.

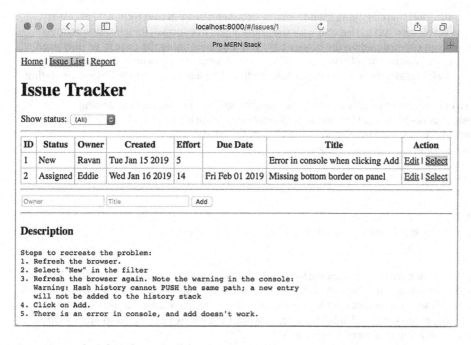

Figure 9-6. *The selected issue and description*

EXERCISE: NESTED ROUTES

1. Instead of using a `Route` while rendering `IssueList`, we could have defined the issue list's route's path as `/issues/:id`, and then displayed the `IssueDetail` passing the ID as part of props. Compare the two methods of achieving the same result. What are the pros and cons?

Answers are available at the end of the chapter.

Browser History Router

We discussed the two kinds of routing—hash-based and browser history-based—at the beginning of this chapter. Hash-based routing was easy to understand and implement if we were to do it ourselves: just changing the anchor part of the URL on transitions would suffice. Also, the server had to return only `index.html` for a request to / and nothing else.

But the downside of using hash-based routing is when the server needs to respond to different URL paths. Imagine clicking refresh on the browser. When hash-based routing is used, the browser makes a request to / from the server, regardless of what follows the # or the actual routing path. If we had to let the server handle this refresh differently, a better strategy would be to use a different URL base (that is, without the # and what follows it) for different routes.

This need (responding differently to different routes from the server itself) arises when we need to support responses to search engine crawlers. That's because, for every link found by the crawler, a new request is made provided the *base* URL is different. If what follows the # is different, the crawler assumes that it's just an anchor within the page, and only a request to / is made regardless of the route's path.

To make our application search engine friendly, using browser history-based routing is necessary. But that's not all, the server also has to respond with the entire page. In contrast, for a browser request, the page would have been constructed on the browser. We'll not be generating the page to be displayed just yet, because it's fairly complex to achieve that and it deserves a chapter of its own. For now, we'll just switch over to the browser history-based router, but assume that the page is constructed by manipulating the DOM only.

The switch to using this new router is as simple as changing the `import` statement and using `BrowserRouter` instead of `HashRouter`. This component achieves routing by using the HTML5 history API (`pushState`, `replaceState`, and `popState`) to keep the UI in sync with the URL.

This change is shown in `App.jsx`, in Listing 9-24.

Listing 9-24. ui/src/App.jsx: Changes for Using Browser History Based Router

```
...
import ReactDOM from 'react-dom';
import { HashRouter BrowserRouter as Router } from 'react-router-dom';
...
```

To test this change, you have to start from the home location, that is, `http://localhost:8000`. The application will seem to work, all the links will lead you to the right pages and views. Also, you'll find that the URLs will be without a #, and simple URLs like `http://localhost:8000/issues` for the Issue List page.

But a refresh on any of the views will fail. For example, while in the Issue List page, if you refresh the browser, you'll get the following message on the screen:

```
Cannot GET /issues
```

That's because the URL in the browser is currently pointing to `/issues` and the browser makes a request to the server for `/issues`, which is not handled by the UI server. To address this, we need to make a change to the UI server, which returns `index.html` for *any* URL that is not handled otherwise. This can be achieved by installing an Express route after all the other routes for the path * which reads the contents of `index.html` and returns it.

The `response` object has a convenience method for this called `sendFile()`. But for security reasons, the file's full absolute path has to be specified—it does not accept relative paths. Let's use `path.resolve()` from the built-in Node.js module `path` for converting a relative path to an absolute path. The changes to `uiserver.js` are shown in Listing 9-25.

Listing 9-25. ui/uiserver.js: Respond with index.html for All Requests

```
...
require('dotenv').config();
const path = require('path');
...

app.get('/env.js', (req, res) => {
  ...
});

app.get('*', (req, res) => {
  res.sendFile(path.resolve('public/index.html'));
});
...
```

If you test the application after making this change, you will find that a refresh on any page works as before. It would also be a good idea to test that other files in the public directory are being served correctly, notably, app.bundle.js and vendor.bundle.js.

But in normal development mode, HMR would serve these bundles rather than let the UI server pick them up from the public directory. So, you will need to disable HMR (by setting the environment variable ENABLE_HMR to false), compile the bundles manually using npm run compile, and then start the UI server. Then, on refreshing the application, you should see these files correctly retrieved from the server. Do not forget to revert the changes to HMR after you are done with the test.

There is still one change left to be done that affects the functioning of HMR. Webpack has a configuration option called publicPath under output. This is an important option when using on-demand-loading or loading external resources like images, files, etc. But we have not used these thus far and not having set this to any value did not affect the functioning of the application. The value defaults to an empty string, which means the same location as the current page.

It turns out that Webpack uses the value of publicPath to fetch update information for modules when they change and are recompiled by HMR. Thus, if you change a source file while you are at a location such as /edit/1 or /issues/1, you will find that HMR calls fail. If you look at the Network tab of developer tools, you'll find that these requests return the contents of index.html instead of the module update information.

You could compare the two requests and responses by looking at what happens when a source file is changed, while you have the browser pointed to /issues and then /issues/1. In the first case, you'll see a request to a resource like /f3f397176a7b9c3237cf.hot-update.json, which succeeds. Whereas in the second case, it will be like /edit/f3f397176a7b9c3237cf.hot-update.json, which fails. That's because Webpack is making a request *relative* to the current location. This request could not be matched by the hot middleware, so it fell through to the catch-all Express route, which returned the contents of index.html.

We did not face this problem when using the hash-based router because the page's location was always /, the route was effected by the anchor part of the URL. The correct request should have been without the /edit prefix. To make this happen, we'll have to change webpack.config.js to set the publicPath configuration. The changes for this are shown in Listing 9-26.

Listing 9-26. ui/webpack.config.js: Changes to Add publicPath

```
...
  output: {
    filename: '[name].bundle.js',
    path: path.resolve(__dirname, 'public'),
    publicPath: '/',
  },
...
```

After this change, you'll find that HMR works fine from any page in the application.

EXERCISE: BROWSER HISTORY ROUTER

1. If we had used hrefs instead of Links for the hyperlinks in the application, would the transition to use BrowserRouter have been as simple? What other changes would have had to be done?

2. Let's now compare using an href and a Link based on their effect. Add an href in addition to the Link for navigating to Edit in the Issue table. Click on these two links and compare what happens. (Hint: Use the Developer Tools' Network tab to inspect network traffic.)

   Now, do the same comparison with HashHistory (Note: You have to use /#/edit in the href, /edit will not work.) Now, is there a difference? Try to explain what you see. (Remember to revert the experimental changes after the exercise.)

Answers are available at the end of the chapter

Summary

In this chapter, you learned how to implement client-side routing, that is, show different pages depending on links in a menu or a navigation bar. The React Router library helped with this.

You also learned how to connect the URL in the browser with what is shown in the page, and how parameters and query strings can be used to tweak the page contents. Implementing routing correctly is key to giving the user a natural feel when clicking on hyperlinks and using the back/forward buttons in the browser. Further, connecting the URL in the browser to the contents on the page not only helps us think about different pages or views in an organized manner, but also helps the user to bookmark links and use the browser's refresh button.

In the next chapter, we'll explore how to deal with a very common occurrence in enterprise applications: forms, the React way. As we do that, we'll also complete the CRUD for the Issues object by implementing Update and Delete operations for issues.

Answers to Exercises
Exercise: Simple Routing

1. If the exact property is removed from the Redirect component, you'll see that the contents section is blank, regardless of the hyperlink that is clicked. This is because *all* URLs now match the first route. Since there is no component defined for the route, the page is blank. Further, you'll also see an error in the console saying that you're trying to redirect to the same route. This is because even on navigation, the same route (the Redirect) is the one that matches.

   You can almost achieve the required behavior by reordering the routes: the redirect can be placed after the two routes and before the catch-all. Now, the /issues and /report paths will match the first two routes and stop there. If neither of them match, then any other route will match / and will redirect to /issues. This is not exactly the same behavior as before, because instead of showing Page Not Found, it will always redirect to /issues.

2. If you replace `<Switch>` with a `<div>`, you'll find that the Page Not Found message is always shown in addition to the issue list or the report placeholder. This is because the matching does not stop at the first match, but instead shows *all* the components from the routes that matched. The `NotFound` component's path (empty) matches any path, and thus shows always.

3. The URL `/#/issues000` shows a Page Not Found, whereas `/#/issues/000` shows the issue list without an `exact` property, and Page Not Found otherwise. This demonstrates that a non-exact route matches full segments of the path, each segment being separated by a `/`. It is not a simple prefix match.

Exercise: Query Parameters

1. When properties are changed in a component, a `render()` is automatically called by React. When a change in properties only affects rendering, we don't need to do anything further.

   The difference in the issue list was that the change in properties caused a change in the state. This change had to be triggered somewhere, and we chose the lifecycle method `componentDidUpdate()` to do that. Eventually, even in Issue Edit page, when we load the issue details in an asynchronous call to the server, we will have to implement the `componentDidUpdate()` method.

2. Without the check for old and new properties being the same, it will result in an endless loop. This is because a new state is also considered an update to the component, thus calling `componentDidUpdate()` again and the cycle will continue endlessly.

3. Any change in a parent component will trigger a render in the child, because it is assumed that the state of the parent can affect the child as well. Normally, this is not a performance problem, because it is only the virtual DOM that is recalculated. Since the old and the new virtual DOMs will be identical, the actual DOM will not be updated.

   Updates to the virtual DOM are not that expensive, because they are no more than data structures in memory. But, in rare cases, especially when the component hierarchy is very deep and the number of components affected is very large, just the act of updating the virtual DOM may take some time. This can be optimized by hooking into the lifecycle method `shouldComponentUpdate()` and determining if a render is warranted.

Exercise: Links

1. If you use `NavLinks`, you will observe that all links are always highlighted. That's because `Link` only matches the *paths* of the URL and the link, and does not consider the query string as part of the path. Since the path is `/issues` for all the links, they will always match.

   Compared to route parameters, query parameters aren't expected to be a finite set, and therefore, not encouraged for use for navigation links. If the filters were navigation links, we should use route parameters as we did for the main navigation bar.

2. The `activeClassName` property for the `NavLink` component determines the class that is added when the link is active. You could set this property to the `current` value to have the desired effect.

Exercise: Programmatic Navigation

1. The `history.replace()` method could have been used, which replaces the current URL so that the history does not have the old location. On the other hand, `router.push()` ensures that the users can use the back button to go back to the previous view.

   Replacing can be used when the two routes are not really different. It is analogous to a HTTP redirect, where the contents of the request are the same, but available at a different location. In this case, remembering the first location as part of the browser's history is not useful.

2. On a refresh, the dropdown resets to the default value, `All`. But the list is filtered on the previous selection of the dropdown, and this is reflected in the URL as part of the query string. We'll synchronize the dropdown value and the query string when we discuss forms in the next chapter.

   If the dropdown value is changed to select the original status, the developer console shows a warning:

```
Hash history cannot PUSH the same path; a new entry will not be added to the history stack.
```

   Since the path is the same, hash history refuses to push the path, and the component is not updated.

3. The wrapper function `withRouter` is a bit hard to understand. The other options are easily understood, and may even seem simpler. But imagine a more nested hierarchy where `IssueFilter` is more than one level inside `IssueList`. In such a case, the `history` object will have to be passed through all intermediate components, increasing the coupling among all these components.

   Letting `IssueFilter` directly manipulate the URL reduces coupling and lets each component deal with a single responsibility. For `IssueFilter`, it is one of setting the URL, and for `IssueList`, it is one of using the query string from the URL, regardless of how it was set.

Exercise: Nested Routes

1. The difference between the two methods is not much, and could also be a matter of consistency. All `Route` does anyway is match the URL and display a component if it matches. Since the match has happened as part of `IssueList`, the nested route does not add much, at least in this case. So, displaying the `IssueDetail` component wrapped in an `if` condition (on the presence of an ID) will work just fine.

Another consideration is how deeply nested in the hierarchy the child component is. In case of IssueDetail, it was just one level deep, and passing in the ID from IssueList to IssueDetail was straightforward. If the nested-routed component is very deeply nested, then the ID would have to be passed through multiple other components, so it's perhaps easier for the IssueDetail to get this parameter from the URL via the router itself.

Exercise: Browser History Router

1. If we had not used Links, we would have had to change all the hrefs to remove the #/ prefix. This is one advantage of using Links as compared to plain hrefs.

2. When using BrowserHistory, an href causes the browser to navigate to another URL, thus initiating a request to the server, fetching a page and then rendering it. In comparison, a Link does not cause a new request to the server; it simply changes the URL in the browser and deals with the change programmatically, by replacing the component that needs to be displayed for the new route.

    When using HashHistory, the two methods are not visibly different because the base URL is always the same (/). The browser does not make a new request to the server even when clicking on the href because the base URL does not change.

## CHAPTER 10

React Forms

User input is an important part of any web application, and the Issue Tracker application is no different. We created a form and user input to create a new issue. But it was very rudimentary, and it did not demonstrate how forms are supposed to be dealt with in React.

In this chapter, we'll start taking in a lot more user input. We will convert the hard-coded filter to something more flexible with user input, and then we'll fill in the Edit page with a form. Finally, we'll add the ability to delete issues from the Issue List page, though this is not necessarily a form.

To be able to do all this, we'll also have to modify the back-end APIs to support these functions. We'll modify the List API to take more filter options, and we'll create new Update and Delete APIs. We'll thus complete implementing all of the CRUD operations.

Controlled Components

One of the challenges that a declarative style of programming faces is user interaction in form inputs, especially if they contain a value that is used to display the initial value from the model. If, like, conventional HTML code, the value of a text <input> is set to a string, it means that the value is *always* that string because it was declared so. On the other hand, if user edits were allowed to change that value, any re-rendering destroys user changes.

We did not have this problem with the IssueAdd component and form because the form did not have any initial values, that is, it performed the function of only taking in user input. So, the internal state of the component could be left *uncontrolled* by its parent, the IssueAdd component. Whenever the value of the input is required, for example when the user clicks the Add button, it can be determined by looking at its value using conventional HTML functions.

To be able to show a value in the input, it has to be *controlled* by the parent via a state variable or props variable. This is done simply by setting the value of the input to that state or props variable. Thus, the input will directly reflect that value, and the React component that renders the form will also control what happens in that form on subsequent user input. An input form element whose value is controlled by React in this way is called a *controlled component*.

If you recollect, in the previous chapter, we postponed the displaying of the currently active filter in the dropdown. Let's take that up now. Let's set the value of the dropdown to the value of the status filter. For this, we'll use URLSearchParams and extract its current value during render() in the IssueFilter component. The changes for this are shown in Listing 10-1.

Listing 10-1. ui/src/IssueFilter.jsx: Status Filter as a Controlled Component

```
...
import React from 'react';
import URLSearchParams from 'url-search-params';
...
  render() {
    const { location: { search } } = this.props;
    const params = new URLSearchParams(search);
    return (
      ...
        <select value={params.get('status') || ''} onChange={this.onChangeStatus}>
...
```

At this point, if you test the application, you will find that, unlike before, a refresh shows the current value of the filter rather than the default value All.

Controlled Components in Forms

The Status filter is now a simple controlled component, but this does not work in all cases. Let's now add more filters (which we will, soon). We'll need a form for the filter and we'll let the user make changes and then apply them all using an Apply button. Let's start by adding an Apply button with an apply handler.

```
...
        <select value={params.get('status') || ''} onChange={this.onChangeStatus}>
          ...
        </select>
        {' '}
        <button type="button" onClick={this.applyFilter}>Apply</button>
...
```

Now, in the onChangeStatus method, we need to remove the code that pushes the new filter to the history, because that's going to be part of the applyFilter method:

```
...
  onChangeStatus(e) {
    const status = e.target.value;
    const { history } = this.props;
    history.push({
      pathname: '/issues',
      search: status ? `?status=${status}` : '',
    });
  }
...
```

At this point in time (you may ignore the ESLint errors, because we'll soon fill in the required code for this method), if you test the application, you will find that you cannot change the value of the dropdown! This is because the value of the select is still the original value. Until that value is changed, the dropdown cannot show a new status.

The solution many other frameworks (for example, Angular) offer is *two-way binding* out of the box. The components are not just bound to the value in the state, but also vice versa. Any user input automatically changes the state variable too.

But in React, unidirectional data flow is important, and it does not support two-way binding as part of the library. In order to let the user's changes flow back into the form input component, the new value has to set in the input. To get hold of the new value, the onChange() event has to be trapped, which will have the event as an argument, and as part of the event, we can get the new value that the user has selected.

This also means that rather than the URL Parameters, we need a store for the input's value, which can be changed to reflect the new value in the dropdown. The state is the ideal place to store this value. When the user changes the value, the state variable can be updated with the new value using setState() within the onChange() event handler so that it is reflected back as the value for the input.

Let's first create this state variable and, in the constructor, initialize it to the URL value.

```
...
  constructor({ location: { search } }) {
    super();
    const params = new URLSearchParams(search);
    this.state = {
      status: params.get('status') || ",
    };

    this.onChangeStatus = this.onChangeStatus.bind(this);
  }
...
```

And then, let's use this state variable as the value of the dropdown input during render().

```
...
  render() {
    const { status } = this.state;
    ...
        <select value={status} onChange={this.onChangeStatus}>
...
```

As part of handling the onChange, we can set the state variable to the new value, which is supplied as part of the event argument to the handler, as event.target.value.

```
...
  onChangeStatus(e) {
    this.setState({ status: e.target.value });
  }
...
```

Now, you will find that you are able to change the value of the dropdown. What's more, the value is always available as part of the state, so to access the current value, all we need to do is access this.state. status. Let's do that in applyFilter and use the history to push the new status filter (which we removed from the dropdown's onChange handler), and then bind this new method to this in the constructor.

```
...
  constructor({ location: { search } }) {
    ...
    this.onChangeStatus = this.onChangeStatus.bind(this);
    this.applyFilter = this.applyFilter.bind(this);
  }
...
```

```
applyFilter() {
  const { status } = this.state;
  const { history } = this.props;
  history.push({
    pathname: '/issues',
    search: status ? `?status=${status}` : ",
  });
}
...
```

At this point, you will find that the Apply button works by changing the URL and thus getting a new filter to be applied. But there is still one minor issue. When a filter is applied and the filter is changed via a Link, for example by clicking on Issue List in the navigation bar, the new filter is not reflected. This is because when the link is clicked, only the props for the component are changed. The component is not constructed again and the state is not modified.

To make the new filter reflect when the link is clicked, we need to hook into one of the lifecycle methods that tells us that a property has changed and show the filter again. We'll use the same method as we've used before to look for changes to properties: componentDidUpdate. And, showing the filter involves just setting the new value in the state, just as in the constructor, based on the search parameters.

```
...
constructor() {
  ...
}

componentDidUpdate(prevProps) {
  const { location: { search: prevSearch } } = prevProps;
  const { location: { search } } = this.props;
  if (prevSearch !== search) {
    this.showOriginalFilter();
  }
}

onChangeStatus(e) {
  ...
}

showOriginalFilter() {
  const { location: { search } } = this.props;
  const params = new URLSearchParams(search);
  this.setState({
    status: params.get('status') || ",
  });
}
...
```

Finally, let's also indicate a difference between the state where the user has selected a new filter, but is yet to apply the new filter. At the same time, let's give the user an option to reset the filter so that the user can see the original filter that the displayed list is using. We can do this by adding a Reset button that is enabled when there are any changes, and on clicking the Reset button, the original filter is shown. We'll need to introduce a state variable called changed for this purpose and we'll disable the button based on this variable.

```
...
  render() {
    const { status, changed } = this.state;
    return (
      ...
        <button type="button" onClick={this.applyFilter}>Apply</button>
        {' '}
        <button
          type="button"
          onClick={this.showOriginalFilter}
          disabled={!changed}
        >
          Reset
        </button>
...
```

The state variable will need to be set to true within onChange, and to false in the constructor and when the original filter is shown again via a reset. Further, since the method showOriginalFilter is now being called from an event, we'll have to bind it to this.

```
...
  constructor({ location: { search } }) {
    ...
    this.state = {
      status: params.get('status') || ",
      changed: false,
    };
    ...
    this.showOriginalFilter = this.showOriginalFilter.bind(this);
  }
...

  onChangeStatus(e) {
    this.setState({ status: e.target.value, changed: true });
  }
...

  showOriginalFilter() {
    ...
    this.setState({
      status: params.get('status') || ",
      changed: false,
    });
  }
```

All of these changes are shown in Listing 10-2.

Listing 10-2. ui/src/IssueFilter.jsx: Changes for Using Controlled Components in Forms

```
...

  constructor({ location: { search } }) {
    super();
    const params = new URLSearchParams(search);
    this.state = {
      status: params.get('status') || ",
      changed: false,
    };

    this.onChangeStatus = this.onChangeStatus.bind(this);
    this.applyFilter = this.applyFilter.bind(this);
    this.showOriginalFilter = this.showOriginalFilter.bind(this);
  }
...

  componentDidUpdate(prevProps) {
    const { location: { search: prevSearch } } = prevProps;
    const { location: { search } } = this.props;
    if (prevSearch !== search) {
      this.showOriginalFilter();
    }
  }

  onChangeStatus(e) {
    const status = e.target.value;
    const { history } = this.props;
    history.push({
      pathname: '/issues',
      search: status ? `?status=${status}` : ",
    });
    this.setState({ status: e.target.value, changed: true });
  }

  showOriginalFilter() {
    const { location: { search } } = this.props;
    const params = new URLSearchParams(search);
    this.setState({
      status: params.get('status') || ",
      changed: false,
    });
  }

  applyFilter() {
    const { status } = this.state;
    const { history } = this.props;
    history.push({
      pathname: '/issues',
```

```
      search: status ? `?status=${status}` : ",
  });
}

render() {
  const { location: { search } } = this.props;
  const params = new URLSearchParams(search);
  const { status, changed } = this.state;
  return (
      ...
      <select value={params.get('status') || "} onChange={this.onChangeStatus}>
      <select value={status} onChange={this.onChangeStatus}>
        ...
      </select>
      {' '}
      <button type="button" onClick={this.applyFilter}>Apply</button>
      {' '}
      <button
        type="button"
        onClick={this.showOriginalFilter}
        disabled={!changed}
      >
        Reset
      </button>
    </div>
  );
...
```

■ **Note** Although no effort has been spared to ensure that all code listings are accurate, there may be typos or even corrections that did not make it into the book before it went to press. So, always rely on the GitHub repository (`https://github.com/vasansr/pro-mern-stack-2`) as the tested and up-to-date source for all code listings, especially if something does not work as expected.

With this set of changes, when you test the application, you will find that the filter is applied only on clicking the Apply button (as opposed to selecting a new value in the dropdown). Further, refreshing the browser will retain the filter that is being shown, if any, and the Reset button gets enabled when any changes to the filter are made. You can revert to the original filter by clicking the Reset button. A screenshot of the new changed filter form is shown in Figure 10-1.

Figure 10-1. *The new filter form*

More Filters

Now that we have a form for the filter, we are in a position to add more ways to filter the list of issues. A useful filter in the real application would be one on the Assignee field. But this is not so interesting from the point of view of learning about forms, as it is a text field and quite straightforward—we'd have to add a text input, and in its onChange, we'd have to update a state variable and use that in the filter.

A more interesting field to filter on would be a non-text field, which is not so straightforward. So, let's add a filter on the Effort field, as that is a number. We'll need two fields for this, a minimum and a maximum value to filter on, both of which are optional. To start, let's change the API to implement this filter and test it using the Playground.

Let's first change the schema to add two more arguments to the issueList API, both integers, called effortMin and effortMax. The changes to schema.graphql are shown in Listing 10-3.

Listing 10-3. api/schema.graphql: Changes for More Filter Options

```
type Query {
  about: String!
  issueList(status: StatusType): [Issue!]!
  issueList(
    status: StatusType
    effortMin: Int
    effortMax: Int
  ): [Issue!]!
  issue(id: Int!): Issue!
}
```

Handling the new values is not as simple as that for handling the status, since we have to check for greater than and less than rather than a equality comparison. The effort property of the MongoDB filter has to be created only if either of the options are present, and then the $gte and $lte options have to be set, if not defined. The changes to issue.js are shown in Listing 10-4.

Listing 10-4. api/issue.js: Changes for Filter on Effort

```
async function list(_, { status, effortMin, effortMax }) {
  ...
  if (status) filter.status = status;

  if (effortMin !== undefined || effortMax !== undefined) {
    filter.effort = {};
    if (effortMin !== undefined) filter.effort.$gte = effortMin;
    if (effortMax !== undefined) filter.effort.$lte = effortMax;
  }
  ...
}
```

To test the new filter in the issueList API, you can use the Playground with a named query as follows:

```
query issueList(
  $status: StatusType
  $effortMin: Int
  $effortMax: Int
) {
  issueList(
    status: $status
    effortMin: $effortMin
    effortMax: $effortMax
  ) {
    id
    title
    status
    owner
    effort
  }
}
```

You can give various values for effortMin and effortMax in the Query Variables section at the bottom to test it.

EXERCISE: MORE FILTERS

1. Add a few issues using the Add form in the Issue Tracker application. Now, if you run a query in the Playground with effortMin as 0, you will find that the added documents are not returned. This is true for any value of effortMin. Why?

2. How would you modify the filter if you wanted all documents with an undefined effort to be returned regardless of the query? Hint: Look up the MongoDB $or query operator at https://docs.mongodb.com/manual/reference/operator/query/or.

Answers are available at the end of the chapter.

Typed Input

In this section, we will change the UI to add two inputs for the effort filter. Since these two inputs need to accept only numbers, we'll add a filter to the user's keystrokes so that only numbers are accepted.

But before that, let's modify IssueList so that the new filter values are used while loading data. The changes involve getting the two extra filter parameters from the URL's search parameters and using them in a modified GraphQL query to fetch the list of issues. Since the values from the URL are strings, these have to be converted to integer values using parseInt(). The changes for this are shown in Listing 10-5.

Listing 10-5. ui/src/IssueList.jsx: Using Effort Filters in Issue List

```
...
  async loadData() {
    ...
    if (params.get('status')) vars.status = params.get('status');

    const effortMin = parseInt(params.get('effortMin'), 10);
    if (!Number.isNaN(effortMin)) vars.effortMin = effortMin;
    const effortMax = parseInt(params.get('effortMax'), 10);
    if (!Number.isNaN(effortMax)) vars.effortMax = effortMax;

    const query = `query issueList($status: StatusType) {
    const query = `query issueList(
      $status: StatusType
      $effortMin: Int
      $effortMax: Int
    ) {
      issueList (status: $status) {
      issueList(
        status: $status
        effortMin: $effortMin
        effortMax: $effortMax
      ) {
        ...
      }
    }`;
...
```

At this point in time, you'll be able to test the effect of these changes by typing the filter parameters in the URL. The next step is to add two state variables for the inputs for the new filter fields in the IssueFilter component. Let's do that.

```
...
  constructor({ location: { search } }) {
    ...
    this.state = {
      status: params.get('status') || ",
      effortMin: params.get('effortMin') || ",
      effortMax: params.get('effortMax') || ",
      changed: false,
    };
```

```
    ...
  }
...
```

At the same time, let's also add these in showOriginalFilter, which is a similar change. (The changes are trivial and not highlighted here for brevity. Refer to Listing 10-6 if needed.) Note that we are using strings in the state to represent these values, which are actually numbers. The convenience it gives us is that we don't need to convert between number and strings when manipulating or reading from the URL parameters.

Now, let's add input fields for these values in the Filter form. We'll just add two <input> fields with type text after the dropdown for status in the IssueFilter component. We'll use their values from the corresponding variables in the state. We'll also set the onChange handler for these two onChange methods.

```
...
  render() {
    const { status, changed } = this.state;
    const { effortMin, effortMax } = this.state;
    return (
      ...
        <select value={status} onChange={this.onChangeStatus}>
          ...
        </select>
        {' '}
        Effort between:
        {' '}
        <input
          size={5}
          value={effortMin}
          onChange={this.onChangeEffortMin}
        />
        {' - '}
        <input
          size={5}
          value={effortMax}
          onChange={this.onChangeEffortMax}
        />
        ...
...
```

Until this point, the changes were quite similar to what we did for the status dropdown. But this being a numeric input, we'll have to validate that the value is indeed a number. Instead, let's prevent the user from typing in non-numeric characters. Normally, we'd have set the state variable to event.target.value in the onChange handler. Instead, we'll test to see if the resulting text can be converted to a number, and if so, we'll discard the change rather than set the state variable. Here is the onChange handler for the effortMin field, which achieves this by using a regex to match the input to contain only digit characters (\d).

```
...
  onChangeEffortMin(e) {
    const effortString = e.target.value;
    if (effortString.match(/^\d*$/)) {
      this.setState({ effortMin: e.target.value, changed: true });
    }
  }
}
...
```

Let's add a similar handler for onChangeEffortMax and bind these methods to this in the constructor. (Refer to Listing 10-6 for this simple change.)

Finally, we can use the state variables in applyFilter to set the new location in the history. Since there are more variables, let's use URLSearchParams to construct the query string rather than use plain string templates.

```
...
  applyFilter() {
    const { status, effortMin, effortMax } = this.state;
    const { history } = this.props;
    history.push({
      pathname: '/issues',
      search: status ? `?status=${status}` : ",
    });

    const params = new URLSearchParams();
    if (status) params.set('status', status);
    if (effortMin) params.set('effortMin', effortMin);
    if (effortMax) params.set('effortMax', effortMax);

    const search = params.toString() ? `?${params.toString()}` : ";
    history.push({ pathname: '/issues', search });
  }
...
```

The complete set of changes in the IssueFilter component to add these two filter fields is shown in Listing 10-6.

Listing 10-6. ui/src/IssueFilter.jsx: Changes for Adding Effort Filters

```
...
  constructor({ location: { search } }) {
    ...
      status: params.get('status') || ",
      effortMin: params.get('effortMin') || ",
      effortMax: params.get('effortMax') || ",
    ...
    this.onChangeStatus = this.onChangeStatus.bind(this);
    this.onChangeEffortMin = this.onChangeEffortMin.bind(this);
    this.onChangeEffortMax = this.onChangeEffortMax.bind(this);
  }
...

  onChangeStatus(e) {
    ...
  }

  onChangeEffortMin(e) {
    const effortString = e.target.value;
    if (effortString.match(/^\d*$/)) {
      this.setState({ effortMin: e.target.value, changed: true });
    }
  }
```

```
  onChangeEffortMax(e) {
    const effortString = e.target.value;
    if (effortString.match(/^\d*$/)) {
      this.setState({ effortMax: e.target.value, changed: true });
    }
  }
...

  showOriginalFilter() {
    ...
      status: params.get('status') || ",
      effortMin: params.get('effortMin') || ",
      effortMax: params.get('effortMax') || ",
    ...
  }

  applyFilter() {
    const { status, effortMin, effortMax } = this.state;
    const { history } = this.props;
    history.push({
      pathname: '/issues',
      search: status ? `?status=${status}` : ",
    });

    const params = new URLSearchParams();
    if (status) params.set('status', status);
    if (effortMin) params.set('effortMin', effortMin);
    if (effortMax) params.set('effortMax', effortMax);

    const search = params.toString() ? `?${params.toString()}` : ";
    history.push({ pathname: '/issues', search });
  }

  render() {
    const { status, changed } = this.state;
    const { effortMin, effortMax } = this.state;
    ...
        </select>
        {' '}
        Effort between:
        {' '}
        <input
          size={5}
          value={effortMin}
          onChange={this.onChangeEffortMin}
        />
        {' - '}
        <input
          size={5}
```

```
        value={effortMax}
        onChange={this.onChangeEffortMax}
    />
    ...
}
...
```

With this set of changes, you'll be able to test the application with various combinations of filters. The filter values should also be seen in the URL bar. To clear the filter, you can click on the Issue List link in the navigation bar. A screenshot of the new filter applied with a maximum effort of 10 points is shown in Figure 10-2.

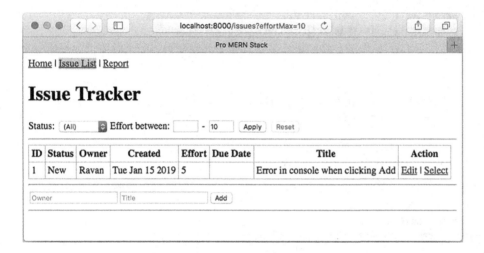

Figure 10-2. *The issue list showing effort filters*

EXERCISE: TYPED INPUTS

1. Let's say we don't convert the values of `effortMin` and `effortMax` to integers, that is, we use the string values as is in the GraphQL query variables. What do you expect to happen? Try it and confirm your answer.

2. Try using `<input type="number">` rather than the default text type. Test it on different browsers, say, Chrome, Safari, and Firefox. Type possibly valid number characters such as . (dot) and E. What do you observe? Why? Hint: Add some `console.log` statements within the change handler and observe the logs.

Answers are available at the end of the chapter.

Edit Form

We had a placeholder for the Edit page all this while. Now that you've learned about components, especially controlled components, let's try to create a complete form for the Edit page in `IssueEdit.jsx`, displaying all the fields of an issue in input fields that can be changed by the user. We'll also have a Submit button, but we will not handle the submission of the form yet. We'll leave that for the following sections, after we have implemented an API to update an existing issue.

Let's start by defining the state for this component. At the minimum, we'll need to store the current value of each input, which correspond to the fields of the issue being edited. In the constructor, let's define an empty object for the issue. (For the sake of brevity, I am omitting obvious new code such as imports. Refer to the listings that follow for the complete set of changes. The code snippets that follow are meant to be for explanation.)

```
...
export default class IssueEdit extends React.Component {
  constructor() {
    super();
    this.state = {
      issue: {},
    };
...
```

We will replace the empty issue with the issue fetched from the server. Let's do that in a method called loadData() using the issue API to load the data asynchronously. The GraphQL query for this is straightforward; it takes in the ID as an argument (from the props) and specifies that all possible fields need to be returned.

```
...
  async loadData() {
    const query = `query issue($id: Int!) {
      issue(id: $id) {
        id title status owner
        effort created due description
      }
    }`;

    const { match: { params: { id } } } = this.props;
    const data = await graphQLFetch(query, { id });
}
...
```

But since all input fields' contents are strings, the state fields also need to be strings. We can't use the result of the API call directly. So, after loading data, we'll have to convert the natural data types of the fields of issue into strings. Further, we'll need to add a null check for all the optional fields and use the empty string as the value instead. If the API failed (indicated by data being null), we'll just use an empty issue in the state.

```
...
    if (data) {
      const { issue } = data;
      issue.due = issue.due ? issue.due.toDateString() : ";
      issue.effort = issue.effort != null ? issue.effort.toString() : ";
      issue.owner = issue.owner != null ? issue.owner : ";
      issue.description = issue.description != null ? issue.description : ";
      this.setState({ issue });
    } else {
      this.setState({ issue: {} });
    }
  }
...
```

Now, we can code the `render()` method. In this method, each of the fields' values could be set to the corresponding value in the state. For example, the owner input field would look like this:

```
...
  const { issue: { owner } } = this.state;
  <input value={owner} />
...
```

But during the period where the component has been constructed and the `loadData()` has returned data, we have the issue object as an empty one. The same is true if an issue with the given ID doesn't exist. To take care of these two cases, let's check for the presence of an `id` field in the issue object and avoid rendering the form. If the `id` field in props is invalid, we'll show an error message that there exists no issue with that ID. If not, we'll assume the page is in the middle of completing `loadData()` and return null in the `render()` method.

```
...
    const { issue: { id } } = this.state;
    const { match: { params: { id: propsId } } } = this.props;
    if (id == null) {
      if (propsId != null) {
        return <h3>{`Issue with ID ${propsId} not found.`}</h3>;
      }
      return null;
    }
...
```

If these two conditions did not match, we can render the form. Note that we used the double-equals rather than the triple-equals, which matches anything that *seems* like null, which includes undefined. We'll use a table with two columns to show a label for the field name in the first column, and the input (or a read-only label for ID and created date) as the value. The form will need a submit button in addition to all the fields, and a submit handler, which we'll name `handleSubmit()`.

Also, to test that the form works correctly when a new issue object is loaded without going to another page or changing the URL manually, let's add links for the previous and next issue objects. Since this is just for a test, we'll not disable the links when the next or previous ID is not a valid one; we'll let the page show an error instead. These links can be added toward the end of the form.

```
...
    return (
      <form onSubmit={this.handleSubmit}>
        <h3>{`Editing issue: ${id}`}</h3>
        <table>
          <tbody>
            <tr>
              <td>Created:</td>
              <td>{created.toDateString()}</td>
            </tr>

            ...

            <tr>
              <td />
              <td><button type="submit">Submit</button></td>
            </tr>
```

```
      </tbody>
    </table>
    <Link to={`/edit/${id - 1}`}>Prev</Link>
    {' | '}
    <Link to={`/edit/${id + 1}`}>Next</Link>
  </form>
);
```
...

As with the filter form, we also need an onChange event handler for each of the inputs. But this can get tedious and repetitive due to the number of fields in this form. Instead, let's take advantage of the fact that the event's target has a property called name, which will reflect the name of the input field in the form. Let's use the field's name in the issue object as the name of the input. Then, let's use a common onChange event handler for all the inputs. For example, the owner input row would now look like this:

...
```
        <tr>
          <td>Owner:</td>
          <td>
            <input
              name="owner"
              value={owner}
              onChange={this.onChange}
            />
          </td>
        </tr>
```
...

For the rest of the input fields, refer to Listing 10-7.

And, in the onChange() method, we'll get the name of the field from the event's target, use that to set the value of the property in the issue object (a copy is needed from the current state), and set the new state. Note that it is not advisable to use this.state directly when arriving at the new state, as it may not accurately reflect the real current value when other setState calls have been made but are yet to take effect. The recommended way is to supply a callback to the setState method that takes in the previous state and returns a new state. Here's the onChange() event handler with these issues taken into account.

...
```
  onChange(event) {
    const { name, value } = event.target;
    this.setState(prevState => ({
      issue: { ...prevState.issue, [name]: value },
    }));
  }
```
...

■ **Note** We used the ES2015+ spread operator ... to *spread* the values of the issue object as if they were all mentioned individually, like { id: prevState.issue.id, title: prevState.issue.title }, etc. This is a simpler way of copying an object compared to Object.assign(). Then the property with name as the *value* of the variable name is used to override the properties that were expanded.

Finally, we need the lifecycle methods componentDidMount() and componentDidUpdate() to load the data. Also, in the handleSubmit() method, let's just display the contents of the issue on the console for now. The complete listing of the IssueEdit file, including these additional methods and cosmetic properties to some of the input fields, is shown in Listing 10-7. The removed code has not been shown for the sake of brevity.

Listing 10-7. ui/src/IssueEdit.jsx: New Contents for Showing an Edit Form

```
import React from 'react';
import { Link } from 'react-router-dom';

import graphQLFetch from './graphQLFetch.js';

export default class IssueEdit extends React.Component {
  constructor() {
    super();
    this.state = {
      issue: {},
    };
    this.onChange = this.onChange.bind(this);
    this.handleSubmit = this.handleSubmit.bind(this);
  }

  componentDidMount() {
    this.loadData();
  }

  componentDidUpdate(prevProps) {
    const { match: { params: { id: prevId } } } = prevProps;
    const { match: { params: { id } } } = this.props;
    if (id !== prevId) {
      this.loadData();
    }
  }

  onChange(event) {
    const { name, value } = event.target;
    this.setState(prevState => ({
      issue: { ...prevState.issue, [name]: value },
    }));
  }

  handleSubmit(e) {
    e.preventDefault();
    const { issue } = this.state;
    console.log(issue); // eslint-disable-line no-console
  }

  async loadData() {
    const query = `query issue($id: Int!) {
      issue(id: $id) {
        id title status owner
```

```
      effort created due description
    }
  }`;

  const { match: { params: { id } } } = this.props;
  const data = await graphQLFetch(query, { id });
  if (data) {
    const { issue } = data;
    issue.due = issue.due ? issue.due.toDateString() : ";
    issue.effort = issue.effort != null ? issue.effort.toString() : ";
    issue.owner = issue.owner != null ? issue.owner : ";
    issue.description = issue.description != null ? issue.description : ";
    this.setState({ issue });
  } else {
    this.setState({ issue: {} });
  }
}

render() {
  const { issue: { id } } = this.state;
  const { match: { params: { id: propsId } } } = this.props;
  if (id == null) {
    if (propsId != null) {
      return <h3>{`Issue with ID ${propsId} not found.`}</h3>;
    }
    return null;
  }

  const { issue: { title, status } } = this.state;
  const { issue: { owner, effort, description } } = this.state;
  const { issue: { created, due } } = this.state;

  return (
    <form onSubmit={this.handleSubmit}>
      <h3>{`Editing issue: ${id}`}</h3>
      <table>
        <tbody>
          <tr>
            <td>Created:</td>
            <td>{created.toDateString()}</td>
          </tr>
          <tr>
            <td>Status:</td>
            <td>
              <select name="status" value={status} onChange={this.onChange}>
                <option value="New">New</option>
                <option value="Assigned">Assigned</option>
                <option value="Fixed">Fixed</option>
                <option value="Closed">Closed</option>
              </select>
            </td>
```

```
      </tr>
      <tr>
        <td>Owner:</td>
        <td>
          <input
            name="owner"
            value={owner}
            onChange={this.onChange}
          />
        </td>
      </tr>
      <tr>
        <td>Effort:</td>
        <td>
          <input
            name="effort"
            value={effort}
            onChange={this.onChange}
          />
        </td>
      </tr>
      <tr>
        <td>Due:</td>
        <td>
          <input
            name="due"
            value={due}
            onChange={this.onChange}
          />
        </td>
      </tr>
      <tr>
        <td>Title:</td>
        <td>
          <input
            size={50}
            name="title"
            value={title}
            onChange={this.onChange}
          />
        </td>
      </tr>
      <tr>
        <td>Description:</td>
        <td>
          <textarea
            rows={8}
            cols={50}
            name="description"
            value={description}
            onChange={this.onChange}
          />
```

```
          </td>
        </tr>
        <tr>
          <td />
          <td><button type="submit">Submit</button></td>
        </tr>
      </tbody>
    </table>
    <Link to={`/edit/${id - 1}`}>Prev</Link>
    {' | '}
    <Link to={`/edit/${id + 1}`}>Next</Link>
  </form>
);
  }
}
```

The Edit page can now be tested by clicking on the Edit link for any of the issues in the Issue List page. You can see that the field values reflect what is saved in the database. Clicking on Submit will display the edited values on the console, but these will be strings rather than natural data types. A screenshot of the Edit page is shown in Figure 10-3.

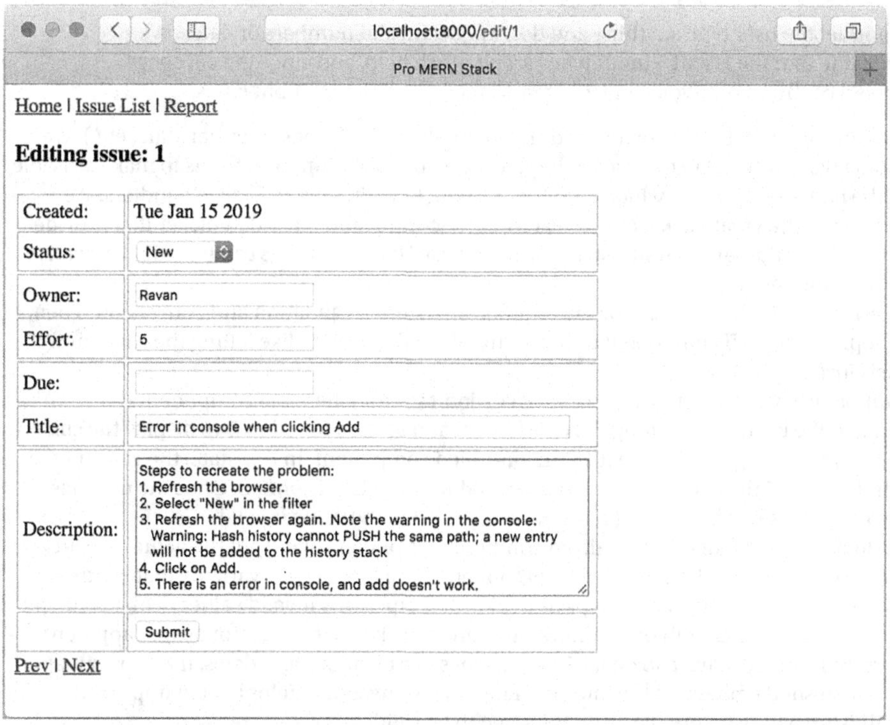

Figure 10-3. *The Edit page*

EXERCISE: EDIT PAGE

---

1. What happens if we don't convert a null value in a string field to an empty string? Try this yourself by removing the line that checks for null and assigns an empty string for the description field. Do this on an issue that has the description field missing rather than a value, even an empty string.

Answers are available at the end of the chapter.

Specialized Input Components

Although we saved some repetitive code by combining all of the onChange() handlers into one handler, it should be immediately obvious that the approach has some scope for improvement.

- When dealing with non-string data types, when it is required that the value is validated (for example, check if the completion date is not before today), it has to be converted to the natural data type. The same conversion is needed before sending the modified issue to the server.

- If there is more than one input of the same type (number or date), the conversions for each input need to be repeated.

- The inputs let the user type anything and don't reject invalid numbers or dates. We already found that the HTML5 input types aren't much help, and since the onChange handler is a common one, you can't add masks there for different input types.

Ideally, we want the form's state to store the fields in their natural data types (number, date, etc.). We also want all of the data type conversion routines to be shared. A good solution to all this is to make reusable UI components for the non-string inputs, which emit natural data types in their onChange handlers. We could very well use some of the great packages like react-numeric-input and react-datepicker that provide these UI components. But for the sake of understanding how these UI components can be built, let's create our own, minimalistic components.

We'll first create a simple UI component for the number with simple validation and conversion. Then, we'll create a more sophisticated UI component for the date, which does more, like letting the user know if and when the value is invalid.

In all these components, we'll take the approach of a disjoint state—where the component is a controlled one as long as the user is not editing the component and its only function is to display the current value. When the user starts editing, we'll make it an uncontrolled component. In this state, the value in the parent will not be updated, and the two values (current and edited) will be disjointed. Once the user has finished editing, the two values will be brought back in sync, provided the value is valid.

Another way to look at this is that the specialized component is uncontrolled, but the actual <input> element is controlled. That is, within the specialized component, we'll have a state variable that controls the value in the input element. This approach helps us deal with temporarily invalid values, which in many cases are needed when transitioning from one valid value to another. The need may not be that apparent with simple numbers. But when you have to deal with data types like decimals and dates, there are situations where the user has not finished typing and the intermediate value is invalid. It helps a lot in improving usability if the user finishes typing before the input is judged to be valid or not.

Number Input

The first specialized input component we'll create is for number inputs. We'll use this for the effort field in the Edit page in place of a plain <input> element. Let's call this component NumInput and use a new file under ui/src/ directory called NumInput.jsx for this.

Let's first define the conversion functions that take in a string and convert to a number and vice versa. As part of these, we'll use an empty string to correspond to the null value for the number.

```
...
function format(num) {
  return num != null ? num.toString() : ";
}

function unformat(str) {
  const val = parseInt(str, 10);
  return Number.isNaN(val) ? null : val;
}
...
```

In the unformat() function, we returned null if the string doesn't represent a number. Since we'll check for valid characters in the user's keystrokes, a non-numeric entry can happen only if the string is empty, so this is good enough.

Next, in the constructor of the component, let's set a state variable (which we will use as the value for the <input> element) after converting the value passed in as props to a string.

```
...
  constructor(props) {
    ...
    this.state = { value: format(props.value) };
  }
...
```

In the onChange() of the input, we'll check for the input containing valid digits and set the state if it is, as we did in the filter form.

```
...
  onChange(e) {
    if (e.target.value.match(/^\d*$/)) {
      this.setState({ value: e.target.value });
    }
  }
...
```

For the changes to take effect in the parent, we'll have to call the parent's onChange(). We won't do this as part of the onChange() method of the component; instead we'll call the parent's onChange() when the input loses focus. The input element's onBlur() property can be used to handle losing of focus. While calling the parent's onChange(), we'll pass the value in the natural data type as a second argument. This is so that we can let the parent handle the original event (the first argument) of onChange() if required.

```
...
  onBlur(e) {
    const { onChange } = this.props;
    const { value } = this.state;
    onChange(e, unformat(value));
  }
...
```

In the render() method, we'll just render an <input> element with the value set to the state's variable and the onChange() and onBlur() handlers of the component class. These methods have to be bound to this in the constructor since these are event handlers. Further, we'll copy over all other properties that the parent may want to supply as part of props for the actual <input> element (for example, the size property). Let's use the spread operator to do this seamlessly, using the syntax {...this.props}.

The render() function and the binding of onBlur() and onChange() are shown in the complete listing of this new file in Listing 10-8.

Listing 10-8. ui/src/NumInput.jsx: New Specialized Input Component for Numbers

```
import React from 'react';

function format(num) {
  return num != null ? num.toString() : ";
}

function unformat(str) {
  const val = parseInt(str, 10);
  return Number.isNaN(val) ? null : val;
}

export default class NumInput extends React.Component {
  constructor(props) {
    super(props);
    this.state = { value: format(props.value) };
    this.onBlur = this.onBlur.bind(this);
    this.onChange = this.onChange.bind(this);
  }

  onChange(e) {
    if (e.target.value.match(/^\d*$/)) {
      this.setState({ value: e.target.value });
    }
  }

  onBlur(e) {
    const { onChange } = this.props;
    const { value } = this.state;
    onChange(e, unformat(value));
  }

  render() {
    const { value } = this.state;
    return (
```

```
    <input
      type="text"
      {...this.props}
      value={value}
      onBlur={this.onBlur}
      onChange={this.onChange}
    />
  );
  }
}
```

Now, let's use this new UI component in the Issue Edit page. The first change is replacing <input> with <NumInput> in the IssueEdit component.

```
...
            <td>Effort:</td>
            <td>
              <input NumInput
...
```

Then, let's change the onChange() handler to include the value in the natural data type that the component *may* send us as the second argument. But we also have regular HTML components, which will not supply the second argument as the natural value. So, a check to see if this value is supplied is needed. If not supplied, we can use the string value from the event itself.

```
...
  onChange(event, naturalValue) {
    const { name, value: textValue } = event.target;
    const value = naturalValue === undefined ? textValue : naturalValue;
    ...
  }
...
```

After these changes, if you test the application, it will seem to work fine as long as you navigate from the issue list to any of the Edit pages. But if you use the Next/Prev buttons, you'll find that the value in the effort field doesn't change, instead, it retains the original issue's effort value. It would remain blank if the first issue that was displayed had an empty effort.

This is due to the fact that we only copy the value from props to the NumInput component's state when constructing the component. After that, when using the Next/Prev buttons, the props for the component change, but the state remains the old one since the old component is reused. We have the following options to solve the issue:

- We could hook into the lifecycle method componentWillReceiveProps() (deprecated) or getDerivedStateFromProps() to reinitialize the state. But these methods can also be called when there is no change in the props, but the parent is being re-rendered for some reason. We can check for change in the props value, but what about when the Next/Prev issue has the same effort value?

- We could use the lifecycle method componentDidUpdate() to replace the state. But as the ESLint errors suggest when you try to do this, it is not a good idea to set the state synchronously in this method.

- We could trap the onFocus() event to set the state for editing along. Otherwise, we can display the props value converted to a string. But even this will not work in corner cases when the issue being shown is replaced with another while the input has focus. (It can happen if the issue being displayed is changed as part of a timer like in a slideshow.)

- We could redraw the page when a new issue is loaded. This can be done, for instance, by introducing a "loading" state while loadData() is in progress and rendering a message or null instead of the form. This will force a reconstruction of the component when the issue object changes. But this will cause a flicker when a new issue is loaded because the entire form disappears temporarily.

Any of these options can work with some assumptions or some workarounds. But let's use the recommended way of dealing with the situation. What is essentially needed is a way to *construct* the component again with a new initial property. The best way to do this is to assign a key property to the component that changes when a new issue is loaded. React uses this property to indicate that a component object cannot be reused if the key is different; a new one has to be constructed.

Since the issue's ID is unique, we can use it as the key to the input component as well. So let's do that. Further, we can now remove the replacement of null to an empty string for the effort field, as nulls will be seamlessly handled by the NumInput component. With these changes, the final modifications to the IssueEdit component are shown in Listing 10-9.

Listing 10-9. ui/src/IssueEdit.jsx: Changes for Using NumInput

```
...
import graphQLFetch from './graphQLFetch.js';
import NumInput from './NumInput.jsx';
...

  onChange(event, naturalValue) {
    const { name, value: textValue } = event.target;
    const value = naturalValue === undefined ? textValue : naturalValue;
    ...
  }
...

  async loadData() {
    ...
    if (data) {
      issue.due = issue.due ? issue.due.toDateString() : '';
      issue.effort = issue.effort != null ? issue.effort.toString() : '';
      ...
    }
  }
...

  render() {
    ...
              <td>Effort:</td>
              <td>
                <input NumInput
                  name="effort"
                  value={effort}
                  onChange={this.onChange}
```

```
                key={id}
            />
    ...
  }
  ...
```

Now, if you test the application, you should be able to edit the effort field and see that the value changes according to the issue object when you click on Next/Prev. Also, when you click Submit, you should be able to see that the value of effort in the issue object is indeed a number (there will be no quotes around the value).

Date Input

In the Number input specialized component, we did not have to worry about the validity of user input, because we prevented any invalid values from being typed by the user. We cannot do this with the Date input because the validity cannot be determined purely by the characters that are allowed in a date. For example, although all digits are allowed, something like 999999 is not a valid date.

Essentially, for a date, the validity can be determined only when the user has finished typing the date. Losing focus from the input element can be used as the signal that the editing has completed. So, in the onBlur() handler, we'll have to check for validity of the date typed by the user, then inform the parent on the change in validity (if any) of the new value, and the new value, if it is valid. To inform the parent of the new validity, let's use a new optional callback named onValidityChange(). Let's also save the focused state and the validity in new state variables called focused and valid. Here's the new onBlur() method, including all these:

```
...
  onBlur(e) {
    const { value, valid: oldValid } = this.state;
    const { onValidityChange, onChange } = this.props;
    const dateValue = unformat(value);
    const valid = value === " " || dateValue != null;
    if (valid !== oldValid && onValidityChange) {
      onValidityChange(e, valid);
    }
    this.setState({ focused: false, valid });
    if (valid) onChange(e, dateValue);
  }
...
```

Note that we allowed an empty string to be a valid date, along with any other string that could be converted to a date object using the unformat() method, which we'll just use the Date(string) constructor for.

Let's also separate the display format and the editable format of the date. For displaying, it's convenient to show the date string as per the locale that the method toDateString() converts the date to. But while editing, let's force the user to enter an unambiguous YYYY-MM-DD format. So, rather than have a single format() function as in NumInput, we'll have two functions, one for display and the other for editing.

```
...
function displayFormat(date) {
  return (date != null) ? date.toDateString() : ";
}
```

```
function editFormat(date) {
  return (date != null) ? date.toISOString().substr(0, 10) : ";
}

function unformat(str) {
  const val = new Date(str);
  return Number.isNaN(val.getTime()) ? null : val;
}
...
```

In the onChange() method, we'll check for valid characters, which are just digits and the dash (-) character. All other characters will be disallowed. The regex we'll use for this check is /^[\d-]*$/.

In the render() method, let's display the user typed-in value as is if it is invalid, or if the user is editing it. Otherwise, let's display the display format or the editable format converted from the original value of the date.

```
...
    const displayValue = (focused || !valid) ? value
      : displayFormat(origValue);
    render() {
     <input
        ...
        value={displayValue}
      ...
    }
...
```

Let's also use a CSS class to signify invalid values, but only when the input is not in the focused state, that is, the user is not in the middle of editing it.

```
...
    const className = (!valid && !focused) ? 'invalid' : null;
...
```

The code of the DateInput component, with all these additions, the cosmetic properties for the <input> element, and the complete constructor—is shown in Listing 10-10.

Listing 10-10. ui/src/DateInput.jsx: New File for the DateInput Component

```
import React from 'react';

function displayFormat(date) {
  return (date != null) ? date.toDateString() : ";
}

function editFormat(date) {
  return (date != null) ? date.toISOString().substr(0, 10) : ";
}

function unformat(str) {
  const val = new Date(str);
  return Number.isNaN(val.getTime()) ? null : val;
}
```

```
export default class DateInput extends React.Component {
  constructor(props) {
    super(props);
    this.state = {
      value: editFormat(props.value),
      focused: false,
      valid: true,
    };
    this.onFocus = this.onFocus.bind(this);
    this.onBlur = this.onBlur.bind(this);
    this.onChange = this.onChange.bind(this);
  }

  onFocus() {
    this.setState({ focused: true });
  }

  onBlur(e) {
    const { value, valid: oldValid } = this.state;
    const { onValidityChange, onChange } = this.props;
    const dateValue = unformat(value);
    const valid = value === " || dateValue != null;
    if (valid !== oldValid && onValidityChange) {
      onValidityChange(e, valid);
    }
    this.setState({ focused: false, valid });
    if (valid) onChange(e, dateValue);
  }

  onChange(e) {
    if (e.target.value.match(/^[\d-]*$/)) {
      this.setState({ value: e.target.value });
    }
  }

  render() {
    const { valid, focused, value } = this.state;
    const { value: origValue, name } = this.props;
    const className = (!valid && !focused) ? 'invalid' : null;
    const displayValue = (focused || !valid) ? value
      : displayFormat(origValue);
    return (
      <input
        type="text"
        size={20}
        name={name}
        className={className}
        value={displayValue}
        placeholder={focused ? 'yyyy-mm-dd' : null}
        onFocus={this.onFocus}
        onBlur={this.onBlur}
```

```
      onChange={this.onChange}
    />
  );
 }
}
```

To use this new component in IssueEdit, let's change the due field to a DateInput component. Further, we'll have to add a new method for storing the validity status of each of the inputs in a state variable called invalidFields. Let's use an object that has an entry for every invalid field set to the value true. We'll just delete the property if the field is valid, so that it's convenient to check the presence of any invalid field.

```
...
  onValidityChange(event, valid) {
    const { name } = event.target;
    this.setState((prevState) => {
      const invalidFields = { ...prevState.invalidFields, [name]: !valid };
      if (valid) delete invalidFields[name];
      return { invalidFields };
    });
  }
...
```

In the constructor and in the method loadData(), we'll have to set the state variable invalidFields to an empty object to initialize it for any new issue that's being loaded.

In the render() method, we can now add a new variable to compute a message that shows the presence of any invalid fields. We'll initialize this message only if there are any invalid fields, which can be calculated by looking at the length of the invalidFields state variable. Let's also use a class to emphasize error messages, called error.

```
...
    const { invalidFields } = this.state;
    let validationMessage;
    if (Object.keys(invalidFields).length !== 0) {
      validationMessage = (
        <div className="error">
          Please correct invalid fields before submitting.
        </div>
      );
    }
...
```

We can then use this element in the form to display the message if there are any invalid inputs as part of the Edit page.

```
...
      </table>
      {validationMessage}
      <Link to={`/edit/${id - 1}`}>Prev</Link>
...
```

These changes, and some more cosmetic changes such as binding methods to `this` in the `IssueEdit` component, are shown in Listing 10-11.

Listing 10-11. ui/src/IssueEdit: Changes to Use the New DateInput Component

```
...
import NumInput from './NumInput.jsx';
import DateInput from './DateInput.jsx';
...

  constructor() {
    ...
    this.state = {
      ...
      invalidFields: {},
    };
    ...
    this.onValidityChange = this.onValidityChange.bind(this);
  }
...

  onValidityChange(event, valid) {
    const { name } = event.target;
    this.setState((prevState) => {
      const invalidFields = { ...prevState.invalidFields, [name]: !valid };
      if (valid) delete invalidFields[name];
      return { invalidFields };
    });
  }
...

  async loadData() {
    ...
    if (data) {
      ...
      issue.due = issue.due ? issue.due.toDateString() : “;
      ...
      this.setState({ issue, invalidFields: {} });
    } else {
      this.setState({ issue: {}, invalidFields: {} });
    }
  }
...

  render() {
    ...
    if (id == null) {
      ...
    }

    const { invalidFields } = this.state;
    let validationMessage;
```

297

```
  if (Object.keys(invalidFields).length !== 0) {
    validationMessage = (
      <div className="error">
        Please correct invalid fields before submitting.
      </div>
    );
  }
  ...
              <input DateInput
                name="due"
                value={due}
                onChange={this.onChange}
                onValidityChange={this.onValidityChange}
                key={id}
              />
  ...
      </table>
      {validationMessage}
      <Link to={`/edit/${id - 1}`}>Prev</Link>
  ...
  }
...
```

We need some changes in the stylesheet to show error messages in a highlighted manner (say, in red font) and to show inputs with errors in a different manner (say, a red border instead of a plain one). These changes to index.html are shown in Listing 10-12.

Listing 10-12. ui/public/index.html: Style Changes for Error Messages and Error Inputs

```
...
  <style>
    ...
    input.invalid {border-color: red;}
    div.error {color: red;}
  </style>
...
```

The style change will need a browser refresh because HMR does not handle changes to index.html. Once you do that, you can test the new Date input field. When you enter a valid value and click Submit, you'll see the actual date object being stored and displayed in the console. For all invalid values, you should see a red bordered input as well as an error message in red. For these invalid inputs, you'll see the original or any previous valid value entered by the user on clicking Submit.

Text Input

A textual input may seem unnecessary because there is no validation or conversion that needs to be done. But to let a component handle null values for input fields would be quite convenient. Otherwise, for every optional text field, we'll need to handle the null check and use an empty string while loading data.

Thus, very similar to the NumInput component, let's create a TextInput component, with some differences. The format() and unformat() will exist simply for converting to and from null values. In the onChange() method, we'll not have masks for valid user inputs: any input will be allowed. Lastly, to handle variations in the HTML element name (we could have textarea and input, both handling textual data), let's not hard-code the element tag in the component, instead let's pass it in as an optional tag property that we can default to input. To be able to do this, we will have to fall back to the React.createElement() method instead of using JSX, as the tag name is a variable.

The full source code of the TextInput component is shown in Listing 10-13.

Listing 10-13. ui/src/TextInput.jsx: New Text Input Component

```
import React from 'react';

function format(text) {
  return text != null ? text : ";
}

function unformat(text) {
  return text.trim().length === 0 ? null : text;
}

export default class TextInput extends React.Component {
  constructor(props) {
    super(props);
    this.state = { value: format(props.value) };
    this.onBlur = this.onBlur.bind(this);
    this.onChange = this.onChange.bind(this);
  }

  onChange(e) {
    this.setState({ value: e.target.value });
  }

  onBlur(e) {
    const { onChange } = this.props;
    const { value } = this.state;
    onChange(e, unformat(value));
  }

  render() {
    const { value } = this.state;
    const { tag = 'input', ...props } = this.props;
    return React.createElement(tag, {
      ...props,
      value,
      onBlur: this.onBlur,
      onChange: this.onChange,
    });
  }
}
```

In the IssueEdit component, we can replace all textual input elements to TextInput, and the description element to TextInput with the property for tag set to textarea. We'll have to use the key property to ensure that the component is reconstructed when switching from editing one issue to another. Finally, we can remove all the null to empty string conversions and load the issue as is in the state of the IssueEdit component.

The final set of changes to IssueEdit is shown in Listing 10-14.

Listing 10-14. ui/src/IssueEdit.jsx: Changes for Using TextInput Component

```
...
import DateInput from './DateInput.jsx';
import TextInput from './TextInput.jsx';
...

  async loadData() {
    ...
    if (data) {
      const { issue } = data;
      issue.owner = issue.owner != null ? issue.owner : ";
      issue.description = issue.description != null ? issue.description : ";
      this.setState({ issue, invalidFields: {} });
    } else {
      this.setState({ issue: {}, invalidFields: {} });
    }
    this.setState({ issue: data ? data.issue : {}, invalidFields: {} });
  }
...

  render() {
            ...
            <td>Owner:</td>
            <td>
              <input TextInput
                name="owner"

                ...
                key={id}
            </td>
            ...
            <td>Title:</td>
            <td>
              <input TextInput
                name="title"

                ...
                key={id}
            </td>
            ...
            <td>Description:</td>
            <td>
              <textarea TextInput
                tag="textarea"

                ...
                key={id}
            </td>
            ...
  }
...
```

Now, you can test all text inputs and see if empty strings input by the user are converted to `null` values when clicking on Submit and vice versa: null values in the database should appear as empty strings in the UI.

Update API

Now that we have the Edit page's user interface working well, let's prepare for saving the edited issue to the database. We'll, of course, need an Update API, and that's what we'll implement in this section. Updating can be done in two different ways:

- Updating one or more fields in the document: This can use the MongoDB `update` command and use the `$set` operator to set the new values of fields.

- Replacing the entire document with new values: This would be similar to creating a new issue, by supplying all the values (changed as well as unchanged) for the fields in the document. The MongoDB `replace` command can be used for replacing the document with a new one.

In the case of the Issue Tracker, the `id` and `created` fields are special, as they are initialized only when the issue is created and never modified after that. A replace approach would necessarily mean that the original object be read and merged with the new values supplied by the API's input, otherwise the `id` and `created` fields would get *new* values as in the `create` API. The same input data type `IssueInputs` can be used for the replace operation as well.

If we use the update approach, where only some fields are supplied, we'll have to maintain this list of fields that can be updated in the GraphQL schema. This data type is quite similar to the `IssueInputs` data type, except that all fields are optional. The downside is that a change in the list of input fields needs a change in `IssueInputs` and this new data type.

But there is some flexibility the update approach offers. It allows the UI to update individual fields very easily. We'll add a feature to close an issue directly from the issue list in the following sections, and you can see how this approach supports both use cases well: replacing an issue from the Edit page as well as changing a single field from the Issue List page.

In other situations, supporting a replace operation may work better, but the presence of the `created` field makes supporting only the update operation more appealing. A replace in this case can be seen as an update of *all* modifiable fields.

So let's implement an API that updates an issue, just like the MongoDB `update()` command, using the `$set` operator. Let's first change the schema to reflect this new API: we first need a new input data type with all possible fields that can be changed, and all of them optional. Let's call this `IssueUpdateInputs`. Then, we need a new mutation entry point, let's call that `updateIssue`. This will return the new modified issue. The changes to `schema.graphql` are shown in Listing 10-15.

Listing 10-15. api/schema.graphql: Update API and Its Input Data Type

```
...
type IssueInputs {
  ...
}


"""Inputs for issueUpdate: all are optional. Whichever is specified will
be set to the given value, undefined fields will remain unmodified."""
input IssueUpdateInputs {
  title: String
  status: StatusType
  owner: String
```

```
  effort: Int
  due: GraphQLDate
  description: String
}
...

type Mutation {
  ...
  issueUpdate(id: Int!, changes: IssueUpdateInputs!): Issue!
}
```

Then, let's connect the API to its resolver in api_handler.js. This change is shown in Listing 10-16.

Listing 10-16. api/api_handler.js: New API Endpoint and Resolver for updateIssue

```
...
const resolvers = {
  ...
  Mutation: {
    ...
    issueUpdate: issue.update,
  },
...
```

Now, we can implement the actual resolver in issue.js, in a function called update(). In this function, we'll need to validate the issue based on the new inputs. The easiest way is to fetch the full object from the database, merge the changes supplied to the API, and run the same validation that we used for adding an issue. Let's also run the validation only if the fields that affect the validity are changing: Title, Status, or Owner. Once the validation succeeds, we can proceed to use the updateOne() MongoDB function with the $set operation to save the changes.

Finally, we'll need to export the update() function along with the other exported functions in module.exports. All these changes are shown in Listing 10-17.

Listing 10-17. api/issue.js: Resolver for the Update API

```
async function update(_, { id, changes }) {
  const db = getDb();
  if (changes.title || changes.status || changes.owner) {
    const issue = await db.collection('issues').findOne({ id });
    Object.assign(issue, changes);
    validate(issue);
  }
  await db.collection('issues').updateOne({ id }, { $set: changes });
  const savedIssue = await db.collection('issues').findOne({ id });
  return savedIssue;
}

module.exports = { list, add, get };
  list,
  add,
```

```
  get,
  update,
};
...
```

Now, you can test these changes by using the Playground. You could use the following named query for this purpose:

```
mutation issueUpdate($id: Int!, $changes: IssueUpdateInputs!) {
  issueUpdate(id: $id, changes: $changes) {
    id title status owner
    effort created due description
  }
}
```

To change the status and the owner for the issue with ID 2, you could use a query variable like this:

```
{ "id": 2, "changes": { "status": "Assigned", "owner":"Eddie" } }
```

You can also test for invalid changes—such as a title with fewer than three characters, or a null owner when status is set to Assigned—and ensure that the changes are rejected with an error.

Updating an Issue

Now that we have a functional Update API, we can write the handleSubmit() method to make the call to the API to save the changes made by the user.

We can use the named query as in the Playground test used in the previous section. As for the query variable called changes, we'll need to strip off the fields that cannot be changed from the issue object and copy it. The fields that cannot be changed are id and created. This can be done like this:

```
...
    const { id, created, ...changes } = issue;
...
```

■ **Note** We used the ES2015+ rest operator ... to collect the *rest* of the values of the issue object into the changes variable after the destructuring assignment to the id and created variables.

After the object is saved using the GraphQL API using the named query, let's replace the current issue being displayed with the returned issue value. This just requires a setState() call with the returned issue, if any. Let's also show an alert message to indicate success of the operation, since there is no other visible change in the UI.

```
...
    const data = await graphQLFetch(query, { changes, id });
    if (data) {
      this.setState({ issue: data.issueUpdate });
```

```
      alert('Updated issue successfully'); // eslint-disable-line no-alert
  }
...
```

Further, let's return without doing anything if there are invalid fields in the form. For this, we can apply the same check that we used for displaying the invalid fields message. The complete changes for updating an issue from the Edit Issue page are shown in Listing 10-18.

Listing 10-18. ui/src/IssueEdit.jsx: Changes for Saving Edits to the Database

```
...
  async handleSubmit(e) {
    e.preventDefault();
    const { issue, invalidFields } = this.state;
    console.log(issue); // eslint-disable-line no-console
    if (Object.keys(invalidFields).length !== 0) return;

    const query = `mutation issueUpdate(
      $id: Int!
      $changes: IssueUpdateInputs!
    ) {
      issueUpdate(
        id: $id
        changes: $changes
      ) {
        id title status owner
        effort created due description
      }
    }`;

    const { id, created, ...changes } = issue;
    const data = await graphQLFetch(query, { changes, id });
    if (data) {
      this.setState({ issue: data.issueUpdate });
      alert('Updated issue successfully'); // eslint-disable-line no-alert
    }
  }
...
```

Now, you can test the application to save any changes to the issue in the database. The changes should be seen in the Edit and Issue List pages.

Updating a Field

Let's now use the same API to update a single field rather than the entire issue object in one go. Let's say we need a quick way to close an issue (that is, set its status to Closed) from the Issue List page itself.

To achieve this, we'll need a button in every row to initiate the operation. Let's change the IssueTable component to add this button as part of the Actions column. On click of this button, we'll need to initiate a close action, which can be a function passed in as a callback in the props. The callback needs to be passed from IssueList via IssueTable to IssueRow. Further, to identify *which* issue to close, we'll also have to receive the index of the issue in the table as another value in the props. The index can be computed in the IssueTable component itself, while iterating over the list of issues.

The changes to the IssueRow and IssueTable components are shown in Listing 10-19.

Listing 10-19. ui/src/IssueTable.jsx: Changes for Adding a Close Button

```
...
const IssueRow = withRouter((({ issue, location: { search } }) => {
  issue,
  location: { search },
  closeIssue,
  index,
}) => {
  ...
        <NavLink to={selectLocation}>Select</NavLink>
        {' | '}
        <button type="button" onClick={() => { closeIssue(index); }}>
          Close
        </button>
  ...
});

export default function IssueTable({ issues, closeIssue }) {
  const issueRows = issues.map((issue, index) => (
    <IssueRow key={issue.id} issue={issue} />
      key={issue.id}
      issue={issue}
      closeIssue={closeIssue}
      index={index}
    />
  ));
  ...
}
...
```

Now, let's implement the closeIssue() method in the IssueList component. Let's have a named query called closeIssue that takes in an issue ID as a query variable. In the implementation of the query, we'll call the issueUpdate API similar to the regular update call, but with the changes hard-coded to setting the status to closed.

```
...
    const query = `mutation issueClose($id: Int!) {
      issueUpdate(id: $id, changes: { status: Closed }) {
        ...
      }
    }`;
...
```

After the query is executed, if the execution is successful, let's replace the issue at the same index with the issue in the returned value. Since the state is immutable, we'll have to make a copy of the issue state variable. Also, since we are using the rest of the existing state to copy from, we'll have do the recommended thing of using a callback for this.setState() that takes in the previous state. If the execution is unsuccessful, we'll just reload the entire data.

```
...
    if (data) {
      this.setState((prevState) => {
        const newList = [...prevState.issues];
        newList[index] = data.issueUpdate;
        return { issues: newList };
      });
    } else {
      this.loadData();
    }
...
```

Other changes to the IssueList component are passing the closeIssue() method as a callback in the props to IssueTable and binding the closeIssue() method to this. The complete set of changes, including these in the IssueList component, are shown in Listing 10-20.

Listing 10-20. ui/src/IssueList.jsx: Changes for Handling Click of Close Button

```
...
  constructor() {
    ...
    this.closeIssue = this.closeIssue.bind(this);
  }
...
  async createIssue(issue) {
    ...
  }

  async closeIssue(index) {
    const query = `mutation issueClose($id: Int!) {
      issueUpdate(id: $id, changes: { status: Closed }) {
        id title status owner
        effort created due description
      }
    }`;
    const { issues } = this.state;
    const data = await graphQLFetch(query, { id: issues[index].id });
    if (data) {
      this.setState((prevState) => {
        const newList = [...prevState.issues];
        newList[index] = data.issueUpdate;
        return { issues: newList };
      });
    } else {
      this.loadData();
    }
  }
...
```

```
render() {
  ...
    <IssueTable issues={issues} closeIssue={this.closeIssue} />
  ...
}
...
```

This set of changes can be tested by clicking on the Close button in any of the rows in the issue list. The status of the issue in that row should change to `Closed`.

EXERCISE: UPDATING A FIELD

1. Could we have called the update API from `IssueRow` itself? What are the ramifications of doing that?

Answers are available at the end of the chapter.

Delete API

To complete the CRUD set of operations, let's implement the last of these operations, Delete. Let's first implement a Delete API. To start, we'll modify the schema to include the Delete API, which just takes the ID of the field to be deleted. We'll return a Boolean value to indicate successful deletion. This change is shown in Listing 10-21.

Listing 10-21. api/schema.graphql: Changes for Adding a Delete API

```
...
type Mutation {
  ...
  issueDelete(id: Int!): Boolean!
}
...
```

Next, we'll connect the API to its resolver within `issue.js` in the API handler. We'll call the function in `issue.js` simply `delete`. This change is shown in Listing 10-22.

Listing 10-22. api/api_handler.js: Changes for Adding a Delete API

```
...
const resolvers = {
  ...
  Mutation: {
    ...
    issueDelete: issue.delete,
  },
  ...
};
...
```

Now, let's implement the Delete API's resolver. Rather than just deleting the record for the given ID, let's do what usually happens when a file is deleted in a computer: it is moved to trash. This is so that we have a chance to recover it at a later point in time. Let's use a new collection called `deleted_issues` to store all deleted issues. We may decide to purge this table periodically, so let's also add a `deleted` field to save the date and time of deletion, which can come in handy (for example, to purge all issues deleted more than 30 days old).

To achieve this, we'll retrieve the issue based on the given ID from the `issues` collection, add the `deleted` field, save it to `deleted_issues`, and then delete it from the `issues` collection. Note that we cannot name the function `delete` because `delete` is a reserved keyword in JavaScript. So, we'll name the function `remove()`, but we'll export it using the name `delete`. The changes for implementing the resolver are shown in Listing 10-23.

Listing 10-23. api/issue.js: Addition of Resolver for the Delete API

```
...
async function update(_, { id, changes }) {
  ...
}

async function remove(_, { id }) {
  const db = getDb();
  const issue = await db.collection('issues').findOne({ id });
  if (!issue) return false;
  issue.deleted = new Date();

  let result = await db.collection('deleted_issues').insertOne(issue);
  if (result.insertedId) {
    result = await db.collection('issues').removeOne({ id });
    return result.deletedCount === 1;
  }
  return false;
}

module.exports = {
  list,
  add,
  get,
  update,
  delete: remove,
};
...
```

Finally, let's also initialize this collection as part of the initialization script. This involves two things: cleaning up the collection to begin with, and then creating an index on the ID field for easier retrieval. The changes for this are shown in Listing 10-24.

Listing 10-24. api/scripts/init.mongo.js: Initialization of deleted_issues Collection

```
...
db.issues.remove({});
db.deleted_issues.remove({});
...
```

```
db.issues.createIndex({ created: 1 });

db.deleted_issues.createIndex({ id: 1 }, { unique: true });
...
```

Now, you can test the Delete API using the Playground. You could use a mutation like the following to delete an issue with ID 4:

```
mutation {
  issueDelete(id: 4)
}
```

If the issue with ID 4 exists, it will be deleted and the API will return true. Otherwise, the API will return false. You could inspect the contents of the collection deleted_issues using the MongoDB shell to verify that the issue has been backed up in this collection.

Deleting an Issue

The UI changes for deleting an issue will be quite similar to the changes we did for updating a field using the Close button.

Let's first add the button and pass the necessary callbacks through IssueTable to IssueRows. Let's use the name deleteIssue for the callback, which we will implement in IssueList soon. Just as with the closeIssue callback, we'll need to delete the index of the issue. We already have the index being passed in for this purpose, so we'll use the same here.

The changes to IssueTable and IssueRows are shown in Listing 10-25.

Listing 10-25. ui/src/IssueTable.jsx: Changes for Delete Button and Handling It

```
...
const IssueRow = withRouter((({
  ...
  deleteIssue,
  index,
}) => {
  ...
        <button type="button" onClick={() => { closeIssue(index); }}>
          Close
        </button>
        {' | '}
        <button type="button" onClick={() => { deleteIssue(index); }}>
          Delete
        </button>
  ...
});

export default function IssueTable({ issues, closeIssue, deleteIssue }) {
  const issueRows = issues.map((issue, index) => (
    <IssueRow
      ...
```

```
      deleteIssue={deleteIssue}
      index={index}
   />
...
```

The next set of changes is in the IssueList component. Again, the changes are quite similar to what we did for the Close button: a deleteIssue() method takes the index of the issue to be deleted, calls the Delete API using this ID in the query variable, and *removes* the issue from the issues state variable if the API succeeded. If not, it reloads the data. Further, there is a possibility that the user is deleting the selected issue. In this case, let's revert to an unselected view, that is, navigate back to /issues (i.e., without the ID suffix).

Other changes are to bind the new method to this and pass the method as a callback to the IssueTable component.

These changes are shown in Listing 10-26.

Listing 10-26. ui/src/IssueList.jsx: Changes for Implementing Delete Functionality

```
...
  constructor() {
    ...
    this.deleteIssue = this.deleteIssue.bind(this);
  }
...

  async closeIssue(index) {
    ...
  }

  async deleteIssue(index) {
    const query = `mutation issueDelete($id: Int!) {
      issueDelete(id: $id)
    }`;
    const { issues } = this.state;
    const { location: { pathname, search }, history } = this.props;
    const { id } = issues[index];
    const data = await graphQLFetch(query, { id });
    if (data && data.issueDelete) {
      this.setState((prevState) => {
        const newList = [...prevState.issues];
        if (pathname === `/issues/${id}`) {
          history.push({ pathname: '/issues', search });
        }
        newList.splice(index, 1);
        return { issues: newList };
      });
    } else {
      this.loadData();
    }
  }

  render() {
    ...
        <IssueTable issues={issues} closeIssue={this.closeIssue} />
```

```
        issues={issues}
        closeIssue={this.closeIssue}
        deleteIssue={this.deleteIssue}
      />
  }
...
```

Now, if you test the application, you'll find an additional button in the Action column for Delete. If you click on Delete, you should find that issue removed from the list. At this point, we're not asking for a confirmation for deleting, because eventually we'll add an Undo button that will restore the deleted issue. That way, if the users click on Delete by mistake, they can undo their action. The Issue List page with the Delete button will look like the screenshot shown in Figure 10-4.

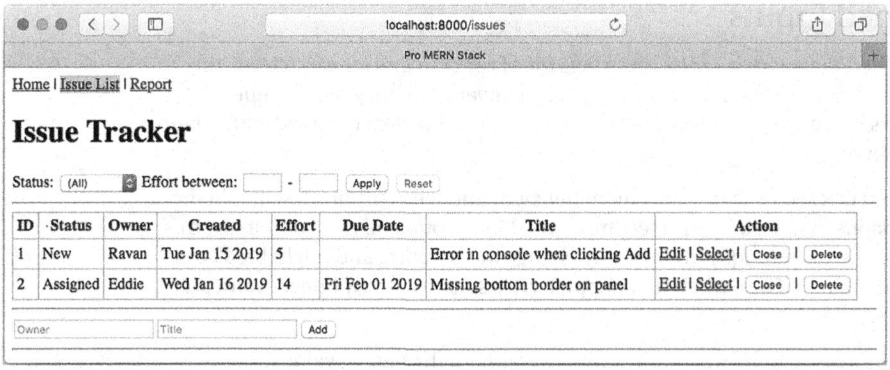

Figure 10-4. The issue list with a Delete button

Summary

We used the Edit page to explore forms and look at the difference between controlled and uncontrolled form components. We also added new APIs to cater to the needs of the new form and completed the CRUD paradigm by adding a Delete operation. Importantly, we created specialized input components that could deal with different data types that one expects in most applications.

While we did all this, a thought must have crossed your mind: can we make all this, especially the Edit page, look better in the browser? That's exactly what we'll set out to do in the next chapter. We'll use a popular CSS library adapted to React to add some polish to the UI.

Answers to Exercises

Exercise: More Filters

1. MongoDB is strict with respect to data types. This also means that for a field that has no value, it cannot determine the type, thus the match cannot occur if the field has a filter criterion. Any field with null values will be ignored and not returned if there is *any* filter on that field.

2. If we do need to return documents with the effort field missing, we'll have to create a condition that includes the original filter, as well as a condition that says the effort is undefined. The $or operator takes an array of filters and matches the document against any of the filter conditions.

To match a document where the effort field is not defined, we must use {$exists: false} as the criterion for the field. Here's an example in the mongo shell:

```
> db.issues.find({$or: [
  {effort: {$lte: 10}},
  {effort: {$exists: false}}
]});
```

Exercise: Typed Inputs

1. Even when the query is sent with strings for effortMin and/or effortMax, the server seems to accept it and automatically convert it to integers. The query works as it does when converting the effort fields to integers before sending them to the server.

Although this seems to be convenient behavior and it is tempting to not add the conversions in the UI, it is not recommended for a couple of reasons. Firstly, this behavior of the graphql-js library may change in the future and might break our implementation if and when that happens. It is safer to supply integer values as integers.

Secondly, the UI ignores any non-numeric values if the parsed value is not a number. So, the application works as if no filter were supplied. On the other hand, if the value was not parsed, the text input would be sent to the server causing an error (this can be tested by typing these non-numeric values in the browser's URL directly).

2. If you set the input's type as a number, you find that (a) it behaves differently on different browsers, (b) masking does not work on some browsers, and (c) when it does allow invalid characters, you don't see them in onChange. This is because as per the HTML specification, when the type is specified and the input does not conform to the specification, the value of the input is supposed to return an empty string. It is also up to the browser how to deal with invalid values; for example, some browsers may display the fact that the input is invalid, whereas others may prevent an invalid entry.

When using React, it is best not to use the type attribute of input fields, instead it's best to deal with the validation or masking yourself (or use packages that do it for you). This lets the behavior be predictable across browsers, as well as allows you to make informed decisions on what to do with invalid input, especially input that is invalid temporarily in order to get to a valid value.

Exercise: Edit Page

1. If the value of a controlled component is set to null, a warning is shown on the console by React:

Warning: 'value' prop on 'textarea' should not be null. Consider using an empty string to clear the component or 'undefined' for uncontrolled components.

The warning is because a null value is a signal to React that the component is uncontrolled. Controlled components must have a non-null value.

Exercise: Updating a Field

1. Although initiating the API can be done from the IssueRow component itself, signaling the success and updating the issue list can only be done within the IssueList component, as the state resides there. Further, this would cause the IssueRow component to stop being a pure function. It would also need a handler for the close action within the component, making it necessary to define it as a class.

Since the state resides in the IssueList component, it's best to let the same component manipulate the state as well.

## CHAPTER 11

React-Bootstrap

CSS frameworks like Bootstrap (https://getbootstrap.com) and Foundation (https://foundation.zurb.com/) have changed the way people build their websites. These tools make it a lot easier to make a web application look professionally styled and be responsive (that is, make it adapt to mobile screens nicely). Of course, the downside is that these existing frameworks may not give you fine-grained customizability, and your application will look like many others. But, even if you do have the luxury or the capability to create your own end-to-end custom styles, I suggest that you start off with these frameworks. That's because there's a lot to learn from the patterns these frameworks use.

Since we are using React as the UI library, we need to choose something that fits into and plays well with React. I evaluated React + Foundation, Material UI, and React-Bootstrap because they appeared the most popular, based on Google searches.

React + Foundation didn't appear to be very different from React-Bootstrap in terms of capability, but Bootstrap itself is far more popular. Material UI has an interesting CSS-in-JS and inline-style approach of styling that fits well into React's philosophy of isolating everything needed by a component, with the component itself. But this framework is much less popular and seems to be a work in progress. And, perhaps the inline-style approach is too drastic a deviation from convention.

React-Bootstrap is a safe alternative that is built on top of the very popular Bootstrap and fits our needs (except for the lack of a date picker). I thus chose React-Bootstrap for this book. In this chapter, we'll look at how to make the application look professionally styled using React-Bootstrap. I won't be covering how to make custom themes and other advanced topics, but you'll learn just enough to appreciate what React-Bootstrap is all about, so you can go further easily if and when required.

Bootstrap Installation

In this section, we'll install React-Bootstrap and confirm that it works by making a small change that is visible in the UI. Let's first install React-Bootstrap:

```
$ cd ui
$ npm install react-bootstrap@0
```

React-Bootstrap contains a library of React components and has no CSS styles or themes itself. It requires Bootstrap stylesheet to be included in the application to use these components. The version or mechanism of including the stylesheet is left to us, but the version that we need to use is Version 3. The latest version of Bootstrap (Version 4) is not yet supported by React-Bootstrap. So, let's include Version 3 of the bootstrap stylesheet. The easiest way is to include it from a CDN directly in index.html, as recommended by the React-Bootstrap "Getting Started" page (https://react-bootstrap.github.io).

But since we have other third-party JavaScript dependencies locally installed, let's to do the same for Bootstrap as well. Let's install bootstrap using npm so that its distribution files are available and can be served from the server directly, like index.html and other static files.

```
$ npm install bootstrap@3
```

The next step is to include the Bootstrap stylesheet in the application. One way to do this is by using Webpack's style and CSS loaders. This can be done using an import (or require) statement to include CSS files just like other React or JavaScript modules. Then, Webpack would build the dependency tree and include all the styles that have been imported in the bundle that is created. This is done by creating a string within the JavaScript bundle containing all the styles. When the application is loaded, the string is placed into the DOM as a <style> node.

To get this to work, we need to install the CSS and style loaders for Webpack. Then, we need to add pattern matches in the Webpack configuration that triggers these loaders based on the file extension. We will also need loaders for the icons and fonts that the stylesheet may include. Finally, we need a single import statement that imports bootstrap.css, maybe just in App.jsx.

I find that for our needs, all of this is overkill. The purpose of Webpack's CSS and style loaders is to be able to modularize stylesheets just as we modularized the React code. If every component had its own set of styles separated into their own CSS files, this method would work great. But the fact is that Bootstrap is shipped as a monolithic stylesheet. Even if only a single component is being used, the entire CSS has to be included. So why not just include the entire stylesheet as is? That's what we'll do.

We'll just keep a symbolic link to the Bootstrap distribution under the public directory and include the CSS just like the other static files such as index.html. The command to achieve this is on a Mac or a Linux-based computer is:

```
$ ln -s ../node_modules/bootstrap/dist public/bootstrap
```

On a Windows PC, the command line tool mklink can be used to do the same, with the /J option to create a *junction* for the directory.

```
> mklink /J public\bootstrap node_modules\bootstrap\dist
```

Alternatively, you can copy the entire dist directory under the Bootstrap library into the public directory.

If you now explore the new directory, you'll find three subdirectories: css, fonts, and js. The js directory will not be used because that's what React-Bootstrap replaces. In index.html, we'll add a link to the main Bootstrap stylesheet, which is under the css sub-directory of the directory that we linked or copied. We won't include the optional theme file, just the main minified Bootstrap style like this:

```
...
  <link rel="stylesheet" href="/bootstrap/css/bootstrap.min.css">
...
```

At this point in time, if you test the application, you should see a different looking application because of the new bootstrap stylesheet. For example, you should see a sans-serif font (Helvetica or Arial) in place of a serif font (Times New Roman) as the default font.

Let's now test this on a mobile device and see the effect of the Bootstrap's responsive design. One way to do this is to actually use a mobile phone and connect to the server that's running on your desktop. But this won't work unless you change the environment variable UI_API_ENDPOINT to the IP address of your computer. Alternatively, you'll have to use the proxy configuration so that all requests are routed via the UI server.

An easier way is to use the mobile emulation mode of the web browsers to see how it looks. I found that only Chrome accurately reflects what happens in a real mobile device. Safari (using the responsive mode under Develop menu) and Firefox (in the dev tools) only simulate a change of screen size. What you'd see on a real mobile device or on Chrome's mobile emulator is shown in Figure 11-1. Note that the outline or the device frame may not be seen for some devices. Also, the Show Device Frame option needs to be turned on in the Developer Tools settings to see the device frame.

Figure 11-1. *The app in a mobile emulator*

As you can see, the screen looks really squished or zoomed out. You could zoom by pinching (use Shift-drag in the mobile emulator) to vary the zoom, but we'd really like it to use the smaller screen width by default. The reason the mobile browser does not take the device width is roughly like this: it assumes that the page has not been designed for mobile screens, so it picks an arbitrary width that would be appropriate for a desktop, uses that, and then zooms out the page so that it fits the screen.

We need to let the mobile browser that the application knows how to handle small screens, so that it doesn't do all that extra work to try to fit a desktop website into the mobile screen. The way to do so is by adding a meta tag in the main page, called `viewport`, the content of which specifies an initial width equal to the device's width and an initial zoom of 100%. This change, and the stylesheet inclusion in `index.html`, are shown in Listing 11-1.

Listing 11-1. ui/public/index.html: Changes for Bootstrap and Mobile Device Compatibility

```
...
<head>
  ...
  <title>Pro MERN Stack</title>
  <link rel="stylesheet" href="/bootstrap/css/bootstrap.min.css" >
  <meta name="viewport" content="width=device-width, initial-scale=1.0">
...
```

With this change, the screen should look much better, with the screen filling the entire device width, as shown in Figure 11-2.

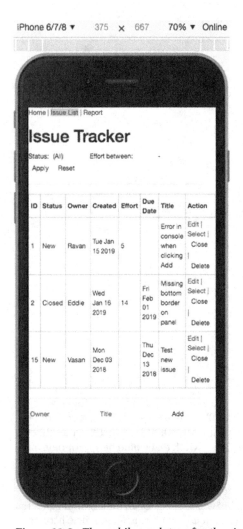

Figure 11-2. *The mobile emulator after the viewport setting*

Well, we tested the Bootstrap stylesheet taking effect and checked it in a mobile browser. Now let's also test that the components of React-Bootstrap are usable. For this, let's use a simple React-Bootstrap component. The list of components available is found in the React-Bootstrap documentation at `https://react-bootstrap.github.io/components/alerts/`. Let's choose the `<Label>` component, which is a simple one that shows the text in a highlighted manner. Let's use this inside the Issue List's title and ensure that it renders as expected. The change for this is made in the `IssueList` component and is shown in Listing 11-2.

Listing 11-2. ui/src/IssueList.jsx: Change the App Title to Use React-Bootstrap's Label Component

```
...
import { Route } from 'react-router-dom';
import { Label } from 'react-bootstrap';
...

  render() {
    ...
    return (
      <React.Fragment>
        <h1><Label>Issue Tracker</Label></h1>
    ...
  }
...
```

Now, if you test the application, you will find that the title in the Issue List page is shown with a dark background and a white foreground. A screenshot of this is shown in Figure 11-3.

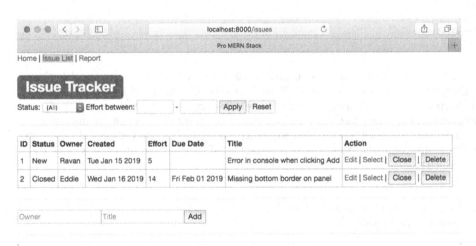

Figure 11-3. *The Issue List page with a Bootstrap label*

Buttons

To get familiar with the way React-Bootstrap works with components, let's start with a simple component: Button. Let's replace the Apply and Reset buttons in the Issue Filter with Bootstrap buttons.

A simple text-based button can be created using the `<Button>` component. Apart from all the properties the regular `<button>` component supports, the `<Button>` component uses the `bsStyle` property to make buttons look distinct. Apart from the default, which shows the button with a white background, the allowed styles are `primary`, `success`, `info`, `warning`, `danger`, and `link`. Let's use the `primary` style for the Apply button and the default for the Reset button. Thus for the Reset button, the only change is in the tag name from `button` to `Button`. The changes to the Apply button are the tag name and the addition of `bsStyle="primary"`.

These changes are shown in Listing 11-3.

Listing 11-3. ui/src/IssueFilter.jsx: Replace Buttons with Bootstrap Buttons

```
...
import { withRouter } from 'react-router-dom';
import { Button } from 'react-bootstrap';
...

      <button type="button" onClick={this.applyFilter}>Apply</button>
      <Button bsStyle="primary" type="button" onClick={this.applyFilter}>
        Apply
      </Button>
      {' '}
      <button
      <Button
        ...
      >
        Reset
      </button>
      </Button>
...
```

As a next step, let's use icons instead of text for the buttons in the Issue Table for closing and deleting issues. Instead of the text in the `<Button>` element, we'll need to use the `Glyphicon` component of React-Bootstrap. A list of icons that this component recognizes is available at the Bootstrap website at https:// getbootstrap.com/docs/3.3/components/. Let's use the `remove` icon for the Close action and the `trash` icon for the Delete action in the `IssueRow` component to replace the regular buttons. Let's also use a smaller sized button so that the table continues to look compact, using the `bsSize` property. The code for the Close action is as follows, which retains the original `onClick()` event.

```
...
      <Button bsSize="xsmall" onClick={() => { closeIssue(index); }}>
        <Glyphicon glyph="remove" />
      </Button>
...
```

A similar change can be made to the button for the Delete action. But since the icons' intended actions are not too obvious, it's good to have a tooltip that is shown on hovering over the button. The HTML property `title` can be used for this purpose, but let's use Bootstrap's stylized `Tooltip` component. But using this is not as simple as setting a `title` property. The `Tooltip` component has to be shown or hidden on mouse over and mouse out. In regular Bootstrap (that is, without React), jQuery would be used for injecting these handlers, but in React, we need a cleaner mechanism that fits in the component's hierarchy.

The way to do this is using the OverlayTrigger component that wraps the button and takes in the Tooltip component as a property. The Tooltip itself is simple: the children of the element are the contents to show. Further, since default placement of the tooltip is to the right of the button and this can get obscured if the button is close to the edge of the screen, let's change the placement to above the button. For this, we can specify the placement property as top.

```
...
  const closeTooltip = (
    <Tooltip id="close-tooltip" placement="top">Close Issue</Tooltip>
  );
...
```

The id property is needed to make the component accessible. Now, this variable can be used as a property in the OverlayTrigger component that we'll wrap the button for the tooltip effect. Also, let's customize the delay after which the tooltip is shown since the default is very short and intrusive. This can be done using the delayShow property of OverlayTrigger.

```
...
        <OverlayTrigger delayShow={1000} overlay={closeTooltip}>
          <Button bsSize="xsmall" onClick={() => { closeIssue(index); }}>
            <Glyphicon glyph="remove" />
          </Button>
        </OverlayTrigger>
...
```

A similar set of components for the Delete action, and the import statements, etc. to complete the changes to the IssueTable.jsx file, are shown in Listing 11-4.

Listing 11-4. ui/src/IssueTable.jsx: Changes for Buttons with Icons and Tooltip

```
...
import { Link, NavLink, withRouter } from 'react-router-dom';
import {
  Button, Glyphicon, Tooltip, OverlayTrigger,
} from 'react-bootstrap';

const IssueRow = withRouter(({
  ...
  const selectLocation = { pathname: `/issues/${issue.id}`, search };
  const closeTooltip = (
    <Tooltip id="close-tooltip" placement="top">Close Issue</Tooltip>
  );
  const deleteTooltip = (
    <Tooltip id="delete-tooltip" placement="top">Delete Issue</Tooltip>
  );
  return (
    ...
        <button type="button" onClick={() => { closeIssue(index); }}>
          Close
        </button>
```

```
        <OverlayTrigger delayShow={1000} overlay={closeTooltip}>
          <Button bsSize="xsmall" onClick={() => { closeIssue(index); }}>
            <Glyphicon glyph="remove" />
          </Button>
        </OverlayTrigger>
        {' ' | ' '}
        {' '}
        <OverlayTrigger delayShow={1000} overlay={deleteTooltip}>
          <Button bsSize="xsmall" onClick={() => { deleteIssue(index); }}>
            <Glyphicon glyph="trash" />
          </Button>
        </OverlayTrigger>
      </td>
   ...
});
...
```

■ **Note**   Although no effort has been spared to ensure that all code listings are accurate, there may be typos or even corrections that did not make it into the book before it went to press. So, do always rely on the GitHub repository (https://github.com/vasansr/pro-mern-stack-2) as the tested and up-to-date source for all code listings, especially if something does not work as expected.

We'll leave the Edit and Select links to be converted to icons for later. That's because, being links, they need to work nicely with React Router and handle the <Link> and <NavLink> elements seamlessly. If you test the application with the current changes, you should find that the Issue List page looks similar to the screenshot in Figure 11-4.

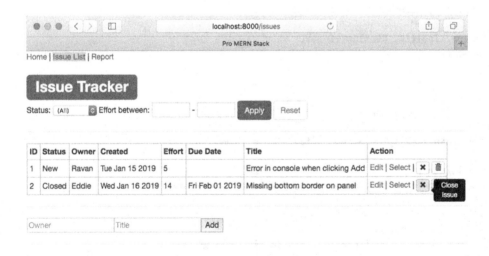

Figure 11-4. *The Issue List with Bootstrap buttons and a hover tooltip on a Close button*

Navigation Bar

In this section, we'll style the navigation links in the header and add a footer that is visible on all pages.

For the navigation bar, let's start with the application title. We'll move it out of the Issue List page to the navigation bar, where it belongs. The Home, Issue List, and Report links can appear as styled navigation links to the right of the title. Let's also, on the right side, have an action item for creating a new issue (we'll move the in-page Add form to a modal in later sections) and an extended dropdown menu for any other actions that may be added in the future. For now, the extended menu will have just one action, called About (which will do nothing for now).

The starting component to create a navigation bar is Navbar. Let's first address the layout of the navigation bar and the components required to implement it. Each item is a NavItem. These items can be grouped together in a Nav. Thus, we'll need two Nav elements, one for the left side of the navigation bar and another for the right side. The right side Nav can be aligned to the right using the pullRight property.

```
...
  <Navbar>
    <Nav>
      <NavItem>Home</NavItem>
      <NavItem>Issue List</NavItem>
      <NavItem>Report</NavItem>
    </Nav>
    <Nav pullRight>
      ...
    </Nav>
  </Navbar>
...
```

As for the application title, let's use Navbar.Header and Navbar.Brand as suggested by the documentation. This should appear before all the Nav elements.

```
...
  <Navbar>
    <Navbar.Header>
      <Navbar.Brand>Issue Tracker</Navbar.Brand>
    </Navbar.Header>
...
```

On the right side, we'll first need an icon-based item for the Create Issue action. We'll use the Glyphicon component inside the NavItem to achieve this. Further, to add a tooltip to the icon, let's use the OverlayTrigger like we used for the action buttons in the Issue List page.

```
...
    <Nav pullRight>
      <NavItem>
        <OverlayTrigger ...
          <Glyphicon glyph="plus" />
        </OverlayTrigger>
      </NavItem>
...
```

As for the extended menu, we need a dropdown. The React-Bootstrap component `NavDropdown` can be used to create a dropdown menu, with each menu item being a `MenuItem` component. The dropdown needs a title, usually text. But since the menu is generic, we'll just use a vertically oriented set of three dots to indicate that an extended menu is available. Normally, when text is used, a caret will indicate a dropdown. But since we're using an icon that already indicates a dropdown, we'll remove the caret by specifying `noCaret` as a property.

```
...
      <NavDropdown
        id="user-dropdown"
        title={<Glyphicon glyph="option-vertical" />}
        noCaret
      >
        <MenuItem>About</MenuItem>
      </NavDropdown>
...
```

Now, let's add the actions that the navigation items should take. The `NavItem` component can take an `href` as a property, or an `onClick` event handler. Now, we have the following options:

- Use an `href` property on the `NavItem`: This has the problem that React Router's `<Link>` will not be used, and clicking on the `href` will cause a full browser refresh.

- Use React Router's `<Link>` instead of `NavItem`: This will mess up the styling and not align properly, as `<Link>` uses an anchor tag (`<a>`) and there's no way to change that component class.

Either of these options introduces a problem. The recommended way to break this impasse is to use the `react-router-bootstrap` package, which provides a wrapper called `LinkContainer` acting as the React Router's `NavLink`, at the same time letting its children have their own rendering. We can place a `NavItem` without an `href` as a child to the `LinkContainer` and let the parent `LinkContainer` deal with the path to the route.

Let's install the package to use the `LinkContainer`:

```
$ cd ui
$ npm install react-router-bootstrap@0
```

Now, we can wrap all the left-side navigation items with a `LinkContainer` (after importing the package) with the path to the route it needs to point to. The `LinkContainer` component supports all properties that the React Router component `NavLink` does.

```
...
      <LinkContainer to="/issues">
        <NavItem>Issue List</NavItem>
      </LinkContainer>
...
```

Let's also add a simple footer that shows a link to the GitHub repository for this book. Including this change, the entire contents of the `Page.jsx` file are shown in Listing 11-5. I have excluded removed lines of code for brevity, and these removed lines are just the original `NavLinks` and the corresponding import statements.

Listing 11-5. ui/src/Page.jsx: New NavBar-Based Header and Trivial Footer

```
import React from 'react';
import {
  Navbar, Nav, NavItem, NavDropdown,
  MenuItem, Glyphicon, Tooltip, OverlayTrigger,
} from 'react-bootstrap';
import { LinkContainer } from 'react-router-bootstrap';

import Contents from './Contents.jsx';

function NavBar() {
  return (
    <Navbar>
      <Navbar.Header>
        <Navbar.Brand>Issue Tracker</Navbar.Brand>
      </Navbar.Header>
      <Nav>
        <LinkContainer exact to="/">
          <NavItem>Home</NavItem>
        </LinkContainer>
        <LinkContainer to="/issues">
          <NavItem>Issue List</NavItem>
        </LinkContainer>
        <LinkContainer to="/report">
          <NavItem>Report</NavItem>
        </LinkContainer>
      </Nav>
      <Nav pullRight>
        <NavItem>
          <OverlayTrigger
            placement="left"
            delayShow={1000}
            overlay={<Tooltip id="create-issue">Create Issue</Tooltip>}
          >
            <Glyphicon glyph="plus" />
          </OverlayTrigger>
        </NavItem>
        <NavDropdown
          id="user-dropdown"
          title={<Glyphicon glyph="option-vertical" />}
          noCaret
        >
          <MenuItem>About</MenuItem>
        </NavDropdown>
      </Nav>
    </Navbar>
  );
}
```

```
function Footer() {
  return (
    <small>
      <p className="text-center">
        Full source code available at this
        {' '}
        <a href="htttps://github.com/vasansr/pro-mern-stack-2">
          GitHub repository
        </a>
      </p>
    </small>
  );
}

export default function Page() {
  return (
    <div>
      <NavBar />
      <Contents />
      <Footer />
    </div>
  );
}
```

Now that the application title is part of the navigation bar, let's remove it from the Issue List page. The changes for this are shown in Listing 11-6.

Listing 11-6. ui/src/IssueList.jsx: Removal of Application Title

```
...
import { Route } from 'react-router-dom';
import { Label } from 'react-bootstrap';
...

      <React.Fragment>
        <h1><Label>Issue Tracker</Label></h1>
...
```

Now, if you test the application, you should see the Issue List page as in the screenshot in Figure 11-5. You should also be able to use the navigation bar to switch between the Issue List page and Report page, and the navigation bar should be visible in the Edit screen as well. The items on the right side of the navigation bar are still dummy items with no effect. We'll implement these in later chapters.

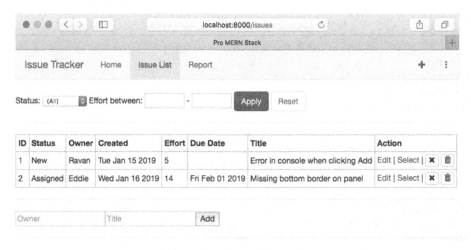

Figure 11-5. *The Issue List page with a navigation bar*

EXERCISE: NAVIGATION BAR

1. The documentation for React-Bootstrap's Navbar at https://react-bootstrap.github.io/components/navbar/ lists support for a property called fixedTop. It's meant to keep the NavBar at the top when scrolling vertically. Try this out. You may have to go to the Edit page and/or reduce the screen height to make the vertical scrollbar appear. Do you see a problem? How would you fix it? Hint: Refer to Bootstrap's Navbar documentation at https://getbootstrap.com/docs/3.3/components/#navbar-fixed-top. (Remember to revert these experimental changes after the exercise.)

Answers are available at the end of the chapter.

Panels

Until now, we've used horizontal rules (the <hr> element) to demarcate sections within a page. For example, in the Issue List page we used it to separate the filter from the Issue Table. Further, after the inclusion of Bootstrap, you'd have noticed that the left margin has disappeared, causing all the contents of the Issue List page to appear starting right at the window edge on the left side.

Bootstrap's Panel component is a great way to show sections separately using a border and an optional heading. Let's use this to decorate the Filter section in the Issue List page. We'll make changes to the IssueList component by adding a panel around the IssueFilter instance in the render() method.

The Panel component consists of an optional heading (Panel.Heading) and a panel body (Panel.Body). The panel body is where we'll place the <IssueFilter /> instance.

```
...
        <Panel>
          ...
          <Panel.Body>
            <IssueFilter />
          </Panel.Body>
        </Panel>
...
```

As for the heading, let's add a heading with the text Filter for it. Rather than using plain text, wrapping it inside a Panel.Title component, meant for panel titles, makes it stand out.

```
...
        <Panel.Heading>
          <Panel.Title>Filter</Panel.Title>
        </Panel.Heading>
...
```

Now, in order to save space, let's collapse the panel. When the users want to apply a filter, they can click on the header and display and manipulate the filter. The way to do this is by adding the collapsible property to the Panel.Body and making the panel title control the collapse behavior by setting its toggle property.

```
...
        <Panel.Heading>
          <Panel.Title toggle>Filter</Panel.Title>
        </Panel.Heading>
        <Panel.Body collapsible>
...
```

The complete changes to implement a collapsible panel around the Issue Filter are shown in Listing 11-7. The panel can be collapsed/expanded by clicking on the title, Filter.

Listing 11-7. ui/src/IssueList.jsx: Changes for Adding a Panel Around the Issue Filter

```
...
import { Route } from 'react-router-dom';
import { Panel } from 'react-bootstrap';
...

  render() {
    ...
    return (
      <React.Fragment>
        <Panel>
          <Panel.Heading>
            <Panel.Title toggle>Filter</Panel.Title>
          </Panel.Heading>
          <Panel.Body collapsible>
            <IssueFilter />
          </Panel.Body>
        </Panel>
```

```
      <IssueTable
      ...
    </React.Fragment>
  );
}
...
```

Even with a panel around the Issue Filter, on testing the application you will find that there is no left margin. The grid system of Bootstrap is the one that adds the margins. Although we won't use a grid yet, we'll need to wrap the body of the page with a <Grid> component to add margins. Rather than do this for each page, let's add the grid component around the Contents component instance in Page.jsx.

There are two kinds of grid containers in Bootstrap: a fluid one, which fills the entire page, and a fixed one (the default), which has a fixed size, but one that adapts to the screen size. Let's use a fluid grid using the fluid property to match the navigation bar, because it would be nice to let the list of issues fill the screen for better readability.

This change is shown in Listing 11-8.

Listing 11-8. ui/src/Page.jsx: Wrapping Page Contents with a Grid to Add Margins

```
...
import {
  ...
  Grid,
} from 'react-bootstrap';
...

export default function Page() {
      <Grid fluid>
        <Contents />
      </Grid>
  );
}
...
```

When you try this set of changes, you'll find that it's not obvious that the panel heading is clickable. Firstly, the cursor does not change to something that shows that it's clickable. Also, the only place you can click is on the text. For the sake of usability, what we'd really like is the cursor to indicate that it's clickable and let the entire header area be clickable.

If you inspect the DOM using Safari's or Chrome's inspectors, you can see that there is an <a> element that is added by React-Bootstrap when the heading is made collapsible. Unfortunately, we don't have a way of configuring the panel to either not add the <a> (and let you specify a clickable node yourself for the header), or to tell it to fill the horizontal space. The only way we can do this is by using a style that makes the <a> a block element that fills the space and set the cursor.

Let's add this style in index.html. This change is shown in Listing 11-9.

Listing 11-9. public/index.html: Style for Making Entire Panel Heading Clickable

```
...
  <style>
    ...
    .panel-title a {display: block; width: 100%; cursor: pointer;}
  </style>
...
```

Now, on testing, you will find that there are margins to separate the content of the page from the edge of the window. You will have to refresh the browser since index.html, which has the updated style, is not automatically updated by HMR. You'll also find that there is a clickable panel heading that opens the filter form on clicking. A screenshot of this is shown in Figure 11-6.

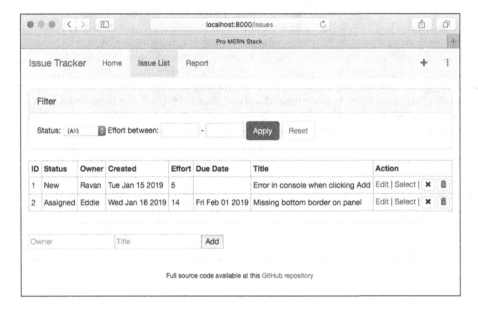

Figure 11-6. *The Issue Filter within a collapsible panel*

EXERCISE: PANELS

1. Let's say we'd like the panel to be shown in an expanded state on a browser refresh. How would you achieve this? To make it more interesting, let's say we want the panel to be expanded if any filter other than the default of all statuses and all effort is in effect. How would you achieve this? Hint: Look up the properties of the Panel component in the React-Bootstrap documentation at https://react-bootstrap.github.io/components/panel/#panels-props-accordion.

Answers are available at the end of the chapter.

Tables

Bootstrap can add some niceties to tables apart from styling them. In this section, we'll convert the plain table into a Bootstrap table, which looks better, expands to fit the screen, and highlights a row on hover. Further, we'll make the entire row clickable to select the issue so that its description is displayed in the Details section. This will replace the Select link in the Action column. We'll use the LinkContainer component from react-router-bootstrap to achieve this. We'll also convert the Edit link into a button, which we couldn't do along with the other two action buttons because we hadn't discovered the LinkContainer component then.

In this section, we'll be using the new components `LinkContainer` and `Table` in the `IssueTable.jsx` file, so let's import them first:

```
...
import { LinkContainer } from 'react-router-bootstrap';
import {
  Button, Glyphicon, Tooltip, OverlayTrigger, Table,
} from 'react-bootstrap';
...
```

Converting the table to a Bootstrap table is as simple as replacing the `<table>` tag with React-Bootstrap's `<Table>` component tag. While we do this, let's also add a few properties that are documented in the React-Bootstrap's Table page at `https://react-bootstrap.github.io/components/table/`.

- `striped`: Highlights alternate rows with a different background. This could interfere with showing the selected row, so let's not use this.

- `bordered`: Adds a border around the rows and cells. Let's use this.

- `condensed`: The default size has too much white space around the text, so let's use the condensed mode.

- `hover`: Highlights the row under the cursor. Let's use this.

- `responsive`: On smaller screens, makes the table horizontally scrollable instead of reducing the width of the columns. Let's use this as well.

The new table component in the `render()` function of the `IssueTable` component will now look like this:

```
...
    <table className="bordered-table">
    <Table bordered condensed hover responsive>
      ...
    </table>
    </Table>
...
```

Next, to replace the `Select` link with the entire row, let's use a `LinkContainer` to wrap the entire row and let it navigate to the same location as in the `Select` link using the `to` property. Note that `LinkContainer` also automatically adds the `active` class to the wrapped element like `NavLink` if the route matches the link path. Bootstrap automatically highlights such rows with a gray background. Thus, instead of returning the `<tr>` element in the `render()` method of the `IssueRow` component, let's assign it to a constant. Then, let's return the same element wrapped around a `LinkContainer`.

```
...
  return (
  const tableRow = (
    <tr>
      ...
        <NavLink to={selectLocation}>Select</NavLink>
        {' | '}
      ...
    </tr>
  );
```

```
return (
  <LinkContainer to={selectLocation}>
    {tableRow}
  </LinkContainer>
);
...
```

Now, let's convert the Edit link to a button with an icon. Let's use the Button and Glyphicon components and use a Tooltip and OverlayTrigger as we did for the Close and Delete buttons, except for the onClick() event handler:

```
...
const selectLocation = { pathname: `/issues/${issue.id}`, search };
const editTooltip = (
  <Tooltip id="close-tooltip" placement="top">Edit Issue</Tooltip>
);
...
        <Link to={`/edit/${issue.id}`}>Edit</Link>
        {' | '}
        <OverlayTrigger delayShow={1000} overlay={editTooltip}>
          <Button bsSize="xsmall">
            <Glyphicon glyph="edit" />
          </Button>
        </OverlayTrigger>
...
```

Now, instead of the onClick() event handler, let's wrap the button with a LinkContainer; the to property is copied from the to property of the original Link component:

```
...
        <LinkContainer to={`/edit/${issue.id}`}>
          <OverlayTrigger delayShow={1000} overlay={editTooltip}>
            ...
          </OverlayTrigger>
        </LinkContainer>
...
```

At this point in time, the changes will seem to work, but a click on the Close or Delete buttons will also have the side-effect of selecting the row. This is because we now have an onClick() handler on the row (installed by the LinkContainer component), and this is invoked when clicking these buttons. To prevent the event from propagating from the buttons to the contained row, we'll need to call e.preventDefault() in the handlers. Let's separate the event handlers into explicit functions (as opposed to anonymous functions within the onClick property) and use the function names instead.

For the Delete button, these are the changes:

```
...
function onDelete(e) {
  e.preventDefault();
  deleteIssue(index);
}
```

```
const tableRow = (
  ...
        <Button bsSize="xsmall" onClick={() => { deleteIssue(index); }}>
        <Button bsSize="xsmall" onClick={onDelete}>
);
...
```

We'll need to make a similar change to the Close button (not shown for the sake of brevity). The complete changes to the IssueTable.jsx file are shown in Listing 11-10.

Listing 11-10. ui/src/IssueTable.jsx: Changes for Using Bootstrap Table, Clickable Rows, and Edit Button

```
...
import { Link, NavLink, withRouter } from 'react-router-dom';
import { LinkContainer } from 'react-router-bootstrap';
import {
  Button, Glyphicon, Tooltip, OverlayTrigger, Table,
} from 'react-bootstrap';

const IssueRow = withRouter(({
  ...
  const selectLocation = { pathname: `/issues/${issue.id}`, search };
  const editTooltip = (
    <Tooltip id="close-tooltip" placement="top">Edit Issue</Tooltip>
  );
  ...
  const deleteTooltip = (
    ...
  );

  function onClose(e) {
    e.preventDefault();
    closeIssue(index);
  }

  function onDelete(e) {
    e.preventDefault();
    deleteIssue(index);
  }

  return (
  const tableRow = (
    ...
        <Link to={`/edit/${issue.id}`}>Edit</Link>
        {' | '}
        <LinkContainer to={`/edit/${issue.id}`}>
          <OverlayTrigger delayShow={1000} overlay={editTooltip}>
            <Button bsSize="xsmall">
              <Glyphicon glyph="edit" />
            </Button>
          </OverlayTrigger>
        </LinkContainer>
```

```
      </LinkContainer>
      {' '}
      <NavLink to={selectLocation}>Select</NavLink>
      {' | '}
  ...
        <Button bsSize="xsmall" onClick={() => { closeIssue(index); }}>
        <Button bsSize="xsmall" onClick={onClose}>
  ...
        <Button bsSize="xsmall" onClick={() => { deleteIssue(index); }}>
        <Button bsSize="xsmall" onClick={onDelete}>
  ...
    );

  return (
    <LinkContainer to={selectLocation}>
      {tableRow}
    </LinkContainer>
  );
});
...

export default function IssueTable({ issues, closeIssue, deleteIssue }) {
  ...
  return (
    <table>
    <Table bordered condensed hover responsive>
      ...
    </table>
    </Table>
    ...
  );
}
...
```

Let's also give an indication that the table rows are clickable by changing the cursor to a pointer. Also, we can now remove the styles we used for setting borders to the original table, as well as show the NavLinks highlighted when active. These changes to the style are shown in Listing 11-11.

Listing 11-11. ui/public/index.html: Removal of Old Styles and New Style for Table Rows

```
...
  <style>
    table.bordered-table th, td {border: 1px solid silver; padding: 4px;}
    table.bordered-table {border-collapse: collapse;}
    a.active {background-color: #D8D8F5;}
    table.table-hover tr {cursor: pointer;}
...
```

If you test the application now, you will find that the table looks different. It now fills the screen horizontally, and the row under the cursor is highlighted. You can click on the row to select rather than use the old select link. Clicking on the Close or Delete button should *not* select the issue. A quick test using the mobile emulator should also confirm that the table is horizontally scrollable. A screenshot of the new Issue List page is shown in Figure 11-7.

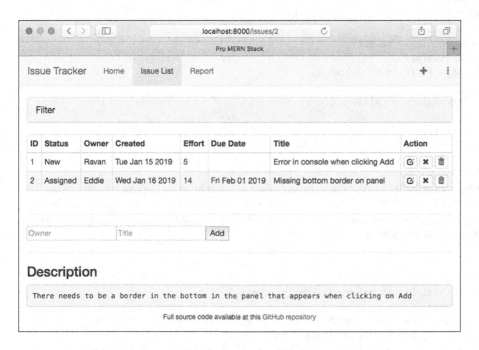

Figure 11-7. *The Issue List page with the Bootstrap table*

Forms

Forms can be styled and laid out in a variety of ways using Bootstrap. But before getting into laying out forms, let's first use the basic components that the library provides to replace the simple <input> and <select> options with the React-Bootstrap equivalents and the labels for these. Let's do this in the Issue Filter form.

In this section, we'll be using many new React-Bootstrap components. Let's import them first in IssueFilter.jsx.

```
...
import {
  ButtonToolbar, Button, FormGroup, FormControl, ControlLabel, InputGroup,
} from 'react-bootstrap';
...
```

Using React-Bootstrap, the common input types are instantiated using a FormControl. By default, it uses a regular <input> type to render the actual element. The componentClass property can be used to change this default to any other element type, for example, select. The rest of the properties, like value and onChange, are the same for a form control as for the regular <input> or <select> elements.

335

A label can be associated with the form control using the ControlLabel component. The only child of this component is the label text. To keep the label and the control together, they need to be put together under a FormGroup. For example, the dropdown for the status filter and its label can be rewritten like this:

```
...
        <FormGroup>
          <ControlLabel>Status:</ControlLabel>
          <FormControl
            componentClass="select"
            value={status}
            onChange={this.onChangeStatus}
          >
            <option value="">(All)</option>
            ...
          </FormControl>
        </FormGroup>
...
```

The Effort inputs are not that straightforward since they're made up of two inputs. We can use an InputGroup to enclose the two FormControls, but by itself, it will cause the two inputs to appear one below the other. The InputGroup.Addon component can be used to display the inputs next to each other, as well as show the dash between the two inputs.

```
...
        <FormGroup>
          <ControlLabel>Effort between:</ControlLabel>
          <InputGroup>
            <FormControl value={effortMin} onChange={this.onChangeEffortMin} />
            <InputGroup.Addon>-</InputGroup.Addon>
            <FormControl value={effortMax} onChange={this.onChangeEffortMax} />
          </InputGroup>
        </FormGroup>
...
```

We used a space character between the two buttons. A better way to do this (and keep the buttons together) is to use the ButtonToolbar component.

```
...
        <ButtonToolbar>
          <Button ...>
            Apply
          </Button>
          {' '}
          <Button
            ...
          >
            Reset
          </Button>
        </ButtonToolbar>
...
```

The complete changes to the IssueFilter component are shown in Listing 11-12.

Listing 11-12. ui/src/IssueFilter.jsx: Replace Inputs with Bootstrap Form Controls

```
...
import { Button } from 'react-bootstrap';
import {
  ButtonToolbar, Button, FormGroup, FormControl, ControlLabel, InputGroup,
} from 'react-bootstrap';
...

  render() {
    ...
    return (
      <div>
        Status:
        {' '}
        <select value={status} onChange={this.onChangeStatus}>
          <option value="">(All)</option>
          ...
        </select>
        <FormGroup>
          <ControlLabel>Status:</ControlLabel>
          <FormControl
            componentClass="select"
            value={status}
            onChange={this.onChangeStatus}
          >
            <option value="">(All)</option>
            ...
          </FormControl>
        </FormGroup>
        {' '}
        Effort between:
        {' '}
        <input
          size={5}
          value={effortMin}
          onChange={this.onChangeEffortMin}
        />
        {' - '}
        <input
          size={5}
          value={effortMax}
          onChange={this.onChangeEffortMax}
        />
        <FormGroup>
          <ControlLabel>Effort between:</ControlLabel>
          <InputGroup>
            <FormControl value={effortMin} onChange={this.onChangeEffortMin} />
            <InputGroup.Addon>-</InputGroup.Addon>
```

```
                <FormControl value={effortMax} onChange={this.onChangeEffortMax} />
              </InputGroup>
            </FormGroup>
            {'  '}
            <ButtonToolbar>
              <Button ...>
                Apply
              </Button>
              {'  '}
              <Button ...>
                Reset
              </Button>
            </ButtonToolbar>
        </div>
      );
    }
...
```

After these changes to use Bootstrap form controls, there should be no change in the functionality of the application. The filter will now look different, as shown in the screenshot in Figure 11-8.

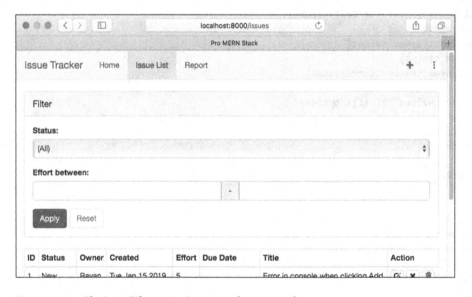

Figure 11-8. *The Issue Filter using Bootstrap form controls*

The Grid System

The default way the form gets laid out in the Issue Filter is not great, as it occupies a lot of space vertically, and the input controls are unnecessarily wide. But this may work well for narrow screens or narrow sections within a page.

A better way to deal with this is to use Bootstrap's grid system and let each field (and that includes the label) float, that is, occupy the space next to its precedent, or below its precedent if the width of the screen doesn't allow it. The Issue Filter is a good use case for this behavior, because we'd like to see it laid out horizontally, but on smaller screens, one below the other.

The grid system works this way: the horizontal space is divided into a maximum of 12 columns. A cell (using the component Col) can occupy one or more columns and a different number of columns at different screen widths. The cells wrap if there are more than 12 column-space cells within a row (Row component). A new row is required if there's a need to force a break in the flow of cells. When it comes to forms, the best way to use the grid system is to have a single row and specify how many columns each form control (one cell) occupies at different screen widths. For example:

```
...
<Grid fluid>
  <Row>
    <Col xs={4}>...</Col>
    <Col xs={6}>...</Col>
    <Col xs={3}>...</Col>
  </Row>
</Grid>
...
```

This grid has one row with three cells, occupying four, six, and three columns each. The xs property denotes an "extra small" screen width, therefore, these cell widths are applicable only to a mobile device. The width allocation for other screen sizes can be specified using sm, md, and lg, which stand for small, medium, and large screens, respectively. If not specified, the value applicable to the screen size *lesser* than this size will be used. Thus, using xs only will mean the same cell widths are used for all screen sizes.

Bootstrap then takes care of laying them out and deciding how to fit the cells at different screen widths. In the filter, we have three cells of roughly equal width: status input (with its label), effort inputs (with their label), and the buttons (together). We don't want to break either the effort inputs or the buttons into multiple lines even on very small screens, so we'll treat them as one cell each.

Let's start with the smallest screen size: a mobile device. Let's use half the screen width per cell. This will mean that we'll have Status and Effort on one line, and the buttons on the next. This can be achieved by specifying xs={6}, that is, half the total available 12 columns. You may wonder how three cells of six columns each, totaling 18 columns, can fit a row of 12 columns. But the fact is that the grid system wraps the last six columns into another line (not row, mind you).

It's best to compare the fluid grid system with paragraphs and lines. Rows are like paragraphs rather than lines. A paragraph (row) can contain multiple lines. As the paragraph width (screen width) reduces, it will need more lines. It's only when you want to break two sets of sentences (sets of cells) that you really need another paragraph (row). Most people take some time to appreciate this aspect of the fluid grid system, because many popular examples show rows and columns in a fixed grid rather than a fluid one, and therefore lay out the screen in multiple rows.

Next, let's consider a slightly bigger screen: a tablet, in landscape mode. The property for this size is sm. Let's fill the screen width with all three cells in one line. We must use a width of four columns for each, thus specifying sm={4} for these cells. If we had more cells, then this too would wrap into multiple lines but since we have exactly three, this will fit the screen in one line.

On larger screens like desktops, we can let each cell continue to occupy four columns each, which doesn't require any more property specifications. But I think it looks ungainly if the form controls stretch too much, so let's reduce the width of the cells using md={3} and lg={2}. This will cause the trailing columns on larger screens to be unoccupied.

Bootstrap's grid system usually starts with a `<Grid>`, but our entire content is already wrapped by a grid, so we don't need another. We can directly add a `<Row>`, within which we can add `<Col>`s, which will hold each of the FormGroups or ButtonToolbar. Let's first import these two components.

```
...
import {
  ...
  Row, Col,
} from 'react-bootstrap';
...
```

Now, we can add a single Row to replace the `<div>` and three Cols within it, which will wrap the form groups and the button toolbar.

```
...
    <Row>
      <Col xs={6} sm={4} md={3} lg={2}>
        <FormGroup>
          ...
        </FormGroup>
      </Col>
      <Col xs={6} sm={4} md={3} lg={2}>
        <FormGroup>
          ...
        </FormGroup>
      </Col>
      <Col xs={6} sm={4} md={3} lg={2}>
        <ButtonToolbar>
          ...
        </ButtonToolbar>
      </Col>
    </Row>
...
```

But this will show a problem in the alignment. Since the height of the first two cells includes the label, it is larger than that of the button toolbar. The contents being center aligned vertically, the buttons will appear above the line of the dropdown and the input fields. To set this right, we'll need to add a FormGroup for the button toolbar as well, with a blank label using .

```
...
        <FormGroup>
          <ControlLabel> </ControlLabel>
          <ButtonToolbar>
            ...
          </ButtonToolbar>
        </FormGroup>
...
```

The final changes for the Issue Filter are shown in Listing 11-13. (Note that changes to indentation are not highlighted.)

Listing 11-13. ui/src/IssueFilter.jsx: Using the Grid System for Issue Filter

```
...
import {
  ...
  Row, Col,
} from 'react-bootstrap';
...

  render() {
    ...
    return (
      <div>
      <Row>
        <Col xs={6} sm={4} md={3} lg={2}>
          <FormGroup>
            <ControlLabel>Status:</ControlLabel>
            ...
          </FormGroup>
        </Col>
        <Col xs={6} sm={4} md={3} lg={2}>
          <FormGroup>
            <ControlLabel>Effort between:</ControlLabel>
            ...
          </FormGroup>
        </Col>
        <Col xs={6} sm={4} md={3} lg={2}>
          <FormGroup>
            <ControlLabel> </ControlLabel>
            <ButtonToolbar>
            ...
            </ButtonToolbar>
          </FormGroup>
        </Col>
      </Row>
      </div>
    );
  }
```

If you test these changes, you should not find any difference in behavior except the layout of the form. The screenshots for a very small and a small screen size are shown in Figure 11-9 and Figure 11-10, respectively.

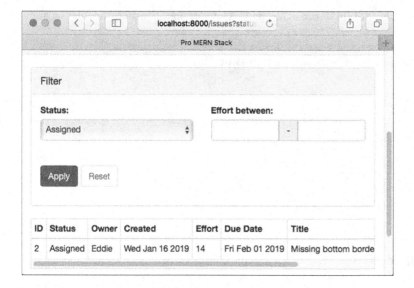

Figure 11-9. *The Issue Filter with grid system in a very small screen*

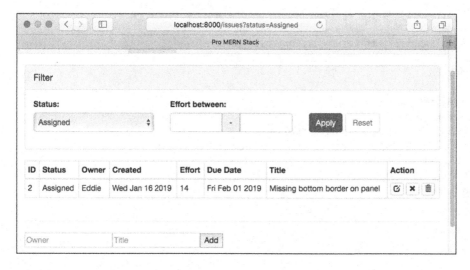

Figure 11-10. *The Issue Filter with grid system in a small screen*

```
                    EXERCISE: GRID SYSTEM
```

1. Let's say the cells are larger and you need the cells to (a) on very small screens, appear one below the other, (b) on small screens, have a max of two cells per line, (c) on medium sized screens, together fit the width, and (d) on large screens, together occupy two-thirds the screen width. What would be the width specifications for the columns in this case?

2. Although great for mobile devices, the input controls look a bit oversized on a desktop browser. What can be done to make them look smaller? Hint: Look up the React-Bootstrap documentation for forms at `https://react-bootstrap.github.io/components/forms/` and look for a property that controls the size. You may find multiple options, so choose the one that you think is best.

Answers are available at the end of the chapter.

Inline Forms

Sometimes we want the form controls next to each other, including the labels. This is ideal for small forms with two or three inputs that can all fit in one line and are closely related. This style will suit the Issue Add form. Let's also replace the placeholders with labels to make them more obvious, which means we'll have to use FormGroups and ControlLabels as we did for the Filter form.

For the grid-based forms, we didn't have to enclose the controls or the groups within a <Form>, since the default behavior of the groups was a vertical layout (one below the other, including labels). For inline forms, we need a <Form> with the inline property to wrap around the form controls. This also comes in handy because we need to set the other attributes of the form: name and submit handler.

Unlike the grid-based form, an inline form needs no columns and rows. The FormGroup elements can be placed one after the other. Further, the button does not need a FormGroup around it, and there are no alignment implications if a ControlLabel is not given for a button. As for spacing between the elements, we need to manually add space using { ' ' } between the label and the control, as well as between form groups.

These are the only changes for converting the Issue Add form to a Bootstrap inline form. These are shown in Listing 11-14.

Listing 11-14. ui/src/IssueAdd.jsx: Changes for Conversion to an Inline Form

```
...
import PropTypes from 'prop-types';
import {
  Form, FormControl, FormGroup, ControlLabel, Button,
} from 'react-bootstrap';
...

  render() {
    return (
      <form Form inline name="issueAdd" onSubmit={this.handleSubmit}>
        <input type="text" name="owner" placeholder="Owner" />
        <input type="text" name="title" placeholder="Title" />
```

```
        <button type="submit">Add</button>
        <FormGroup>
          <ControlLabel>Owner:</ControlLabel>
          {' '}
          <FormControl type="text" name="owner" />
        </FormGroup>
        {' '}
        <FormGroup>
          <ControlLabel>Title:</ControlLabel>
          {' '}
          <FormControl type="text" name="title" />
        </FormGroup>
        {' '}
        <Button bsStyle="primary" type="submit">Add</Button>
      </form>
      </Form>
  );
}
...
```

This is perhaps a good time to remove the horizontal rules from the Issue List page since the tables and forms themselves have a distinct separation. The footer does need a separation from the rest of the page, so let's add a horizontal rule in the footer. These changes are shown in Listing 11-15 and Listing 11-16.

Listing 11-15. ui/src/IssueList.jsx: Removal of Horizontal Rules

```
...
        <IssueTable
          ...
        >
        <hr />
        <IssueAdd createIssue={this.createIssue} />
        <hr />
...
```

Listing 11-16. ui/src/Page.jsx: Addition of Horizontal Rule Above the Footer

```
...
function Footer() {
  return (
    <small>
      <hr />
      <p className="text-center">
...
```

You will find, on testing the application now, that the changes are only visual. Do ensure that the functionality has not changed. A screenshot of the new screen is shown in Figure 11-11.

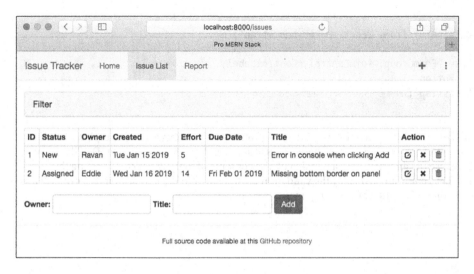

Figure 11-11. *The Issue Add form as an inline form*

EXERCISE: INLINE FORMS

1. Try viewing the new `IssueAdd` form on a very small screen. What do you see? What does it tell you about Bootstrap and forms?

2. Let's say you did not change to use labels for the controls. Do you still need a `FormGroup`? Try it out, especially in very small screen size.

3. The widths of the two controls are identical, and it seems we have no control over this. The `bsSize` property seems to affect only the height. If we want to show a wider Title Input, what can be done?

Answers are available at the end of the chapter.

Horizontal Forms

The next type of form we will explore is the horizontal form, where the label appears to the left of the input, but each field appears one below the other. Typically, the input fills the parent container until the right edge, giving it an aligned look. Let's change the Issue Edit page to use a horizontal form, since this form has a lot of fields and this kind of form will suit it. While we are at it, let's also use the validation states that Bootstrap provides to highlight invalid input rather than our own rudimentary method to display validation error in the Date input.

Let's first import the new components that we'll be using in `IssueEdit.jsx`.

```
...
import { LinkContainer } from 'react-router-bootstrap';
import {
  Col, Panel, Form, FormGroup, FormControl, ControlLabel,
  ButtonToolbar, Button,
} from 'react-bootstrap';
...
```

To lay out a horizontal form, we need the horizontal property, therefore, we need to replace a plain
<form> with Bootstrap's <Form> and set this property. Let's also move the <h3> showing the ID of the issue
being edited and enclose the entire form in a panel, with the contents of the original <h3> forming the
header of the panel. Let's continue to display the validation message within the panel, after the form. All this
is in the render() method of the IssueEdit component.

```
...
    return (
      <Panel>
        <Panel.Heading>
          <Panel.Title>{`Editing issue: ${id}`}</Panel.Title>
        </Panel.Heading>
        <Panel.Body>
          <Form horizontal onSubmit={this.handleSubmit}>
            ...
          </Form>
          {validationMessage}
        </Panel.Body>
      </Panel>
    )
...
```

Within the form, we can have the usual FormGroups for each of the editable fields. Within that, we'll
have the control label and the actual control. But that's not all. We also need to specify how much width the
label and the input will occupy. For this, we need to enclose the <ControlLabel> and the <FormControl>
within <Col>s and specify the column widths. Since we want it to fill the screen in most cases, we won't
use different widths for different screen sizes, just one specification for the small screen width using the sm
property that splits the label and the input in some proportion. The grid system will use the same ratio for
bigger screen widths. As for the very small screen width, it will cause it to collapse to a single column. Let's
choose a 3-9 split between the two columns.

For example, the owner field *could* look like this:

```
...
              <FormGroup>
                <Col sm={3}>
                  <ControlLabel>Owner</ControlLabel>
                </Col>
                <Col sm={9}>
                  <FormControl name="owner" ... />
                </Col>
              </FormGroup>
...
```

Enclosing the `<FormControl>` with a `<Col>` works great, but for a `<ControlLabel>`, this does not have the intended effect of right-aligning the label. The suggested method in the Bootstrap documentation is to set the `componentClass` of the `<Col>` to `ControlLabel` instead. This has the effect of rendering a single element with the combined classes of a `ControlLabel` and a `Col` rather than a label within a `<div>`.

Recall that we can specify our own component classes for the `FormInput` as well. This lets us use the custom components `NumInput`, `DateInput`, and `TextInput` in place of a regular `<input>` where we need them. The final code for the Owner field thus is as follows:

```
...
        <FormGroup>
          <Col componentClass={ControlLabel} sm={3}>Owner</Col>
          <Col sm={9}>
            <FormControl
              componentClass={TextInput}
              name="owner"
              value={owner}
              onChange={this.onChange}
              key={id}
            />
          </Col>
        </FormGroup>
...
```

All other controls can be written similarly, with the `componentClass` for the Status dropdown being `select`, for the Owner, Title, and Description fields `TextInput`, for Effort `NumInput`, and for Due `DateInput`. All the other properties that the original controls used can be retained as such. For changes to these other controls, refer to Listing 11-17; I am not calling out these changes here for the sake of brevity.

As for the Created Date field, React-Bootstrap provides a static control in the form of the component `FormControl.Static`. Let's use that.

```
...
            <FormControl.Static>
              {created.toDateString()}
            </FormControl.Static>
...
```

For the Submit button, we can convert it to a Bootstrap `Button` component using the `primary` style. But the usual expectation is that there needs to be a Cancel operation following any Submit action. Since this is not a dialog, let's use a link back to the Issue List in place of the Cancel operation. This can be achieved by a `LinkContainer` surrounding the new Back button, which is styled as a link.

```
...
        <ButtonToolbar>
          <Button bsStyle="primary" type="submit">Submit</Button>
          <LinkContainer to="/issues">
            <Button bsStyle="link">Back</Button>
          </LinkContainer>
        </ButtonToolbar>
...
```

Now, since the buttons don't need a label, we could us the same trick as before, supplying an empty label in the first cell. But a better way to do this, now that we have columns within a grid, is to specify an offset to where the column starts.

```
...
            <FormGroup>
              <Col smOffset={3} sm={6}>
                <ButtonToolbar>
                  ...
                </ButtonToolbar>
              </Col>
            </FormGroup>
...
```

We can retain the Next and Prev links, but let's use a Panel footer to place them in, right after the end of the panel body.

```
...
        </Panel.Body>
        <Panel.Footer>
          <Link to={`/edit/${id - 1}`}>Prev</Link>
          {' | '}
          <Link to={`/edit/${id + 1}`}>Next</Link>
        </Panel.Footer>
...
```

Bootstrap's form controls support displaying invalid input fields in a distinctive manner. To achieve this, the validationState property can be used in any FormGroup. A value of error for this property makes it display the label and the control in red, as well as an red cross icon to indicate the same within the form control.

We only have the date input Due field, which can have an invalid state in this form. Let's use the state variable invalidFields and look for the property with this field's name to be present in that object to determine the validity.

```
...
            <FormGroup validationState={
              invalidFields.due ? 'error' : null
            }
            >
              <Col componentClass={ControlLabel} sm={3}>Due</Col>
...
```

The complete changes to the IssueEdit.jsx file are shown in Listing 11-17. For the sake of readability, the entire render() method is shown rather than the lines removed and added as struck-through and bold, respectively. The only other change is in the imports, which are shown using the regular convention.

Listing 11-17. ui/src/IssueEdit.jsx: render() Method Rewritten to Use a Bootstrap Horizontal Form

```
...
import { Link } from 'react-router-dom';
import { LinkContainer } from 'react-router-bootstrap';
```

```
import {
  Col, Panel, Form, FormGroup, FormControl, ControlLabel,
  ButtonToolbar, Button,
} from 'react-bootstrap';
...

    return (
      <Panel>
        <Panel.Heading>
          <Panel.Title>{`Editing issue: ${id}`}</Panel.Title>
        </Panel.Heading>
        <Panel.Body>
          <Form horizontal onSubmit={this.handleSubmit}>
            <FormGroup>
              <Col componentClass={ControlLabel} sm={3}>Created</Col>
              <Col sm={9}>
                <FormControl.Static>
                  {created.toDateString()}
                </FormControl.Static>
              </Col>
            </FormGroup>
            <FormGroup>
              <Col componentClass={ControlLabel} sm={3}>Status</Col>
              <Col sm={9}>
                <FormControl
                  componentClass="select"
                  name="status"
                  value={status}
                  onChange={this.onChange}
                >
                  <option value="New">New</option>
                  <option value="Assigned">Assigned</option>
                  <option value="Fixed">Fixed</option>
                  <option value="Closed">Closed</option>
                </FormControl>
              </Col>
            </FormGroup>
            <FormGroup>
              <Col componentClass={ControlLabel} sm={3}>Owner</Col>
              <Col sm={9}>
                <FormControl
                  componentClass={TextInput}
                  name="owner"
                  value={owner}
                  onChange={this.onChange}
                  key={id}
                />
              </Col>
            </FormGroup>
```

```
<FormGroup>
  <Col componentClass={ControlLabel} sm={3}>Effort</Col>
  <Col sm={9}>
    <FormControl
      componentClass={NumInput}
      name="effort"
      value={effort}
      onChange={this.onChange}
      key={id}
    />
  </Col>
</FormGroup>
<FormGroup validationState={
  invalidFields.due ? 'error' : null
}
>
  <Col componentClass={ControlLabel} sm={3}>Due</Col>
  <Col sm={9}>
    <FormControl
      componentClass={DateInput}
      onValidityChange={this.onValidityChange}
      name="due"
      value={due}
      onChange={this.onChange}
      key={id}
    />
    <FormControl.Feedback />
  </Col>
</FormGroup>
<FormGroup>
  <Col componentClass={ControlLabel} sm={3}>Title</Col>
  <Col sm={9}>
    <FormControl
      componentClass={TextInput}
      size={50}
      name="title"
      value={title}
      onChange={this.onChange}
      key={id}
    />
  </Col>
</FormGroup>
<FormGroup>
  <Col componentClass={ControlLabel} sm={3}>Description</Col>
  <Col sm={9}>
    <FormControl
      componentClass={TextInput}
      tag="textarea"
      rows={4}
      cols={50}
      name="description"
      value={description}
```

```
            onChange={this.onChange}
            key={id}
          />
        </Col>
      </FormGroup>
      <FormGroup>
        <Col smOffset={3} sm={6}>
          <ButtonToolbar>
            <Button bsStyle="primary" type="submit">Submit</Button>
            <LinkContainer to="/issues">
              <Button bsStyle="link">Back</Button>
            </LinkContainer>
          </ButtonToolbar>
        </Col>
      </FormGroup>
    </Form>
    {validationMessage}
  </Panel.Body>
  <Panel.Footer>
    <Link to={`/edit/${id - 1}`}>Prev</Link>
    {' | '}
    <Link to={`/edit/${id + 1}`}>Next</Link>
  </Panel.Footer>
</Panel>
  );
}
...
```

At this point, if you test the application, you will find that the date field is not filling the width of the screen. It also looks quite differently styled from the other inputs. The reason is that we are setting the class for the input within DateInput to either 'null' or 'invalid', depending on the validation state. Bootstrap would have normally set a class for the input, and our setting, especially the null, overwrites it.

What we need within the DateInput class is to retain the class that Bootstrap would have set to the <input>. One option is to replace the className with this.props.className. But there could be other properties being passed through, apart from className. So it is safer to use the rest of the properties and pass them through to the <input> element. Also, we don't need to set the class to invalid, as Bootstrap's validationState replaces that.

The changes to DateInput are shown in Listing 11-18.

Listing 11-18. ui/src/DateInput.jsx: Pass Through Class and Other Properties from Parent

```
...
  render() {
    const { valid, focused, value } = this.state;
    const { value: origValue, name } = this.props;
    const className = (!valid && !focused) ? 'invalid' : null;
    const { value: origValue, onValidityChange, ...props } = this.props;
    const displayValue = (focused || !valid) ? value
      : displayFormat(origValue);
    return (
      <input
        type="text"
```

351

```
      size={20}
      name={name}
      className={className}
      {...props}
      value={displayValue}
      placeholder={focused ? 'yyyy-mm-dd' : null}
      onFocus={this.onFocus}
    ...
  }
...
```

After this change, the form will look as it should when you test it. A screenshot of this form is shown in Figure 11-12, which includes the validation message and error indication for the Due field, which shows a red border and a red X.

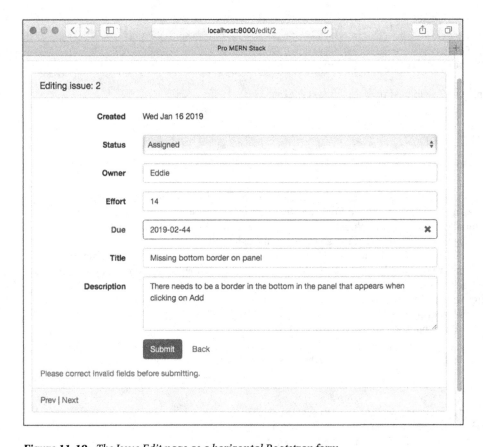

Figure 11-12. *The Issue Edit page as a horizontal Bootstrap form*

EXERCISE: HORIZONTAL FORMS

1. Add a validation for checking if the title is three characters or more using Bootstrap's `validationState`, as we did for the Due field. How is this different in effect from the Due field's validation? How is it different visually? Why?

Answers are available at the end of the chapter.

Validation Alerts

Bootstrap provides nicely styled alerts via the `Alert` component. The first candidate to convert to a Bootstrap-styled alert is the validation message in the Issue Edit page. This could look aligned and styled like the rest of the page. Also it could be subtler. Since the form field itself shows that something is wrong, the error message needn't be displayed until after the users click Submit. We'll also let the users dismiss the message after they've seen it.

React-Bootstraps's `<Alert>` component works well for this. It has different styles for the message like danger and warning, and it also has the ability to show a Close icon. Let's include this component in the list of imports in the `IssueEdit` component.

```
...
import {
  ...
  ButtonToolbar, Button, Alert,
} from 'react-bootstrap';
...
```

Then, let's use this component to construct the validation message.

```
...
    validationMessage = (
      <div className="error">
      <Alert bsStyle="danger">
        Please correct invalid fields before submitting.
      </Alert>
      </div>
...
```

But its visibility needs to be handled by the parent component: the message should be shown conditionally based on a state variable in `IssueEdit`. Let's add this state variable.

```
...
  constructor() {
    ...
    this.state = {
      ...
      showingValidation: false,
    };
...
```

Let's use this new state variable to control the contents of validationMessage while initializing this variable.

```
...
    const { invalidFields, showingValidation } = this.state;
    let validationMessage;
    if (Object.keys(invalidFields).length !== 0 && showingValidation) {
      validationMessage = (
        ...
      );
    }
...
```

The Close icon is part of <Alert> and to cause that icon to make the message disappear, we have to pass in a handler that modifies the visibility state. The Alert component takes in a callback named onDismiss to achieve this. This callback is called when the user clicks the Close icon. Let's now define two methods to toggle the state of the validation message's visibility and bind them to this in the constructor (refer to Listing 11-19 for the bind statements).

```
...
  showValidation() {
    this.setState({ showingValidation: true });
  }

  dismissValidation() {
    this.setState({ showingValidation: false });
  }
...
```

The second method can be passed as the onDismiss property to the Alert component.

```
...
      <Alert bsStyle="danger" onDismiss={this.dismissValidation}>
...
```

Now, the validation message's visibility is always false. As we'd decided, let's start showing the message when the user clicks Submit. This can be done by calling showValidation() unconditionally in the submit handler. If there are no errors, the validation message is suppressed.

```
...
  async handleSubmit(e) {
    e.preventDefault();
    this.showValidation();
    ...
  }
...
```

Let's also move the validation message from outside the form to align with the Submit button in a new form group, right after the FormGroup containing the Submit button. We'll use the same strategy as for the button toolbar in specifying an offset to start the validation message's column.

```
...
        <FormGroup>
          <Col smOffset={3} sm={9}>{validationMessage}</Col>
        </FormGroup>
      </Form>
      {validationMessage}
...
```

The complete changes to the IssueEdit component are shown in Listing 11-19.

Listing 11-19. ui/src/IssueEdit.jsx: Showing Validation Using Bootstrap Alert Component

```
...
import {
  ...
  ButtonToolbar, Button, Alert,
} from 'react-bootstrap';
...

  constructor() {
    ...
    this.state = {
      ...
      showingValidation: false,
    };
  }
...

  async handleSubmit(e) {
    e.preventDefault();
    this.showValidation();
    ...
  }
...

  async loadData() {
    ...
  }

  showValidation() {
    this.setState({ showingValidation: true });
  }

  dismissValidation() {
    this.setState({ showingValidation: false });
  }
...
```

```
render() {
  ...
  const { invalidFields, showingValidation } = this.state;
  let validationMessage;
  if (Object.keys(invalidFields).length !== 0 && showingValidation) {
    validationMessage = (
      <div className="error">
      <Alert bsStyle="danger" onDismiss={this.dismissValidation}>
        Please correct invalid fields before submitting.
      </Alert>
      </div>
    );
  }
  ...
          <FormGroup>
            <Col smOffset={3} sm={9}>{validationMessage}</Col>
          </FormGroup>
        </Form>
        {validationMessage}
  }
...
```

At this point in time, we can get rid of some styles that were being used to show these errors in red font. The changes to the stylesheet are shown in Listing 11-20.

Listing 11-20. ui/public/index.html: Removal of Old Styles

```
...
  <style>
    ...
    input.invalid {border-color: red;}
    div.error {color: red;}
    ....
  </style>
...
```

Now, if you test the application, you will find that errors in the Due field are prevented from being submitted. The stylized error message is shown only after you click Submit, and the error message can be dismissed using the red X on the top-right corner of the alert message. A screenshot of the Issue Edit page with an error in the Due field is shown in Figure 11-13.

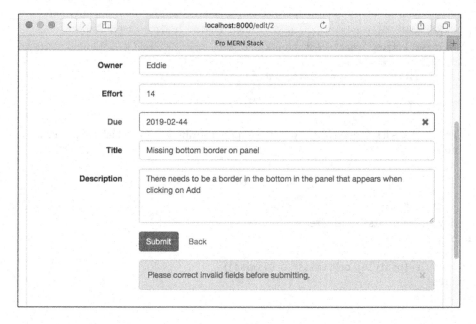

Figure 11-13. *A validation message using Bootstrap Alert in danger style*

Toasts

Let's now look at result messages and informational alerts, that is, the reporting of successes and failures of an operation. These messages are intended to be unobtrusive, so let's make them disappear after a few seconds automatically rather than make the users close them. We'll also let the messages overlay the page as well as transition in and out like the Toast messages in the Android OS.

Since many pages have the need to show such messages, let's create a new custom component for this that can be reused. Let's name this new component Toast after the Android OS's Toast message. We'll model the interface on the Alert component itself: the visibility will be controlled by the parent, which passes an onDismiss property, which can be called to dismiss it. In addition to the Close icon's click calling this onDismiss callback, there will also be a timer that calls onDismiss() when it expires. The message it shows can be specified as children to the component.

Here's an example of this component, which can be placed anywhere in the DOM hierarchy in the parent because it will be absolutely positioned outside the layout of the parent.

```
...
    <Toast
      showing={this.state.showingToast}
      onDismiss={this.dismissToast}
      bsStyle="success"
    >
...
```

Let's start implementing the Toast component in a new file called Toast.jsx under the ui/src directory. We'll start with the basic import of React and the React-Bootstrap components we'll use: Alert and Collapse and the definition of the class itself.

```
...
import React from 'react';
import { Alert, Collapse } from 'react-bootstrap';

export default class Toast extends React.Component {
}
...
```

In the render() method, we'll first add an alert with the required attributes, all of which are passed in from the parent as props.

```
...
  render() {
    const {
      showing, bsStyle, onDismiss, children,
    } = this.props;
    return (
        <Alert bsStyle={bsStyle} onDismiss={onDismiss}>
          {children}
        </Alert>
    );
  }
...
```

Let's position the alert message close to the bottom-left corner of the window, overlaying any other UI elements. To do this, we can enclose the alert within a <div> that is absolutely positioned using the style position: fixed.

```
...
      <div style={{ position: 'fixed', bottom: 20, left: 20 }}>
        <Alert ... />
      </div>
...
```

To show and hide the alert, we'll use React-Bootstrap's Collapse component. This component takes in a property called in which determines whether its child element fades in or out. When set to true, the child element shows (fades in) and when set to false, it hides (fades out). We can directly use the passed-in property showing for this purpose.

```
...
      <Collapse in={showing}>
        <div ... />
      </Collapse>
...
```

Now, let's set up an automatic dismiss after five seconds. Since we expect the Toast to be constructed with showing set to false, we can expect a componentDidUpdate() call whenever the Toast is being shown. So, within this lifecycle method, lets add a timer and call onDismiss on its expiry.

```
...
componentDidUpdate() {
    const { showing, onDismiss } = this.props;
    if (showing) {
      setTimeout(onDismiss, 5000);
    }
  }
...
```

But the timer may fire even if the user has navigated away from the page, so it's a good idea to dismiss the timer when the component is unmounted. So, let's save the timer in an object variable called dismissTimer and clear this timer when the component is being unmounted. Let's also clear the same timer before setting up a new one.

```
...
  componentDidUpdate() {
    ...
    if (showing) {
      clearTimeout(this.dismissTimer);
      this.dismissTimer = setTimeout(onDismiss, 5000);
    }
  }

  componentWillUnmount() {
    clearTimeout(this.dismissTimer);
  }
...
```

The complete source code of Toast.jsx is shown in Listing 11-21.

Listing 11-21. ui/src/Toast.jsx: New Component to Show a Toast Message

```
import React from 'react';
import { Alert, Collapse } from 'react-bootstrap';

export default class Toast extends React.Component {
  componentDidUpdate() {
    const { showing, onDismiss } = this.props;
    if (showing) {
      clearTimeout(this.dismissTimer);
      this.dismissTimer = setTimeout(onDismiss, 5000);
    }
  }

  componentWillUnmount() {
    clearTimeout(this.dismissTimer);
  }

  render() {
    const {
      showing, bsStyle, onDismiss, children,
    } = this.props;
```

```
    return (
      <Collapse in={showing}>
        <div style={{ position: 'fixed', bottom: 20, left: 20 }}>
          <Alert bsStyle={bsStyle} onDismiss={onDismiss}>
            {children}
          </Alert>
        </div>
      </Collapse>
    );
  }
}
```

To use the Toast component, we'll have to make changes to all the components that need to show a success or error message. But there is also the data-fetching function in graphQLFetch.js that shows alerts on any error. Since this is not a component, let's make it so that the calling component passes in a callback to show errors. We'll also make this callback optional, so that the caller can choose to suppress the showing of errors and handle it by looking at the return value. We can also remove the comment that disables ESLint errors due to the presence of alert() function calls, because we'll no longer have these. The changes to graphQLFetch.js are shown in Listing 11-22.

Listing 11-22. ui/src/graphQLFetch.js: Changes for Replacing Alerts with a Callback

```
...
/* eslint "no-alert": "off" */
...

export default async function
graphQLFetch(query, variables= {}, showError = null) {
  ...
    if (result.errors) {
        ...
        alert(`${error.message}:\n ${details}`);
        if (showError) showError(`${error.message}:\n ${details}`);
    } else if (showError) {
        alert(`${error.extensions.code}: ${error.message}`);
        showError(`${error.extensions.code}: ${error.message}`);
    }
  }
  ...
  } catch (e) {
    alert(`Error in sending data to server: ${e.message}`);
    if (showError) showError(`Error in sending data to server: ${e.message}`);
    ...
  }
}
...
```

Next, let's change the components IssueDetail, IssueEdit, and IssueList to use the Toast. The changes for each of these components is very similar. Let's start with importing the component and the changes to the state. We need a variable for the visibility, another for the message, and one for the type of Toast (error, success, warning, etc.).

```
...
import Toast from './Toast.jsx';
...
  constructor() {
    this.state = {
      ...
      toastVisible: false,
      toastMessage: '',
      toastType: 'success',
    };
    ...
  }
...
```

Then, let's create three convenience functions: one to display a success message, one to display an error message, and one to dismiss the Toast. All these do is to set the state with new values for the Toast variables.

```
...
  showSuccess(message) {
    this.setState({
      toastVisible: true, toastMessage: message, toastType: 'success',
    });
  }

  showError(message) {
    this.setState({
      toastVisible: true, toastMessage: message, toastType: 'danger',
    });
  }

  dismissToast() {
    this.setState({ toastVisible: false });
  }
...
```

(These will have to be bound to this, the code for which I am not showing explicitly here. Refer to Listing 11-23.)

The method dismissToast() will be passed to the Toast component. We can replace any alerts with the showSuccess() method, for example in the IssueEdit component in handleSubmit:

```
...
    if (data) {
      this.setState({ issue: data.issueUpdate });
      alert('Updated issue successfully'); // eslint-disable-line no-alert
      this.showSuccess('Updated issue successfully');
    }
...
```

As for errors, we can pass the method this.showError to the function call of graphQLFetch():

```
...
    const data = await graphQLFetch(query, { ... }, this.showError);
...
```

The Toast component can be rendered anywhere, but let's choose to do it at the very end of the JSX, just before the final closing tag. In the case of IssueEdit, it will be just before the closing tag for the panel.

```
...
  render() {
    ...
    const { toastVisible, toastMessage, toastType } = this.state;

    return (
      <Panel>
        ...
        <Toast
          showing={toastVisible}
          onDismiss={this.dismissToast}
          bsStyle={toastType}
        >
          {toastMessage}
        </Toast>
      </Panel>
    );
...
```

The actual changes to each of the components is shown in the following listings, with minor variations in each component. In the IssueList component, let's add a success message on successful deletion of an issue in addition to the previous changes. In the IssueDetail component, there is no need for a success message, so that method and its binding are not included.

The changes to each of these components are shown in Listing 11-23, Listing 11-24, and Listing 11-25.

Listing 11-23. ui/src/IssueEdit.jsx: Changes for Using Toast Component

```
...
import TextInput from './TextInput.jsx';
import Toast from './Toast.jsx';
...

  constructor() {
    ...
    this.state = {
      ...
      toastVisible: false,
      toastMessage: '',
      toastType: 'success',
    };
    ...
```

```
    this.showSuccess = this.showSuccess.bind(this);
    this.showError = this.showError.bind(this);
    this.dismissToast = this.dismissToast.bind(this);
  }
  ...

  async handleSubmit(e) {
    ...
    const data = await graphQLFetch(query, { changes, id }, this.showError);
    if (data) {
      this.setState({ issue: data.issueUpdate });
      alert('Updated issue successfully'); // eslint-disable-line no-alert
      this.showSuccess('Updated issue successfully');
    }
  }

  async loadData() {
    ...
    const query = `query issue($id: Int!) {
      ...
    }`;

    const data = await graphQLFetch(query, { id }, this.showError);
    ...
  }
...

  dismissValidation() {
    ...
  }

  showSuccess(message) {
    this.setState({
      toastVisible: true, toastMessage: message, toastType: 'success',
    });
  }

  showError(message) {
    this.setState({
      toastVisible: true, toastMessage: message, toastType: 'danger',
    });
  }

  dismissToast() {
    this.setState({ toastVisible: false });
  }
...

  render() {
    ...
    const { toastVisible, toastMessage, toastType } = this.state;
```

```
    return (
      <Panel>
        ...
        <Toast
          showing={toastVisible}
          onDismiss={this.dismissToast}
          bsStyle={toastType}
        >
          {toastMessage}
        </Toast>
      </Panel>
    );
  }
...
```

Listing 11-24. ui/src/IssueDetail.jsx: Changes for Including Toast Component

```
...
import graphQLFetch from './graphQLFetch.js';
import Toast from './Toast.jsx';
...

  constructor() {
    this.state = { issue: {} };
      issue: {},
      toastVisible: false,
      toastMessage: '',
      toastType: 'info',
    };

    this.showError = this.showError.bind(this);
    this.dismissToast = this.dismissToast.bind(this);
  }
...
  componentDidUpdate(prevProps) {
    ...
  }

  showError(message) {
    this.setState({
      toastVisible: true, toastMessage: message, toastType: 'danger',
    });
  }

  dismissToast() {
    this.setState({ toastVisible: false });
  }
```

```
  async loadData() {
    ...
    const data = await graphQLFetch(query, { id }, this.showError);
    ...
  }

  render() {
    ...
    const { toastVisible, toastType, toastMessage } = this.state;
    return (
      <div>
        ...
        <Toast
          showing={toastVisible}
          onDismiss={this.dismissToast}
          bsStyle={toastType}
        >
          {toastMessage}
        </Toast>
      </div>
    );
  }
...
```

Listing 11-25. ui/src/IssueList.jsx: Changes for Including Toast Message

```
...
import graphQLFetch from './graphQLFetch.js';
import Toast from './Toast.jsx';
...

  constructor() {
    ...
    this.state = { issues: [] }
      issues: [],
      toastVisible: false,
      toastMessage: '',
      toastType: 'info',
    };
    ...
    this.showSuccess = this.showSuccess.bind(this);
    this.showError = this.showError.bind(this);
    this.dismissToast = this.dismissToast.bind(this);
  }
...

  async loadData() {
    ...
    const data = await graphQLFetch(query, vars, this.showError);
    ...
  }
```

```
async createIssue(issue) {
  ...
  const data = await graphQLFetch(query, { issue }, this.showError);
  ...
}

async closeIssue(index) {
  ...
  const data = await graphQLFetch(query, { id: issues[index].id },
    this.showError);
  ...
}

async deleteIssue(index) {
  ...
  const data = await graphQLFetch(query, { id }, this.showError);
  ...
  if (data && data.issueDelete) {
    ...
    this.showSuccess(`Deleted issue ${id} successfully.`);
  }
  ...
}

showSuccess(message) {
  this.setState({
    toastVisible: true, toastMessage: message, toastType: 'success',
  });
}

showError(message) {
  this.setState({
    toastVisible: true, toastMessage: message, toastType: 'danger',
  });
}

dismissToast() {
  this.setState({ toastVisible: false });
}

render() {
  const { issues } = this.state;
  const { toastVisible, toastType, toastMessage } = this.state;
  ...
  return (
    <React.Fragment>
      ...
      <Toast
        showing={toastVisible}
        onDismiss={this.dismissToast}
        bsStyle={toastType}
      >
```

```
      {toastMessage}
    </Toast>
  </React.Fragment>
 );
}
...
```

Now we've gotten rid of all alerts in the UI code and replaced them with Toast messages. You can test error messages by creating or updating an issue with invalid values such as the title being less than three characters. You can test success Toast messages by saving an Issue in the Edit page and deleting an issue. A screenshot of a success Toast message in the Edit page after saving changes is shown in Figure 11-14.

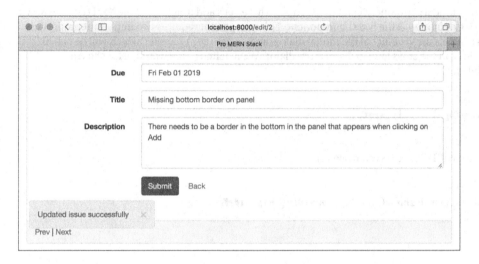

Figure 11-14. The Toast message in the Edit page

Modals

In this section, we'll replace the in-page IssueAdd component with a modal dialog that is launched by clicking the Create Issue navigation item in the header. This is so that the user can create an issue from anywhere in the application, not just from the Issue List page. Further, when the new issue is submitted, we'll show the newly created issue in the Issue Edit page, because this can be done regardless of where the dialog was launched from.

Instead of a modal dialog, the Create Issue can also be a separate page. But a modal works better when the number of required fields is small; the user can quickly create the issue and later fill up more information if required.

When a modal is rendered, it is rendered outside the main <div> of the DOM that holds the page. Thus, in terms of code placement, it can be placed anywhere in the component hierarchy. In order to launch or dismiss the modal, the Create Issue navigation item is the controlling component. So, let's create a component that is self-contained: it displays the navigation item, launches the dialog and controls its visibility, creates the issue, and routes to the Issue Edit page on a successful creation. Let's call this new component IssueAddNavItem and place it in a file called IssueAddNavItem.jsx.

Let's first move the NavItem for Create Issue from the navigation bar to this new component and add an onClick() handler that shows the modal dialog by calling a method showModal(), which we'll define a little later.

367

```
...
  render() {
    return (
      <React.Fragment>
        <NavItem onClick={this.showModal}>
          ...
        </NavItem>
      </React.Fragment>
    );
  }
...
```

Next, since the modal component can be placed anywhere, let's add it right after the NavItem. The root of the modal dialog definition is the Modal component. This component requires two important properties: showing, which controls the visibility of the modal dialog, and an onHide() handler, which will be called when the user clicks on the cross icon to dismiss the dialog. We'll define a state variable for showing to control the visibility.

```
...
    const { showing } = this.state;
    return (
      ...
        <NavItem onClick={this.showModal}>
          ...
        </NavItem>
        <Modal keyboard show={showing} onHide={this.hideModal}>
        </Modal>
    );
...
```

The showModal() and hideModal() methods need only set the state variable appropriately.

```
...
  showModal() {
    this.setState({ showing: true });
  }

  hideModal() {
    this.setState({ showing: false });
  }
...
```

Within the Modal component, let's use the header (Modal.Header) to show the title of the modal. The closeButton property can be used to show a cross icon that can be clicked to cancel the dialog.

```
...
        <Modal keyboard show={showing} onHide={this.hideModal}>
          <Modal.Header closeButton>
            <Modal.Title>Create Issue</Modal.Title>
          </Modal.Header>
        </Modal>
...
```

368

Then, within the body, let's add a vertical form (the default) with two fields, Title and Owner. This will just be two FormGroups as in the original Add inline form, but without any spacing between them.

```
...
        <Modal.Body>
          <Form name="issueAdd">
            <FormGroup>
              <ControlLabel>Title</ControlLabel>
              <FormControl name="title" autoFocus />
            </FormGroup>
            <FormGroup>
              <ControlLabel>Owner</ControlLabel>
              <FormControl name="owner" />
            </FormGroup>
          </Form>
        </Modal.Body>
...
```

We'll use the modal's footer (Modal.Footer) to show a button toolbar with a Submit and a Cancel button styled as Primary and Link, respectively. We'll let the Submit button click call the method handleSubmit(), and the Cancel button hide the modal dialog.

```
...
        <Modal.Footer>
          <ButtonToolbar>
            <Button
              type="button"
              bsStyle="primary"
              onClick={this.handleSubmit}
            >
              Submit
            </Button>
            <Button bsStyle="link" onClick={this.hideModal}>Cancel</Button>
          </ButtonToolbar>
        </Modal.Footer>
...
```

In the handleSubmit() method, we'll need to combine the two functions of reading the form's values (from the file IssueAdd.jsx) and submitting the values by calling the Create API (from IssueList.jsx). We'll also need to close the Modal dialog when the user clicks on Submit. On success, we'll show the Issue Edit page by pushing the Edit page's link to the history.

```
...
  async handleSubmit(e) {
    e.preventDefault();
    this.hideModal();
    const form = document.forms.issueAdd;
    const issue = {
      owner: form.owner.value,
      title: form.title.value,
      due: new Date(new Date().getTime() + 1000 * 60 * 60 * 24 * 10),
    };
```

```
  const query = `mutation issueAdd($issue: IssueInputs!) {
    issueAdd(issue: $issue) {
      id
    }
  }`;

  const data = await graphQLFetch(query, { issue }, this.showError);
  if (data) {
    const { history } = this.props;
    history.push(`/edit/${data.issueAdd.id}`);
  }
}
...
```

To handle errors in the graphQLFetch call, we'll need to show a Toast message. So, we'll define the Toast state variables and a showError() method as in the previous sections. The contents of the new file IssueAddNavItem.jsx, including the Toast message additions, are shown in Listing 11-26.

Listing 11-26. ui/src/IssueAddNavItem.jsx: New File for Adding an Issue

```
import React from 'react';
import { withRouter } from 'react-router-dom';
import {
  NavItem, Glyphicon, Modal, Form, FormGroup, FormControl, ControlLabel,
  Button, ButtonToolbar, Tooltip, OverlayTrigger,
} from 'react-bootstrap';

import graphQLFetch from './graphQLFetch.js';
import Toast from './Toast.jsx';

class IssueAddNavItem extends React.Component {
  constructor(props) {
    super(props);
    this.state = {
      showing: false,
      toastVisible: false,
      toastMessage: '',
      toastType: 'success',
    };
    this.showModal = this.showModal.bind(this);
    this.hideModal = this.hideModal.bind(this);
    this.handleSubmit = this.handleSubmit.bind(this);
    this.showError = this.showError.bind(this);
    this.dismissToast = this.dismissToast.bind(this);
  }

  showModal() {
    this.setState({ showing: true });
  }
```

```
hideModal() {
  this.setState({ showing: false });
}

showError(message) {
  this.setState({
    toastVisible: true, toastMessage: message, toastType: 'danger',
  });
}

dismissToast() {
  this.setState({ toastVisible: false });
}

async handleSubmit(e) {
  e.preventDefault();
  this.hideModal();
  const form = document.forms.issueAdd;
  const issue = {
    owner: form.owner.value,
    title: form.title.value,
    due: new Date(new Date().getTime() + 1000 * 60 * 60 * 24 * 10),
  };
  const query = `mutation issueAdd($issue: IssueInputs!) {
    issueAdd(issue: $issue) {
      id
    }
  }`;

  const data = await graphQLFetch(query, { issue }, this.showError);
  if (data) {
    const { history } = this.props;
    history.push(`/edit/${data.issueAdd.id}`);
  }
}

render() {
  const { showing } = this.state;
  const { toastVisible, toastMessage, toastType } = this.state;
  return (
    <React.Fragment>
      <NavItem onClick={this.showModal}>
        <OverlayTrigger
          placement="left"
          delayShow={1000}
          overlay={<Tooltip id="create-issue">Create Issue</Tooltip>}
        >
          <Glyphicon glyph="plus" />
        </OverlayTrigger>
      </NavItem>
```

371

```
        <Modal keyboard show={showing} onHide={this.hideModal}>
          <Modal.Header closeButton>
            <Modal.Title>Create Issue</Modal.Title>
          </Modal.Header>
          <Modal.Body>
            <Form name="issueAdd">
              <FormGroup>
                <ControlLabel>Title</ControlLabel>
                <FormControl name="title" autoFocus />
              </FormGroup>
              <FormGroup>
                <ControlLabel>Owner</ControlLabel>
                <FormControl name="owner" />
              </FormGroup>
            </Form>
          </Modal.Body>
          <Modal.Footer>
            <ButtonToolbar>
              <Button
                type="button"
                bsStyle="primary"
                onClick={this.handleSubmit}
              >
                Submit
              </Button>
              <Button bsStyle="link" onClick={this.hideModal}>Cancel</Button>
            </ButtonToolbar>
          </Modal.Footer>
        </Modal>
        <Toast
          showing={toastVisible}
          onDismiss={this.dismissToast}
          bsStyle={toastType}
        >
          {toastMessage}
        </Toast>
      </React.Fragment>
    );
  }
}

export default withRouter(IssueAddNavItem);
```

In order to use this new component, we'll need to replace the NavItem in Page.jsx with this new component's instance. The changes to Page.jsx are shown in Listing 11-27.

Listing 11-27. ui/src/Page.jsx

```
...
import {
  ...
  MenuItem, Glyphicon, ~~Tooltip, OverlayTrigger,~~
  Grid,
}
import IssueAddNavItem from './IssueAddNavItem.jsx';


...
function NavBar() {
  ...
      <Nav pullRight>
        <NavItem>
          ...
        </NavItem>
        <IssueAddNavItem />
        ...
      </Nav>
  ...
}
...
```

In the IssueList component, we can remove the rendering of IssueAdd and the createIssue function, now that the issue is being created directly from the modal. The changes to IssueList.jsx are shown in Listing 11-28.

Listing 11-28. ui/src/IssueList.jsx: Changes to Remove IssueAdd and createIssue

```
...
import IssueTable from './IssueTable.jsx';
~~import IssueAdd from './IssueAdd.jsx';~~
...
  constructor() {
    ...
    this.createIssue = this.createIssue.bind(this);
    ...
  }
...

  ~~async createIssue(issue) {~~
    ...
  ~~}~~

  render() {
    ...
      ~~<IssueAdd createIssue={this.createIssue} />~~
    ...
  }
...
```

After these changes, if you click on the + icon in the right side of the navigation bar, you should see a modal dialog as in Figure 11-15. You should be able to create new issues using this dialog, and on success, you should be shown the Edit page of the newly created issue.

Figure 11-15. *The Create Issue modal dialog*

Summary

Adding styles and themes to an application in a MERN stack is no different from any other stack because the important part is the CSS and how styles are handled by various browsers. And they don't vary depending on the chosen stack. Bootstrap, a pioneer in this area, enabled browser independence and a responsive behavior out of the box. React-Bootstrap replaced the separate JavaScript code that dealt with the Bootstrap elements and made self-contained components possible.

We could have used Material-UI or any other framework to achieve what was required, but the take-away from this chapter should be a peek into how you can design your own styled reusable UI components if and when required. It would also be good if you took a look at the documentation of React-Bootstrap at https://react-bootstrap.github.io/getting-started/introduction and Bootstrap itself at http://getbootstrap.com/docs/3.3/ to get a grasp of the kinds of components that these two libraries offer.

At this point in time, the application may look complete except for some advanced features. But if the application needed search engine bots to be able to index the pages naturally, it will need the ability to serve fully constructed pages directly from the server, as they would appear in the browser. This is because search engines usually do not run the JavaScript in the pages that they crawl, and for an SPA, this is essential to construct the pages in the browser.

In the next chapter, you'll learn how to do construct the HTML on the server and respond to the client and, more importantly, how to do this using the same codebase on the client as well as the UI server.

Answers to Exercises

Exercise: Navigation Bar

1. Just using the `fixedTop` property will cause the navigation bar to overlay the top portion of the content. To fix it, you'll need to add a padding to the body tag as suggested in the Bootstrap documentation.

   Often, you will need to refer to the Bootstrap documentation in addition to the React-Bootstrap documentation because React-Bootstrap is based on Bootstrap. When you do that, remember to choose the Version 3.3 documentation rather than the latest version 4 documentation of Bootstrap.

Exercise: Panels

1. The `defaultExpanded` property controls whether the panel's initial state is expanded or closed. Setting this property to `true` (or just specifying the property) will have the effect of showing the filter open when the browser is refreshed. In order to make this behavior dependent on the presence of a filter, you could check for the search property of location not being an empty string to calculate the value of this property, as shown in this code snippet:

```
...
    const hasFilter = location.search !== '';
    return (
      <React.Fragment>
        <Panel defaultExpanded={hasFilter}>
        ...
...
```

Exercise: Grid System

1. If the cells were larger, a specification of `xs={12}` `sm={6}` `md={4}` `lg={3}` would work best. On very small and small screens, you'll see multiple lines, and on medium and large screens, the cells will fit into a single line.

2. To make the controls look smaller, you can use the `bsSize="small"` property on the `FormGroups`. It could be done on the `FormControls` too, but using it on the `FormGroup` makes it affect the labels too. But this does not work for buttons—we must specify the property for each button instead.

Exercise: Inline Forms

1. On a very small screen, the controls look like a default form, the labels as well as the controls one below the other. The React-Bootstrap Form component has media-queries that make this transition, just like the columns in the grid system.

2. No, a form group is not really required to show the form controls inline, next to one another. But without a form group, on a very small screen, the controls are too close together and not visually appealing. Thus, even when not using labels, it is best to surround the controls with a FormGroup.

3. To specify an exact width, you must use an inline style, like style={{ width: 300 }}. Without a width specification, the control fills the width of the screen on very small screens. With a width, it takes the width specified on all screen sizes. In effect, if we do set the width, it's better to set the size on all controls rather than some.

Exercise: Horizontal Forms

1. The way to add a validation indication is using the following property in the FormGroup corresponding to the Title field:

```
...

        <FormGroup validationState={title.length < 3 ? 'error' : null}>
...
```

Although this does show the error (using red borders around the control and the label in red font), a submit is not prevented. This is because we have not let TextInput handle length errors and notify the IssueEdit component so that it can update invalidFields.

Visually, you'll find that the red X is absent in case of invalid input in the Title field. The reason is the same as that for the DateInput before we made changes to this section: we have not passed through props such as class that Bootstrap could be adding to the component.

CHAPTER 12

Server Rendering

In this chapter, we'll explore another cornerstone of React, the ability to generate HTML on the server in addition to being able to render directly to the DOM. This enables creation of *isomorphic* applications, that is, applications that use the same codebase on the server as well as the client to do either task: render to the DOM or create HTML.

Server rendering (also known as server-side rendering or SSR for short) is the opposite of what characterizes an SPA: rather than fetch data via APIs and construct the DOM on the browser, the entire HTML is constructed on the server and sent to the browser. The need for it arises when the application needs to be indexed by search engines. Search engine bots typically start from the root URL (/) and then traverse all the hyperlinks present in the resulting HTML. They do not execute JavaScript to fetch data via Ajax calls and look at the changed DOM. So, to have pages from an application be properly indexed by search engines, the server needs to respond with the same HTML that will result after the Ajax call in componentDidMount() methods and subsequent re-rendering of the page.

For example, if a request is made to /issues, the HTML returned should have the list of issues in the table prepopulated. The same goes for all other pages that can be bookmarked or have a hyperlink pointing to them. But this defeats the purpose of SPAs, which provide a better user experience when the user navigates within the application. So, the way we'll make it work is as follows:

- The first time any page is opened in the application (e.g., by typing in the URL in the browser, or even choosing refresh on the browser when already in any page in the application), the entire page will be constructed and returned from the server. We'll call this *server rendering*.

- Once any page is loaded and the user navigates to another page, we'll make it work like an SPA. That is, only the API will be made and the DOM will be modified directly on the browser. We'll call this *browser rendering*.

Note that this is true for any page, not just for the home page. For example, the user could type in the URL of the Edit page of an issue in the browser, and that page will be constructed at the server and returned too.

Since the steps to achieve all this are not simple, we'll create a new simple page—the About page—for mastering the techniques required. We'll start with a static page, then add complexity by using an API to fetch the data it renders. Once we've perfected the technique to render the About page at the server, we'll extend the changes required to all other pages.

A note of caution: not all applications need server rendering. If an application does not need to be indexed by search engines, the complexity introduced by server rendering can be avoided. Typically, if the pages do not have public access, they don't need search engine indexing. The performance benefits alone do not justify the complexity of server rendering.

V. Subramanian, *Pro MERN Stack*, https://doi.org/10.1007/978-1-4842-4391-6_12

New Directory Structure

Until now, we didn't give too much attention to the directory structure for the UI. That's because all the code under the src directory was meant to be compiled into a bundle and served to the browser. This is no longer going to be the case. What we'll need instead is three sets of files:

- All the shared files, essentially, all the React components.

- A set of files used to run the UI server using Express. This will import the shared React components for server rendering.

- A starting point for the browser bundle, one that includes all the shared React components and can be sent to the browser to execute.

So, let's split the current source code into three directories, one for each set of files. Let's keep the shared React components in the src directory. As for the browser-specific and server-specific files, let's create two directories called browser and server respectively. Then, let's move the browser-specific file App.jsx into its directory and the server-specific file uiserver.js into the server directory.

```
$ cd ui
$ mkdir browser
$ mkdir server
$ mv src/App.jsx browser
$ mv uiserver.js server
```

This change will also require that the linting, compiling, and bundling configurations change to reflect the new directory structure. Let's start with the linting changes. Let's have four .eslintrc files, one at the base (ui), and one in each of the sub-directories—the src, browser, and server directories—so that each of these inherits from the one at the root. At the .eslintrc in the ui directory, all we need to do is specify the rule set to inherit from, that is, airbnb. The changes for this are shown in Listing 12-1.

Listing 12-1. ui/.eslintrc: Changes to Keep Only the Base

```
...
{
  "extends": "airbnb-base",
  "env": {
    "node": true
  },
  "rules": {
    "no-console": "off"
  }
}
...
```

Next, in the shared src folder, let's add node: true for the environment, to indicate that these set of files are meant to be run in Node.js as well as in the browser. We'll also remove the extends specification since that will be inherited from the parent directory's .eslintrc. The changes for this are shown in Listing 12-2.

Listing 12-2. ui/src/.eslintrc: Changes to Add Node

```
...
{
  "extends": "airbnb",
  "env": {
    "browser": true,
    "node": true
  },
  rules: {
  ...
}
...
```

Now, let's create a new .eslintrc in the browser directory, which is the same as the original .eslintrc in the src directory, without the Node.js environment. This new file is shown in Listing 12-3.

Listing 12-3. ui/browser/.eslintrc: New ESLint Configuration for Browser Source Files

```
{
  "env": {
    "browser": true
  },
  rules: {
    "import/extensions": [ 'error', 'always', { ignorePackages: true } ],
    "react/prop-types": "off"
  }
}
```

As for the server .eslintrc, it's a copy of the original one in the ui directory, specifying just the environment (Node.js only) and allowing console messages. This is shown in Listing 12-4.

Listing 12-4. ui/server/.eslintrc: New ESLint Configuration for Server Source Files

```
{
  "env": {
    "node": true
  },
  "rules": {
    "no-console": "off"
  }
}
```

As a next step, let's add a .babelrc in the browser directory, which is a copy of the one in the shared src directory.

```
$ cd ui
$ cp src/.babelrc browser
```

We'll also need to change the location of imported/required files in App.jsx and uiserver.js. These are shown in Listings 12-5 and 12-6.

Listing 12-5. ui/browser/App.jsx: New Location of Page.jsx

```
...
import Page from '../src/Page.jsx';
...
```

Listing 12-6. ui/server/uiserver.js: New Location of Webpack Config File

```
...
const config = require('./webpack.config.js');
const config = require('../webpack.config.js');
...
```

Finally, we'll need to change the entry points in package.json for the new location of the UI server start-up file and webpack.config.js for the location of App.jsx. These are shown in Listings 12-7 and 12-8.

Listing 12-7. ui/package.json: Changes for Entry Point of uiserver.js

```
...
  "scripts": {
    "start": "nodemon -w uiserver.js -w .env uiserver.js",
    "start": "nodemon -w server -w .env server/uiserver.js",
    ...
  }
...
```

Listing 12-8. ui/webpack.config.js: Changes for Entry Point of the Bundle

```
...
module.exports = {
  ...
  entry: { app: ['./src/App.jsx'] },
  entry: { app: ['./browser/App.jsx'] },
  ...
}
```

After these changes, the application should work just as before. You should test both with HMR enabled as well as HMR disabled and manually compile the browser bundle using npm run compile before starting the server.

Basic Server Rendering

We used the ReactDOM.render() method to render a React element into the DOM. The counterpart method that is to be used to create an HTML on the server side is ReactDOMServer.renderToString(). Although the method itself is a simple one, the changes that we need to make in order to use it are not. So, let's use a simple About component to get familiar with the fundamentals. Then, in later sections, we'll use the same technique for the other components in the application.

The code for the very basic About component is shown in Listing 12-9.

Listing 12-9. ui/src/About.jsx: New About Component

```
import React from 'react';

export default function About() {
  return (
    <div className="text-center">
      <h3>Issue Tracker version 0.9</h3>
      <h4>
        API version 1.0
      </h4>
    </div>
  );
}
```

Let's include the new component in the application so that it's shown when the extended menu item About is clicked. The first change needed for this is in the set of routes, so that /about loads the About component. This change to Contents.jsx is shown in Listing 12-10.

Listing 12-10. ui/src/Contents.jsx: Include About Component in the Application

```
...
import IssueEdit from './IssueEdit.jsx';
import About from './About.jsx';
...
    <Switch>
      ...
      <Route path="/report" component={IssueReport} />
      <Route path="/about" component={About} />
      ...
    </Switch>
...
```

We also need to change the menu item so that instead of a dummy, it links to /about. This change to Page.jsx is shown in Listing 12-11.

Listing 12-11. ui/src/Page.jsx: Include About in the Navigation Bar

```
...
function NavBar() {
  return (
    ...
        <LinkContainer to="/about">
          <MenuItem>About</MenuItem>
        </LinkContainer>
    ...
  );
}
...
```

Now, if you point your browser to http://localhost:8000/ and navigate to the new page by clicking on the About extended menu item, you should see the About page, just like any of the other pages in the application. A screenshot of this page is shown in Figure 12-1.

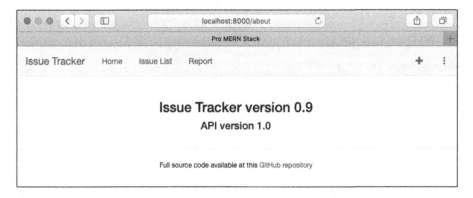

Figure 12-1. *The About page*

But in this case, the component was *browser rendered*, just as all other components were being rendered until now. A sequence diagram of the events that lead to the About page being displayed using browser rendering is shown in Figure 12-2.

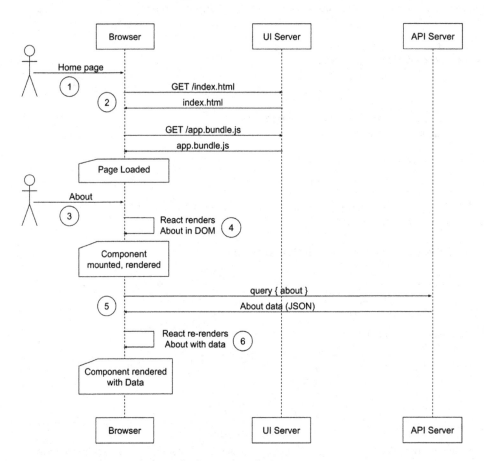

Figure 12-2. *Sequence diagram for browser rendering*

Here's an explanation of what happens during browser rendering. The explanation and the diagram are for the About page, but the sequence is identical for any other page:

1. The user types in the URL of the home page or refreshes the browser at the home page.

2. The UI server returns index.html, which has a reference to the JavaScript app. bundle.js. That is also fetched, and it contains the react components, including the About component. Now, the page is considered loaded. (The Issue List component will also be mounted, but that's not of importance at the moment.)

3. The user clicks on the link to the About page.

4. React mounts and renders the About component, whose code is part of the JavaScript bundle. At this point, all the static text in the component is seen.

5. Once the initial mount is completed, componentDidMount() is called, which will trigger a call to the API server to fetch the data for the component. We have not implemented this yet, but you should be able to appreciate this by considering the other pages that we have implemented, for example, the Issue List page.

6. On successful fetch of the data using the API call, the component is re-rendered with the data.

Next, let's render the About component on the server. Since the server is yet to use JSX compilation, we'll need to compile it manually to pure JavaScript so that the server can include it:

```
$ cd ui
$ npx babel src/About.jsx --out-dir server
```

This will result in a file called About.js in the server directory. Now, on the server, after importing About.js, we can render a string representation of the component using the following code snippet:

```
...
  const markup = ReactDOMServer.renderToString(<About />);
...
```

But this is going to produce only the markup for the About component. We still need the rest of the HTML such as the <head> section, with the component inserted in the contents <div>. So, let's make a template out of the existing index.html that can accept the contents of the <div> and return the complete HTML.

Powerful templating languages such as pug can be used for this, but our requirement is quite simple, so we'll just use the ES2015 template strings feature. Let's place this function in a file called template.js under the server directory. The template string is the same as the contents of index.html, except that the <script> tags have been removed. This entire contents of this file are shown in Listing 12-12. The changes highlighted are differences from index.html.

Listing 12-12. ui/server/template.js: Template for Server Rendered HTML

```
function template(body) {
  return `<!DOCTYPE HTML>
<html>

<head>
  <meta charset="utf-8">
  <title>Pro MERN Stack</title>
```

```
    <link rel="stylesheet" href="/bootstrap/css/bootstrap.min.css" >
    <meta name="viewport" content="width=device-width, initial-scale=1.0">

    <style>
      table.table-hover tr {cursor: pointer;}
      .panel-title a {display: block; width: 100%; cursor: pointer;}
    </style>
  </head>

  <body>
    <!-- Page generated from template. -->
    <div id="contents">${body}</div>

    <script src="/env.js"></script>
    <script src="/vendor.bundle.js"></script>
    <script src="/app.bundle.js"></script>
  </body>

</html>
`;
}

module.exports = template;
```

We'll eventually add the scripts, but for the moment, it's better to test the changes without this complication. As for import of the About component and rendering it to string, let's do this in a new file in the server directory, in a function called render(). The function will take in a regular request and response like any Express route handler. It will then send out the template as a response, with the body replaced by the markup created from ReactDOMServer.renderToString().

Since the code in the server directory is still pure JavaScript (there's no compilation step yet), let's not use JSX to instantiate the About component. Instead, let's use React.createElement:

```
...
  const body = ReactDOMServer.renderToString(
    React.createElement(About),
  );
...
```

There's one more minor incompatibility between the code in src and server directories. These use different ways of including other files and modules. You may recall from Chapter 8, "Modularization and Webpack," that the React code uses the import/export paradigm rather than the require/module. exports way of including modules as in the server code. Fortunately, the two are compatible, with a minor change. The Babel compiler places any variables exported using the export default keywords also in module.exports, but using the property default. Thus, we'll have to add default after importing the About component using require():

```
...
const About = require('./About.js').default;
...
```

The complete code for this new file is shown in Listing 12-13.

Listing 12-13. ui/server/render.js: New File for Rendering About

```
const React = require('react');
const ReactDOMServer = require('react-dom/server');

const About = require('./About.js').default;
const template = require('./template.js');

function render(req, res) {
  const body = ReactDOMServer.renderToString(
    React.createElement(About),
  );
  res.send(template(body));
}

module.exports = render;
```

Now, in uiserver.js, we can set this function as the handler for the route with the /about path. Let's add this route just before the catch-all route that returns index.html. This change, along with the import statement for including render.js, is shown in Listing 12-14.

Listing 12-14. ui/server/uiserver.js: New Route for /About to Return Server-Rendered About

```
...
const proxy = require('http-proxy-middleware');

const render = require('./render.js');
...

app.get('/about', render);

app.get('*', (req, res) => {
  ...
});
...
```

At this point, About.js needs to be compiled manually. Do that using the npx babel command and then restart the server. If you point your browser to http://localhost:8000/about, you should see the About component without any adornment of the navigation bar. This is because we replaced the placeholder ${body} with the About component and have not the routed Page component. A screenshot of this plain About page rendered at the server is shown in Figure 12-3.

Issue Tracker version 0.9
API version 1.0

Figure 12-3. *The server rendered About page*

Although this is a bit different from the browser-rendered version (which we'll fix in later sections), it is good enough to demonstrate that the *same* component can be rendered at the server as well as the browser. The sequence diagram in Figure 12-4 explains in detail what happens during server rendering, which includes a step where data is fetched from the API server that we've yet to implement.

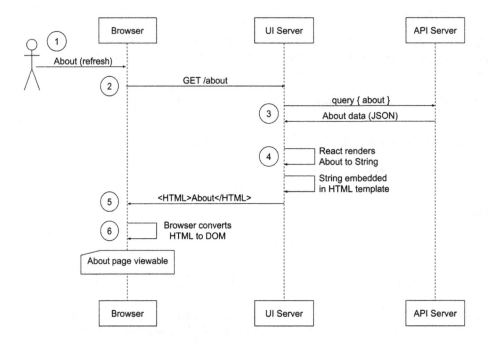

Figure 12-4. *Sequence diagram for server rendering*

Here is an explanation of the sequence of steps that lead to server rendering:

1. The user types in the URL for the About page (or chooses refresh in the browser while on the About page).

2. The browser sends a request to /about to the UI server.

3. The UI server fetches the data required for the page from the API server using a GraphQL API call. We'll implement this in later sections in this chapter.

4. On the UI server, ReactDOM.renderToString() is called with the About component and its data.

5. The server returns an HTML, with the markup for the About page included in it.

6. The browser converts the HTML to the DOM and the About page is visible in the browser.

EXERCISE: BASIC SERVER RENDERING

1. Let's say the string representation of the component rendered in the server was quite large. Creating a string from the template in memory would take up a lot of memory and be slow. What option do you have in this case? Hint: Look up the documentation of `ReactDOMServer` at https://reactjs.org/docs/react-dom-server.html to see what other methods are available.

Answers are available at the end of the chapter.

Webpack for the Server

At this point, we just have a simple About component. We'll need it to get data by calling the about API and rendering it on the server. We'll do all that in the following sections, but before that, let's deal with the inconvenience of having to compile About.js manually from About.jsx. Soon, we'll have to compile all the files under the src directory for inclusion in the server side, and a manual compilation can become unviable.

Further, you also saw that the import/export paradigm and require/module.exports paradigm, although compatible, are not convenient when mixed. One needs to remember adding the .default after every require() of a file that uses the import/export paradigm.

It turns out that Webpack can be used for the server as well, and it can compile JSX on the fly. This will also let us consistently use the import/export paradigm in the UI server codebase. Webpack works quite the same as with the front-end code, but for one difference. Many server-side Node packages such as Express are not compatible with Webpack. They import other packages dynamically, making it hard for Webpack to follow the dependency chain. So, we'll have to exclude the third-party libraries from the bundle and rely on node_modules to be present in the UI server's file system.

The first thing we'll do is add a new section in the webpack.config.js file for the server configuration. Webpack allows an array of configurations to be exported. When it encounters an array, Webpack executes all configurations in this array. The outline of the new webpack.config.js file is like this:

```
...
const browserConfig = {
  mode: 'development',
  entry: { app: ['./browser/App.jsx'] },
  ...
}

const serverConfig = {
  mode: 'development',
  entry: { server: ['./server/uiserver.js'] },
  ...
}

module.exports = [browserConfig, serverConfig];
...
```

The `browserConfig` variable contains the original configuration contents. One issue of using shared files between the server and the browser is that we can't use the same Babel configuration. When compiling for Node.js, the target is Node's latest version alone, whereas when compiling for the browser, it needs a list of browser versions. So, let's get rid of `.babelrc` in the `src` and `browser` directories and instead configure Babel options via Webpack. That way, we can tell Babel what options to use based on the target: browser or server.

```
$ cd ui
$ rm src/.babelrc browser/.babelrc
```

Now, in the `browserConfig` section of `webpack.config.js`, we can specify these options like this:

```
...
        use: 'babel-loader',
        use: {
          loader: 'babel-loader',
          options: {
            presets: [
              ['@babel/preset-env', {
                targets: {
                  ie: '11',
                  ...
                },
              }],
              '@babel/preset-react',
            ],
          },
        },
      },
...
```

For the server configuration, we'll need an output specification. Let's compile the bundle into a new directory called `dist` (short for distribution) and call the bundle `server.js`.

```
...
const serverConfig = {
  ...
  output: {
    filename: 'server.js',
    path: path.resolve(__dirname, 'dist'),
    publicPath: '/',
  },
...
```

As for the Babel configuration for the server, let's compile all `js` and `jsx` files to target Node.js version 10 and include the React preset.

```
...
const serverConfig = {
  ...
  module: {
    rules: [
      {
```

```
      test: /\.jsx?$/,
      use: {
        loader: 'babel-loader',
        options: {
          presets: [
            ['@babel/preset-env', {
              targets: { node: '10' },
            }],
            '@babel/preset-react',
          ],
        },
      },
    },
  ],
},
...
```

This configuration is not going to work because it does not exclude the modules in node_modules. We could use the same strategy as we did for the browser configuration, but the recommended way to do this on the server is to use the webpack-node-externals module, which works better. Let's install that package.

```
$ cd ui
$ npm install --save-dev webpack-node-externals@1
```

Now, in the Webpack configuration, we can import this package and use it in the server part of the configuration like this:

```
...
const path = require('path');
const nodeExternals = require('webpack-node-externals');


...
const serverConfig = {
  ...
  target: 'node',
  externals: [nodeExternals()],
  output: {
...
```

The final contents of webpack.config.js are shown in Listing 12-15. This includes a source-map specification that I have not explicitly mentioned for the server configuration. Also, I have not shown the deleted code for the sake of brevity: the entire contents of the file are listed.

Listing 12-15. ui/webpack.config.js: Full Listing of File for Including Server Configuration

```
const path = require('path');
const nodeExternals = require('webpack-node-externals');

const browserConfig = {
  mode: 'development',
  entry: { app: ['./browser/App.jsx'] },
  output: {
```

```javascript
      filename: '[name].bundle.js',
      path: path.resolve(__dirname, 'public'),
      publicPath: '/',
    },
    module: {
      rules: [
        {
          test: /\.jsx?$/,
          exclude: /node_modules/,
          use: {
            loader: 'babel-loader',
            options: {
              presets: [
                ['@babel/preset-env', {
                  targets: {
                    ie: '11',
                    edge: '15',
                    safari: '10',
                    firefox: '50',
                    chrome: '49',
                  },
                }],
                '@babel/preset-react',
              ],
            },
          },
        },
      ],
    },
    optimization: {
      splitChunks: {
        name: 'vendor',
        chunks: 'all',
      },
    },
    devtool: 'source-map',
};

const serverConfig = {
  mode: 'development',
  entry: { server: ['./server/uiserver.js'] },
  target: 'node',
  externals: [nodeExternals()],
  output: {
    filename: 'server.js',
    path: path.resolve(__dirname, 'dist'),
    publicPath: '/',
  },
  module: {
    rules: [
      {
```

```
        test: /\.jsx?$/,
        use: {
          loader: 'babel-loader',
          options: {
            presets: [
              ['@babel/preset-env', {
                targets: { node: '10' },
              }],
              '@babel/preset-react',
            ],
          },
        },
      },
    ],
  },
  devtool: 'source-map',
};

module.exports = [browserConfig, serverConfig];
```

Now, we are ready to convert all the `require()` statements to `import` statements. But before we do that, since we are deviating from the norm of not specifying extensions in imports, we'll have to disable the ESLint setting for this. This change to the server-side `.eslintrc` is shown in Listing 12-16.

Listing 12-16. ui/server/.eslintrc: Disable Import Extensions Rule

```
...
  "rules": {
    "no-console": "off",
    "import/extensions": "off"
  }
...
```

Let's first change `template.js` to use the import/export paradigm. The changes for this are shown in Listing 12-17.

Listing 12-17. ui/server/template.js: Use Import/Export

```
...
export default function template(body) {
  ...
}
...

module.exports = template;
...
```

As for `render.js`, let's change all `require()` statements to `import` statements. Also, now that we can handle JSX at the server side as part of the bundling process, let's replace `React.createElement()` with JSX and change the file's extension to reflect this fact.

```
$ cd ui
$ mv server/render.js server/render.jsx
```

The new contents of the render.jsx file are shown in Listing 12-18.

Listing 12-18. ui/server/render.jsx: New File for Rendering, Using JSX

```
import React from 'react';
import ReactDOMServer from 'react-dom/server';

import About from '../src/About.jsx';
import template from './template.js';

function render(req, res) {
  const body = ReactDOMServer.renderToString(<About />);
  res.send(template(body));
}

export default render;
```

In the main server file uiserver.js, apart from the require() statement to import changes, we will also need to change the HMR initialization routine that loads up the initial configuration. Now that the configuration exports an array, we'll use the first configuration in that array rather than use the configuration as is.

```
...
  const config = require('../webpack.config.js')[0];
...
```

Since we are now executing a bundle, when any error is encountered on the server, the line numbers that are shown in stack traces are that of the bundle's. This is not at all convenient when we encounter errors. The source-map-support module solves this problem. On the front-end, the source-map support module also made it convenient to add breakpoints. On the back-end, all it does is make error messages more readable.

Let's install the source-map-support package:$ cd ui
$ npm install source-map-support@0

We can now install this support in the main server file uiserver.js like this:...
import SourceMapSupport from 'source-map-support';
...
SourceMapSupport.install();
...

The final changes to uiserver.js are shown in Listing 12-19.

Listing 12-19. ui/server/uiserver.js: Changes for Using Import, Source Maps, and Webpack Config Array Element

```
...
require('dotenv').config();
const path = require('path');
const express = require('express');
const proxy = require('http-proxy-middleware');

const render = require('./render.js');
```

```
import dotenv from 'dotenv';
import path from 'path';
import express from 'express';
import proxy from 'http-proxy-middleware';
import SourceMapSupport from 'source-map-support';

import render from './render.jsx';

const app = express();

SourceMapSupport.install();
dotenv.config();
...

  const config = require('../webpack.config.js')[0];
...
```

Let's change the scripts section in package.json to use the bundle to start the server instead of the file uiserver.js. Let's also change the ESLint command to reflect the new directory structure. These changes are shown in Listing 12-20.

Listing 12-20. ui/package.json: Changes for Scripts

```
...
  "scripts": {
    ...
    "start": "nodemon -w server -w .env server/uiserver.js",
    "start": "nodemon -w dist -w .env dist/server.js",
    ...
    "lint": "eslint . --ext js,jsx --ignore-pattern public",
    "lint": "eslint server src browser --ext js,jsx",
    ...
  }
...
```

The manually generated About.js file is no longer needed, so let's clean it up.

```
$ cd ui
$ rm server/About.js
```

The server bundle can be built using the following manual compilation command:

```
$ cd ui
$ npx webpack
```

Now, you can start the application using npm start and check it out. There should be no changes in the application's behavior. You can try the About page, both directly and by loading /issues and navigating from there. The two avatars will continue to be different since we are yet to return an HTML with the navigation bar, etc. while rendering from the server.

HMR for the Server

Although using Webpack for the server does simplify the compilation process, you'll find that during development, you still need to restart the server for every change. You could use the nodemon wrapper by running npm start, but even there you'll find that the front-end HMR doesn't work. This is because, on a restart, the HMR middleware is reinstalled, but the browser tries to connect to the original HMR, which is no longer there.

The solution to all this is to automatically reload the modules even in the back-end, using HMR. Since we are using Webpack to bundle the server, this should work. But the fact is that the Express already has stored references to any existing modules and it needs to be told to replace these modules when accepting HMR changes. Although it can be done, setting this up is quite complex.

So, let's take the easy way out: we'll only reload changes to modules based on the shared folder. As for changes to uiserver.js itself, we expect these to be very few and far between, so let's restart the server manually when this file is changed and use HMR for the rest of the code that it includes.

Let's start by creating a new Webpack configuration that enables HMR for the server. This configuration should be different from the one used to create a production bundle. For the browser, we added HMR dynamically as part of the UI server (by loading the configuration and modifying it in the server code). But since we don't have a server to serve the bundle in the case of the server code, we'll have to create a separate configuration file. Rather than copy the entire configuration file and make changes to it, let's instead base it on the original configuration and *merge* the changes required for HMR. A package called webpack-merge comes in handy for this.

```
$ cd ui
$ npm install --save-dev webpack-merge@4
```

Let's use this to merge HMR changes on top of the server configuration in a new file called webpack. serverHMR.js. In this file, let's first load up the base configuration from the main configuration file. Note that the server configuration is the second element in the array.

```
...
const serverConfig = require('./webpack.config.js')[1];
...
```

Then, let's merge the serverConfig with new changes: we'll add a new entry point that polls for changes, and we'll add the HMR plugin to this configuration. The complete new file is shown in Listing 12-21.

Listing 12-21. ui/webpack.serverHMR.js: Merged Configuration for Server HMR

```
/*
  eslint-disable import/no-extraneous-dependencies
*/
const webpack = require('webpack');
const merge = require('webpack-merge');
const serverConfig = require('./webpack.config.js')[1];

module.exports = merge(serverConfig, {
  entry: { server: ['./node_modules/webpack/hot/poll?1000'] },
  plugins: [
    new webpack.HotModuleReplacementPlugin(),
  ],
});
```

Now, the server bundle can be rebuilt on changes if you run Webpack with this file as the configuration with the watch option. Also, it will let the running server listen for changes and load up the changed modules. The command to run Webpack with this configuration is as follows:

```
$ cd ui
$ npx webpack -w --config webpack.serverHMR.js
```

But, HMR is not going to work because the server is not (yet) accepting changes. As discussed, let's only accept changes to render.jsx. Thus, in uiserver.js, we can add the following at the end of the file:

```
...
if (module.hot) {
  module.hot.accept('./render.jsx');
}
...
```

But, this has the effect only of loading the changed module and replacing the variable render in this file to reference the new changed module. The Express route for /about still has a handle to the old render function. Ideally, we should tell the Express route that there is a new render function, perhaps like this:

```
...
if (module.hot) {
  module.hot.accept('./render.jsx', () => {
    app.get('/about', render);
  });
}
```

Unfortunately, this ends up installing another route instead of replacing the existing one. There is also no way to *unmount* a route in Express. To get around this, instead of passing a reference to the function to the Express route handler, let's create a function wrapper and call render() explicitly within this. This way, the render function that is called is always the latest one. This change, along with the module accept change, is shown in Listing 12-22.

Listing 12-22. ui/server/uiserver.js: Changes for HMR

```
...
app.get('/env.js', (req, res) => {
  ...
});

app.get('/about', render);
app.get('/about', (req, res, next) => {
  render(req, res, next);
});
...

app.listen(port, () => {
  ...
});
```

```
if (module.hot) {
  module.hot.accept('./render.jsx');
}
...
```

Finally, let's change package.json's script section to add convenience scripts for starting the UI server. We can now change the start script to remove nodemon (since HMR will load the modules automatically). Then, let's replace the watch script with a watch-server-hmr script that runs the webpack.serverHMR.js configuration in the watch mode. Since both this and the start script are needed for starting the UI server in development mode, let's add a script called dev-all that does both, one after the other.

In npm scripts, multiple commands can be combined using the & operator. The commands are started up simultaneously. Just to safeguard the server.js bundle being built before the npm start command is run, it's good to have a sleep command before the npm start command. The amount of time to wait can vary depending on how fast your computer is and how long it takes to compile the server files. To start off, you could use a sleep timer of five seconds and customize this based on your needs.

The changes to the package.json scripts are shown in Listing 12-23, but the script dev-all works only on MacOS and Linux.

Listing 12-23. ui/package.json: Changes to Scripts for HMR

```
...
  "scripts": {
    ...
    "start": "nodemon -w dist -w .env dist/server.js",
    "start": "node dist/server.js",
    ...
    "#watch": "Compile, and recompile on any changes.",
    "watch": "webpack --watch"
    "#watch-server-hmr": "Recompile server HMR bundle on changes.",
    "watch-server-hmr": "webpack -w --config webpack.serverHMR.js",
    "#dev-all": "Dev mode: watch for server changes and start UI server",
    "dev-all": "rm dist/* && npm run watch-server-hmr & sleep 5 && npm start"
  },
...
```

On a Windows PC, you may need to create your own batch file with equivalent commands or execute npm watch-server-hmr and npm start on different command windows.

Now, you can stop all other UI server commands and restart it using the single npm run dev-all command. The application should work just as before, but most changes should automatically reflect without having to restart this command.

Server Router

The way the About page was rendered from the server was different from the way it was rendered by navigating to it from /issues. In the first case, it was displayed without the navigation bar, and in the second, with it.

The reason this happened is as follows. On the browser, App.jsx mounted the Page component on to the contents div. But, on the server, the About component was rendered directly within the contents div, by stuffing it in the template.

On the server, wrapping a Router around the page, or using Switch or NavLinks, will throw up errors. This is because the Router is really meant for the DOM, where on clicking of a route's link, the browser's history is manipulated and different components are loaded based on the routing rules.

On the server, React Router recommends that we use a StaticRouter in place of a BrowserRouter. Also, whereas the BrowserRouter looks at the browser's URL, the StaticRouter has to be supplied the URL. Based on this, the router will choose an appropriate component to render. StaticRouter takes a property called location, which is a *static* URL that the rest of the rendering will need. It also needs a property called context, whose purpose is not obvious right now, so let's just supply an empty object for it.

Let's then modify render.js to render the Page component instead of the About component, but wrapped around by a StaticRouter. The changes for this are shown in Listing 12-24.

Listing 12-24. ui/server/render.jsx: Changes to Render Page Instead of About Directly

```
...
import { StaticRouter } from 'react-router-dom';

import About from '../src/About.jsx';
import Page from '../src/Page.jsx';
...

function render(req, res) {
  const body = ReactDOMServer.renderToString(<About />);
  const element = (
    <StaticRouter location={req.url} context={{}}>
      <Page />
    </StaticRouter>
  );
  const body = ReactDOMServer.renderToString(element);
  res.send(template(body));
}
...
```

Now, if you test the application, you will find that both server rendering and browser rendering are identical for the About page: the navigation bar will appear in both cases. To test server rendering, you will need to press refresh on the browser while on the About page. As for browser rendering, you will need to refresh the browser in another page, say the Issue List page, and then navigate to the About page using the extended menu. Refer to the screenshot in Figure 12-1 to recap how it looks.

Note that at this point, except for the About page, the other pages are only being rendered on the browser, even when refreshing. We will address that soon, once we perfect the About page server rendering.

EXERCISE: SERVER ROUTER

1. Press refresh on the browser while on the About page, to display the page using server rendering. Try to create a new issue by clicking on the Create Issue menu item (+ icon) in the navigation bar. What happens? Can you explain this? Hint: (a) Try to put a breakpoint in showModal() method in IssueAddNavItem and then (b) inspect the + icon using the browser's Developer Tools. Check out the event listeners attached to it. Try these after clicking on the Home menu and note the difference.

2. Press refresh on the browser while on the About page, to display the page using server rendering. Use the Developer Tools to inspect the network calls and then navigate to any other page, say the Issue List page. Do the same by starting at the Report page rather than the About page. What differences do you see, and why?

Answers are available at the end of the chapter.

Hydrate

Although the page looks as it is supposed to now, there is still a problem with it. If you tried the exercise at the end of the previous section, you will realize that what was rendered was pure HTML markup, without any JavaScript code or event handlers. Thus, there is no user interaction possible in the page.

In order to attach event handlers, we have to include the source code and let React take control of the rendered page. The way to do this is by loading React and letting it render the page as it would have done during browser rendering using the ReactDOM.render(). Since we have not included the JavaScript bundles in the template, this is not being called and therefore, React did not get control of the page. So let's add the scripts to the served page, just as in index.html, and see what happens. The changes to the template are shown in Listing 12-25.

Listing 12-25. ui/server/template.js: Include Browser Bundles

```
...
<body>
  <!-- Page generated from template. -->
  <div id="contents">${body}</div>

  <script src="/env.js"></script>
  <script src="/vendor.bundle.js"></script>
  <script src="/app.bundle.js"></script>
</body>
...
```

Now, if you test the application by refreshing the About page, you'll find that the + button works! This means event handlers have been attached. But you'll also see a warning on the console to this effect:

Warning: render(): Calling ReactDOM.render() to hydrate server-rendered markup will stop working in React v17. Replace the ReactDOM.render() call with ReactDOM.hydrate() if you want React to attach to the server HTML.

So, React makes a distinction between rendering the DOM to replace a DOM element and attaching event handlers to the server-rendered DOM. Let's change render() to hydrate() as recommended by the warning. This change to App.jsx is shown in Listing 12-26.

Listing 12-26. ui/browser/App.jsx: Change Render to Hydrate

```
...
ReactDOM.render hydrate(element, document.getElementById('contents'));
...
```

When testing with this change, you will find that the warning has disappeared and that all event handlers have been installed. You can see the effect not only when you click on the + button, but also when navigating to other tabs in the navigation bar. Earlier, these would have caused browser refreshes whereas now these navigations will load the appropriate component into the DOM directly, with React Router doing its magic.

This step completes the server rendering sequence of events, and the sequence diagram for server rendering needs this last step for the sake of completion. The new sequence diagram is shown in Figure 12-5.

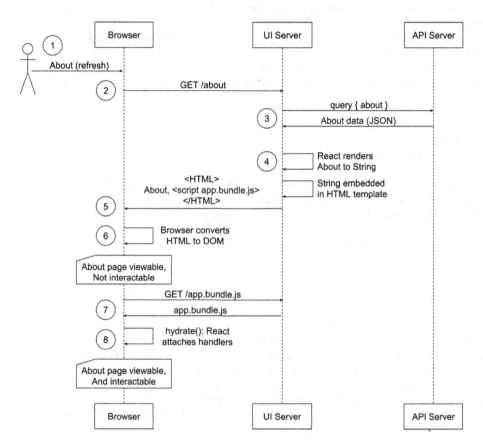

Figure 12-5. *Server rendering sequence diagram updated with Hydrate*

The changes to the diagram are outlined in the following steps:

1. Rather than the plain About component, the server returns script tags for the application and React and other library source code bundles.

2. The About page is viewable, but not interactive. There is no real change in the execution here, only that the diagram explicitly states that the page is not interactive.

3. The browser fetches the JavaScript bundles and executes them. As part of this, ReactDOM.hydrate() is executed with the routed page as the root element.

4. ReactDOM.hydrate() causes event handlers to be attached to all components, and now the page is viewable *and* interactive.

Data from API

We used a hard-coded message in the About component to get off the ground. In reality, this string should come from the API server. Specifically, the about API's result should be displayed in place of the hard-coded version string for the API.

If we were to follow the same pattern as the other components that loaded up data from the API, we would have implemented the data fetching in the lifecycle method componentDidMount() and set the state of the component. But in this case, we really need the API's return value to be available when the component is being rendered on the server.

This means that we'll need to be able to make requests to the API server via graphQLFetch() from the server as well. All this while this function assumed that it was being called from the browser. This needs a change. Firstly, we'll need to replace the whatwg-fetch module with something that can be used both on the browser as well as Node.js. The package called isomorphic-fetch is what we'll use to achieve this. So let's replace the package.

```
$ cd ui
$ npm uninstall whatwg-fetch
$ npm install isomorphic-fetch@2
```

Now, we can replace the import whatwg-fetch with isomorphic-fetch. But the import is currently within App.jsx, which is browser specific. Let's remove it there and add isomorphic-fetch where it is really required: graphQLFetch.js. The change to App.jsx is shown in Listing 12-27.

Listing 12-27. ui/browser/App.jsx: Removal of whatwg-fetch Import

```
...
import 'whatwg-fetch';
...
```

In graphQLFetch.js, we currently have the API endpoint specification in window.ENV.UI_API_ ENDPOINT. This will not work on the server because there is no variable called window. We'll need to use process.env variables. But we don't have anything to indicate whether the function is being called in the browser or in Node.js. Webpack's plugin called DefinePlugin can be used to define global variables that are available at runtime. We had discussed this plugin briefly at the end of Chapter 8, "Modularization and Webpack," but did not use it. Let's now use this plugin to define a variable called __isBrowser__ that is set to true in a browser bundle, but false in the server bundle. The changes for defining this variable in webpack. config.js are shown in Listing 12-28.

Listing 12-28. ui/webpack.config.js: DefinePlugin and Setting __isBrowser__

```
...
const webpack = require('webpack');
...
const browserConfig = {
  ...
  plugins: [
    new webpack.DefinePlugin({
      __isBrowser__: 'true',
    }),
  ],
  devtool: 'source-map',
};
```

```
const serverConfig = {
  ...
  plugins: [
    new webpack.DefinePlugin({
      __isBrowser__: 'false',
    }),
  ],
  devtool: 'source-map',
};
```

In the uiserver.js file, let's set up the variable in process.env if it's not set already. This is so that other modules can get this configuration variable without having to worry about the default value. Further, in the proxy mode of operation, the browser and the server API endpoints need to be different. The browser would need to use the UI server for the APIs, which will get proxied to the API server, whereas the server needs to call the API server directly. Let's introduce a new environment variable for the API endpoint for the UI server, called UI_SERVER_API_ENDPOINT. We can default this to the same endpoint as the UI_API_ENDPOINT if it was not specified. The changes for this are shown in Listing 12-29.

Listing 12-29. ui/server/uiserver.js: Set process.env Variable If Not Set

```
...
if (apiProxyTarget) {
  ...
}

const UI_API_ENDPOINT = process.env.UI_API_ENDPOINT
  || 'http://localhost:3000/graphql';
const env = { UI_API_ENDPOINT };

if (!process.env.UI_API_ENDPOINT) {
  process.env.UI_API_ENDPOINT = 'http://localhost:3000/graphql';
}

if (!process.env.UI_SERVER_API_ENDPOINT) {
  process.env.UI_API_ENDPOINT = process.env.UI_API_ENDPOINT;
}

app.get('/env.js', (req, res) => {
  const env = { UI_API_ENDPOINT: process.env.UI_API_ENDPOINT };
  res.send(`window.ENV = ${JSON.stringify(env)}`);
});
...
```

You could add the new environment variable to your .env file, but since we're using the non-proxy mode of operation, you can leave it commented out. The same change is shown in sample.env in Listing 12-30.

Listing 12-30. ui/sample.env: Addition of Environment Variable for API Endpoint for Use by the UI Server

```
...
UI_API_ENDPOINT=http://localhost:3000/graphql
# UI_SERVER_API_ENDPOINT=http://localhost:3000/graphql
...
```

Now, we can change graphQLFetch.js to get the correct API endpoint from process.env or from window.ENV depending on whether it's being run on Node.js or on the browser. The changes to this file are shown in Listing 12-31.

Listing 12-31. ui/src/graphQLFetch.js: Using Isomorphic-Fetch and Conditional Configuration

```
...
import fetch from 'isomorphic-fetch';
...

export default async function
graphQLFetch(query, variables = {}, showError = null) {
  const apiEndpoint = (__isBrowser__) // eslint-disable-line no-undef
    ? window.ENV.UI_API_ENDPOINT
    : process.env.UI_SERVER_API_ENDPOINT;
  try {
    const response = await fetch(window.ENV.UI_API_ENDPOINT apiEndpoint, {
      ...
    }
  ...
}
...
```

Now, we are in a position to call graphQLFetch() from the server. Just before calling renderToString(), we can make a call to get the data from the About API like this:

```
...
async function render(req, res) {
  const resultData = await graphQLFetch('query{about}');
...
```

But then, how do we pass this information down to the About component while it's being rendered? One way to do this is by passing it to the Page component as props, which in turn can pass it along to the Contents component, and then finally to About. But this is a hindrance and causes excess coupling between components—neither Page nor Contents need to know about the data that is of relevance only to About.

The solution to this is to use a *global* store for all data that is needed for the hierarchy of components that need to be rendered. Let's create this store as a module in the shared directory, in a file called store.js. The implementation of this store is simple: just an empty object that is exported. The users of this module can just assign key values that will be available globally by importing this module. The contents of the new file are shown in Listing 12-32.

Listing 12-32. ui/src/store.js: New Global Generic Storage Module (Complete Source)

```
const store = {};

export default store;
```

Now, the results of the API call can be saved in this store. This change to render.jsx, and the call to graphQLFetch() for getting the initial data, are shown in Listing 12-33.

Listing 12-33. ui/src/render.jsx: Changes for Saving the Data from an API Call

```
import template from './template.js';
import graphQLFetch from '../src/graphQLFetch.js';
import store from '../src/store.js';

async function render(req, res) {
  const initialData = await graphQLFetch('query{about}');
  store.initialData = initialData;
  ...
}
...
```

With the data being available in the global store, we can now change the About component to read it off the global store to display the *real* API version. Let's also guard this by checking if the store exists; this could be useful when constructing the same component in the browser. This change to About.jsx is shown in Listing 12-34.

Listing 12-34. ui/src/About.jsx: Use Version Obtained from the API Call Via a Global Store

```
...
import React from 'react';
import store from './store.js';

export default function About() {
  ...
      <h4>
        API version 1.0
        {store.initialData ? store.initialData.about : 'unknown'}
      </h4>
  ...
}
...
```

If you test this, you'll be surprised to find that the About page shows the API version as "unknown" instead of the value fetched from the API. Do take a look at the page's source (use Developer Tools to inspect the page source), and you will find that the HTML indeed has the API version string from the server. Then, why does it not show up in the screen?

If you look at the Developer Console, you'll see an error message like this:

```
Warning: Text content did not match. Server: "Issue Tracker API v1.0" Client: "unknown"
```

That should give you a hint as to the underlying problem. We'll address this issue in the next section.

Syncing Initial Data

The error message in the previous section says that there was a difference between the DOM that ReactDOM. hydrate() generated and what was rendered by the server. From the server, we used the result of the API call to set the version, but when React tried to attach event handlers using hydrate() on the browser, it did not find any value in the store, and thus the error. Here's a quote from the React documentation:

> React expects that the rendered content is identical between the server and the client. It can patch up differences in text content, but you should treat mismatches as bugs and fix them. In development mode, React warns about mismatches during hydration. There are no guarantees that attribute differences "patched up in case of mismatches. This is important for performance reasons because in most apps, mismatches are rare, and so validating all markup would be prohibitively expensive.

If you think about it, it makes a lot of sense. When hydrating (or attaching event handlers to the DOM), things can get ambiguous if the tree generated by the hydrate() call doesn't match the tree that is already there, rendered by the server. Note that hydrate() is just a variation of render()—it really creates a virtual DOM with event handlers that can be synced to the actual DOM.

What is needed is to make the browser render identical to the server render. But this requires that the same data be used to render the component on the server as well as the browser. An API call during the browser render (for example, in the lifecycle method componentDidMount()) will not cut it because it is asynchronous. We need the data when the component is being rendered for the *first time*.

The recommended way to do this is to pass the same initial data resulting from the API call to the browser in the form of a script and use that to initialize the global store. This way, when the component is being rendered, it will have the same data as the component that was rendered at the server.

The first thing to do is to change the template so that it takes an additional argument (the initial data) and sets it in a global variable in a <script> section. Since we've to convert any object to a string representation that can be valid JavaScript, let's use JSON.stringify() to convert the data to a string. Let's call this global variable __INITIAL_DATA__. The double-underscore signifies that this is a special global variable and that it is unlikely to collide with any other global variable because of other modules. The changes to template.js are shown in Listing 12-35.

Listing 12-35. ui/server/template.js: Include Initial Data as a Script

```
...
export default function template(body, data) {
  ...
  <div id="contents">${body}</div>
  <script>window.__INITIAL_DATA__ = ${JSON.stringify(data)}</script>
  ...
}
...
```

At the time of rendering at the server, we can now pass the initial data to the browser via this template, the same data that was used in the rendering of the page on the server. The changes for this in render.jsx are shown in Listing 12-36.

Listing 12-36. ui/server/render.jsx: Changes for Sending Initial Data to the Browser

```
...
async function render(req, res) {
  ...
  const body = ReactDOMServer.renderToString(element);
  res.send(template(body, initialData));
}
...
```

At the browser, we'll need to set this value to the global store before anything else, so that when the component is rendered, it has access to the initial data in the global store. We can do this global store initialization where the browser rendering starts, in App.jsx. This change is shown in Listing 12-37.

Listing 12-37. ui/browser/App.jsx: Use Initial Data to Initialize the Store

```
...
import Page from '../src/Page.jsx';
import store from '../src/store.js';

// eslint-disable-next-line no-underscore-dangle
store.initialData = window.__INITIAL_DATA__;
...
```

Now, when the component is rendered in the browser, it will have the same initial data in the store as it did when it was rendered on the server. If you test the application by refreshing the browser while in the About page, you will find that the React error message is no longer shown. This indicates that the result of the browser rendering matched the server rendering, allowing React to attach event handlers without any mismatches.

The other pages will still show an error, for example, the /issues URL will throw the following error in the console:

```
Warning: Expected server HTML to contain a matching <div> in <div>.
```

The original index.html is being returned for the URL /issues, which just has an empty <div> in the body, because it was not server-rendered like in the case of the About page. When React renders the DOM in the browser during the call to hydrate(), the actual page is rendered. Thus, there is a mismatch in what the server rendered and what the browser rendered, and therefore the error. We'll address this in later sections in this chapter, when we synchronize the server and browser data for all pages in a generic manner.

Common Data Fetcher

At this point, although refreshing the browser with the URL pointing at /about works well, you'll find that navigating to the About page after starting from any other page, say /issues, does not show the API version from the API server. That's because we never added a data fetcher in the About component that could be used to populate its message to take care of the case where it is mounted only on the browser.

So, just like for the other components, let's add a componentDidMount() method in the About component. It will now need to be converted to a regular component from a stateless function. Let's use a state variable to store and display the API version. We'll call this variable apiAbout. Let's initialize this variable in the constructor from the global store, if it has the initial data.

```
...
  constructor(props) {
    super(props);
    const apiAbout = store.initialData ? store.initialData.about : null;
    this.state = { apiAbout };
  }
...
```

This will set the state variable to `null` if the initial data was missing, as would be the case when the `/issues` page was loaded and the user navigated to the About page. We could use this fact to initiate an API call within `componentDidMount()`. But since we have the same API call being made in `render.jsx`, let's use a common function to fetch the data that can be shared by the About component as well as by the `render.jsx` file. The best place for this is in the About component itself, as a static function.

```
...
  static async fetchData() {
    const data = await graphQLFetch('query {about}');
    return data;
  }
...
```

Now, in `componentDidMount()`, data can be fetched and set in the state if the state variable `apiAbout` has not been initialized by the constructor.

```
...
  async componentDidMount() {
    const { apiAbout } = this.state;
    if (apiAbout == null) {
      const data = await About.fetchData();
      this.setState({ apiAbout: data.about });
    }
  }
...
```

Finally, in the `render()` method, we can use the state variable rather than the variable from the store. The complete source code of `About.jsx` after all these changes is shown in Listing 12-38.

Listing 12-38. ui/src/About.jsx: Replaced Contents of About.jsx for Loading Data

```
import React from 'react';
import store from './store.js';
import graphQLFetch from './graphQLFetch.js';

export default class About extends React.Component {
  static async fetchData() {
    const data = await graphQLFetch('query {about}');
    return data;
  }

  constructor(props) {
    super(props);
    const apiAbout = store.initialData ? store.initialData.about : null;
```

```
    this.state = { apiAbout };
  }

  async componentDidMount() {
    const { apiAbout } = this.state;
    if (apiAbout == null) {
      const data = await About.fetchData();
      this.setState({ apiAbout: data.about });
    }
  }

  render() {
    const { apiAbout } = this.state;
    return (
      <div className="text-center">
        <h3>Issue Tracker version 0.9</h3>
        <h4>
          {apiAbout}
        </h4>
      </div>
    );
  }
}
```

Now, the GraphQL query in render.jsx can be replaced by a call to About.fetchData(). This change is shown in Listing 12-39.

Listing 12-39. ui/server/render.jsx: Use Common Data Fetcher from About.jsx

```
...
import graphQLFetch from '../src/graphQLFetch.js';
import About from '../src/About.jsx';
...

async function render(req, res) {
  const resultData = await graphQLFetch('query{about}');
  const resultData = About.fetchData();
...
```

After this change, you can test the application, in particular, load the home page or /issues and then navigate to the About page. You should see the correct API version being shown. You can also confirm that a call to the API is being made by inspecting the Network tab of the Developer Tools.

Generated Routes

In this section, we'll fix the mismatch errors that React is showing for the rest of the pages. We'll also lay down the framework that deals with fetching data in a generic manner, so that we can remove the call to About.fetchData() in render.jsx, and make it fetch data that is appropriate for the component that will actually be rendered within the page.

First, instead of returning index.html, let's return the server-rendered HTML using the template for all the pages. The change for this is in the Express route that deals with the path /about. Let's replace this with a * to indicate *any* path should return the templated HTML, rather than the file index.html from the public directory. This change is shown in Listing 12-40.

Listing 12-40. ui/server/uiserver.js: Return Templated HTML for Any Path

```
...
import path from 'path';
...

app.get('/about', (req, res, next) => {
app.get('*', (req, res, next) => {
  render(req, res, next);
});

app.get('*', (req, res) => {
  res.sendFile(path.resolve('public/index.html'));
});
```

Since index.html is no longer required, we can remove this file.

```
$ cd ui
$ rm public/index.html
```

This change will need a restart of the server since HMR does not handle changes to uiserver.js itself. On testing the application, you will find that the React error for mismatched <div> for all the pages is no longer seen. If you inspect the page source, you will find that the server returns a full page with the navigation bar, etc., but without the data.

For example, when you refresh the page /issues, you will see that the table header is present, but the table itself is not populated with issues. It matches the browser rendering because even in the browser, the initial render starts with an empty set of issues. Only during componentDidMount() is the list of issues fetched from the API and populated in the table. We'll address this in the following sections. For now, let's ensure that we have the ability to determine what data needs to be fetched based on the matching route.

The main problem we need to solve is that the data required via API calls needs to be available *before* rendering is initiated on the server. The only way this can be done is by keeping a common source of truth for the list of routes available. Then, we could match the request's URL against each route and figure out which component (and therefore, which fetchData() method) will match. The same source of truth should also be responsible for generating the actual <Route> components during a render.

Let's keep this list of routable pages in a JavaScript array in a new file called routes.js. This can be a simple array with the path to the route and the component that needs to be rendered if the route is matched with the URL. This new file is shown in Listing 12-41.

Listing 12-41. ui/src/routes.js: New File to Store Route Metadata

```
import IssueList from './IssueList.jsx';
import IssueReport from './IssueReport.jsx';
import IssueEdit from './IssueEdit.jsx';
import About from './About.jsx';
import NotFound from './NotFound.jsx';

const routes = [
  { path: '/issues', component: IssueList },
  { path: '/edit/:id', component: IssueEdit },
```

```
  { path: '/report', component: IssueReport },
  { path: '/about', component: About },
  { path: '*', component: NotFound },
];

export default routes;
```

We've imported and used NotFound as a component, but this is defined as part of Contents.jsx, and that won't work. Let's separate it and create a new file for it, as shown in Listing 12-42.

Listing 12-42. ui/src/NotFound.jsx: New File for the Page Not Found Component

```
import React from 'react';

function NotFound() {
  return <h1>Page Not Found</h1>;
}

export default NotFound;
```

We can now modify Contents.jsx to generate the <Route> components from this array of routes metadata. Let's just map the array and return a <Route> for each component, with the attributes the same as the properties of each object in the array. React also needs a unique key for every element in an array, and this can be the path of the route since that has to be unique. The changes to this file are shown in Listing 12-43.

Listing 12-43. ui/src/Contents.jsx: Changes to Generate Routes from routes.js Array

```
...
import IssueList from './IssueList.jsx';
import IssueReport from './IssueReport.jsx';
import IssueEdit from './IssueEdit.jsx';
import About from './About.jsx';

const NotFound = () => <h1>Page Not Found</h1>;
import routes from './routes.js';

export default function Contents() {
  return (
    <Switch>
      <Redirect exact from="/" to="/issues" />
      <Route path="/issues" component={IssueList} />
      <Route path="/edit/:id" component={IssueEdit} />
      <Route path="/report" component={IssueReport} />
      <Route path="/about" component={About} />
      <Route component={NotFound} />
      {routes.map(attrs => <Route {...attrs} key={attrs.path} />)}
    </Switch>
  );
}
...
```

While rendering, both on the server as well as the browser, one of the routes will be chosen for rendering based on the URL. On the browser, the history object of BrowserRouter will supply the URL for matching, and on the server, we've supplied it via the location property of the StaticRouter, which we used to wrap the page.

We still need to replace the call to About.fetchData() with something more generic. To do that, we need to determine which of the components would match the current URL that is passed in via the request object in render.jsx. React Router exposes a function called matchPath(), which is meant exactly for this purpose: it matches a given JavaScript object, which is a route specification as in the array in routes.js like this:

```
...
  const match = matchPath(urlPath, routeObject)
...
```

The routeObject object is expected to contain the properties path, exact, and strict, just as you would define a <Route> component. It returns a match object if the route matches the supplied urlPath. Thus, we can iterate over the array of routes from routes.js and find the matching route.

```
...
import routes from '../src/routes.js';
import { StaticRouter, matchPath } from 'react-router-dom';
...
  const activeRoute = routes.find(
    route => matchPath(req.path, route),
  );
...
```

If there was a match, we can peek into the matched route object's component property and see if there is a static function defined in the component to fetch data for it. If there is one, we can call that function to get the initial data.

```
...
  let initialData;
  if (activeRoute && activeRoute.component.fetchData) {
    initialData = await activeRoute.component.fetchData();
  }
...
```

This initial data can now replace the hard-coded call to About.fetchData(). This change, and the changes to render.jsx, are shown in Listing 12-44.

Listing 12-44. ui/server/render.jsx: Changes for Fetching the Initial Data Depending on the Matched Route

```
...
import { StaticRouter, matchPath } from 'react-router-dom';
...
import About from '../src/About.jsx';
import store from '../src/store.js';
import routes from '../src/routes.js';
...

async function render(req, res) {
  const initialData = About.fetchData();
```

```
const activeRoute = routes.find(
  route => matchPath(req.path, route),
);

let initialData;
if (activeRoute && activeRoute.component.fetchData) {
  initialData = await activeRoute.component.fetchData();
}
...
}
```

With these changes, we have managed to get rid of the hard-coding of the data that needs to be fetched based on the component that *will* be rendered for the matched route. But we've not yet implemented the fetching of data in many of the components. For example, refreshing the browser on /issues will continue to render an empty table that's later filled with the list of issues fetched from an API call in the browser. This is not what is needed: a request to /issues should result in a page replete with the list of issues that match the filter. But there are nuances that are different from what we did for the About component: these API calls vary depending on parameters. As we set out to implement the data fetcher in each of the existing components, we'll explore how these parameters can be passed through for use in rendering.

Data Fetcher with Parameters

In this section, we'll make the IssueEdit component render from the server with the data that it requires prepopulated.

To start, let's separate the data fetcher into a static method as we had done in the About component. This method relies on the ID of the issue to fetch the data. The most generic entity that has this information is the match object that the component has access to automatically while rendering on the browser.

While rendering on the server, the result of the matchPath() call gives us the same information. So, let's change the prototype of the fetchData() function to include the match. Further, since the method for showing errors on the browser and the server is different, let's also take the function to show errors, showError, as an argument. And then, let's move the GraphQL query to this function from the loadData() function and execute it with the issue's ID obtained from the match object.

```
...
static async fetchData(match, showError) {
  const query = `...`;

  const { params: { id } } = match;
  const result = await graphQLFetch(query, { id }, showError);
  return result;
}
...
```

As part of the constructor, we can check if there is any initial data and use that to initialize the state variable issue. Further, instead of having an empty issue object, let's set the state variable to null to indicate that it was not preloaded from the server. Now that we have multiple components looking at initial data, it is possible that the constructor of a component rendered on the browser confuses the initial data to be meant for itself. So, let's delete the data from the store once we've consumed it.

411

```
...
  constructor() {
    super();
    const issue = store.initialData ? store.initialData.issue : null;
    delete store.initialData;
    this.state = {
      issue: {},
...
```

In the `componentDidMount()` method, we can now look for the presence of the state variable. If it is not `null`, it means that it was rendered from the server. If it's `null`, it means that the user navigated to this component in the browser from a different page that was loaded from the server. In this case, we can load the data using `fetchData()`.

```
...
  componentDidMount() {
    const { issue } = this.state;
    if (issue == null) this.loadData();
  }
...
```

In the `loadData()` method, we'll replace the original call to `graphQLfetch()` with a call to `fetchData()`.

```
...
  async loadData() {
    const { match } = this.props;
    const data = await IssueEdit.fetchData(match, this.showError);
    this.setState({ issue: data ? data.issue : {}, invalidFields: {} });
  }
...
```

Now that we're setting the `issue` object value to `null` to indicate a preinitialized state, let's return `null` in the `render()` method if the issue state variable is `null`.

```
...
  render() {
    const { issue } = this.state;
    if (issue == null) return null;

    const { issue: { id } } = this.state;
    ...
  }
...
```

The complete changes to the `IssueEdit` component are shown in Listing 12-45.

Listing 12-45. ui/src/IssueEdit.jsx: Changes to Use a Common Data Fetcher

```
...
import Toast from './Toast.jsx';
import store from './store.js';
...

export default class IssueEdit extends React.Component {
  static async fetchData(match, showError) {
    const query = `query issue($id: Int!) {
      issue(id: $id) {
        id title status owner
        effort created due description
      }
    }`;

    const { params: { id } } = match;
    const result = await graphQLFetch(query, { id }, showError);
    return result;
  }

  constructor() {
    super();
    const issue = store.initialData ? store.initialData.issue : null;
    delete store.initialData;
    this.state = {
      issue: {},
      issue,
      invalidFields: {},
      ...
    }
    ...
  }
  ...

  componentDidMount() {
    const { issue } = this.state;
    if (issue == null) this.loadData();
  }
  ...

  async loadData() {
    const query = `query issue($id: Int!) {
      ...
    }`;

    const { match: { params: { id } } } = this.props;
    const data = await graphQLFetch(query, { id }, this.showError);
    const { match } = this.props;
    const data = await IssueEdit.fetchData(match, this.showError);
    this.setState({ issue: data ? data.issue : {}, invalidFields: {} });
  }
  ...
```

```
  render() {
    const { issue } = this.state;
    if (issue == null) return null;
    ...
  }
  ...
}
...
```

Since we also have the About component creating the initial data, let's delete this data after using it, as we have done in IssueEdit. The changes for this are shown in Listing 12-46.

Listing 12-46. ui/src/About.jsx: Add Deletion of initialData After Consumption

```
...
  constructor(props) {
    ...
    const apiAbout = store.initialData ? store.initialData.about : null;
    delete store.initialData;
    ...
  }
...
```

The next step is to pass in the match parameter at the time of server rendering, in render.jsx. We could save the result of matchPath() during the find() routine, but I've chosen to reevaluate this value after matching. The changes to render.jsx are shown in Listing 12-47.

Listing 12-47. ui/server/render.jsx: Changes to Include the Match Object in a Call to fetchData()

```
...
  if (activeRoute && activeRoute.component.fetchData) {
    const match = matchPath(req.path, activeRoute);
    initialData = await activeRoute.component.fetchData(match);
  }
...
```

At this point, if you navigate to the Edit page of any issue and refresh the browser, you will find errors in the Developer Console like this:

```
Uncaught TypeError: created.toDateString is not a function
```

This is because we wrote out the contents of the issue object using JSON.stringify(), which converts dates to strings. When we made an API call via graphQLFetch, we used a JSON date reviver function to convert strings to date objects, but the script that initializes the data does not use JSON.parse(). The script is executed as is. You can take a look at the source file using View Page Source in your browser, and you'll find that the key created is set to a string.

The solution is to serialize the contents of the initialize data so that it is proper JavaScript (and the property created will be assigned with new Date(...)). To do this, there is a package called serialize-javascript, which we can install now:

```
$ cd ui
$ npm install serialize-javascript@1
```

Now, let's replace JSON.stringify() in template.js with the serialize function. The changes for this are shown in Listing 12-48.

Listing 12-48. ui/server/template.js: Use Serialize Instead of Stringify

```
...
import serialize from 'serialize-javascript';
...

  <script>window.__INITIAL_DATA__ = ${JSON.stringify serialize(data)}</script>
...
```

If you test the application after this change, you will find that the error message is gone, and the Issue Edit page shows the issue properly, including the date fields. Further, if you navigate to the About page, you should see that it loads the API version from the API server (the Network tab of the Developer Tools will show this). This proves that the initial data for one page does not affect the rendering of another page.

EXERCISE: DATA FETCHER WITH PARAMETERS

1. Is there a way to use the JSON date reviver strategy for the initial data also? How about the reverse: Is there a way to use serialize() instead of JSON.parse() for the API calls? Should we do it?

Answers are available at the end of the chapter

Data Fetcher with Search

In this section, we'll implement the data fetcher in the IssueList component. In the IssueEdit component, we dealt with the fact that the data fetcher needed the parameters of the matching route. In IssueList, we'll deal with the fact that the search (query) string part of the URL is needed for fetching the correct set of issues.

Let's pass the query string (React Router calls this search) in addition to the match object to fetchData(). In the server, we don't have direct access to this, so we'll have to search for the ? character and use a substring operation on the request's URL to get this value. The changes for this in render.jsx are shown in Listing 12-49.

Listing 12-49. ui/server/render.jsx: Include Search String in fetchData() Calls

```
...
  if (activeRoute && activeRoute.component.fetchData) {
    const match = matchPath(req.path, activeRoute);
    const index = req.url.indexOf('?');
    const search = index !== -1 ? req.url.substr(index) : null;
    initialData = await activeRoute.component.fetchData(match, search);
  }
...
```

Due to this change, we'll also have to modify `IssueEdit` to include this new argument in its static `fetchData()` method. The changes for this are shown in Listing 12-50.

Listing 12-50. ui/src/IssueEdit: Changes for Change in fetchData() Prototype

```
...
export default class IssueEdit extends React.Component {
  static async fetchData(match, search, showError) {
    ...
  }
  ...
  async loadData() {
    ...
    const data = await IssueEdit.fetchData(match, null, this.showError);
    ...
  }
  ...
}
...
```

Now, let's create the data fetcher in the `IssueList` component. We'll move the required piece of code from the `loadData()` method into this new static method. The following changes are in comparison to the original code in the `loadData()` method. For a full listing of this method, refer to Listing 12-51.

```
...
  static async fetchData(match, search, showError) {
    const { location: { search } } = this.props;
    const params = new URLSearchParams(search);
    ...

    const query = `query issueList(
      ...
    }`;

    const data = await graphQLFetch(query, vars, this.showError);
    return data;
  }
...
```

The `loadData()` method will now use this data fetcher instead of making the query directly. The code that has moved to `fetchData()` is not shown as deleted explicitly; this is the complete code for this method.

```
...
  async loadData() {
    const { location: { search } } = this.props;
    const data = await IssueList.fetchData(null, search, this.showError);
    if (data) {
      this.setState({ issues: data.issueList });
    }
  }
...
```

416

In the constructor, we'll use the store and the initial data to set the initial set of issues and delete it once we have consumed it.

```
...
  constructor() {
    super();
    const issues = store.initialData ? store.initialData.issueList : null;
    delete store.initialData;
    this.state = {
      issues: [],
      issues,
...
```

When the component is mounted, we can avoid loading the data if the state variable has a valid set of issues, i.e., it is not null.

```
...
  componentDidMount() {
    const { issues } = this.state;
    if (issues == null) this.loadData();
  }
...
```

Finally, as in the IssueEdit component, let's skip rendering if the state variable issues is set to null. The complete set of changes to this component, including this last change, are shown in Listing 12-51.

Listing 12-51. ui/src/IssueList.jsx: Changes for Data Fetcher Using Search

```
...
import Toast from './Toast.jsx';
import store from './store.js';
...

export default class IssueList extends React.Component {
  static async fetchData(match, search, showError) {
    const params = new URLSearchParams(search);
    const vars = {};
    if (params.get('status')) vars.status = params.get('status');

    const effortMin = parseInt(params.get('effortMin'), 10);
    if (!Number.isNaN(effortMin)) vars.effortMin = effortMin;
    const effortMax = parseInt(params.get('effortMax'), 10);
    if (!Number.isNaN(effortMax)) vars.effortMax = effortMax;

    const query = `query issueList(
      $status: StatusType
      $effortMin: Int
      $effortMax: Int
    ) {
      issueList(
        status: $status
        effortMin: $effortMin
```

```
        effortMax: $effortMax
      ) {
        id title status owner
        created effort due
      }
    }`;

    const data = await graphQLFetch(query, vars, showError);
    return data;
  }

  constructor() {
    super();
    const issues = store.initialData ? store.initialData.issueList : null;
    delete store.initialData;
    this.state = {
      issues: [],
      issues,
      ...
    };
    ...
  }
  ...

  componentDidMount() {
    const { issues } = this.state;
    if (issues == null) this.loadData();
  }
  ...

  async loadData() {
    const { location: { search } } = this.props;
    const params = new URLSearchParams(search);
    ...
    const data = await graphQLFetch(query, vars, this.showError);
    const data = await IssueList.fetchData(null, search, this.showError);
    if (data) {
      this.setState({ issues: data.issueList });
    }
  }
  ...

  render() {
    const { issues } = this.state;
    if (issues == null) return null;
    ...
  }
  ...
}
```

If you test the application, especially the Issue List page now, you should find that a refresh on the Issue List shows the issues filled in the table. This can be confirmed by inspecting the source of the page: you should find that the table is prefilled. Also, if you watch the Network tab of the Developer Tools, you should not see any API call being made to fetch the list of issues on a refresh, whereas the API call will be made when navigating from any other page. Do also test with different values of filters to ensure that the search string is being used correctly.

Nested Components

We still have one more component to deal with: IssueDetail. At this juncture, the component will seem to work, both when clicking on an issue row in the list and when the browser is refreshed with the URL containing an issue ID such as /issues/1. But you'll find that the detail is being fetched *after* mounting the component and not as part of the server rendered HTML. As discussed, this is not good. We really need the detail part also to be rendered in the server.

Although React Router's dynamic routing works great when navigating via links in the UI, it is quite inconvenient when it comes to server rendering. We cannot easily deal with nested routes. One option is to add nesting of routes in routes.js and pass the nested route object to the containing component so that it can create a <Route> component at the appropriate place based on this.

Another alternative is the one we discussed in the "Nested Routes" exercise in Chapter 9. In this alternative, the route specification for IssueList includes an optional Issue ID, and this component deals with the loading of the detail part too. This has the following advantages:

- The route specification remains simple and has only the top-level pages in a flat structure, without any hierarchy.

- It gives us an opportunity to combine two API calls into one in the case where the Issue List is loaded with a selected issue.

Let's choose this alternative and modify the component IssueList to render its contained detail as well. This will cause the IssueDetail component to be greatly simplified, reducing it to a stateless component, which only renders the detail. The complete code for the new IssueDetail component is shown in Listing 12-52.

Listing 12-52. ui/src/IssueDetail.jsx: Replaced Contents with a Stateless Component

```
import React from 'react';

export default function IssueDetail({ issue }) {
  if (issue) {
    return (
      <div>
        <h3>Description</h3>
        <pre>{issue.description}</pre>
      </div>
    );
  }
  return null;
}
```

Let's also modify the route to specify the ID parameter, which is optional. The way to specify that the parameter is optional is by appending a ? to it. The changes to routes.js are shown in Listing 12-53.

Listing 12-53. ui/src/routes.js: Modification of /issues Route to Include an Optional Parameter

```
...
const routes = [
  { path: '/issues/:id?', component: IssueList },
  ...
];
...
```

Now, in the IssueList component, we'll find the ID of the selected issue in props.match. Also, in fetchData(), we'll use the match object to find the ID of the selected issue and use it. If there exists a selected ID, we'll fetch its details along with the issue list in a *single* GraphQL call. GraphQL allows adding multiple named queries within a query, so we'll take advantage of this. But since the second call for the issue's details is optional, we'll have to execute this conditionally. We can use the @include directive of GraphQL to achieve this. We'll pass an extra variable hasSelection, and we'll include the second query if the value of this is true.

```
  ...
  static async fetchData(match, search, showError) {
    const params = new URLSearchParams(search);
    const vars = { hasSelection: false, selectedId: 0 };
    ...

    const { params: { id } } = match;
    const idInt = parseInt(id, 10);
    if (!Number.isNaN(idInt)) {
      vars.hasSelection = true;
      vars.selectedId = idInt;
    }

    const query = `query issueList(
      ...
      $hasSelection: Boolean!
      $selectedId: Int!
    ) {
      issueList(
        ...
      }
      issue(id: $selectedId) @include (if : $hasSelection) {
        id description
      }
    }`;

    const data = await graphQLFetch(query, vars, showError);
    return data;
  }
  ...
```

Now, the returned data object will have two properties in it when hasSelection is set to true: issueList and issue. The same will appear in store.initialData, so let's use the additional issue object to set the initial state in the constructor.

```
...
  constructor() {
    ...
    const selectedIssue = store.initialData
      ? store.initialData.issue
      : null;
    delete store.initialData;
    this.state = {
      issues,
      selectedIssue,
      ...
    };
...
```

We need to make similar changes to loadData(): pass the match to fetchData(), then use the result to set the state variable selectedIssue in addition to issues.

```
...
  async loadData() {
    const { location: { search }, match } = this.props;
    const data = await IssueList.fetchData(nullmatch, search, this.showError);
    if (data) {
      this.setState({ issues: data.issueList, selectedIssue: data.issue });
    }
  }
...
```

Now we can use the new state variable selectedIssue in the render() function to display the details at the desired location instead of a <Route>.

```
...
  render() {
    ...
    const { match } = this.props;
    const { selectedIssue } = this.state;
    return (
      ...
        <Route path={`${match.path}/:id`} component={IssueDetail} />
        <IssueDetail issue={selectedIssue} />
      ...
    );
  }
...
```

At this point, refreshing the issue list and changing the filter will work, but selecting a new issue row will not reflect the changes in the detail section. That's because componentDidUpdate() checks only for changes in the search and reloads the data. We need also to check for changes in the ID of the selected issue to reload.

```
...
  componentDidUpdate(prevProps) {
    const { location: { search: prevSearch } } = prevProps;
    const {
      location: { search: prevSearch },
      match: { params: { id: prevId } },
    } = prevProps;
    const { location: { search }, match: { params: { id } } } = this.props;
    if (prevSearch !== search || prevId !== id) {
      this.loadData();
    }
  }
...
```

The complete set of changes to the IssueList component are shown in Listing 12-54.

Listing 12-54. ui/src/IssueList.jsx: Pull Up IssueDetail Into IssueList

```
...
import URLSearchParams from 'url-search-params';
import { Route } from 'react-router-dom';
...

  static async fetchData(match, search, showError) {
    ...
    const vars = { hasSelection: false, selectedId: 0 };
    ...
    if (!Number.isNaN(effortMax)) vars.effortMax = effortMax;

    const { params: { id } } = match;
    const idInt = parseInt(id, 10);
    if (!Number.isNaN(idInt)) {
      vars.hasSelection = true;
      vars.selectedId = idInt;
    }

    const query = `query issueList(
      ...
      $hasSelection: Boolean!
      $selectedId: Int!
    ) {
      issueList(
        ...
      }
      issue(id: $selectedId) @include (if : $hasSelection) {
        id description
      }
    }`;
    ...
```

```
    }
...

  constructor() {
    ...
    const selectedIssue = store.initialData
      ? store.initialData.issue
      : null;
    delete store.initialData;
    this.state = {
      issues,
      selectedIssue,
      ...
    };
...

  componentDidUpdate(prevProps) {
    const { location: { search: prevSearch } } = prevProps;
    const {
      location: { search: prevSearch },
      match: { params: { id: prevId } },
    } = prevProps;
    const { location: { search }, match: { params: { id } } } = this.props;
    if (prevSearch !== search || prevId !== id) {
      this.loadData();
    }
  }
...

async loadData() {
    const { location: { search }, match } = this.props;
    const data = await IssueList.fetchData(nullmatch, search, this.showError);
    if (data) {
      this.setState({ issues: data.issueList, selectedIssue: data.issue });
    }
  }
...

render() {
    ...
    const { match } = this.props;
    const { selectedIssue } = this.state;
    return (
      ...
        <Route path={`${match.path}/:id`} component={IssueDetail} />
        <IssueDetail issue={selectedIssue} />
      ...
    );
  }
...
```

423

If you test the Issue List page now, especially with any one issue selected and refreshing the browser, you'll find the detail of the selected issue loaded along with the list of issues. If you change the selected issue by clicking on another row, you will see in the Network tab of the Developer Tools that a single GraphQL call is fetching both the list of issues as well as the details of the selected issue.

EXERCISE: NESTED COMPONENTS

1. When changing the selected issue, although it's a single GraphQL call, the entire issue list is being fetched. This is not required and adds to the network traffic. How would you optimize for this?

Answers are available at the end of the chapter

Redirects

We still have one last thing to take care of: a request to the home page, that is, /, returns an HTML from the server that contains an empty page. It seems to work because after rendering on the browser, React Router does a redirect to /issues *in the browser history*. What we really need is for the server itself to respond with a 301 Redirect so that the browser fetches /issues instead from the server. This way, search engine bots also will get the same contents for a request to / as they get for /issues.

React Router's StaticRouter handles this by setting a variable called url in any context that is passed to it. We've been passing an empty, unnamed context to StaticRouter. Instead, let's pass a named object, though empty, to it. After rendering to string, if the url property is set in this object, it means that the router matched a redirect to this URL. All we need to do is send a redirect in the response instead of the templated response.

The changes to render.jsx to handle the redirect are shown in Listing 12-55.

Listing 12-55. ui/server/render.jsx: Handle Redirects on the Server

```
...
  store.initialData = initialData;
  const context = {};
  const element = (
    <StaticRouter location={req.url} context={{}context}>
      <Page />
    </StaticRouter>
  );
  const body = ReactDOMServer.renderToString(element);

  if (context.url) {
    res.redirect(301, context.url);
  } else {
    res.send(template(body, initialData));
  }
...
```

Now, if you enter http://localhost:8000/ in your browser, you should see that the Issue List page loads without any flicker. In the Network tab, you will find the very first request resulting in a redirect to /issues, which then follows the regular path of rendering the issue list at the server.

Summary

This chapter may have been a little heavy since we used complex constructs and patterns to implement server rendering. Hopefully, using the About page eased the complexity and helped you understand the fundamental concepts for server rendering.

It must also be evident by now that React itself, not being a framework, does not dictate each of the additional parts that complete the application. React Router helped us a bit with front-end routing, but some of it did not work for server rendering. We had to invent our own patterns of generated routes and that of data fetchers as static methods in each of the routed components to deal with data associated with server rendered pages.

As we move on to the next chapter, we won't focus on one single feature or concept. Instead we'll implement features that are common to many applications. As we do this, we'll see how the MERN stack satisfies the needs of these advanced features.

Answers to Exercises

Exercise: Basic Server Rendering

1.   The ReactDOMServer method renderToNodeStream() can be considered to replace renderToString(). This method returns a stream that can be piped to the Express response stream. Instead of a template, we'll need pre- and a post-body strings that we can write to the response before and after piping the node stream, respectively.

Exercise: Server Router

1.   When the About page is rendered using server rendering, you will find that clicking on the + menu item does nothing. There are no event handlers attached to the menu item, further, you will find that there is no code where you can put a breakpoint. The reason is that the template does not include the JavaScript bundles that contained both the component as well as React library code.

2.   In a browser-rendered navigation bar, clicking on a link does not load the page from the server. Only XHR calls are made to get the data and the DOM is constructed on the browser. In a server-rendered navigation bar, clicking on a link loads the page from the server, just like a normal href would have done. The reason is the same as in the previous exercise: in a server-rendered page, there are no event handlers attached that trap the click event and make changes on the DOM within the browser. In a server-rendered page, the links behave as pure href links do: they make the browser load a new page.

Exercise: Data Fetcher with Parameters

1.   You could use JSON.parse(), but it needs a string as its argument. Since the string representation of the initial data itself has a lot of double quotes, they need to be escaped, or you could use single quotes around it. Another strategy used by some is to use a hidden textarea or a div to store the string and read it off the DOM and call JSON.parse() on that string. I find that serialize is a much more concise and clearer option.

As for the reverse, the caller of the API will need to use an eval() instead of JSON.parse() on the resulting data. This is quite dangerous because it would allow new functions to be installed as a result, if the data contained any. If the API server has somehow been compromised, this can enable malicious code to be injected into the browser. Further, this strategy assumes that the caller works on JavaScript, and this may not be a valid assumption.

Exercise: Nested Components

1. A good strategy to optimize the data being fetched is to write another method that fetches the selected issue alone via a different GraphQL query. This method, say loadSelectedIssue(), can be called from componentDidUpdate() if the search did not change but the ID parameter changed.

CHAPTER 13

■ ■ ■

Advanced Features

In this chapter, we'll take a look at features common to many applications. These features cut across the different technologies (front-end, back-end, database) that the MERN stack consists of, and requires us to put together changes in all of them to make them work.

We'll first refactor the UI code to reuse common code across many components that display the Toast messages. We'll move most of the repeated code in the components into new file using a pattern common to React. Then, we'll implement the Report page that has until now been a placeholder. This will require us to use the aggregate function of MongoDB. Then we'll implement pagination in the Issue List page to deal with large lists. This will exercise another feature of MongoDB: the skip and offset options of find().

We'll then implement an Undo operation when deleting issues to resurrect them. Finally, we'll display a search bar in which the users can type keywords and look for issues matching the keywords.

Higher Order Component for Toast

A fair bit of code is repeated across the main views for showing and managing Toast messages. This includes the following:

- The state variables that are used for the Toast: showing state, the message, and the message type

- The methods showError(), showSuccess(), and dismissToast()

- The placement of the Toast component within the render() function

In many other languages, these would have been addressed by inheriting the actual views from a base class that had these methods and variables implemented. But the authors of React recommend composition over inheritance for reusing code across components. So, let's create a new component that wraps each of the main views to add the Toast functionality. Let's call this class ToastWrapper. We'll thus *compose* a wrapped component using ToastWrapper and any of the view components, say, IssueList. This is what the views' parent needs to use instead of the plain view component. Here's the skeleton of ToastWrapper's render() method:

```
...
  render() {
    return (
      <React.Fragment>
        <IssueList />
        <Toast />
      </React.Fragment>
    );
  }
...
```

Now, we can move all the state variables relating to the Toast into the ToastWrapper component and the dismissToast method. Within render, we can use the state variables to control the display of the Toast, moving the code out of IssueList.

```
...
    constructor(props) {
      super(props);
      this.state = {
        toastVisible: false, toastMessage: ", toastType: 'success',
      };
      this.dismissToast = this.dismissToast.bind(this);
    }

    dismissToast() {
      this.setState({ toastVisible: false });
    }

    render() {
      const { toastType, toastVisible, toastMessage } = this.state;
      return (
        <React.Fragment>
          <IssueList />
          <Toast
            bsStyle={toastType}
            showing={toastVisible}
            onDismiss={this.dismissToast}
          >
            {toastMessage}
          </Toast>
        </React.Fragment>
      );
    }
...
```

Within the original component IssueList, we need a way to show the error, and if required, dismiss it. Let's create the showError and showSuccess methods in ToastWrapper and pass them as props to IssueList. Further, let's include any other props that the parent may want to pass through to IssueList.

```
...
    showSuccess(message) {
      this.setState({ toastVisible: true, toastMessage: message, toastType: 'success' });
    }

    showError(message) {
      this.setState({ toastVisible: true, toastMessage: message, toastType: 'danger' });
    }
...
    render() {
      ...
        <IssueList
          showError={this.showError}
```

```
      showSuccess={this.showSuccess}
      dismissToast={this.dismissToast}
      {...this.props}
    />
...
```

We still need to parameterize the view rather than hard-code the IssueList. Creating this class for every view that needs to show a Toast message would defeat the purpose of reusing code. One way to do this is by passing the original component as a child of the wrapper in the parent, like this:

```
...
  <ToastWrapper>
    <IssueList .../>
  </ToastWrapper>
...
```

And, in the ToastWrapper class, instead of hard-coding IssueList, we can use props.children. For the other views, IssueEdit and IssueAddNavItem, we'll need similar wrapped components. This could work in some cases, but if you take a look at where these components are being used, you'll notice that we need to supply a component *class*, not an instance. Here's the snippet from routes.js.

```
...
  { path: '/issues/:id?', component: IssueList },
...
```

What we really need is something that creates a new component *class* from the existing component classes: IssueList, IssueEdit, and IssueAddNavItem. Let's create a function called withToast to do just this, like React Router's withRouter function. It will take in the original component as an argument and return a class that uses the ToastWrapper and wraps the original component.

```
...
export default function withToast(OriginalComponent) {
  return class ToastWrapper extends React.Component {
    ...
    render() {
        <OriginalComponent
          ...
          {...this.props}
        />
  };
}
...
```

Now, wherever IssueList is referred, we can simply use withToast(IssueList) instead. This pattern of creating a new component class from an existing component class and injecting into it additional functionality is called *Higher Order Component* (HOC). The full code of the new HOC is shown in Listing 13-1.

Listing 13-1. ui/src/withToast.jsx: New HOC for Adding Toast Functionality to a Component

```
import React from 'react';
import Toast from './Toast.jsx';

export default function withToast(OriginalComponent) {
  return class ToastWrapper extends React.Component {
    constructor(props) {
      super(props);
      this.state = {
        toastVisible: false, toastMessage: '', toastType: 'success',
      };
      this.showSuccess = this.showSuccess.bind(this);
      this.showError = this.showError.bind(this);
      this.dismissToast = this.dismissToast.bind(this);
    }

    showSuccess(message) {
      this.setState({ toastVisible: true, toastMessage: message, toastType: 'success' });
    }

    showError(message) {
      this.setState({ toastVisible: true, toastMessage: message, toastType: 'danger' });
    }

    dismissToast() {
      this.setState({ toastVisible: false });
    }

    render() {
      const { toastType, toastVisible, toastMessage } = this.state;
      return (
        <React.Fragment>
          <OriginalComponent
            showError={this.showError}
            showSuccess={this.showSuccess}
            dismissToast={this.dismissToast}
            {...this.props}
          />
          <Toast
            bsStyle={toastType}
            showing={toastVisible}
            onDismiss={this.dismissToast}
          >
            {toastMessage}
          </Toast>
        </React.Fragment>
      );
    }
  };
}
```

Now, to use this new function, the following could be done in `routes.js`:

```
...
  { path: '/issues/:id?', component: withToast(IssueList) },
...
```

But this increases the coupling between the two modules: `routes.js` now needs to know which components need the Toast functionality. Instead, just like we did for `withRouter` wrapping, let's encapsulate this wrapper within the components themselves (such as `IssueList`) and export the modified component class, for example:

```
...
export default class IssueList extends React.Component {
  ...
}

export default withToast(IssueList);
...
```

But this has one side-effect: it would hide the static method `fetchData()`, which is being called from outside this component. We'll have to copy the reference of the component's static methods to the wrapped component too, to make it visible.

```
...
const IssueListWithToast = withToast(IssueList);
IssueListWithToast.fetchData = IssueList.fetchData;

export default IssueListWithToast;
...
```

The other changes needed for the `IssueList` component to use `withToast` are removal of state variables, Toast-related method definitions, and replacing class methods for Toast functions with the ones received via props. The complete set of changes in the `IssueList` component is shown in Listing 13-2.

Listing 13-2. ui/src/IssueList.jsx: Changes for Using the withToast HOC

```
...
import Toast from './Toast.jsx';
import withToast from './withToast.jsx';
...

export default class IssueList extends React.Component {
  ...
  constructor() {
    ...
    this.state = {
      ...
      toastVisible: false,
      toastMessage: '',
      toastType: 'info',
    };
    ...
```

```
    this.showSuccess = this.showSuccess.bind(this);
    this.showError = this.showError.bind(this);
    this.dismissToast = this.dismissToast.bind(this);
  }
...

  async loadData() {
    const { location: { search }, match, showError } = this.props;
    const data = await IssueList.fetchData(match, search, this.showError);
    ...
  }
...
  async closeIssue(index) {

    ...
    const { showError } = this.props;
    const data = await graphQLFetch(query, { id: issues[index].id },
      this.showError);
    ...
  }
...

  async deleteIssue(index) {

    ...
    const { showSuccess, showError } = this.props;
    ...
    const data = await graphQLFetch(query, { id }, this.showError);
    if (data && data.issueDelete) {
      ...
      this.showSuccess(`Deleted issue ${id} successfully.`);
    }
    ...
  }
...

  showSuccess(message) {
    ...
  }

  showError(message) {
    ...
  }

  dismissToast() {
    ...
  }

  render() {
    ...
    const { toastVisible, toastType, toastMessage } = this.state;
    ...
      <Toast
```

```
      ...
      >
        {toastMessage}
      </Toast>
    ...
  }
...
```

```
const IssueListWithToast = withToast(IssueList);
IssueListWithToast.fetchData = IssueList.fetchData;

export default IssueListWithToast;
...
```

A similar set of changes to the component IssueEdit is shown in Listing 13-3.

Listing 13-3. ui/src/IssueEdit.jsx: Changes for Using the withToast HOC

```
...
import Toast from './Toast.jsx';
import withToast from './withToast.jsx';
...

export default class IssueEdit extends React.Component {
  ...
  constructor() {
    ...
    this.state = {
      ...
      toastVisible: false,
      toastMessage: '',
      toastType: 'info',
    };
    ...
    this.showSuccess = this.showSuccess.bind(this);
    this.showError = this.showError.bind(this);
    this.dismissToast = this.dismissToast.bind(this);
  }
...

  async handleSubmit(e) {
    ...
    const { showSuccess, showError } = this.props;
    const data = await graphQLFetch(query, { changes, id }, this.showError);
    if (data) {
      ...
      this.showSuccess('Updated issue successfully');
    }
  }
```

```
  async loadData() {
    const { match, showError } = this.props;
    const data = await IssueEdit.fetchData(match, null, this.showError);
    ...
  }

...

  showSuccess(message) {
    ...
  }

  showError(message) {
    ...
  }

  dismissToast() {
    ...
  }

  render() {
    ...
    const { toastVisible, toastType, toastMessage } = this.state;
    ...
        <Toast
          ...
        >
          {toastMessage}
        </Toast>
    ...
  }
...

const IssueEditWithToast = withToast(IssueEdit);
IssueEditWithToast.fetchData = IssueEdit.fetchData;

export default IssueEditWithToast;
...
```

The changes to the component IssueAddNavItem are similar with a minor variation. This component does not have a fetchData() method, so we don't need to copy that method to the wrapped component. Further, the component is already wrapped with withRouter(), so we'll need to add the withToast() wrapper in addition to that. The changes are shown in Listing 13-4.

Listing 13-4. ui/src/IssueAddNavItem.jsx: Changes for Using the withToast HOC

```
...
...
import Toast from './Toast.jsx';
import withToast from './withToast.jsx';
...
```

```
class IssueAddNavItem extends React.Component {
  ...
  constructor() {
    ...
    this.state = {
      ...
      toastVisible: false,
      toastMessage: '',
      toastType: 'info',
    };
    ...
    this.showError = this.showError.bind(this);
    this.dismissToast = this.dismissToast.bind(this);
  }
...

  showError(message) {
    ...
  }

  dismissToast() {
    ...
  }
...

  async handleSubmit(e) {
    ...
    const { showError } = this.props;
    const data = await graphQLFetch(query, { issue }, this.showError);
    ...
  }
...

  render() {
    ...
    const { toastVisible, toastType, toastMessage } = this.state;
    ...
        <Toast
          ...
        >
          {toastMessage}
        </Toast>
    ...
  }
...

export default withToast(withRouter(IssueAddNavItem));
...
```

With these changes, the application should continue to behave as before. You can test it by testing each of the error or success messages that these components show.

■ **Note** Although no effort has been spared to ensure that all code listings are accurate, there may be typos or even corrections that did not make it into the book before it went to press. So, do always rely on the GitHub repository (https://github.com/vasansr/pro-mern-stack-2) as the tested and up-to-date source for all code listings, especially if something does not work as expected.

MongoDB Aggregate

We had left a placeholder for reports in the navigation bar until now. In preparation for implementing this page in the next two sections, let's explore what MongoDB provides in terms of getting summary data of a collection, that is, *aggregates*.

First, let's create a lot of issues in the database so that summaries can look meaningful. A simple MongoDB shell script to generate a set of issues randomly distributed across dates, owners, and statuses is shown in Listing 13-5.

Listing 13-5. api/scripts/generate_data.mongo.js: Mongo Shell Script to Generate Some Data

```
/* global db print */
/* eslint no-restricted-globals: "off" */

const owners = ['Ravan', 'Eddie', 'Pieta', 'Parvati', 'Victor'];
const statuses = ['New', 'Assigned', 'Fixed', 'Closed'];

const initialCount = db.issues.count();

for (let i = 0; i < 100; i += 1) {
  const randomCreatedDate = (new Date())
    - Math.floor(Math.random() * 60) * 1000 * 60 * 60 * 24;
  const created = new Date(randomCreatedDate);
  const randomDueDate = (new Date())
    - Math.floor(Math.random() * 60) * 1000 * 60 * 60 * 24;
  const due = new Date(randomDueDate);

  const owner = owners[Math.floor(Math.random() * 5)];
  const status = statuses[Math.floor(Math.random() * 4)];
  const effort = Math.ceil(Math.random() * 20);
  const title = 'Lorem ipsum dolor sit amet, ${i}';
  const id = initialCount + i + 1;

  const issue = {
    id, title, created, due, owner, status, effort,
  };

  db.issues.insertOne(issue);
}

const count = db.issues.count();
db.counters.update({ _id: 'issues' }, { $set: { current: count } });

print('New issue count:', count);
```

Let's run this script once to populate the database with 100 new issues. The command to do this if you are using mongo on your localhost is:

```
$ cd api
$ mongo issuetracker scripts/generate_data.mongo.js
```

MongoDB provides the collection method aggregate() to summarize and perform various other read tasks on the collection using a *pipeline*. A pipeline is a series of transforms on the collection before returning the result set. In fact, the default call to aggregate() without any arguments is identical to a call to find(), that is, it returns the entire list of documents in the collection, without any manipulation.

The MongoDB aggregation pipeline consists of stages. Each stage transforms the documents as they pass through the pipeline. For example, a match stage will act like a filter on the list of documents from the previous stage. To simulate a find() with a filter, a single match stage in the pipeline can be used. To transform the document, a project stage can be used. This, unlike the projection in find(), can even add new calculated fields to the document using expressions.

Each stage does not have to produce a one-to-one mapping of the previous stage. The group stage is one such stage that produces a summary rather than replicate each document. The unwind stage is something that does the opposite: it expands array fields into one document for each array element. The same stage can appear multiple times—for example, you could start with a match, then a group, and then another match to filter out some documents after the grouping.

For a full listing of all available stages, refer to the MongoDB documentation on the pipeline stages at https://docs.mongodb.com/manual/reference/operator/aggregation/. I'll only discuss in depth the two stages match (based on the filter) and group (to summarize the counts) that are needed to implement the Report page in the Issue Tracker application.

The aggregate() method takes a single parameter, an array of pipeline stage specifications. Each stage specification is an object with a key indicating the type of the stage and the value holding the parameters for the stage. A match stage takes in the filter, as you would specify in a find() method. Thus, the following command (issued in the MongoDB shell) will return all open issues:

```
> db.issues.aggregate([ { $match: { status: 'New' } } ])
```

The group stage is a little more involved. It consists of a set of fields that need to be created, and a specification of how they need to be created. In the object specification, the key is the name of the field, and the value specifies how the field's value is to be constructed. The values are typically based on existing fields in the document (in fact the results of the previous stage), and to refer to these fields, one needs to use a $ prefix, without which it will be taken as a literal.

The _id field is mandatory and has a special meaning: it is the value that the results are grouped by. Typically, you use an existing field specification for this, the grouping will be done on this field's value. For the rest of the fields in the output, you can specify an aggregation function to construct their values.

For example, if you need the sum and average effort of all issues grouped by the owner, you use the following aggregate() command (which has a single stage in the pipeline):

```
> db.issues.aggregate([
  { $group: {
    _id: '$owner',
    total_effort: { $sum: '$effort' },
    average_effort: {$avg: '$effort' },
  } }
])
```

This command will produce output like this:

```
{ "_id" : "Victor", "total_effort" : 232, "average_effort" : 10.08695652173913 }
{ "_id" : "Pieta", "total_effort" : 292, "average_effort" : 12.166666666666666 }
{ "_id" : "Parvati", "total_effort" : 212, "average_effort" : 11.157894736842104 }
{ "_id" : "Eddie", "total_effort" : 143, "average_effort" : 8.9375 }
{ "_id" : "Ravan", "total_effort" : 213, "average_effort" : 10.65 }
```

If the entire collection needs to be grouped into a single value, that is, you don't need a grouping field; you can use a literal value for the _id, typically null. Also, there is no special count function—you just need to sum the number 1 to get a count of all matched documents. Thus, another way to count the number of documents in a collection using the aggregate() method is

```
> db.issues.aggregate([ { $group: { _id: null, count: { $sum: 1 } } }])
```

This will produce output like this:

```
{ "_id" : null, "count" : 102 }
```

To use a filter before grouping the output, a match can be used as the first element in the array, followed by the group stage. So, to count the number of issues with status as New, the following aggregate command can be used:

```
> db.issues.aggregate([
  { $match: { status: 'New' } },
  { $group: { _id: null, count: { $sum: 1 } } },
])
```

This would result in a much lower count number compared to all the issues in the collection, something like this:

```
{ "_id" : null, "count" : 31 }
```

You could verify that the count is indeed correct by issuing a count command.

```
> db.issues.count({ status: 'New' })
```

For the Report page, let's create a pivot table (or a cross-tab) output that shows the counts of issues assigned to various owners, further grouped by statuses. For this, we need two grouped by fields, the owner and the status. Multiple group fields can be specified by setting the _id field to an object instead of a string. This object needs to contain the name of the output and the field identifier for each of the fields. Then, in the output, rather than a string as the value of _id, an object will be returned, each returned row with a different combination of the two fields.

So, to get a count of issues grouped by owner and status, this is the command to use:

```
> db.issues.aggregate([
  { $group: {
    _id: { owner: '$owner',status: '$status' },
    count: { $sum: 1 },
```

```
  } }
])
```

This should result in an array of documents, with one document for every owner-status combination, which is the key or _id.

```
{ "_id" : { "owner" : "Eddie", "status" : "Closed" }, "count" : 2 }
{ "_id" : { "owner" : "Parvati", "status" : "Closed" }, "count" : 2 }
{ "_id" : { "owner" : "Victor", "status" : "Closed" }, "count" : 6 }
{ "_id" : { "owner" : "Victor", "status" : "Assigned" }, "count" : 6 }
{ "_id" : { "owner" : "Parvati", "status" : "Fixed" }, "count" : 6 }
...
```

To add a filter before grouping the results, a match stage can be used. For instance, to get a count of issues where the effort is more than 4, the command would be:

```
> db.issues.aggregate([
  { $match: { effort: { $gte: 4 } } },
  { $group: {
    _id: { owner: '$owner',status: '$status' },
    count: { $sum: 1 },
  } }
])
```

That's the final structure of the query that we will use in the next section to implement the API that will help build the Report page.

Issue Counts API

As part of the Issue Counts API implementation, we will need to make the aggregate query to MongoDB, as discussed in the previous section. It would have been quite convenient to return the data received from MongoDB as is, but let's try to make it a bit more usable for the caller. In the array that is returned, let's have one element per owner rather than one element for each owner-status combination, and one property each for the count of each status. In the GraphQL schema, let's define this as a new type.

```
...
type IssueCounts {
  owner: String!
  New: Int
  Assigned: Int
  Fixed: Int
  Closed: Int
}
...
```

The query itself will take as input a filter specification (as in the issueList query) and return an array of IssueCounts objects. The applicable changes to schema.graphql are shown in Listing 13-6.

Listing 13-6. api/schema.graphql: Changes for Issue Counts API

```
...
type Issue {
  ...
}

type IssueCounts {
  owner: String!
  New: Int
  Assigned: Int
  Fixed: Int
  Closed: Int
}
...
type Query {
  ...
  issue(id: Int!): Issue!
  issueCounts(
    status: StatusType
    effortMin: Int
    effortMax: Int
  ): [IssueCounts!]!
}
...
```

We'll place the implementation of the API or the resolver in issue.js along with other resolvers related to this object. We'll call the new function counts(), which will take in a filter specification, the same as for the list function. Let's copy the filter construction part from the list function and use it in the query, which is nothing but what we finalized in the end of the previous section. We'll then process each of the documents returned by the database and update an object called stats. We'll locate the object with the key as the owner (if not found, we'll create one), and then set the value for the status key to the count.

```
...
  const stats = {};
  results.forEach((result) => {
    // eslint-disable-next-line no-underscore-dangle
    const { owner, status: statusKey } = result._id;
    if (!stats[owner]) stats[owner] = { owner };
    stats[owner][statusKey] = result.count;
  });
...
```

But we need to return an array to the caller. We can do this by simply calling Object.values(stats). Finally, we need to add the new function as another exported value, along with the other exports. The entire set of changes to issue.js is shown in Listing 13-7.

Listing 13-7. api/issue.js: Changes for Issue Counts API

```
...
async function remove(_, { id }) {
  ...
}

async function counts(_, { status, effortMin, effortMax }) {
  const db = getDb();
  const filter = {};

  if (status) filter.status = status;

  if (effortMin !== undefined || effortMax !== undefined) {
    filter.effort = {};
    if (effortMin !== undefined) filter.effort.$gte = effortMin;
    if (effortMax !== undefined) filter.effort.$lte = effortMax;
  }

  const results = await db.collection('issues').aggregate([
    { $match: filter },
    {
      $group: {
        _id: { owner: '$owner', status: '$status' },
        count: { $sum: 1 },
      },
    },
  ]).toArray();

  const stats = {};
  results.forEach((result) => {
    // eslint-disable-next-line no-underscore-dangle
    const { owner, status: statusKey } = result._id;
    if (!stats[owner]) stats[owner] = { owner };
    stats[owner][statusKey] = result.count;
  });
  return Object.values(stats);
}

module.exports = {
  list,
  add,
  get,
  update,
  delete: remove,
  counts,
};
...
```

Now, to tie the new function to the GraphQL schema, let's make changes to api_handler.js that specify the resolver for the endpoint issueCounts. The appropriate changes are shown in Listing 13-8.

441

Listing 13-8. api/api_handler.js: Changes for Issue Counts API

```
...
const resolvers = {
  Query: {
    ...
    issueCounts: issue.counts,
  },
  ...
};
...
```

You can now test the API using the Playground. A simple query with a filter for a minimum effort will look like this:

```
query {
  issueCounts(effortMin: 4) {
    owner New Assigned Fixed Closed
  }
}
```

Upon running this query, you should see results like this:

```
{
  "data": {
    "issueCounts": [
      {
        "owner": "Eddie",
        "New": 4,
        "Assigned": 2,
        "Fixed": 4,
        "Closed": 1
      },
      {
        "owner": "Parvati",
        "New": 4,
        "Assigned": 3,
        "Fixed": 6,
        "Closed": 2
      },
      ...
    ]
  }
}
```

EXERCISE: ISSUE COUNTS API

1. Rather than converting the `stats` object to an array, could we have returned the `stats` object as is? How would the schema look? Hint: Look up the Apollo GraphQL issue at https://github.com/apollographql/apollo/issues/5.

Answers are available at the end of the chapter.

Report Page

Now that we have a working API, let's construct the UI for the Report page. We'll use a format that is popularly known as a cross-tab or a pivot table: a table with one axis labeled with the statuses and the other axis with owners.

Since the number of owners can be many and there are a limited number of statuses, let's line up the statuses on the horizontal axis (table row header) and use one row per owner to show the count of issues assigned to that owner. This way, we could handle a large number of owners easily. Let's replace the stateless component placeholder in `IssueReport` with a regular component inherited from `React.component` and start with the `render()` method. We'll use a collapsible panel and place the `IssueFilter` component here, just like we did for the Issue List. Following this, let's show a table with the report, one row for every value in the data returned by the API.

But we can't use the `IssueFilter` component as is. That's because its Apply button is hard-coded to navigate to the route `/issues`, with the filter set as the search string. Let's first address that, by passing in the base URL as props to this component. From the Issue List, this can be passed as `/issues` and from the Report page, it can be passed as `/report`. The changes for this in the `IssueFilter` component are shown in Listing 13-9.

Listing 13-9. ui/src/IssueFilter.jsx: Changes for Customizable Base URL

```
...
  applyFilter() {
    ...
    const { history, urlBase } = this.props;
    ...
    history.push({ pathname: '/issues' urlBase, search });
  }
...
```

Let's also make a change in `IssueList` for passing in the new property. This change is shown in Listing 13-10.

Listing 13-10. ui/src/IssueList.jsx: Changes to Customizable Base URL in IssueFilter

```
...
  render() {
    ...
        <Panel.Body collapsible>
          <IssueFilter urlBase="/issues" />
        </Panel.Body>
    ...
  }
}
...
```

Now, let's start with the render() method in the IssueReport component, with a collapsible filter and a table. We'll soon fill in the headerColumns and statRows variables.

```
...
    return (
      <>
        <Panel>
          <Panel.Heading>
            <Panel.Title toggle>Filter</Panel.Title>
          </Panel.Heading>
          <Panel.Body collapsible>
            <IssueFilter urlBase="/report" />
          </Panel.Body>
        </Panel>
        <Table bordered condensed hover responsive>
          <thead>
            <tr>
              <th />
              {headerColumns}
            </tr>
          </thead>
          <tbody>
            {statRows}
          </tbody>
        </Table>
      </>
    );
...
```

■ **Note** The syntax <> is a JSX shortcut for <React.Fragment>.

While generating the header columns for each status, rather than specify each status individually, let's create an array of all statuses that we can iterate over. Using this, we'll generate one <th> for each status in the header.

```
...
const statuses = ['New', 'Assigned', 'Fixed', 'Closed'];
...

  render() {
    const headerColumns = (
      statuses.map(status => (
        <th key={status}>{status}</th>
      ))
    );
    ...
  }
...
```

As for the rows themselves, we need to iterate over the data received by calling the API. Let's store this data in a state variable called stats. If this variable is not initialized (which would be the case when the asynchronous API call has not yet returned), let's return a blank page. The rows can now be generated like this:

```
...
  render() {
    const { stats } = this.state;
    if (stats == null) return null;
    ...

    const statRows = stats.map(counts => (
      <tr key={counts.owner}>
        <td>{counts.owner}</td>
        {statuses.map(status => (
          <td key={status}>{counts[status]}</td>
        ))}
      </tr>
    ));
    ...
  }
...
```

Let's now implement the data fetching static method, fetchData(). The initial portion of creating the query variables from the filter can be copied over from IssueList.jsx, except for the hasSelection and selectedID variables. The query for GraphQL is what we used in the Playground for testing, but with the filter parameters as the variables.

```
...
  static async fetchData(match, search, showError) {
    const params = new URLSearchParams(search);
    const vars = { };
    ...
    if (!Number.isNaN(effortMax)) vars.effortMax = effortMax;

    const query = `query issueList(
      $status: StatusType
      $effortMin: Int
      $effortMax: Int
    ) {
      issueCounts(
        status: $status
        effortMin: $effortMin
        effortMax: $effortMax
      ) {
        owner New Assigned Fixed Closed
      }
    }`;
    const data = await graphQLFetch(query, vars, showError);
    return data;
  }
...
```

For the rest of the implementation of this component, let's follow the same pattern as in the other main views. We'll need to add the following:

- A constructor to fetch the initial data from the store and delete it after consumption

- A componentDidMount() method to load the data in case it has not been loaded yet

- A componentDidUpdate() method to check if the search string has changed, and if so, reload the data

- A loadData() method that these two lifecycle methods can call to load it and set the state

- A Toast wrapper, which will need to be exported rather than the original class

The final complete code of the IssueReport page is shown in Listing 13-11.

Listing 13-11. ui/src/IssueReport.jsx: New Report Page

```
import React from 'react';
import { Panel, Table } from 'react-bootstrap';

import IssueFilter from './IssueFilter.jsx';
import withToast from './withToast.jsx';
import graphQLFetch from './graphQLFetch.js';
import store from './store.js';

const statuses = ['New', 'Assigned', 'Fixed', 'Closed'];

class IssueReport extends React.Component {
  static async fetchData(match, search, showError) {
    const params = new URLSearchParams(search);
    const vars = { };
    if (params.get('status')) vars.status = params.get('status');

    const effortMin = parseInt(params.get('effortMin'), 10);
    if (!Number.isNaN(effortMin)) vars.effortMin = effortMin;
    const effortMax = parseInt(params.get('effortMax'), 10);
    if (!Number.isNaN(effortMax)) vars.effortMax = effortMax;

    const query = `query issueList(
      $status: StatusType
      $effortMin: Int
      $effortMax: Int
    ) {
      issueCounts(
        status: $status
        effortMin: $effortMin
        effortMax: $effortMax
      ) {
        owner New Assigned Fixed Closed
      }
    }`;
    const data = await graphQLFetch(query, vars, showError);
    return data;
  }
```

```
constructor(props) {
  super(props);
  const stats = store.initialData ? store.initialData.issueCounts : null;
  delete store.initialData;
  this.state = { stats };
}

componentDidMount() {
  const { stats } = this.state;
  if (stats == null) this.loadData();
}

componentDidUpdate(prevProps) {
  const { location: { search: prevSearch } } = prevProps;
  const { location: { search } } = this.props;
  if (prevSearch !== search) {
    this.loadData();
  }
}

async loadData() {
  const { location: { search }, match, showError } = this.props;
  const data = await IssueReport.fetchData(match, search, showError);
  if (data) {
    this.setState({ stats: data.issueCounts });
  }
}
render() {
  const { stats } = this.state;
  if (stats == null) return null;

  const headerColumns = (
    statuses.map(status => (
      <th key={status}>{status}</th>
    ))
  );

  const statRows = stats.map(counts => (
    <tr key={counts.owner}>
      <td>{counts.owner}</td>
      {statuses.map(status => (
        <td key={status}>{counts[status]}</td>
      ))}
    </tr>
  ));

  return (
    <>
      <Panel>
        <Panel.Heading>
          <Panel.Title toggle>Filter</Panel.Title>
        </Panel.Heading>
```

```
          <Panel.Body collapsible>
            <IssueFilter urlBase="/report" />
          </Panel.Body>
        </Panel>
        <Table bordered condensed hover responsive>
          <thead>
            <tr>
              <th />
              {headerColumns}
            </tr>
          </thead>
          <tbody>
            {statRows}
          </tbody>
        </Table>
      </>
    );
  }
}

const IssueReportWithToast = withToast(IssueReport);
IssueReportWithToast.fetchData = IssueReport.fetchData;

export default IssueReportWithToast;
```

If you now test the Report page, you should see a page similar to the one in Figure 13-1. You can use the collapsible filter panel to change the filter and see its effect too.

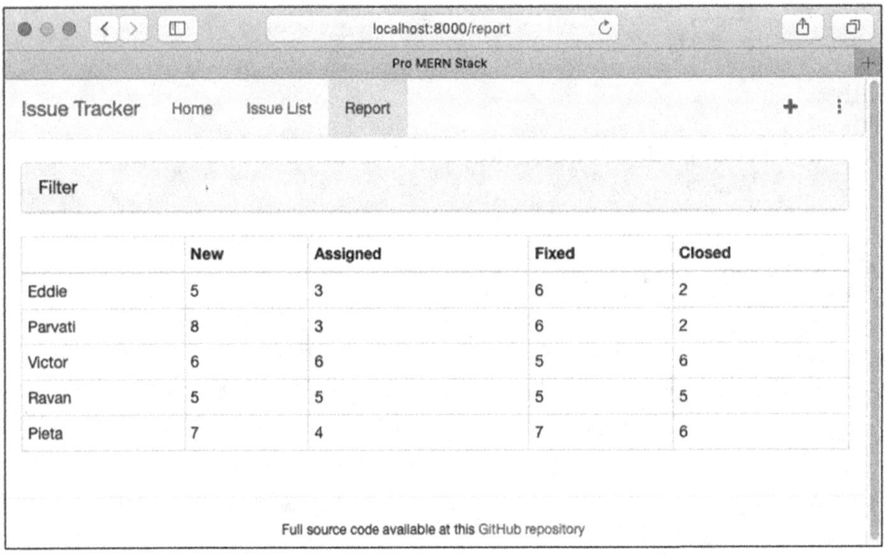

localhost:8000/report
Pro MERN Stack
Issue Tracker
Home
Issue List
Report
Filter
New
Assigned
Fixed
Closed
Eddie 5 3 6 2
Parvati 8 3 6 2
Victor 6 6 5 6
Ravan 5 5 5 5
Pieta 7 4 7 6
Full source code available at this GitHub repository

Figure 13-1. *The Report page*

EXERCISE: REPORT PAGE

1. Let's say you needed row totals. How would you go about implementing this? Try it out.

2. How about column totals? How can these be implemented?

Answers are available at the end of the chapter.

List API with Pagination

You perhaps by now have noticed that the Issue List page has become unwieldy because it displays all the issues in the database. In this and the next section, we'll implement pagination so that the user is shown a limited set of issues and can navigate to other pages. Let's keep the UI for the next section and modify the List API to support pagination in this section.

In order to show a pagination bar, we'll also need the total count of pages for the list. So, let's first modify the schema to add a count of pages in addition to the list of issues. Instead of returning the list of issues directly, we'll need to return an object that contains the list as well as a page count. Then, in addition to the filter specification, we need to specify *which* page to fetch.

The changes in the schema are shown in Listing 13-12.

Listing 13-12. api/schema.graphql: Addition of Page Count to List API

```
...
type IssueCounts {
  ...
}

type IssueListWithPages {
  issues: [Issue!]!
  pages: Int
}
...

type Query {
  ...
  issueList(
    ...
    page: Int = 1
  ): [Issue!]! IssueListWithPages
  ...
}
...
```

■ **Note**   It's not a good practice to change a GraphQL API in a real-life project, because it would break the UI application. The recommended practice is to create a new API, for example, a query called issueListWithPages for this purpose, especially if the application is already in production. But I'm modifying the existing API so that the final code is concise.

In the API implementation, we'll have to use the new parameter page to skip to the given page and limit the number of objects returned. The MongoDB cursor method skip() can be used to get the list of documents starting at an offset. Further, the limit() cursor method can be used to limit the output to a certain number. We'll use the PAGE_SIZE constant for the number of documents in a page.

```
...
const PAGE_SIZE = 10;
...
  const issues = await db.collection('issues').find(filter).
    .skip(PAGE_SIZE * (page - 1))
    .limit(PAGE_SIZE)
    .toArray();
...
```

Whenever we use an offset into a list, we also need to ensure that the list is in the same order when queried multiple times. Without an explicit sort order, MongoDB does not guarantee any order in the output. The order of the documents may vary between two queries (although it appears to always be the order of insertion). To guarantee a certain order, we need to include a sort specification. Since the ID is a natural key to sort on (since it matches the insertion order), and it is an indexed field (that is, there is no penalty for requesting the list to be sorted in this order), let's use it as the sort key.

```
...
  const issues = await db.collection('issues').find(filter).
    .sort({ id: 1 })
    ...
...
```

Now, we also need a count of pages, which needs the count of documents matching this filter. Instead of making another query to get the count, MongoDB lets us query the cursor itself for the number of documents it matched. So, instead of converting the cursor that find() returns to an array, let's keep the cursor and query it for the count first, and then convert it to an array and return it.

```
...
  const cursor = db.collection('issues').find(filter)
    ....

  const totalCount = await cursor.count(false);
  const issues = cursor.toArray();
  const pages = Math.ceil(totalCount / PAGE_SIZE);
...
```

Note that the count() method is asynchronous, but this ends up evaluating the cursor's contents. So, the next call on the cursor toArray() can be synchronously invoked. The argument to the count() function takes in a Boolean that determines whether the count to be returned takes into account the effect of skip() and limit() or not. Using the argument's value as false gives us the total count of objects that would have matched the filter. This is the count that we need.

Now, we can return both the issues list as well as the page count in the return value. The entire set of changes, including this change in the API implementation, is shown in Listing 13-13.

Listing 13-13. api/issue.js: Add Pagination Support to List API

```
...
const PAGE_SIZE = 10;

async function list(_, {
  status, effortMin, effortMax, page,
}) {
  ...
  const issues = await db.collection('issues').find(filter).toArray();
  const cursor = db.collection('issues').find(filter)
    .sort({ id: 1 })
    .skip(PAGE_SIZE * (page - 1))
    .limit(PAGE_SIZE);

  const totalCount = await cursor.count(false);
  const issues = cursor.toArray();
  const pages = Math.ceil(totalCount / PAGE_SIZE);
  return issues;
  return { issues, pages };
}
...
```

Since the return value in the schema has changed, we'll also need to change the caller, the IssueList component to accommodate the change. Instead of using the value issueList directly from the data, we'll need to use it as issueList.issues. We'll not implement pagination just yet; this change is only to ensure that the Issue List page continues to work, by showing the first 10 issues.

The changes to this component are shown in Listing 13-14.

Listing 13-14. ui/src/IssueList.jsx: Changes to Account for API Change

```
...
  static async fetchData(match, search, showError) {
    ...
    const query = `query issueList(
      ...
      issueList(
        ...
      ) {
        issues {
          id title status owner
          created effort due
        }
      }
      ...
  }
...

  constructor() {
    super();
    const issues = store.initialData
```

```
      ? store.initialData.issueList.issues : null;
    ...
  }
...

  async loadData() {
    ...
    if (data) {
      this.setState({
        issues: data.issueList.issues,
        ...
      });
    }
  }
...
```

The API changes can be tested in the Playground. You can use the following query to test the page parameter:

```
query {
  issueList(page: 4) {
    issues { id title }
    pages
  }
}
```

This should return 10 issues and the total page count. If you had 102 issues (the original two from init.mongo.js and 100 more from generate_data.mongo.js), the page count should be returned as 11 as follows:

```
{
  "data": {
    "issueList": {
      "issues": [
        {
          "id": 31,
          "title": "Lorem ipsum dolor sit amet, 28"
        },
        ...
        {
          "id": 40,
          "title": "Lorem ipsum dolor sit amet, 37"
        }
      ],
      "pages": 11
    }
  }
}
```

Further, you can test the Issue List page to ensure that the API changes haven't broken anything, except that you should now be seeing only the first page (that is, 10 issues) rather than all the 100 or so issues.

Pagination UI

Let's now use the new API that we coded in the previous section to display a bar of pages.

React-Bootstrap has support for the pagination presentation, but this is a pure presentation component. In order to calculate the pages to be displayed, especially if there are to be pages of pages (let's call them sections), the calculations to be done are not part of any out-of-the-box component. According to the documentation at https://react-bootstrap.github.io/components/pagination/#pagination, previous versions supported such a component, which is now in a separate repository as @react-bootstrap/pagination. But I am not choosing this library for the following reasons:

- The npm page says that it is not actively maintained.

- The resulting page items are buttons and not links, making it hard for search engine bots to index them. What we should prefer is a <Link> or equivalent that works well with React Router.

So, let's create our own minimalistic pagination bar that shows pages in chunks of five. To go to the next or previous section, let's use the > and < indicators at the each end of the bar. The math required for this is simple and good enough to demonstrate what can be done.

To start, let's modify the data fetcher in the IssueList component to include the total count of pages in the query and save it in the state.

```
...
  static async fetchData(match, search, showError) {
    const params = new URLSearchParams(search);
    ...

    let page = parseInt(params.get('page'), 10);
    if (Number.isNaN(page)) page = 1;
    vars.page = page;

    const query = `query issueList(
      ...
      $page: Int
    ) {
      issueList(
        ...
        page: $page
      ) {
        issues {
          ...
        }
        pages
      }
      ...
    }`;
  }
...
```

453

Now, `data.issueList.issues` will have a list of issues and `data.issueList.pages` will have the total count of pages for this. Let's use all these to set state variables that'll come in handy to render the pagination bar. We need to do this in the constructor as well as the `loadData()` method where state is initialized or modified.

```
...
  constructor() {
    super();
    const issues = store.initialData
      ? store.initialData.issueList.issues : null;
    const selectedIssue = store.initialData
      ? store.initialData.issue
      : null;
    const initialData = store.initialData || { issueList: {} };
    const {
      issueList: { issues, pages }, issue: selectedIssue,
    } = initialData;
    ...
    this.state = {
      ...
      pages,
    };
    ...
  }
...
  async loadData() {
    ...
    if (data) {
      this.setState({
        ...
        pages: data.issueList.pages,
      });
    }
  }
...
```

Now, in the `render()` function, we can start laying out the pagination bar. But each link in the bar also needs to encode the currently active filter, in addition to using a `LinkContainer` to create the actual link. To ease this out, let's create a new component called `PageLink` in this file itself. This will wrap whatever is being passed in as the display object with a link, based on the search `params` that are passed, the page number to link to, and the current page to determine if the link needs to be highlighted as active. We'll use page number 0 to indicate an unavailable page.

```
...
function PageLink({
  params, page, activePage, children,
}) {
  params.set('page', page);
  if (page === 0) return React.cloneElement(children, { disabled: true });
  return (
```

```
    <LinkContainer
      isActive={() => page === activePage}
      to={{ search: `?${params.toString()}` }}
    >
      {children}
    </LinkContainer>
  );
}
...
```

Now, in the render() function, we can generate a series of page links. The actual link component that we will use is the React-Bootstrap's Pagination.Item component. I will not explain the details of the math used in the following, but the overall logic is that the pages are split into sections of SECTION_SIZE pages each, and all we need to do is display the pages in that section. The < and > indicators will move to the previous and next section, which are nothing but SECTION_SIZE pages before and after the start page for this section. If previous and next are not available, being less than the first page or more than the last page, we'll specify 0 as the page to navigate to, so that it is disabled.

```
...
    const params = new URLSearchParams(search);
    let page = parseInt(params.get('page'), 10);
    if (Number.isNaN(page)) page = 1;

    const startPage = Math.floor((page - 1) / SECTION_SIZE) * SECTION_SIZE + 1;
    const endPage = startPage + SECTION_SIZE - 1;
    const prevSection = startPage === 1 ? 0 : startPage - SECTION_SIZE;
    const nextSection = endPage >= pages ? 0 : startPage + SECTION_SIZE;

    const items = [];
    for (let i = startPage; i <= Math.min(endPage, pages); i += 1) {
      params.set('page', i);
      items.push((
        <PageLink key={i} params={params} activePage={page} page={i}>
          <Pagination.Item>{i}</Pagination.Item>
        </PageLink>
      ));
    }
...
```

Finally, let's display this set of items in the returned JSX, as part of the pagination bar. To start the bar, we use the Pagination component and display each clickable link as a Pagination.Item component inside this, wrapped by a PageLink. The complete changes, including this last change for displaying the pagination in the IssueList component, are shown in Listing 13-15.

Listing 13-15. ui/src/IssueList.jsx: Changes for Pagination UI

```
...
import { Panel, Pagination } from 'react-bootstrap';
import { LinkContainer } from 'react-router-bootstrap';
...

const SECTION_SIZE = 5;
```

```
function PageLink({
  params, page, activePage, children,
}) {
  params.set('page', page);
  if (page === 0) return React.cloneElement(children, { disabled: true });
  return (
    <LinkContainer
      isActive={() => page === activePage}
      to={{ search: `?${params.toString()}` }}
    >
      {children}
    </LinkContainer>
  );
}

class IssueList extends React.Component {
  static async fetchData(match, search, showError) {
    const params = new URLSearchParams(search);
    ...

    let page = parseInt(params.get('page'), 10);
    if (Number.isNaN(page)) page = 1;
    vars.page = page;

    const query = `query issueList(
      ...
      $page: Int
    ) {
      issueList(
        ...
        page: $page
      ) {
        issues {
          ...
        }
        pages
      }
      ...
    }`;
  }

  constructor() {
    super();
    const issues = store.initialData
      ? store.initialData.issueList.issues : null;
    const selectedIssue = store.initialData
      ? store.initialData.issue
      : null;
    const initialData = store.initialData || { issueList: {} };
    const {
      issueList: { issues, pages }, issue: selectedIssue,
    } = initialData;
    ...
```

```
    this.state = {
      ...
      pages,
    };
    ...
  }
...
  async loadData() {
    ...
    if (data) {
      this.setState({
        ...
        pages: data.issueList.pages,
      });
    }
  }
...

  render() {
    ...

    const { selectedIssue, pages } = this.state;
    const { location: { search } } = this.props;

    const params = new URLSearchParams(search);
    let page = parseInt(params.get('page'), 10);
    if (Number.isNaN(page)) page = 1;

    const startPage = Math.floor((page - 1) / SECTION_SIZE) * SECTION_SIZE + 1;
    const endPage = startPage + SECTION_SIZE - 1;
    const prevSection = startPage === 1 ? 0 : startPage - SECTION_SIZE;
    const nextSection = endPage >= pages ? 0 : startPage + SECTION_SIZE;

    const items = [];
    for (let i = startPage; i <= Math.min(endPage, pages); i += 1) {
      params.set('page', i);
      items.push((
        <PageLink key={i} params={params} activePage={page} page={i}>
          <Pagination.Item>{i}</Pagination.Item>
        </PageLink>
      ));
    }

    return (
      <React.Fragment>
        ...
        <Pagination>
          <PageLink params={params} page={prevSection}>
            <Pagination.Item>{'<'}</Pagination.Item>
          </PageLink>
          {items}
          <PageLink params={params} page={nextSection}>
            <Pagination.Item>{'>'}</Pagination.Item>
```

```
        </PageLink>
      </Pagination>
    </React.Fragment>
  );
}
...
```

If you test the application now, you will find that the home page redirects to the complete list of issues, which has 11 pages, divided into three sections of five pages each. The < and > links will take you to the previous and next section respectively, and they should appear disabled if the operation is unavailable due to section boundaries having been reached. A screenshot of the Issue List page with the pagination bar is shown in Figure 13-2.

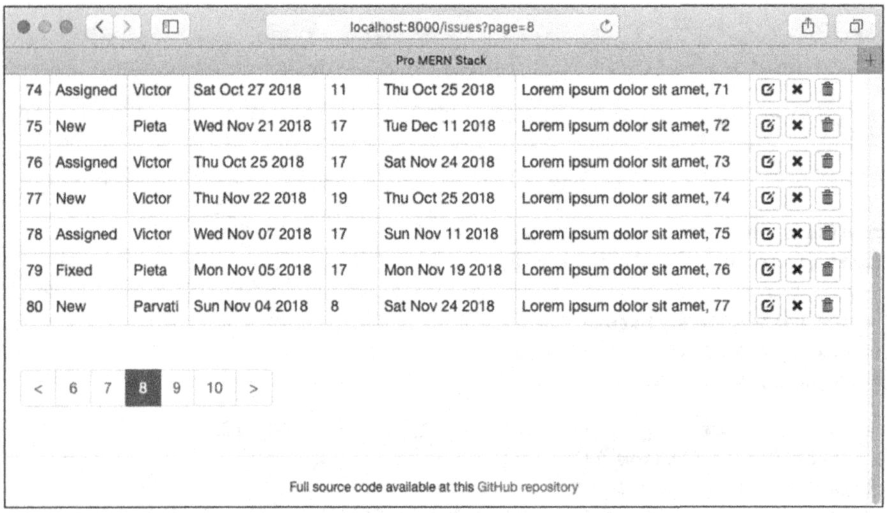

Figure 13-2. *Issue List screen with the pagination bar on page 8*

But there is still one minor issue left: The pagination, especially the active button, has a style with a z-index of 3. This is set by Bootstrap. By itself, it's okay, but when displaying Toast messages, the pagination buttons hide the message. To overcome this, let's set the z-index of the Toast message to something higher so that it always appears on top. The changes to Toast.jsx are shown in Listing 13-16.

Listing 13-16. ui/src/Toast.jsx: Set the Toast's Z-Index So It Always Shows on Top

```
...
      <Collapse in={showing}>
        <div style={{
          position: 'fixed', bottom: 20, left: 20, zIndex: 10,
        }}
        >
...
```

A far more intuitive and creative pagination can be created based on the current page, which also lets the users go to the end or the beginning of the pages. But this should have given you the basic building blocks of how to go about implementing pagination in the MERN stack.

Pagination Performance

The approach of using the same cursor to fetch the count was okay for small data sets, but it can't be used for larger data sets. The problem with a pagination that knows the number of pages is that it needs the total count of documents in the filtered set.

The fact is that in any database, counting the number of matches is expensive. The only way it can be done is by applying the filter and visiting every document to check whether it matches the filter. Unless, of course, you have indexes for every possible filter combination, which either means limiting the kind of filters you want to allow the user, or spending enormous storage capacity for indexing all combinations.

I find that, practically, it isn't of much use to show the exact number of pages or count of matched records, when the result is possibly very large. If it's indeed hundreds of pages long, it is highly unlikely that the user will want to go to exactly the 97th page, or even the last page. In such cases, it's advisable to just show the Previous and Next links and not query the total count in every request. React-Bootstrap's Pager component will work well for this approach.

If a user (or a search engine bot) is unlikely to go beyond the few initial pages, this approach will surely work. But it so happens that even a skip() operation has to traverse all the documents that are being skipped to get to the start of the page being displayed. If there were a million documents, for example, and the user (or a search engine bot) were to traverse all the way to the last page, it would mean that the last page would retrieve all the million documents before returning the list corresponding to the last page.

The ideal strategy to use with these large sets is to return a value in the API's return that indicates where the next page starts, in terms of an indexed field value. In the case of the Issue Tracker application, the ID field is ideal for this. With this strategy, you wouldn't use the skip() operation; instead, you use the ID as a filter to start from, using the $gte operator. Since the ID field is indexed, the database wouldn't have to *skip* so many documents to arrive at this ID; it would directly reach the document and traverse from thereon to fetch one page of documents. The disabling of previous and next buttons becomes non-trivial in these cases and is beyond the scope of this book.

EXERCISE: PAGINATION UI

1. The currently active page had to be calculated from the search string, once in fetchData() method and again in the render() method. In this case, it was perhaps a simple operation, but in cases where this may require lots of code and/ or be computationally expensive, should you consider saving this value in the state? What are the pros and cons? Hint: Look up the "Thinking in React" page at https://reactjs.org/docs/thinking-in-react.html#step-3-identify-the-minimal-but-complete-representation-of-ui-state.

Answers are available at the end of the chapter.

Undo Delete API

The next feature that we'll implement is an undo action on the delete operation. The older convention for destructive operations such as a delete was to ask for confirmation from the user. But usability is enhanced if we don't ask for confirmation, because it is quite rare that the user answers "No" to an "Are you sure?" question. If the user mistakenly deletes the issue, providing an undo feature works far better.

In the next section, we'll implement the undo feature's UI for deleting issues. To start, in this section, we'll implement the API required for this, one that restores a deleted issue. The first change we need to make is in the schema. We'll add a new mutation for this purpose and call it issueRestore. The changes to the schema are shown in Listing 13-17.

Listing 13-17. api/schema.graphql: Changes to the Restore API

```graphql
...
type Mutation {
  ...
  issueRestore(id: Int!): Boolean!
}
...
```

Next, the actual implementation of the API is somewhat similar to the Delete API itself. The difference is that, instead of moving from the `issues` collection to the `deleted_issues` collection, the restore API has to transfer an issue in the reverse direction: from the `deleted_issues` collection to the `issues` collection. Let's copy the code from the `remove()` function and swap these two collection names.

The changes for adding the `restore` function are listed in Listing 13-18.

Listing 13-18. api/issue.js: New Restore API Implementation

```javascript
...
async function remove(_, { id }) {
  ...
}

async function restore(_, { id }) {
  const db = getDb();
  const issue = await db.collection('deleted_issues').findOne({ id });
  if (!issue) return false;
  issue.deleted = new Date();

  let result = await db.collection('issues').insertOne(issue);
  if (result.insertedId) {
    result = await db.collection('deleted_issues').removeOne({ id });
    return result.deletedCount === 1;
  }
  return false;
}
...

module.exports = {
  ...
  restore,
  counts,
};
...
```

Finally, we have to tie the resolver to the API endpoint in the API handler. This change is shown in Listing 13-19.

Listing 13-19. api/api_handler.js: Changes to Restore API

```
...
const resolvers = {
  ...
  Mutation: {
    ...
    issueRestore: issue.restore,
  },
  ...
};
...
```

You can test the new API using the Playground. You could delete an issue using the Delete button in the Issue List page. Then, in the Playground, you could execute the following mutation, with the ID replaced with the ID of the issue you just deleted:

```
mutation {
  issueRestore(id: 6)
}
```

It should return a success value, and if you refresh the browser, you should see that the deleted issue has been restored.

Undo Delete UI

The best place to initiate an undo of a delete operation is in the Toast message that shows that the issue has been deleted. Within the Toast message indicating the success of the delete operation, let's include a button that can be clicked to initiate the undo. This needs to be done in the IssueList component.

Then, when the button is clicked, we'll need to call the Restore API. This is best done by using a method in the IssueList class for restoring an issue, one that takes in the ID of the issue to be restored. The Undo button can now set its onClick property to this method. The changes for this are shown in Listing 13-20.

Listing 13-20. ui/src/IssueList.jsx: Changes for Including an Undo Button

```
...
import { Panel, Pagination, Button } from 'react-bootstrap';
...

async deleteIssue(index) {
  ...
    showSuccess('Deleted issue ${id} successfully.');
    const undoMessage = (
      <span>
        {`Deleted issue ${id} successfully.`}
        <Button bsStyle="link" onClick={() => this.restoreIssue(id)}>
          UNDO
        </Button>
      </span>
    );
```

```
        showSuccess(undoMessage);
    ...
  }

  async restoreIssue(id) {
    const query = `mutation issueRestore($id: Int!) {
      issueRestore(id: $id)
    }`;
    const { showSuccess, showError } = this.props;
    const data = await graphQLFetch(query, { id }, showError);
    if (data) {
      showSuccess(`Issue ${id} restored successfully.`);
      this.loadData();
    }
  }
}
...
```

Now, when you click on the Delete button on any row in the Issue List, the Toast message will include an Undo button (a link in fact). Clicking on this should result in the deleted issue being restored. A screenshot of the Issue List page with the Toast message that has the Undo link is shown in Figure 13-3. You should be able to click on the Undo link and see that the deleted issue is back in the list of issues.

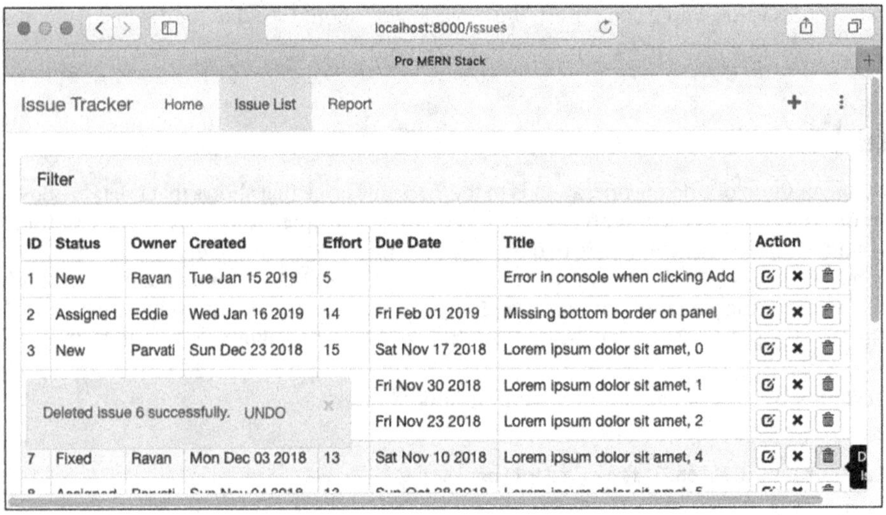

Figure 13-3. *The Delete success Toast with an Undo link*

Text Index API

A search bar in most applications lets you find documents by just typing in some words. We'll implement this not like a search filter, but as an autocomplete that finds all issues matching the words typed, and lets the user pick one of them to directly view. We'll add this search in the navigation bar since the user should be able to jump to a particular issue, no matter which page they are viewing.

Assuming that the number of issues is large, it wouldn't perform well if we were to apply a filter criterion like a regex on all the issues. That's because to apply the regex, MongoDB would have to scan all the documents and apply the regex to see if it matches the search term.

MongoDB's text index, on the other hand, lets you quickly get to all the documents that contain a certain term. A text index gathers all the terms (words) in all the documents and creates a lookup table that, given a term (word), returns all documents containing that term (word). You can create such an index using all the words in the title with the following MongoDB shell command:

```
> db.issues.createIndex({ title: "text" })
```

Now, if you look for issues with any term in the title, it will return matching documents. The syntax for using the text index is as follows:

```
> db.issues.find({ $text: {$search: "click" } })
```

This should return one document that has the word click in the title. But this may not be enough, we may need the ability to search in the description as well, for the same term. So, let's recreate the index by including the description text in the index. To drop the created index, let's first determine which indexes are currently in existence.

```
> db.issues.getIndexes()
```

You should find one index with the name property set to title_text. We need to drop this index and recreate it with the description field included.

```
> db.issues.dropIndex('title_text')
> db.issues.createIndex({ title: "text", description: "text" })
```

If you now execute the same find() query to look for documents containing the word click, you should find that it returns two issues, the first one because the term "clicking" was there in the title. The second will also be returned because the description has the term "clicking" in it. Note that this is not a pattern search, for example, searching for the term "clic" is not going to match any documents, even though it partially matches the text in the documents. Also, you will find that common words (known as stop words) like "in", "when," etc. are not indexed, and searching for these will result in no matches.

Let's save this index in init.mongo.js so that next time the DB is initialized, the index will be created. The changes are shown in Listing 13-21.

Listing 13-21. api/scripts/init.mongo.js: Addition of Text index

```
...
db.issues.createIndex({ created: 1 });
db.issues.createIndex({ title: 'text', description: 'text' });
...
```

The next change is in the GraphQL schema. Let's add one more filter option for the search string. The changes are shown in Listing 13-22.

Listing 13-22. api/schema.graphql: Addition of Search in Filter

```
...
type Query {
  ...
  issueList(
    ...
    search: String
    page: Int = 1
```

```
  ): IssueListWithPages
  ...
}
...
```

Now, let's change the `list` resolver in `issue.js` to use the new parameter to search for documents. All that is needed is to add the search string as an additional filter if it exists. The changes are shown in Listing 13-23.

Listing 13-23. api/issue.js: Changes to Add a Search Filter

```
...
async function list(_, {
  status, effortMin, effortMax, search, page,
}) {
  ...
  if (search) filter.$text = { $search: search };

  const cursor = db.collection('issues').find(filter)
  ...
}
...
```

To test these changes, you can use the Playground and use the terms that we used in the mongo shell. Here is an example query:

```
query {
  issueList(search: "click") {
    issues { id title description }
    pages
  }
}
```

This query should return two documents in the result, the same as when it was executed in the mongo shell. In the next section, we'll add the UI to use this API and search for documents using a search bar. Note that although the API allows for combining other filter values with the search query, the UI will use only one or the other.

Search Bar

Instead of implementing the search component ourselves, let's use one of the popular controls available. I have chosen React Select (https://react-select.com/home), as it fits the purpose nicely: after the user types in a word, the requirement is to asynchronously fetch results and show them in a dropdown, one of which can be selected. This component's `Async` variation lets us achieve this effect easily.

Let's first install the package that has the component.

```
$ cd ui
$ npm install react-select@2
```

Let's also create a new component within the UI source directory that will display a React Select and implement the methods required to fetch the documents using the new search filter in the List API. React Select needs two callbacks to show the options: `loadOptions` and `filterOptions`. The first is an asynchronous method that needs to return an array of options. Each option is an object with the properties `label` and `value`, the `label` being what the user sees and the `value` being a unique identifier. Let's choose the issue ID as the `value`, and for the `label`, let's combine the ID and the issue title.

Let's implement the `loadOptions()` method first and fetch a list of issues that match the search term using the `graphQLFetch()` function. Let's limit the API to be fired only for words that are longer than two letters.

```
...
  async loadOptions(term) {
    if (term.length < 3) return [];
    const query = `query issueList($search: String) {
      issueList(search: $search) {
        issues {id title}
      }
    }`;

    const data = await graphQLFetch(query, { search: term });
    return data.issueList.issues.map(issue => ({
      label: `#${issue.id}: ${issue.title}`, value: issue.id,
    }));
  }
...
```

The next callback, `filterOption`, is expected to be called for each of the returned options to determine whether or not to show the option in the dropdown. This can be useful in other cases, but since the options that were retrieved using `loadOptions()` are already the matched ones, we can just return `true` in the callback. If we don't supply this function, React Select will apply its own matching logic and that's not what we want. So, within the `render()` method, we can return the React Select with these two callbacks as follows:

```
...
import SelectAsync from 'react-select/lib/Async';
...
  render() {
    return (
      <SelectAsync
        loadOptions={this.loadOptions}
        filterOption={() => true}
      />
    );
  }
...
```

The next step is to take an action when the user selects one of the displayed issues. React Select provides an onChange property, which is a callback that is called when the user selects an item, with the value of the selected item as an argument. Let's display the Edit page for that issue when this happens, as that page shows an issue completely. To be able to do this, we need React Router's history to be available, so we will eventually need to use `withRouter` to export this component.

```
...
  onChangeSelection({ value }) {
    const { history } = this.props;
    history.push(`/edit/${value}`);
  }
...
  render() {
    return (
      <SelectAsync
        ...
        onChange={this.onChangeSelection}
      />
    );
  }
...
```

We'll add a few more useful properties to the React Select control:

- An instanceId is useful for React Select to identify the control in case there are multiple React Selects being used on the same page. Let's set this to search-select. Without this ID, you will find that React Select auto-generates these IDs and an error in the console will be shown saying that the server-rendered ID and the client-rendered ID do not match.

- We don't need the dropdown indicator (down arrow on the right side of the control) that can be used to pull down the list of pre-loaded options. Since there are no pre-loaded options, this is not needed. There is no direct option for this, rather, React Select allows each of the components within React Select to be customized using the components property. We'll just set the DropdownIndicator component to null, indicating that nothing needs to be shown.

- The React Select component is designed for selecting and *showing* the selection once selected. We really don't need to show the selected item, so let's just set the value property to an empty string to achieve this.

Finally, in case of errors when calling the API, it would be good to show an error. So, let's wrap the component with withToast and supply the showError function to the GraphQL fetch function. With all these changes, the complete code of the new component is shown in Listing 13-24.

Listing 13-24. ui/src/Search.jsx: New File and Component for the Search Bar

```
import React from 'react';
import SelectAsync from 'react-select/lib/Async'; // eslint-disable-line
import { withRouter } from 'react-router-dom';

import graphQLFetch from './graphQLFetch.js';
import withToast from './withToast.jsx';

class Search extends React.Component {
  constructor(props) {
    super(props);
```

```
    this.onChangeSelection = this.onChangeSelection.bind(this);
    this.loadOptions = this.loadOptions.bind(this);
  }

  onChangeSelection({ value }) {
    const { history } = this.props;
    history.push('/edit/${value}');
  }

  async loadOptions(term) {
    if (term.length < 3) return [];
    const query = `query issueList($search: String) {
      issueList(search: $search) {
        issues {id title}
      }
    }`;

    const { showError } = this.props;
    const data = await graphQLFetch(query, { search: term }, showError);
    return data.issueList.issues.map(issue => ({
      label: `#${issue.id}: ${issue.title}`, value: issue.id,
    }));
  }

  render() {
    return (
      <SelectAsync
        instanceId="search-select"
        value=""
        loadOptions={this.loadOptions}
        filterOption={() => true}
        onChange={this.onChangeSelection}
        components={{ DropdownIndicator: null }}
      />
    );
  }
}

export default withRouter(withToast(Search));
```

To integrate this in the navigation bar, we can add the component between the two `<Nav>`s in `Page.jsx`.

```
...
import Search from './Search.jsx';
...
    <Nav>
      ...
    </Nav>
    <Search />
    <Nav pullRight>
      ...
    </Nav>
...
```

Although functionally this will work, you will see that the alignment of the search bar in the header is not proper; the search control occupies the entire width of the header and pushes the right side Nav to the next row. To avoid this, we'll need to wrap the Search component with a `<div>` or something that restricts the width. Instead of a fixed width, let's use React-Bootstrap's Col component, which will flexibly change its width depending on the screen size. Further, as suggested in the React-Bootstrap's Navbars documentation at `https://react-bootstrap.github.io/components/navbar/?no-cache=1#navbars-form`, to get the control to properly align within the Nav, we need to enclose it within a `Navbar.Form` component.

The complete set of changes in the navigation bar is shown in Listing 13-25.

Listing 13-25. ui/src/Page.jsx: Changes to Include the Search Control in the Navigation Bar

```
...
import {
  ...
  Grid, Col,
} from 'react-bootstrap';
...
import IssueAddNavItem from './IssueAddNavItem.jsx';
import Search from './Search.jsx';
...

function NavBar() {
    ...
    <Nav>
      ...
    </Nav>
    <Col sm={5}>
      <Navbar.Form>
        <Search />
      </Navbar.Form>
    </Col>
    <Nav pullRight>
      ...
    </Nav>
}
...
```

At this point, the application will work and so will the search control. You should be able to type in terms and see a dropdown with the matched issues that can be selected. For example, if you type in the word "click," two issues will be shown in the dropdown. On selecting any of them, the page should switch to editing the issue selected. A screenshot of the search control with the dropdown is shown in Figure 13-4.

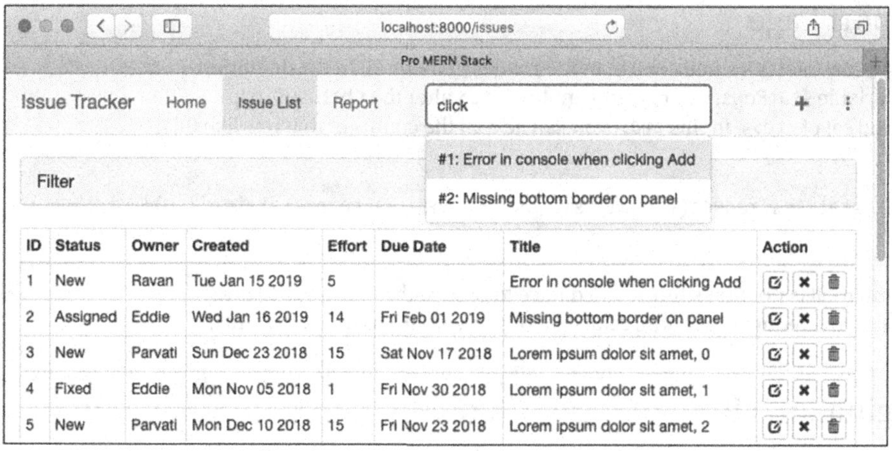

Figure 13-4. *Search control in the Issue List page*

Summary

In this chapter, we explored a variety of techniques and concepts that you can use to implement common features that make the application more usable.

You first learned about a common React pattern for reusable code: Higher Order Components (HOCs). You then saw how to use MongoDB's aggregate framework to summarize or even expand the data fetched from collections. You saw how to implement common features, how to use third-party components for undoing a delete and adding pagination, and how to use a search control for finding issues based on a text index in MongoDB.

In the next chapter, we'll discuss how to go about implementing authentication and authorization for the Issue Tracker application. We'll use Google Sign-in to let users sign in to the Issue Tracker application. While most of the application will continue to be available for everyone, including those who have not signed in, we'll make it so that only signed-in users can make any modifications to the data.

Answers to Exercises

Exercise: Issue Counts API

1. GraphQL schema does not allow a variable schema, or objects with fields that are not named in the schema itself. If we return the object stats as is, it would amount to every object having a key (value of the owner field) that is not predefined. There is no way we could define such a schema. GraphQL is all about being able to specify which keys are important to the caller and using a variable key will make it impossible.

Exercise: Report Page

1. Adding a row total is a small change in the `render()` method. In the definition of the variable `statRows`, you can add another `<td>` after the `statuses.map` generated set of `<td>`s. In this `<td>`, you can add all the counts of that row like this:

```
...
    <td>{statuses.reduce((total, status) => total + counts[status], 0)}</td>
...
```

2. A column total is not that simple, you'd have to reduce the entire `stats` array, and within the reducer function, return an object with totals for each status.

Exercise: Pagination UI

1. As the documentation suggests, it's not a good idea to store computed values in the state. Instead, computing them from the original source of truth whenever required is recommended. In cases where the computation can become expensive, utilities such as `memorize` can be used to cache computed values.

CHAPTER 14

Authentication

Most applications need to identify and authenticate users. Instead of creating a custom sign-up and authentication mechanism, we'll integrate with one of the social sign-ins. We'll only implement one (Google Sign-In for Websites). This will serve as a good example for other integrations, since it uses the OAuth2 mechanism, which most other authentication integrations also use.

We'll make it so that users can view all information without signing in, but in order to make any change, they will have to sign in. We'll use a modal dialog that lets the user sign in with Google from anywhere in the application. Once signed in, the application will let the user stay on the same page, so that they can perform the edit functions after having signed in.

In all this, we won't lose sight of server rendering. We'll ensure that entire pages can be rendered at the UI server even though they are authenticated pages.

Sign-In UI

Let's start by building the necessary user interface for signing in users. Although we won't do any authentication in this section, we will ensure that all the ground work in terms of UI is in place for adding it in later sections.

In the navigation bar, on the right side, let's have an item with the label "Sign In". On clicking this, let's show a modal dialog that lets the user sign in using a button labeled Sign In. For the Issue Tracker application, we'll have only one sign-in button, but this approach allows you to add multiple sign-in options like Facebook, GitHub, etc. On successful sign-in, let's show the user's name instead of the Sign In menu item, with a dropdown menu that lets the user sign out.

To achieve all this, let's create a new component called `SignInNavItem` similar to `IssueAddNavItem`, which can be placed in the navigation bar. The complete code for this component is shown in Listing 14-1 and I'll discuss a few important snippets here.

The state variables and some methods for showing the modal are very similar to the component `IssueAddNavItem`: the `showModal` and `hideModal` methods control the visible state of the modal using a variable called `showing`. Further, let's have a state variable object called `user` to save the signed-in status (`signedIn`) as well as the name of the user (`givenName`). If the state variable indicates that the user is already signed in, the `render()` method returns just a dropdown and a menu item to sign out the user.

```
...
  if (user.signedIn) {
    return (
      <NavDropdown title={user.givenName} id="user">
        <MenuItem onClick={this.signOut}>Sign out</MenuItem>
      </NavDropdown>
    );
...
```

© Vasan Subramanian 2019

V. Subramanian, *Pro MERN Stack*, https://doi.org/10.1007/978-1-4842-4391-6_14

If the user is not signed in, the render() method returns the menu item for signing in as well as a modal dialog to show a Sign In button.

```
...
      <NavItem onClick={this.showModal}>
        Sign in
      </NavItem>
      <Modal keyboard show={showing} onHide={this.hideModal} bsSize="sm">
        ...
        <Modal.Body>
          <Button block bsStyle="primary" onClick={this.signIn}>
            Sign In
          </Button>
        </Modal.Body>
        ...
      </Modal>
...
```

On clicking the Sign In button in the modal, all we'll do is set the given name of the user to "User1" and the signed in state to true. On signing out, we'll reverse this. For these, we have the handlers signIn and signOut in the component. Finally, we'll need to add a bind(this). The final source code for this component including all this is shown in Listing 14-1.

Listing 14-1. ui/src/SignInNavItem.jsx: New Component for Signing In

```
import React from 'react';
import {
  NavItem, Modal, Button, NavDropdown, MenuItem,
} from 'react-bootstrap';

export default class SigninNavItem extends React.Component {
  constructor(props) {
    super(props);
    this.state = {
      showing: false,
      user: { signedIn: false, givenName: '' },
    };
    this.showModal = this.showModal.bind(this);
    this.hideModal = this.hideModal.bind(this);
    this.signOut = this.signOut.bind(this);
    this.signIn = this.signIn.bind(this);
  }

  signIn() {
    this.hideModal();
    this.setState({ user: { signedIn: true, givenName: 'User1' } });
  }

  signOut() {
    this.setState({ user: { signedIn: false, givenName: '' } });
  }
```

```
  showModal() {
    this.setState({ showing: true });
  }

  hideModal() {
    this.setState({ showing: false });
  }

  render() {
    const { user } = this.state;
    if (user.signedIn) {
      return (
        <NavDropdown title={user.givenName} id="user">
          <MenuItem onClick={this.signOut}>Sign out</MenuItem>
        </NavDropdown>
      );
    }

    const { showing } = this.state;
    return (
      <>
        <NavItem onClick={this.showModal}>
          Sign in
        </NavItem>
        <Modal keyboard show={showing} onHide={this.hideModal} bsSize="sm">
          <Modal.Header closeButton>
            <Modal.Title>Sign in</Modal.Title>
          </Modal.Header>
          <Modal.Body>
            <Button block bsStyle="primary" onClick={this.signIn}>
              Sign In
            </Button>
          </Modal.Body>
          <Modal.Footer>
            <Button bsStyle="link" onClick={this.hideModal}>Cancel</Button>
          </Modal.Footer>
        </Modal>
      </>
    );
  }
}
```

Let's change the navigation bar to insert this new navigation item right after the IssueAddNavItem component. This change to Page.jsx is shown in Listing 14-2.

Listing 14-2. ui/src/Page.jsx: Inclusion of the Sign In Menu in the Navigation Bar

```
...
import SignInNavItem from './SignInNavItem.jsx';
...
    <Nav pullRight>
      <IssueAddNavItem />
      <SignInNavItem />
      ...
    </Nav>
...
```

With these changes, you'll find that clicking on Sign In will show a modal dialog with a single button, as shown in the screenshot in Figure 14-1. Clicking on the button will replace the menu item with a dropdown titled "User1". On clicking Sign Out, the UI should go back to the initial state with the menu item Sign In.

Figure 14-1. *The Sign In modal dialog*

Google Sign-In

Now that we've got most of the UI in place, let's replace the Sign In button with a button to sign in using Google. Once signed in, we'll use Google to retrieve the user's name and show it instead of the hard-coded "User1".

The various options for integrating with Google Sign-In are listed in the "Guides" section at https://developers.google.com/identity/sign-in/web/sign-in. As a preparatory measure, we need a console project and a client ID to identify the application. Follow the instructions in the guide to create your own project and client ID. As for the origin URI, use http://localhost:8000, which is where the Issue Tracker application resides as of now. Once you have done that, save the client ID in your .env file in the UI server directory; this will be needed in the UI code for initializing the Google library. A sample entry in sample.env is shown in Listing 14-3. You will have to use your own client ID in place of YOUR_CLIENT_ID.

■ **Note** The button in the guide automatically creates a project called My Project in the API console. If you want finer control of the names that will be used, create an OAuth2 client ID in the API console at https://console.cloud.google.com/apis/credentials instead.

Listing 14-3. ui/src/sample.env: Configuration for the Google Client ID

```
...
# ENABLE_HMR=true
GOOGLE_CLIENT_ID=YOUR_CLIENT_ID.apps.googleusercontent.com
...
```

In the recommended method for integration listed in the guide, the library itself renders the button and handles its enabled and signed-in states. Unfortunately, this doesn't work well with React because the Google library needs a handle to the button and needs it to be permanent. If you try to use the button within a React-Bootstrap modal, the Google library throws errors. That's because, on closing the modal, the button is destroyed and recreated when the modal is opened again. The library apparently doesn't like this. So, we must display the button ourselves by following the guide titled "Customize the Sign-In Button".

Let's start with including the Google library. We'll do this in `template.js` along with all other scripts that the UI needs. The library we'll use is the one that allows us to customize the sign-in button, and it is specified in the code listing under "Building a Custom Graphic". The changes for this are shown in Listing 14-4.

Listing 14-4. ui/server/template.js: Changes for Including Google Library

```
...
  <meta name="viewport" content="width=device-width, initial-scale=1.0">

  <script src="https://apis.google.com/js/api:client.js"></script>

  <style>
...
```

We'll need to use the Google client ID while initializing the library. To be able to access this in the UI code, we'll need to pass it along as we passed along the configuration variable UI_API_ENDPOINT, using a request to /env.js. Let's call this new configuration variable GOOGLE_CLIENT_ID. The change to the UI server to let the UI code access this new variable is shown in Listing 14-5.

Listing 14-5. ui/server/uiserver.js: Changes to Send Google Client ID to the UI

```
...
app.get('/env.js', (req, res) => {
  const env = {
    UI_API_ENDPOINT: process.env.UI_API_ENDPOINT,
    GOOGLE_CLIENT_ID: process.env.GOOGLE_CLIENT_ID,
  };
  res.send(`window.ENV = ${JSON.stringify(env)}`);
});
...
```

Now we are ready to use the library and implement Google Sign-In within `SignInNavItem`. The complete set of changes for this component can be found in Listing 14-6, some snippets of which I'll discuss next.

Let's start by initializing the library. This can be done within `componentDidMount` of the component `SignInNavItem`. This component will be called only once, as it's in the header and always visible. The code for this is taken from the "Building a Custom Graphic" section of the guide. We'll set a state variable `disabled` (initialized to `true`) on successful initialization of the library. We'll use this state to enable the sign-in button only after successful initialization.

```
...
  componentDidMount() {
    const clientId = window.ENV.GOOGLE_CLIENT_ID;
    if (!clientId) return;
    window.gapi.load('auth2', () => {
      if (!window.gapi.auth2.getAuthInstance()) {
        window.gapi.auth2.init({ client_id: clientId }).then(() => {
          this.setState({ disabled: false });
        });
      }
    });
  }
...
```

Within the modal dialog, let's replace the plain text button with a button that follows Google's branding guidelines (this is described in the integration guide). This is a must for any application in production. For testing you may just use the plain text button, though. I have shortened the URL for a publicly available image (https://developers.google.com/identity/images/btn_google_signin_light_normal_web.png) to https://goo.gl/4yjp6B and used that.

```
...
              <img src="https://goo.gl/4yjp6B" alt="Sign In" />
...
```

If the client ID is missing (which is possible if the deployment's .env or environment does not have this variable), let's show an error message when the Sign In menu item is clicked. Otherwise, let's continue to show the modal dialog. Being able to show an error using a Toast message requires that we use withToast to wrap the component before exporting it, which we'll add soon.

```
...
  showModal() {
    const clientId = window.ENV.GOOGLE_CLIENT_ID;
    const { showError } = this.props;
    if (!clientId) {
      showError('Missing environment variable GOOGLE_CLIENT_ID');
      return;
    }
    this.setState({ showing: true });
  }
...
```

Finally, in the signIn handler, let's call the auth2.signin() method. This method is not described in the guide, but you can find a description in the "Reference" section. On a successful sign in, we'll set the username from the profile obtained from the result of the sign in. Also, the signIn handler now needs to be an async function due to the await calls within.

```
...
      const auth2 = window.gapi.auth2.getAuthInstance();
      const googleUser = await auth2.signIn();
      const givenName = googleUser.getBasicProfile().getGivenName();
      this.setState({ user: { signedIn: true, givenName } });
...
```

The complete set of changes, including error handling and Toast-related changes, are shown in Listing 14-6.

Listing 14-6. ui/src/SignInNavItem.jsx: Changes for Google Sign-In

```
...
import withToast from './withToast.jsx';

export default class SigninNavItem extends React.Component {
  constructor(props) {
    ...
    this.state = {
      showing: false,
      disabled: true,
      ...
    };
    ...
  }
...

  componentDidMount() {
    const clientId = window.ENV.GOOGLE_CLIENT_ID;
    if (!clientId) return;
    window.gapi.load('auth2', () => {
      if (!window.gapi.auth2.getAuthInstance()) {
        window.gapi.auth2.init({ client_id: clientId }).then(() => {
          this.setState({ disabled: false });
        });
      }
    });
  }

  async signIn() {
    this.hideModal();
    this.setState({ user: { signedIn: true, givenName: 'User1' } });
    const { showError } = this.props;
    try {
      const auth2 = window.gapi.auth2.getAuthInstance();
      const googleUser = await auth2.signIn();
      const givenName = googleUser.getBasicProfile().getGivenName();
      this.setState({ user: { signedIn: true, givenName } });
    } catch (error) {
      showError(`Error authenticating with Google: ${error.error}`);
    }
  }
...

  showModal() {
    const clientId = window.ENV.GOOGLE_CLIENT_ID;
    const { showError } = this.props;
    if (!clientId) {
      showError('Missing environment variable GOOGLE_CLIENT_ID');
      return;
    }
```

```
      this.setState({ showing: true });
  }
...

  render() {
    ...
    const { showing, disabled } = this.state;
    ...
            <Button
              block
              disabled={disabled}
              bsStyle="primary"
              onClick={this.signIn}
            >
              <img src="https://goo.gl/4yjp6B" alt="Sign In" />
            </Button>
    ...
  }
...

export default withToast(SigninNavItem);
...
```

Due to the changes to the .env file, the UI server needs to be restarted using npm run dev-all. Once you do that and click on the Sign In menu item, you'll find the Google button in the modal dialog. Clicking on that will pop up a new window, controlled by Google. This will let you sign in to any of your own Google accounts. A screenshot of the modal dialog with the Google Sign-In button is shown in Figure 14-2.

Figure 14-2. *The Sign In modal dialog with Google button*

Once you sign in with Google, you'll find that the menu item should be replaced with your given name, and on clicking that, a Sign Out menu item should appear that signs you out as well. A screenshot of this is shown in Figure 14-3.

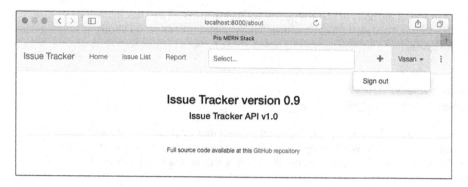

Figure 14-3. *The application after signing in*

EXERCISE: GOOGLE SIGN-IN

1. Say we wanted to show the user's profile picture after signing in. Do you think this can be done? How? Hint: Look up the guide for getting profile information in the Google developer site at `https://developers.google.com/identity/sign-in/web/people`.

Answers are available at the end of the chapter.

Verifying the Google Token

Just authenticating with Google is not enough; we'll need to do something with the authentication. In this section, we'll ensure that the credentials are verified at the back-end. We'll also get the user's name from the back-end to verify that we use only verified authentication information. Later, we'll establish a session for a logged-in user and keep it persistent across browser refreshes.

Validating a token at the back-end is required as a measure of security. That's because the back-end cannot trust the UI to have done the authentication, as it is public and can also respond to any HTTP request, not just from the Issue Tracker UI. The technique to do this is described in the guide "Authenticate with a Backend Server," at `https://developers.google.com/identity/sign-in/web/backend-auth`. Essentially, the client authentication library returns a token on successful authentication, which can be verified at the back-end using Google's authentication library for Node.js. We'll need to send this token from the UI to the back-end for it to be verified.

Let's create a new file called `auth.js` in the API server to hold all authentication-related functions. Also, let's not use GraphQL to implement the signing-in API. One reason is that it is not straightforward to set and access cookies within GraphQL resolvers and we'll be using cookies in later sections to maintain a session. Another reason is to keep the implementation flexible, and if required, use third-party libraries such as Passport, which hook directly in to Express rather than GraphQL.

So, in `auth.js`, we'll implement a series of endpoints as Express routes. We'll export these routes, which we'll later mount in the main Express app. The complete code for this file is shown in Listing 14-7, from which I'll discuss some snippets.

Since we'll need to access the body of POST requests, we'll have to install a parser that allows us to do this and use that in the routes. Further, we'll need to install the Google authentication library as suggested in the Google guide for sign-in.

```
$ cd api
$ npm install body-parser@1
$ npm install google-auth-library@2
```

The first thing we'll need to do in auth.js is construct a router that we'll export. Let's also install the body-parser middleware in this. We'll accept only a JSON document in our endpoints. For this, bodyParser.json() can be used which will make the JSON document accessible via req.body.

```
...
const Router = require('express');
const bodyParser = require('body-parser');

const routes = new Router();

routes.use(bodyParser.json());
...

module.exports = { routes };
...
```

In this section, we'll implement just one route, '/signin'. Within this route implementation, we'll retrieve the supplied Google token from the request body and verify it using the Google authentication library.

```
...
const { OAuth2Client } = require('google-auth-library');
...

routes.post('/signin', async (req, res) => {
  const googleToken = req.body.google_token;
  ...

  const client = new OAuth2Client();
  let payload;
  try {
    const ticket = await client.verifyIdToken({ idToken: googleToken });
    payload = ticket.getPayload();
  } catch (error) {
    res.status(403).send('Invalid credentials');
  }

  ...
});
...
```

Once we have the payload based on the verified token, we can extract various fields such as name and email from the payload. Let's extract these and respond with a JSON object that contains these, as well as a Boolean to indicate that the sign in was successful. The complete code of auth.js, including the response, is shown in Listing 14-7.

Listing 14-7. api/auth.js: New File for Auth-Related Code and Routes

```
const Router = require('express');
const bodyParser = require('body-parser');
const { OAuth2Client } = require('google-auth-library');

const routes = new Router();

routes.use(bodyParser.json());

routes.post('/signin', async (req, res) => {
  const googleToken = req.body.google_token;
  if (!googleToken) {
    res.status(400).send({ code: 400, message: 'Missing Token' });
    return;
  }

  const client = new OAuth2Client();
  let payload;
  try {
    const ticket = await client.verifyIdToken({ idToken: googleToken });
    payload = ticket.getPayload();
  } catch (error) {
    res.status(403).send('Invalid credentials');
  }

  const { given_name: givenName, name, email } = payload;
  const credentials = {
    signedIn: true, givenName, name, email,
  };
  res.json(credentials);
});

module.exports = { routes };
```

Now, to use this new set of routes in the main application, we'll need to mount the routes in the main app. Let's do that at the path /auth to separate the namespace from /graphql. Thus, to access the signin endpoint, the full path to use will be /auth/signin. This change is made in server.js, as shown in Listing 14-8.

Listing 14-8. api/server.js: Changes for Mounting Auth Routes

```
...
const auth = require('./auth.js');

const app = express();

app.use('/auth', auth.routes);

installHandler(app);
...
```

At this point, the API can be tested, but it's not very convenient to do so. You'll have to add a breakpoint right after the variable googleUser is initialized in SignInNavItem. On a successful sign in, execution will stop at this breakpoint. Now, in the JavaScript console, you can execute the following to extract the token:

```
> googleUser.getAuthResponse().id_token;
```

This will print out a very long token which you can copy. If you are using bash, you use this token to initialize an environment variable called token by pasting it, for example:

```
$ token="eyJhbGciOiJSUzI1NiI...."
```

Now, you can test the new signin API by executing the following curl command in MacOS and Linux:

```
$ curl http://localhost:3000/auth/signin -X POST \
  --data "{ \"google_token\": \"$token\" }" \
  -H "Content-Type: application/json"
```

In the output, you should see the details of the profile, for example:

```
{"signedIn":true,"givenName":"Vasan","name":"Vasan Subramanian","email":
"vasan.XXXXX@gmail.com"}
```

Now, since we have a new endpoint prefix /auth, we'll need a new configuration variable for it so that the UI can send requests to it. This will need to be passed from the server to the UI, just like the API endpoint configuration variable UI_API_ENDPOINT. Let's call the new configuration variable UI_AUTH_ENDPOINT. Also, in the case of a proxy configuration, we'll need to proxy this new endpoint prefix, in addition to the /graphql endpoint prefix. These two additions are in uiserver.js, as shown in Listing 14-9.

Listing 14-9. ui/server/uiserver.js: Changes for New /Auth Endpoint Prefix

```
...
if (apiProxyTarget) {
  app.use('/graphql', proxy({ target: apiProxyTarget }));
  app.use('/auth', proxy({ target: apiProxyTarget }));
}
...

if (!process.env.UI_AUTH_ENDPOINT) {
  process.env.UI_AUTH_ENDPOINT = 'http://localhost:3000/auth';
}
```

```
app.get('/env.js', (req, res) => {
  ...
    UI_API_ENDPOINT: process.env.UI_API_ENDPOINT,
    UI_AUTH_ENDPOINT: process.env.UI_AUTH_ENDPOINT,
    GOOGLE_CLIENT_ID: process.env.GOOGLE_CLIENT_ID,
  ...
});
...
```

This change will require a restart and a browser refresh (since changes to uiserver.js are not handled by HMR). Now we are ready to send the Google token to the new API. The token itself can be obtained by a call to googleUser.getAuthResponse().id_token, as we saw when manually extracting the token. Then, we'll need to pass this token to the signin API, gather its resultant JSON, and use the givenName field from there to set the state variable givenName.

The changes, all in the component SignInNavItem, are shown in Listing 14-10.

Listing 14-10. ui/src/SignInNavItem: UI Changes for Verifying Google Token at the Back-End

```
...
  async signIn() {
    ...
    let googleToken;
    try {
      ...
      const givenName = googleUser.getBasicProfile().getGivenName();
      this.setState({ user: { signedIn: true, givenName } });
      googleToken = googleUser.getAuthResponse().id_token;
    } catch (error) {
    ...

    try {
      const apiEndpoint = window.ENV.UI_AUTH_ENDPOINT;
      const response = await fetch(`${apiEndpoint}/signin`, {
        method: 'POST',
        headers: { 'Content-Type': 'application/json' },
        body: JSON.stringify({ google_token: googleToken }),
      });
      const body = await response.text();
      const result = JSON.parse(body);
      const { signedIn, givenName } = result;

      this.setState({ user: { signedIn, givenName } });
    } catch (error) {
      showError(`Error signing into the app: ${error}`);
    }
  }
...
```

Now, if you try to sign in, you will get the following error, assuming you are not running in the proxy mode.

```
Access to fetch at 'http://localhost:3000/auth/signin' from origin 'http://localhost:8000'
has been blocked by CORS policy:
```

All the GraphQL APIs were successfully executed because Apollo Server enabled CORS, as we discussed in Chapter 7. But, this was applicable only to the endpoint prefix /graphql. For the new endpoint prefix /auth, we'll need to handle it separately. But that's not all. Since we are going to be setting a cookie in the next section, we'll need a more elaborate configuration to make this work.

Rather than do all that right now, let's switch to the proxy mode of operation, since it's simpler to get it working in this mode. Once all authentication- and authorization-related changes have been made, we'll switch back to the non-proxy mode and configure CORS correctly in later sections.

To switch to the proxy mode, you will have to make the changes in your .env file (or set environment variables manually). The modified sample.env file is shown in Listing 14-11, which you can use to copy-paste lines. Since we will be switching back and forth between the proxy and non-proxy modes, it's good to keep both configurations handy, but commented out.

Listing 14-11. ui/sample.env: Switching to Proxy Mode

```
...
UI_SERVER_PORT=8000
UI_API_ENDPOINT=http://localhost:3000/graphql
# UI_SERVER_API_ENDPOINT=http://localhost:3000/graphql
# API_PROXY_TARGET=http://localhost:3000
# ENABLE_HMR=true
GOOGLE_CLIENT_ID=YOUR_CLIENT_ID.apps.googleusercontent.com

# Regular config
# UI_API_ENDPOINT=http://localhost:3000/graphql
# UI_AUTH_ENDPOINT=http://localhost:3000/auth

# Proxy Config
UI_API_ENDPOINT=http://localhost:8000/graphql
UI_AUTH_ENDPOINT=http://localhost:8000/auth
API_PROXY_TARGET=http://localhost:3000
UI_SERVER_API_ENDPOINT=http://localhost:3000/graphql
...
```

This change too will require the UI server to be restarted. After the restart, if you test the sign-in process, you'll find that the API call to /auth/signin now succeeds (use the Network tab in the Developer Console to verify this) and you'll find your given name (based on the Google user that you used to sign in) reflected in the navigation bar, as in the previous section. But the difference is that the name is now *verified* and can also be used in the back-end.

JSON Web Tokens

Although we verified the token and used the name from the back-end, we did not persist the information. This means that on a browser refresh, the information about the sign-in would disappear, forcing the user to log in again. Further, any calls to the other APIs will not carry any authentication information, preventing the APIs from applying any authorization restrictions.

One way to persist the authentication information is by creating a session on the back-end, identified by a cookie. This can easily be done by using the middleware `express-session`, which adds a property in the request called `req.session`. On this session, variables can be set and retrieved, for example the user's ID and email. The middleware maintains, in memory, a mapping between the session variable and the cookie, which is also automatically sent to the browser by the middleware.

But using such an in-memory session is not considered scalable for several reasons:

- If the server instance were not a single one (for reasons of scaling or for high availability), the session information will not be shared among the instances, requiring the user to sign in to all of them separately.

- The session information is opaquely encoded and cannot be shared across different services, especially those written in different languages or using different technologies.

- A server restart will lose the login.

JSON Web Tokens (JWT) solve this problem by encoding all the session information that needs to be stored in a token. This is very similar to the Google token that we received after authenticating with Google. The token string by itself has all the information, that is, the user's name, email ID, etc. But the information is encrypted so that it cannot be snooped upon or impersonated.

Why not use the Google token itself? Why do we need to generate one of our own? The reason is that if and when you need to introduce other forms of authentication, it is better to have a single token that identifies the user to the Issue Tracker application, uniformly. Further, creating our own token lets us add more variables, for example, a role identifier can be added to the session information and that can be quickly retrieved to apply authorization rules.

In this section, we'll establish a session that persists even across server restarts. We'll use JWT to generate a token and send it back to the browser. On every API call that the UI makes, this token will need to be included, identifying the signed-in user.

There are various ways in which the token can be saved and sent back to the back-end on API calls:

- The UI can keep it in *memory* and attach the token as a header with every API call request. The common header that is used for this is the `Authorization:` header. This will work great as long as the user uses the application as an SPA and doesn't refresh the browser. But on a browser refresh, since the page is reloaded, all JavaScript memory will be reinitialized, making the token unavailable.

- The token can be saved in the browser's *local storage* or session storage instead of memory, so that it is persisted. But this can be insecure if there exists an cross-site-scripting (XSS) vulnerability in the application. You can read more about this in the OWASP website: `https://www.owasp.org/index.php/Cross-site_Scripting_` `(XSS)`. Essentially, an XSS vulnerability is created by forgetting to escape HTML special characters when generating a page, allowing a malicious user to inject code into the application. Since it is not escaped, the code can get executed rather than displayed, allowing access to the local storage data programmatically.

  Most modern UI frameworks, including React, avoid XSS by making it extremely hard for a programmer to generate HTML without encoding. But, we have included a few third-party UI libraries such as React-Bootstrap and React-Select, and we can't be sure how well these have been fortified against XSS attacks.

- The token can be sent across as a *cookie,* and to avoid XSS, we can prevent the cookie from being read programmatically by setting the HttpOnly flag on the cookie. The downside is that the amount of information that can be saved in a cookie is limited to 4KB. Further, there are many restrictions that browsers place on cross-site cookies. Since the Issue Tracker UI and the API servers are different, it is almost impossible to make cookies work if the two servers are under different domains.

  You may also read on the Internet that cookies expose your application to Cross-Site Request Forgery (XSRF), and that you need an XSRF token with every request to avoid this. But this is true only for conventional HTML forms.

A summary of these choices is shown in Table 14-1.

Table 14-1. *Comparison of JWT Storage Methods*

Storage Method	Pros	Cons
In-memory	Secure; No size limit	Session is not persistent; Including the token in all requests has to be programmatically managed
Local storage	No size limit	May be vulnerable to XSS attacks; Storage and token inclusion has to be programmatically managed
Cookie	Simple to implement	Size Limit on data; Cross-domain limitations; Vulnerable to XSRF in HTML forms

Using cookies to store JWT seems the best option, provided the information stored in the JWT is small enough and the UI and API servers are part of the same domain. Also, we need to store very little information (just the name and email ID, and maybe the role in the future), and most applications are deployed with the UI and the API being sub-domains of the main domain. Further, since the Issue Tracker application has no conventional HTML forms, and the GraphQL API does not accept anything other than application/json as the content type in POST requests, it is not vulnerable to XSRF. But it allows API calls using the GET method, which is vulnerable to XSRF. We'll need to disable this method of access since the UI does not use it.

Let's start by generating the JWT in the signin API. The jsonwebtoken package has a convenient way to do this, so let's install it. Also, since we'll be using cookies, let's install a cookie parser as well.

```
$ cd api
$ npm install jsonwebtoken@8
$ npm install cookie-parser@1
```

We'll need to set and retrieve cookies not just in auth.js, but also in GraphQL resolvers (in the future, when we implement authorization). So, let's install the cookie parser globally for all routes. This change to server.js is shown in Listing 14-12.

Listing 14-12. api/server.js: Include Cookie Parser in All Routes

```
...
const express = require('express');
const cookieParser = require('cookie-parser');
...
```

```
app.use(cookieParser());
app.use('/auth', auth.routes);
...
```

We'll be making multiple changes to auth.js, which are all shown in Listing 14-13. The first thing to do is generate a JWT in the signin API and set it as a cookie. The jsonwebtoken package provides a simple function called sign that takes in a JavaScript object and encrypts it using a secret key. We'll then set a cookie called jwt with the value as the signed token.

```
...
const jwt = require('jsonwebtoken');
...
routes.post('/signin', async (req, res) => {
  ...
  const token = jwt.sign(credentials, JWT_SECRET);
  res.cookie('jwt', token, { httpOnly: true });

  res.json(credentials);
}
...
```

Next, let's create a new API to get the current logged-in status. This will do both the jobs of verifying the JWT as well as extracting the username, etc. Let's call this API endpoint /user under the /auth set of routes. Within this, we'll retrieve the JWT from the cookie and call jwt.verify(), which does the reverse of sign: gets back the credentials. We'll also separate this retrieval of the credentials into a separate function, because in the future we'll need to do this for every request when we implement authorization.

```
...
function getUser(req) {
  const token = req.cookies.jwt;
  if (!token) return { signedIn: false };

  try {
    const credentials = jwt.verify(token, JWT_SECRET);
    return credentials;
  } catch (error) {
    return { signedIn: false };
  }
}
...

routes.post('/user', (req, res) => {
  res.send(getUser(req));
});
...
```

As for the JWT_SECRET variable, we'll need a configuration variable in the environment. Let's use an environment variable called JWT_SECRET for this. You should generate your own random string as the value for this variable, especially when deploying the application in production.

In the absence of this variable, let's just use a default value, but only in development mode. In production we'll disable authentication if the secret key is missing. Including this change, the complete changes to auth.js are shown in Listing 14-13.

Listing 14-13. api/auth.js: Changes for JWT Generation and Verification

```
...
const { OAuth2Client } = require('google-auth-library');
const jwt = require('jsonwebtoken');

let { JWT_SECRET } = process.env;

if (!JWT_SECRET) {
  if (process.env.NODE_ENV !== 'production') {
    JWT_SECRET = 'tempjwtsecretfordevonly';
    console.log('Missing env var JWT_SECRET. Using unsafe dev secret');
  } else {
    console.log('Missing env var JWT_SECRET. Authentication disabled');
  }
}

const routes = new Router();

routes.use(bodyParser.json());

function getUser(req) {
  const token = req.cookies.jwt;
  if (!token) return { signedIn: false };

  try {
    const credentials = jwt.verify(token, JWT_SECRET);
    return credentials;
  } catch (error) {
    return { signedIn: false };
  }
}

routes.post('/signin', async (req, res) => {
  if (!JWT_SECRET) {
    res.status(500).send('Missing JWT_SECRET. Refusing to authenticate');
  }
  ...

  const credentials = {
    ...
  };

  const token = jwt.sign(credentials, JWT_SECRET);
  res.cookie('jwt', token, { httpOnly: true });

  res.json(credentials);
});
```

```
routes.post('/user', (req, res) => {
  res.send(getUser(req));
});
...
```

To ensure that on a browser refresh we continue to maintain the signed-in status, let's fetch the authentication information using the /auth/user endpoint API. The only component as of now that uses the user information is the SignInNavItem component. So, let's load this data in that component's componentDidMount() method and set the user information in its state.

We'll use the usual pattern of a loadData() function that's called within componentDidMount(). In this function, we'll make a call to the /auth/user API, retrieve the user information, and set the state. Note that we have to use the fetch() API rather than a GraphQL API, since there is no GraphQL API for getting the current user information yet. The changes for this are shown in Listing 14-14.

Listing 14-14. ui/src/SignInNavItem.jsx: Changes to Use Persist and Use Authentication Info from the Back-End

```
...
  async componentDidMount() {
    const clientId = window.ENV.GOOGLE_CLIENT_ID;
    if (!clientId) return;
    window.gapi.load('auth2', () => {
      if (!window.gapi.auth2.getAuthInstance()) {
        window.gapi.auth2.init({ client_id: clientId }).then(() => {
          this.setState({ disabled: false });
        });
      }
    });
    await this.loadData();
  }

  async loadData() {
    const apiEndpoint = window.ENV.UI_AUTH_ENDPOINT;
    const response = await fetch(`${apiEndpoint}/user`, {
      method: 'POST',
    });
    const body = await response.text();
    const result = JSON.parse(body);
    const { signedIn, givenName } = result;
    this.setState({ user: { signedIn, givenName } });
  }
...
```

Now, you can test the application and you'll find that the signed-in information persists across browser refreshes. It would also be a good idea to check if the JWT is being sent across on every GraphQL request as well. You can do this by navigating to a different page and using the Developer Console to inspect the network traffic. You should see that the cookie named jwt is being sent to the server on every request. Also on a browser refresh, you should see a request going out to /auth/user and the menu item in the navigation bar change from "Sign In" to the user's given name.

If you click on Sign Out, the menu item will change back to Sign In, but on a browser refresh, you will find that the username is back on the menu item. That's because the cookie is still active, and that indicates a signed-in state.

Signing Out

Signing out requires two things: the JWT cookie in the browser needs to be cleared and the Google authentication needs to be forgotten.

Since we've set the HttpOnly flag in the cookie, it's not programmatically accessible from the front-end code. To clear it, we'll have to rely on the server. For this purpose, let's implement another API under /auth to sign out, which will essentially just clear the cookie. This change to auth.js is shown in Listing 14-15.

Listing 14-15. api/auth.js: Sign-Out API

```
...
routes.post('/signout', async (req, res) => {
  res.clearCookie('jwt');
  res.json({ status: 'ok' });
});

routes.post('/user', (req, res) => {
  ...
});
...
```

Let's call this API from the UI and replace the trivial signOut() function in the component SignInNavItem with a call to this. Further, let's also call the Google authentication API's signOut() function, which is part of the authInstance. The changes to SignInNavItem component are shown in Listing 14-16.

Listing 14-16. ui/src/SignInNavItem.jsx: Changes for Signing Out from the Back-End and Google

```
...
  async signOut() {
    const apiEndpoint = window.ENV.UI_AUTH_ENDPOINT;
    const { showError } = this.props;
    try {
      await fetch(`${apiEndpoint}/signout`, {
        method: 'POST',
      });
      const auth2 = window.gapi.auth2.getAuthInstance();
      await auth2.signOut();
      this.setState({ user: { signedIn: false, givenName: '' } });
    } catch (error) {
      showError(`Error signing out: ${error}`);
    }
  }
...
```

After this set of changes, even on a browser refresh, you should find that the signed-out status doesn't change. To confirm, you could inspect the network traffic to ensure that the cookie is not being sent on any request. Another way to confirm this is by looking at the cookie data in your browser and ensuring that the site localhost does not have the jwt cookie after a sign-out.

Authorization

Now that we've identified a user who is accessing the Issue Tracker application, let's put this information to use. A typical enterprise application will have roles and users belonging to roles. The roles will specify what operations are allowed for the user. Rather than implement all that, we'll just implement a simple authorization rule that suffices to demonstrate how this can be done.

The rule that we will implement is thus: if a user is signed in, the user is allowed to make changes. Unauthenticated users can only read the issues. Thus, we'll prevent any API under mutation from being accessed by unauthenticated users. We'll also need to change the UI to disable operations that are unavailable, but let's reserve that for the next section. In this section, we'll only ensure that the back-end APIs are secure and prevent unauthorized modification. The APIs will report an error when an unauthorized operation is attempted.

Apollo Server provides a mechanism by which a *context* can be passed through to all resolvers. Until now, we only used the first two arguments in any resolver, for example:

```
...
async function add(_, { issue }) {
...
```

The GraphQL library in fact passes a third argument, the context, which can be customized to the application's requirements.

```
...
async function add(_, { issue }, context) {
...
```

The context can be set to any value that can be derived from the request. We can set the user information as the context and let each resolver check whether the credentials are good enough to serve the request. Given our simple rule, this could look like:

```
...
async function add(_, { issue }, user) {
  if (!user || !user.signedIn) {
    throw new AuthenticationError('You must be signed in');
  }
  ...
}
...
```

Let's first create the context that holds user information and is passed on to each resolver as the third argument. The place to do it is during initialization of the Apollo server. Along with the typedefs and the resolvers, we need to specify a function that takes in an object, with req as one property, and returns the context that will be supplied to all resolvers.

```
...
const server = new ApolloServer({
  typeDefs: ...
  resolvers,
  context: getContext,
});
...
```

Since we already have a function that returns the user credentials given a request object as part of auth.js, it would be quite simple to implement getContext() using that. With that change, the final changes to api_handler.js are shown in Listing 14-17.

Listing 14-17. api/api_hander.js: Set the User as Context in All Resolver Calls

```
...
const issue = require('./issue.js');
const auth = require('./auth.js');
...

function getContext({ req }) {
  const user = auth.getUser(req);
  return { user };
}

const server = new ApolloServer({
  typeDefs: ...
  resolvers,
  context: getContext,
  ...
});
...
```

Now, rather than include the context in each resolver function and check for a valid user in all of them, let's try to reuse that code. What we need is something that takes in an existing resolver and returns a function that does this check before executing that resolver. Let's create such a function in auth.js and export it. Let's also export getUser because that is needed in api_handler, within getContext(). These changes are shown in Listing 14-18.

Listing 14-18. api/auth.js: Common Function for Simplistic Authorization Check

```
...
const jwt = require('jsonwebtoken');
const { AuthenticationError } = require('apollo-server-express');

...
function mustBeSignedIn(resolver) {
  return (root, args, { user }) => {
    if (!user || !user.signedIn) {
      throw new AuthenticationError('You must be signed in');
    }
    return resolver(root, args, { user });
  };
}

module.exports = { routes, getUser, mustBeSignedIn };
...
```

Now, to prevent unauthenticated users from calling protected APIs, let's replace their exports with a mustBeSignedIn wrapped function. The change for protecting setAboutMessage is shown in Listing 14-19.

Listing 14-19. api/about.js: Prevent Unauthenticated Access to setAboutMessage

```
...
const { mustBeSignedIn } = require('./auth.js');

let aboutMessage = 'Issue Tracker API v1.0';
...

module.exports = { getMessage, setMessage: mustBeSignedIn(setMessage) };
...
```

A similar set of changes for all the issue-related APIs is shown in Listing 14-20.

Listing 14-20. api/issue.js: Prevent Unauthenticated Access to Issue Methods

```
...
const { getDb, getNextSequence } = require('./db.js');
const { mustBeSignedIn } = require('./auth.js');
...

module.exports = {
  list,
  add: mustBeSignedIn(add),
  get,
  update: mustBeSignedIn(update),
  delete: mustBeSignedIn(remove),
  restore: mustBeSignedIn(restore),
  counts,
};
...
```

Now, if you try to access any of the functionality from the UI that makes a call to any of these APIs, you should find that they fail with an error, "UNAUTHENTICATED: You must be signed in." For example, clicking on the + button to create an issue and clicking Submit in the modal dialog will result in the error message as a Toast.

EXERCISE: AUTHORIZATION

1. If we needed to prevent unauthenticated users from accessing *any* functionality, that is, the entire application needs to have protected access, how could the GraphQL APIs be changed for this? Ignore the UI changes that would be needed to let users sign in. Focus on the APIs alone. Hint: Look up Apollo Authentication documentation at https://www.apollographql.com/docs/apollo-server/features/authentication.html.

Answers are available at the end of the chapter.

Authorization-Aware UI

It's great to prevent users from executing unauthorized operations, but it would be even better to prevent access to these operations at the UI rather than check for them at the back-end alone. In this and the next section, we'll make the UI aware of the signed-in status.

We'll use two mechanisms to do this. In this section, we'll disable the Create Issue button in the navigation bar by conventional means. We'll lift the state up to a common ancestor and let the state flow down as props that can be used in the children. In the next section, we'll use a different technique that's more suitable for passing props to components very deep in the hierarchy.

Let's choose the Page component as the component in the hierarchy where the user signed-in state will reside. To do this, we'll have to convert the component into a regular component, that is, not a stateless component. Then, we'll move the state variable user from SignInNavItem to Page. Instead of separate methods for signing in and out, let's use a single method called onUserChange, as this makes it easier to pass it down as props. We'll pass this method and the user variable down to the navigation bar (and later, further down the hierarchy).

We'll also need to load the state in componentDidMount() by making a call to the API /auth/user. This piece of code can be copied over from SignInNavItem. The changes to the Page component are shown in Listing 14-21.

Listing 14-21. ui/src/Page.jsx: Lift User State Up to Page

```
...
export default function class Page () extends React.Component {
  constructor(props) {
    super(props);
    this.state = { user: { signedIn: false } };

    this.onUserChange = this.onUserChange.bind(this);
  }

  async componentDidMount() {
    const apiEndpoint = window.ENV.UI_AUTH_ENDPOINT;
    const response = await fetch(`${apiEndpoint}/user`, {
      method: 'POST',
    });
    const body = await response.text();
    const result = JSON.parse(body);
    const { signedIn, givenName } = result;
    this.setState({ user: { signedIn, givenName } });
  }

  onUserChange(user) {
    this.setState({ user });
  }

  render() {
    const { user } = this.state;
    return (
      <div>
        <NavBar user={user} onUserChange={this.onUserChange} />
        <Grid fluid>
```

```
        <Contents />
      </Grid>
      <Footer />
    </div>
  );
  }
}
...
```

Now that the navigation bar has a prop variable for the signed-in user, let's pass that down to the NavItems that need them: Create Issue and the Sign In menu items. Also, the Sign In menu item needs the onUserChange property to call back when there is a change to the signed-in status. so let's pass that as well. These changes are shown in Listing 14-22.

Listing 14-22. ui/src/Page.jsx: Passing Through User Properties to Navigation Items

```
...
function NavBar({ user, onUserChange }) {
  ...
    <Nav pullRight>
      <IssueAddNavItem user={user} />
      <SignInNavItem user={user} onUserChange={onUserChange} />
      ...
    </Nav>
  ...
}
...
```

Showing the Create Issue navigation item in a disabled state is straightforward: we'll check for the signedIn flag and disable the NavItem if it is false. This change to the IssueAddInNavItem component is shown in Listing 14-23.

Listing 14-23. ui/src/IssueAddNavItem.jsx: Disable the Item When Not Signed In

```
...
  render() {
    const { showing } = this.state;
    const { user: { signedIn } } = this.props;
    return (
      <React.Fragment>
        <NavItem disabled={!signedIn} onClick={this.showModal}>
        ...
    );
  }
...
```

In the SignInNavItem component, we'll remove the state variable for the user and use new props being passed in instead. Also, we'll no longer need to load the data on component mount, as this is being done along with the state in the Page component. These changes are shown in Listing 14-24.

Listing 14-24. ui/src/SignInNavItem.jsx: Moving User State Out

```
...
  constructor(props) {
    this.state = {
      ...
      user: { signedIn: false, givenName: '' },
    };
  }
...

  async componentDidMount() {
    ...
    await this.loadData();
  }

  async loadData() {
    ...
  }

  async signIn() {
    ...
      this.setState({ user: { signedIn, givenName } });
      const { onUserChange } = this.props;
      onUserChange({ signedIn, givenName });
    ...
  }

  async signOut() {
    ...
      this.setState({ user: { signedIn: false, givenName: '' } });
      const { onUserChange } = this.props;
      onUserChange({ signedIn: false, givenName: '' });
    ...
  }
...

  render() {
    const { user } = this.state props;
    ...
  }
...
```

Now, on testing, you will find that the SignInNavItem retains its behavior of showing the username when signed in and a Sign In label when not. Further, the Create Issue button gets disabled when the user is not signed in.

Although this seemed like a lot of work for very little effect, this becomes necessary when common properties are shared among sibling components. Note that we could have moved the state up to the navigation bar component NavBar, but since we'll need the user state passed down to other components that are not under the NavBar, it was more convenient to move it to the Page component.

React Context

In this section, we'll make other components aware of the authentication status. We'll disable the Close and Delete buttons in the Issue Table and then we'll disable the Submit button in the Edit page.

But doing this in the same manner as we did for the navigation menu items will not only make it tedious (passing the user property through many components in the hierarchy), but it also poses a challenge. In the Contents component, we are generating the routes from an array, and it's not clear how to pass props to the component that will be rendered.

So, in this section, I'll introduce the React Context API that can be used to pass properties across the component hierarchy without making intermediate components aware of it. The React Context is designed to share data that is to be considered global. The authenticated user does fall under the global category, so it's not a bad idea to use the context for this purpose.

To start using the context, we'll first need to create a context using the `React.createContext()` method. This takes in an argument, the default value of the context that will be passed through to all components that need it. Since we need to pass a user object, let's use that as the context variable and set its default value to an initial state where the user is not signed in. We'll also need to share the context across components where its value is being set as well as where it is being used. So, let's create a separate JavaScript module called UserContext for this. This new module is shown in Listing 14-25.

Listing 14-25. ui/src/UserContext.js: A React Context for Storing User State

```
import React from 'react';

const UserContext = React.createContext({
  signedIn: false,
});

export default UserContext;
```

The created context exposes a component called Provider under it, which needs to be wrapped around any component hierarchy that needs the context. The component takes in a prop called value, which needs to be set to the value that the context will be set to in all descendent components. As an example, look at the following code:

```
<UserContext.Provider value={{ givenName: 'User1' }}>
  <IssueList />
</UserContext>
```

This will make the UserContext available to the IssueList component in the form of this.context, and all descendants of IssueList. But to make it explicit that it is the UserContext that needs to be consumed, we'll have to specify the context type as a static variable in the component in any of the descendants wishing to consume the context. Thus, to use the user context, say, in the IssueTable component, we'll need to do the following:

```
class IssueTable extends React.Component {
  render() {
    const user = this.context;
    ...
  }
}

IssueTable.contextType = UserContext;
```

Note that since `IssueTable` is a child of `IssueList`, it will receive the user context without having to pass it explicitly through the `IssueList` component. Also, we don't necessarily have to set the value of the context in the provider to a static one, as shown. It can be set to the value of a state variable, which will then have the effect of re-rendering all child components when the state changes, with the new value in the context.

So, let's set the user state as the value in the provider and wrap the provider around the `Contents` component in Page. The change for this is shown in Listing 14-26.

Listing 14-26. ui/src/Page.jsx: Providing the User Context

```
...
import Search from './Search.jsx';
import UserContext from './UserContext.js';
...

  render() {
    const { user } = this.state;
    return (
      ...
          <UserContext.Provider value={user}>
            <Contents />
          </UserContext.Provider>
      ...
    );
  }
```

Now, all descendants of `Contents` can access the user context. Let's first consume it in the `IssueEdit` component. As discussed earlier, we'll need to define the static variable `contextType` and set it to the object `UserContext`. Then, the user will be available as `this.context`, which we'll use to get the `signedIn` property and disable the Submit button based on that. These changes are shown in Listing 14-27.

Listing 14-27. ui/src/IssueEdit.jsx: Changes to Disable the Submit Button Based on User Context

```
...
import UserContext from './UserContext.js';

class IssueEdit extends React.Component {
  render() {
    ...
    const user = this.context;

    return (
      ...
                  <Button
                    disabled={!user.signedIn}
                    bsStyle="primary"
                    type="submit"
                  >
      ...
    );
  }
}

IssueEdit.contextType = UserContext;
...
```

498

This change can be tested independently—you should be able to see that the Submit button in the Edit page is disabled until you sign in.

The next component that needs a change to incorporate the user context is the IssueRow component. But unfortunately, stateless components do not have a this variable, and therefore, the context is not available through this. Earlier versions of React passed the context as an additional parameter to functional components, and it can be done using the Legacy Context API. But this is not recommended, because the old API is deprecated.

Another option is to consume the context at the nearest parent that is not a stateless component and pass the variable down as props. But this defeats the purpose of creating a context in the first place. So, let's instead convert the IssueRow component to a regular (that is, *not* stateless) component and consume the context.

There is also another complexity: we're wrapping the component using withRouter. This causes the wrapped component to inherit the static variable contextType from the inner component (the component that's being wrapped), and consequently causes an error in the Developer Console. This is because the wrapped component happens to be a stateless component.

To prevent it from throwing this error, we need to delete the contextType static variable in the wrapped component, leaving it in the inner component alone. This issue is present in React Router as of writing this book, but it is possible that it has been resolved at the time you are reading this book and trying it out. Do refer to the details of this issue at https://stackoverflow.com/questions/53240058/use-hoist-non-react-statics-with-withrouter for more information.

To do all this, we'll need to create a different name for the inner component so that it can be accessed independently. Let's call it IssueRowPlain, and the component wrapped with the router as IssueRow, as before. The changes for converting to a regular component as well as for consuming the context are shown in Listing 14-28. Indentation changes are not shown for the sake of brevity.

Listing 14-28. ui/src/IssueTable.jsx: IssueRow Converted to Regular Component for Consuming User Context

```
...
import UserContext from './UserContext.js';

const IssueRow = withRouter(({
  issue, location: { search }, closeIssue, deleteIssue, index,
}) => {
// eslint-disable-next-line react/prefer-stateless-function
class IssueRowPlain extends React.Component {
  render() {
    const {
      issue, location: { search }, closeIssue, deleteIssue, index,
    } = this.props;
    const user = this.context;
    const disabled = !user.signedIn;

    const selectLocation = { pathname: `/issues/${issue.id}`, search };
    ...
            <Button disabled={disabled} bsSize="xsmall" onClick={onClose}>
      ...
            <Button disabled={disabled} bsSize="xsmall" onClick={onDelete}>
    ...

  }
}
```

```
IssueRowPlain.contextType = UserContext;
const IssueRow = withRouter(IssueRowPlain);
delete IssueRow.contextType;
...
```

With this change, you should be able to see that the Close and Delete buttons are disabled by default until you sign in. You could, if you prefer, revert the changes to the navigation items to use the context instead of passing the user as props via the NavBar component.

EXERCISE: REACT CONTEXT

1. We avoided passing props to the components constructed by <Route>s. In the case of the user context, we could do this because the user information can indeed be considered a global variable. What if you need to pass something through to the routed component, but it is not a global variable? In other words, how does one pass props to routed components? Hint: Look up this blog post: https://tylermcginnis.com/react-router-pass-props-to-components/.

Answers are available at the end of the chapter.

CORS with Credentials

When we added verification of the Google token, we had to switch to the proxy mode of operation because CORS blocked the request from being sent to /auth/signin. In this section, we'll see how we can get the application to work in the non-proxy mode by relaxing the CORS options, at the same time maintaining security.

The reason the request was blocked is that when the origin of the application (where the starting page, /index.html, is fetched from) is not the same as the target of any XHR call, the browser blocks it, deeming it unsafe. In the Issue Tracker application, the starting page was fetched from http://localhost:8000 but the API calls were being made to http://localhost:3000. At this point, it would help for you to read the section titled "Proxy-Based Architecture" in Chapter 7, "Architecture and ESLint," as a recap on CORS.

Let's first switch back to the non-proxy mode. If you were using an .env based on the sample.env, you could make the changes as shown in Listing 14-29. The lines in the Regular config are uncommented and the lines in the Proxy Config are commented out to affect this change.

Listing 14-29. ui/sample.env: Switch Back to Non-Proxy Mode

```
...
# Regular config
#-UI_API_ENDPOINT=http://localhost:3000/graphql
#-UI_AUTH_ENDPOINT=http://localhost:3000/auth

# Proxy Config
# UI_API_ENDPOINT=http://localhost:8000/graphql
# UI_AUTH_ENDPOINT=http://localhost:8000/auth
# API_PROXY_TARGET=http://localhost:3000
# UI_SERVER_API_ENDPOINT=http://localhost:3000/graphql
...
```

A server restart is required to read in the new environment variables. At this point, if you try signing in, you will find that signing in fails with the following error message in the Developer Console:

```
Access to fetch at 'http://localhost:3000/auth/user' from origin 'http://localhost:8000'
has been blocked by CORS policy: No 'Access-Control-Allow-Origin' header is present on the
requested resource. If an opaque response serves your needs, set the request's mode to
'no-cors' to fetch the resource with CORS disabled.
```

The default configuration of the Apollo Server enabled CORS and allowed requests to /graphql. But since it was not done on /auth, it was blocked. Let's try to enable CORS for the /auth set of routes. The cors package lets us do this very easily. All we need to do is install a middleware in the route which will deal with setting up the necessary headers in the preflight requests to the API server. Let's first install the package in the api directory.

```
$ cd api
$ npm install cors@2
```

Then, we'll need to import this package and add a middleware in auth.js.

```
...
const cors = require('cors');
...
routes.use(bodyParser.json());
routes.use(cors());
...
```

Now, a sign-in will seem to succeed and you'll be able to see the Sign In menu item changed to reflect the given name. So, adding the default middleware did work, and the browser is sending API requests to /auth routes as well. But there is a caveat. If you refresh the browser, you will find that the authentication information has disappeared!

If you inspect the Network tab of the Developer Tools, you will find that the jwt cookie is not being sent in further requests to the server, and therefore a request to /auth/user returns the signedIn flag as false. But you can see that the cookie was indeed set in the response to /auth/signin.

So, the default CORS configuration seems to allow requests, but does not allow cookies to be sent for cross-origin requests. This makes sense as a safe default because any public resource should be accessible anyway; it is only the authenticated requests that have any user credentials that must be blocked.

To let credentials also be passed to cross-origins, the following must be done:

1. All XHR calls (that is, calls using the API fetch()) must include the header credentials: 'include'. Otherwise, cookies will be stripped from these calls.

2. Including credentials using this method is forbidden if cross-origin requests from a wildcard origin are allowed by the server. If you noticed in the request headers, there is a header Access-Control-Allow-Origin: *. This is the default CORS configuration, and for good reason, including credentials from *any* origin should be disallowed. We'll need to change this to allow requests with origin *only* from the UI server. Thus, the CORS middleware should include an origin as a configuration option, for example:

```
...
routes.use(cors({ origin: 'http://localhost:8000' }));
...
```

If this is not done, you will find a helpful message in the Developer Console like this:

```
Access to fetch at 'http://localhost:3000/auth/user' from origin 'http://localhost:8000'
has been blocked by CORS policy: The value of the 'Access-Control-Allow-Origin' header in
the response must not be the wildcard '*' when the request's credentials mode is 'include'.
```

3. It's not enough if the browser is instructed to send credentials; the server must also explicitly allow it. This is done by another CORS configuration option called credentials, which must be set to true.

Let's first make the change to auth.js to set these CORS configuration options. Also, rather than hard-code the origin, let's use an environment variable called UI_SERVER_ORIGIN for this. You could save this in your .env file, similar to the change to sample.env shown in Listing 14-30.

Listing 14-30. api/sample.env: Option for UI Server's Origin

```
...
# ENABLE_CORS=false

UI_SERVER_ORIGIN=http://localhost:8000
...
```

In auth.js, let's use this environment variable and set the CORS options to include the origin and credentials. The final set of changes to auth.js is shown in Listing 14-31.

Listing 14-31. api/auth.js: Changes to Include CORS with Correct Configuration Options

```
...
const cors = require('cors');
...
routes.use(bodyParser.json());

const origin = process.env.UI_SERVER_ORIGIN || 'http://localhost:8000';
routes.use(cors({ origin, credentials: true }));
...
```

We'll also need to include credentials in all API calls to /auth. Let's do this within SignInNavItem first. This is shown in Listing 14-32.

Listing 14-32. ui/src/SignInNavItem.jsx: Include Credentials in Fetch Calls

```
...
  async signIn() {
    ...
      const response = await fetch(`${apiEndpoint}/signin`, {
        method: 'POST',
        credentials: 'include',
        ...
      });
    ...
  }
```

```
async signOut() {
  ...
    await fetch(`${apiEndpoint}/signout`, {
      method: 'POST',
      credentials: 'include',
    });
  ...
}
...
```

Then, in Page.jsx, when we fetch the user credentials, we'll have to include the credentials. This change is shown in Listing 14-33.

Listing 14-33. ui/src/Page.jsx: Include Credentials in Fetch Calls

```
...
  async componentDidMount() {
    ...
    const response = await fetch(`${apiEndpoint}/user`, {
      method: 'POST',
      credentials: 'include',
    });
  ...
```

Now, on testing you will find that a browser refresh does indeed maintain the logged-in status. But all the GraphQL API calls use the original CORS configuration, which don't have the credentials yet. This will cause the APIs to reject any modifications from the application. For example, a Create Issue even when you are signed in will fail, saying you need to be logged in.

For the GraphQL API calls to allow these, we'll need to set the CORS configuration options in the Apollo Server as well. Apart from the true and false values, the CORS option when creating the Apollo Server can also take in the CORS configuration itself. This is what we'll use to set the CORS configuration.

In addition to allowing only the configured origin, we'll also restrict the methods allowed to POST only. That's because the Apollo Server allows GET requests by default, and as discussed in the section titled "JSON Web Tokens," this can be a cause for XSRF vulnerability. The application itself does not use any method other than POST, so it is safe to add this restriction. The changes for CORS configuration in the GraphQL API are shown in Listing 14-34.

Listing 14-34. api/api_handler.js: CORS Configuration for Apollo Server

```
...
function installHandler(app) {
  ...
  console.log('CORS setting:', enableCors);
  let cors;
  if (enableCors) {
    const origin = process.env.UI_SERVER_ORIGIN || 'http://localhost:8000';
    const methods = 'POST';
    cors = { origin, methods, credentials: true };
  } else {
    cors = 'false';
  }
```

```
    server.applyMiddleware({ app, path: '/graphql', cors: enableCors });
}
...
```

Since all GraphQL API calls are routed through graphQLFetch function, the only place we'll need to add the credentials: 'include' header is in graphQLFetch.js. This change is shown in Listing 14-35.

Listing 14-35. ui/src/graphQLFetch.js: Include Credentials in Fetch Calls

```
...
    const response = await fetch(apiEndpoint, {
      method: 'POST',
      credentials: 'include',

      ...
    });
...
```

With all these changes, you will find that credentials are being sent to the server for all GraphQL calls as well. At this point, the application should work as it was working in the proxy mode of operation at the end of the previous section. You should also take a look at the Network tab in the Developer Tools and verify that the cookie is being set on an authentication response and sent to the API server for /auth and /graphql calls.

Server Rendering with Credentials

Until now, we did not handle the server rendering of pages including the authenticated user information. The effect of this is that on a browser refresh, the page is loaded as if the user has not signed in. The menu item says "Sign In". Then, after the user credentials are fetched asynchronously and the user state is updated, the menu changes to the given name of the signed-in user.

In practice, at least for the purpose of search engine bots, this is perfectly fine. That's because there is no way search engines are going to sign in as a user and crawl the site's pages. It is only the publicly available set of pages that a bot crawls.

But if you don't like the (slightly) ungainly flicker which transitions from an unsigned-in state to a signed-in state, or, if you like all pages to behave consistently whether or not the user is signed in, you may want to consider rendering the page at the server that includes the credentials.

There are essentially three challenges that server rendering with credentials poses, which is different from the regular pattern of server rendering that we used for the routed views.

- The initial data fetched for the user credentials goes to the /auth endpoint rather than the /graphql endpoint. Server rendering relies on the fact that all data fetching calls go through graphQLFetch(), where we make critical decisions based on whether the call is made from the browser or the UI server.

- When the user data is fetched, the API call made by the UI server to fetch the data must include the cookie. When called from the UI, the browser would have added this cookie automatically. But in the UI server, we'll need to manually include the cookie. Otherwise, the call will behave as if the user is not signed in.

- The initial data that is fetched needs to be *in addition* to any other data fetched prior to rendering using fetchData() functions in the views. Also, this data is not fetched by any view which is part of the routes: it is fetched at a much higher level, in the Page component.

To address the first challenge, let's introduce a new GraphQL API for the authenticated user credentials. We used the /auth set of routes because GraphQL resolvers could not set cookies, as they did not have access to the Express response object. But fetching the signed-in user's credentials only requires access to the Express *request* object, and as we saw in the Authorization section previously, this should be feasible.

To start implementing this API, let's change the schema. This change is shown in Listing 14-36.

Listing 14-36. api/schema.graphql: User Credentials API

```
...
type IssueListWithPages {
  ...
}

type User {
  signedIn: Boolean!
  givenName: String
  name: String
  email: String
}
...

type Query {
  about: String!
  user: User!
  ...
}
...
```

As for the resolver, let's introduce a resolver function as part of auth.js that just returns the context. You will recall that we set the GraphQL context for all resolvers to nothing but the user object, so that's all we need as the return value. The change to auth.js is shown in Listing 14-37.

Listing 14-37. api/auth.js: GraphQL Resolver for Returning User Credentials

```
...
function resolveUser(_, args, { user }) {
  return user;
}

module.exports = {
  routes, getUser, mustBeSignedIn, resolveUser,
};
...
```

Let's tie this new resolver in to the API Handler. This change is shown in Listing 14-38.

Listing 14-38. api/api_handler.js: Add Resolver for User API

```
...
onst resolvers = {
  Query: {
    about: about.getMessage,
    user: auth.resolveUser,
    ...
  },
  ...
};

...
```

To test the API, you could use the Playground. But now that we have protected APIs, the Playground will not work for these by default. You need to ensure that cookies are sent across in the API queries. There is a setting in the Playground that can be used to allow this, called request.credentials. The default value for this is "omit", which you will need to change to "include". Then, all requests will include cookies. So, after signing in to the application, the following query should return the given name of the user who is signed in.

```
query { user { givenName } }
```

The next challenge is to let the user credentials pass through to the API calls via the UI server. You will recall that a server rendered page will be returned when a request is made from the browser to a routed URL such as /issues or /about to the UI server. The UI server then makes API calls to the API server and prefills the page using the data. So, the cookie received in the first step by the UI server needs to be replicated in calls to the API server.

Essentially, any call to graphQLFetch() made as part of rendering from the server needs to include the JWT cookie that was received in initiating the request. The way we can do this is by letting all fetchData() static functions receive an optional parameter cookie, which can be passed through when any function calls graphQLFetch().

Let's now change graphQLFetch.js to have the ability to include a cookie in the API request. This change is shown in Listing 14-39.

Listing 14-39. ui/src/graphQLFetch.js: Changes to Pass Through Cookies

```
...
export default async function
graphQLFetch(query, variables = {}, showError = null, cookie = null) {
  const apiEndpoint = (__isBrowser__) // eslint-disable-line no-undef
    ? window.ENV.UI_API_ENDPOINT
    : process.env.UI_API_ENDPOINT;
  try {
    const headers = { 'Content-Type': 'application/json' };
    if (cookie) headers.Cookie = cookie;
    const response = await fetch(apiEndpoint, {
      method: 'POST',
      credentials: 'include',
      headers: { 'Content-Type': 'application/json' },
      body: JSON.stringify({ query, variables }),
    });
...
```

Since this function is being used both on the server as well as on the browser, we'll have to ensure that the cookie argument is passed *only* for calls from the server rendering routines, that is, from render.jsx. For calls from the browser, the cookie will automatically be included by the browser.

Using this, let's change the Page component to load data as part of a static fetchData() function as we did for the other routed components. We'll replace the call to /auth/user with the new GraphQL API as well. Here's the new static function, where the cookie is optional. We'll need to pass in the cookie for server-side requests, so the function needs to take the cookie as an argument.

```
...
  static async fetchData(cookie) {
    const query = `query { user {
      signedIn givenName
    }}`;
    const data = await graphQLFetch(query, null, null, cookie);
    return data;
  }
...
```

In the constructor, let's do the check for the global store containing the value for the user credentials, just as we did for the routed components, and use it if it exists. We'll signal its absence by storing a null value in the state variable, which componentDidMount() can check for and load the data. Rather than use store.initialData, we'll need to use a different variable since the user data is *in addition* to other data required for rendering the routed components. Let's use a new variable called userData for this purpose.

```
...
  constructor(props) {
    ...
    const user = store.userData ? store.userData.user : null;
    delete store.userData;
    this.state = { user };
    ...
  }
...
```

Note that since the Page component is always being rendered, there cannot be a case where the server does not include the user data as part of rendering. But to be consistent and allow this component to be mounted on the server by navigating as well, let's ensure that the data is loaded in componentDidMount(), like we did for the views. This call need not include any cookies, as the browser will automatically attach them.

```
...
  async componentDidMount() {
    const { user } = this.state;
    if (user == null) {
      const data = await Page.fetchData();
      this.setState({ user: data.user });
    }
  }
...
```

507

Finally, in the render() method, let's check for the user state variable being null and return null, to keep it consistent with other views, even though this case is not going to occur. This change and the other changes to Page.jsx are shown in Listing 14-40.

Listing 14-40. ui/src/Page.jsx: Changes for fetchData Separation, Using graphQLFetch and Global Store

```
...
import UserContext from './UserContext.js';
import graphQLFetch from './graphQLFetch.js';
import store from './store.js';
...

export default class Page extends React.Component {
  static async fetchData(cookie) {
    const query = `query { user {
      signedIn givenName
    }}`;
    const data = await graphQLFetch(query, null, null, cookie);
    return data;
  }

  constructor(props) {
    super(props);
    const user = store.userData ? store.userData.user : null;
    delete store.userData;
    this.state = { user: { signedIn: false } };
    ...
  }

  async componentDidMount() {
    const apiEndpoint = window.ENV.UI_AUTH_ENDPOINT;
    ...
    this.setState({ user: { signedIn, givenName } });
    const { user } = this.state;
    if (user == null) {
      const data = await Page.fetchData();
      this.setState({ user: data.user });
    }
  }
...

  render() {
    const { user } = this.state;
    if (user == null) return null;
    ...
  }
...
```

We don't really need to change all the other fetchData() calls such as IssueList.fetchData to include the cookie. That's because the presence of a cookie does not make a difference to the result of these publicly available APIs. There may be cases where this is required, for example, if the list of issues returned depends on the currently signed-in user. In such cases, the relevant fetchData() functions also need to be modified to be able to pass through any cookies.

To address the next challenge of fetching the user data *in addition* to other data required for routed views, let's decide that all global data fetches such as user credentials will have to be hard-coded while rendering on the server. We will not make this as generic and flexible as what we did for the routed components. So, while rendering on the server, let's make a call to Page.fetchData() explicitly to fetch the global data and include it in the store.

The first change we need for this is in the template, where we'll create a new variable for user data just as we did for initial data. We'll also rename the parameter for initial data to make it more explicit. This is shown in Listing 14-41.

Listing 14-41. ui/server/template.js: Include User Data

```
...
export default function template(body, data initialData, userData) {
  ...
  <script>
    window.__INITIAL_DATA__  = ${serialize(data initialData)}
    window.__USER_DATA__ = ${serialize(userData)}
  </script>
    ...
}
...
```

And, in the browser, to transfer this data to the store, we'll need to change App.jsx. The changes are shown in Listing 14-42.

Listing 14-42. ui/browser/App.jsx: Transfer User Data to Store

```
...
import store from '../src/store.js';

// eslint-disable-next-line no-underscore-dangle
/* eslint-disable no-underscore-dangle */
store.initialData = window.__INITIAL_DATA__;
store.userData = window.__USER_DATA__;
...
```

Next, during the server rendering call, let's fetch the user data and supply it to the template for constructing the user data variable to be available in the browser. While doing this, we'll have to pass the cookie from the request headers through to the fetchData() calls. The changes for server rendering are shown in Listing 14-43.

Listing 14-43. ui/server/render.jsx

```
...
  if (activeRoute && activeRoute.component.fetchData) {
    ...
    initialData = await activeRoute.component
    .fetchData(match, search, req.headers.cookie);
  }
```

```
const userData = await Page.fetchData(req.headers.cookie);

store.initialData = initialData;
store.userData = userData;
...

    res.send(template(body, initialData, userData));
...
```

Note that we included the cookie in *all* fetchData() requests, including the active routed component's fetchData() call. As discussed, this is not required because these calls will not be affected by the presence of credentials. Yet, to keep it consistent and to let future modifications of views that may use the credentials display the contents differently, let's keep this.

Now, if you test the application, you will find that the flicker of the menu item is no longer there. Although this is not a great use case to be solved with all the complexity that was introduced, it could serve as a pattern that can be used to include truly global data at the time of server rendering.

Cookie Domain

In the previous two sections I glossed over an important aspect of cookies, which can come into play when the APIs are accessed directly from the browser. Since we used localhost as the domain to access the application, it worked seamlessly.

It is important to note that cookies and CORS work slightly differently when it comes to cross-site requests. Whereas CORS recognizes even a port difference as a different origin, a cookie set by the server is tied to the *domain*, and all requests to the same domain from the browser will include the cookie. For example, a cookie set by localhost:3000 will be sent to localhost:8000 as well. The cookie policy ignores differences in ports.

If you inspect the network traffic in the developer tools, you will find that the JWT cookie is being passed to requests to localhost:8000 (the UI server) even though it was set by the signin API by the API server on port 3000. This is what made it possible for us to pass the credentials through the UI server to the API server during server rendering.

To test whether this works for real domains as well, you'll need to create a domain and two subdomains, both of which point to the localhost. This can be done by editing the hosts file and adding the following line:

```
...
127.0.0.1 api.promernstack.com ui.promernstack.com
...
```

(On MacOS and Linux, this file can be found at /etc/hosts, and it's found at c:\Windows\System32\ Drivers\etc\hosts on a Windows PC.)

Now, you can set environment variables and configure your UI server so that the API endpoint is based on api.promernstack.com:3000 and then use ui.promernstack.com:8000 to access the application. The changes to sample.env in the ui directory are shown in Listing 14-44.

Listing 14-44. ui/sample.env: Changes for Using Domain Names

```
...
# Regular config
# UI_API_ENDPOINT=http://localhost:3000/graphql
# UI_AUTH_ENDPOINT=http://localhost:3000/auth

# Regular config with domains
UI_API_ENDPOINT=http://api.promernstack.com:3000/graphql
UI_AUTH_ENDPOINT=http://api.promernstack.com:3000/auth
...
```

You will also need to add the UI server's URL ui.promernstack.com in the Allowed Origins list in your Google Developer Console to test this; otherwise, you will not be able to sign in using Google. Further, the API server needs to set the CORS origin to the new URL for the UI: ui.promernstack.com:8000.

```
...
UI_SERVER_ORIGIN=http://ui.promernstack.com:8000
...
```

After this, you'll find that authentication and authorization still do not work. In particular, a sign-in will work, but a browser refresh will lose the credentials.

That's because the default domain setting for the cookie domain is the host part of the URL, that is, api. promernstack.com. The cookie will *not* be sent as part of the request in a call to ui.promernstack.com (as you can see in the Developer Tools Network tab). To let the two applications share the cookie, we'll need to set the cookie's domain as the base domain name, that is, without either of the sub-domain api or ui. Let's do that in the res.cookie() call in the response to /signin. Let's get the domain from an environment variable called COOKIE_DOMAIN. This is shown in Listing 14-45.

Listing 14-45. api/auth.js: Changes for Setting Cookie Domain

```
...
res.cookie('jwt', token, { httpOnly: true, domain: process.env.COOKIE_DOMAIN });
...
```

As for setting the variable itself, you should do it in your .env file. A sample change is shown in Listing 14-46, along with the change for the UI_SERVER_ORIGIN, which we did previously.

Listing 14-46. api/sample.env: New Variable for COOKIE_DOMAIN and Setting UI_SERVER_ORIGIN

```
...
UI_SERVER_ORIGIN=http://localhost:8000
UI_SERVER_ORIGIN=http://ui.promernstack.com:8000

COOKIE_DOMAIN=promernstack.com
...
```

Now (after restarting the servers, since the environment variables have changed), you will find that the authentication works fine, because cookies set in the API calls are used in requests to the UI server.

But, if you need different domains, for example, if you need to access the application using `localhost:8000` while the API is at `api.promernstack.com:3000`, you will find that the credentials are *not* sent to the API server. This is because the domains are different (`localhost` vs. `promernstack.com`). It is going to be extremely rare to require that the two servers be on two different domains (not sub-domains). But if it is really needed, the best option you have is to use the proxy mode of operation, where the browser sees only one domain for both the API and the UI.

Summary

There are many ways to authenticate users and different applications have different needs. For the Issue Tracker application, we used Google to authenticate a user. A different approach would be needed for signing up and authenticating users using say, a user ID, but once authenticated, the rest of the concepts you learned in this chapter would still be applicable.

You saw how JWT can be used to persist session information in a stateless, yet secure manner. Then, you saw how authorization works with GraphQL APIs and how it can be extended to perform different authorization checks based on the application's needs. You also saw how CORS and cookie handling restrictions on the browser come into play when the browser accesses the APIs directly.

All this while you hosted the application on your own computer. To make the application available to other users, it needs to be hosted on an external server. In the next chapter, we'll take a look at how this can be done using a Platform as a Service (PaaS) on the cloud, Heroku.

Answers to Exercises

Exercise: Google Sign-In

1. Yes, the profile picture is available and can be obtained by a call to the `getImageUrl()` function of the basic profile.

Exercise: Authorization

1. As the section titled "Schema Authorization" explains, a simple way to achieve this is to throw an exception in the `getContext()` function itself, if the user is not signed in.

```
...
function getContext({ req }) {
  const user = auth.getUser(req);
  if (!user || !user.signedIn) throw new AuthenticationError('you must be logged
in');
  return { user };
},
...
```

This way, the call doesn't even reach any resolver function.

Exercise: React Context

1. As suggested in the blog post, you will need to use the render property of the Route component rather than the component property. The render property takes in a function with props as an argument. Using the props supplied, you can construct a component by passing in these props, and any other additional props that you need to pass through. Thus, if you had to pass user as props, this is how the code in Context.jsx would look.

    ```
    ...
        {routes.map(attrs => (
          <Route path={attrs.path} key={attrs.path}
            render={(props) => <attrs.component {...props} user={user} />}
          />
        ))}
    ...
    ```

CHAPTER 15

Deployment

There are quite a number of ways to deploy the Issue Tracker on the cloud. You have do-it-yourself options such as firing up your own Linux-based instances on Amazon AWS, Google Cloud, and Microsoft Azure and running Node.js and MongoDB on them just like you did on your local computer throughout this book.

But I find that Platform-as-a-Service (PaaS) options are far easier to deploy to and maintain. So, in this chapter, I have chosen one of the most popular PaaS, Heroku. There is a free tier that you can experiment with before making a choice for your production application. In this chapter, I'll guide you through deploying the Issue Tracker application on Heroku.

Git Repositories

The simplest way to deploy an app on Heroku is using a Git repository. Until now, we haven't discussed how the Issue Tracker source code can be controlled and shared among a team for collaboration. You'd have created all the files on your local computer and very likely not used a repository as yet. Now is a good time to do that, since we'll need to do that anyway for deploying on Heroku. You could use CVS, SVN, Git, or any other modern source code control system, but since Heroku needs Git, we'll use the same for the Issue Tracker application's collaboration needs as well.

The repositories we are about to create should not be confused with the repository accompanying this book, at https://github.com/vasansr/pro-mern-stack-2. The book's repository has been organized in a manner to make it convenient to follow the code changes in the book and it is not ideal for real-life applications. So, do not clone or fork this repository; instead, start fresh with the code that we have written until this point.

You could use GitHub or BitBucket or any cloud Git service, or even your own hosted Git server. I have assumed GitHub for the instructions that follow. The instructions for the other services will be similar, if not identical.

Let's start by creating these repositories in GitHub. Log in to GitHub at https://github.com (create an account if you don't have one) and, using the user interface, explore how to create repositories. We have two deployable applications: the API server and the UI server. We will need two repositories, one for each of these. Let's call them tracker-api and tracker-ui. You will also need the Git command line utility: git. I will not go into the details of how to install git or set it up for accessing GitHub. There are different options to do these, and you will find a number of resources on the Internet as well the GitHub website itself that will help you get set.

There are two options to access the GitHub repository from the Git command line: using SSH or using HTTPS. In the following instructions, I will assume that you have set up Git for access using SSH. If you prefer HTTPS, you will have to change the remote URL for the repository in the following commands accordingly.

After creation of the repositories, let's initialize them with the current codebase. First, let's deal with the API codebase. To start, we'll need to initialize Git in the API directory. The following commands will get the job done:

```
$ cd api
$ git init
```

Next, we'll need to add all the files to be managed by Git. You could add each file manually. But it's easier to specify which files to exclude using a file called .gitignore, so let's do that. The contents of this file in the API directory are shown in Listing 15-1.

Listing 15-1. api/.gitignore: List of Files to Exclude from Git Management

```
node_modules
.env
```

Now, to add all the files in the API directory, excluding the ones shown in Listing 15-1, let's do the following:

```
$ git add .
$ git commit -m "First commit"
```

In this chapter, there will be many situations where you need to use your GitHub username. It would be convenient to define an environment variable so that commands can be copy-pasted from either the book or the book's GitHub repository without modification. Let's use an environment variable called GITHUB_USER for this purpose. At this point in time, you'll need to set this variable to your GitHub username.

The following commands assume a Linux computer or a Mac, and the environment variable is accessed using $GITHUB_USER. On a Windows PC, you will need to use %GITHUB_USER% instead, or replace the variable name with your GitHub username. The same applies to other variables that we will be using in this chapter.

Now, let's push the code to GitHub:

```
$ git remote add origin git@github.com:$GITHUB_USER/tracker-api.git
$ git push -u origin master
```

Adding a *remote* in Git sets up a linkage between the local repository and a remote repository, which in this case is on GitHub. After it succeeds, you should be able to see the source code in the GitHub website. Check it out and make sure all the code, including the script subdirectory, has been created.

A similar set of steps is needed for the UI directory. But the files to be excluded are different. Apart from the directory node_modules and the file .env, we also have files generated by compilation that need not be checked in to the Git repository. These are the entire dist directory and the .js and .js.map files in the public directory. Let's include these and create a .gitignore file, the contents of which are listed in Listing 15-2.

Listing 15-2. ui/.gitignore: Files to Exclude from the UI Directory

```
dist
node_modules
.env
public/*.js
public/*.js.map
```

Now, to initialize, add files, and push the UI directory to GitHub, let's execute the following commands as described in the GitHub prompt that appears after creating a repository:

```
$ cd ui
$ git init
$ git add .
$ git commit -m "First commit"
$ git remote add origin git@github.com:$GITHUB_USER/tracker-ui.git
$ git push -u origin master
```

At this point, you could browse the UI repository online on GitHub to ensure that the files have indeed been pushed to GitHub.

MongoDB

Before we deploy the servers on Heroku, let's first ensure that we have a MongoDB database on the cloud. Do revisit the section entitled "Installation" in Chapter 6, "MongoDB". If you have already been using a MongoDB database on the cloud, there is nothing more to be done. If not, choose one of the cloud options described in that chapter and follow the instructions to create a database on the cloud.

It would be convenient to have the connection URL along with the user ID and password handy, so let's set an environment variable called DB_URL for that and use that in the commands that follow. If you have just transitioned from a local database to a new database on the cloud, you will need to initialize the database as well. Use the following commands for this purpose:

```
$ cd api
$ mongo $DB_URL scripts/init.mongo.js
$ mongo $DB_URL scripts/generate_data.mongo.js
```

Heroku

The first thing to do is create a Heroku account, if you don't already have one. This can be done starting at https://heroku.com. Once you have a login account, you can install the Heroku CLI from https://devcenter.heroku.com/articles/heroku-cli#download-and-install. Most of the commands that we'll be executing for deploying are also available from the Heroku web user interface. But using the CLI, it's easier to follow the instructions in this book and execute commands.

The first thing to do to use the CLI after installing it is log in.

```
$ heroku login
```

This should respond with the following prompt, which will open the browser to get the login information.

```
heroku: Press any key to open up the browser to login or q to exit:
```

If you are already logged into Heroku via the web user interface, the login should be automatic. Otherwise, it may prompt you for your user ID and password. Once you log in, you should see the following in the console.

```
Logging in... done
Logged in as YOUR_MAIL_ID
```

In the following sections, we'll create and deploy the API application and then the UI application on Heroku.

The API Application

Deploying the API application requires a few changes to the application, because of what Heroku expects.

Firstly, the port on which the application can listen is dynamically allocated by Heroku. The reason is that each application is deployed in a *container* rather than a dedicated host. Thus, Heroku assigns a port to the application and sends traffic to that port for the application. But, on the Internet, the same port is reflected as an HTTP (80) or an HTTPS (443) port. There's a firewall in Heroku that does this. Heroku then sets an environment variable to let the application know which port the traffic will be received in the container. This environment variable is called simply PORT. And that's the port the application must listen on.

So, let's change the environment variable that we've been using, API_SERVER_PORT, to just PORT. The change in server.js is shown in Listing 15-3.

Listing 15-3. api/server.js: Change in Environment Variable Name for Server Port

```
...
const port = process.env.API_SERVER_PORT || 3000;
...
```

If you have been using a .env, a similar change has to be made in that file too, but this is only for testing on your local computer. It does not affect a Heroku deployment because the environment variables are not set using .env in Heroku. The same change in the sample .env file is shown in Listing 15-4.

Listing 15-4. api/sample.env: Change in Variable Name for Server Port

```
...
## Server Port
API_SERVER_PORT=3000
...
```

Apollo server disables the Playground by default when it's run in a production environment. But it's good to have the Playground available, and since the data is public anyway, let's enable it. This requires a code change to set the options while creating the Apollo server, as shown in Listing 15-5.

Listing 15-5. api/api_handler.js: Enable GraphQL Playground in Production

```
...
const server = new ApolloServer({
  ...
  playground: true,
  introspection: true,
});
...
```

Heroku deploys applications and determines the environment, language, etc. using an auto-detection algorithm. The presence of package.json in the repository is good enough for Heroku to detect that it's a Node. js environment. But since there are different versions of Node.js engines available that Heroku can use, we'll need to tell Heroku the particular version we need our application to run on. Further, since we're going to be installing packages just before running, we'll need to specify the version of npm that we'd like to use as well. The way to do this is by setting the engines property in package.json. This change is shown in Listing 15-6.

Listing 15-6. api/package.json: Engine Specification for Heroku

```
...
  "engines": {
    "node": "10.x",
    "npm": "6.x"
  },
  "scripts": {
...
```

To make these changes permanent, let's commit them. But a commit will affect only the local repository. It's a good idea to push these changes to the GitHub remote as well, so that others in your team can also get the changes.

```
$ cd api
$ git commit -am "Changes for Heroku"
$ git push origin master
```

Now, we're ready to deploy the app on Heroku. As recommended in the Heroku documentation, we'll first need to create and initialize the application. The Heroku CLI command create needs to be used for this. The application's name needs to be universal, so let's use your GitHub username as part of the application name, minimizing the chances that the chosen name is unavailable.

```
$ heroku create tracker-api-$GITHUB_USER
```

```
Creating tracker-api-GITHUB_USER... done
https://tracker-api-GITHUB_USER.herokuapp.com/ |
https://git.heroku.com/tracker-api- GITHUB_USER.git
```

Instead, if it shows an error that the application name is already in use, you will have to try different names for the application. When it succeeds, the creation will add a Git remote repository on Heroku, which will be referred to locally as heroku, pushing to which will have the effect of deploying the application.

But before that, let's set the environment variables that are needed by the API server. We need the DB URL and the JWT Secret. As for the cookie domain, let's set it to the common part of the API server and the UI server's domain, which is herokuapp.com.

```
$ heroku config:set \
  DB_URL=$DB_URL \
  JWT_SECRET=YOUR_SPECIAL_SECRET \
  COOKIE_DOMAIN=herokuapp.com
```

This command assumes a Linux or a Mac computer. When using a Windows PC, you will have to use the %DB_URL% syntax for variables and type the entire command in one line rather than use multiple lines with the \ character at the end.

Note that we don't need to set the PORT variable because it's set by Heroku when starting the application, and that's the only port we can use. Now, we can deploy the application on the cloud by doing a simple Git push operation to the Heroku remote.

```
$ git push heroku master
```

This should show an output on the console roughly like this:

```
remote: Compressing source files... done.
remote: Building source:
remote:
remote: -----> Node.js app detected
remote:
remote: -----> Creating runtime environment
...

remote: -----> Installing binaries
remote:        engines.node (package.json):  10.x
remote:        engines.npm (package.json):   6.x
remote:
...

remote:
remote: -----> Building dependencies
remote:        Installing node modules (package.json + package-lock)
...

remote: -----> Pruning devDependencies
remote:        removed 126 packages and audited 2780 packages in 6.746s
remote:        found 0 vulnerabilities
...

remote: -----> Build succeeded!
remote:        Released v4
remote:        https://tracker-api-$GITHUB_USER.herokuapp.com/ deployed to Heroku
remote:
remote: Verifying deploy... done.
```

You should go through the messages and ensure that there's nothing amiss or unexpected. Of particular interest at this point is the message:

```
remote:        Installing node modules (package.json + package-lock)
```

This means that Heroku, after copying over the files from the Git repository, has also run npm install on the target directory. Since we have package.json and package-lock.json files also in the Git repository, the versions that it installs will also automatically match what you have used during development.

> ■ **Note** Heroku installs packages listed in devDependencies also, but later prunes these, as can be seen by the message Pruning devDependencies.

If everything works okay, you should see the last line that says that the deployment is verified and done. Now you can test the API by using the Playground. This will also ensure that the API server can connect to the MongoDB server on the cloud. To access the Playground, browse to https://tracker-api-$GITHUB_USER.herokuapp.com/graphql (replace $GITHUB_USER with your GitHub user ID).

You could also just type heroku open in the console, and a browser tab or window should open with the previous URL, but without the /graphql path, resulting in a message "Cannot GET /". You will need to append /graphql once the window opens to access the Playground.

If things don't seem to work, to troubleshoot, you could look at the console output of the server by executing the following command line:

```
$ heroku logs
```

A normal successful start of the API server should look something like this:

```
2018-12-30T12:20:34.841550+00:00 app[web.1]: > pro-mern-stack-2-api@1.0.0 start /app
2018-12-30T12:20:34.841552+00:00 app[web.1]: > nodemon -e js,graphql -w . -w .env server.js
2018-12-30T12:20:35.498072+00:00 app[web.1]: [nodemon] 1.18.9
2018-12-30T12:20:35.500474+00:00 app[web.1]: [nodemon] to restart at any time, enter `rs`
2018-12-30T12:20:35.501650+00:00 app[web.1]: [nodemon] watching: *.* .env
2018-12-30T12:20:35.502464+00:00 app[web.1]: [nodemon] starting `node server.js`
2018-12-30T12:20:37.028765+00:00 app[web.1]: CORS setting: true
2018-12-30T12:20:38.639869+00:00 heroku[web.1]: State changed from starting to up
2018-12-30T12:20:38.512917+00:00 app[web.1]: Connected to MongoDB at mongodb+srv://UUU:PPP@
XXX.mongodb.net/issuetracker?retryWrites=true
2018-12-30T12:20:38.523184+00:00 app[web.1]: API server started on port 46837
```

The UI Application

A similar set of steps in the UI server is required for UI server. First, let's change the name of the variable that sets the port to listen on. The changes needed are shown in Listings 15-7 and 15-8.

Listing 15-7. ui/server/uiserver.js: Change in Name of PORT Environment Variable

```
...
const port = process.env.UI_SERVER_PORT || 8000;
...
```

Listing 15-8. ui/sample.env: Change in Name of PORT Environment Variable

```
...
UI_SERVER_PORT=8000
...
```

In the API application, the source code was enough for the server to start and run the server. The UI application is a different because it needs compilation before the files needed to start the server are ready. There is also the need to link or copy Bootstrap's static CSS and JavaScript files to the public directory.

There are two npm scripts that this can be done in. The script postinstall is one that is run right after npm install finishes. This is a Node.js specific script, and it will be run automatically by npm. Thus, it takes effect both when a developer runs npm install locally as well as after Heroku runs npm install after deployment. The other script is heroku-postbuild, which is specific to Heroku. That is, this script is run only on Heroku deployments, and not when a developer runs npm install on the local computer.

For developers, running a compile after installation would be a waste of time since they would normally use HMR via Webpack. Also, linking the Bootstrap files to public will mean that we have to assume it is a Mac or Linux computer. So, let's do these two steps in the script heroku-postbuild only. Further, we need a change in package.json for specifying the Node.js and npm versions, as we did for the API server. All these changes to package.json are shown in Listing 15-9.

Listing 15-9. ui/package.json: Changes for Specifying engine, postinstall, and post-build

```
...
  "main": "index.js",
  "engines": {
    "node": "10.x",
    "npm": "6.x"
  },
...
    "dev-all": "rm dist/* && npm run watch-server-hmr & sleep 5 && npm start",
    "heroku-postbuild": "npm run compile && ln -fs ../node_modules/bootstrap/dist ↵
    public/bootstrap"
...
```

To make the changes permanent, let's commit them to the local Git repository and push them to the GitHub remote.

```
$ cd ui
$ git commit -am "Changes for Heroku"
$ git push origin master
```

Now, we're ready to deploy the UI server, but first we need to create the application on Heroku. Let's call this application tracker-ui-GITHUB_USER and create it.

```
$ heroku create tracker-ui-$GITHUB_USER
```

Before we start the server by pushing it to the Heroku remote, we'll need to configure the API and authentication endpoints that the UI server needs. We already have the GITHUB_USER environment variable set in the shell, so using that, let's set these configuration variables. For Google authentication, let's also set another variable, called GOOGLE_CLIENT_ID. Set this variable to the Google Client ID that you obtained from the Google developer console.

```
$ heroku config:set \
  UI_API_ENDPOINT=https://tracker-api-$GITHUB_USER.herokuapp.com/graphql \
  UI_AUTH_ENDPOINT=https://tracker-api-$GITHUB_USER.herokuapp.com/auth \
  GOOGLE_CLIENT_ID=$GOOGLE_CLIENT_ID
```

Deploying the server is the same as we did for the API server. We'll need to push the repository to the Heroku remote.

```
$ git push heroku master
```

In the deployment logs, you should see messages very similar to the API server deployment. But importantly, you should also be seeing a compilation step like this:

```
...
remote: -----> Building dependencies
remote:        Installing node modules (package.json + package-lock)
...

remote:        Running heroku-postbuild
remote:
remote:        > pro-mern-stack-2-ui@1.0.0 heroku-postbuild ↲ /tmp/build_605a3a265a979f27ab
                 6e5296a8297eb9
remote:        > npm run compile && ln -fs ../node_modules/bootstrap/dist public/bootstrap
remote:
remote:
remote:        > pro-mern-stack-2-ui@1.0.0 compile ↲ /tmp/build_605a3a265a979f27ab6e5296a82
                 97eb9
remote:        > webpack --mode production
remote:
remote:        Hash: 0288037a5cd24d5397fc7b520cbaa24cafcace5c
...

remote: -----> Caching build
remote:        - node_modules
remote:
remote: -----> Pruning devDependencies
remote:        removed 454 packages and audited 3507 packages in 8.764s
remote:        found 0 vulnerabilities
remote:
...

remote: -----> Launching...
remote:        Released v1
remote:        https://tracker-ui-$GITHUB_USER.herokuapp.com/ deployed to Heroku
remote:
remote:        Verifying deploy... done.
```

Once the app is up and running, you should be able to view the main issues page. But on navigating to any other page, you should see a CORS error. That's because the API server has not been set to the UI_SERVER_ORIGIN and it would be defaulted to http://localhost:8000. Let's set that in the API server, now that we know the URL of the UI server.

```
$ cd api
$ heroku config:set \
  UI_SERVER_ORIGIN=https://tracker-ui-$GITHUB_USER.herokuapp.com
```

Now, if you browse to the applications URL (or, simply type heroku open while in the ui directory), you should see the Issue Tracker UI with the initial set of issues loaded. You should also be able to navigate to other pages successfully. These other pages should also work on a browser refresh while on that page.

But you will find that this works only for unauthenticated users. Signing in at this point will not work because of the new domain being used and due to CORS and cookie considerations. But before we address that, let's see if the proxy mode works.

Proxy Mode

The proxy mode should seem to work normally because there are no CORS or cookie considerations. Let's set up the proxy mode by setting the corresponding environment variables.

```
$ cd ui
$ heroku config:set \
  UI_API_ENDPOINT=https://tracker-ui-$GITHUB_USER.herokuapp.com/graphql \
  UI_AUTH_ENDPOINT=https://tracker-ui-$GITHUB_USER.herokuapp.com/auth \
  UI_SERVER_API_ENDPOINT=https://tracker-api-$GITHUB_USER.herokuapp.com/graphql \
  API_PROXY_TARGET=https://tracker-api-$GITHUB_USER.herokuapp.com
```

Now, if you try the application, the first page load will succeed, but on navigating to other views, you will see browser-rendered requests will time out, and in the Network tab of the developer tools, you will find that the API calls are failing. If you try the Playground using the proxied URL https://tracker-ui-$GITHUB_USER.herokuapp.com/graphql, you will be shown an error page, again because proxied requests to the API server fail. This happen because of how Heroku routes HTTP requests.

In reality, many web applications share the same resources on Heroku. Not just computing resources, they also share IP addresses. Because of this, it is necessary for every request to specify *which* application the request should land on so that it can be routed to the appropriate application. This is done using the Host header in the HTTP request. The technique is referred to as *Name Based Virtual Hosting*, which is also supported by popular web servers such as Apache and nginx.

Browsers automatically set this header to the hostname part of the URL, so any request to the API server or the UI server from the browser was routed by Heroku to the correct application. But when proxying requests, the http-proxy-middleware does not automatically do this. What it does by default is use the original Host header that was received from the browser and copy it to the request to the API server.

Thus, the following sequence of events happen when the browser initiates a request to say, https://tracker-ui-$GITHUB_USER.herokuapp.com/graphql:

1. The browser resolves the IP address of tracker-ui-$GITHUB_USER.herokuapp.com, which is one of many common IP addresses shared by all Heroku applications.

2. The browser sets the Host header to tracker-ui-$GITHUB_USER.herokuapp.com.

3. Heroku looks at the Host header and routes a request to the UI server.

4. The proxy middleware intercepts the request (because the target is /graphql), and tries to forward this to tracker-api-$GITHUB_USER.herokuapp.com.

5. The proxy middleware resolves the host for the API server, which also results in a common IP address.

6. The proxy middleware forwards to the IP address, the *same* request, that is, with the Host header as tracker-ui-$GITHUB_USER.herokuapp.com.

7. Heroku receives the request, looks at the Host header, and routes this to the UI server! This leads to an infinite loop until the request times out.

The reason proxy mode worked when we tried it on our local computer is that there was no virtual host based routing. All requests to `http://localhost:3000` directly landed in the API server and it did not cause any problem.

The remedy for making it work correctly in Heroku is to change the behavior of `http-proxy-middleware`. We need it so that the `Host` header is set the same as the target URL rather than the original header. The flag `changeOrigin` in the options for the proxy middleware controls this behavior, and all we need to do is set this to `true`. The changes to `uiserver.js` for this fix are shown in Listing 15-10.

Listing 15-10. ui/server/uiserver.js: Change Origin When Proxying Requests

```
...
if (apiProxyTarget) {
  app.use('/graphql', proxy({ target: apiProxyTarget, changeOrigin: true }));
  app.use('/auth', proxy({ target: apiProxyTarget, changeOrigin: true }));
}
...
```

Now, if you commit these changes and push them to Heroku using `git push heroku master`, you will find that the application works great. You should confirm that authentication works and is persisted on a browser refresh.

Non-Proxy Mode

The non-proxy mode of operation doesn't work even though the two applications have the same domain (`heroku.com`). The browser does not share the cookie between these two applications because `heroku.com` is listed in the Public Suffix List. This list is meant exactly for situations like this, and you can learn more about this at `https://publicsuffix.org/learn/`.

Although it seems inconvenient at first, you probably realize by now that if your two applications could share the same cookie, it would also be shared among *all* other applications on Heroku, even those belonging to other Heroku users. Surely, this is not secure at all. So, Heroku has ensured that the domain `herokuapp.com` is considered on par with a top-level domain by adding it to the Public Suffix List. This causes the browser to reject a `set-cookie` header with the domain as `herokuapp.com`.

The only way to share cookies between the UI and the API server is by using a custom domain. Then, sub-domains on that domain can be used as the UI and API servers, thus enabling sharing of cookies to make the non-proxy mode of operation work. So, you will have to create a custom domain for yourself to try out the non-proxy mode of operation on Heroku.

There are many ways to register your own domain, including free ones. Pick one and create a domain. Once you have done that, create an environment variable called `CUSTOM_DOMAIN` and set it to that domain. For example, if you have registered `myfreedomain.tk` as your custom domain, set `CUSTOM_DOMAIN` to `myfreedomain.tk`, including the top-level domain `.tk`. We'll use `ui.$CUSTOM_DOMAIN` and `api.$CUSTOM_DOMAIN` as the UI and API application's sub-domains in the commands that follow.

One downside of using custom domains is that Heroku does not enable SSL for these by default, or for free. You will need to upgrade to a paid account on Heroku to be able to enable SSL for your custom domain. So, for the rest of this chapter, we'll use `http://` rather than `https://` based URLs.

Firstly, you will have to authorize the new domain-based URL as an authorized JavaScript origin in the Google Developer project. The origin will be `http://ui.$CUSTOM_DOMAIN`. This will also require you to add an authorized domain as `$CUSTOM_DOMAIN` in the Google developer console in the OAuth Consent screen tab. Note that after adding the JavaScript origin, it takes some time for it to take effect. If you plan on using SSL in the future, it may be a good idea to add the `https://` version of the origin now itself.

Next, we'll need to add these domains to Heroku so that it recognizes these domains and directs HTTP traffic addressed to these domains to the Heroku applications that we've created. Let's do that first in the UI application.

```
$ cd ui
$ heroku domains:add ui.$CUSTOM_DOMAIN
```

This will show an output such as the following:

```
Adding ui.$CUSTOM_DOMAIN to tracker-ui-$GITHUB_USER ... done
 ▶    Configure your app's DNS provider to point to the DNS Target
 ▶    sheltered-tor-u2t67pge87ki9sbr6iqw1h.herokudns.com.
 ▶    For help, see https://devcenter.heroku.com/articles/custom-domains
```

As the console output instructs, you need to configure DNS so that a request to ui.$CUSTOM_DOMAIN lands at the Heroku hosted UI application. This needs to be done in your domain provider, using their UI. You will need to create a CNAME record, which creates an alias for a domain. Essentially, you'll need to map the custom domain as an alias for the real domain, for example, sheltered-tor-u2t67pge87ki9sbr6iqw1h. herokudns.com, that Heroku automatically assigned for the application.

Then, we need to add the domain for the API application to Heroku:

```
$ cd api
$ heroku domains:add api.$CUSTOM_DOMAIN
```

And then, you need to set the DNS alias mapping in your domain provider's records, just like you did for the UI server. If you are using GoDaddy to host your domain, you should end up in a screen similar to Figure 15-1 in the Domain Manager.

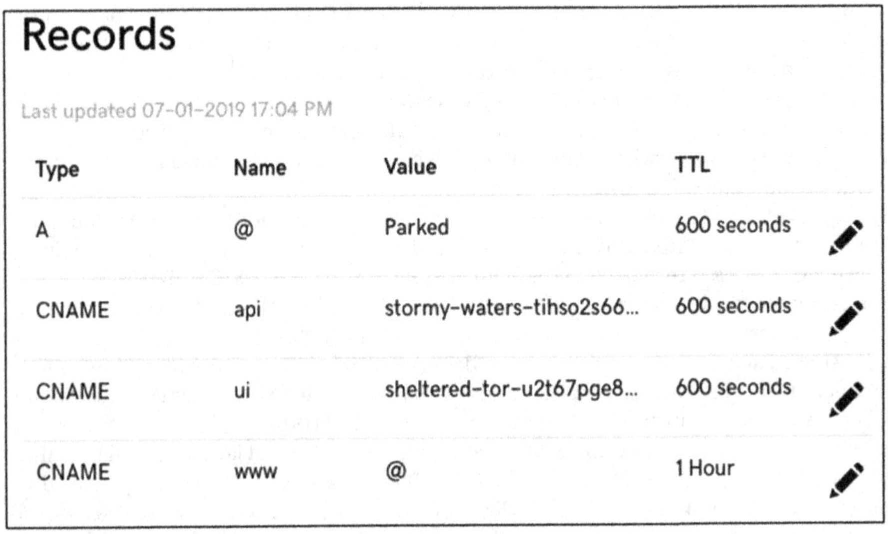

Records

Last updated 07-01-2019 17:04 PM

Type	Name	Value	TTL	
A	@	Parked	600 seconds	✎
CNAME	api	stormy-waters-tihso2s66…	600 seconds	✎
CNAME	ui	sheltered-tor-u2t67pge8…	600 seconds	✎
CNAME	www	@	1 Hour	✎

Figure 15-1. *Screenshot of Domain Manager after creating a record for ui and api*

Next, let's set the API and auth endpoints for the UI application to the new custom-domain based API server's URL, while we switch to the non-proxy mode of operation.

```
$ cd ui
$ heroku config:set \
  UI_API_ENDPOINT=http://api.$CUSTOM_DOMAIN/graphql \
  UI_SERVER_API_ENDPOINT=http://api.$CUSTOM_DOMAIN/graphql \
  UI_AUTH_ENDPOINT=http://api.$CUSTOM_DOMAIN/auth
$ heroku config:unset \
  API_PROXY_TARGET
```

Finally, for CORS to work correctly and for the cookies to shared between the UI and the API apps, we'll need to configure the API server as follows:

```
$ cd api
$ heroku config:set \
  UI_SERVER_ORIGIN=http://ui.$CUSTOM_DOMAIN \
  COOKIE_DOMAIN=$CUSTOM_DOMAIN
```

The servers would now be automatically restarted, and if you test the application, it should work seamlessly as it did in the proxy mode.

Summary

Although we made the Issue Tracker application work on your local computer, deploying it to the cloud, especially to a Platform-as-a-Service, introduced some challenges.

In the proxy mode, we had to set up the http-proxy-middleware correctly to change the Host header when proxying requests. In the non-proxy mode, you learned that using the default application domain does not work, and we had to use a custom domain. We also had to make changes to the code, but these changes were compatible with the application for local development as well.

We touched upon Git and version control, and we used two remotes for the repository: one for team collaboration on GitHub and another for Heroku. This is just one way of managing versions and releases. If you are working in a team and want to collaborate, you would do so in the GitHub remote, and when the time comes to release, you would push it to the Heroku remote. I did not delve into other options for managing releases, as these are both specific to your project as well as not really a MERN subject.

As we come to the end of this book, let's wrap up by discussing what more can be done with the MERN stack in the next chapter. We'll stop changing the application and just look at other techniques and libraries that are related and could be useful to you in your MERN project.

CHAPTER 16

Looking Ahead

I hope by now that I have succeeded in planting the fundamentals of the MERN stack in your mind. More importantly, I hope I have equipped you to take it all to the next level, because this is by no means the end of the Issue Tracker application, or anything else you had in mind as a project. If you'd really tried answering the exercises in each chapter, you should now be familiar with where to get more information when needed.

There are many more features that can be added and more technologies that can be used to help you going forward. In this chapter, I'll touch upon some of the technologies that you may want to consider if you decide to use MERN in real-life projects. But this will only be a brief introduction to what's possible; we won't be adding any code to the application we've created until now.

Do note that these new things may not necessarily suit your application. You need to evaluate them carefully if and when you hit a roadblock or want to automate some repetitive code as your application grows. The previous chapters in this book should have given you enough confidence that you can use the MERN stack and solve all problems by hand, or yourself. But in many a case, others have faced similar problems and created libraries to solve them. I suggest that you look for an existing solution, but wait until you are clear about what is it that you want solved.

Mongoose

Most technology stacks using relational databases can be supplemented with Object Relation Mapping (ORM) libraries. These add a layer of abstraction and let the developer see objects as such and not as tables with rows and columns.

When it comes to MongoDB, at first glance it doesn't seem necessary to map relations to the way the database stores into objects in memory, as the objects naturally map to MongoDB documents without an intermediate layer of conversion. But there are other things an Object Document Mapping (ODM) layer can provide. Mongoose (`https://mongoosejs.com`) is one such popular ODM library for MongoDB, which gives you the following:

- *Schema definitions*: This is useful since MongoDB does not enforce a schema, unlike SQL databases. With SQL databases, a schema error will be automatically caught by the database, whereas we ignored schema validations for the Issue Tracker application. Using Mongoose, you can define schemas and have new documents automatically validated against it. As of version 3.6, MongoDB itself supports schemas, but the support seems primitive compared to Mongoose.

- *Validations*: Mongoose has built-in validators over and above what GraphQL does in terms of required checks and data type checks. These include string lengths and minimum and maximum checks for numbers. Further, you can add custom validators such as email ID validators and reuse them across object types.

- *Isomorphic*: There's a browser component that lets the schema validations be used in the browser. This can help usability by showing errors in the UI *before* the user submits a form.

- *Models*: Although we encapsulated all code related to issues in `issue.js`, we did not attach functions to the Issue object. Using Mongoose, you can write truly object-oriented models that can encapsulate data as well as methods in the objects. Models also let the developer write code more intuitively, for instance, use `Object.save()` rather than `db.collection.insertOne()`.

For smaller projects such as the Issue Tracker, Mongoose was probably not needed. You could easily extract and share the validations in `issue.js` to reuse code if required. But for larger projects with multiple people working in a team, using Mongoose will definitely avoid errors in the development process and serve as documentation for the object schema, which is especially helpful for newcomers to the team.

Flux

If you have read about React, it is very likely that you have also heard about Redux and/or the Flux pattern. Due to its popularity, it's very tempting to dive right in and start using it. But let's first look at opportunities for improvement before we find solutions for them.

When we added user sign-in, we found that we had to transfer user information and the sign-in action up the component hierarchy and back down to the components that had use for it. It seems a little wasteful (and an unwanted increase in coupling) for the components somewhere in between, that don't need to know the information. For example, the component `NavBar` by itself had little use for the user's name or signed-in state. All it did was pass the knowledge down to `SignInNavItem`.

We solved the problem by using React Context for truly global state variables. Further, for initialization, we also created a global `store` object. If you do run into cases where there is a need to share the state among many components, yet, the state is not really global, you will feel the need to add more and more into the `store` object. But anything that's global needs some restrictions or contracts to avoid havoc caused by uncontrolled changes. This is what the Flux architectural pattern tries to define.

Flux embraces a unidirectional data flow, so that all changes to the state are channeled through a dispatcher, which controls the order of changes and thus avoids infinite loops because of interdependencies. Although this pattern was invented by the same people who developed React (that is, Facebook), the pattern is not restricted to be used only in React. Here is a very succinct, yet complete, description of Flux that I'm quoting from Facebook's React blog:

> When a user interacts with a React view, the view sends an action (usually represented as a JavaScript object with some fields) through the dispatcher, which notifies the various stores that hold the application's data and business logic. When the stores change state, they notify the views that something has updated. This works especially well with React's declarative model, which allows the stores to send updates without specifying how to transition views between states.

Essentially, the pattern consists of formally defined actions, for example, Create Issue, initiated by the user. The action is dispatched to a store. This affects the store's state. Typically, a function called a reducer is used to describe the effect of an action on the state: the new state is a function of the current state and the action.

Redux and Mobx are two popular choices recommended by the authors of React that can be used for global state management, and they follow the concepts of the Flux pattern largely. The effect of these frameworks or the Flux pattern is that you will have to write a lot of boilerplate code, that is, code that looks very much like some other code, seemingly unnecessarily. For every user action, you must formally define an action, a dispatcher, and a reducer that, given the current state, returns the contents of a new state.

Let's take the action of deleting an issue as an example. You must define a set of formal actions, including a constant like DELETE_ISSUE. Then, you must define a reducer, which is a function that takes in various actions and their parameters and returns a new state (a switch-case for each different action). Then, you must create a dispatcher, which converts the action and parameters into a real action, such as sending the request to the server.

All of this is worth it if the state machine in your application is very complicated, like say, if a delete request can be initiated from several different places in the UI (and even from outside the UI, as in some other user's action), and it has many other implications besides just removing a row in a table. Not many applications face this kind of complexity.

I can assure you with reasonable confidence that there'll be a point in time when your application will grow big enough within a single page (imagine your Facebook page) and you'll know you need Redux or Mobx, and why. Until that point in time, it may be wiser to get things done using just the basics and fundamentals while continuing to learn about these new patterns.

Create React App

We did a lot of work to set up the React compilation and development environment using Webpack and Babel. If you are not interested in setting up all this or do not want finer control of optimizing and customizing it, you may want to consider application initializers.

One such application initializer is Create React App. This can help you get started quickly and set up all the necessary tools such as Webpack and Babel for a pure react application. This could suffice for almost all the requirements of the Issue Tracker UI server. The following commands could have created the initial version:

```
$ npx create-react-app tracker-ui
```

Note that we did not have to install any Node.js modules. The command line npx temporarily installed whatever was necessary to run the command line create-react-app and ran it. Now, within the directory tracker-ui, you will find an src directory with two files: a JavaScript file and a CSS file. This is just a starter; you can add more files here to write code for your project. Now, to start the application, you can use the familiar start script:

```
$ npm start
```

This will not only compile and serve the bundle, but also automatically open a browser tab and point it to the application's URL, http://localhost:3000/. You can take a look at the User Guide of Create React App at https://facebook.github.io/create-react-app/docs/getting-started. A few things that you must remember before relying on this tool for your project:

- This creates a *pure* React application, that is, it has no server-side components. What this means is that there is no Express server created and, therefore, you cannot do things that the Issue Tracker UI server did: proxying requests and rendering on the server.

- This can be used for the UI server only. The API server will need to remain the way it is in the Issue Tracker application.

- If you do need the proxy server and server rendering, you could start with Create React App and "eject" the resulting application, by executing npm run eject and customizing the configuration by installing Express, etc. Ejecting the created app has the effect of making all the configuration visible and allowing customization, but it prevents you from easily upgrading to newer versions of Create React App.

- Create React App uses Webpack for handling all assets, including CSS. Since the Issue Tracker relied on React-Bootstrap and we don't have modularized CSS, this is not quite ideal, though it can be made to work by including bootstrap's CSS file. For an example, see in the source file index.js, how index.css has been included.

Thus, if your requirement is a pure React application, or if you are comfortable making configuration changes to include Express for the UI server, you could use Create React App as your starting point. Or, you could check out some of the popular alternatives to consider based on the type of your project, at https://github.com/facebook/create-react-app#popular-alternatives.

mern.io

If you want to get a good head start on most of the popular practices followed in a MERN stack application, it's handy to start with a project that's already crafted with all of the boilerplate code, as well as an example set of objects that you can tweak or copy to get your job done quickly.

A scaffolding tool built just for the MERN stack can be found at http://mern.io. This project includes a nifty utility that you can use to create the skeleton of a MERN application. The package itself is called mern-cli, a command line utility that creates an application based on the MERN stack. The commands to create your new MERN application (only on Linux or MacOS) are as follows:

```
$ npm install -g mern-cli
$ mern init mernApp
```

If your Node.js version is 10, you will probably get some compiler warnings that you can safely ignore for now. You will find that you have an entire functional application under the directory mernApp. To quickly see if it really works, all you need to do is navigate to the directory, install all the required packages (using npm install), and then run npm start:

```
$ cd mernApp
$ npm install
$ npm start
```

There will be more warnings since the project uses older versions of npm packages, which now have been found to have some vulnerabilities. If you ignore these warnings and point your browser to http://localhost:8000, you will see a functional application that can create and delete blog posts. The differences between what we've done in the Issue Tracker application and mernApp are as follows:

- The application mernApp does not use Bootstrap or React-Bootstrap. It has its own style sheets for styling its content. But including Bootstrap is not that hard, and it can be done following the steps that we did as part of the chapter on React-Bootstrap (Chapter 11).

- mernApp uses Mongoose and Redux, two technologies we discussed in previous sections, but did not use in the Issue Tracker application.

- There is no authentication or session handling in the mernApp.

- The code is organized as modules, which are cohesive pieces of code that work together to expose a significant functionality. The only module that is created by default is the Post module and you can create more modules as necessary.

- The server is a single server, unlike the Issue Tracker, where we had separate API and UI servers.

- mernApp uses REST-based APIs, and not GraphQL.

Despite all these differences, the project does show promise. But it's a bit outdated, does not work on Windows, many warnings are thrown up during creation of the application, and it is not actively maintained. But version 3.0 is in the making. Perhaps when the new version is released, it could become *the* application initializer for MERN-based applications.

Passport

When you need to integrate more authentication providers such as Facebook or Twitter, if you follow the approach we took in Chapter 14, "Authentication," you'd have to write different branches of code for each authentication option.

The Node.js package Passport (http://www.passportjs.org/) solves this problem by creating a single framework into which multiple authentication *strategies* can be plugged. Passport by itself only dictates the framework and the interface to the application developer. Each strategy (for example, the Google Strategy) is implemented as a separate package.

Note that Passport is a back-end-only package. All authentication requests from the UI will need to be passed through the back-end. This is unlike what we implemented as part of the Google Sign-in in the Issue Tracker, where we used Google's client-side libraries to initiate the authentication request directly to Google's authentication engine. Once authentication succeeded, we passed the Google Authentication token *from the UI* to the back-end where it was verified.

In contrast, Passport uses the Open ID Connect protocol that Google supports as an alternative (https://developers.google.com/identity/protocols/OpenIDConnect). In this approach, the UI makes a call for authentication to the application's back-end and not Google's authentication engine. The user is then *redirected* to the Google Accounts page, as opposed to it being a pop-up. Then, using a set of callback URLs to the application's back-end, success and failure of authentication needs to be handled.

The Open ID approach suits server-rendered applications and applications where the user needs to be logged in from the start. For an SPA like the Issue Tracker, this will cause a few refreshes of the application's page. In comparison, the direct approach used in the Issue Tracker application causes no browser refreshes and the authentication information is updated within the page. But this is a minor inconvenience compared to all the ease of implementation that Passport provides when dealing with multiple authentication providers.

That's All Folks!

I hope it has been a fun sail through the waters of the MERN stack for you, as it has been for me. I have learned a lot by just contemplating on the programming model, the paradigm, and the new thinking that the MERN stack has opened my eyes to.

I made sure we got into the nuts and bolts of each piece in the MERN stack and the accompanying tools rather than use frameworks like Passport or Create React App that could have made the job easier. I hope you enjoyed getting your hands dirty and the consequent learning that came out of it all, though it was harder to get the job done.

But this is nowhere close to the end. In a few months, I am reasonably certain that things won't be the same. Who knows? Browsers may themselves adapt or incorporate the virtual DOM technique, making React mostly redundant! Or, you'll see a new framework (not a library) that anchors React as the View part in an MVC offering. Or, a new version of a library that we used may come up with a totally new way of doing things.

The key thing is to keep looking for these new developments, yet be very, very analytical about why they do or do not work for *your* application and your team.

Here's to looking ahead to the *more* awesome future.

Index

Printed in the United States
By Bookmasters